Counseling and Psychotherapy

Counseling and Psychotherapy

SECOND EDITION

Les Parrott III
Seattle Pacific University

THOMSON

BROOKS/COLE

Australia • Canada • Mexico • Singapore • Spain
United Kingdom • United States

THOMSON
™
BROOKS/COLE

Editor: *Julie Martinez*
Marketing Manager: *Caroline Concilla*
Marketing Assistant: *Mary Ho*
Assistant Editor: *Shelley Gesicki*
Editorial Assistant: *Mike Taylor*
Project Editor: *Kim Svetich-Will*
Production Service: *Carlisle Communications*

Manuscript Editor: *Karen Bankston*
Permissions Editor: *Karyn Morrison*
Cover Design: *Cheryl Carrington*
Cover Art: *Pierre-Yves Goavec/Getty Images*
Print Buyer: *Nancy Panziera*
Compositor: *Carlisle Communications*
Printing and Binding: *Phoenix Color Corp*

For more information about our products, contact us at:
Thomson Learning Academic Resource Center
1-800-423-0563

For permission to use material from this text,
contact us by: **Phone:** 1-800-730-2214
Fax: 1-800-730-2215

Web: http://www.thomsonrights.com

Library of Congress Cataloging-in-Publication Data
Parrott III, Les.
    Counseling and psychotherapy / by Les Parrott III.
    —2nd ed. p. cm.
    Includes bibliographical references and index.
    ISBN 0-534-59337-2
    1. Counseling. 2. Psychotherapy. I. Title.
BF637.C6 P275 2002
158'.3—dc21   2002020072

Brooks/Cole/Thomson Learning
511 Forest Lodge Road
Pacific Grove, CA 93950
USA

Asia
Thomson Learning
5 Shenton Way #01-01
UIC Building
Singapore 068808

Australia
Nelson Thomson Learning
102 Dodds Street
South Melbourne, Victoria 3205
Australia

Canada
Nelson Thomson Learning
1120 Birchmount Road
Toronto, Ontario M1K 5G4
Canada

Europe/Middle East/Africa
Thomson Learning
High Holborn House
50/51 Bedford Row
London WC1R 4LR
United Kingdom

Latin America
Thomson Learning
Seneca, 53
Colonia Polanco
11560 Mexico D.F.
Mexico

Spain
Paraninfo Thomson Learning
Calle/Magallanes, 25
28015 Madrid, Spain

To Leslie,
My Soul Mate

About the Author

Les Parrott, Ph.D., is Professor of Psychology at Seattle Pacific University. With his wife, Dr. Leslie Parrott, he also codirects the Center for Relationships Development on the campus of Seattle Pacific University, a goundbreaking program dedicated to teaching the basics of good relationships. Les received his Ph.D. in clinical psychology from the Graduate School of Psychology at Fuller Theological Seminary. His clinical training included work at the University of Southern California Medical Center and a two-year postdoctoral fellowship at the University of Washington School of Medicine. The author of more than 50 articles, Les has also written several books, including *How to Write Psychology Papers, Helping the Struggling Adolescent, High-Maintenance Relationships, Becoming Soul Mates,* and the award-winning *Saving Your Marriage Before It Starts.* For further information on Dr. Parrott and his work go to www.RealRelationships.com.

Contents

Chapter 11

Transactional Analysis   230

Chapter 12

Behavior Therapy   266

Chapter 13

Rational-Emotive Therapy and Other Cognitively Based Theories   301

Chapter 14

Reality Therapy   340

CHAPTER 15

Marriage and Family Therapy   365

CHAPTER 16

Conclusion: Comparing the Major Therapeutic Theories   396

APPENDIX A

Divisions of the American Counseling Association   417

Preface

A WORD TO STUDENTS

"All beginnings are hard." So reads the first sentence of Chaim Potok's novel *In the Beginning*. He elaborates through his main character, David, who as a nine-year-old boy, burst into tears because a passage of a Bible commentary had proved too difficult for him to understand. But David's mentor spoke to him in a gentle voice: "Be patient, David, you cannot swallow all the world at one time."

As a teacher, I resonate with that sentiment. And I hope that as a beginning counseling student you do, too. Perhaps you have already decided on a career in counseling. Maybe you are still considering such a decision. Or maybe you are interested in the study of professional counseling because an introductory knowledge of this field will augment other endeavors. Whatever your aspirations and position, I trust that you are beginning this journey one step at a time. For truly, the art and science of counseling cannot be swallowed whole.

Along with your professor, this book will help you break the field of counseling into manageable pieces that can be more easily studied, critiqued, and eventually assimilated into your own understanding and application of an approach to counseling and psychotherapy. I hope that along the way you will seriously consider the limitations and contributions of the various therapeutic systems this book presents and that you will slowly start to acquire the foundation of a counseling style that fits your values and personality. This will require keeping an open mind as you read, and not jumping to conclusions or making assumptions before fully grasping each therapeutic approach.

The truth is, it takes most professional counselors many years of study and experience before developing a sound rationale for systematically adhering to certain therapeutic concepts and techniques. Avoid the temptation to advocate one approach to the exclusion of all others at this beginning stage. An introductory course in counseling is not enough to make that kind of decision, and there is no reason to unduly limit yourself to a single theory when you can draw on many other fruitful approaches. You will soon discover that each and every theory offers a unique approach to understanding human predicaments and provides the counselor with healing tools for resolving them.

While it may be difficult, I encourage you to not judge each theory as "right" or "wrong." Instead, make it your goal to learn from them all, and in time your own personal theory of psychotherapy will develop and emerge, one step at a time.

HOW THIS BOOK IS ORGANIZED

This text is divided into two parts. "Part I: The Practice of Counseling and Psychotherapy" provides a foundation for understanding the field of counseling. This includes exploring the realm of counseling (where counseling comes from and what counselors do), the qualities of effective counseling, the legal and ethical issues in counseling, and contemporary issues in counseling, such as cross-cultural counseling.

"Part II: Major Therapeutic Theories" presents the basic concepts of the most influential theories of modern counseling. An overview of the divergent forms of counseling and therapy will allow you to evaluate the unique contributions and limitations of each therapeutic system, applying it to psychological struggles.

In writing this book, I have included a number of features to help you understand and better remember the material.

- Each chapter begins with an outline of the main points. I suggest that you read the outline first to gain a concept of how the chapter is organized.
- Special boxes are used at various points in the text to amplify and enrich the main narrative. To avoid having them perceived merely as extras, I refer to each box at the point in the text where it is most relevant to the topic under discussion.
- Many chapters include a glossary of key terms to explain technical language. The key terms are readily accessible in the chapter you are studying rather than at the end of the book.
- Notable quotes by many famous counselors, psychotherapists, and others are highlighted in the margins throughout the text.
- References are cited in the text by authors' last names and dates of publication (e.g., Freud, 1940). This method of citation not only documents the various sources of information cited in the text but is also useful for consultation when pursuing particular topics in more detail.

- The Subject Index and Name Index, appearing at the end of the text, provide you with an alphabetized listing of all terms, subject matter, and people's names along with their page citations.
- A Study Guide accompanies the textbook. It contains many helpful exercises and suggestions for studying to promote learning.

ACKNOWLEDGMENTS

Many people have been extremely helpful in reading one or more chapters of the book. I would like to thank the following people who have read and commented on the second edition of *Counseling and Psychotherapy:* Barbara Boccaccio, Tunxis Community College; T. K. Daugherty, Winthrop College; Daisy B. Ellington, Wayne State University; Joshua Gold, University of South Carolina; Elizabeth Kincade, Indiana University of Pennsylvania; Robin Lewis, California Polytechnic State University, San Luis Obispo; Beverly Palmer, California State University, Dominguez Hills; and Ann Puryear, Northern Arizona University.

It is now time to conclude introductory remarks and embark on your journey. As you study modern counseling and psychotherapy, the persons, places, and perspectives will be filled in with greater understanding by the student who stays the course. My best.

Les Parrott, III

Advice is like snow; the softer it falls, the longer it dwells upon, and the deeper it sinks into the mind. —**Samuel Taylor Coleridge**

The Practice of Counseling

Knowledge is the eye of desire and can become the pilot of the soul. —**Will Durant**

1 CHAPTER | The Realm of Counseling

CHAPTER OUTLINE

Vienna and Beyond
The Deep Roots of Counseling
What Is Counseling?
Counseling or Psychotherapy?
Functions of Counselors
Therapeutic Training and Settings
Professional Growth and Development
Summary
Key Terms
References

Following the mayhem of the American and French Revolutions in the late 18th century, a revolution began in 19th-century Europe without firing guns, leading troops, or seizing political power. It began with a single man who irreversibly changed the way Western civilization thinks. He provided new paradigms on which a great number of other ideas and behavior patterns are based. He defined issues that are points of reference for modern women and men. He set in place the frameworks on which decisions for educating children are made, people are evaluated, events interpreted, values determined, actions motivated, documents negotiated. For better or for worse, almost nothing in life has escaped his influence. The intellectual giant who revolutionized the thinking of the Western World was a neurologist-turned-psychiatrist whose life is forever identified with Vienna, Austria. His name is Sigmund Freud (1856–1939).

Freud is a household name on both sides of the Atlantic today. Who has not heard of a "Freudian slip" or an "unconscious motive"? He established the unconscious as a motivator and believed that human personality is built like a block wall, one brick at a time. A flawed personality is the result of imperfect bricks buried in a hidden tier far below the capstone, the fault of the brick layer rather than of the troubled adult.

Freud ranks among the most influential thinkers in history. His theories changed the way Western civilization thinks about human nature. His work on the origin and treatment of mental illness has formed the point of departure, if not the basis, for 20th-century psychiatry. His theories on sexual development have led to the open discussion of the subject in modern media. His theories on sex and violence as basic factors in personality have had a major impact on the writing of novels, the making of movies, and much of daytime and evening television fare, to say nothing of billboard advertising and magazine content. It is difficult to find a part of our lives Freud has not touched.

It is equally difficult to understand modern counseling and psychotherapy without exploring—if only briefly—its origins. The first few pages of this text are devoted to an excavation, if you will, of some of the most influential developments. Even the deep roots of healing that predate Freud will be exposed for your examination. We begin with an excavation site rich in artifacts that will soon take us to several intriguing locales beyond the borders of Western culture.

VIENNA AND BEYOND

As Athens was the cultural center of the Greek world, Rome the capital of the Empire, and Jerusalem the Holy City for Jews and Christians, Vienna, on the south bank of the Danube at the foot of the Austrian Alps, is considered by many to be the birthplace of psychiatry, psychoanalysis, and psychotherapy and the source from which other counseling methods have taken root, developed, and spread.

Sigmund Freud and Alfred Adler (1870–1937) lived in Vienna. They attended medical school there. And it was in Vienna that they honed their therapeutic skills and developed their theories based on research from their patient relationships. Even Victor Frankl, the Jewish psychiatrist who at age 26 was sent to a Nazi death camp during World War II and who survived to develop and practice his Logo Therapy, was president of the same Vienna medical association that Freud once headed.

Freud's influence moved out from over Vienna to hover above other great centers of learning dedicated to the greater understanding of the mind and its healing. Carl Jung (1875–1961) received his medical degree from the University of Zurich and began his practice and research in Basel, the town of his birth. As an early disciple of Freud, Jung later broke with him over his mentor's excessive focus on sexual instincts. Their friendship ended, but Jung stayed in his hometown to become a professor of medical psychology at the University of Basel.

In 1938 Freud moved to London to escape the wrath of the Germans who had overrun Austria, and it was in London that his daughter, Anna Freud (1895–1982), continued her work after her father's death. Inevitably the influence of Freud's work in psychotherapy crossed the Atlantic and came to rest in New York, where existentialists like Rollo May and humanists like Carl Rogers did some of their work. Eventually, the working places of leaders in the field of mind healing spread widely to include such locales as San Francisco (Eric Berne), Mexico City (Eric Fromm), and Johannesburg in the Republic of South Africa (Frederick Perls, who later moved to California).

All of these diverse places have some things in common. They are cities instead of rural settings. This means there were many people who needed their services, and costs could be covered by people who could afford it or by enlightened government agencies that made funds available. Each of these cities have strong medical schools with a bias toward research. The concentration of these groundbreaking practitioners in geographical centers made interaction among themselves possible and afforded access for the aggregate of followers who needed to be near their leader. From these centers of leadership in psychotherapy and research, the practice of those who followed the various schools of thought spread out to cover the Western world and beyond.

As a result, today we take the "talking cure" for granted. Counseling and psychotherapy have reached nearly every part of the modern globe. From great metropolises to small towns on nearly every continent, the healing craft begun by Freud in Vienna is being conducted, in one form or another, by thousands of practitioners. If the truth be known, however, Freud and the other theorists you will study in this text were not the first to offer therapeutic help. Counseling has a long, long past.

THE DEEP ROOTS OF COUNSELING

In reality, the desire to help others—to counsel—is as old as time and not limited to Western cultures. To a considerable extent, the contemporary history of psychotherapy has been developmentally blind to its heritage and culturally bound by its borders. Because its roots are deeply embedded in the rich soil of European-American thought and theory, modern counseling has developed without significant contribution from healers and thinkers who represent the non-Western world. In fact, it has been estimated that more than 90 percent of all psychologists who have ever lived are from the Western world (Lonner & Malpass, 1994). Even today, for a variety of reasons, some members of ethnic minority groups choose informal sources of help for emotional problems (Mays & Albee, 1993; Sue & Sue, 1999). Help is sought, not from a professional counselor, but from acupuncturists, herbalists, family physicians, clergy, friends, and family members who share a world view with the person—and who are thus culturally sensitive.

> Inherent in every form of psychotherapy is an attempt by the therapist to help clients translate their problems into more hopeful and less demoralizing terms.
>
> —Jerome Frank

Even before Freud, then, there were ancient counterparts to today's counselors, many of them beyond the borders of Europe. The chieftains of old tribal societies, for example, offered counsel to those in need (Gibson & Mitchell, 1986). The American Indian and other tribal groups relied on the shaman, believing much more in spiritual and holistic healing than in a conventional "counselor." Historically, Asia, Africa, and South America all looked to various kinds of mind healers. Although psychological theory and elaborate counseling techniques were not necessarily developed and systematized, these individuals were sought out for their intuitive wisdom and insight.

From the classical Greek and Roman eras to early modern times, counselors were philosophers, physicians, or priests. Plato (427–347 B.C.), one of the first to organize psychological insights into a systematic theory, dealt with questions about children, parenting, education, decision making, attitudes, and so on. Plato's most famous student, Aristotle (384–323 B.C.), also contributed to what was to become therapeutic understanding. Hippocrates and other Greek physicians contributed insight into the helping professions as well.

The ancient Hebrew people accepted the importance of personal identity and responsibility. The first-century Christian societies emphasized humanistic ideals that were later basic to the counseling movement. In the Middle Ages therapeutic interventions—wise or unwise—were increasingly implemented by the Church.

While many modern historians point to Freud as the founder and catalyst of psychotherapy, a number of people who preceded Freud, in addition to the ancients, made significant contributions to counseling as we know it. One European antecedent to Freud was Paul Dubois (1848–1918), a Swiss physician and psychotherapist who treated psychotic patients by talking with them in a reasonable manner. At about the time Freud was beginning his work, Pierre Janet (1848–1947), a well-known and respected psychotherapist, founded a new system of "dynamic psychiatry" (Corsini & Wedding, 1995). And it was Josef Breuer (1842–1925), a well-known Viennese physician 14 years older than Freud, who taught him about **catharsis,** a method of removing hysterical symptoms through "talking them out." The emergence of counseling as a psychologically based profession also owes a debt to Wilhelm Wundt, who distinguished psychology as a separate science in 1879 by opening his Psychological Institute at the University of Leipzig, thereby launching a systematic inquiry into human behavior. The beginning of psychiatry as a specialty of medicine was another important development of this period (Gibson & Mitchell, 1986).

It should also be pointed out that early in the evolution of psychoanalysis, women such as Ruth Mack Brunswick, Marie Bonaparte, Helene Deutsch, Edith Jacobson, and Theresa Benedek developed new understandings of the psychology of women that went beyond the early psychoanalytic focus on sexuality. Other women, including Karen Horney and Clara Thompson, would later challenge the givens of the Freudian psychoanalytic scheme that had contributed to myths about women. All of these factors, from ancient societies' reliance on "counselors" to European antecedents, contributed to the birth and growth of Freud's psychoanalysis and the general emergence of the practice of counseling and psychotherapy, eventually leading to its explosive growth in the United States.

1.1 | **Therapy on Wheels**

Hurtling down life's fast lane, executives and professionals often don't have time to bare their souls to a psychotherapist. Enter Dr. Ursula Strauss and Dr. Shelley Lennox, two psychologists who have come up with a scheme as original to psychology as takeout food and the Big Mac were to the culinary arts. They chauffeur their patients to work and analyze them all at the same time.

For $175 a session, a uniformed driver and either Dr. Strauss or Dr. Lennox pick up the executive at a suburban home in a van with an interior customized as a therapist's office—a burgundy couch faced by two bucket seats, a small coffee table graced by fresh flowers, and a clock on the wall. As Dr. Strauss or Dr. Lennox listen to the patients' problems, the driver, who is sealed off from the therapeutic conversations, heads to the executive's Manhattan office.

Neither the honks of a log-jammed Long Island Expressway nor the jolts of Manhattan's cratered streets seems to distract their patients, the psychologists say. For executives who cannot spare the rush hour, the psychologists are willing to do lunch scheduling, parking near the patient's building and saving the trip to a therapist's office. They will even schedule a session on the way to an airport.

Their business, Mobile Psychological Services, has grown to 50 patients, 6 therapists, 3 drivers and 4 vans and they are already thinking franchises.

As America entered the 20th century, life became more complex, and the demands for psychological adjustment, more intense. The changing values, increased pace, and contradictions in rural versus metropolitan norms of the early 20th century created the backdrop for the development of professional counseling. Pastors who had considered the pulpit as the center of their work now needed training for the proper use of their new counseling rooms. Doctors who thought their work was medicine suddenly learned that people were their business. Teachers were called on, not simply to teach, but to understand children. The revolution was on, and professional counselors were helping to see it through.

The common thread uniting these historical eras even beyond the borders of Western civilization is the concept of the psychotherapist as the "doctor of the interior" (Cushman, 1992, p. 22). This is true not only for psychodynamic theories but also for the diverse post-World War II era modalities included in this book: humanistic, behavioral, cognitive, and so on. Counselors shape, maintain, and facilitate healing in the private quarters that make up every individual.

Today therapeutic interventions are being welcomed everywhere from prisons to churches. The variety of approaches, theories, and fads has grown at a bewildering rate; by now there are more than 200 different psychotherapeutic

The American Psychological Association knows of no other enterprise quite like this, and a spokesman, Doug Fizel, said he has heard no particular criticisms or endorsements of the idea.

"There's greater concern about therapy over the phone, therapy over radio, therapy on television," he said. "At least in a van the therapist is there. With the other forms of therapy, there's no direct contact and the therapist can't pick up non-verbal cues from the patient."

Dr. Strauss and Dr. Lennox feel they are filling an unmet need. "There were these patients who always had the same problem: they had to cancel, they had to be out of town," said Dr. Strauss, who still spends most of her week, seeing patients in her Bronx and Westchester offices, which have no wheels.

For patients who are in emotional crisis, Dr. Strauss and Dr. Lennox prefer to use their offices, but the van, they say, is fine for routine psychotherapy and for helping people with problems like substance abuse or phobias.

Stockbrokers, bankers, and lawyers, she said, are often Type A personalities who work hard and work others hard and come to her to learn "how to handle it all," Of course, she said, she is aware that her service is feeding their neuroses, gratifying their need to squeeze everything into their pressured life style. "It's an irony that's not lost on us," she said. "But as one of the patients said, 'It's either this or nothing.'"

As a result of van treatment, Dr. Lennox added, the patients should learn to "appreciate the importance of providing the time for a therapy session," and forgo the van.

By Joseph Berger, *The New York Times*, January 13, 1995. Reprinted with permission.

systems (Gabbard, 1995). New strategies and techniques are developing in unexpected forms and at a rapid pace. The future of counseling and psychotherapy reaches to the horizon and beyond.

WHAT IS COUNSELING?

With a brief overview of counseling's historical roots, it is appropriate that we define, as much as possible, exactly what counseling is and how most practitioners understand their various functions.

Counseling is a word everyone understands, but no two people understand it in quite the same way. It is easier to practice the art and science of counseling than it is to describe it (London, 1964; Meehl, 1993). Conventional dictionaries offer little help. If you look up counseling, you'll find something like "the art of advising." The definition is not particularly wrong; it is simply too broad to be useful. Many people advise. Psychologists, social workers, salespeople, psychics, school guidance personnel, pastors, attorneys,

A word means what you want it to mean.
—Lewis Carroll

camp leaders, dentists, bartenders, and even friends advise. Professional counseling is more than merely the art of giving advice.

Consider the variety of definitions provided by scholars. The similarities and differences in these references indicate how difficult it is to locate a succinct definition of counseling. Here is a small sampling of the hundreds we have to choose from:

- Counseling is the artful application of scientifically derived psychological knowledge and techniques for the purpose of changing human behavior (Burke, 1989).
- Counseling is a helping relationship that includes someone seeking help and someone willing to give help who is trained to help in a setting that permits help to be given and received (Cormier & Hackney, 1987).
- Counseling consists of whatever ethical activities a counselor undertakes in an effort to help the client engage in those types of behavior which will lead to a resolution of the client's problems (Krumboltz, 1965).
- Psychotherapy is a situation in which two people interact and try to come to an understanding of one another, with the specific goal of accomplishing something beneficial for the complaining person (Bruch, 1981).

A commonly accepted and easily remembered definition of counseling does not exist because counseling is a dynamic, ever evolving profession. The term itself is value-laden and therefore "responsive to a nexus of interlocking pressures and concerns" (Belkin, 1988, p. 120). The numerous attempts to define counseling, however, have revealed many of its consistent and fundamental elements. In his insightful work *Persuasion and Healing,* Jerome Frank (1973) describes common factors that cut across the spectrum of counseling and psychotherapy. Common features include the counselor having a personal commitment to help clients; being given a certain degree of authority and thus inspiring faith and hope in clients; acting as a mediator between suffering clients and the larger society; helping clients release emotions, rethink problems, and restore morale simply by listening in an empathic manner; offering a framework for change by providing an explanatory scheme that helps clients understand suffering; and being actively involved in the process of change, usually over a number of sessions.

Other scholars have also highlighted common features in the diverse pool of counseling definitions (see Gottman and Markman, 1978). Most assume, for example, that counselors are *trained as professionals.* They have a base of knowledge and a bank of proven techniques and procedures as resources for their work. Counselors do not rely upon folk wisdom or intuition, the way one does over an informal cup of coffee with a friend. Competent counselors are in touch with current developments in their profession, and they have a repertoire of professional skills that have been gained through education and application (Beutler & Kendall, 1995).

Another common notion is that counseling is *an art as well as a science.* Professional counselors may rely upon research to direct their practice and inform their effectiveness, but they balance their scientific knowledge with the art of warm relationships. They see people, not as subjects or cases, but as people. In the same vein, professional counselors maintain high *ethical standards in their prac-*

tices. They recognize the need for clear-cut codes of ethical conduct and a means of accountability. They hold high moral standards and values. They understand the importance of clients' rights and act in full recognition of their professional limits. Of course, all of this is *directed toward positive change*. The desired results of therapy are behavioral, emotional, or attitudinal change. Counselors help clients learn and practice new ways of thinking and living. They help clients make choices and act on them. Effective counseling results in improved relationships, better coping skills, and personal growth (Cavaliere, 1995).

1.2 │ Are You Reluctant to Seek Help?

Society encourages people to be independent and autonomous when they experience emotional struggles. Consequently, the decision to see a counselor or psychotherapist compounds some people's stress. How willing are you to seek professional help during periods of inner conflict?

The following scale was developed to assess a person's willingness to see a counselor. Read each statement carefully and indicate your degree of agreement using this scale. In responding, please be completely candid.

0 = Disagreement
1 = Probable Disagreement
2 = Probable Agreement
3 = Agreement

_____ 1. Although there are clinics for people with psychological troubles, I would not have much faith in them.

_____ 2. If a good friend asked my advice about a mental health problem, I might recommend that he or she see a counselor.

_____ 3. I would feel uneasy going to a psychologist because of what some people would think.

_____ 4. A person with a strong character can get over psychological conflicts by him- or herself, and would have little need of a professional counselor.

_____ 5. There are times when I have felt completely lost and would have welcomed professional advice for a personal or emotional problem.

_____ 6. Considering the time and expense involved in psychotherapy, it would have doubtful value for a person like me.

_____ 7. I would willingly confide intimate matters to an appropriate person if I thought it might help me or a member of my family.

_____ 8. I would rather live with certain psychological struggles than go through the ordeal of getting professional treatment.

_____ 9. Emotional difficulties, like many things, tend to work out by themselves.

_____ 10. There are certain problems that should not be discussed outside of one's immediate family.

_____ 11. A person with a serious emotional disturbance would probably feel most secure in a good mental hospital.

(continued)

| **1.2** | **Are You Reluctant to Seek Help?** (continued) |

_____ 12. If I believed I was having a mental breakdown, my first inclination would be to get professional attention.

_____ 13. Keeping one's mind on a job is a good solution for avoiding personal worries and concerns.

_____ 14. Having been a psychiatric patient is a blot on a person's life.

_____ 15. I would rather be advised by a close friend than by a psychologist, even for an emotional problem.

_____ 16. A person with an emotional problem is not likely to solve it alone; he or she *is* likely to solve it with professional help.

_____ 17. I resent a person—professionally trained or not—who wants to know about my personal difficulties.

_____ 18. I would want to get psychiatric attention if I were worried or upset for a long period of time.

_____ 19. The idea of talking about problems with a psychologist strikes me as a poor way to get rid of emotional conflicts.

_____ 20. Having been mentally ill carries with it a burden of shame.

_____ 21. There are experiences in my life I would not discuss with anyone.

_____ 22. It is probably best not to know *everything* about oneself.

_____ 23. If I were experiencing a serious emotional crisis at this point in my life, I would be confident that I could find relief in psychotherapy.

_____ 24. There is something admirable in the attitude of a person who is willing to cope with his or her conflicts and fears *without* resorting to professional help.

_____ 25. At some future time I might want to have psychological counseling.

COUNSELING OR PSYCHOTHERAPY?

There is a line in *The Music Man:* "People from Iowa can stand toe to toe, for days and days, and never see eye to eye." The same could be said of scholars who debate the distinctive features of counseling and psychotherapy. Some believe the distinction between counseling and psychotherapy is vital. Others see it as useless. Although we will use the terms more or less interchangeably in this text, it is helpful to understand the common perceptions of the two terms.

Counseling has traditionally been viewed as less intensive than psychotherapy. It has focused more on preventive mental health, while psychotherapy has concerned itself with reparative intervention. The goals of counseling have been oriented toward education and developmental concerns, while the goals of psychotherapy have generally been remedial. Work settings have

> A word is not a crystal, transparent and unchanged, it is the skin of a living thought and may vary greatly in color and content according to the circumstances and the time in which it is used.
> —Oliver Wendell Holmes

_____ 26. A person should work out his or her own problems; getting psychological counseling would be a last resort.

_____ 27. Had I received treatment in a mental hospital, I would not feel that it had to be "covered up."

_____ 28. If I thought I needed psychiatric help, I would get it no matter who knows about it.

_____ 29. It is difficult to talk about personal affairs with highly educated people such as doctors, teachers, and clergymen.

Scoring procedure: Begin by reversing the numerical value for items 1, 3, 4, 6, 8, 9, 10, 13, 14, 15, 17, 19, 20, 21, 22, 24, 26, and 29; that is, 0 earns 3 points, 1 earns 2 points, 2 earns 1 point and 3 earns 0 points. After reversing the scores of these items, add the numbers for all 29 items.

Interpreting your score: Low scores of 29 to 49 express a negative attitude toward seeking professional help. This does not mean that you presently have problems that require professional help; it simply means if you did, you would be reluctant to see a therapist. You may feel that a social stigma is attached to seeking help or that it is a sign of personal weakness. Medium scores of 50 to 63 indicate that you believe professional help can be useful, but you are somewhat unsure about whether you would actually use it. A high score of 64 to 87 suggests that you have a positive attitude toward seeking a counselor or psychotherapist for help.

If you expect to counsel others, the experience of being a client can give you firsthand knowledge of what your clients are likely to undergo. In addition, personal therapy can help you come to grips with unresolved situations, blind spots, unfinished business, and interpersonal conflicts. As a future counselor, you can learn few things more important than how you carry old feelings into present situations.

Fischer, E., & Turner, J. (1970). Attitudes toward seeking professional help: Development and research utility of an attitude scale. _Journal of Consulting and Clinical Psychology, 35,_ 82–83. Copyright © 1970 American Psychological Association. Reprinted by permission of the author.

also been used to distinguish between counseling and psychotherapy. Psychotherapists, according to traditional expectations, are more apt to work in hospital settings or in private practice, while counselors are more likely to work in educational settings (George and Cristiani, 1994). Some consider the number of interventions to be a deciding factor (Gelso, 1998; Gelso & Fretz, 1992). About 12 to 15 sessions constitute counseling, whereas interventions beyond that point are psychotherapy.

Some view the difference as a matter of degree on a continuum, with counseling and psychotherapy at opposite ends (Brammer, Abrego, & Shostrom, 1993). Counseling is characterized by such terms as "educational," "vocational," "supportive," "situational," "problem-solving," "conscious," and "oriented in the present," with emphasis on "normal" and "short-term." Psychotherapy, on the other end of the continuum, can be characterized by such terms as "reconstructive," "in-depth," "oriented in the past," "analytical," "emphasis on dysfunction," and "long-term." But in the middle range of this continuum, where the interventions are less defined, the terms *counseling* and *psychotherapy* are often options for describing the same thing.

Despite efforts and the desire to make distinctions, however, current trends are blurring the fine lines between counseling and psychotherapy (Lipsey & Wilson, 1993). Counselors, for example, are now working with more severe populations in such places as hospitals, mental health agencies, and correctional institutions. In some states, counselors are moving more and more into private practice. There is so much overlap that broad generalizations about differences between the two are of little value. Despite attention to particular differences, most professionals in the field agree that counselors practice what psychotherapists consider psychotherapy, and psychotherapists practice what counselors consider counseling. Thus clear-cut distinctions between counseling and psychotherapy are virtually impossible to defend (Moldawsky, 1990). Patterson (1973) flatly states *"there are no essential differences between counseling and psychotherapy"* (italics in original, p. xiv).

FUNCTIONS OF COUNSELORS

With a cursory examination of counseling's roots and an attempt to more clearly define what counseling is, we now turn to what counselors do. You see, contemporary counselors do more than "counsel." They function as consultants, trainers, and supervisors. Blocher (2000) outlines several distinct counselor "delivery modes." Along with traditional one-to-one counseling, for example, counselors provide assistance to their clients through group *therapy,* which has become increasingly popular. At one time, groups were considered a time-saving way of providing service to more people. Today, group therapy is often used as a treatment of choice for clients whose struggles revolve around dysfunctional interpersonal relationships or problems in communication. A group setting can have advantages over one-to-one counseling. Groups more closely simulate a person's natural social situation, and they can provide the type of social support individual counseling may not offer.

Consultation is another rapidly growing delivery mode used by counselors. For example, counselors frequently consult with parents, teachers, school administrators, youth workers, ministers, police officers, and others who work or live with troubled people. They may also consult with volunteer workers in such organizations as Big Brothers or Big Sisters. In each of these cases the counselor works with a person who is attempting to help another person who is not seen by the counselor. Some call it "indirect helping" (Blocher & Biggs, 1983) or "triadic consultation" (Tharp & Wetzel, 1969). Blocher (2000) notes several advantages of such consultation. First, it is an effective means of reaching hard-to-reach clients, people who simply will not see a counselor directly but can receive help through others. Consultation allows counselors to meet those needs indirectly. Second, consultation multiplies the scope of a counselor's services. Consulting with teachers in a school, for example, increases the number of people who are served. People working collaboratively with a counselor can affect many lives. Finally, consultation has a ripple effect, often reaching beyond the identified client, benefiting others who encounter the person with whom the counselor consulted. Consultation with a parent about one child, for example, may ultimately benefit the entire family.

Another important service provided by many effective counselors is **training.** Not every psychological problem is the result of deep-seated, intrapsychic conflict or dysfunction. Clients' emotional struggles are often the result of not practicing basic coping strategies and skills. Some people never learn how to contend with stressful situations. Their problems are not the result of pathology, but of a lack of understanding of essential life skills (Gazda, 1984). Counselors can "give psychology away" by converting psychological principles into teachable skills and disseminating these skills through training efforts (Larson, 1984, p. 2). Teaching and training people in coping skills is sometimes the most preferred method of treatment (Carkhuff, 1971, 2000; Phillips, 1978).

Organizational development is another increasingly used mode of intervention. Counselors are concerned with the healthy development of organizations because organizations shape the lives of clients in significant ways. Children, for example, spend thousands of hours in schools. Adults spend many of their waking hours in company environments. It is not surprising, then, that the problems people bring to counselors often arise out of stresses originating in organizations. The competent counselor recognizes the importance of developing organizational environments that further human goals and fulfill human needs effectively (Jewell, 1985). Counselors in a school setting, for example, can work with teachers and administrators in implementing everything from curricular changes to the physical structure of the classroom. The goal of organizational development is "to improve the quality of the environment of a given organization in order both to improve the performance of the organization and to enhance the psychological development and well-being of its members" (Blocher, 2000, p. 10).

Supervision allows established counselors to advance their profession by training new and less experienced counselors (Bernard & Goodyear, 1994; Osipow, Walsh, & Tosi, 1984). In supervision, master counselors evaluate the skills of other counselors and provide them with constructive comments. Every competent training program places counseling students in observational settings such as practicums and internships, where they work with a supervisor who evaluates their performance. For this reason, many established counselors are likely to eventually provide supervision for novice counselors. For some counselors it is a part of their job description. Directors of counseling agencies, for example, often supervise junior-level counselors who work under them.

It should be clear, then, that the contemporary counselor does more than counsel. While one-on-one, face-to-face counseling is still a predominant mode of service delivery, today's counselors are not limited to a single treatment strategy. Group therapy, consultation, training, organizational development, and supervision are becoming standard specialties in the counseling profession.

THERAPEUTIC TRAINING AND SETTINGS

We come now to a critically important issue: how persons become a specific type of counselor and the settings in which they do their work.

> To be ignorant of what occurred before you were born is to remain always a child.
> —Marcus Tullius Cicero

A study at the University of Montana revealed that people are confused about the role and training of professional people-helpers (Warner & Bradley, 1991). When asked about the difference between a psychologist and a psychiatrist, for example, many people are at a loss. There are a great variety of professional therapists, trained at numerous levels and working in diverse settings. It is no wonder that students of counseling need a clearer understanding of the types of mental health service providers.

Most professional counselors or psychotherapists earn either a master's degree or a doctoral degree in counseling or clinical psychology. Interdisciplinary in substance and scope, counseling is typically taught in graduate programs by a diverse group of specialized professionals (Belkin, 1988; Christensen & Jacobson, 1994). The faculty of a typical counseling department may include clinical psychologists, counseling psychologists, school and family counselors, psychiatric social workers, psychometricians, philosophers of education, community psychologists, vocational counselors, and social workers.

Cormier and Cormier (1997) suggest that counselors in training typically demonstrate growth and proficiency in *self-development*—that is, in a heightened awareness of attitudes and behaviors that may facilitate or interfere with a helping relationship; in *skill development*—in counseling techniques, strategies, and style; and in *process development*—in becoming aware of the effect of particular counseling interventions on clients. Each of these areas is crucial to effective counseling and is therefore the focus of most counselor training programs.

> There are some things which cannot be learned quickly, and time, which is all we have, must be paid heavily for their acquiring.
> —Ernest Hemingway

Of course, the type of degree and the specialization within the program will determine what kind of professional one becomes. Since there is considerable overlap among the various concentrations in all mental health professions, it is important to understand the legal and functional distinctions that makes each unique. In brief, mental health practitioners are classified by the following descriptions.

Psychiatrists are medical doctors who have advanced training in mental health and psychopathology. Some psychiatrists specialize in prescribing psychotropic medication and have had little training in psychotherapy or counseling, while others do psychotherapy in addition to or instead of using medication. Still others are trained in psychoanalysis and have gone through the process themselves. Certification in psychiatry by the American Board of Psychiatry and Neurology is preferred but not required in all situations.

Psychoanalysts are trained specifically in Freudian psychoanalysis. Reputable institutes of psychoanalytic training require at least three years of training. Many insist that the trainee be licensed as a psychologist or psychiatrist.

Psychologists hold a Ph.D., Ed.D., or Psy.D. from an approved institution of higher education. Not all psychologists are trained as counselors or psychotherapists, however. Many psychologists specialize in a range of related studies, including animal behavior, social psychology, life-span development, geriatrics, and organizational psychology.

Clinical psychologists are trained in helping people solve major psychological problems. Their doctoral work includes internship training in psychological assessment and psychotherapy. Although requirements vary from state to state, generally clinical psychologists are required to pass comprehensive written and oral examinations. Licensed by the states in which they practice, clinical psychologists work in a number of settings, including hospitals, prisons, clinics, and private practice.

Counseling psychologists are usually trained at the doctoral level to help people solve psychological problems related to such areas as personal adjustment, marriage, family, career, and school. They are licensed in the same way as clinical psychologists but usually do not work with more severe forms of psychological disturbance. Counseling psychologists often work in school settings and in private practice.

School psychologists are often trained at the doctoral level and work with educators and others to promote the intellectual, social, and emotional growth of school-age children. They may evaluate and treat children, generate programs, and consult with teachers and school officials. Their work settings include schools, nurseries, and day care centers.

Industrial/organizational psychologists are trained at the doctoral level and are concerned with developing general theories or models that increase the effectiveness of organizations and make sense of the often confusing and complex patterns of interaction in the workplace. They use theories and experience in solving specific work behavior problems such as absenteeism or low productivity.

Marriage and family therapists earn a master's or doctorate in marital and family therapy and in most states become licensed as Marriage, Family, and Child Counselors (MFCC). Their training and practice is based on a theory of systems (i.e., interactions between a person and his or her social environment) rather than a model of individual therapy.

Social workers usually earn a bachelor of social work degree from an accredited undergraduate school and then a master's degree in social work. In many states they must become licensed to practice as a clinical social worker, a specialty focusing primarily on individual and family treatment. Social workers practice in a number of environments, including medical settings, rehabilitative centers, correctional centers, private practice, and facilities for both the mentally and physically challenged.

Psychiatric nurses earn an associate's or baccalaureate degree, pass a comprehensive examination, and specialize in psychiatric services. They provide front-line care in psychiatric hospitals, community mental health clinics, day treatment centers, and other settings. In many states a nurse with an M.S.N. and psychiatric/mental health certification is also considered third party reimbursable and can provide private practice (they cannot do this with a B.S.N.).

Pastoral counselors are ministers who have been trained primarily in theology but have also acquired education and experience in counseling. They maintain a vision of spiritual wholeness rooted in their belief in the healing power of God. Many have been trained in one of more than 350 clinical pastoral education centers in the United States.

Vocational counselors usually earn a master's degree. Concerned with much more than matching a person with a specific job, they work with people in helping them choose, enter, and progress in their vocations.

Occupational counselors may earn a B.A. or a master's degree and gain clinical experience through an internship. They primarily help children and adults suffering from physical challenges to make the most of their resources.

School counselors earn an advanced degree in counseling psychology and work primarily with people needing to clarify educational and career issues. They work primarily, but not exclusively, in school settings.

Substance abuse counselors earn a B.A. or a master's degree and help individuals suffering from addictions to drugs and alcohol. They usually work in treatment centers for substance abuse.

Paraprofessional counselors have intensive but limited training in helping approaches. They have gained some supervised field experience and almost always work under the direct supervision of a professional.

1.3 | Sources of Therapeutic Services

Therapists work in a variety of organizational settings. Foremost among them are the following:

- *Private practitioners*—Self-employed therapists are listed in the Yellow Pages under their professional category, such as psychologists or psychiatrists. Private practitioners tend to be relatively expensive, but they also tend to be highly experienced therapists.
- *Community mental health centers*—These centers have salaried psychologists, psychiatrists, and social workers on staff. The centers provide a variety of services and often have staff available on weekends and at night to deal with emergencies. These centers may be the only resource for clients with limited funds because many provide treatment for clients on a sliding fee schedule.
- *Hospitals*—Several kinds of hospitals provide therapeutic services. There are both public and private mental hospitals that specialize in the care of people with psychological disorders. Many general hospitals have a psychiatric unit, and those that do not usually have psychiatrists and psychologists on staff and on call. Although hospitals tend to concentrate on inpatient treatment, many provide outpatient therapy as well.
- *Human service agencies*—Various social service agencies employ therapists to provide short-term counseling. Depending on your community, you may find agencies that deal with family problems, juvenile problems, drug problems, and so forth.
- *Schools and workplaces*—Most high schools and colleges have counseling centers where students can get help with personal problems. Similarly, some large businesses offer in-house counseling to their employees.

Reprinted from Weiten, Lloyd, & Lashley, *Psychology Applied to Modern Life: Adjustment in the 90s* (3rd ed.). Monterey, CA: Brooks/Cole.

PROFESSIONAL GROWTH AND DEVELOPMENT

Before concluding this introductory chapter, it is important to make one more point clear: Competent counselors are dedicated to lifelong professional development. They recognize that the completion of a degree, even a doctorate, does not signal the end of personal and professional growth; only continuing education will enable them to maintain a vital and satisfying career in counseling. While these academic milestones are important and worthy of celebration, proficient counselors maintain involvement in organizations that keep them accountable and current in their profession. Even counselors who have endured years of graduate courses, internships, post-doctoral fellowships, and a rigorous licensure exam come to understand the old adage, "The more I learn, the more I need to I know."

> An education isn't how much you have committed to memory, or even how much you know. It's being able to differentiate between what you do know and what you don't.
>
> —Anatole France

Counselors have many opportunities to sharpen their skills and further their understanding of counseling (Davison & Lazarus, 1994). Each year books are published for practicing counselors. But one of the best resources for professional development is membership in a counseling organization that provides resources through news publications, scholarly journals, workshops, and conventions.

Established more than 100 years ago, the American Psychological Association (APA) is the oldest organization of this kind and serves more than 70,000 members. The APA is composed of more than 50 divisions covering a range of interests (see Appendix for a listing of current divisions). The Division for Counseling Psychology (Division 17) publishes the *Journal of Counseling Psychology,* the *Journal of Vocational Behavior,* the *Journal of Professional Psychology,* and the *Counseling Psychologist.* Membership dues and fees include subscriptions to the *APA Monitor,* psychology's newspaper, and the *American Psychologist,* the official journal of the APA.

In 1951 several professional associations for counselors and student personnel workers joined to form the American Personnel and Guidance Association. In 1984 it became the American Association for Counseling and Development, and in 1992 it again changed its name to the American Counseling Association (ACA). Boasting a membership of more than 55,000 from all fields of counseling, the ACA is made up of 16 divisions that include such specialties as multicultural counseling and development, career development, and mental health. The ACA disseminates counseling news and research through the *Journal of Counseling and Development* and the newsletter *Counseling Today.* In addition, most of the ACA divisions publish journals dedicated specifically to concerns of that division.

The ACA and the APA hold annual regional and national conventions. The national meetings are large, with workshops, paper sessions, and symposia scheduled almost every hour. Joining these organizations and attending their conventions is an important part of a counselor's professional development and accountability. In order to keep counselors in check, both the APA and the ACA

1.4 | ## Periodicals Related to Counseling and Psychotherapy

An excellent way to learn more about the field of counseling is to discover its journals. The following is not an exhaustive list of periodicals related to counseling and psychotherapy. It is intended to indicate the scope of the field, and it includes many of the professional resources available in university libraries. Journals are the main disseminators of counseling research, news, and professional development.

American Journal of Psychiatry
American Journal of Psychotherapy
American Psychological Association Monitor
American Psychologist
American Vocational Journal
Career Development Quarterly
Clinical Psychology Review
Counseling and Values
Counseling Psychologist
Counselor Education and Supervision
Elementary School Guidance and Counseling
International Journal of Family Counseling
Journal for Specialists in Group Work
Journal of Clinical Psychology
Journal of Consulting and Clinical Psychology
Journal of Counseling and Development
Journal of Counseling Psychology
Journal of Cross Cultural Counseling
Journal of Employment Counseling
Journal of Family Counseling
Journal of Marriage and the Family
Journal of Multicultural Counseling and Development
Journal of Offender Counseling
Journal of Psychology and Theology
Measurement and Evaluation in Counseling and Development
Psychotherapy: Theory, Research & Practice
Rehabilitation Counseling Bulletin
School Counselor
Women and Therapy

also have specific ethical guidelines, which will be addressed specifically in the chapter on Legal and Ethical Issues.

Students planning on an advanced degree in counseling or clinical psychology can begin their lifelong process of professional accountability and development by joining these professional organizations as student affiliates. For a fraction of the cost of professional membership, students can receive special newsletters and reduced rates on journals. The address for APA is: 750 First St., N.E., Washington, DC 20002-4242 (www.apa.org). Students interested in the ACA can write to: ACA Student Membership, 5999 Stevenson Ave., Alexandria, VA 22304-3303 (www.americancounseling.org).

SUMMARY

The study of counseling is like following the flow of a great river where territorial conflicts are fought, bridges are constructed for commercial advantage, and alliances are made with various tributaries that serve the purposes of the main stream. But in the meanwhile, most of life is lived on the banks of the river by people who have learned how to adjust to circumstances beyond their control as they make a living, raise families, and strive to keep order in their lives. It is on these banks, among these people, that qualified professional counselors find their fullest opportunities for service. It is also here that most become fulfilled by the rewards of a profession that truly can make a difference.

> We have a choice: to plow new ground or let the weeds grow.
> —Jonathan Westover

Before moving on to the next chapter, review what counseling is. Set your mind free from misunderstandings, conflicts, and overlapping of the various kinds of counseling within the total realm, and satisfy yourself on what counselors do. This process will take time, but it is worth the effort before turning to the important issues in the next chapter.

Key Terms

Catharsis Method of alleviating hysterical symptoms by "talking them out."

Clinical psychologist Counselor trained to help people solve major psychological problems.

Consultation Delivering counseling by consulting with parents, teachers, school administrators, youth workers, ministers, police officers, and others who work or live with troubled people.

Counseling psychologist Professional trained at the doctoral level to help people solve psychological problems related to such areas as personal adjustment, marriage, family, career, and school.

Industrial/organizational psychologist Professional trained at the doctoral level to develop general theories or models that increase the effectiveness of organizations and make sense of complex patterns of interaction in the workplace.

Marriage and family therapists Counselors trained to master's or doctoral level based on a theory of systems rather than a model of individual therapy.

Occupational counselor Professional who helps children and adults suffering from physical challenges make the most of their resources.

Organizational development Mode of intervention at the organizational level; counselors work with schools, workplaces, and other organizations to enhance the psychological development and well-being of the people within those groups.

Paraprofessional counselor Counselor with intensive but limited training in helping approaches.

Pastoral counselor Minister trained in theology, with education and experience in counseling.

Psychiatric nurses Nurses with specialty in psychiatric services, working in front-line care in psychiatric hospitals, community mental health clinics, day treatment centers, and other settings.

Psychiatrist Medical doctor with advanced training in mental health in psychopathology.

Psychoanalyst Counselor specifically trained in Freudian psychoanalysis.

Psychologist Professional who has earned a Ph.D., Ed.D., or Psy.D. and who may work as a counselor, psychotherapist, or specialist in such studies as animal behavior, social psychology, or organizational psychology.

School counselor Professional with advanced degree in counseling psychology who works primarily with people needing to clarify educational and career issues.

School psychologist Professional trained at the doctoral level to work with educators and others to promote the intellectual, social, and emotional growth of school-age children.

Social worker Professional who practices primarily individual and family treatment in a variety of settings, including medical and rehabilitative centers, correctional centers, private practice, and facilities for the mentally and physically challenged.

Substance abuse counselor Professional trained to counsel individuals suffering from addiction to drugs or alcohol.

Supervision Evaluating the skills of other counselors and providing them with constructive comments.

Training Service provided by counselors to help clients learn basic coping strategies and other life skills.

Vocational counselor Professional who works with people in helping them choose, enter, and progress in their vocations.

References

Belkin, G. (1988). *An introduction to counseling* (3rd ed.). Dubuque, IA: Wm. C. Brown.

Bernard, J. M., & Goodyear, R. K. (1994). *Fundamentals of clincial supervision.* New York: Allyn and Bacon.

Beutler, L. E., & Kendall, P. C. (1995). Introduction to the special section: The case for training in the provision of psychological therapy. *Journal of Consulting and Clinical Psychology, 63,* 179–181.

Blocher, D. H. (2000). *Counseling: A Developmental Approach*. New York: Macmillan.

Blocher, D. H., & Biggs, D. (1983). *Counseling psychology in community settings*. New York: Springer.

Brammer, L. M., Abrego, P. J., & Shostrom, E. L. (1993). *Therapeutic counseling and psychotherapy* (6th ed.). Englewood Cliffs, NJ: Prentice Hall.

Bruch, H. (1981). Teaching and learning of psychotherapy. *Canadian Journal of Psychiatry, 26*, 86–92.

Burke, J. F. (1989). *Contemporary approaches to psychotherapy and counseling: The self-regulation and maturity model*. Pacific Grove, CA: Brooks/Cole.

Carkhuff, R. R. (1971). Training as a preferred mode of treatment. *Journal of Counseling Psychology, 13*, 123–131.

Carkhuff, R. R. (2000). *The art of helping in the 21st century*. New York: HRD Press.

Cavaliere, F. (1995, June). APA brochure offers tips on choosing a psychologist. *The APA Monitor, 9*.

Christensen, A., & Jacobson, N. S. (1994). Who (or what) can do psychotherapy: The status and challenge of nonprofessional therapies. *Psychological Science, 5*, 8–14.

Cormier, W. H., & Cormier, L. S. (1997). *Interviewing strategies for helpers*. Monterey, CA: Brooks/Cole.

Cormier, L. S., & Hackney, H. (1987). *The professional counselor: A process guide to helping*. Englewood Cliffs, NJ: Prentice Hall.

Corsini, R. J., & Wedding, D. (1995). *Current psychotherapies* (5th ed.). Itasca, IL: F. E. Peacock.

Cushman, P. (1992). Psychotherapy to 1992: A historically situated interpretation. In D. K. Freedheim, H. J. Freudenberger, J. W. Kessler, S. B. Messner, D. R. Peterson, H. H. Strupp, & P. L. Wachtel (Eds.), *A history of psychotherapy: A century of change*. Washington, DC: American Psychological Association.

Davison, G. C., & Lazarus, A. A. (1994). Clinical innovation and evaluation: Integrating practice with inquiry. *Clinical Psychology: Science and Practice, 1*, 157–168.

Frank, J. (1973). *Persuasion and healing*. New York: Schocken Books.

Gabbard, G. (1995). Are all psychotherapies equally effective? *The Menninger Letter, 3*, 1–2

Garfield, S., & Bergin, A. (1986). Introduction and historical overview. In S. Garfield & A. Bergin (Eds.), *Handbook of psychotherapy and behavior change*. New York: Wiley.

Gazda, G. M. (1984). Multiple impact training: A life skills approach. In D. Larson (Ed.), *Teaching psychological skills*. Monterey, CA: Brooks/Cole.

Gelso, C. J. (1998). *The psychotherapy relationship: Theory, research and practice*. New York: John Wiley and Sons.

Gelso, C. J., & Fretz, B. R. (1992). *Counseling psychology*. Fort Worth, TX: Harcourt Brace Jovanovich.

George, R. L., & Cristiani, T. S. (1994). *Counseling theory and practice* (4th ed.). New York: Prentice Hall.

Gibson, R. L., & Mitchell, M. H. (1986). *Introduction to counseling and guidance* (2nd ed.). New York: Macmillan.

Gottman, J., & Markman, H. (1978). Experimental designs in psychotherapy research. In S. Garfield & A. Bergin (Eds.), *Handbook of psychotherapy and behavior change: An empirical analysis*. New York: Wiley.

Jewell, L. N. (1985). *Contemporary industrial/organizational psychology*. New York: West Publishing.

Krumboltz, J. D. (1965). Behavioral counseling: Rationale and research. *Personnel and Guidance Journal, 44*, 383–387.

Larson, D. (1984). *Teaching psychological skills*. Monterey, CA: Brooks/Cole.

Lipsey, M., & Wilson, D. (1993). The efficacy of psychological, education, and behavioral treatment: Confirmation from meta-analysis. *American Psychologist, 48*, 1181–1209.

London, P. (1964). *The modes and morals of psychotherapy*. Washington, DC: Hemisphere.

Lonner, W. J., & Malpass, R. (1994). *Psychology and culture*. New York: Allyn and Bacon.

Mays, V. M., & Albee, G. W. (1993). Psychotherapy and ethnic minorities. In D. K. Freedheim (Ed.), *History of psychotherapy*. Washington, DC: American Psychological Association.

Meehl, P. E. (1993). If Freud could define psychoanalysis, why can't ABPP do it?

Psychoanalysis and Contemporary Thought, 16, 299–326.

Moldawsky, S. (1990). Is solo practice really dead? *American Psychologist, 45*, 544–546.

Osipow, S. H., Walsh, W. B., & Tosi, D. J. (1984). *A survey of counseling methods* (Rev. ed.). Homewood, IL: Dorsey Press.

Patterson, C. H. (1973). *Theories of counseling and psychotherapy* (2nd ed.). New York: Harper and Row.

Phillips, L. (1978). *The social skills basis of psychopathology*. New York: Grune & Stratton.

Sue, D. W., & Sue, D. (1999). *Counseling the culturally different: Theory & practice,* (3rd ed.). New York: Wiley.

Tharp, R. G., & Wetzel, R. J. (1969). *Behavior modification in the natural environment.* New York: Academic Press.

Warner, D. L., & Bradley, J. R. (1991). Undergraduate psychology students' views of counselors, psychiatrists, and psychologists: A challenge to academic psychologists. *Professional Psychology: Research and Practice, 22*, 138–140.

A failure is not always a mistake: it may simply be the best one can do under the circumstances. —**B. F. Skinner**

Becoming an Effective Counselor

CHAPTER 2

CHAPTER OUTLINE

Personal Qualities of Effective Counselors
Common Pitfalls Faced by Beginning Counselors
Summary
References

Karl Wallenda, a great tightrope aerialist, fell to his death in 1978, while walking a 75-foot-high wire in downtown San Juan, Puerto Rico. Shortly after this tragedy, his wife, also an aerialist, discussed that fatal walk. She recalled that all Karl thought about for three straight months prior to his attempt was falling. It was the first time he'd ever thought about failure in his work and, from her point of view, he put all his energies into *not falling* rather than walking the tightrope. Karl was virtually destined to make a mistake.

The counselor who focuses more on his or her potential for failure, like Karl Wallenda, than on success is also likely to fall. The counselor in training is especially tempted to invest a disproportionate amount of time and energy in trying to avoid mistakes instead of focusing on what it takes to be effective. Do you have a secret fear of making therapeutic blunders? If so, you are not alone. In this chapter we attempt to alleviate this kind of anxiety by exploring the personal qualities of effective counselors by paying attention not so much to *what* they do as to *who* they are. We then turn our attention to some of the most common mistakes the beginning therapist makes. The goal is to help you become aware of these pitfalls, avoid them, and put your energy into becoming the most effective counselor you can be.

PERSONAL QUALITIES OF EFFECTIVE COUNSELORS

What makes counselors effective? Is it their theoretical orientation? Their therapeutic techniques and skills? Not as much as you might guess. After reviewing nearly 100 studies on the effectiveness of counselors, Truax and Mitchell (1971) concluded that therapeutic techniques can be useful only when the counselor's personality is "inherently helpful." In other words, a counselor's *personal qualities* are at least as essential to therapeutic outcomes as the counselor's knowledge, theory, and skill (Jevne, 1981). Theoretical orientation, interviewing skills, and even professional experience are not the critical determinants for effective therapy. The counselor's personality is the single most important criterion for effectiveness (Perez, 1979; Seligman, 1995).

> Good counselors lack no clients.
>
> —Shakespeare

Before developing this point further, however, a word of caution is in order: a person's traits cannot compensate for inadequate knowledge or poor therapeutic skills. "A helpful personality that lacks knowledge and helping skills is like a good driver who operates an unsafe car" (Cavanaugh, 2001, p. 72). Although personal qualities cannot substitute for adequate training, the point is that the most effective practitioners possess certain personal qualities that transcend their therapeutic techniques and cut across theoretical lines (Small, 1990).

Which qualities make a difference? A classic four-year study conducted with counselors who worked with hospital patients reported that patients improved when their therapists showed high levels of warmth, genuineness, and empathy, regardless of their theoretical orientation. When these qualities were lacking, the hospital patients grew worse (Rogers, Genlin, Kiesler, & Truax, 1967). These early findings have been bolstered by subsequent research, both with patients and with counselees who were not hospitalized (see Corrigan, Dell, Lewis, & Schmidt, 1980; Gelso & Carter, 1994; Loesch, Crane, & Rucker, 1978; Rowe, Murphy, & DeCsipkes, 1975).

Through the years numerous studies have contributed to the list of basic qualities shared by effective counselors. In fact, discovering these qualities is one the most popular of dissertation topics among students seeking advanced degrees in therapy (Patterson & Eisenberg, 1983). Perhaps because of this extensive research on the subject, the list of personal qualities that improve the possibilities of healing keeps growing. Many authors, including Corey and Corey (1982), Carkhuff and Berenson (1977), Trotzer (1977), Kottler (1983), Patterson and Eisenberg (1983), and Sexton and Whiston (1994) have compiled several lists that include such qualities as a sense of humor, a high energy level, self-confidence, neutrality, flexibility, analytical thinking, creativity, enthusiasm, compassion, and honesty. The following, however, is an annotated list of what seem to be, according to the studies, the eight most important qualities in an effective counselor. Of course, perfection in these personal qualities is not required, only an awareness of one's own personality and a willingness to confront what is detrimental and to cultivate what is needed. These eight qualities are psychological health, genuine interest in others, empathic ability, personal warmth, personal power, self-awareness, tolerance of ambiguity, and an awareness of values.

Psychological Health

No one expects professional counselors to be paragons of psychological health; the crucial factor is the counselor's sense of well-being and his or her willingness to be in process. Counselors are models of behavior. If they do not demonstrate psychological health, they become part of the problem rather than part of the solution (Cavanaugh, 2001). Of all the personality variables studied in positive mental health research, meaning and purpose are most predictive of well-being. Counselors need a positive philosophy for living, a sense of meaning and purpose that gives them inner strength to adjust to circumstances beyond their control. Abraham Maslow, who turned psychology on its heels by being the first to study personal health, said, "Human beings need values and a philosophy of life to live by in the same sense that they need sunlight, calcium, or love." A positive philosophy of life helps generate the strength to overcome the unavoidable struggles along the way—not that people with optimum mental health are immune to difficulties, failures, and tragedies, but they possess the capacity to incorporate meaning into their struggles and to rise above them.

Another mark of mental health is a sense of personal responsibility. Some experts view an avoidance of personal responsibility as the essence of *all* emotional disturbance. When people avoid responsibility for themselves, they either blame selected people or they generalize the blame on the nebulous "they," whether the government, General Motors, or a special interest group such as environmentalists or loggers. Either way, they become unnecessarily dependent by making someone else responsible for their needs, their pain, or their failure. Healthy counselors are not passive victims looking to lay the blame on someone else; rather, they are on a quest for more mastery in their lives. They model responsibility and avoid the attitude of "You think *you've* got problems!" Albert Bandura (1977) calls this ability to be in control of one's life "perceived self-efficacy." Studies have shown that the greater one's perceived self-efficacy, the better one's general psychological adjustment (Heppner & Anderson, 1985; Seligman, 1990).

Psychological health is also marked by being at peace in the present. Maslow said: "Some people spend their entire lives indefinitely preparing to live." This is not true, however, for people who enjoy positive mental health. These individuals find joy in the journey toward their destination; they are not simply waiting to "arrive." Healthy people have launched themselves fully into the stream of life and find it stimulating, meaningful, and enjoyable (Rogers, 1961). They read, write, travel, and play. They enjoy the company of diverse friends as well as the privacy of being alone (Cavanaugh, 2001). In summary, while ineffective counselors are relatively uneasy with the character of their inner life, effective counselors are on relatively good terms with their own emotional experience (Allen, 1967; Gurman, 1972).

Genuine Interest in Others

One's desire to be a professional counselor can be equated with an authentic interest in helping people, the emphasis being as much on the word "authentic" as on the phrase "helping people." Unfortunately, some persons pursue the profession of counseling for wrong reasons. As T. S. Eliot wrote in his play, *Murder in the Cathedral,* "The last temptation is the greatest treason; to do the right deed for the wrong reason." There are many self-serving reasons for would-be counselors to enter the helping profession: for personal advancement, for recognition, or even because of a need for self-therapy (Pietrofessa, Hoffman, & Splete, 1984).

> The counselor's personality is the fulcrum on which are balanced knowledge of behavior dynamics and therapeutic skill.
> —Michael E. Cavanaugh

Effective counselors, on the other hand, are authentic; they are genuinely interested in helping people gain better mental health. Carl Rogers (1951) called this quality of authenticity "congruence" and defined it as consistency between a counselor's real self and what a counselor says and does. A counselor cannot fake authenticity. It is not something you do, but something you are.

Genuine concern for others is part of a lifestyle (Egan, 2001). It is integral to the persona, to the role one chooses to play in life, as Carl Jung put it. It cannot be mustered up for the moment like a manufactured smile. Being genuine means stripping away masks and being real. It means not playing a role (MacDevitt, 1987). The point is that energy spent on role playing or keeping a facade on straight absorbs energy that might have been used in alleviating problems. Counselors cannot help clients achieve authenticity without being authentic themselves. Burdened with the lack of honesty in the "outside" world, clients do not want to relate to another un-

2.1 | The Self-Actualizing Therapist

The ideal outcome of counseling is to help clients become more self-actualizing or more fully functioning. If this is a goal for clients, some writers (e.g., Carkhuff & Berenson, 1977) believe it should be an objective for counselors as well. You can only lead someone as far as you have traveled yourself. Maslow's quest to discover the characteristics of highly functioning people revealed the following traits (Patterson, 1985):

- *Reality-based.* The self-actualizing person detects phoniness and has an accurate, nondistorted perception of reality.
- *Accepting of self, others, and nature.* Self-actualizing persons respect and esteem themselves and others.
- *Spontaneous.* Self-actualizing persons are not conformists, but neither are they anti-conformist for the sake of being so.
- *Problem-centered.* Self-actualizing persons have a sense of mission in their lives.
- *A need for privacy.* Self-actualizing persons enjoy solitude.
- *Autonomous.* Self-actualizing persons do not depend on others or their culture for satisfaction.
- *Continued freshness of appreciation.* Self-actualizing persons experience pleasure and wonder in their everyday world.
- *Mystical.* Self-actualizing persons have meaningful experiences of ecstasy and awe.
- *Compassionate.* Self-actualizing persons have strong feelings of sympathy and regard for other human beings in general.
- *Relational.* Self-actualizing persons have a circle of deep friendships with other healthy persons.
- *Nondiscriminatory.* Self-actualizing persons are humble and ready to learn from anyone.
- *Highly ethical.* Self-actualizing persons clearly distinguish means from ends.
- *Sense of humor.* Self-actualizing persons have a spontaneous and thoughtful sense of humor that is neither hostile nor sarcastic.
- *Creative.* Self-actualizing persons have a fresh creative way of looking at things.

Effective counselors are on a quest toward self-actualization to better help others in their self-actualizing journey. It is not expected that counselors rate high on each of these qualities, but rather that they are aware of where they are in the process and what they must do to move on.

---

real person who is playing the role of counselor (Dreyfus, 1967). They cannot be open, trusting, and honest with a counselor who does not mirror these same qualities. Genuineness underlies the entire counseling relationship, and it is at the core of an effective counselor's being. Only when those who hope to practice counseling appreciate the centrality of genuineness can they apply therapeutic theories and techniques effectively (Pietrofessa, Hoffman, & Splete, 1984).

2.2 | **Being "Role-Free"**

Effective therapists do not take refuge in the role of playing counselor. They do not use the facade of being a "counselor" to substitute for competence or to fool the client. Gibb (1968, 1978) suggests several ways counselors can become "role-free." Here are a few of his suggestions:

- Communicate without distorting your messages.
- Listen to others without distorting their messages.
- Reveal your true motivations.
- Be spontaneous and free in your communications.
- Strive for interdependence rather than dependence with clients.
- Be concrete in your communications.
- Be willing to commit yourself to others.

Empathic Abilities

Empathy is the ability to put oneself in the shoes of other people and see the world as they see it. Unlike sympathy, which merely projects feelings onto other people, empathy allows one to sensitively enter another's feelings and accurately understand them. Sympathy is standing on the shore, seeing a person struggling in the water and throwing out a life-ring. Empathy, on the other hand, is jumping into the water and risking one's own safety to help the struggling person. Empathy is risky because it will change you. Once you empathize with an alcoholic, for example, you won't look at alcoholism in the same way again (Parrott, 1994).

Contemporary writers view empathy in a number of ways. Empathy has been described as thinking "*with,* rather than *for* or *about* the client" (Brammer & Shostorm, 1982, p. 160) or as the process of grasping with great clarity the meaning clients want to convey (Tyler, 1969). Some have said that empathy is "the ability to understand and to accurately communicate the meanings of the client's cognitive and affective responses about his or her self and the environment" (Osipow, Walsh, & Tosi, 1984, p. 18). One of the best explanations of empathy comes from Carl Rogers (1957), who said empathy is "to sense the client's private world as if it were your own, but without ever losing the 'as if' quality—that is empathy" (p. 99).

Studied extensively, empathy has proven to be crucial to positive outcomes in counseling (Aspey, 1975; Barrett-Lennard, 1962; Ridley, Mendoza, & Kanitz, 1994). It helps build rapport, elicit information from clients, and foster their goals (Egan, 2001). Carkhuff (1969) developed a "Discrimination Inventory" that presents a scale for assessing a counselor's level of empathy. On their scale, a counselor's responses are rated on the following five levels:

Level 1: The counselor communicates no awareness of even the most obvious, expressed surface feelings of clients.

Level 2: The counselor may communicate some awareness of obvious, surface feelings of clients, but the level of meaning is distorted.

Level 3: The counselor responds with accurate understandings of the surface feelings of clients, but may not respond to or may misinterpret the deeper feelings.

Level 4: The counselor communicates an understanding of the expressions of clients at a level deeper than they were expressed, enabling them to experience and express those feelings at a deeper level.

Level 5: The counselor is "tuned in" to clients and responds with accuracy to all their deeper as well as surface feelings.

Empathy conveys: "If I were her I would act as she does." According to Carkhuff (2000), empathy is the key ingredient in a helping relationship[1]. "Without an empathic understanding of the helpee's world and his difficulties as he sees them, there is no basis for helping" (p. 173).

Personal Warmth

Personal warmth refers to one's psychological climate and the conditions of the therapeutic interview. But a significant distinction can be made between the liberation of personal warmth and the oppressiveness of "humidity" that can suffocate potential: "The warm counselor is caring and freeing; the humid counselor is needy and possessive" (Cavanagh, 1990, p. 85). A counselor with personal warmth shows interest, concern, and attention but allows for personal space as well. His or her caring is nonpossessive and does not judge or evaluate (Bergin & Garfield, 1971; Rausch & Bordin, 1957; Truax & Carkhuff, 1967). Rogers (1951) called this quality *unconditional positive regard,* the complete acceptance of clients' characteristics and behaviors.

> Anyone with a modicum of human warmth, common sense, some sensitivity to human problems, and a desire to help can benefit many candidates for psychotherapy.
> —Jerome D. Frank

The purpose of nonpossessive warmth is to preserve clients' self-respect and to provide a trusting and safe atmosphere. Warmth stimulates clients' trust and helps them recognize that they can be "liked" in spite of unattractive characteristics (Bergin & Garfield, 1971; Osipow et al., 1984). Clients count on the therapist being consistently nonjudgmental. This stability allows them to express themselves freely without fearing a reaction of disapproval, shock, or criticism. In addition, warmth begets warmth, melting human defenses. "It is a rare human being who does not respond to warmth with warmth and to hostility with hostility. It is probably the most important principle for the beginning therapist to understand" (Truax & Carkhuff, 1967, p. 36).

An attitude of warmth accepts what is, rather than demands what should be. It is the capacity to suspend critical judgment (Egan, 2001). The opposite of contempt, an accepting attitude involves neither approval nor disapproval of clients' personality characteristics or behavior. In acceptance there are no reservations, conditions, evaluations, and judgments of clients' feelings (Boy & Pine, 1982). This kind of acceptance is often revealed through nonverbal behaviors (Cavanagh, 1990; Gazda, 1973; LaCrosse, 1975). Smiles, head nods, hand gestures, eye contact, and a slight forward tilt of the body can all contribute to counselors being judged as warm by their clients. In other words, clients are very much aware of their counselors' nonverbal behaviors and use these signals to interpret their warmth.

Whatever specific approach a counselor uses, the likelihood of his or her success in the counseling dialog is strengthened by a capacity for personal warmth (Kanfer & Goldstein, 1991). According to Goldstein and Higginbotham (1991), without the expression of warmth, particular strategies and helping interventions may be "technically correct but therapeutically impotent" (p. 48).

 ## Nonverbal Cues of Personal Warmth and Coldness

Warmth is communicated primarily through nonverbal behaviors such as voice tone, eye contact, facial expressions, gestures, and touch. It is important to remember that clients from non-Western cultures may perceive these North American nonverbal signals of warmth and cold differently.

Nonverbal cue	Warmth	Coldness
Tone of voice	Soft, soothing	Callous, reserved, hard
Facial expression	Smiling, interested	Poker-faced, frowning, disinterested
Posture	Relaxed, leaning toward the other person	Tense, leaning away from the other person
Eye contact	Looking directly into the other person's eyes	Avoiding eye contact
Touching	Touching the other softly and discreetly	Avoiding all touch
Gestures	Open, welcoming	Closed, as if guarding oneself
Physical proximity	Close	Distant

Self-Awareness

The ancient dictum of Socrates to "know thyself" is critical to becoming an effective counselor. Self-knowledge allows counselors to identify personal limits and become more objective. It empowers counselors to know "what they are doing, why they are doing it, which problems are theirs, and which belong to the client" (Cavanaugh, 2001, p. 73). When counselors know themselves and are comfortable with themselves, they are more at ease in working with others (Baldwin & Satir, 1987; Brennan & Piechowski, 1991). Self-awareness keeps counselors from allowing themselves to interfere with the therapeutic process. For this reason, many graduate training programs in counseling rightly encourage their students to undergo personal therapy themselves. Counselors in training can also become more self-aware by keeping a journal, in which they can record thoughts, feelings, experiences, stories, poems, dreams, and drawings. Our written expressions are often different from what we might disclose verbally, and they can teach us much about who we are (Watson & Tharp, 1993). Cormier and Cormier (1985) say "it is just as important to keep track of our own personal growth as it is to keep track of what technique or change program we are using with a client" (p. 13).

Regardless of the means for achievement, there is no debating that counseling is more effective when counselors are aware of their personal issues. Belkin (1988) points to three critical areas deserving of self-study for the counselor: security, trust, and courage. A responsible self-examination can lead to heightened self-awareness by asking questions that target these important areas of the inner self. To begin, ask, "Do I feel secure?" Counselors who are secure have little need to pass judgment on others, and they are confident enough to allow clients to develop at their own rates and in their own directions. It has also been found that insecure therapists are less accurate in their ability to recall words and feelings expressed in counseling interviews (Milliken & Kirchner, 1971). Next, ask yourself, "Do I trust other people?" The counselor who is suspicious and cynical is not likely to relate to clients in ways that are conducive to healthy change and growth. Mistrustful counselors project feelings and ideas onto clients that do not exist. For example, a therapist who is feeling angry projects this feeling onto the client and asks, "Why are you so negative today?" The third question in this self-study trilogy is, "Do I have the courage to confront challenges?" Counselors must have the courage to confront themselves—to examine their true motives, feelings, and limitations. Counselors must also have the courage to confront their clients and be willing, at times, to subjugate their own feelings and desires to be liked, respected, and admired in favor of the therapeutic process of the clients.

Tolerance of Ambiguity

Much of the counselor's world is abstract and ambiguous. Clients are often not fully aware of their real problems, and they sometimes complain of vague, indefinable symptoms. Their feelings may vacillate daily without reason. On top of these ambiguities, other uncertainties are endemic to the practice of counseling.

The light of the body is the eye.

—Matthew 6:22

For instance, there is no single way of approaching a given therapeutic issue. The counselor cannot prescribe a proven antidote the way a physician can scribble out a prescription on a pad. The path to healing is often unique to a particular client, and there are no precise road maps for the counselor to follow. The uncertainty of the journey requires stamina, poise, and a high tolerance for ambiguity.

According to a German proverb, "Patience is a bitter plant, but it bears sweet fruit." Counselors who have a high tolerance for ambiguity understand this principle of patience, and their therapeutic labors show it.

Don't judge another person until you have walked a mile in their moccasins.

—Native American Saying

Effective counselors—those who are tolerant of ambiguity—consistently practice patience with their clients, gently working to move the process along. At times, they abandon their search for cause and effect and come to terms with the ambiguity of diagnostic changes and the uncertainty of tentative treatment plans (Tramel, 1981). In short, less successful counselors are less tolerant of ambiguous material in the counseling interview than are more effective counselors.

Awareness of Values

More than 50 years ago, in a classic study in nursery-school, children were shown a poker chip and then asked to compare the size of the chip to the size of an adjustable circle of light, until the chip and the circle of light were perceived as being the same size. The children were then told they could exchange their poker chips for candy. After the children understood this proposition, they were again asked to compare the size of the chips to a circle of light. This time, the chips seemed much larger to the children (Lambert, Solomon, & Watson, 1949). Quite clearly, our personal values color our perceptions.

Values are the convictions or beliefs that determine our goals and how we attempt to meet them. They guide our actions and prescribe our outlook on life. If

The deepest principle in human nature is the craving for appreciation.

—William James

you value success and accomplishment, for example, you will probably be a hard worker, striving for advancement. If you place a high value on social activities, you are more likely to seek a work setting requiring a minimal commitment. Becoming aware of one's values is critically important to being an effective counselor. A particular combination of values constitutes a world view, which will influence counseling activities in numerous ways.

To begin with, effective counselors have thought through their values and live by them. Carl Rogers (1969, 1977) found that most people who seek out therapy follow external value judgments that are not necessarily their own. They deny their own personal convictions in favor of convictions others have taught them to hold. This is not true, however, of the effective counselor, who is particularly aware of personal convictions and has the courage to uphold them. A review of research related to a variety of helping professionals, in-

cluding teachers, clergy, school counselors, and counselors in training, concluded that the helper's awareness of values is a significant factor in predicting
the effectiveness of the help (Combs, 1986; Kelly, 1990). Of course, the effective counselor also strives to understand and appreciate the values of others.
After all, it was Eric Fromm who said that the test of love is loving the stranger
at our gates—the individual with values different from our own.

2.4 | **What Do You Value?**

A few years ago three sociologists designed a television program called *The Great
American Values Test* to conduct an experiment on the possible influence of television on values. To take their test, study the list and place a number to the left of each
value that describes its importance to you (1 = most important; 18 = least important). In completing this test, think carefully and work slowly. If you change your
mind, don't hesitate to change your answer.

Rank	*Value*
_____	Beautiful world
_____	Comfortable life
_____	Equality
_____	Exciting life
_____	Family security
_____	Freedom
_____	Happiness
_____	Inner harmony
_____	Mature love
_____	National security
_____	Pleasure
_____	Recognition from others
_____	Salvation
_____	Self-respect
_____	Sense of accomplishment
_____	True friendship
_____	Wisdom
_____	World peace

You may find it interesting to compare your rankings with a sample of adults
in the state of Washington who responded to this test. From top to bottom, they responded: 15, 8, 12, 17, 1, 3, 5, 11, 14, 13, 16, 18, 10, 4, 7, 9, 6, 2.

The Great American Values Test: "Can Television Alter Basic Beliefs?" by S. J. Ball-Rokeach, M.
Rokeach, and J. W. Grube, (1984). *Psychology Today, 18,* 34–41.

Of course, not all values have an impact on the helping process. Cormier and Cormier (1985), for example, suggest that "the counselor who values sailing can probably work with a client who values being a landlubber without any problem" (p. 17). It is those values that reflect morality, ethics, and lifestyle that have a greater probability of entering into the helping process.

Can counselors avoid conveying these values to their clients? Should they? Some professionals believe that counselors should communicate no value orientation to clients, that they should strive to be morally neutral in their counseling and focus only on the clients' values. They believe that the influence of the counselor's values would prevent clients from constructing their own internalized values (George & Cristiani, 1990; Ibrahim, 1991).

At the same time, some professionals have long called for an abandonment of this position (e.g., Patterson, 1958; Rosenthal, 1955; Samler, 1960; Williamson, 1958). They believe counselors cannot escape their values, that they cannot pretend to abandon or lack a value system in a counseling setting (George and Cristiani, 1990)—in short, that it is impossible to be "value-free" with clients (Cormier & Cormier, 1985). The counselor's values will be a part of the therapeutic work, either consciously or unconsciously (Coonerty, 1991; Rokeach & Regan, 1980). Okun (1982) asserts that "in an interpersonal relationship, whether or not it is a helping relationship, values are transmitted either covertly or overtly between the participants" (p. 229). In other words, values may sometimes be communicated in subtle ways, but they *are* communicated. Nonverbal cues of approval and disapproval, for example, convey value messages whether or not the therapist intends to or not (Corey, Corey, & Callanan, 1984). Given this inevitable communication of values, many professionals favor an open and explicit value orientation in counseling. They treat changing values of clients as part of the counseling process and argue that, no matter how passive and valueless the counselor may appear, the value systems of clients are influenced and gradually become congruent with the counselor's system of values.

In fact, while many counselors believe their values should be kept out of therapy as much as possible, research indicates that clients who improve most perceptibly tend to conform their values with those of the counselor. According to one study, when clients were grouped by how similar their values were to the values of the counselor, it was found that clients in a medium similarity group improved more than those in either high similarity or low similarity groups (Cook, 1966). These and other findings suggest that seeing themselves as too similar or too different from the other has an adverse effect on their interactions.

Since values are an integral part of personality, they are blended into the counselor's formula for effectiveness. Counselors who hold world views radically different from those of their clients and who are unaware of these differences "are most likely to impute negative traits to their clients" (Sue, 1978, p. 458). The effective counselor who is aware of personal values and respects clients' welfare when those values clash may be expected to refer clients to a more compatible therapist.

These qualities of an effective counselor—psychological health, genuine interest in others, empathic ability, personal warmth, self-awareness, tolerance of ambiguity, and an awareness of values—take time to acquire. Perhaps the word *becoming* in the title of this chapter should be underlined. Becoming effective as a counselor is not a product, but a process. No one is error free. Nevertheless, the remainder of this chapter is devoted to the identification of the most probable hurdles in a counselor's path and how they may be avoided.

COMMON PITFALLS FACED BY BEGINNING COUNSELORS

When a promising young executive at IBM lost more than $10 million in a venture under his authority, both he and his immediate bosses were understandably devastated. When IBM's founder and president, Tom Watson, called the shattered executive into his office for a review of what happened, the man blurted out, "I guess you want my resignation?" "You can't be serious," Watson replied. "We've just spent $10 million educating you!"

Thankfully, most mistakes are not as costly as the one this IBM executive made. And most schools and counseling centers can't absorb $10 million mistakes. Still, there is no such thing as learning without making mistakes. As a counselor in training, you will be expected to make mistakes, and you will be expected to learn from your failures (Gambrill, 1990). Learning to counsel is like learning to ski: if you're not falling down, you're not learning.

The following is not an exhaustive list of blunders made by beginning counselors, nor is it a catalog of the worst possible therapeutic errors. Rather, this list is representative of some of the most common mistakes made by beginning therapists. The list is designed to stimulate your thinking and heighten your awareness of difficulties that may lie around the corner.

Premature Problem Solving

Like a complex puzzle with interlocking pieces, a client's struggle cannot normally be diagnosed and cured in a brief time. A problem that has been escalating for years cannot be understood and healed in minutes. Trying to solve the problem before it is fully understood, however, is one of the most common therapeutic mistakes.

Consider Traci, a college student with a 3.8 GPA who says, "I'm really depressed and I think it's because I bombed my English mid-term." As her counselor reviewed her symptoms, the self-assessment seemed accurate. Traci expected to receive high marks, and falling short had indeed been traumatic for her. The counselor mused silently over the signs of an overachiever whose academic performance was unrealistic. The therapist searched gently, asking questions and listening for answers that might or might not enforce the hypothesis. The student admitted she was impatient with herself. She wanted to be valedictorian. The counselor seemed to have nailed the problem squarely, and it was time in the counseling process to dispute her

> We understand only that which we love.
>
> —Goethe

unrealistic goal of valedictorian. She had obviously inflicted herself with disquieting pressure that caused mild depression, and the counselor spent the next five sessions trying to whittle away at her unrealistic standards. It seemed progress was underway. Later in the week, however, the counselor received a message on the office answering machine that changed everything. It was from Traci's roommate, who said, "I know I probably shouldn't be calling you, but I was afraid that Traci hadn't told you she's bulimic." All of a sudden, the counselor's theory about Traci's overachieving disintegrated.

A seasoned counselor knows it is normally not easy, in one or two sessions, to identify clearly and to diagnose the underlying problems in a dysfunctional person. It may take that long for clients to trust the counselor enough to share the most revealing factors in their situation. The effective counselor is therefore continually asking, "Is there something else I may be missing?"

Setting Limits

In an effort to be understanding and tolerant, most beginning counselors have difficulty setting their own personal limits and dealing appropriately with such issues as repeated calls on the phone by clients, missed appointments, and clients not paying fees on time. Another potential problem area is the amount of time the counselor spends with clients in each session. Some clients may attempt to test the limits by continuing to talk past the appointed end of the session. But giving clients 60 or 70 minutes when 50 were promised may raise questions in their minds. Clients will wonder if you are strong enough to be their therapist if you can't handle their end-of-session ramblings. Do not be afraid to set limits and courteously hold to them (Cloud & Townsend, 1992).

Fear of Silence

The inexperienced counselor is often afraid of silence. The compulsion to say something during an awkward silence is natural and part of the human need to fill the gaps of everyday conversation. In counseling, however, silence is not a sign that the counselor needs to say something. Silence does not mean that something has gone wrong. When the counselor senses that the "wheels of thought and feeling" are turning, he or she should give clients time to reflect and contemplate. The effective counselor allows this process to happen without interruption. A nervous counselor who gets anxious during silence, on the other hand, will derail a train of thought by interrupting the productive silence.

Many clients have difficulty expressing themselves on sensitive subjects, and interrupting them before they have finished what they are trying to say is degrading. The effective counselor rehearses what he or she is going to say

> We can only know ourselves through knowing others and we can only know others through knowing ourselves.
>
> —Sydney Harris

next, but holds it in check until clients have fully completed the momentary struggle of thinking and talking about something that probably makes them feel very vulnerable.

There are times, of course, when silence is not productive. Some clients, for example, may be socially anxious and, for this reason, they may be unable to express themselves easily. Naive about how therapy works, other clients may expect the therapist to do all the talking. But more often, silence works to a positive purpose. Some of counseling's most therapeutic moments occur during periods of quiet contemplation. The inexperienced counselor needs to remember that it takes clients much longer to incorporate what you have said than the time it took you to say it. When clients are quiet they are often in the therapeutic process. Become comfortable with silence and learn to maintain eye contact with your clients, nodding your head as a nonverbal expression of listening and understanding (Brammer & MacDonald, 1996).

Interrogating

By relying too heavily on asking questions, the inexperienced counselor may cause clients to feel interrogated rather than understood. But interrogation and counseling are not synonymous: little therapeutic help takes place during an inquisition. Counselors in training, therefore, need to learn to refrain from subjecting clients to a barrage of questions. Excessive probing can make them feel beleaguered, and eventually they may clam up.

It is important to understand that good information can be obtained without interrogation. In response to a client who says, "My father was angry at me for most of the afternoon," numerous questions could follow: How often does your father become angry? What does he do when he is angry? How does that make you feel? A therapist can obtain much of this information and more by saying something like, "I get the impression you have experienced your father's anger more than once." An open-ended statement like this lets clients know they are understood, and it invites further disclosure without the risk of putting them on the spot.

The point is that it is possible for the skilled counselor to elicit information without a series of threatening questions. When he or she actively tries to understand clients' experiences, this helps them genuinely open up. Relevant information then becomes more readily accessible, and a stronger therapeutic alliance is built.

Impatience

Every therapist watches with hope for signs of progress. Every counselor wants clients to improve as soon as possible. Impatience among inexperienced counselors shows up in an eagerness to push unprepared clients into a treatment strategy before their time has come. Although there are certain "aha" moments in counseling, most therapeutic improvement is gradual, often slow. Gradual change is not an indicator of poor therapy (Cunningham, Davis, Bremner, Dunn, & Rzasa, 1993). Transformation in the mind takes time. A person who is grieving the loss of a loved one, for example, cannot be forced to "snap out of it." Nor can a person struggling with an eating disorder be expected to reverse habits quickly that have been building for a long time. The problem may be radical, but it is inevitable that the cure will be gradual.

In fact, clients who are rushed into making rapid changes will be set up for further failure. Being pushed to show signs of improvement too soon may result in extreme defensiveness, regression, or a premature termination of therapy all together. Thus, the beginning counselor must be sensitive to issues of personal impatience, for most clients cannot and will not make dramatic changes quickly. Nor should they.

Moralizing

Therapists are not required to compromise their convictions or relinquish their beliefs, values, and morals. Nevertheless, regardless of clients' behaviors, a professional counselor must refrain from passing judgment on the personhood of the clients. A primary goal of therapy is not to condemn, but to understand. Understanding, of course, does not in and of itself condone behavior; it does not mean the therapist becomes amoral. Understanding means simply accepting people by keeping an open, nonjudgmental mind. Research has shown that the counselor who is not open-minded continues to believe incorrect things about clients, even in light of new and different information (Anderson, Lepper, & Ross, 1980).

Clients are rarely helped by a moralizing counselor. In fact, in the majority of cases passing moral judgment decreases the probability of healthy change. "When you criticize me," Carl Rogers once said, "I intuitively dig in to defend myself. However, when you accept me like I am, I suddenly find I am willing to change" (1961, p. 90). While holding firm to personal convictions, the effective counselor does not mistake preaching for counseling. When a counselor cannot seem to refrain from personal judgment of a client, referral may be an appropriate option.

Reluctance to Refer

No counselor is expected to work with all the potential clients who come for help. The beginning counselor must learn, early on, that referral to another competent counselor is a part of doing good therapeutic work. If for any reason—shortage of time, skill, or capacity to be emotionally present—a counselor is unable to meet clients' needs, referral is not only a necessity but an ethical obligation.

> The unexamined life is not worth living.
> —Socrates

Careful referral involves more than giving clients the name of another counselor, however. Clients should be given a choice among therapists who are qualified to deal with their problems. And to protect against abandonment, the counselor should follow up on the referral to determine whether or not the appropriate connection was made.

SUMMARY

Fear of failure is one of the greatest obstacles that confronts the inexperienced counselor. Every therapist, regardless of experience and training, will make mistakes. Even Freud, Rogers, Ellis, and all the great theorists with whom we will become acquainted in this text were not immune to error. The counselor in training needs space to make mistakes that can turn into lessons. No supervisor expects to see a perfect set of attitudes and techniques from an intern, even one with a diploma in hand. Thus, the inexperienced counselor needs to learn to be patient, as he or she initially struggles to gain professional momentum.

Consider the genius and inventor Thomas Edison, who was one day faced with two dejected assistants telling him, "We've just completed our seven hundredth experiment and we still don't have a light bulb. We have failed." But Edison did not agree. "We haven't failed," he said. "We now know seven hundred things not to do. We are becoming experts."

Edison's wisdom applies to beginning counselors. Each "mistake" you make brings you one step closer to reaching your goal. Hopefully you will avoid the mistakes outlined in the latter half of this chapter and journey closer to qualities of effectiveness noted in the first half, but you are certain to stumble from time to time. After all, counseling is a serious business. What you do as a future counselor can make a significant difference in the lives of your clients. For this reason you can accept your anxieties as normal. As you log more and more counseling experience and as you progress in counselor education, your errors will decrease and your confidence will increase.

References

Allen, T. (1967). Effectiveness of counselor trainees as a function of psychological openness. *Journal of Counseling Psychology, 14,* 35–40.

Anderson, C. A., Lepper, M. R., & Ross, L. (1980). Perseverance of social theories. The role of explanation in the persistence of discredited information. *Journal of Personality and Social Psychology, 39,* 1037–1049.

Aspey, D. N. (1975). Empathy. *The Counseling Psychologist, 5,* 10–14.

Baldwin, M., & Satir, V. (1987). *The use of self.* New York: Hawthorn Press.

Bandura, A. (1977). Self-efficacy: Toward a unifying theory of behavioral change. *Psychological Review, 84,* 191–215.

Barrett-Lennard, G. T. (1962). Dimensions of therapist response as causal factors in therapeutic change. *Psychological Monographs, 76* (43, Whole no. 562).

Belkin, G. S. (1988). Introduction to Counseling. (3rd ed.). Dubuque, IA: Wm. C. Brown.

Bergin, A. E., & Garfield, S. L. (Eds.). (1971). *Handbook of psychotherapy and behavior change: An empirical analysis.* New York: Wiley.

Bergin, A. E., & Lambert, M. J. (1978). The evaluation of therapeutic outcomes. In S. L. Garfield & A. E. Bergin (Eds.), *Handbook of psychotherapy and behavior change: An empirical analysis* (pp. 139–189). New York: Wiley.

Boy, A., & Pine, G. (1982). *Client-centered counseling: A renewal*. Boston: Allyn and Bacon.

Brammer, L. M., and MacDonald, G. (1996). *The helping relationship: Process and skills* (6th ed.). Englewood Cliffs, NJ: Prentice Hall.

Brammer, L. M., and Shostorm, E. L. (1982). *Therapeutic psychology: Fundamentals of counseling and psychotherapy* (4th ed.). Englewood Cliffs, NJ: Prentice Hall.

Brennan, T. P., & Piechowski, M. M. (1991). A developmental framework for self-actualization: Evidence from case studies. *Journal of Humanistic Psychology, 31*, 43–64.

Carkhuff, R. R. (2000). *The art of helping in the 21st century*. New York: HRD Press.

Carkhuff, R. R., & Berenson, B. G. (1977). *Beyond counseling and therapy* (2nd ed.). New York: Holt, Rinehart & Winston.

Cavanaugh, M. E. (1990). The counseling experience. Prospect Heights, IL: Waveland Press.

Cavanaugh, M. E. (2001). *The counseling experience* (2nd ed.). Prospect Heights, IL: Waveland Press.

Cloud, H., & Townsend, J. (1992). *Boundaries: When to say yes and when to say no*. Grand Rapids, MI: Zondervan.

Combs, A. (1986). What makes a good helper. *Person-Centered Review, 1*, 51–61.

Cook, R. E. (1966). A comparative study of motivational intentions associated with the committing of problem behaviors. Dissertation Abstracts International, 27 (3-A), 666–667.

Coonerty, S. M. (1991). Change in the change agent's growth in the capacity to heal. In R. C. Curtis & G. Stricker (Eds.), *How people change: Inside and outside therapy* (pp. 81–97). New York: Plenum.

Corey, G., & Corey, M. (1982). *Groups: Process and practice* (2nd ed.). Monterey, CA: Brooks/Cole.

Corey, G., Corey, M., & Callanan, P. (1984). *Professional and ethical issues in counseling and psychotherapy* (2nd ed.). Monterey, CA: Brooks/Cole.

Cormier, L. S., & Hackney, H. (1987). *The professional counselor: A process guide to helping*. Englewood Cliffs, NJ: Prentice Hall.

Cormier, W. H., & Cormier, L. S. (1985). *Interviewing strategies for helpers* (2nd ed.). Monterey, CA: Brooks/Cole.

Corrigan, J. D., Dell, D. M., Lewis, K. N., and Schmidt, L. D. (1980). Counseling as a social influence process: A review. *Journal of Counseling Psychology, 27*, 395–441.

Cunningham, C., Davis, J. R., Bremner, R., Dunn, K. W., & Rzasa, T. (1993). Coping modeling problem solving versus mastery modeling: Effects on adherence, in-session process, and skill acquisition in a residential parent-training program. *Journal of Consulting and Clinical Psychology, 23*.

Dreyfus, E. A. (1967). Humanness: A therapeutic variable. *Personnel and Guidance Journal, 45*, 573–628.

Egan, G. (2001). *The skilled helper: A systematic approach to effective helping* (7th ed.). Monterey, CA: Brooks/Cole.

Gambrill, E. (1990). *Critical thinking in clinical practice*. San Francisco: Jossey-Bass.

Gazda, G. (1973). *Human relations development: A manual for educators*. Boston: Allyn and Bacon.

Gelso, C. J., & Carter, J. A. (1994). Components of the psychotherapy relationship: Their interaction and unfolding. *Journal of Counseling Psychology, 41*, 296–309.

Gendlin, E. (1962). *Experiencing and the creation of meaning*. New York: Free Press.

George, R. L., & Cristiani, T. S. (1990). *Counseling theory and practice* (3rd ed.). New York: Prentice Hall.

Gibb, J. R. (1968). The counselor as a role-free person. In C. A. Parker (Ed.), *Counseling theories and counselor education*. Boston: Houghton Mifflin.

Gibb, J. R. (1978). *Trust: A new view of personal and organizational development*. Los Angeles: The Guild of Tutors Press.

Goldstein, A. P., & Higginbotham, H. N. (1991). Relationship-enhancement methods. In F. H. Kanfer & A. P. Goldstein (Eds.), *Helping people change* (pp. 20–69). New York: Pergamon Press.

Gurman, A. S. (1972). Therapists' mood patterns and therapeutic facilitativeness. *Journal of Counseling Psychology, 19*, 169–170.

Heppner, P. P., & Anderson, W. P. (1985). The relationship between problem-solving self appraisal and psychological adjustment. *Cognitive Therapy and Research, 9*, 415–427.

Ibrahim, F. (1991). Contributions of cultural worldview to generic counseling and development. *Journal of Counseling and Development, 70,* 13–19.

Jevne, R. (1981). Counselor competencies and selected issues in a Canadian counselor education program. *Canadian Counselor, 15,* 57–63.

Kanfer, F. H., & Goldstein, A. P. (1991). *Helping people change: A textbook of methods* (4th ed.). New York: Pergamon Press.

Kelly, T. A. (1990). The role of values in psychotherapy: A critical review of process and outcome effects. *Clinical Psychology Review, 10,* 171–186.

Kottler, J. A. (1983). *Pragmatic group leadership.* Monterey, CA: Brooks/Cole.

LaCrosse, M. B. (1975). Nonverbal behavior and perceived counselor attractiveness and persuasiveness. *Journal of Counseling Psychology, 22,* 563–566.

Lambert, W. W., Solomon, R. L., & Watson, P. D. (1949). Reinforcement and extinction as factors in size estimation. *Journal of Experimental Psychology, 39,* 637–641.

Loesch, L. C., Crane, B. B., & Rucker, B. B. (1978). Counselor trainee effectiveness: More puzzle pieces. *Counselor Education and Supervision, 17,* 195–204.

MacDevitt, J. W. (1987). Therapist's personal therapy and professional self-awareness. *Psychotherapy, 24,* 693–703.

Milliken, R. L., & Kirchner, R. (1971). Counselor's understanding of student's communication as a function of the counselor's perceptual defense. *Journal of Counseling Psychology, 18,* 14–18.

Okun, B. F. (1982). *Effective helping: Interviewing and counseling techniques* (2nd ed.). Monterey, CA: Brooks/Cole.

Osipow, S. H., Walsh, W. B., & Tosi, D. J. (1984). *A survey of counseling methods.* Homewood, IL: The Dorsey Press.

Parrott, L. (1994). *Love's unseen enemy.* Grand Rapids, MI: Zondervan.

Patterson, C. (1958). The place of values in counseling and psychotherapy. *Journal of Counseling Psychology, 5,* 216–223.

Patterson, C. H. (1985). *The therapeutic relationship: Foundations for an eclectic psychotherapy.* Monterey, CA: Brooks/Cole.

Patterson, L. E., & Eisenberg, S. (1983). *The counseling process* (3rd ed.). Boston: Houghton Mifflin.

Perez, J. F. (1979). *Family counseling: Theory and practice.* New York: Van Nostrand.

Pietrofessa, H. H., Hoffman, A., & Splete, J. J. (1984). *Counseling: An introduction* (2nd ed.). Boston: Houghton Mifflin.

Rausch, H. L., & Bordin, E. S. (1957). Warmth in personality development and in psychotherapy. *Psychiatry, 20,* 351–363.

Ridley, C. R., Mendoza, D., & Kanitz, B. (1994). Multicultural training: Reexamination, operationalization, and integration. *The Counseling Psychologist, 22,* 227–289.

Rogers, C. R. (1951). *Client-centered therapy.* Boston: Houghton Mifflin.

Rogers, C. R. (1957). The necessary and sufficient conditions of therapeutic personality change. *Journal of Consulting Psychology, 21,* 95–103.

Rogers, C. R. (1961). *On becoming a person: A therapist's view of psychotherapy.* Boston: Houghton Mifflin.

Rogers, C. R. (1969). *Freedom to learn.* Columbus, OH: Charles E. Merrill.

Rogers, C. R. (1977). *Carl Rogers on personal power.* New York: Delacorte Press.

Rogers, C. R., Genlin, G. T., Kiesler, D. V., & Truax, C. B. (1967). *The therapeutic relationship and its impact.* Madison: University of Wisconsin Press.

Rokeach, M. (1973). *The nature of human values.* New York: Free Press.

Rokeach, M., & Regan, J. F. (1980). The role of values in the counseling situation. *Personnel and Guidance Journal, 58,* 576–582.

Rosenthal, R. (1995). Progress in clinical psychology: Is there any? *Clinical Psychology Science and Practice, 2*(2), 183–192.

Rowe, W., Murphy, H. B., & DeCsipkes, R. A. (1975). The relationship of counseling characteristics and counseling effectiveness. *Review of Educational Research, 45,* 231–246.

Samler, J. (1960). Change in values: A goal in counseling. *Journal of Counseling Psychology, 7,* 32–39.

Seligman, M. E. (1990). *Learned optimism.* New York: Knopf.

Seligman, M. E. (1995). The effectiveness of psychotherapy: The Consumer Reports Study. *American Psychologist, 50,* 965–974.

Sexton, T. L., & Whiston, S. C. (1994). The status of a counseling relationship: An empirical review. *The Counseling Psychologist, 22,* 6–78.

Small, J. (1990). *Becoming naturally therapeutic.* New York: Bantam.

Sue, D. W. (1978). World views and counseling. *Personnel and Guidance Journal, 22,* 458–462.

Tramel, D. (1981). A lesson from the physicists. *Personnel and Guidance Journal, 59,* 425–429.

Trotzer, J. P. (1977). *The counselor and the group.* Monterey, CA: Brooks/Cole.

Truax, C. B., & Carkhuff, R. R. (1967). *Toward effective counseling and psychotherapy.* Chicago: Aldine.

Truax, C. B., & Mitchell, K. M. (1971). Research on certain therapist interpersonal skills in relation to process and outcome. In A. E. Bergin & S. Garfield (Eds.), *Handbook of psychotherapy and behavior change* (pp. 299–344). New York: Wiley.

Tyler, L. E. (1969). *The work of the counselor.* New York: Appleton-Century-Crofts.

Watson, D. L., & Tharp, R. G. (1993). *Self-directed behavior: Self-modification for personal adjustment* (6th ed.). Pacific Grove, CA: Brooks/Cole.

Williamson, E. (1958). Value orientation in counseling. *Personnel and Guidance Journal, 36,* 520–528.

*Whatsoever I shall see or hear in the course of my profession
in my intercourse with men, if it be what should not be
noised abroad, I will never divulge, holding such things to be
holy secrets.* —**Hippocratic Oath**

Legal and Ethical Issues for the Beginning Counselor

CHAPTER OUTLINE

Foundations of Legal and Ethical Practice
The Client/Counselor Relationship
Confidentiality and Privileged Communication
When in Doubt
Ethical Principles and Guidelines
Summary
Key Terms
References

Construction on the Golden Gate Bridge, that great engineering feat which was to connect San Francisco with Marin County, was interrupted by outrage from people over the frequent fatalities and maimings of workers who fell from the span to the icy waters of the bay several hundred feet below. Newspapers fanned the public flame with gruesome pictures and heartrending stories of the men and the impact of their deaths on their widows and fatherless children. The bridge was less than half finished, and there had already been 24 such accidents.

The sponsors and underwriters responded to the widespread distress by installing a configuration of strong nets beneath the working area. Accidental deaths were reduced to only four during the remainder of the construction. This was good, but there was also an unexpected result. Knowing the safety net was there, the physical confidence of the men increased, their equilibrium was substantially improved, and the total number of accidents of all kinds was greatly reduced.

43

The same idea applies in the counseling room. Counselors work with more personal confidence and will protect themselves from relational disasters when they are aware of the configuration of safety nets provided for those who work within the legal and ethical guidelines of their profession. Both the therapist and the client are protected by these nets.

Few professions are more vulnerable to encountering potential legal troubles and ethical dilemmas than counselors (Cohen, 1992; Remley & Herlihy, 2000; Wilson & Ranft, 1993). The voluminous numbers of articles and books on the subject are a silent witness to the perils. In this chapter, you will learn the basic legal and ethical issues pertaining to the counselor-client relationship.

FOUNDATIONS OF LEGAL AND ETHICAL PRACTICE

A legal and ethical counseling practice is grounded on something counselors *are,* not something counselors *do.* The bedrock of legal and ethical counseling is *virtue*—a term rarely heard in psychology (Gelso & Fretz, 1992). Virtue should not be confused with a principle or rule, "rather it is a habit, disposition, or trait that a person may possess or aspire to possess. A moral virtue is an acquired habit or disposition to do what is morally right or praiseworthy" (Beauchamp & Childress, 1983, p. 261). The virtuous counselor, however, does not acquire ethical behavior through good intentions. The counselor with character begins by being legally and ethically competent. A sound counseling practice is built on knowing the law and understanding client rights (Hatton, Balente, & Rink, 1977). Virtue is nourished by deep roots anchored in the bedrock of the self. Virtue is grounded in an enlightened knowledge of the law, a clearly understood set of ethical, professional standards that are securely anchored from within, and personal values and beliefs that drive the morality of client relationships (Cooper, 1992).

> Perfect virtue is to do unwitnessed that which we should be capable of doing before all the world.
>
> —François de La Rochefoucauld

Jordan and Meara (1990) present the idea of *virtue ethics,* which focuses on *being* as much as on *doing.* Virtuous counselors emphasize "not so much what is permitted as what is preferred" (p. 112). Personal values of the counselor are a basis for empowering the practice of ethical behavior (Remley & Herlihy, 2000; Wrenn, 1962). A counselor's ethical behavior involves more than subscribing to a code of ethics. For good ethics are built on a genuine concern for the client's welfare (Corey, Corey, & Callanan, 1997).

Counselors have an obligation to their clients and to their profession to be accountable for the quality of the professional services they offer. Legally, the therapist must possess the degree of learning, skill, and ability that others similarly situated ordinarily possess; exercise reasonable care and diligence in the application of knowledge and skill to the patient's needs; and use his or her best judgment in the treatment and care of patients (*Stone v. Procter* 1963; quoted in Furrow, 1980, p. 23). Effective counselors are transparent and fully honest with themselves about the limits of their expertise (Pope & Vasquez, 1998). The American Psychological Association requires professionals to "provide services and only use techniques for which they are qualified by training and experience" (APA, 1992, p. 390). Being competent as a therapist does not mean being able to treat every person that needs counseling. A responsible therapist will only accept clients that can benefit from the training and skill the therapist has acquired. Research has shown that inept counseling can indeed be worse than no treatment at all (Bergin, 1963). Competency includes knowing what issues you cannot treat because you are not qualified by training and experience. Simply reading a book or attending a weekend workshop devoted to a particular topic does not qualify a counselor to begin unsupervised therapy in a new treatment area. If a counselor wishes to expand an area of professional competence, supervision from a clearly qualified professional is essential. Failure to practice at a reasonable level of competence may result in accusations of malpractice (Jobes & Berman, 1993). Generally, malpractice is defined as "a failure to meet prevailing, professionally accepted standards of practice" (Blocher, 2000, p. 30).

When a counselor recognizes that a client's needs are beyond his or her expertise, the counselor is responsible to make referrals to other qualified counselors (Remley & Herlihy, 2000). In making referrals of clients, counselors need to help clients understand the reasons for the referral and the distinctive qualifications of the professional to whom the referral is made. If, for example, a counselor is referring a depressed client to a psychiatrist who specializes in psychotropic medication, the counselor should explain that the psychiatrist is practicing a medical specialty and may prescribe much needed medication to help the client better manage the depressive symptoms (Cormier & Cormier, 1997).

THE CLIENT/COUNSELOR RELATIONSHIP

The essential element in a therapeutic relationship is trust. Counseling deals with deeply personal issues and requires a high level of risk taking on the part of clients. Without a reasonable level of trust, the therapeutic relationship cannot be effective. Counselor effectiveness is proportionate to the level of trustworthiness between therapist and clients. As trust is diminished so is healing.

Informed consent is the basis of a trusting relationship and a cornerstone of counselor ethics. Through informed consent, clients are told what can be expected during treatment, how long it may take, and how much it will probably cost. They are also informed of their right to agree or decline to participate in any aspect of counseling (Green, 1993). The information is communicated, not in professional jargon, but in language that is easily understood. Informed consent also gives clients opportunities to ask questions. According to Schutz (1982), a therapist should "describe the therapeutic program recommended, indicating also the anticipated benefits of the program, the foreseeable material risks of treatment, and the likely results of no treatment" (p. 24).

> You can fool some of the people all the time, and all of the people some of the time, but you cannot fool all of the people all the time.
>
> —Abraham Lincoln

3.1 | Sex in the Forbidden Zone

It is, in a way, the ideal setting for extraordinary intimacy. Patient and therapist are isolated from the world, focused on each other intently, exploring long-buried emotions. In successful psychotherapy, patients usually undergo something called **transference,** in which they come to see the therapist as an all-loving parent they can trust completely. The process can stir feelings in the therapist, too; power is a potent aphrodisiac. Freud warned that therapists should struggle against such "countertransference" and not abuse the patient's longing for love. Yet even some of his closest disciples couldn't withstand the temptations of the couch. Carl Jung took two patients as his mistresses. Otto Rank had a long affair with a patient.

History is replete with such indiscretions between psychotherapists and patients, and they've become the standard plot line for popular films from "The Prince of Tides" to "Basic Instinct." Books like *Sex in the Forbidden Zone* and *Sex in the Therapy Hour* have explored therapeutic sexual ethics in detail. Nobody knows how widespread sex between therapists and clients really is, but one thing is certain: A number of widely publicized cases is forcing the therapeutic profession to take stronger action. "A lot more cases are being reported," says Shirley Siegel, cofounder of the group Stop Abuse By Counselors in Seattle. "Women are much more willing to come forward and report embarrassing situations." Eight states have enacted laws making sex between patients and therapists a crime, and several more are weighing criminal sanctions. Professional associations are also getting tougher about disciplining ethics abuse. The APA now publicizes the fact that in the last 10 years, it has expelled or suspended 113 members, mostly for sexual misconduct.

Almost inevitably, patients who sleep with their therapists end up more emotionally scarred than when they began treatment. Sexually abused patients "look very much like incest survivors," says psychiatrist Nanette Gartrell. Many find it difficult to trust subsequent therapists, and most blame themselves for the encounter. In one national survey, it was found that 11 percent of patients who had sex with their therapists were hospitalized as a result; 14 percent attempted suicide and 1 percent succeeded. "When a therapist engages in sex with a patient, he or she is engaging in a potentially homicidal activity," former chairman of the APA's ethics committee Kenneth Pope says, "far more than getting into a car drunk and driving."

According to Hackney and Cormier (2000), counselors are responsible for providing the following information to clients at the outset of counseling:

1. A description of their role and qualifications as counselor
2. An explanation of the process of counseling and any particular procedures or approaches to be used, and their purpose
3. A description of any discomfort or risks that may evolve
4. A description of any reasonably expected benefits
5. A disclosure of other approaches or strategies that also may be useful
6. An offer to answer inquiries about counseling or procedures at any time
7. A statement that the client can withdraw consent and discontinue participation in a procedure or in therapy at any time

Psychotherapy continues to battle the mistaken notion that therapists have "magical" powers, that therapists are latter-day miracle workers. Much of the public must be educated regarding the realities of counseling and professionals need to help dispel erroneous thinking about counseling. "Therapists," says Schutz (1982), "should attempt to create reasonable expectations for the public about what psychotherapy can and cannot do" (p. 95).

What about associating with clients outside of the therapeutic setting? "Deep down in his mind," according to Freda Fromm-Reichmann (1950), "no patient wants a nonprofessional relationship with his therapist, regardless of the fact that he may express himself to the contrary" (p. 46). A relationship with a client outside of the therapeutic context will almost always complicate treatment (Borys & Pope, 1989). It leads to a tangled web of dual or multiple roles. To protect the welfare of clients, counselors must avoid dual relationships (Newman, 1993; Otero & O'Meara, 1991). Otherwise, he or she will run the risk of clouding objectivity and interfering with the therapeutic process. Dual relationships also increase the probability of sexual intimacies in psychotherapy so often publicized (Cornell, 1994; Pope, 1990; Williams, 1992).

CONFIDENTIALITY AND PRIVILEGED COMMUNICATION

A 15-year-old sat in the office of an inexperienced counselor. "Look, I need your help," he said. "Can I tell you a secret without you telling anyone else?" Sensing something serious and wanting the adolescent to open up, the new counselor agreed to keep quiet.

"My dad is a total jerk, and I can't handle it anymore. I got a ticket to California, and I'm gone, man. I want you to give me a week and then give my mom this." He handed over two folded sheets of white notebook paper, stapled shut.

The counselor tried to change the boy's mind or at least get him to talk with his father first. He offered to mediate the conversation, but, standing firm, the boy finally left unconvinced. Even though the counselor had agreed not to break the secret, she wondered if she shouldn't tell someone.

Problems of confidentiality are the most frequent source of ethical dilemmas for counselors (Pope & Vetter, 1992). **Confidentiality** can be defined as a relationship built on trust in which a client reveals private or secret information to a counselor with confidence it will not be passed on to anyone. Confidentiality assumes the counselor, "having grown powerful as a result of such knowledge, discloses the information to others only at the behest or with the consent of the [client]" (Dulchin & Segal, 1982, p. 13). This means that counselors do not talk to anyone about a client or even reveal that they are seeing a client without prior written permission from the client (Knapp & VandeCreek, 1987; VandeCreek & Jackson, 2000).

> Law is reason free from passion.
> —Aristotle

There is no justifiable excuse for inadvertent slips that reveal information shared in confidence. Even nondamaging information must be protected (Abeles, 1992; Kompf, 1993). It is unethical, for example, to show a client's IQ test results to a counseling center receptionist—even if they are the highest IQ scores you have ever seen. Gelso and Fretz (1992) state that "any information obtained in professional relationships is to be treated confidentially" (p. 56). Clients deserve to have their personal information protected by strict confidentiality. It frees clients from worrying over who might hear the private information they discuss with the therapist. Confidentiality protects clients from having confessional gossip or tidbits about themselves revealed. Pure confidentiality is a hallmark of professional counseling (Sheeley & Herlihy, 1986).

Confidentiality, however, does have limits (Denkowski & Denkowski, 1982; MacNair, 1992). Confidentiality is an ethical principle rather than a legal statute. Confidentiality, according to Siegel (1979), involves "professional ethics rather than any legalism and indicates an explicit promise or contract to reveal nothing about an individual except under conditions agreed to by the source or subject" (p. 251). Legally, the concept of confidentiality is known as *privileged communication*. It spells out the legal conditions for breaking confidence with a client (DeKraai & Sales, 1982; Herlihy & Sheeley, 1987). Shah (1969) defines privileged communication as "the legal right which exists by statute and which protects the client from having his confidences revealed publicly from the witness stand during legal proceedings without his permission" (p. 57). Lawyers, physicians, ministers, and psychologists are among the few professionals who have a legal right to claim privileged communication.

> You may be deceived if you trust too much, but you will live in torment if you don't trust enough.
> —Frank Crane

Ethical dilemmas, like the one at the beginning of this section, also arise because of a conflict between what is best for the client and what is best for other involved people. Blocher (2000) states that "when a counselor encourages a client to believe that a communication will be held in full and complete confidence, the only ethical ground for breaking that confidence is danger to human life" (p. 27). In other words, privileged communication does not hold up in cases where the counselor has reasonable cause to believe that the person is in such a psychological state as to be dangerous to himself (i.e., suicidal) or to the person or property of another. For example, health and mental health professionals have a duty to warn the sexual partners of clients with AIDS if the clients refuse to do so themselves (Cohen, 1990; Harding, Gray & Neal, 1993; Lamb, Clark, Drumheller, Frizzell, & Surrey, 1989). The next chapter will have much more to say about AIDS as a counseling issue.

In such cases, counselors have a "duty to warn" by disclosing information that can prevent a threatened danger (Gehring, 1982; Leslie, 1983). Berger (1982) concludes that a confidence should be broken when the client is a danger to himself or others, when the client is engaged in criminal actions, when the counselor is so ordered by the court, and when it is in the best interests of a child or an elder who is a victim of abuse.

3.2 Privilege and Public Peril: The Duty to Warn

In August 1969 Prosejit Poddar informed his counselor that he was planning to kill his girlfriend. Poddar was a voluntary outpatient at the Cowell Memorial Hospital on the Berkeley campus of University of California. The therapist later called the campus police and told them of this threat. He asked the campus police to observe Poddar and watch for danger signs that might require psychiatric hospitalization.

The campus officers did take Poddar into custody for questioning, but they later released him because he was "rational." Poddar's counselor followed up his call with a formal letter requesting the assistance of the chief of campus police. Later, the counselor's supervisor asked that the letter be returned, ordered that the letter and the therapist's case notes be destroyed, and asked that no further action be taken in the case. No warning was given, either to the intended victim or to her parents, of Tatiana's peril.

Two months later, on October 27, 1969, Poddar killed Tatiana Tarasoff. In what is now a landmark court case referred to as the Tarasoff decision, Tatiana Tarasoff's parents filed suit against the Board of Regents and employees of the university for failing to notify the intended victim of the threat. A lower court dismissed the suit, the parents appealed, and the California Supreme Court ruled in favor of the parents in 1976 and held that a failure to warn the intended victim was irresponsible.

This case resulted in the establishment of laws requiring psychotherapists to warn individuals when they become aware of intentions to harm: "We conclude that the public policy favoring protection of the confidential character of patient-psychotherapist communication must yield to the extent that exposure is essential to avert danger to others. The protection privilege ends where the public peril begins" (Beauchamp & Childress, 1983, p. 283).

Clients should be apprised of the limits of confidentiality at the outset of therapy. Counselors should also obtain client permission before tape recording a session or sharing information with a supervisor (McGuire, Graves, & Blau, 1985). Of course, supervisors, like counselors, are obligated to respect the confidentiality of client communication. "When a clear policy exists and is explained to the client before confidences are accepted, many ethical and professional problems can be avoided" (Blocher, 2000, p. 26).

WHEN IN DOUBT

Few things damage social dignity as much as physically stumbling over some unseen object. Missing a step is humiliating. But, assuming no one is hurt, it is always humorous to onlookers when the elegantly dressed stumble and fall. When a professional and proper musician, for example, steps onto a platform with music in hand, stumbles, and sends sheets of music into the air, it takes a good emcee to recover from the embarrassment and have the audience laughing with him instead of at him. Unfortunately, when qualified counselors stumble professionally, it is never a laughing matter. Misjudgment occurs when counselors do not use accessible resources for understanding and practicing the legal and ethical standards of counseling—consultation with other colleagues.

When in doubt, consult an experienced colleague. Legal and ethical considerations can be complex and confusing, so effective counselors regularly consult with other professionals on issues that are unclear (Sileo & Kopala, 1993; Taylor & Gazda, 1991). This can take the form of a brief phone call or be as extensive as bringing in a colleague to observe your sessions. Counselors can also obtain guidance by phone consultations with state and national counseling associations like the American Counseling Association or the American Psychological Association.

In addition to consulting with professional colleagues, competent counselors will also commonly make referrals to other counselors who can meet the needs of a particular client more effectively than themselves. MacDonald (2000) has compiled a list of situations likely to call for referral (based on Cormier & Cormier, 1997; Seligman, 1986). A referral may be necessary when the following situations arise:

> Doubt is the beginning, not the end, of wisdom.
> —George Iles

- Your client wishes to pursue matters that are contrary to your value system, to professional ethics, or to legal codes.
- You lack essential knowledge and/or skills for the best modes of treatment for each client.
- Personality differences between you and your client prevent working together effectively.
- Interpersonal connections with the client outside of counseling might create a conflict of interest (e.g., being asked to counsel a family member of an associate).
- You and your client are making little progress toward treatment goals and prospects for making greater progress are dim.

In addition, it is a good idea to refer a person for a thorough physical examination as part of the counseling evaluation (Cavanagh, 1990). It can also be helpful to enlist the aid of a minister, priest, or rabbi, especially when the person communicates a need for spiritual comfort during crisis interventions. Referral to a counselor of the same sex may help a client feel more comfortable. A woman who has been sexually abused may make more progress, for example, with a female therapist. Referral can be appropriate and helpful in a number of situations, both for ancillary work with the primary counselor and for a final referral when the counselor is doubtful about his or her ability to meet the needs of the client effectively.

ETHICAL PRINCIPLES AND GUIDELINES

Determining what is or is not ethical behavior is often difficult for the experienced practitioner as well as the novice counselor. Thankfully, the helping professions offer several guidelines and codes of ethical behavior to lead practioners through perplexing ethical dilemmas. These codes include the *Code of Ethics* published in 1989 by the National Board of Certified Counselors (NBCC); the *AAMFT Code of Ethics* (1991) adopted by the American Association for Marriage and Family Therapists; *Code of Ethics for Mental Health Counselors* adopted in 1987 by the American Mental Health Counselors Association (AMHCA) and supported by the National Academy for Certified Clinical Mental Health Counselors (NACCMHC); *Ethical Guidelines for Group Counselors* approved in 1989 by the Association for Specialists in Group Work (ASGW); *Ethical Principles of Psychologists and Code of Conduct Standards* adopted in 1988 by the American Counseling Association; and *Ethical Standards for School Counselors* adopted in 1984 by the American School Counselors Association (ASCA). Not only have these national professional groups provided ethical guidelines for their members, but many state counseling and psychological associations have also adopted their own versions of ethical standards.

Perhaps the most widely used guidelines for ethical behavior come from the American Psychological Association (1992) and the American Counseling Association (1995). These documents should be consulted by any practitioner in doubt about specific ethical questions. Both sets of guidelines are reprinted in the study guide that accompanies this book.

> Where law ends,
> tyranny begins.
> —William Pitt

SUMMARY

Unlike many in other professions, counselors are particularly vulnerable to legal troubles and ethical dilemmas. For this reason it is essential that students of counseling become familiar with the basic legal and ethical issues pertaining to the field. The bedrock of legal and ethical standing in counseling is virtue—a disposition to do what is morally right. A sound counseling practice is built on knowing the law and understanding client rights. Counselors have an obligation to their clients and to their profession to be accountable for the quality of the professional services they offer.

The essential element in a therapeutic setting is trust. It forms the basis of the client-counselor relationship. As trust is diminished so is healing. To build trust the counselor is responsible for providing to clients a description of his or her role as a counselor, an explanation of the process of counseling, a description of any risks that may evolve, and other useful information.

Problems of confidentiality are the most frequent source of ethical dilemmas for counselors. In a relationship built on trust, a client reveals private or secret information to a counselor with confidence it will not be passed on to anyone. Confidentiality, however, does have limits. It is an ethical principle rather than a legal statute. Legally, it is known as privileged communication.

The helping professions offer several codes of ethical behavior, and it is imperative that counselors become familiar with them.

Key Terms

Confidentiality   The counselor's obligation not to reveal private or secret information shared by a client; legally, the concept of confidentiality is known as *privileged communication.*

Informed consent   Telling clients what can be expected during treatment, how long it may take, and how much it will probably cost; this communication forms the basis of a trusting relationship between counselor and client.

References

Abeles, N. (1992). An ethical dilemma: Disclosure of test items to parents. *Psychotherapy in Private Practice, 10,* 23–26.

American Association for Counseling and Development. (1981). *Ethical standards.* Alexandria, VA: Author.

American Association for Marriage and Family Therapy. (1991). *AAMFT code of ethics.* Washington, DC: Author.

American Counseling Association. (1988). *Ethical standards.* Alexandria, VA: Author.

American Counseling Association. (1992). *ACA legal series* (T. Remley, Ed.). Alexandria, VA: Author.

American Mental Health Counselors Association. (1987). *Code of ethics for mental health counselors.* Alexandria, VA: Author.

American Psychological Association. (1992). Ethical principles of psychologists. *American Psychologist, 47,* 1597–1611.

American School Counselors Association. (1984). *Ethical standards for school counselors.* Washington, DC: Author.

Association for Specialists in Group Work. (1989). *Ethical guidelines for group counselors.* Alexandria, VA: Author.

Bates, C. M., & Brodesky, A. M. (1989). *Sex in the therapy hour: A case of professional incest.* New York: Guilford Press.

Beauchamp, T. L., & Childress, J. S. (1983). *Principles of biomedical ethics* (2nd ed.). New York: Oxford University Press.

Berger, M. (1982). Ethics and the therapeutic relationship. In M. Rosenbaum (Ed.), *Ethics and values in psychotherapy* (67–95). New York: Free Press.

Bergin, A. E. (1963). The effects of psychotherapy: Negative effects revisited. *Journal of Counseling Psychology, 10,* 244–249.

Blocher, D. H. (2000). *Counseling: A developmental approach*. New York: John Wiley and Sons.

Borys, D. S., & Pope, K. S. (1989). Dual relationships between therapist and client: A national study of psychologists, psychiatrists, and social workers. *Professional Psychology: Research and Practice, 20*, 283–293.

Cavanaugh, M. E. (1990). The counseling experience. Prospect Heights, IL: Waveland Press, Inc.

Cavanaugh, M. E. (2001). *The counseling experience*. Prospect Heights, IL: Waveland Press.

Cohen, E. D. (1990). Confidentiality, counseling, and clients who have AIDS: Ethical foundations of a model rule. *Journal of Counseling and Development, 68*, 282–286.

Cohen, K. (1992). Some legal issues in counseling and psychotherapy. *British Journal of Guidance and Counseling, 20*, 10–26.

Cooper, G. F. (1992). Ethical issues in counseling and psychotherapy: The background. *British Journal of Guidance and Counseling, 20*, 1–9.

Corey, G., Corey, M. S., & Callanan, P. (1997). *Issues and ethics in the helping professions* (5th ed.). Pacific Grove, CA: Brooks/Cole.

Cormier, W. H., & Cormier, L. S. (1997). *Interviewing strategies for helpers* (4th ed.). Monterey, CA: Brooks/Cole.

Cornell, W. F. (1994). Dual relationships in transactional analysis: Training, supervision, and therapy. *Transactional Analysis Journal, 24*, 21–30.

DeForest, C., & Stone, G. L. (1980). Effects of sex and intimacy level on self-disclosure. *Journal of Counseling Psychology, 27*, 93–96.

DeKraai, M. B., & Sales, B. D. (1982). Confidential communications of psychotherapists. *Psychotherapy, 21*, 293–318.

Denkowski, K. M., & Denkowski, G. C. (1982). Client-counselor confidentiality: An update of rationale, legal status, and implications. *Personnel and Guidance Journal, 60*, 371–375.

Dulchin, J., & Segal, A. J. (1982). The ambiguity of confidentiality in a psychoanalytic institute. *Psychiatry, 45*, 13–25.

Fromm-Reichmann (1950). Principles of intensive psychotherapy. Chicago: University of Chicago Press.

Furrow, B. R. (1980). *Malpractice in psychotherapy*. Lexington, MA: Lexington Books.

Gehring, D. D. (1982). The counselor's "duty to warn." *Personnel and Guidance Journal, 61*, 208–210.

Gelso, C. J., & Fretz, B. R. (1992). *Counseling psychology*. Fort Worth, TX: Harcourt Brace Jovanovich.

Green, S. W. (1993). Long-term psychotherapy and informed consent. *Hospital and Community Psychiatry, 44*, 1005–1006.

Hackney, H., & Cormier, L. S. (2000). *The professional counselor: A process guide to helping* (4th ed.). Englewood Cliffs, NJ: Prentice Hall.

Harding, A. K., Gray, L. A., & Neal, N. (1993). Confidentiality limits with clients who have HIV: A review of ethical and legal guidelines and professional policies. *Journal of Counseling and Development, 71*, 297–305.

Hatton, C. L., Balente, S. M., & Rink, A. (1977). *Suicide: Assessment and intervention*. Englewood Cliffs, NJ: Prentice Hall.

Hendrick, S. S. (1981). Self-disclosure and marital satisfaction. *Journal of Personality and Social Psychology, 40*, 1150–1159.

Herlihy, B., & Sheeley, B. L. (1987). Privileged communication in selected helping professions: A comparison among statutes. *Journal of Counseling and Development, 65*, 479–483.

Jobes, D. A., & Berman, A. L. (1993). Suicide and malpractice liability: Assessing and revising policies, procedures, and practice in outpatient settings. *Professional Psychology: Research & Practice, 24*, 91–99.

Jordan, A. E., & Meara, N. M. (1990). Ethics and the professional practice of psychologists: The role of virtues and principles. *Professional Psychology Research and Practice, 21*, 107–114.

Knapp, S., & VandeCreek, L. (1987). *Privileged communications in the mental health professions*. New York: Van Nostrand Reinhold.

Kompf, M. (1993). Ethical considerations in teacher disclosure: Persons and methods. *Teaching & Teacher Education, 9*, 519–528.

Lamb, D. H., Clark, C., Drumheller, P., Frizzell, K., & Surrey, L. (1989). Applying Tarasoff to AIDS-related psychotherapy issues. *Professional Psychology: Research and Practice, 20*, 37–43.

Leslie, R. (1983). Tarasoff decision extended. *California Therapist,* November/December 6.

MacDonald, D. (2000). *Making effective referrals.* Unpublished manuscript.

MacNair, R. R. (1992). Ethical dilemmas of child abuse reporting: Implications for mental health counselors. *Journal of Mental Health Counseling, 14,* 127–136.

McGuire, J. M., Graves, S., & Blau, B. (1985). Depth of self-disclosure as a function of assured confidentiality and videotape recording. *Journal of Counseling and Development, 64,* 259–263.

National Board of Certified Counselors. (1989). *Code of ethics.* Alexandria, VA: Author.

Newman, J. L. (1993). Ethical issues in consultation. *Journal of Counseling and Development, 72,* 148–156.

Otero, Z. T. M., & O'Meara, D. P. (1991). Mental injury litigation: The roles of the lawyer and the psychologist. *Medical Psychotherapy: An International Journal, 4,* 17–26.

Pope, K. S. (1988). How clients are harmed by sexual contact with mental health professionals: The syndrome and its prevalence. *Journal of Counseling and Development, 67,* 222–226.

Pope, K. S. (1990). Therapist-patient sexual involvement: A review of the research. *Clinical Psychology Review, 10,* 477–490.

Pope, K. S., & Vasquez, M. J. T. (1998). *Ethics in psychotherapy and counseling: A practical guide for psychologists* (2nd ed.). San Francisco: Jossey-Bass.

Pope, K. S., & Vetter, V. A. (1992). Ethical dilemmas encountered by members of the American Psychological Association. *American Psychologist, 47,* 397–411.

Remley, T., & Herlihy, B. (2000). *Ethical, legal and professional issues in counseling.* New York: Prentice Hall.

Rutter, P. (1989). *Sex in the forbidden zone: When men in power—therapists, doctors, clergy, teachers and others—betray women's trust.* Los Angeles: Jeremy P. Tarcher.

Schutz, B. (1982). *Legal liability in psychotherapy.* San Francisco: Jossey-Bass.

Seligman, L. (1986). *Diagnosis and treatment planning in counseling.* New York: Human Sciences.

Shah, S. (1969). Privileged communications, confidentiality, and privacy: Privileged communications. *Professional Psychology, 1,* 56–69.

Sheeley, V. L., & Herlihy, B. (1986). The ethics of confidentiality and privileged communication. *Journal of Counseling and Human Service Professions, 1,* 141–148.

Siegel, M. (1979). Privacy, ethics and confidentiality. *Professional Psychology, 10,* 249–258.

Sileo, F. J., & Kopala, M. (1993). An A-B-C-D-E worksheet for promoting beneficence when considering ethical issues. *Counseling & Values, 37,* 89–95.

Taylor, R. E., & Gazda, G. M. (1991). Concurrent individual and group therapy: The ethical issues. *Journal of Group Psychotherapy, Psychodrama & Sociometry, 44,* 51–59.

VandeCreek, L., & Jackson, T. (2000). *Innovations in clinical practice.* New York: Professional Resources.

Williams, M. H. (1992). Exploitation and inference: Mapping the damage from therapist-patient sexual involvement. *American Psychologist, 47,* 412–421.

Wilson, L. S., & Ranft, V. A. (1993). The state of ethical training for counseling psychology doctoral students. *Counseling Psychologist, 21,* 445–456.

Wrenn, C. G. (1962). The culturally encapsulated counselor. *Harvard Educational Review, 32,* 444–449.

It is change, continuing change, inevitable change, that is the dominant factor in society today. No sensible decision can be made any longer without taking into account not only the world as it is, but the world as it will be. —Isaac Asimov

Contemporary Issues in Counseling

CHAPTER 4

CHAPTER OUTLINE

Multicultural Counseling
Gender Differences
The Differently Abled
Religious Clients
AIDS
Older Adults
Summary
Key Terms
References

Professional counseling is forever changing as the emphasis on certain concerns within society shifts. For example, changing gender roles, innovations in media and technology, changing insurance policies, poverty, AIDS, homelessness, religious clients, and aging are among the concerns that will and are changing the face of psychotherapy (Hackney & Wrenn, 1990). This chapter explores some of the most current issues in the realm of professional counseling: multicultural issues, gender differences, the physically challenged, AIDS, and counseling of older adults. To be clear, this is an introduction, a brief overview, of these issues, not an in-depth analysis.

MULTICULTURAL COUNSELING

Culture consists of everything people have learned to do, believe, value and enjoy in their collective lives. According to Sue and Sue (1999), it is the totality of ideals, beliefs, skills, tools, customs, and institutions into which each member of society is born. Contemporary counselors have come to understand that a client's culture must be carefully understood and considered if counseling is to be effective (Atkinson, Morten, & Sue, 1997; Devore & Schlesinger, 1991; Goldrick, Pearce, & Giordano, 1996; Lee & Richardson, 1996; Sue & Sue, 1999). Racial and ethnic factors, for example, can prevent counselors from establishing a therapeutic relationship with clients from different cultures (Carter, 1991; Ridley, 1995). "Ethnicity," according to Aponte (1990, p. 3) "can be part of the solution or the problem for the client."

> In times of change, the learners inherit the earth while the learned find themselves beautifully equipped to live in a world that no longer exists.
>
> —Eric Hoffer

Research indicates that ethnic-minority clients often do not take advantage of counseling services, and when they do, they frequently terminate the therapeutic relationship prematurely. For example, the termination rate for Asian Americans, African Americans, Hispanics, and Native Americans has been found to be 50 percent after only the first counseling session. The termination rate for Anglo clients in the same situation is 30 percent (Sue, 1977; Sue, Fujino, Hu, Takeuchi, & Zane, 1991; Sue & McKinney, 1975; Sue, McKinney, Allen, & Hall, 1974). Clients of counselors who have received training in cross-cultural counseling, however, are less likely to terminate from therapy prematurely (Lopez, Lopez, & Fong, 1991; Wade & Bernstein, 1991).

Cross-cultural counseling has been defined as a relationship in which the client and counselor do not share the same cultural background, values, norms, roles, lifestyle, and/or methods of communicating (Ponterotto, Casas, Suzuki, & Alexander, 2001). To be a culturally skilled counselor, Sue and Sue (1999, pp. 167–168) have identified the following characteristics they see as vital:

1. Culturally skilled counselors have moved from being culturally unaware to being aware and sensitive to their own cultural heritage and to valuing and respecting differences. Rather that being "ethnocentric" and believing in the superiority of one's own cultural heritage, there is acceptance and respect for cultural differences.
2. Culturally skilled counselors are aware of their own values and biases and how they may affect clients of different cultures. These counselors try not to hold preconceived notions about people of other cultures. They actively avoid unwarranted labeling and stereotyping.
3. Culturally skilled counselors are comfortable with differences that exist between themselves and their clients in terms of race and beliefs. They do not see differences as being deviant. Every person, regardless of culture or differences, is equally human.
4. Culturally skilled counselors are sensitive to circumstances that may dictate referral of a client to a member of his or her own culture or to another counselor in general. They are not threatened by the prospect of referring

a client to someone else because of their own limitations in cross-cultural counseling.

5. Culturally skilled counselors acknowledge their own prejudicial attitudes, beliefs, and feelings. They do not deny that they have been socialized in a racist society and they accept responsibility for their own racism.

Certain factors present themselves in cross-cultural counseling that are not operative in other counseling relationships. Counselors, regardless of ethnic background, who plan to work with those whose cultural heritage is different from their own must take seriously these factors and learn to deal with them effectively (Pedersen, 1994; Sue, Arredondo, & McDavis, 1992).

GENDER DIFFERENCES

Just as race or national origin can be a hurdle for counselors in helping relationships, so can gender differences. A feminist counseling approach has arisen precisely because male therapists often do not take into account women's issues, and it has made the counseling profession painfully aware of sexist notions applied to therapy (Worell, 2001). Important differences in the therapeutic treatment received by men and women are often overlooked. For instance, women are more likely than men to seek professional counseling (Gove & Tudor, 1973; Williams, 1987; Worell & Remer, 1992). In part, this may reflect a higher rate of mental illness among women for some disorders (e.g., abuse survival, depression, severe anxieties, phobias, and eating disorders), but it is also likely that women are more willing than men to admit that they have psychological problems and that they need help in solving them (Hubbard, 1992). In fact, some studies indicate that women engage in more open and personal self-disclosure than do men; and, of course, this is to their advantage (Antill & Cotton, 1986; DeForest & Stone, 1980; Good, Gilbert, & Scher, 1990; Greenblatt, Hasenauer, & Freimuth, 1980; Hendrick, 1981; O'Brien, 1988).

> A little philosophy inclineth men's minds to atheism, but depth in philosophy bringeth men's minds about to religion.
>
> —Francis Bacon

The counseling profession has only recently begun to consider the importance of gender differences. Most counseling theories were developed by males and most therapists are male. As a result women in therapy may be encouraged, directly or indirectly, to adopt traditional, male-oriented views. For example, there may be a tendency for male therapists to encourage women to adapt, adjust, or conform to their surroundings passively (Broverman, Broverman, Clarkson, Rosenkrantz, & Vogel, 1970; Hare-Mustin, 1983; Schlossberg & Pietrofesa, 1973). This inhibition of activity and the resulting suppression of anger, in fact, may predispose women to depression more than men. Inadvertently or not, counseling has fostered a societal context that put women at increased risk for emotional distress.

Male therapists are often not sufficiently sensitive to how much some of the stress women experience derives from the world in which they live (APA, 1975; Asher, 1975; Scher & Good, 1990). Specific life experiences of women, such as domestic abuse, sexual harassment, menstrual cycle, and menopause, have not been incorporated into mental health theory or treatment. In response to these concerns, gender-sensitive therapists have attempted to help their clients become more aware of the extent to which their problems derive from external controls, female physiology, and inappropriate sex roles. They help them become more conscious of their own needs and goals and help them avoid passively accepting the status quo by developing a sense of pride in their womanhood (Williams, 1987).

The American Psychological Association (1978) provides several guidelines regarding the treatment of women in psychotherapy. For example, therapy should be free of constrictions based on gender-defined roles, and the options explored between client and practitioner should be free of sex role stereotypes. Therapists should recognize the reality, variety, and implications of sex-discriminatory practices in society and should facilitate client examination of options in dealing with such practices. They should not only be knowledgeable about current empirical findings on sex roles, sexism, and individual differences resulting from the client's gender-defined identity, their theoretical concepts should be free of sex bias and sex role stereotypes. A therapist's language should be free of derogatory labels involving women. If authoritarian processes are employed as a technique, the therapy should not have the effect of maintaining or reinforcing stereotypic dependency of women. The therapist whose female client is subjected to violence in the form of physical abuse or rape should recognize and acknowledge that the client is the victim of a crime (Worell, 2001).

THE DIFFERENTLY ABLED

Persons with disabilities face issues with which good counselors must be prepared to deal. Like clients of different cultures, persons with disabilities often feel singled out and isolated from the general population. The basic skills and procedures that form the core of any helping relationship are integral to counseling these persons and, from this perspective, they are no different from the general population (Cristiani & Sommers, 1978; Hosie, 1979; Vandergriff & Hosie, 1979). However, from a psychosocial point of view a number of factors can make these clients exceptional (Perlman & Kirk, 1991).

Differently abled people are challenged by at least three significant hurdles: (1) the physical condition that renders them exceptional in the first place, (2) the unreal perception that many people have of them because of their disability, and (3) the impact of these interpersonal responses—their own physical condition and the public perception of them—on their own self-perceptions. These combined factors expose disabled people to stressors most of the general population cannot comprehend (Rusalem & Cohen, 1975; Van Hasseld, Strain, & Hersen, 1988).

> It is a high privilege to be able to share the experiences of so many different people; counselors are in an enviable role because they are able to interact with a very wide range of unique individuals.
>
> —Susan K. Gilmore

Counselors are typically unaware of the complexity of being physically challenged. They are too often ill-prepared to provide effective services for the physically challenged because they carry biases, prejudices, and values regarding handicapping conditions (Filer, 1982; Nathanson, 1979).

Counselors, therefore, should not only be familiar with the psychosocial needs of differently abled individuals, they should be informed of specific counseling strategies to deal with such special needs as self-concept, body image, frustration, anger, dependency, and motivation (McDowell, Coven, & Eash, 1979).

Not every counselor may be able to work with the physically or developmentally challenged client. State and federal regulations are constantly changing and those therapists who specialize in this population are most apt to be current in the field and thus better prepared to do this work. However, every counselor in training should be aware of some basic guidelines and factors in working with physically challenged clients (Hosie, 1979). For example, counselors must be aware of the rights of handicapped children and their parents as well as the skills necessary to advise parents on how to exercise those rights. The growth and development process, characteristics, and impediments of the disabled and the skills necessary to relate this knowledge to developmental learning tasks and strategies are also important information. Of course the characteristics and development of the learning disabled and the skills necessary to diagnose why the individual is failing tasks cannot be overlooked. Nor can sensory impairments, speech disorders, and communication deficits, along with their effect on diagnosis and remediation, and the skills necessary to overcome or lessen their effect in learning and counseling settings.

Contemporary counselors must understand the characteristics of differently abled persons related to employment skills, training programs, and potential occupational and educational opportunities and the skills necessary to assist these clients in career decision making and development (Parrott & Parrott, 1995). This is accomplished, in part, by knowing the ability, learning rates, and modes of learning of the disabled and the skills necessary to use these factors in recommending educational placements and environments.

RELIGIOUS CLIENTS

A recent poll indicates that two thirds of the population of the United States consider religion to be "important" or "very important" in their lives. People seeking help from psychotherapists are increasingly presenting problems that involve spiritual and religious issues and overtones (Butler, 1990; *Religion in America*, 1985; Miller, 1999; Richards & Bergin, 1997, 2000; Shafranske, 1996). As a result, counselors are being confronted with calls for help in areas that were formerly the primary domain of the clergy. The challenge is how to handle the spiritual and religious issues in a way that assures ethical integrity for the therapist as well as the client.

"The possibility for greater empathy with religious clients," writes Bergin (1991, p. 396), "is suggested by the substantial but professionally unexpressed religiosity that exists among therapists." Bergin is talking about the unexpected personal investment psychotherapists have in religion. Almost half of the professional counseling community agrees with the statement, "My whole approach to life is based on my religion," and almost 80 percent agree with the statement, "I try hard to live by my religious beliefs."

Given the value that both clients and therapists place on spirituality and religion, it is surprising that these issues are only recently showing up in the counseling room as major themes of concern. For most of counseling's history, religion has been seen as irrational and equivalent to emotional disturbance (Ellis, 1980; Freud, 1927). Gladding (1999), however, points to three events that brought spirituality more to the forefront of professional contemporary counseling. First, spiritual factors are incorporated in Alcoholics Anonymous and other 12-step programs. Second, M. Scott Peck's book, *The Road Less Traveled*, bridged the gap between traditional psychotherapy and religion. The final event Gladding cites for the increase in spiritual awareness is the series of interviews Bill Moyers had with Joseph Campbell, who "gave respectability to the spiritual-psychological quest itself, even in modern-times" (Butler, 1990, p. 30). Even Albert Ellis has recently been more open to a religious approach to his Rational Emotive Behavior Therapy (see Ellis, 2000).

> Wisdom lies neither in fixity nor in change, but in the dialectic between the two.
>
> —Octavio Paz

Perhaps another contributing factor has been the growing success of professional organizations devoted to religion and psychology. The Association for Religious and Value Issues in Counseling (ARVIC), a division within the American Counseling Association, is one of the fastest growing divisions. The same is true for Psychology of Religion, Division 36 of the American Psychological Association. In 1992, the American Association of Christian Counselors (AACC) began with less than 300 members; its membership in 2001 is more than 40,000. Professionals associated with organizations like these are providing the counseling community with descriptive evidence of the usefulness of spiritual dimensions for enhancing change (e.g., Bradford & Spero, 1990; Collins, 1993; Malony, 1988; Stern, 1985; Worthington, 1989). In addition, several professional schools of psychology are fully accredited by APA and teaching students to integrate their faith seriously with the practice of psychotherapy. The Fuller Graduate School of Psychology in Pasadena, California, and the Rosemead Graduate School of Psychology at Biola University in La Mirada, California, are two of the most visible and influential.

Regardless of the causes, the issue of religiosity in the contemporary counseling office cannot be ignored. The religious client must be taken seriously and, as Richards (1991) cautions, counselors need to avoid stereotypical assumptions that religiously devout clients are more emotionally disturbed than other clients. Spiritual and religious issues are expressed in beliefs and behavior. As part of a person's total functioning, religious feelings and values should be considered as part of therapeutic treatment for religious and spiritual persons (Browning, Jobe, & Evison, 1990; Richards & Bergin, 1997, 2000; Tan, 1996). Religiously oriented counseling and psychotherapy should be conducted in an ethically sensitive, professionally competent and clinically helpful way (Tan, 1994, 1999).

AIDS

No disease in modern times has received more attention or produced such concern as AIDS (acquired immunodeficiency syndrome). It is a disease that results in the body's immune system breaking down and is caused by the human immunodeficiency virus (HIV). People infected with HIV may appear completely healthy, but they may also develop many health problems that signal the onset of AIDS, including extreme weight loss, severe pneumonia, a form of cancer (Kaposi's sarcoma), and damage to the nervous system. The AIDS epidemic constitutes a worldwide public health threat whose magnitude continues to grow. In some areas of the United States, it is the number one cause of premature death (Hearst & Hulley, 1988 Joint United Nations Programme on HIV/AIDS, 2001) and it is nearly impossible for contemporary counselors to avoid clients whose lives have not been touched, directly or indirectly, by AIDS (Newman, Durrance, & Fell, 1993).

While thousands of researchers are involved in an unprecedented, worldwide effort to understand and ultimately cure and/or prevent AIDS, a committee of knowledgeable scientists commissioned by the National Research Council has predicted that the AIDS virus will be around for many years (Byrne, 1989). Today's counselors, therefore, cannot afford to neglect understanding this disease and its relationship to counseling. Counselors must be prepared with practical information about when, where, and why a client should obtain testing for HIV. The disease, of course, restricts personal freedom, subdues pleasure with fear, and calls for discipline of desires. As a result, counselors will face some belligerence, from time to time, when dealing with clients who are filled with denial and expressing anger and confusion toward this "inconvenient disease" (Albers, 1990). However, if today's counselors do not break through this hardened emotional shell, these clients will suffer and others may lose their lives.

> You could not step twice into the same rivers; for other waters are ever flowing on to you.
>
> —Heraclitus

On the other hand, some clients will be overly concerned about whether they should be tested for AIDS. Sexual contacts before 1980, casual contact with possible AIDS patients, excessive fears of HIV in the environment, and many other irrational reasons for asking for testing are often given. Counselors should always listen to these concerns and acknowledge them as real, but not everyone need be recommended for medical consultation and HIV testing. Once educated about the virus, if there is unrealistic concern that will not be dissuaded with education, or if there is need for absolute confirmation with a negative test, counselors should be firm in suggesting the patient have his or her blood tested. The fear of knowing one's HIV status is greatly outweighed by the benefits of testing, no matter what the result is, and blood testing for HIV is now very common and inexpensive, less than $50 per test.

Anticipatory counseling can benefit clients who are at risk for HIV and about to be tested. Dealing with their present emotional state, the fears, guilts, anxieties, and relationships helps them sort through these confused reactions to their devastating predicament. Personal and psychological ramifications of both a negative test and the dreaded positive test can be explored. When a patient learns he or she is HIV positive, group counseling has proven to be quite effective as the disease progresses (Sorenson, London, Heitzmann, & Gibson, 1994). Participants in one program, for example, have six sessions, each focusing on one right that is felt necessary by dying people: to be in control, to reminisce, to laugh, to feel connected to a family, to have a sense of purpose, and to feel religious or spiritual (Smith, 1994).

Of course, many clients also need counseling for staying free from AIDS. Often a crisis fear of HIV will bring a client to counseling, and education as well as support is needed to keep the client from making the same, risky mistakes again and again. Counselors today must also be prepared to counsel the families of AIDS patients. In addition to the emotional support families can provide clients, they are also the most important source of prevention of AIDS. Families, for example, are becoming involved in educational programs designed to equip young people from getting involved in high-risk behavior, and the counselor can enlist their help in these efforts (Beckerman, 1994).

Another important consideration in AIDS counseling is confidentiality. When a client infected with HIV is sexually irresponsible, threatening others with infection, counselors are placed in a dilemma of preserving the right of con-

4.1 | Facts on AIDS: Acquired Immune Deficiency Syndrome

On June 5, 1981, the U.S. Centers for Disease Control issued a brief report describing five gay men in Los Angeles with a rare form of pneumonia; in time, this pneumonia was determined to be one symptom of AIDS. Today, more than 250,000 Americans have died from AIDS, and the disease has spread to more than 130 countries and has resulted in a global total of more than 1.5 million cases. Here are some of the frequently asked questions about AIDS.

What does HIV-positive mean?

Being HIV-positive means that one has been exposed to HIV (human immunodeficiency virus) but may actually be symptom-free. After initial exposure, the virus may lie dormant for an average of seven to eight years before being reactivated. Once active, the virus progressively destroys the immune system, making the patient vulnerable to life-threatening infections and diseases. Once the symptoms of AIDS are diagnosed, a person has an average life expectancy of about one year.

What are the symptoms of AIDS?

The symptoms vary with the types of infections that inflict a person with AIDS, but commonly include fevers, night sweats, weight loss, loss of appetite, fatigue, swollen lymph nodes, diarrhea, atypical bruising or bleeding, skin rashes, headache, chronic cough, and a whitish coating on the tongue or throat.

How is AIDS transmitted?

The HIV virus survives best in blood tissues and some bodily fluids, such as semen and vaginal fluids. Thus, AIDS is transmitted through sexual contact; by sharing fidentiality of the client or taking action to protect unsuspecting sexual partners from potential harm. The issue is never clear-cut, but measures of action must be taken by the competent counselor to assure that the HIV virus is not spread to unsuspecting persons (Erickson, 1993; Friedman & Hughes, 1994).

In summary, dispelling the myths about this deadly disease becomes the job of every contemporary counselor. A great deal of anxiety in some clients can be relieved simply with accurate information about AIDS. Magazines, tabloids, and broadcasts, to say nothing of the person on the street, add to the general rumor mill, creating hundreds of pieces of misinformation about this disease (Trezza, 1994). Fears create rumors that foster ignorance that create more fear. Even though the disease is dangerous, people's perceptions of their personal risk are often blown out of proportion, and counselors can ease this anxiety with factual information (Batchelor, 1988).

needles for drugs, tattooing, or body piercing; by having had a blood transfusion before 1985 (when a test was developed to detect the HIV virus); or from an infected mother to her unborn child. The most common age group for full-blown AIDS is 20–39 years. Most of these people were infected with the virus several years before they became sick.

How can HIV infection be prevented?

There are two primary areas for protecting oneself against AIDS. First, one should steer clear of injecting drugs since AIDS is commonly spread by sharing needles. Second, because AIDS can be spread through sexual contact, the surest way to avoid it is to abstain from sex. For the noncelibate, a monogamous relationship with a person whose HIV status is negative is the only other sure way of protection. Using latex condoms can decrease the chances of contracting AIDS, but condoms are not guaranteed protection from the disease—they simply decrease the chances.

What is the treatment for AIDS?

At the end of 2001, an estimated 40 million people globally were living with HIV. In many parts of the developing world, the majority of new infections occured in young adults, with young women especially vulnerable. About one-third of those currently living with HIV/AIDS are aged 15–24. Most of them do not know they carry the virus. Many millions more know nothing or too little about HIV to protect themselves against it.

As of this writing, there is no cure for AIDS. Several drugs, such as AZT, appear to slow the progression of AIDS and extend patients' lives.

OLDER ADULTS

The population of the United States is becoming increasingly elderly. In 1994, about one in eight Americans were elderly; by 2030, about one in five will be elderly. (U.S. Census Bureau, 2002). For the most part, this change is due to a declining birth rate accompanied by an increase in life expectancy. In 1900 the average life expectancy was about 48 years. Today more than half of the U.S. population is more than 50 years old, and 44 percent of older persons are more than 75. The American Association of Retired Persons (AARP) currently has a membership of more than 27 million persons. While it was originally formed to promote life insurance and other group benefits, AARP has developed into a powerful political force (Hess, 1991). Inspite of this impressive statistical growth among the aged—the "graying of America," as it is called—professional counselors have yet to devote adequate attention to this overlooked segment in society (Butler & Lewis, 1998; Myers, 1989; Myers, 1990).

> Among all my patients in the second half of life—that is to say, over thirty-five, there has not been one whose problem in the last resort was not that of finding a religious outlook on life. It is safe to say that every one of them fell ill because he had lost that which the living religions of every age have given to their followers and none of them has been really healed who did not regain his religious outlook.
>
> —Carl Gustave Jung

The therapeutic treatment of problems associated with aging starts with an understanding of this segment in the life span. Well-known developmental psychologist Erik Erikson has identified the primary developmental task of older persons as "integrity vs. despair." The positive resolution of this task results in wisdom, which Erikson defines as "informed and detached concern with life itself in the face of death itself" (Erikson, 1987). The negative counterpart of wisdom is despair and disdain, which is basically a bitter rejection of one's place in life, a rejection of the self as finished and helpless. It is in this despair that counseling can help lift older adults and help them adjust to life's losses and changes.

The transitions and role losses in old age greatly affect the vulnerability of the elderly adult. Typical transitional difficulties include relocation, employers' ageist attitudes toward older workers, terminal illness, sexuality, widowhood, grief, loneliness, depression, isolation, and chronic health problems (Glass & Grant, 1983; Lombana, 1976; Simonton, 1990).

The American pioneer in geriatric counseling was Lillien J. Martin. In 1929 she founded the San Francisco Old Age Counseling Center. For the next 15 years she developed her own techniques. The Martin method involved a series of structured interviews emphasizing a directive approach of specific suggestions.

> For everything there is a season, a time for every matter.
>
> —Ecclesiastes 3:13

Although the Martin clinic appeared to be successful, her influence in geriatrics never extended to the mainstream of social work or psychotherapy. Today, however, that is changing. The contemporary counseling profession is being equipped to cope with a wide range of elderly struggles. Many of the problems associated with aging can be

4.2 | Consumer Watch: I'm Okay, You're Online

Diana is juggling the demands of managing a small home business and caring for two young children. Francesca and her husband are dealing with infertility. Jim is a widower. It's hard to imagine three situations more different, and yet Diana, Francesca, and Jim have all sought out a similar source of advice, encouragement, and information: online support groups. Throughout all the major online services and the Internet, informal communities are developing among people with common questions and problems—from health-related concerns, such as a personal illness or a sick friend or family member, to questions about parenting, relationships, and employment problems.

Okay, the cynic in you is probably saying, "That sounds way too touchy-feely for me." But don't write off this new form of help too quickly. Hundreds of people who would never dream of baring their souls to a bunch of strangers face-to-face are doing just that online.

"I feel like I can say more online than I ever would in person," says Francesca, who runs an online support forum for couples dealing with infertility. "It's harder to open up to someone when you're looking them in the eyes," she adds. Francesca and her husband log on together to get information about new treatments, catch up with friends they've made online, and share their thoughts, concerns, and questions with other forum members.

The number and variety of support groups is staggering. America Online, CompuServe, Prodigy, and The Microsoft Network all have dozens of high-traffic groups covering a diverse range of topics. One such area is the Better Health and Medical Network on AOL, founded by Elin Silveous in 1993. About a year earlier, Silveous was diagnosed with multiple sclerosis and logged on to all the online services to research her condition. All she found was a smattering of information that was often difficult for a layperson to understand. Support groups were virtually nonexistent at that time. Figuring there were many people in the same boat, Silveous decided to start an online health forum. Her goal? To provide consumers with a supportive environment where they could get up-to-date, easy-to-understand information. The forum now boasts 50 forums, covering both common and obscure health concerns. It logs roughly 1.7 million new entries each month.

Information Seekers

"When a consumer comes in to one of the [health-related] forums, it's usually because either they or a loved one has been diagnosed with a condition," explains Silveous. "They're confused, often scared, even angry, and looking for information." That's where the message boards come in. "They learn they aren't alone. They post a message, share their situation, and other members reach back," explains Silveous.

(continued)

Consumer Watch: I'm Okay, You're Online
(continued)

That same pattern is repeated over and over again, regardless of the nature of the question or problem that draws someone to an online forum. Diana Ennen, co-host of the Work-at-Home forum on AOL's Parent's Soup, says she started participating in online message areas for two reasons: to discover new ways to cope with her hectic work and family life and to share her experiences as a small-business owner. "It's a great way to get a lot of the frustrations out, and to get motivated," says Ennen.

For many people, the ability to participate anonymously is an important part of online support groups, particularly when it comes to sensitive issues like employment-related problems. Whether it's in a public forum or one-to-one online counseling, participants are able to ask questions about harassment, disagreements with a supervisor, or being laid off, without fear of retribution, backlash, or ridicule, says James Gonyea, founder and host of the America Online Career Center, where he provides career counseling. "It's very comforting to be able to go to a professional counselor who doesn't know who you are," says Gonyea, noting that screen name­ to­ screen name counseling sessions guarantee anonymity and confidentiality.

Many people start by trawling through the message boards, then graduate to one of the live support groups that meet in chat rooms just about every day of the week on all the online services. Jim Lescallette started posting messages on Prodigy's Grief and Death bulletin board after his wife died. "It was a lifesaver for me and has been for many others," says Lescallette, who adds that a small group who met online now meet in person once a year.

mediated and sometimes prevented or postponed through counseling (Afresti, 1992). Preretirement counseling, for example, can help the retiree plan more effectively for a future that is bolstered by good physical and mental health. Family counseling services can enable better communication among family members and can promote acceptance of the adjustment required by the aging process for all involved (Lombana, 1976).

SUMMARY

Counseling and cultural differences, gender differences, the differently abled, religious clients, AIDS, and older adults—each area presents a unique set of issues and special needs. But all are calling to the contemporary counselor for help, and it is the responsibility of today's counselors to wake up and answer the call. It is also the responsibility of counselors-in-training to help the field of counseling respond professionally to these contemporary concerns. The future of counseling depends on it.

Key Terms

Cross-cultural counseling A relationship in which the client and counselor do not share the same cultural background, values, norms, roles, lifestyle, and/or methods of communicating.

References

Afresti, A. A. (1992). Counselor training and ethical issues with older clients. *Counselor Education & Supervision, 31,* 43–50.

Albers, G. R. (1990). *Counseling and AIDS.* Waco, TX: Word.

American Psychological Association. (1975). Report on the task force on sex bias and sex-role stereotyping in psychotherapeutic practice. *American Psychologist, 30,* 1169–1175.

American Psychological Association. (1978). Guidelines for therapy with women. *American Psychologist, 33,* 1122–1123.

Antill, J. K., & Cotton, S. (1986). Self-disclosure between husbands and wives: Its relationship to sex roles and marital happiness. *Australian Journal of Psychology, 39,* 11–24.

Aponte, H. J. (1990). Ethnicity dynamic, important in therapeutic relationships. *Family Therapy News, 21,* 3.

Asher, J. (1975, April). Sex bias found in therapy. *APA Monitor, 1,* 5.

Atkinson, D. R., Morten, G., & Sue, D. W. (1997). *Counseling American minorities: A cross cultural perspective* (5th ed.). New York: McGraw-Hill.

Batchelor, W. (1988). The science and the limits of science. *American Psychologist, 43,* 853.

Beckerman, N. L. (1994). Psychosocial tasks facing parents whose adult child has AIDS. *Family Therapy, 21,* 209–216.

Bergin, A. E. (1991). Values and religious issues in psychotherapy and mental health. *American Psychologist, 46,* 394–403.

Bradford, D. T., & Spero, M. H. (Eds.). (1990). Psychotherapy and religion [Special issue]. *Psychotherapy, 27* (1).

Browning, D. S., Jobe, T., & Evison, I. S. (1990). *Religious and ethical factors in psychiatric practice.* Chicago: Nelson-Hall.

Broverman, I. K., Broverman, D. M., Clarkson, F. E., Rosenkrantz, P., & Vogel, S. R. (1970). Sex role stereotypes and clinical judgments of mental health. *Journal of Consulting and Clinical Psychology, 34,* 1–7.

Butler, K. (1990). Spirituality reconsidered. *Family Therapy Networker, 14,* 226–237.

Butler, R. N., & Lewis, M. I. (1998). *Aging and mental health* (5th ed.). New York: Macmillan.

Byrne, G. (1989). AIDS panel urges new focus. *Science, 243,* 887.

Carter, R. T. (1991). Cultural values: A review of empirical research and implications for counseling. *Journal of Counseling and Development, 70,* 164–173.

Collins, G. R. (1993). *The Biblical basis of Christian counseling for people helpers.* Colorado Springs, CO: NavPress.

Cristiani, T., & Sommers, P. (1978). The counselor's role in mainstreaming the handicapped. *Viewpoints in Teaching and Learning, 54,* 20–28.

Devore, W., & Schlesinger, E. G. (1991). *Ethnic-sensitive social work practice* (3rd ed.). New York: Macmillan.

Ellis, A. (1980). Psychotherapy and atheistic values: A response to A. E. Bergin's "Psychotherapy and religious values." *Journal of Consulting and Clinical Psychology, 48,* 635–639.

Ellis, A. E. (2000). Can Rational Emotive Behavior Therapy (REBT) be effectively used with people who have devout beliefs in God and religion? *Professional Psychology: Research and Practice, 31,* 29–33.

English, A. (1991). Runaway and street youth at risk for HIV infection: Legal and ethical issues in access to care. *Journal of Adolescent Health, 12,* 504–510.

Erikson, E. H. (1987). A way of looking at things: Selected papers from 1930 to 1980. New York: Norton.

Erickson, S. H. (1993). Ethics and confidentiality in AIDS counseling: A professional dilemma. *Journal of Mental Health Counseling, 15,* 118–131.

Filer, P. (1982). Counselor trainees' attitudes toward mainstreaming the handicapped. *Counselor Education and Supervision, 22,* 61–69.

Freud, S. (1927). The future of an illusion. *Standard Edition, 21,* 5–56.

Friedman, A. L., & Hughes, R. B. (1994). AIDS: Legal tools helpful for mental health counseling interventions. *Journal of Mental Health Counseling, 16,* 291–303.

Gladding, S. T. (1999). *Counseling: A comprehensive profession* (4th ed.). New York: Merrill.

Glass, J., & Grant, K. (1983). Counseling in the later years: A growing need. *Personnel and Guidance Journal, 62,* 210–213.

Goldrick, M., Pearce, J. K., & Giordano, J. (1996). *Ethnicity & family therapy* (2nd ed.). New York: Guilford Press.

Good, G. E., Gilbert, L. A., & Scher, M. (1990). Gender aware therapy: A synthesis of feminist therapy and knowledge about gender. *Journal of Counseling and Development, 68,* 376–380.

Gove, W. R., & Tudor, J. F. (1973). Adult sex roles and mental illness. In J. Huber (Ed.), *Changing women in a changing society* (pp. 50–73). Chicago: University of Chicago Press.

Greenblatt, L., Hasenauer, J. E., & Freimuth, V. G. (1980). Psychological sex type and androgyny in the study of communication variables: Self-disclosure and communication apprehension. *Human Communication Research, 6,* 117–129.

Hackney, H., & Wrenn, C. G. (1990). The contemporary counselor in a changed world. In H. Hackney (Ed.), *Changing contexts for counselor preparation in the 1990s* (pp. 1–20). Alexandria, VA: Association for Counselor Education and Supervision.

Hare-Mustin, R. T. (1983). An appraisal of the relationship between women and psychotherapy: 80 years after the case of Dora. *American Psychologist, 38,* 593–601.

Hearst, N., & Hulley, S. (1988). Preventing the heterosexual spread of AIDS. *Journal of the American Medical Association, 259,* 2428–2432.

Hendrick, S. S. (1981). Self-disclosure and marital satisfaction. *Journal of Personality and Social Psychology, 40,* 1150–1159.

Hess, B. B. (1991). Growing old in the 1990s. In B. B. Hess & E. W. Markson (Eds.), *Growing old in America* (4th ed., pp. 5–22). New Brunswick, NJ: Transaction Books.

Hosie, T. (1979). Preparing counselors to meet the needs of the handicapped. *Personnel and Guidance Journal, 58,* 271–275.

Hubbard, M. G. (1992). *Women: The misunderstood majority.* Waco, TX: Word.

Kunins, H., Hein, K., & Futterman, D. (1993). Guide to adolescent HIV/AIDS program development. *Journal of Adolescent Health, 14,* 140.

Lee, C. C., & Richardson, B. L. (1996). *Multicultural issues in counseling* (2nd ed.). Alexandria, VA: AACD.

Lombana, J. H. (1976). Counseling the elderly: Remediation plus prevention. *Personnel and Guidance Journal, 55,* 143–144.

Lopez, R., Lopez, A., & Fong, K. (1991). Mexican Americans' initial preferences for counselors: The role of ethnic factors. *Journal of Counseling Psychology, 38,* 487–496.

Malony, H. N. (1988). The clinical assessment of optimal religious functioning. *Review of Religious Research, 30,* 3–17.

McDowell, W., Coven, A., & Eash, U. (1979). The handicapped: Special needs and strategies for counseling. *Personnel and Guidance Journal, 58,* 228–232.

Miller, W. M. (ed.) (1999). Integrating Spirituality into Treatment: Resources for Practitioners. Washington, DC: American Psychological Association.

Myers, J. E. (1989). *Infusing gerontological counseling into counselor preparation.* Alexandria, VA: AACD.

Myers, J. E. (1990). Aging: An overview for mental health counselors. *Journal of Mental Health Counseling, 12,* 245–259.

Nathanson, R. (1979). Counseling parents with disabilities: Are the feelings, thoughts, and behaviors of helping professionals helpful? *Personnel and Guidance Journal, 58,* 233–237.

Newman, S., Durrance, P., & Fell, M. (1993). Counseling in HIV and AIDS. *British Journal of Clinical Psychology, 32,* 117–119.

O'Brien, M. (1988). Men and fathers in therapy. *Journal of Family Therapy, 10,* 109–123.

Parrott, L., & Parrott, L. (1995). *The career counselor.* Dallas, TX: Word.

Pedersen, P. (Ed.). (1994). *Handbook of cross-cultural counseling and therapy.* Westport, CT: Greenwood Publishing Group.

Perlman, L. G., & Kirk, F. S. (1991). Key disability and rehabilitation legislation. *Journal of Applied Rehabilitation Counseling, 22,* 21–27.

Ponterotto, J. G., Casas, J. M., Suzuki, L. A., & Alexander, C. M. (2001). *Handbook of multicultural counseling* (2nd ed.). Thousand Oaks, CA: Sage.

Religion in America. (1985). Report No. 236. Princeton, NJ: Gallup Organization.

Richards, P. S. (1991). Religious devoutness in college students: Relations with emotional adjustment and psychological separation from parents. *Journal of Counseling Psychology, 38,* 189–196.

Richards, P. S., & Bergin, A. E. (1997). A Spiritual Strategy for Counseling and Psychotherapy. Washington, DC: APA.

Richards, P. S., & Bergen, A. E. (2000). *Handbook of psychotherapy and religious diversity.* Washington, DC: American Psychological Association.

Ridley, C. R. (1995). *Overcoming unintentional racism in counseling and therapy: A practitioner's guide to intentional intervention.* Thousand Oaks, CA: Sage.

Rusalem, H., & Cohen, J. (1975). Guidance of the exceptional student. In William M. Cruickshank and G. Orville Johnson (Eds.), *Education of exceptional children and youth* (pp. 613–622). Englewood Cliffs, NJ: Prentice Hall.

Schafranske, E. P. (ed.) (1996). Religion and the clinical practice of psychology. Washington, DC: American Psychological Association.

Scher, M., & Good, G. E. (1990). Gender and counseling in the twenty-first century: What does the future hold? *Journal of Counseling & Development, 68,* 388–391.

Schlossberg, N. K., & Pietrofesa, J. J. (1973). Perspectives on counseling bias: Implications for counselor education. *Counseling Psychologist, 4,* 44–54.

Simonton, D. K. (1990). Creativity in the later years: Optimistic prospects for achievement. *The Gerontologist, 30,* 626–631.

Smith, D. C. (1994). A "last rights" group for people with AIDS. *Journal for Specialists in Group Work, 19,* 17–21.

Sorenson, J. L., London, J., Heitzmann, C., & Gibson, D. R. (1994). Psychoeducational group approach: HIV risk reduction in drug users. *AIDS Education and Prevention, 6,* 95–112.

Stern, E. M. (Ed.). (1985). *Psychotherapy and the religiously committed patient.* New York: Haworth Press.

Sue, D. W. (1977). Counseling the culturally different: A conceptual analysis. *Personnel and Guidance Journal, 55,* 422–425.

Sue, D. W., Arredondo, P., & McDavis, R. J. (1992). Multicultural counseling competencies and standards: A call to the profession. *Journal of Counseling and Development, 70,* 477–486.

Sue, D. W., & Sue, D. (1999). *Counseling the culturally different: Theory & practice* (3rd ed.). New York: Wiley.

Sue, S., Fujino, D. C., Hu, L., Takeuchi, D. T., & Zane, N. W. S. (1991). Community mental health services for ethnic minority groups: A test of the cultural responsiveness hypothesis. *Journal of Consulting and Clinical Psychology, 59,* 533–540.

Sue, S., & McKinney, H. (1975). Asian Americans in the community mental health care system. *American Journal of Orthopsychiatry, 45,* 111–118.

Sue, S., McKinney, H., Allen, D., & Hall, J. (1974). Delivery of community mental health services to black and white clients. *Journal of Consulting and Clinical Psychology, 42,* 794–801.

Tan, S. Y. (1994). Ethical considerations in religious psychotherapy: Unique contributions and potential pitfalls. *Journal of Psychology and Theology, 22,* 389–394.

Tan, S. Y. (1996). Religion in clinical practice: implicit and explicit integration. In E. Shafranske (Ed.), *Religion and the clinical practice of psychology* (pp. 365–387). Washington, DC: American Psychology Association.

Tan, S. Y. (1999). Religion in psychological therapy. *Psychology of Religion Newsletter, 24*(3), 1–7.

Trezza, G. R. (1994). HIV knowledge and stigmatization of persons with AIDS: Implications for the development of HIV education for young adults. *Professional Psychology Research and Practice, 25,* 141–148.

Van Hasselt, V. B., Strain, P. S., & Hersen, M. (1988). *Handbook of developmental and physical disabilities.* New York: Pergamon Press.

Vandergriff, A., & Hosie, T. (1979). PL 94-142: A role change for counselors or just an extension of present role? *Journal of Counseling Services, 3,* 6–11.

Vontress, C. E. (1971). Racial differences: Impediments to rapport. *Journal of Counseling Psychology, 18,* 7–13.

Wade, P., & Bernstein, B. L. (1991). Culture sensitivity training and counselor's race: Effects on black female clients' perceptions and attrition. *Journal of Counseling Psychology, 38,* 9–15.

Williams, J. H. (1987). *Psychology of women: Behavior in a biosocial context* (3rd ed.). New York: W. W. Norton.

Williams, M. H. (1992). Exploitation and inference: Mapping the damage from therapist-patient sexual involvement. *American Psychologist, 47,* 412–421.

Worell, J. (Ed.). (2001). *Encyclopedia of women and gender: Sex similarities and differences and the impact of society on gender.* New York: Academic Press.

Worell, J., & Remer, P. (1992). *Feminist perspectives in therapy: An empowerment model for women.* New York: Wiley.

Worthington, E. L. (1989). Religious faith across the life span: Implications for counseling and research. *The Counseling Psychologist, 17,* 555–612.

Wrenn, C. G. (1958). Psychology, religion, and values for the counselor, Part III, in the symposium, the counselor and his religion. *Personnel and Guidance Journal, 36,* 326–334.

www.unaids.org/epidemic_update/report_dec01/index.html

www.census.gov/population/www/pop-profile/elderpop.html

Anyone with a modicum of human warmth, common sense, some sensitivity to human problems, and a desire to help can benefit many candidates for psychotherapy. —**Jerome D. Frank**

Major Therapeutic Theories

In order to understand anything well, you need at least three good theories. —**William Perry**

5 CHAPTER | Introduction: Your Personal Theory of Therapy

CHAPTER OUTLINE

Why Study Theories?
Discovering the Theory Within You
An Overview of the Chapters
Summary
Key Terms
References

In 585 B.C., a mathematician named Thales of Miletus had a theory about solar activity and, as a result, successfully predicted a solar eclipse, but only after he had made an embarrassing mistake. While contemplating the stars, it seems Thales lost his footing and fell head over heels into a deep hole. While his amazing prediction won popular acclaim, he was also remembered as an absent-minded, bumbling theorist. Someone reportedly asked him, "How can thou knowest what is doin in the heavens, when thou seest not what is at thy feet?" That's a good question. There is danger in lofty and speculative theorizing. But a good theory can reveal truth and lead to valuable benefits—especially good theories about how to practice psychotherapy.

Aristotle was the first to make a distinction between theory and practice. His terms were *theoria* and *praxis*. According to Aristotle, praxis follows analysis and has to do with "doing." Praxis is the application of theoretical knowledge. Each of the theories in this book is designed to lead eventually to praxis. For this reason, they are practical theories, tested in the comprehensive laboratories of counseling and confirmed when social scientists throw out parts of theories that do not continue to make sense over time and retain those that do. In the words of Kurt Lewin, "There is nothing so practical as a good theory."

The theories covered in this text—the theories of Freud, Adler, Rogers, and all the rest—have been studied, evaluated, critiqued, compared, and scrutinized. Yet they continue to stand tall. Some are more popular than others, but each offers significant insight and salient strategies for the helping profession.

The goal of this text is not to convert anyone to a specific theory of psychotherapy. Neither is it the purpose of this text to guide students into choosing and committing themselves henceforth to the assumptions and techniques of any one theory. The goal of this text, however, is to make you, as a prospective counselor, aware of the most important approaches to psychotherapy. Truth be known, few counselors today are theoretical purists, ascribing to only one approach. Human pain and suffering in contemporary society is far too complex for universal and strict formulas broadly applied. For this reason, a pragmatic rather than a dogmatic approach to counseling is affirmed throughout this text. Each theory in this book was carefully selected to undergird your future counseling with professional knowledge, human understanding, and the application of useful techniques for the counseling relationship.

After studying the various theories, you may find yourself gravitating toward one or two theories in particular, dedicating your focus to them exclusively. Or perhaps, like many, you will view the successive presentation of these theories more as a smorgasbord from which to choose main entrées and side dishes that will please the pallet of hurting people. Whatever the result, it is important that you become knowledgeable of each of these theories that hold historical, conceptual, and pragmatic significance to the entire field of counseling.

WHY STUDY THEORIES?

"The way we think about problems determines to a large degree what we will do about them," says Krumboltz (1966, p. 4). Therefore, it is important for therapists (1) to know how their decision-making process functions in *analyzing* human problems, (2) to understand what *assumptions* about counseling they believe are really true, and (3) to discover what they see as the best features in the theories they tend to *accept* as good. "Analyze," "assume," and "accept"— the triple As—are three important verbs counselors must think about in the

The prospect of preparing an overview of psychotherapy in America today is enough to make the most stout-hearted quail.

—Jerome D. Frank

development of their personal approach to therapy. Our thinking, our assumptions, and our beliefs form the foundation of what we do as counselors.

It is safe to assume that every counselor believes a therapeutic intervention has the potential for helping a client. Therapists believe that therapy is a worthy enterprise. Beyond this fundamental and essential assumption are a great many hypotheses, or questions about the helping process. And each and every question requires its own answer. Throughout the chapters in this section, students will encounter a number of questions requiring reflection and personal exploration (Brammer, 1973):

- How is human personality structured?
- What is my responsibility to others?
- What motivates people to behave as they do?
- How do people get the way they are?
- How do people change?
- How does thinking influence behavior?
- What are the relationships of thinking, feeling, and behaving?
- Where do our values come from?
- How do people make choices?
- How do people learn?
- How can I facilitate change?
- Does our personality influence the environment or is it the other way around?

Theories help answer these and many other questions. They help us formulate beliefs and values. Historically, many counselors took refuge in the comforting notion that a counselor's values could and should be kept out of the therapeutic relationship. However, in the late 1950s and early 1960s, therapists began to express the philosophy that counselors, rather than remaining neutral, tend to bring goals and techniques into the counseling relationship that are products of their personal values. For instance, theorists such as Lowe (1976) described the counselor as one who provides the client with a moral meaning and direction for life. Patterson (1959) found a direct relationship between the counselor's values and his or her style of counseling. For this reason it is imperative that counselors explore a variety of theories that will help you discover your own approach to psychotherapy.

DISCOVERING THE THEORY WITHIN YOU

Michelangelo attempted 44 statues in his life, but finished only 14 of them. They include such masterpieces as David in the Piazza of Florence, the Pieta in the Vatican basilica, and Moses in another of Rome's great churches. Michelangelo's 30 unfinished sculptures, however, are, in their own way, just

I have constructed three thousand different theories in connection with the electric light. . . . Yet in only two cases did my experiments prove the truth of my theory.
—Thomas A. Edison

as interesting as those that became classics. They are preserved in one of Italy's many museums. Each is a huge chunk of marble from which Michelangelo sculpted only an elbow or the beginning of a wrist. One mass of marble reveals a leg, thigh, knee, calf, and foot. The rest of the body is locked forever into the stone. The person Michelangelo had in mind will never step forth.

The following brief questionnaire is designed to help chip away at the theory of therapy developing inside you. Every potential counselor holds beliefs and values, still under construction, that will one day meld into a personal theory about the human condition and how to best help it. Take time to reflect and respond thoughtfully to these questions. You can take this simple step in revealing your values and sculpting your own theory of counseling.

T   F   1. Therapists should work only with clients whom they really like and care for.

T   F   2. My values should be kept out of the therapy process.

T   F   3. Giving advice is possibly the most important function of a therapist.

T   F   4. Confidentiality is an absolute, and I would never disclose anything a client revealed during therapy.

T   F   5. My own mental health is probably the most important variable that determines the success or failure of counseling.

T   F   6. Counseling is basically for people who are not coping with life well.

T   F   7. I should be completely open, honest, and transparent with my clients.

T   F   8. It is essential to know the origin and causes of a problem before a person can truly change.

T   F   9. To be effective as a counselor I need to have an attitude of total acceptance toward my client.

T   F   10. Intellectual insight is necessary for a person to change.

T   F   11. Asking questions is generally helpful as a therapeutic technique.

T   F   12. A therapist should rarely allow long moments of uncomfortable silence to occur.

T   F   13. As a counselor my job is basically that of a teacher. I am reeducating clients with better coping skills.

T   F   14. Confrontation generally causes great pain or discomfort, and it is better to let clients confront themselves when they are ready.

T   F   15. In a counseling session, my needs as a counselor are not important.

T   F   16. To be effective in counseling, one must be fairly good at persuasion.

T   F   17. A good therapist is born, not made.

T F 18. One of the most valuable gifts a client can receive is a word of solid advice.

T F 19. Counseling should focus on the present more than the past.

T F 20. The primary purpose of counseling is to provide solutions to problems.

T F 21. The primary purpose of counseling is to change behavior.

T F 22. The primary purpose of counseling is help people think rationally.

T F 23. The most effective therapy is done over a long period of time.

T F 24. To be a good counselor, one needs to be undergoing therapy.

T F 25. It is generally best to go with one's instincts as a counselor—your perception of a client's situation is probably correct.

For now, do not seek to "score" this questionnaire. It was not designed to have right and wrong answers. Its sole purpose is to help you begin thinking about how you already approach the practice of psychotherapy. However, after you have studied each of the theories in this book, you may find it quite helpful to come back to these statements and consider them the way a particular theorist would. For example, after reading "Psychoanalytic Therapy," try to answer the question in the way that you believe Freud would and then compare your responses to his. This exercise will help you better internalize Freud's theoretical approach, and it will help you sharpen your personal theory as well.

AN OVERVIEW OF THE CHAPTERS

Your journey through the theories of the following chapters is much like navigating a river. Knowing where the rocks are, estimating strength in the rolls of water off big boulders, determining the power and momentum of the current, and identifying the sink holes that threaten the destruction of the boat are, figuratively, the pieces of information each counselor needs in developing his or her own strategic approach—before launching into the white water rapids of a counseling relationship. To eliminate unexpected turns and to make the trip more pleasurable, each chapter features a consistent structure. Special boxes are also used at various points in the text to enhance your journey. But the basic outline in the chapters remains constant: brief biography, historical development, view of human nature, development of maladaptive behavior, function of the therapist, goals of therapy, major methods and techniques, application, critical analysis, current status, key terms, chapter summary, and recommended reading.

> All practicing therapists should know at least two or three theories of therapy well, and have nodding acquaintance with several others.
> —Janet Moursund

Brief Biography

It is difficult to separate the theory from the theorist. Serious students of psychotherapeutic theories will enhance and expand their understanding of a particular theory by studying the life of the theorist. Even a brief look into the background of a founding theorist can cast light and shadows onto their theory and provide a deeper understanding of their therapeutic perspective.

Historical Development

"The main thing is to make history, not to write it," wrote Otto von Bismarck. While many of the theorists covered in this book did not "write" the history of their ideas, the historical development of their thinking cannot be overlooked. Marcus Tullius Cicero, the great Roman statesman, declared, "To be ignorant of what occurred before you were born is to remain always a child." In the spirit of this aphorism, the origins and development of major concepts and hypotheses of each theory are explored. In this way, the chapters provide historical hooks on which to hang theoretical concepts.

View of Human Nature

Each of us, knowingly or not, holds personal thoughts on what human beings are really like. In the same way, each theorist holds a concept of the nature of being human. From Freud's determinism to Roger's humanism, each theory reveals the theorist's view of human nature. Thoughtful students of therapeutic theory will delve into this aspect of a particular approach to discover its vital importance. As Mark Twain said, "There is a great deal of human nature in people."

Development of Maladaptive Behavior

The biblical story of King Saul shows how he suffered from episodes of extreme melancholy followed by outbursts of mania. Today his condition is known as bipolar mood disorder. But while maladaptive behavior has been around since ancient days, our understanding of why it occurs still has not been settled. Hippocrates argued that it was not caused by divine intervention, as was commonly believed, but by disturbances in the brain. Thousands of years later, modern scientists study and debate his claim. Each of the theorists in these chapters also has a unique perspective on how and why maladaptive behavior develops. Many of their views may surprise you.

> The only therapy is life.
> —Otto Rank

Function of the Therapist

Each theorist assigns specific and unique duties to the counselors who join their camp. Some require active involvement, while others urge contemplative and minimal interaction with their clients. Some prescribe explicit values, while others assign a counselor role where values are left to personal style. In each chapter, the role and function of the therapist will be explored.

Goals of Therapy

Jean de La Fontaine said, "In everything we ought to look to the end." The theorists in this book have certainly taken his advice. Each theory calls for outcomes or clearly conceived ends. For some the goal of therapy is decidedly specific: "to change irrational thinking," for example. Other goals, when voiced, seem vague and obscure: to "experience one's experience as real." Still others aim to reconstruct a person's entire personality. Regardless of its goals, each theory is dedicated to making outcomes a reality. In the following chapters these goals will be laid out for thorough examination.

Major Methods and Techniques

Eventually, after discussing the ideas of therapeutic intervention, every theory comes to a place of action. In their own ways, each theory echoes the words of another great artist, William Wordsworth: "Thought and theory must precede all salutary action; yet action is nobler in itself than either thought or theory." In these chapters, each theory will be identified with a series of customary therapeutic actions that are appropriate to their outcomes. Each theory packs a therapeutic bag of methods and techniques for healing the human psyche.

Application

There is perhaps no better way of understanding the heart of a particular therapeutic theory than to see it demonstrated. Each chapter will eventually provide you with examples of how and where the theory is often applied, and it will show you exactly how it works through excerpts from actual counseling cases. Many times, these cases will come directly from the files of the founding theorist.

Critical Analysis

Once a thorough exploration of the theory has taken place, you will be challenged to think through what each approach has to offer. What are its major contributions to the field of counseling? Where does it miss the mark? A critique of each theory will be offered as a catalyst for your own further critique. This subsection, by the way, will give special attention to the pluses and minuses of the approach to cross-cultural counseling issues.

Current Status

After exploring the inner corridors of a theory, the chapter will turn briefly to its current status among contemporary counselors. The chapter will note the professional organizations, associations, and publications that keep the theory alive and will suggest sources where students may turn for more information.

SUMMARY

To help you conceptualize and internalize the components of each theory, a chapter summary is offered. Its purpose is in no way to substitute for a thorough study of the chapter itself. It will simply help you refresh your reading by highlighting many of the specific theory's features.

Near the beginning of the nineteenth century, the philosopher Immanuel Kant wrote an essay entitled, "On the Old Saw: It May Work in Theory, But It Won't Work in Practice." The theories that make up this section have all been shown to "work" to some degree or another. Ultimately, though, the effectiveness of any one of them will be up to you, the counselor.

Key Terms

Every field of study has its own professional language. Depending on your previous knowledge of psychology, you may already be familiar with some of the terminology in these chapters. Regardless, a glossary of terms that is specific to that theory is located at the end of each chapter.

References

Brammer, L. (1973). *The helping relationship: Process and skills.* Englewood Cliffs, NJ: Prentice Hall.

Krumboltz, J. D. (1966). Promoting adaptive behavior: Behavioral approach. In J. Krumboltz (Ed.), *Revolution in counseling.* Boston: Houghton-Mifflin.

Lowe, C. M. (1976). *Value orientations in counseling and psychotherapy: The meanings of mental health.* Cranston, RI: Carroll Press.

Patterson, C. H. (1959). The place of values in counseling and psychotherapy. *Journal of Counseling Psychology, 5,* 216–223.

By words one can give to another the greatest happiness or bring about utter despair. —Sigmund Freud

6 CHAPTER | Psychoanalytic Therapy

CHAPTER OUTLINE

Throughout history, scientists have rewritten our place in the universe three times over. Nicolaus Copernicus proved the earth is not the center of the universe but merely one of several planets revolving around the sun. Charles Darwin contributed a major revision when he convinced much of the Western world that humans are not a unique life form but one of the many species that have evolved over millions of years. And according to Sigmund Freud, we are masters not even of our own minds but victims of powerful unconscious motives, seldom recognized and less often understood.

Each of these scientists, Copernicus, Darwin, and Freud, changed the paradigms by which we think. But for the counselor none is more important than Sigmund Freud, an intellectual revolutionary who developed a psychoanalytic theory that sought to help troubled people come to grips with their demons. Freud's explorations led him into previously uncharted territory and allowed him to draw a new map of the human mind. Most social scientists agree that Freud's theory is the "most comprehensive and far-reaching conceptualization of personality, psychopathology, and psychotherapy in existence" (Korchin, 1976, p. 332).

The pervasiveness of psychoanalysis can be seen in nearly every academic discipline, and its direct and indirect influence on the larger public consciousness can hardly be overestimated (Arlow & Brenner, 1988; Jones & Wilson, 1987; Runyan, 1988; Sampson, 1990). Freud's influence is reflected in art, literature, and music, and even in Hollywood, where the Freudian concepts of sex and violence are taken as basic not only to the nature of human beings but to the film industry as well. Along with others who changed the world, Freud stands with Plato, Marx, and Einstein.

BRIEF BIOGRAPHY

Sigmund Freud was born on May 6, 1856, in a German-speaking territory that is now Czechoslovakia. Freud's father, Jakob, a wool merchant, was married the third time to Amalie, who favored Sigmund, calling him her "golden Sigi." She entertained higher hopes for Freud than for her five daughters and two sons born after him. Freud's great grandfather was a rabbi, and Freud himself was raised in the traditions and beliefs of the Jewish religion.

When Freud was three years old, his father moved the family to Vienna, where Freud lived most of his life. A brilliant student, graduating from high school with honors, Freud loved literature, especially Shakespeare, and was proficient in German, French, English, Italian, Spanish, Hebrew, Latin, and Greek (Jones, 1953). Although he dreamed of becoming a Napoleon or a minister of state like Oliver Cromwell, a Jewish boy's choices were limited in late nineteenth-century Vienna. He considered a career in law but eventually chose medicine. After receiving his medical degree from the University of Vienna at age 25, he practiced medicine at Vienna's General Hospital, where he continued his studies in organic diseases of the nervous system.

Freud—the Darwin of the mind.

—Ernest Jones

In 1886 Freud married Martha Bernays, to whom he had been engaged for four years. They had six children, three boys and three girls, the youngest of whom, Anna, became famous in her own right as a psychoanalyst specializing in the treatment of children.

Freud supported his family through his private practice in psychiatry, specializing in nervous diseases. At first he employed conventional treatments of his day: baths, massage, electro-therapy, and rest cures. But gradually Freud's interests moved away from the physical aspects of the nervous system and more toward the psychological factors, a move that may have been prompted by a need to escape the anti-Semitic medical community of Vienna. This shift in focus intensified with each year and resulted in full-time study of the psychological origins of neuroses (Gay, 1988). Eventually acclaim came his way, as did popular attention. He was even offered a job writing an advice column for the lovelorn in *Cosmopolitan* (Clark, 1980).

During the last 16 years of his life, Freud was afflicted with a painful cancer of the mouth and jaw, requiring 33 operations. Often smoking as many as 20 cigars daily, as a physician Freud was well aware of the risks he took and many times tried desperately to stop. A tragic prototype of a tobacco addict, even after his cancer was diagnosed he continued to smoke. "Don't try to live forever," he often said, quoting George Bernard Shaw. "You will not be successful" (Brecher, 1972).

Having abandoned his long-time home in Vienna in 1938 to escape Nazi persecution, Freud died at his son's home in London a year later at age 83. Never lamenting his persecution and illness, Freud waited for death. "It is tragic when a man outlives his body" was his only complaint.

A lucid and prolific writer, Freud continued to publish well into his 70s. On a typical day he was up by eight, saw patients until seven, and often wrote until one in the morning. More than half a century after his death, many of his 23 books are still in print, among them *The Interpretation of Dreams* (1900), *The Psychopathology of Everyday Life* (1901), *Beyond the Pleasure Principle* (1920), *The Ego and the Id* (1923), and *Civilization and Its Discontents* (1930). Sigmund Freud's life has been chronicled and analyzed by many: by his official biographer, Ernest Jones, who wrote the definitive three-volume work (1953, 1955, 1957) and more recently by Ronald W. Clark (1980) and Peter Gay (1988).

HISTORICAL DEVELOPMENT

Although the beginnings of psychoanalysis cannot be restricted to a specific year, its origins are identified with the early 1880s, at the height of the industrial revolution. People swarmed to the cities where sweat shops brutalized the disenfranchised, usually children, women, and immigrants. On both sides of the Atlantic, the Victorian Age set the moral climate of Europe and America, leaving many people torn between behavioral norms and their own inner feelings. Few had addressed the psychological suffering during this troubled era.

The Talking Cure

In late nineteenth-century Vienna, Josef Breuer, the neurologist known as the "doctor with the golden touch," was especially successful in treating hysteria. Freud described him as having a "striking intelligence." "We [shared] all our scientific interests with each other," Freud recalled. "In this relationship the gain was naturally mine" (1935, p. 33).

The seeds of psychoanalysis were sown by Dr. Breuer's patient, Bertha Pappenheim, or as she later came to be known, Anna O. She was a bright young woman who presented a variety of hysterical symptoms, including a nervous cough, anorexia, paralysis, a double personality, and, despite an inability to speak her native German, a proficiency in English. Not surprisingly, Breuer was fascinated by Miss Pappenheim and devoted much of his time to treating her. Each evening they explored the ties between her memories and her symptoms. The paralysis of her arm, for example, first appeared when she hallucinated a large, black snake in her father's bed. She tried to ward the snake off with her arm, but it would not move, and from that time her arm had been paralyzed. Although such recollections were intensely emotional, afterwards she felt cheerful and calm—so calm, in fact, that Breuer spoke of this release of tension as a "catharsis." The effects of this catharsis were welcomed but not expected by Breuer. He began describing his treatment of Bertha Pappenheim as the "talking cure."

> A man who has been the indisputable favorite of his mother keeps for life the feeling of a conqueror.
>
> —Sigmund Freud

Breuer devoted a disproportionate amount of time to his treatment of Bertha, often seeing her twice a day. In time, Breuer's wife became concerned about their relationship and insisted that he end his treatment. Bertha went on to a successful career as Germany's first social worker and was a zealous champion of women's rights.

The Birth of Psychoanalysis

Breuer exchanged his views on the case with the 26-year-old Freud, and they eventually coauthored the landmark *Studies on Hysteria* (Freud & Breuer, 1895). To respect Bertha Pappenheim's privacy, Breuer would refer to her as Fräulein Anna O. This woman, the "best-known of all psychotherapy patients," played an important role in Freud's formulation of psychoanalysis (Hollender, 1980, p. 797).

In 1885 Freud was awarded a grant that allowed him to study hysteria in Paris with the famous French neurologist Jean Charcot. Under hypnosis, Charcot found that some hysterical patients relinquished their symptoms and recalled the traumatic experiences that had generated them. Impressed by Charcot's techniques, Freud quickly recognized the connection to Breuer's work.

After returning from his sojourn in Paris, Freud lost no time in explaining his discoveries to his circle of physicians in Vienna. His advocacy of hypnotic techniques was met with skepticism, but this did not deter him from incorporating it into his treatment of nervous disorders (Jones, 1953).

Together with his interest in Anna O., Freud's work with Charcot lay the groundwork for a revolutionary theory. It was a theory which Freud first referred to as "Breuer's method," then as "psychical analysis," and finally as "psychoanalysis" (Freeman, 1972). Freud first used the term **psychoanalysis** in 1896 (Gay, 1988). While it was only in crude form and far from its ultimate shape, the basic outline of psychoanalysis was in hand, and a view of humans and how to treat them eventually emerged.

VIEW OF HUMAN NATURE

Sigmund Freud painted a vivid portrait of human nature. He believed people were dominated by instinctual, unconscious, and irrational forces, leaving them at war internally and externally. But chief among these drives was aggression and sex, housed within an inner core dominated by the superego. Everyone was highly sexual, he believed, even during years of "childhood innocence."

For Freud, personality was determined entirely by conditions and events beyond personal control. Lying behind every human thought or action was a cause, Freud believed. Thoughts, feelings, and actions did not occur by chance. They were not accidents. Reading the word "breast" when the text says "beast," forgetting a relative's name, or losing a borrowed book may not be in conscious awareness, but each is the hidden expression of a feeling or impulse buried in the mind. Freud believed that these causes could be identified and that undesirable personality traits, their distorted outcomes, could be treated. One need only explore the unconscious to trace and uncover these hidden causes (Pine, 1990).

The Unconscious

At the epicenter of this revolutionary theory is the **unconscious.** "If Freud's discovery had to be summed up in a single word, that word would without a doubt have to be 'unconscious'" (Laplanch and Pontailis, 1973, p. 474). Freud believed a revelation of the unconscious could explain all human thought, feeling, and action. Like woolly mammoths, perfectly preserved in the Arctic tundra, Freud wrote, once the layers of resistance have been laid bare, our past, our memories, still retain their freshness (Wachtel, 1977, p. 28).

Freud's focus on the unconscious, however, was not in the mainstream of turn-of-the-century medical practice. Physicians were, by and large, not attempting to deal with the psychology of disease; few considered the unconscious self a subject deserving of critical scientific study and analysis. At the time the field of psychology was primarily concerned with the perception of objects and other such states of consciousness.

Freud, on the other hand, viewed consciousness as only a small part of the total psyche, the proverbial tip of the iceberg. In traditional psychoanalytic theory there are, in fact, three levels of personality: the visible **consciousness,** which consists of everything within cognitive awareness; the pre-

> The great question that has never been answered . . . is "What does a woman want?"
>
> —Sigmund Freud

conscious, made up of material that is fairly accessible but not immediately within the person's awareness; and then the underlying *unconscious,* which consists of every aspect in human personality of which we are unaware. It was here, in the powerful unconscious drive, that Freud found the most fruitful place to look for explanations of human motivation.

Structure of Personality

Freud (1901, 1924) divided personality, which he called the "scaffold of the mind," into three components: the **id,** which represents the biological self in personality; the **ego,** the partially unconscious drive or psychological center of personality; and the **superego,** the governor, the social controller in the tower that brings behavior within culturally acceptable limits.

Freud's greatest achievement probably consisted in taking neurotic patients seriously.

—Carl Jung

These three aspects, or factors, are not physical parts of the personality. They cannot be located and photographed. They are unseen, but nonetheless real psychological processes of the mind. They interact with one another in dynamic ways that change and influence personality. The id, ego, and superego are in unrelenting contention, each driven to dominate the personality at the expense of the other.

The Id   The id—literally the "it"—is the most basic of the three systems. A reservoir of instincts, of needs and wishes, it is entirely unconscious, being "the dark inaccessible part of personality . . . a cauldron full of seething excitations" (Freud, 1933, p. 73). The id engages in **primary process** thinking, which is as primitive and illogical as a newborn baby instinctually grasping, crying for milk, sleeping, sucking, and urinating. Preoccupied with its own needs and desires, the id is entirely self-centered and selfish. By nature it does nothing for anyone else. Biological in nature and oriented toward the past, the behavior of the id is determined by what Freud called the **pleasure principle,** whose aim is self-gratification.

Freud identified two instincts fundamental to the id, both of them wholly illogical and amoral: life and death. Instincts toward life, called **Eros,** represent energy for preserving oneself and others. The most important aspect of Eros is **libido,** a generalized pleasure drive. Clinical observation of patients who suffered traumatic experiences during the First World War led Freud to add to his recognizable drives the instinct toward death, **Thanatos,** a negative force propelling people toward aggressive and destructive behaviors. This primitive urge to obey the law of entropy, to return to an inorganic state, seemed to Freud to be a primitive urge common to all living things. These life and death instincts, Freud believed, may fuse together or work against each other.

The Ego   Beginning at about age six to eight months, the ego, literally the "I," develops for the purpose of helping the id satisfy its physical and social needs in ways that do not impinge upon others. According to Freud, the ego is "a kind of facade of the id . . . an external, cortical layer of it" (Freud, 1926, p. 18).

Unlike the id, a reservoir of desires and wishes, the ego spans the conscious, preconscious, and unconscious aspects of the mind. Rational and capable of forming realistic plans of action, the ego serves as a liaison between the real world and the hidden world of the id. Psychological in nature and oriented toward the present, the behavior of the ego is guided by reality, and it seeks out the safety of the self.

While the ego has a bent toward pleasure, it can suspend the pleasure drive in favor of the **reality principle.** Whereas the id is subjective, directed internally toward its own wants and needs, the ego is objective, focused outside itself. The ego counsels with reality to determine whether or not it can satisfy the pleasures the id seeks to express without harming itself or others. The ego works to tame the unbridled desires of the id by delaying gratification for a more appropriate time and place. "Like a man on horseback, [the ego] has to hold in check the superior strength of the horse" (Freud, 1923, p. 15).

In the long run, however, the ego seeks to maximize gratification, as does the id. But the ego engages in realistic **secondary process thinking,** which is oriented toward problem solving and self-preservation. The highest function of the ego is decision making, which holds in check the passions of the id or which, in reasonable circumstances, ordains them as realistic. "Such decisions," wrote Freud, "make up the whole essence of worldly wisdom" (1926, p. 27).

Anxiety is caused by the ego's reaction to threatening or destructive urges from the id. To minimize this unpleasant emotional state, which may run from mild to extreme, the ego recruits a variety of internal **defense mechanisms,** which protect the person by blocking unacceptable urges or propositions from ever reaching conscious awareness. These unconscious, involuntary strategies for coping with the threatening instincts of the id serve as a kind of pain reliever to the psychological system. Because all of these defenses not only operate at an unconscious level but also distort one's perception of reality, they reduce the dark sense of anxiety (Freud, 1966).

The Superego   The third component in personality formation, according to Freud, is the superego, which operates according to the **morality principle.** It represents society's views of right and wrong. But, unlike the ego, it is irrational, directing all of its energy toward extinguishing the id's unacceptable expression of sexual and aggressive instincts. Social in nature and oriented toward the past, then, the behavior of the superego is guided by morality, and it seeks perfection.

The content of each person's superego results from **introjection,** a process of incorporating the norms and standards of culture into personality by identifying with significant adults during childhood, when the ego is especially sensitive to potential losses of love. Although these significant role figures may include uncles and aunts, neighbors, clergy, and teachers, parents, of course, are the primary interpreters of society's rules. It is parents especially who convey their values to their children by offering love when they are "good" and, when these standards are not followed, by punishing them when they are "bad." A punished child may or may not be guided toward better behavior, but he or she is certainly pushed toward debilitating feelings of rejection.

6.1 | Major Defense Mechanisms

Denial "Elvis is dead!" "No way!" When circumstances of reality frustrate an id impulse, denial intervenes to protect the ego from the frustration of the real situation. It protects the self from unpleasant reality by refusing to perceive it.

Displacement This defense replaces the object of an impulse with a substitute object. Here's an example: A researcher's grant proposal is rejected for funding. She tells her lab assistant he's been goofing off, who tells his wife she's been ignoring the kids, who tells their six-year-old to pick up his toys, who throws a shoe at the dog, which pees on the kitchen floor.

Intellectualization This process involves escaping one's emotions through a focus on intellectual concepts, abstract and insignificant details, or rational explanation devoid of personal significance. This may be seen in the example of a person who, having suffered a major career setback, discusses with apparent detachment all the ways his debacle could have been more devastating.

Projection This is the process of unconsciously attributing one's own unacceptable impulses, attitudes, and behaviors to other people. Projection enables us to blame someone else for our shortcomings. A student who blames his poor grade on a professor who "can't teach" is an example. A favorite projection of young men who are not admitting their desires is "She wants me."

Rationalization Sometimes referred to as "sour grapes," rationalization is typified by the famous Aesop fable of the fox who tried repeatedly without success to reach a bunch of grapes. The fox finally gave up his attempts, rationalizing that the grapes looked sour anyway. Rationalization allows a person to defend the self's real feeling by creating false motives.

Reaction Formation Sometimes the ego can control or defend against the expression of a forbidden impulse by consciously expressing its opposite. Reaction formation operates in two steps: first, the unacceptable impulse is repressed; next, the opposite is expressed on a conscious level. For example, this process may cover repressed hostility with an overwhelming show of kindness, unconscious desires for sexual promiscuity with celibacy, or great moral restraint.

Regression Regression is a way of alleviating anxiety by retreating to an earlier period of life that was more secure and pleasant. Losing one's temper, pouting, sulking, talking baby talk, rebelling against authority, and other childish behavior are forms of regression. When former television evangelist Jim Baker's illegal dealings were discovered, he clearly demonstrated an extreme form of regression. He was found under his attorney's desk in the fetal position.

Repression Threatening instinctual impulses from the id are removed from consciousness in repression. Visual or auditory perceptions may be distorted or memories associated with painful events may be obliterated completely. For example, an adult may have suffered a terrible act of child abuse in early years. If anger over this toward the abusing parent is fully repressed, leaving no conscious memory of the event or feelings surrounding it, it may seek conscious expression through anger toward some authority or parentlike figure.

Sublimation According to Freud, sublimation is the only healthy way to deal with objectionable impulses because it allows the ego to convert them into socially acceptable forms of expression. A person with a great deal of unrecognized hostility, for example, may sublimate by taking up karate.

The superego is a significant force that the ego must contend with in its struggle to ameliorate the id. Like an inner master, the superego can become an independent and dominant force in one's personality, which is when and how neuroses develop. The superego can work against both the id and the ego by pushing one's personality toward excessive and sometimes irrational conformity to internalized norms. Given free rein, it can lock a person into rigid moral patterns, unrelentingly seeking total perfection in everything it does (Leak & Christopher, 1982). It can take the ego to task, give orders, lay blame, induce guilt, and make threats. On the other hand, when its standards, its **ego ideal,** are met, the superego can offer the personality positive emotional experiences, reinforcing a sense of self-respect.

Although in Freud's model the ego and superego operate at all three levels of awareness—the conscious, the preconscious, and the unconscious—the id is entirely unconscious, expressing its urges at a conscious level through the ego.

Development of Personality

Since Freud believed adult personality is established by about the age of five, the importance of early childhood development is a cornerstone in his theory. Freud theorized that personality development follows a more or less set course from birth, a series of discrete stages defined by **erogenous zones,** those parts of the body that are sensitive to sexual stimulation: the mouth, anus, penis, clitoris, and vagina. Defined broadly, this "sexual" activity encompasses any pleasurable feelings associated with stimulation of the erogenous zones, whether or not the stimulation is directed toward genital sex. (One Freudian example of libidinous satisfaction is the release of tension associated with urination.) Nothing Freud wrote shocked Victorian culture more than his exploration of this mysterious drive. At the turn of the century public discussion of sexuality was abhorrent, but attributing sexual impulses to children seemed monstrous.

> Freud would often say three things were impossible to fulfill completely: Healing, educating, governing. He limited his goals in analytic treatment to bringing a patient to the point where he could work for a living, and learn to love.
>
> —Theodor Reik

According to Freud, every human being experiences the resulting five sequential stages of **psychosexual development:** oral, anal, phallic, latency, and genital.

The Oral Stage   During the first year of life oral functions such as sucking, eating, biting, cooing, and crying are the primary means of a baby's gratification. Mothers have long observed that a baby's gateway to the world is the mouth, through which almost everything that enters the field of consciousness passes.

At about eight months, weaning begins, the breast is withdrawn, and other foods are offered. This shift can be traumatic, especially if it is abrupt or uncaring. If such is the case, vestiges of the **oral stage** may stay with the person throughout life. The more difficult it is for the child to leave the mother's breast (or bottle), the more the libido is **fixated** at the oral stage—that is, the more likely it is that the libido should be developmentally arrested or halted at a particular stage because of excessive satisfaction, frustration, or anxiety. At the oral stage fixation is characterized by excessive concern with eating, drinking, smoking, and kissing.

Psychoanalytic literature identifies two modes of oral expression: receptive (taking in) and aggressive (spitting out). According to Freud, infants who are overindulged will grow up with an *oral-receptive* trait, relying on other people for gratification of their needs. As adults they become dependent on others and overly gullible, swallowing anything they are told. They will also be interested in receiving information and acquiring material goods. The *oral-aggressive* trait is also derived from childhood pleasure associated with the mouth. Chewing, crunching, biting, and use of teeth are dominant expressions of this trait. People of this character type are expected to favor hard candy to soft, hard-stemmed pipes to cigarettes. They chomp the ice in their drinks and chew the end of their pencil. The orally aggressive character is sarcastic and argumentative, making "biting" remarks.

The Anal Stage   Around the age of two or three, the child moves into the anal stage, when libidinal gratifications are met through the region of the anus. Here the child derives sexual gratification in two ways: eliminating feces and retaining them. Toilet training is the highlight of the anal period. From the parent's perspective, the issue is social control. Some parents are rigid and demanding with their two-year-old, which reaps rebellion or passive acceptance in the toddler. An adverse reaction to parental demands takes some form of rebellion, whereas the child who responds positively exhibits cooperation. Some parents are highly permissive in accepting their child's preferences and schedule.

Fixation at the anal stage produces either the anal-retentive or anal-expulsive personality. *Anal-retentive* people delay satisfactions until the last possible moment, "saving" dessert, for example, to eat after others have finished theirs. They are orderly, stingy, and stubborn. In contrast, children who discover social control by means of direct opposition develop an *anal-expulsive* personality. They are expected to express anger by becoming wasteful, disorderly, or messy. Their room, office, or car tends to be unkempt. Good grooming or well organized plans run against the grain in the personality of the anal-expulsive individual.

The Phallic Stage   Around the age of four or five years, the child enters the **phallic stage,** when satisfaction is gained primarily through stimulation of the penis or clitoris. The phallic stage is dominated by the realization that boys have penises whereas girls do not. Freud maintained that this realization is startling to both boys and girls because of their assumption that all persons are supposed to have penises. This discovery, according to Freud, causes **castration anxiety** in boys and **penis envy** in girls. In other words, boys fear losing their highly prized organ of pleasure while girls wish to someday overcome feelings of inferiority by obtaining a penis of their own.

| 6.2 | **Womb Envy** |

The male bias in Freud's theory was questioned by later psychoanalysts who proposed revisions of his ideas (e.g., Horney, 1926; Thompson, 1943). Karen Horney (pronounced HORN-eye) challenged Freud's use of penis envy to explain feminine inferiority and disputed Freud's claim that motherhood's greatest psychological importance for women is as a means of compensating for that inferiority. Horney believed that Freud's image of women was distorted and biased because he based it exclusively on observations of neurotic women.

Most see the origins of Freud's concept of penis envy coming out of social rather than anatomical factors. In other words, revisionists see penis envy as a symbolic reflection of men's greater cultural and economic advantages. But anthropologist Margaret Mead (1974) took it even further by offering a parallel, female-oriented concept of **womb envy.** Mead hypothesized that as boys begin to accept the fact they cannot bear children, they compensate for this inferiority by learning to place a high value on achievement. More recent psychoanalysts echo Mead's complementary concept and emphasize the fascination boys have with childbirth and their mothers' ability to have children (Buie, 1989).

This last and most crucial childhood conflict involves the child's unconscious wish to possess the parent of the opposite sex and, at the same time, to eliminate the parent of the same sex. Up to this stage of development, Freud theorized, boys love their mothers and see their fathers as rivals. Well read in classical mythology, Freud termed this dynamic the **Oedipus complex,** in memory of Oedipus, who killed his father and married his mother (Glenn, 1987). The reverse dynamic for girls, the love of the father and hatred of the mother, was termed the **Electra complex** by Carl Jung.

The Latency Stage   Freud's fourth stage of psychosexual development is notable for its absence of dominant erogenous zones and readily visible events or outcomes. The time between 6 and 12 years of age is marked by repression of sexual impulses and a curbing of oral, anal, and phallic activities that provide pleasure. As its name implies, **latency** is a quiet period of transition from pregenital to genital stages. Incidently, an assumption of a decrease in sexual urges and interest during the ages of 6 through 13 might have suited Victorian children, but it does not fit observations of children in other cultures. A more plausible assumption, and one more difficult to test, is that there are no new developments during this stage in terms of the ways in which children gratify their instincts.

The Genital Stage   With the onset of puberty the child emerges from latency and enters Freud's final stage of development, the **genital stage,** characterized by pleasure provided through the genitals in the course of heterosexual activity. The greater a person's success in reaching the genital stage without large amounts of libido fixated in pregenital stages, the greater will be the person's capacity to lead a "normal" life, free of neurosis.

The genital stage differs from the first three stages by being less selfish and more altruistic. Its energies are directed toward psychoanalytic ideals of personal maturity: love and work. The pursuit of these goals contributes to the fulfillment of Eros's instinctual aim of preserving the self and the species. According to psychoanalytic theory persons unable to make psychological attachments during adolescence and young adulthood will show abnormal personality patterns.

DEVELOPMENT OF MALADAPTIVE BEHAVIOR

According to psychoanalytic thought, we are all "a little neurotic" (Freud, 1901). Maladaptive behavior is universal and inevitable in this model because conflicts and fixations in our formative years are unavoidable. Nobody proceeds through early developmental stages without problems. Specific symptoms of abnormality vary, however, depending upon the psychosexual stage in which the conflicts and fixations first developed and the manner in which defense mechanisms are used to deal with the resulting anxiety (Fromm, 1991; Munroe, 1955).

Operating largely at the unconscious level, anxiety is at the core of all psychopathology. The degree of anxiety depends on the leadership of the ego. When effective, the ego sublimates or blocks dangerous id impulses. It heeds the moral dictates of the superego but checks a conscience that speaks too loudly or an ego ideal that becomes overly perfectionistic.

A weakened ego spends excessive amounts of psychic energy wrestling with the id and superego. Life's inevitable frustrations give the id and superego renewed power while the weak ego is unable to cope. It may allow more libido to regress to earlier points of fixation, resulting in childishness, narcissism, or immorality and destructiveness.

The weak ego may be dominated by a stern superego enforcing rigid defenses that deprive the person of pleasures most people consider socially acceptable. A person is rarely aware of how events are affecting underlying impulses or unresolved conflicts and fixations. As anxiety intrudes on consciousness, the person tends to panic and the full spectrum of psychopathology takes shape.

GOALS OF THERAPY

Freud made rather modest claims for his therapy. He never presented it as a panacea for all psychic ills. He never guaranteed that healing gained through psychoanalysis was permanent or irreversible. Psychoanalysis offers help to those who are willing and able to endure a lengthy, arduous, and often painful process to achieve a resolution for intrapsychic conflicts that will enable them to handle life's other conflicts in a healthier way.

The ultimate goal of psychoanalysis is not the removal of symptoms. Rather, it is the total reconstruction of personality. What Freud tried to accomplish in therapy was a general strengthening of a person's ego so that instinctual aggressive and sexual impulses could be brought under control. Designed to reintegrate previously repressed experiences into the total personality structure, psychoanalysis attempts to make unconscious material accessible to consciousness by identifying and overcoming resistances to its awareness. However, Freud recognized this was an impossible ideal. He believed that a more realistic aim of treatment was the recovery of the patient's "ability and capacity for enjoyment and an active life" (1963, p. 60). Of course, this does not happen quickly. As a consequence, psychoanalysis is a long, intense, and expensive process (Harper, 1975; Nye, 1992).

> Where id was, let ego be.
>
> —Sigmund Freud

FUNCTION OF THE THERAPIST

Freud consistently asserted that compassionate neutrality was the proper mind-set for the analyst during the psychoanalytic session. While attentive, accepting, and nonjudgmental, the analyst is a neutral observer of the therapeutic process, intervening only occasionally to offer interpretations of the client's past experiences.

Typically, the analyst is viewed as extremely passive and detached, repeatedly responding with the famous "Um hum." It is important to recognize that modern psychoanalytic views that see the analyst as being more active have modified the classical conception of the role of the emotionally neutral psychoanalyst (Strupp & Binder, 1984). However, the traditional analyst neither offers advice nor extends sympathy but encourages clients to talk about whatever comes to mind, especially about childhood experiences (Meissner, 1985). To allow patients to talk freely, psychoanalysts often have clients recline on a couch while the analyst sits out of view in a chair behind the client's head.

In classical psychoanalysis the analyst fosters a transference by allowing the client to project unresolved conflicts, feelings, and experiences on to the analyst. Pure Freudian analysts believe that saying little about themselves and rarely sharing their personal reactions leads the client to project on them the feelings they have had toward significant figures in their past. This transference of the client's inaccurate perceptions to the analyst is of central importance in classical psychoanalysis.

Analytically oriented therapists, not pure Freudians, often dispense with the couch and sit in a chair, face to face with the patient and develop a less neutral relationship with their clients. They view transference as important but place a greater focus on outside events in the client's life (Blanck & Blanck, 1968; Meares, 1992). They may use psychoanalytic understandings simply as a flexible guide for the therapeutic process, not as binding law. Whereas a classic psychoanalyst is more concerned with lifting repressions of deeply unconscious material from the past, for example, analytically oriented therapists may concentrate on the conflicts in the present.

Some of the most vocal reformers of traditional psychoanalysis are Franz Alexander and Thomas French (1946), who have argued that Freud fit the client's problems to analytic techniques rather than the techniques to the client's problems. They encouraged the use of nonanalytic techniques and made a distinction between "uncovering therapy" and "supportive therapy." Uncovering therapy, also called insight therapy, is aimed at permanently changing the ego through the insight gained in the emotional resolution of transference. Supportive therapy is not aimed at changing the ego; rather the therapist encourages the client's ego to respond maturely to life's demands. Alexander and French argued that the practice of contemporary psychoanalysis calls for both uncovering and supportive methods. But such alternate forms of psychotherapy only contaminate the psychoanalytic orthodoxy of "pure" analysts. Contemporary psychoanalysts remain divided on the precise function of the therapist (Nemiah, 1984).

MAJOR METHODS AND TECHNIQUES

Psychoanalysts and other contemporary therapists have introduced many treatment variations on the early techniques. Free association, dream analysis, analysis of transference, and analysis of resistance still endure.

Free Association

The cardinal technique of psychoanalysis is to allow the client to say anything and everything that comes to mind, no matter how illogical, silly, painful, or trivial. This "free association has the priority over all other means of producing material in the analytic situation" (Greenson, 1967, p. 32). Through free association the client abandons normal ways of censoring or editing thoughts, although, in harmony with Freud's deterministic position, a client's "free associations" are, of course, not really free at all. **Free association** is predicated on the assumption that one association leads to another that is deeper in the unconscious (Laplanche & Pontailis, 1973). Freud felt such insights into the true nature of a person's problems could only be discovered through this verbal stream of consciousness, a technique which he labeled **catharsis,** from the Greek word meaning "purification."

In free association, nothing the client says is taken at face value. Even a slip of the tongue can reveal hidden wishes. Freud demonstrated how the repressed content of the unconscious inadvertently slips into the spoken word. A woman talking with her therapist about flying home to see her parents, for example, says, "I haven't bought my pain [instead of *plane*] ticket yet"—resulting in what is now known as a **Freudian slip.**

Dream Analysis

In both classical and modern analysis, dreams, which Freud referred to as "the royal road to the unconscious," play a central role. When a person sleeps, the ego relaxes its control over unconscious material. As a result, by uncovering wishes that are unacceptable to the conscious mind, dreams become a window into the unconscious (Abrams, 1992; Lipschitz, 1990).

Analysts encourage clients to report their dreams and free-associate about them. The analyst may also discuss or interpret the meaning of dreams, which are said to contain surface material called the **manifest content** and then the deeper, hidden meaning, the **latent content.** The analyst's job is to discover and interpret the latent dream content.

Freud's attempts to interpret dreams resulted in his monumental study, *The Interpretation of Dreams* (1900/1957). Over the course of his work with patients, Freud found consistent symbols in dreams that signified the same thing for nearly everyone. For example, he said steps, ladders, and staircases represented sexual intercourse; candles, snakes, and tree trunks stood for the penis. In spite of apparent universality of certain symbols, Freud warned that they still have to be interpreted within the context of the individual's life.

Interpretation of Transference

Originally Freud considered **transference,** which occurs when the client responds to the analyst as a significant authority person out of his or her life, an obstacle to treatment. Eventually, however, he realized the phenomenon of transference made treatment and the cure possible. Only when the analyst serves as a surrogate, allowing old reactions and conflicts to be relived, is the nature of childhood difficulties revealed.

Both positive and negative feelings can be transferred. Statements of admiration, anger, or dislike are categories of transference. Because clients' reactions indicate the presence of emotional residues from their past, they are unaware of their functional importance. The therapist, not interpreting the transference immediately, encourages its development to enhance insight into the client's ways of perceiving, feeling, and reacting to significant figures from early life. Orthodox psychoanalysts regard analysis of transference as absolutely vital to the therapeutic process (Winnicott, 1956).

As clients become gradually aware of the true meaning of their transference relationship with the analyst, they gain insight into their past and present experiences. A therapist, however, must be keenly aware of the transference and not take it personally. When this occurs it is called **countertransference.** A certain client may inadvertently touch on issues in a therapist's life that have not been resolved. Dealing with the complexities of countertransference can be difficult and sometimes requires professional outside consultation.

Interpretation of Resistance

As a client's unconscious mind is stirred, resistance arises. Despite consciously desiring to change, a client may unconsciously resist efforts to help eliminate old behavior patterns. **Resistance** is a means of keeping the unconscious conflict intact, thereby impeding any attempts to probe into the real sources of personality problems.

6.3 | The "Inkblot" Test

To a psychoanalyst, the most important conflicts in a personality are buried deep within the unconscious. For obvious reasons, a client cannot discuss these unknown areas directly. To overcome this hurdle, psychoanalysts bypass direct reporting and rely on *projective tests*. These allow the client to project their unconscious conflicts onto a neutral stimulus (such as a cloud). With an ambiguous stimuli, a client simply describes what he or she sees. There are no right or wrong answers. One person may see a bat while another sees an insect or a butterfly.

More than 50 years ago Hermann Rorschach designed a projective test based on inkblots. Known today as the "Rorschach Test," this exercise employs 10 cards, each containing nothing more than a blot of ink. Test takers are instructed to describe what they see in the inkblot. Their responses can be analyzed with any of several scoring systems, but many psychologists rely on their personal insights in interpreting the responses. Unusual answers and recurring themes are of particular interest. For example, if a client is seeing violent acts on nearly every card, it provides the therapist with a definite area of exploration in therapy. The Rorschach, like other projective tests, is often criticized for its subjectivity.

Resistance can be expressed in many ways, such as "forgotten" counseling appointments, difficulty in free association, and dismissal of interpretations.

> The dream is a disguised fulfillment of a repressed wish.
> —Sigmund Freud

Another form of resistance is talking about topics unrelated to the real work of therapy. A client, for example, may talk at length about the economy, the weather, or anything else that is not related to his or her personal issues. The ultimate form of resistance, of course, is for the client to discontinue therapy prematurely. When resistance begins to interfere with the therapeutic process, however, a psychoanalytic therapist will skillfully interpret it, bringing repressed conflicts into the open and ridding the client of unconscious defenses (Hornstein, 1992).

Each of these therapeutic techniques—free association, dream analysis, and the interpretation of transference and resistance—is designed to make the unconscious conscious and help people achieve greater insight into the causes of their distress. Insight alone, however, is not a sufficient condition for behavioral change in the client. In the final stages of treatment, analysts encourage patients to convert their newly discovered insights into their everyday living experiences. This is sometimes called *emotional reeducation*. The whole point is to think, perceive, feel, and behave differently.

APPLICATION

Freud discovered that patients did not always willingly provide free associations or obediently present their dreams for interpretation. They often "resisted" the very methods the analyst assured them would be the way to relief. Why was this so, and how did Freud achieve insight into the explanation that was to serve as a basic credo in psychoanalysis? A brief description of the following case will illustrate Freud's therapeutic work as well as how he came to some of his conclusions (Freud, 1957).

"Dora" was 18 years old. She had threatened suicide and also manifested several hysterical symptoms. She was referred to Freud by her father. At first, everything went well. Dora was bright and took readily to free association. Although she showed quick improvement following Freud's interpretations regarding her infantile sexuality problems, soon after she terminated therapy.

Why did she leave when everything seemed to be going so well? To answer this question, Freud carried out a retrospective analysis of the case and, to his own satisfaction, discovered the reasons. Although Dora's father was often ill,

> Innocent dreams . . . are wolves in sheep's clothing. They turn out to be quite the reverse when we take the trouble to analyze them.
> —Sigmund Freud

his wife's major preoccupation seemed to be keeping the house clean. She had little time for either Dora or her husband. As a result, nursing care for Dora's father fell increasingly to Ms. K, a neighbor who, along with her husband, was a close friend of Dora's parents. Later Dora realized that Ms. K had become not just a nurse but also her father's mistress. For a variety of reasons, Mr. K seemed to sanction the affair. As Dora began to turn into an attractive young woman, she caught the eye of Mr. K, and he began to buy her gifts (including a jewelry box). He also made several amorous advances. Later, Dora remarked in therapy how much she hated the tobacco smell on his breath.

During a summer vacation when Dora, her parents, and Mr. and Ms. K shared a house, Dora and Mr. K were taking a walk when Mr. K complained that his wife "gave him nothing." Dora did not tell her parents about this direct sexual suggestion on the part of Mr. K, but for two weeks afterwards she experienced an unpleasant dream. At that point, she insisted to her parents that she could no longer remain in the vacation house. As a result, she accompanied her father on a business trip and told him about her difficulties with Mr. K. Although her vivid dreams ceased, several hysterical problems arose to take their place. It was at this point that her father had referred her to Freud.

During the analysis Dora's dreams came back: "A house was on fire. My father was standing beside my bed and woke me up. I dressed myself quickly. Mother wanted to stop and save her jewel-case; but father said: I refuse to let myself and my two children be burnt for the sake of your jewel-case. We hurried downstairs, and as soon as I was outside I woke up" (Freud, 1953, p. 64).

Some of the hidden elements of the dream became apparent in Dora's free associations. Represented by the jewel case and the fire, suggesting the smell of tobacco, Mr. K's presence was obvious to Freud. The dream also prompted Dora to recall that at the vacation house she slept in a hallway, which necessitated her dressing hurriedly so that Mr. K would not see her in her nightdress. Freud also deduced that the fire symbolized some of Dora's developing sexual urges. From all this, Freud concluded that Dora was experiencing the conflicting sensations of being attracted to Mr. K while at the same time being fearful of him.

The meaning of the dream was clear to Freud: it signified not only her present, conflict-ridden attraction toward Mr. K but also her earlier attraction for her father during the Oedipal period.

But if this were true, why did Dora flee from therapy? And why did the dream recur during therapy? After further analysis, Freud concluded that his original analysis of the dream had been incomplete. He realized that the dream did not simply revolve around Dora's feelings toward Mr. K. After all, Mr. K was no longer a part of her life. While the original dream had signified something about Mr. K, the recurrence of the dream signified something about Freud himself. Freud smoked many cigars and often discussed a variety of sexual matters with Dora, which could have stirred up numerous threatening urges. Just as before, Dora was fleeing from a relationship with another man who had tobacco on his breath, this time not from a vacation house but from a therapy room.

According to Freud the case of Dora clearly revealed both resistance and transference. Not only did Dora resist confronting her basic conflicts; she also transferred onto Freud some of the chief motives and characteristics of significant people from her past. Of course, Dora is one of Freud's exemplary case studies. The elements of resistance and transference are not always so plain, and the analysis is not always dramatic. See "A Modern-Day Psychoanalytic Therapy Session," which follows, for an example of what the daily work of a psychoanalyst might involve.

6.4   A Modern-Day Psychoanalytic Therapy Session

The following brief excerpt from a post-Freudian analytic session illustrates the type of verbal interchange that takes place between patient and analyst. The patient is a 34-year-old woman.

Patient: I feel uneasy . . . like I'm out of balance or something. . . . I don't really know what to say about it. (18-second pause)

P: Well, I just feel torn apart. If I lose any more control I don't know what would happen. (12-second pause)

P: Of course, I may be exaggerating things. My imagination . . . well, the worst things rarely happen. (30-second pause)

P: Sometimes . . . Sometimes, like right now, I feel as though there is nothing for me to say. (8-second pause)

P: I just, um . . . I feel like I'm just making up stuff to try and fit into the conversation . . . but I'm at a total loss. (12-second pause)

P: It's like a big game of charades or something (laughs). (15-second pause)

Analyst: You know what kind of charade you would play?

P: Not really. (8-second pause)

P: I could just let go, I suppose, and do what comes naturally . . . whatever comes to mind. I have some pretty wild feelings, come to think of it.

A: Hmm-mm.

P: Is that it? Should I just let go and dance and scream if I want to?

A: I'm not asking you to do anything.

P: No, I know you're not. . . . But do you feel that I have unnatural control?

A: You have some doubt about that?

P: No. I just wanted to hear you say so.

There is nothing terribly striking about this excerpt. The patient says nothing extraordinary and the therapist makes no monumental interpretations. Uncovering the roots of the patient's problems is a long, slow process. The excerpt, as mundane as it might appear, is typical. Major breakthroughs come infrequently. The patient does most of the talking, mainly in the form of free association. There are many pauses. After listening to the patient, the analyst interprets what the patient said. The patient then uses the interpretations to begin to gain insight about her feelings.

CRITICAL ANALYSIS

In the entire field of psychology there is perhaps no ongoing issue more controversial than the value of psychoanalytic treatment. The psychiatric literature contains many testimonials to the insights and personality changes achieved through psychoanalysis. But from other quarters, the value of psychoanalytic therapy has been sharply criticized. The contributions and oppositions of psychoanalysis must be weighed carefully.

Freud's theory is comprehensive. The range and diversity of issues Freud sought to understand include more than the treatment of emotional and behavioral disorders. He explored and explained issues related to war, death, humor, marriage, friendship, societal mores, creativity, competition, fairy tales, and absentmindedness. Few scholars would disagree that Freud's thinking led to extraordinarily comprehensive conceptual systems of human understanding.

While Freud's theory is comprehensive, however, its explanatory scheme is highly restricted in nature: sex and aggression are the sole determinants of behavior. Thus, the motivational base of the theory is limited and does not allow for different and more adequate explanations of behavior. Its pessimistic perspective views people as essentially irrational and controlled by amoral forces. Similarly, the structure of personality is divided into only three components, and the interactions among them are presumed to account for all underlying conflicts that hinder a person's functioning. So while his theory is comprehensive, its explanatory scheme is restricted.

Another problem with psychoanalysis is the relative vagueness of its concepts and the difficulties it presents in deriving clear and verifiable hypotheses. Much of the theory is presented in terms that do not lend themselves to precise scientific testing—the life and death instincts, for example. The universal conclusions that Freud drew about human behavior on the basis of extensive observations of a few patients seem naive. Recently, some historians assert that Freud even distorted facts that contradicted his theory (Raymond, 1991; Silverstein, 1989; Storr, 1989). Whatever the reason, it has become plain to see that when psychoanalytic theory is put to the empirical test, gaps quickly emerge.

> Just as for the individual, so also for all mankind, life is hard to bear.
>
> —Sigmund Freud

Eysenck (1952), for instance, conducted an early massive review of the clinical literature to assess the effectiveness of psychoanalysis. After examining more than 7,000 case histories of patients, he concluded that psychoanalytic therapy did not significantly facilitate the recovery of neurotic patients. Although 66 percent of patients treated to completion by means of psychoanalysis were much improved or cured, Eysenck found that 72 percent of patients who were not treated by means of any formal therapy were also much improved or cured within two years of the onset of their illnesses. Thus, approximately two thirds of patients recovered or improved to a marked extent whether they were treated psychoanalytically or not. Although numerous critics have attacked Eysenck's conclusions, reviews of all the evidence show that Eysenck's argument is still essentially valid today (Erwin, 1980; Franks, Wilson, Kendal, & Foreyt, 1990; Rachman, 1971; Stunkard, 1991).

Research exploring the connection between psychoanalytic insight and personal change also raises some questions. The Menninger Foundation conducted an intensive longitudinal study of the psychodynamic therapy of 42 patients beginning in 1952 and following them for 30 years (Wallerstein, 1989). To the researchers' surprise, they found that many patients achieved significant personal change even though they had not achieved a comparable degree of psychoanalytic insight into their problems. What was particularly surprising was that changes persisted, suggesting that other mechanisms in therapy, such as attempts to change interpersonal behavior directly and changes initiated to please the therapist, may be as important as insight.

There has always been a question as to how valid certain aspects of psychoanalytic thought are when applied to women. In many ways it views women as more vain, sensitive, submissive, and dependent than men. These attributes have been seen as part of the biology of being female. Quite bluntly, in Freud's view, women are inferior to men. He believed that the part of their personality that is different from men's comes from defending against and overcompensating for

---

6.5   Feminist Freudians?

The women who came together in the feminist movement of the 1970s were from a variety of backgrounds and often had sharply clashing views. But on one issue, they were as solid as an upraised fist: They had seen the enemy, and he was Freud. It was Sigmund Freud, they agreed, who had helped institutionalize the oppression of women by ratifying the notion that they were innately inferior to men. It was Freud who had suggested that their very development as women, and their demand for equality, were driven mainly by their need to compensate for the lack of a penis.

In recent years some feminists have been advocating not precisely forgiveness but a new circumspection about the man who once described women as "maimed" little creatures lacking "the only proper genital organ." In a stream of books and articles reappraising Freudian texts, they are suggesting that the father of psychoanalysis may have had something useful to say about women after all. Observes Wesleyan College humanities professor Elisabeth Young-Bruehl: "This whole new feminist appropriation of Freud reads him as saying, not 'Women are inferior,' but 'Women *feel* inferior'" in social structures established by men.

Young-Bruehl, who teaches a popular course on the history of psychoanalysis at the Connecticut school, is one of the women cautiously nudging Freud back into the feminist fold by finding new meaning in his writings. In "Freud On Women," she suggests that rather than simply passing judgment on women, Freud was attempting to describe the convoluted course by which their femininity develops.

Adapted from "A Fresh Take on Freud," by David Gelman, *Newsweek,* October 29, 1990.

their inferiority. Exception to the psychoanalytic implications that "biology is destiny" was voiced early on by analyst Karen Horney. She questioned many of Freud's views concerning women and feminine sexuality and more than anyone made room for female figures within its ranks (e.g., Anna Freud, Helene Deutsch, Greta Bibring, Margaret Mahler, Clara Thompson, and Frieda Fromm-Reichman). Freud clearly did not consider cultural factors in his understanding of women, and psychoanalysis is clearly biased as a result (Caplan, 1984).

Psychoanalysis also presents limitations when applied to multicultural counseling. Since the time and money that psychoanalysis requires rules out most people who are not wealthy, it is generally perceived as being based on upper- and middle-class values. In addition, its focus on personality restructuring conflicts with the more fundamental socioeconomic issues of survival and security. Finding resources to solve immediate and pressing problems is not the primary focus. It is not a practical theory for minority clients who might benefit from personality reconstruction only after more pressing issues have been resolved. On the other hand, a strength of psychoanalytic theory is its awareness of countertransference. The value it places on intensive psychotherapy as part of the training of therapists helps therapists of all ethnic and racial backgrounds become aware of their own biases and prejudices (Comas-Diaz & Minrath, 1985).

As a result Freudian thought has come under fire from many sectors: "from the academic psychologist for being unscientific, from humanistic and theistic psychology for being too reductionistic, and from the behaviourists for not being reductionistic enough" (Hurding, 1985, p. 70). Still, despite its critics, the seminal contributions of psychoanalysis to therapy have been an inspiration, in some form, to nearly all other theories of therapy. It is a stimulating theory that has left a permanent imprint not only on psychology, but on literature, art, sociology, history, anthropology, religion, philosophy, and political science as well. Freud's ideas reverberate throughout all of contemporary culture.

> What progress we are making. In the Middle Ages they would have burnt me; nowadays they are content with burning my books.
>
> —Sigmund Freud

CURRENT STATUS

While psychoanalytic purists do exist, contemporary analytic psychotherapies have evolved substantially beyond orthodox analytic thought. Most typically, psychoanalytic therapists take aspects of Freud's work and shape it to their own particular ends (Sampson, 1990; Zucker, 1993).

Psychoanalysts have proposed several variations of Freud's original theory (Liff, 1992). A major issue on which many contemporary analysts differ is the extent to which they adopt Freud's assumption that the infant (as well as adult) is primarily motivated by pleasure seeking. The theories range from those building on traditional Freudian theory (e.g., Kernberg, 1975, 1976; Mahler, 1968) to those replacing it with a whole new view of development (e.g., Fairbairn,

1952; Guntrip, 1969; Klein, 1976; Kohut, 1977, 1984). Other theories accept Freudian theory with modifications (e.g., Modell, 1975).

Contemporary psychoanalytic thinking can be divided into three major camps (Pine, 1988): ego psychology, object-relations theories, and self-psychology.

Ego Psychology

Since the death of Freud in 1939, ego psychology, sometimes dubbed the "American school," arose to give more attention to the conscious adaptive and controlling functions of the ego. It also stressed development of the personality across the life span. In reaction to what is perceived as Freud's excessive attention to the unconscious and the id, in ego psychology the patient and therapist sit face to face, and free association may or may not be invoked. The client's talk is much more reality-based and present-oriented (Blanck & Blanck, 1968). The therapist's job is to create an atmosphere in which clients feel free to delve into feelings of anxiety, guilt, and shame. The goal is to help them know themselves more fully, understand their inner conflicts, and become more aware of ways to respond differently in the future. Beyond the tensions surrounding sex and aggression, issues of identity, intimacy, and integrity become especially salient in this tradition. Heinz Hartman, René Spitz, Margaret Mahler, Anna Freud, Erik Erikson, and David Rapport are among the major theoreticians in this tradition (Prochaska, 1984).

Object Relations

Object-relations theorists from the "the British school," such as W. R. D. Firbairn, Otto Kernberg, and Melanie Klein (1975), have identified more clearly than Freudians how past childhood experience is reflected unconsciously in *object relations,* a technical term roughly translated as "past interpersonal relationships." (Although the term *object* primarily refers to persons, it may also include things.) These theorists point out that we develop our patterns of living from our early relations, particularly with parents—internalized "objects" (St. Clair, 1986). Experiences and relationships in early years leave impressions on the personality that profoundly influence behavior and thought over a life span. These internal objects replace the id, ego, and superego as the structure of personality, so that drives are seen as relational rather than sexual or aggressive. The goal of object-relations therapy is to understand how these childhood patterns are repeated in adult life (Edkins, 1985).

Self-Psychology

Heinz Kohut (1985) developed self-psychology based on the construct of the self. Originating in infancy, the self integrates and develops incrementally to produce either healthy relationships or the opposite, full range of adult psychopathologies. If early relationships are healthy and nurturing, a stable or "true" self will develop that is capable of mature relationships. If the early environment is characterized by emotional deprivation, however, the resulting "false" self remains limited in its capacity for relationship (Tobin, 1990).

Kohut asserted that the id, ego, and superego as well as the Oedipus conflict and penis envy are inadequate to describe the basic infant psyche. The self is the sum of all these entities plus an unnamed integrating function. Kohut's work is presented in two volumes, *The Analysis of the Self* (1971) and *The Restoration of the Self* (1977). Consider this summary on Freudian adaptations:

> Whether we are Freudians or not, as I am not, we are surely all post-Freudians.
> —Rollo May

1. Classical psychoanalysis asserts that people who understand their problems through interpretation will be able to overcome them.
2. Modern psychoanalysis is concerned with helping people meet unmet maturational needs. Greenberg and Mitchell (1983) point out that the three contemporary traditions also view cognitive processes and interpersonal relationships as the building blocks of personality.
3. The ego psychologists modify the classic id-drive model by emphasizing early, formative relationships.
4. A more radical strategy, adopted by the object-relations theorists, requires complete replacement of Freud's drive concept with a strong interpersonal model.
5. Self-psychology has adopted drive model concepts and mixed them with the relational model.

During World War II a number of European analysts moved to the United States, making it the country with the largest number of psychoanalytic adherents. Most of today's analysts are located in large urban settings near psychoanalytic institutes in such cities as New York, Los Angeles, Boston, and Chicago (Nye, 1992). In these institutes the next generation of analysts are being trained.

Despite the criticisms of traditional analysts, who claim that psychoanalysis is being watered down by those who deviate from Freud's basic theory, changes seem inevitable (Cooper, 1987). And it may well be these changes that prevent psychoanalysis from becoming a relic. These updated forms of psychoanalysis are contributing to its good health, as evidenced by the bulk of material being published on the subject (Fine, 1990). Although it has been a century since Breuer and Freud developed the structure of psychoanalysis, it sustains a promising future (Gay, 1989).

Many today still echo the sentiments of W. H. Auden's poetic tribute to the Viennese master, which he wrote a few months after Freud's death in 1939:

> If often he was wrong and at times absurd,
> To us he is no more a person now
> But a whole climate of opinion
> Under whom we conduct our differing lives.

SUMMARY

1. *Biography.* Freud (1856–1939) spent nearly all his life in Vienna. He was an excellent student but his career choices were restricted because of his Jewish heritage. He settled on medicine and at age 26 attained a position at the University of Vienna. By exploring the meaning of his own dreams, he gained insights into the dynamics of personality, and he formulated his clinical theory as he observed the work of his patients in analysis. He had little tolerance for colleagues who diverged from his psychoanalytic doctrines. He died of cancer of the jaw in London.

2. *Historical Development.* The origins of psychoanalysis are identified with the early 1880s. During this time, Josef Breuer's treatment of hysteria (specifically with Anna O.) influenced Freud's thinking. Freud studied under Jean Charcot, exploring the use of hypnotic techniques. These two experiences were instrumental in Freud's first using the term *psychoanalysis* in 1896.

3. *View of Human Nature.* Freud viewed people as being dominated by the instinctual, unconscious, and irrational forces of sex and aggression. For Freud, personality was determined entirely by conditions and events beyond personal control. He viewed consciousness as only a small part of the total psyche. Freud divided personality into three components: id (present at birth, entirely unconscious, and including all innate instincts), ego (developing out of the id at about six to eight months to help the id gain its ends), and superego (developing out of the ego at about age three to five years, including the ego ideal and the conscience). Furthermore, Freud believed adult personality is established by about age five, following a more or less set course through a series of psychosexual stages: oral, anal, phallic, latency, and genital.

4. *Development of Maladaptive Behavior.* Symptoms of abnormality vary in the psychoanalytic thought depending upon the psychosexual stage in which conflicts and fixations first developed and the manner in which defense mechanisms are used to deal with the resulting anxiety. The fixation of excessive amounts of libido at pregenital stages generally results in various character patterns and psychopathology. Libido may also regress to a previous psychosexual stage or to an earlier object choice long since abandoned, usually one that was strongly fixated. Anxiety, operating largely at the unconscious level, is at the core of all psychopathology. The degree of anxiety depends on the leadership of the ego. A weak ego spends excessive amounts of psychic energy wrestling with the id and superego, resulting in maladaptive behavior.

5. *Goals of Therapy.* The ultimate goal of psychoanalysis is not the removal of symptoms. Rather, it is the total reconstruction of personality through making the unconscious conscious. The person's ego is to be strengthened so that aggressive and sexual impulses can be brought under control. It is designed to reintegrate previously repressed experiences in the total personality structure.

6. *Function of the Therapist.* The analyst neither offers advice nor extends sympathy, but encourages clients to talk about whatever comes to mind, espe-

cially about childhood experiences. In classical psychoanalysis the analyst fosters a transference by allowing the client to project unresolved conflicts, feelings, and experiences on to the analyst. This classical conception of the role of the psychoanalyst as an emotionally neutral figure, however, has been modified by modern psychoanalytic views of the analyst as more active.

7. *Major Methods and Techniques.* The most enduring therapeutic techniques of psychoanalysis are free association (the cardinal technique of allowing the client to say whatever comes to mind, no matter how illogical or trivial), dream analysis (interpreting the latent content of the dream primarily through the use of consistent symbols that signify the same thing for nearly everyone), analysis of transference (when the client responds to the analyst as a significant authority person from his or her life, thus revealing the nature of childhood difficulties), and analysis of resistance (the unconscious resisting of efforts to help eliminate old behavior patterns, thereby impeding any attempts to probe into the real sources of personality problems).

8. *Application.* Freud leaned heavily on case studies in the formulation of his theory. The case of "Dora" is one example that illustrated how Freud used resistance and transference to bring about psychological insight. Since the therapeutic goals are so high and difficult to obtain, and the self-defeating patterns so deeply established with the client, it is inevitable that psychoanalytic treatment be intensive and long term. A modern-day excerpt from an analytic session was also depicted in the chapter.

9. *Critical Analysis.* Psychoanalysis has both devoted admirers and strong critics. Among its strengths are its comprehensive nature and its monumental value to spurring on other therapeutic theories. Among its shortcomings are methodological problems, an overemphasis on biological determinants of personality, relative vagueness of concepts, and gender and cultural bias.

10. *Current Status.* Contemporary analytic psychotherapies have evolved substantially beyond orthodox analytic thought. A major issue on which many contemporary analysts differ is the extent to which they adopt Freud's assumption that the infant (as well as adult) is primarily motivated by pleasure seeking. Contemporary psychoanalytic thinking can be divided into ego psychology (present-oriented and reality-based, focusing on issues of identity, intimacy, and integrity), object-relations theories (focusing on early relations and rational drives), and self-psychology (focusing on the construct of the self originating in infancy and its integrating function).

Key Terms

Anal stage The second of Freud's psychosexual stages, during which gratification comes primarily from the elimination process.

Anxiety A feeling of fear and dread without an obvious case.

Castration anxiety A boy's fear during the Oedipal period that his penis will be cut off.

Catharsis The expression of emotions that is expected to lead to their reduction.

Conscious A component of the superego containing behaviors for which the child has been punished.

Countertransference The phenomenon of the therapist transferring feelings, fantasies, and behaviors from a previous relationship onto the client and thus creating an inappropriate therapeutic relationship.

Defense mechanisms A strategy of distorting reality used by the ego to defend itself against the anxiety provoked by the conflicts of everyday life.

Dream analysis A technique involving the interpretation of dreams to uncover unconscious conflicts.

Ego The rational aspect of the personality, responsible for directing and controlling instincts.

Ego ideal A component of the superego containing the moral or ideal behaviors for which a person should strive.

Electra complex The unconscious desire of girls during the phallic stage of psychosexual development for their fathers, accompanied by a desire to replace or destroy their mothers.

Erogenous zones The parts of the body that are sensitive to sexual stimulation: the mouth, anus, penis, clitoris, and vagina.

Fixation The state in which a portion of the libido remains invested in one of the psychosexual stages because of excessive frustration or gratification.

Free association A technique in which the client says whatever comes to mind; a kind of daydreaming out loud.

Freudian slip A slip of the tongue revealing unconscious material.

Genital stage The fifth and final stage in Freud's psychosexual stages, during which a person learns socially appropriate channels for the expression of sexual impulses.

Id The aspect of personality operating according to the pleasure principle and allied with drives.

Introjection A process of incorporating the norms and standards of culture into personality by identifying with significant adults during childhood.

Latency stage The fourth stage of Freud's psychosexual stages, during which satisfaction is gained primarily through exploration of the environment and development of skills and interests.

Latent content The symbolic meaning of events in a dream.

Libido The form of psychic energy manifested by the life instincts that drive a person toward pleasurable behaviors and thoughts.

Manifest content The actual events in a dream.

Morality principle The part of the personality that represents society's views of right and wrong.

Oedipus complex The unconscious desire of boys during the phallic stage of psychosexual development for their mothers, accompanied by a desire to replace or destroy their fathers.

Oral stage The first and most primitive of Freud's psychosexual stages, during which the mouth region is the primary source of gratification.

Penis envy The envy females feel toward males because they possess a penis, accompanied by a sense of loss because females do not have one.

Phallic stage The third of Freud's psychosexual stages during which satisfaction is gained primarily through genital manipulation and exploration.

Pleasure principle The id functions on this principle to avoid pain and to maximize pleasure.

Preconscious Memory accessible to consciousness only after something calls one's attention to it.

Primary process Childlike thinking by which the id attempts to satisfy the instinctual drives.

Psychoanalysis Sigmund Freud's system of therapy.

Psychosexual stages The stages through which children pass and in which instinctual gratification depends on the stimulation of corresponding area of the body.

Reality principle The ego functions on this principle to provide appropriate constraints on the expression of the id instincts.

Resistance A blockage or refusal to disclose painful memories in free association.

Secondary process Mature thought processes needed to deal rationally with the external world.

Superego The moral aspect of personality that has internalized parental and societal values and standards.

Thanatos The unconscious drive toward decay, destruction, and aggression.

Transference The phenomenon of clients placing their unconscious material onto the therapist and experiencing the therapist as if he or she were a previously encountered person.

Unconscious The domain of the psyche that stores repressed urges and primitive impulses.

Womb envy The inferiority experienced by boys in discovering they cannot bear children.

SUGGESTED READING

Translations of Freud's writing are found in many forms by various publishers. Hogarth Press of London has published a complete Standard Edition of his works, consisting of 24 volumes. Other paperbound editions of Freud's works can be found in most bookstores. They include the following:

An outline of psychoanalysis. New York: W. W. Norton.

Beyond the pleasure principle. New York: Bantam Books

Civilization and its discontents. New York: W. W. Norton.

The ego and the id. New York: W. W. Norton.

The interpretation of dreams. New York: Avon Books.

In addition to Freud's own writings there are many helpful books about psychoanalysis:

Brenner, C. (1974). *An elementary textbook of psychoanalysis* (Rev. ed.). Garden City, NY: Doubleday (Anchor).

Gay, P. (1988). Freud: *A life for our time.* New York: Norton.

Jones, E. (1961). *The life and work of Sigmund Freud* (Abridged ed.). New York: Basic Books.

Kline, P. (1984). *Psychology and Freudian theory.* New York: Methuen.

St. Clair, M. (1986). *Objects relations and self psychology: An introduction.* Pacific Grove, CA: Brooks/Cole.

References

Abrams, D. (1992). The dream's mirror of reality. *Contemporary Psychoanalysis, 28,* 50–71.

Alexander, F., & French, T. (1946). *Psychoanalytic therapy.* New York: Ronald Press.

Arlow, J. A., & Brenner, C. (1988). The future of psychoanalysis. *Psychoanalytic Quarterly, 57,* 1–14.

Blanck, G., & Blanck, R. (1968). *Ego psychology: Theory and practice.* New York: Columbia University Press.

Brecher, E. M. (1972). *Licit and illicit drugs.* New York: Consumers Union.

Buie, J. (1989, January). Traditional analysis may be changing. *APA Monitor,* 19.

Caplan, P. J. (1984). The myth of women's masochism. *American Psychologist, 39,* 130–139.

Clark, R. W. (1980). *Freud: The man and the cause.* New York: Random House.

Comas-Diaz, L., & Minrath, M. (1985). Psychotherapy with ethnic minority borderline clients. *Psychotherapy, 22,* 418–426.

Cooper, A. M. (1987). Changes in psychoanalytic ideas: Transference interpretation. *Journal of the American Psychoanalytic Association, 35,* 77–98.

Edkins, W. (1985). Object relations theory. In D. Benner (Ed.), *Baker encyclopedia of psychology* (pp. 796–771). Grand Rapids, MI: Baker.

Erwin, E. (1980). Psychoanalytic therapy: The Eysenck argument. *American Psychologist, 35,* 435–443.

Eysenck, H. J. (1952). The effects of psychotherpay: An evaluation. *Journal of Consulting Psychology, 16,* 319–324.

Fairbairn, W. R. D. (1952). *Psychoanalytic studies of the personality.* London: Tavistock Publications and Routledge & Kegan Paul.

Fine, R. (1990). Freud and psychoanalysis. *Contemporary Psychology, 35,* 775–776.

Franks, C. M., Wilson, G. T., Kendal, P. C., & Foreyt, J. P. (1990). *Review of behavior theory: Theory and practice* (Vol. 12). New York: Guilford Press.

Freeman, L. (1972). *The story of Anna O.* New York: Walker.

Freud, A. (1966). *The ego and the mechanism of defense* (Rev. ed.). New York: International Universities Press.

Freud, S. (1901). *The psychopathology of everyday life.* London: Hogarth Press.

Freud, S. (1923). *The ego and the id.* London: Hogarth Press.

Freud, S. (1924). *A general introduction to psychoanalysis.* New York: Boni and Liveright.

Freud, S. (1926). *Inhibitions, symptoms, and anxiety.* London: Hogarth Press.

Freud, S. (1933). *New introductory lectures on psychoanalysis.* London: Hogarth Press.

Freud, S. (1935). *An autobiographical study* (J. Strachey, Trans.). London: Hogarth Press.

Freud, S. (1957). *The interpretation of dreams.* In J. Strachey (Ed.), *The standard edition of the complete psychological works of Sigmund Freud* (Vol. 12). London: Hogarth. (Originally published 1900).

Freud, S. (1963). *Sigmund Freud: Therapy and technique.* New York: Collier Books.

Freud, S., & Breuer, J. (1895). *Studies on hysteria.* London: Hogarth Press.

Fromm, E. (1991). Causes for the patient's change in analytic treatment. *Contemporary Psychoanalysis, 27,* 581–602.

Gay, P. (1988). *Freud: A life for our time.* New York: Norton.

Gay, P. (1989). *The Freud reader.* New York: Norton.

Glenn, J. (1987). Freud, Birgil, and Aeneas: An unnoticed classical influence on Freud. *American Journal of Psychoanalysis, 47* (3), 279–281.

Greenberg, J., & Mitchell, S. (1983). *Object-relations in psychoanalytic theory.* Cambridge, MA: Harvard University Press.

Greenson, R. R. (1967). *The technique and practice of psychoanalysis,* (Vol. 1). New York: International Universities Press.

Guntrip, H. (1969). *Schizoid phenomena, object relations and the self.* New York: International Universities Press.

Harper, R. (1975). *The new psychotherapies.* Englewood Cliffs, NJ: Prentice Hall.

Hollender, M. H. (1980). The case of Anna O.: A reformulation. *American Journal of Psychiatry, 137,* 787–800.

Horney, K. (1926). The flight from womanhood: The masculinity complex in women as viewed by men and by women. *International Journal of Psychoanalysis, 7,* 324–329.

Hornstein, G. (1992). The return of the repressed: Psychology's problematic relations with psychoanalysis, 1906–1960. *American Psychologist, 47* (2), 245–263.

Hurding, R. (1985). *Roots and shoots.* London: Hodder and Stoughton.

Jones, E. (1953). *The life and work of Sigmund Freud* (Vol. 1). New York: Basic Books.

Jones, E. (1955). *The life and work of Sigmund Freud* (Vol. 2). New York: Basic Books.

Jones, E. (1957). *The life and work of Sigmund Freud* (Vol. 3). New York: Basic Books.

Jones, J., & Wilson, W. (1987). *An incomplete education.* New York: Ballantine.

Kanzer, M., & Glenn, J. (1980). *Freud and his patients.* New York: Aronson.

Kernberg, O. (1975). *Borderline conditions and pathological narcissism.* New York: Aronson.

Kernberg, O. (1976). *Object-relations theory and clinical psychoanalysis.* New York: Aronson.

Klein, G. S. (1976). *Psychoanalytic theory: An exploration of essentials.* New York: International Universities Press.

Klein, M. (1975). *Envy and gratitude and other works, 1946–1963.* London: Hogarth.

Kohut, H. (1971). *The analysis of the self.* Monograph series of the psychoanalytic study of the child (4). New York: International Universities Press.

Kohut, H. (1977). *The restoration of self.* New York: International Universities Press.

Kohut, H. (1984). *How does analysis cure?* Chicago: University of Chicago Press.

Kohut, H. (1985). *Self psychology and the humanities: Reflections on a new psychoanalytic approach.* New York: Norton.

Korchin, S. (1976). *Modern clinical psychology.* New York: Basic Books.

Laplanch, J., & Pontailis, J. (1973). *The language of psychoanalysis.* New York: Norton.

Leak, G. K., & Christopher, S. B. (1982). Freudian psychoanalysis and sociobiology. *American Psychologist, 37,* 313–322.

Liff, Z. A. (1992). Psychoanalysis and dynamic techniques. In D. K. Feedheim (Ed.), *History of psychotherapy: A century of change* (pp. 571–586). Washington, DC: American Psychological Association.

Lipschitz, F. (1990). The dream within a dream: Profliction vs. reflection. *Contemporary Psychoanalysis, 26,* 716–731.

Mahler, M. (1968). *On human symbiosis and the vicissitudes of individuation: Infantile psychosis* (Vol. 1). New York: International Universities Press.

Mead, M. (1974). On Freud's view of female psychology. In J. Strouse (Ed.), *Women and analysis: Dialogues on psychoanalytic views of femininity* (pp. 95–106). New York: Grossman.

Meares, R. (1992). Transference and the play space: Towards a new basic meta-phor. *Contemporary Psychoanalysis, 28,* 32–49.

Meissner, W. (1985). Theories of personality and psychopathology: Classical psychoanalysis. In H. I. Kaplan and B. J. Sadock (Eds.), *Comprehensive textbook of psychiatry* (Vol. 4, pp. 337–418). Baltimore, MD: Williams and Wilkins.

Modell, A. (1975). The ego and the id: 50 years later. *International Journal of Psychoanalysis, 56,* 57–68.

Munroe, R. (1955). *Schools of psychoanalytic thought.* New York: Holt, Rinehart and Winston.

Nemiah, J. C. (1984). Psychoanalysis and individual psychotherapy. In T. B. Karasu (Ed.), *The psychiatric therapies* (pp. 321–346). Washington, DC: American Psychiatric Association.

Nye, R. D. (1992). *Three psychologies: Perspectives from Freud, Skinner, and Rogers* (4th ed.). Monterey, CA: Brooks/Cole

Pine, F. (1988). The four psychologies of psychoanalysis and their place in clinical work. *Journal of the American Psychoanalytic Association, 36,* 571–596.

Pine, F. (1990). *Drive, ego, object and self.* New York: Basic Books.

Prochaska, J. (1984). *Systems of psychotherapy* (2nd ed.). Chicago: Dorsey.

Rachman, S. (1971). *The effects of psychotherapy.* Oxford, England: Pergamon.

Raymond, C. (1991). Study of patient histories suggest Freud suppressed or distorted facts that contradicted his theories. *Chronicle of Higher Education, 37,* A4–A6.

Runyan, W. McK. (Ed.). (1988). *Psychology and historical interpretation.* New York: Oxford University Press.

Sampson, H. (1990). The problem of adaptation to reality in psychoanalytic theory. *Contemporary Psychoanalysis, 26,* 677–691.

Silverstein, S. (1989). Freud's dualistic mind-body interactionism: Implications for the development of his psychology. *Psychological Reports, 64,* 1091–1097.

St. Clair, M. (1986). *Object relations and self psychology.* Belmont, CA: Wadsworth.

St. Clair, M. (1986). *Objects relations and self psychology: An introduction.* Pacific Grove, CA: Brooks/Cole.

Storr, A. (1989). *Freud.* New York: Oxford.

Strupp, H. H., & Binder, J. L. (1984). *Psychotherapy in a new key.* New York: Basic Books.

Stunkard, A. J. (1991). Review of Schwartz, H. J. (Ed.), *Bulimia: Psychoanalytic treatment and theory.* Madison, CT: International Universities Press, 1988. *Psychiatric Annals, 19,* 279.

Thompson, C. (1943). "Penis envy" in women. *Psychiatry, 6,* 123–125.

Tobin, S. A. (1990). Self psychology as a bridge between existential-humanistic psychology and psychoanalysis. *Journal of Humanistic Psychology, 30,* 14–63.

Wachtel, P. L. (1977). *Psychoanalysis and behavior therapy: Toward an integration.* New York: Basic Books.

Wallerstein, R. S. (1989). The psychotherapy research project of the Menninger Foundation: An overview. *Journal of Consulting and Clinical Psychology, 57,* 195–205.

Winnicott, D. W. (1956). On transference. *International Journal of Psycho-Analysis, 37,* 386–388.

Zucker, H. (1993). Reality: Can it be only yours or mine? Conference of the Westchester Center for the Study for Psychoanalysis and Psychotherapy. *Contemporary Psychoanalysis, 29,* 479–486.

I have taken forty years to make my psychology simple. —Alfred Adler

Adlerian Therapy | CHAPTER **7**

CHAPTER OUTLINE

Brief Biography
Historical Development
View of Human Nature
Development of Maladaptive Behavior
Function of the Therapist
Goals of Therapy
Major Methods and Techniques
Application
Critical Analysis
Current Status
Summary
Key Terms
Suggested Reading
References

So influential is Alfred Adler, the first of the Viennese psychoanalysts to break with Freud, that some have called him the "true father of modern psychotherapy" (Ellis, 1970). Their separation occurred in 1911 when it became apparent that their thinking was irreconcilably at odds. Unfortunately, the professional dispute became personal when Freud, who accused the "defector" of being too proud to live in the shadow of a giant, forbade his followers to attend any of Adler's conferences. Undaunted, Adler went on to develop a new society, a new journal, and a new therapeutic approach called **individual psychology.**

Adler holds a significant place in the field of psychology. He influenced neo-Freudians like Karen Horney and Erich Fromm (although some argue they should be called neo-Adlerians) as well as more modern theorists like Carl Rogers and Albert Ellis (Corsini & Wedding, 1989). Not only did he shift the Freudian emphasis on the libido to the ego's striving for power, he also developed a personality model, a theory of psychopathology, the concept of the inferiority complex, and a treatment method (Parrott, 1992).

According to Adler, individuals are victims of neither their genetic endowment nor their social conditioning. Rather, they are responsible for themselves and learn to respond in adaptive, creative ways to their surroundings. Even early in life individuals strive toward an ideal that runs as a major theme throughout their lives (Adler, 1959).

7.1 | Adler's Contribution to Modern Psychology

Adlerian Concept	Modern Counterpart
• Emphasis on the social rather than the sexual aspects of the person	• Socially oriented theories of Fromm, Horney, and Sullivan
• Emphasis on the ego	• Ego psychology of Erikson, Hartmann, and others
• Importance of personal choices and courage in living	• Existential perspective of "being-in-the-world" and facing the fear of nothingness
• Importance of self-esteem and equality in therapy	• Rogers's emphasis on self-esteem and positive regard
• Use of physical movements to reveal a style of life	• "Body language;" Allport's study of expressive behavior
• Equality of women	• Feminist movement
• Self-created style of life	• Kelly's psychology of personal constructs
• Social interest	• A criteria of mental health in Maslow's theory
• Treating children in the company of their parents and establishing child guidance clinics	• Family therapy, group therapy, community psychology
• Face-to-face weekly interviews in psychotherapy	• Almost all modern forms of psychotherapy

Surprisingly, Adler's influence remains largely unrecognized. "It would not be easy," writes Ellenberger, "to find another author from which so much has been borrowed from all sides without acknowledgment, than Adler" (1970, p. 645). Wilder, in his introduction to *Essays in Individual Psychology*, writes, "Most observations and ideas of Alfred Adler have subtly and quietly permeated modern psychological thinking to such a degree that the proper question is not whether one is Adlerian but how much of an Adlerian one is" (Adler & Deutsch, 1959, p. xv).

BRIEF BIOGRAPHY

Born on February 7, 1870, in a suburb of Vienna, Alfred Adler was the second of six children. He grew up in the shadow of a gifted and successful older brother. One of his earliest childhood memories was of sitting on a bench, bandaged and incapacitated by rickets, while his athletic older brother played vigorously. As a young student, Adler tasted early failure. He could not draw well and repeated an arithmetic class. One teacher told his father that the boy should be an apprentice to a shoemaker because he was unfit for anything else.

As a grain merchant, Adler's father provided the family with a comfortable living even though they faced financial difficulties. While Adler's mother, gloomy, rejecting, and self-sacrificing, embodied what her son later called the *martyr complex,* his father was cheerful and self-confident, and Adler identified with him. Understandably, he would later reject Freud's Oedipus complex, so foreign to his own childhood experience. And while Freud, raised in a Jewish ghetto, was at times self-conscious about his minority status, Adler knew few Jewish children. In fact, Adler was so much more immersed in Viennese culture than in his Jewish heritage that at the age of 34 he converted from Judaism to Christianity.

Adler described his childhood as unhappy. There were close encounters with disease and death. At age three, he witnessed the death of a younger brother in the bed next to his. When he was five, he barely survived pneumonia. When he heard the doctor say to his father, "Your boy is lost," he decided to become a doctor himself (Orgler, 1963, p. 16). Twice he was injured in serious street accidents.

> Perhaps there are so few Adlerians because we are all Adlerians.
> —Joseph F. Burke

Despite these personal and family setbacks, at age 25 Adler received a medical degree in 1895 from the University of Vienna. Ironically, he never attended any of the lectures on hysteria given there by a relatively unknown physician, Sigmund Freud. His field of specialization was ophthalmology; his interest in psychiatry would bloom later.

From his clinic in a lower-middle-class neighborhood, Adler worked with a broad range of patients and diseases. Since his office was near an amusement park, his patients were often performers and artists, including acrobats, many of whom, Alder learned, had developed their abilities in reaction to childhood weaknesses or accidents (Furtmuller, 1964). These early investigations first suggested to Adler that the organic and psychological dimensions of disease were not separate, that many high-achieving people with great mental or physical abilities were overcompensating for childhood inferiorities.

At a political rally Adler met his strong-willed future wife, Raissa Epstein, who would shape her husband's views on the equality of women. The daughter of Russian intelligentsia, she had come to Vienna to complete her education. When she returned home, Adler scraped together enough money to visit her in Russia, where they were married in 1897. They had four children, three daughters and a son, two of whom became psychiatrists themselves.

After the First World War Adler was given the task of establishing guidance clinics for the Vienna school system. Every child from 6 to 14 was screened in order to refer for counseling those with learning disabilities, emotional disturbances, or behavioral problems. This project reduced delinquency in a city where it might have been expected to be rampant. More importantly, this work so convinced Adler of the importance of child-rearing practices that his subsequent theories about parent-child relationships would have a lasting effect on modern educational theory and practice.

A short man, inclined to an unpretentious, sometimes slovenly, appearance, Adler was markedly less handsome or charismatic than Freud. Adler first heard Freud lecture in 1899, and he was invited to join Freud's discussion group in 1902. Although Adler was never psychoanalyzed himself, as were other members of the inner circle, he won the respect of his colleagues and was selected as the editor of their journal. In 1910 Adler was elected president of the Vienna Psychoanalytic Society, an honor previously held by Freud, and he came to impress people as a witty and inspiring lecturer.

Adler never considered himself a disciple of Freud, however, and his intellectual independence led to a widening rift between them. "Do you think it gives me such great pleasure to stand in your shadow my whole life long?" he once remarked to Freud (Freud, 1914, p. 51). Seemingly in response, Freud wrote in a letter to Carl Jung that Adler "is always . . . complaining that he is disappearing under my shadow, and forcing me into the unwelcome role of the aging despot who prevents young men from getting ahead" (McGuire, 1974, p. 373). He called Adler a "pygmy." With equal bitterness, Adler called Freud's psychoanalysis "filth" (Roazen, 1975, p. 210). Their breakup was precipitated by the primacy Freud assigned to sexuality. While Adler acknowledged the significance of sexual conflicts, he felt that people's problems stemmed from a variety of social sources. While Freud argued that women find themselves inferior because they lack male genitals, Adler looked not to women's anatomy but to their interactions with society to find the source of their perceptions. Toward the end of their relationship, the two men, Freud and Adler, had little more in common than their mutual appreciation for cigars.

Early in 1911 Adler delivered to Viennese society three lectures that elaborated the differences that distinguished his work from Freud's. This resulted in the formation of the Society for Free Psychoanalysis, which later became known as the Society for Individual Psychology (Orgler, 1963). In 1926 Adler visited the United States for the first time, accepting appointments at Columbia University and later at Long Island College of Medicine. Adler made the United States his permanent home in 1934 in order to flee Nazi Germany. Three years later he died of a heart attack in the midst of a strenuous European lecture tour at the University of Aberdeen in Scotland.

HISTORICAL DEVELOPMENT

The Bible and the Stoic philosophers were among the many influences on Adler's thinking. He drew from writers such as Dostoevsky, Goethe, and Shakespeare, and from Karl Marx, Nietzsche, Henri Bergson, and Immanuel Kant as well. His theory was informed by such Americans as G. Stanley Hall, John Dewey, and William James (Ansbacher, 1992). However, the primary influence on Adler's views came from the philosopher Hans Vaihinger (1924), who taught that none of us can know truth completely. We formulate approximations of reality, Vaihinger wrote, and then live by these con-

> A psychological system has an inseparable connection with the life philosophy of its formulator.
>
> —Alfred Adler

structions as if they were true. Vaihinger's (1911) book, *The Psychology of "As If,"* proposed that people live in accordance with fictional goals they set for themselves. Adler seized upon this notion in order to develop his own concept of a *lifestyle:* the particular arrangement of convictions or conclusions about self, others, and reality we establish early in life. Significantly, Vaihinger's work provided Adler with the grounds for his reaction against Freud's strict determinism. According to Adler, people are motivated not so much by their past experiences as by their future goals, an explanation called **teleology.** Although people are usually unaware of these goals, according to Adler, they are the keys to their unconscious, guiding their striving for superiority.

Others influenced Adler's thinking as well: Janet, who believed that a sense of inferiority is the general cause of neurosis; Nietzsche, whose emphasis on both the importance of the individual and the striving for perfection lay behind much of Adler's concept of the striving for superiority; and Marx, who identified social forces as the prime determinants of human behavior and who urged reforms promoting equal opportunity regardless of birth or gender. It was Marx who allowed Adler to formulate his concern for "social interest" (Brink, 1985). And it was Vaihinger's contention that people are motivated not by reality but by fictions, by goals and interpretations, that inspired Adler's concepts of "guiding fiction" and the subjective "as if."

But the greatest contemporary influence on Adler's individual psychology was, of course, Sigmund Freud, with whom Adler collaborated for almost a decade (1902–1911). Adler adopted Freud's emphasis on the importance of early childhood and parental factors, along with his psychoanalytic perspective that all behavior results from and reflects the underlying personality. However, Adler disputed the claim that neither hereditary nor environmental forces completely determine an individual's personality.

Six years before his death, Adler published a paper that elaborated the differences between Freud's approach to psychoanalysis and his own approach to individual psychology. Unlike Freud, Adler spoke of neither instincts, such as Eros or Thanatos, nor of entities of the mind, such as the id, ego, or superego. Nor did Adler distinguish between the conscious and unconscious, although he used both concepts. Not only was Adler less inclined than Freud to attribute problems to human sexuality, he was also less systematic in his theorizing—his constructs are not particularly well integrated, and there are fewer of them—and he was less methodical in laying out a plan for treatment. Adler placed much more emphasis than Freud on defensive mechanisms and on family relationships, on one's environment, and on learning. And while Freud spoke of the internal drive of the instincts, Adler emphasized the many different goals that motivate human behavior.

VIEW OF HUMAN NATURE

Central to Adler's program is the premise that human beings are irreducibly whole. In fact, so fundamental to Adler's work is this premise, that he called his system of psychotherapy *Individual Psychology,* after the Latin term *individuum*: indivisible, complete, whole. Unlike Freud, Adler saw human nature in holistic rather than reductionistic terms. In other words, the way individuals organize themselves largely determines their response to the outside world (Dinkmeyer, Pew, & Dinkmeyer, 1979).

Inferiority

In *The Neurotic Constitution,* one of Adler's earliest and most influential works, he considered the problem of **organ inferiority**—that is, the role of physical abnormalities or personality deficits in the development of neurosis (1917). "A body which is ill-suited to the environment," wrote Adler, "will usually be felt by the mind as a burden" (1931, p. 34). Adler believed that the resulting sense of inferiority is the source of human striving, the driving force that motivates behavior. All individual progress, growth, and development result from the attempt to **compensate** for our inferiorities, be they imagined or real.

In one of his earliest papers, Adler investigated the issue of inferiority and **compensation** (1907). It was well known that disease often attacks weaker organs in the body, but Adler observed that disease is not the inevitable consequence of a weak organ. Under some circumstances, like a broken bone healing even stronger at its fracture line, the body compensates for this weakness and develops an offsetting strength, either by rebuilding its organ or by increasing its capacity to function in spite of its disability. Adler held that this compensation is achieved because the organic inferiority stimulates the process of rebuilding the affected organ.

Adler, who was an optimist, believed that people could find personal happiness by similarly compensating for emotional inferiority. Studying the functional tendencies of the body in order to unravel the secrets of the mind, Adler turned to history and literature for illustrations of how inferiority can be turned to superiority under favorable environmental conditions. Teddy Roosevelt, for example, a weakling as a child, developed into a hearty and robust adult who led the charge up San Juan hill. He launched the National Park Service, led legislative initiatives to protect the environment, broke up ruthless corporations like Standard Oil, popularized the slogan "Speak softly but carry a big stick," and, significantly, coined the term "rugged individualism."

> To live is to feel inferior.
> —Alfred Adler

Adlerian counseling assumes that individuals are motivated by a striving for superiority. Because all children feel inferior, by virtue of their size and lesser capabilities, Adler believed that the longing for significance, for self-esteem, emerges early. Individuals crave a sense of mastery, purposefulness, and meaning, and this **striving for superiority** is what drives adult life (Adler, 1930). By "striving for superiority" Adler was speaking not of human tendencies toward domination or arrogance, but of the human capacity to turn a deficiency into an advantage. As a synonym for "superiority," he occasionally used the word *perfection*, in the sense of wholeness and completion, from the Latin *perficere*, "to complete" or "to finish."

Finalism

Whereas Freud believed that human behavior is pushed by the past, Adler believed it is pulled by the future. Thus, while Freud considered behavior to be rigidly determined by physiological instincts and experiences of childhood, Adler believed that expectations and goals for the future motivate human activity. It is this final goal of superiority or perfection that explains human motivations. And it is this **finalism**, as Adler termed it, this belief in an ultimate goal, a final state of being, that accounts for our ever present tendency or necessity to move in that direction. What is intriguing about personal goals, according to Adler, is that they do not exist as actualities but as potentialities. We strive for unfulfilled ideals, for the belief, for instance, that people are created equal or that people are basically good. To this notion that such ideals guide the way we perceive and interact with those around us, Adler gave the term **fictional finalism.**

Social Interest

From earliest times, people have congregated in communities, families, tribes, and nations for survival and protection. It has always been necessary for people to cooperate. Adler believed that people are inherently concerned with the welfare of others, a capacity that he labeled *Gemeinschaftsgefuhl,* or **social interest** (O'Connell, 1965). People need to cooperate with and contribute to society in order to realize personal and social goals. Social interest is the engine that drives empathy and altruism. Originally Adler regarded social interest as a force that opposes a striving for superiority, that prevents people from being ruthlessly selfish, but he later combined the two concepts. The enhancement of social interest, Adler came to believe, is the most important goal toward which people strive (Ansbacher, 1980).

In contrast to Freud, who believed that the individual and society are in conflict, Adler believed that the relationship between people and their larger world is harmonious (Adler, 1931). In fact, Adler's concept of social interest encompasses the whole of human actions, thoughts, and emotions (O'Connell, 1965; Mosak, 1991). Included among behaviors associated with social interest are, for example, those that encourage individuals to help and to respect one another; to share, cooperate, and compromise with one another; to encourage; and to empathize with another's thoughts and emotions. But it is not only behaviors that emerge from this social interest, Adler argued. A feeling of ease or communality; a sense of belonging, of being "at home"; a faith in others; a spirit of optimism; the courage to be "imperfect," recognizing that making mistakes is a natural part of being human; even a broader sense of "being human," that is, of feeling a part of humanity, especially in an existential sense—all of these emotions, Adler proposed, grow out of people's need to cooperate with one another, to contribute to the social good. All of these emotions grow out of social interest (Kaplan, 1986; Moschetta, 1993).

> To be human means to feel inferior. At the beginning of every psychological life there is a deep inferiority feeling.
>
> —Alfred Adler

As a result Adler's criterion for mental health includes an intrinsic concern for others. "Social interest is the barometer of the child's normality" (Ansbacher & Ansbacher, 1956, p. 154). The degree to which people successfully contribute to the common good is an indicator of their maturity and psychological health. Without such an interest in the social welfare, maladaptive behavior is inevitable.

DEVELOPMENT OF MALADAPTIVE BEHAVIOR

According to Adler, maladaptive behavior results from discouraging or disappointing circumstances. When people lose the courage to face life's demands directly, when they seem insignificant to themselves, they move from a sense of inferiority to an **inferiority complex.** Unconsciously convinced of their inferiority, people in this disillusioned state develop abnormal behavior to divert attention from their troubles (Ansbacher, 1992).

The seeds for such pathological behavior are planted early in life. Ideally, the child's potential for social interest is brought to fruition by the mother. It is she who administers the initial lesson in cooperation by nursing the baby at her breast, thereby serving as the child's first bridge to social life (Adler, 1964b). And it is she who later helps the child extend relationships to the father and to others. If the mother is clumsy, uncooperative, or untrustworthy, however, the child will learn to resist rather than strive to develop social interest.

The father's role is to instill within the child courage and self-reliance and to stress the need for choosing a satisfying and worthwhile occupation. For Adler, too many parents are poorly prepared for the challenging task of raising their children. Too many parents, Adler believed, shower their children with excessive attention, protection, and assistance. Such **pampering,** the most serious of parental errors, robs children of their independence and initiative, shatters their self-confidence, and creates the impression that the world will not hold them accountable for rules that apply to others.

It is these pampered children who develop an inferiority complex, a pathological condition that often remains concealed until life passes the inevitable milestones of stress and disappointment. Having never learned self-reliance, they try to resolve their problems by making unrealistic demands on other people and by expecting everyone to treat their wishes as law. Rather than focus on the need for social or human cooperation, as adults they approach work and marriage with the same self-centered orientation (Stone, 1993).

On the other hand, when parents fail to provide sufficient care for and attention to their children, they collapse into the opposite error of **neglect,** creating the impression that the world is cold and unsympathetic. Unable to see the need to win affection and esteem by socially approved behavior, children with this mind set regard life, and especially other adults, as the enemy. The resulting inferiority complex is expressed through suspicion, isolation, stubbornness, and maliciousness (Adler, 1931).

Parents contribute to the development of maladaptive behavior in their children in other ways as well: by failing to show them tenderness, for instance, by stigmatizing sentimentality as being ridiculous, or by establishing unattainable standards. Resorting to harsh, nonrehabilitating punishment, which exaggerates the child's helplessness, is just as likely to precipitate an inferiority complex. In fact, Adler was the first to emphasize that any praise or blame of a child should be directed, not toward the person, but toward his or her behavior (Adler, 1931; Nikelly, 1971).

In addition to parenting errors, a significant physical deficiency or severe illness may also trigger strong psychological feelings of helplessness (Adler, 1907). While inferiority need not result in psychopathology, it often presents substantial difficulties, which concerned parents are likely to exacerbate by pampering—by misguided help that only fuels the development of an inferiority complex. If a child is unable to compensate adequately for inferiority, whether brought on by pampering, neglect, or disability, a sense of helplessness becomes more intense and a long-term inferiority complex develops. Adler saw the consequence as "an inability to solve life's problems" (Orgler, 1963, p. 63).

Alternatively, people may attempt to compensate for their sense of inferiority by developing what Adler called a **superiority complex**—that is, by developing an exaggerated opinion of their own abilities and accomplishments, or by finding no need to back up their sense of superiority with accomplishments. In either case their behavior is characterized by boasting, banality, self-centeredness, and a tendency to denigrate others. It should be noted, however, that as a means of compensating for their inferiority, some people become extremely successful.

In summary, abnormal behavior characterizes individuals who develop such a massive sense of inferiority in early childhood that they become discouraged about life. In order to compensate, children develop inappropriate patterns of behavior, frequently manifesting an unrealistic striving for personal superiority. This compensatory, self-centered, self-protective behavior precludes any chance of fulfilling social interest. In and of themselves, such feelings of inferiority are not abnormal. It is only when individuals *act as if* they were inferior that an inferiority complex becomes operative.

FUNCTION OF THE THERAPIST

Identifying and building on strengths the client already demonstrates, Adlerian therapists often function as educators or tutors. They encourage their clients to use their talents for the benefit of others. From the initial contact, Adlerians work to establish and maintain an accepting, caring, cooperative relationship with their clients. Convinced that clients are discouraged when they enter therapy, counselors work to develop a supportive and encouraging relationship. By being humorous rather than anxious, unimpressed by their own mistakes rather than perfectionistic, and curious rather than defensive, they model the behavior they desire for their clients. As educators they realize that much of what clients take with them from the counseling relationship will be caught rather than taught. Adlerian therapists are seldom impassive, sphinxlike persons. They are more likely to be active and talkative.

Nevertheless, while qualities of empathy, warmth, and genuineness are important to Adlerian therapists, the focus is on action-oriented behaviors such as interpretation, confrontation, and concreteness. In addition, Adlerian counselors must be fully aware of their own beliefs and emotions, of their role as a model for the client, and of conditions that are essential to the client's development.

Adlerian practitioners view therapy as a collaborative effort. The counselor and client are partners who work toward goals that are mutually agreed upon and clearly identified. They focus not on the conditions that made the clients what they are, but on what it is that they might become. At times the therapy strategy is spelled out in a written contract, which specifies the goals of the process and the responsibilities of each partner. The counselor then uses the plan as a means of support to maximize assets and minimize deficits. In short, the counselor's energy is invested, not in analysis, but in encouragement.

Since Adlerian therapists view their clients' lives as personal constructs built based on perceptions, beliefs, and feelings, they strive to develop and deepen their understanding of these lifestyles. Once counselors understand the lifestyle, they can help their clients understand how their lifestyle has been influenced by their basic beliefs and perceptions. Since Adler held that beliefs influence emotions, not vice versa, counselors discuss the beliefs that underlie emotions, rather than simply reflect on the emotions themselves. This is, of course, a crucial distinction between Freud and Adler.

Although Adlerian counselors are empathic and accepting, they also confront clients with their basic mistakes, misplaced goals, self-defeating behaviors, and restrictive beliefs. These confrontations help clients to resolve apparent contradictions and realign mistaken goals.

Another important function of Adlerian therapists is to help translate insight into action. Therapists encourage their clients to act upon new alternatives for reaching specific goals. The counselor and counselee "work together to consider alternative attitudes, beliefs, and actions" (Dinkmeyer, Pew, & Dinkmeyer, 1979, p. 98).

GOALS OF THERAPY

Adlerians believe that most people seek therapy because they have low social interest. In these instances, the primary goal of therapy is to increase the clients' social interest, or sense of commonality with all fellow humans. By virtue of our limitations, human solidarity is a universal necessity. We need one another's cooperation in order to live.

In addition to fostering social interest, Adlerian therapy seeks to decrease a sense of inferiority in clients, to overcome discouragement, and to recognize and use their resources. By helping people to contribute, by altering faulty motivations that underlie even acceptable behavior, by encouraging equality—in all these ways, Adlerians seek to change the lifestyles, perceptions, and goals of their clients (Dreikurs, 1971; Kottman & Warlick, 1990; Mosak, 1989; Mosak & Dreidurs, 1973).

Adlerian therapy seeks to develop courageous people who view a task or situation, not in terms of potential threats and dangers, but in terms of possible actions and solutions. For the Adlerian, courage is comprised of self-confidence and the conviction that solutions can be found to cope with life's situations. Courageous people do not feel defeated or inferior (Dinkmeyer & Dreikurs, 1963). It rarely takes longer than a year for an Adlerian therapeutic relationship to achieve its goals; most cases are expected to show at least partial improvement by the third month of treatment (Adler, 1959; Ellenberger, 1970).

MAJOR METHODS AND TECHNIQUES

Adlerians apply a wide variety of therapeutic techniques. After beginning by establishing a warm, caring empathic relationship between the client and the therapist, the therapist will assess the client's goals and lifestyle, generate insight into the client's mistaken thoughts and the resulting maladaptive behaviors, and, finally, effect change in the behavior by reeducating and encouraging the client to act on alternative ways of thinking.

Initiating the Therapeutic Relationship

Establishing rapport between clients and practitioners is a process characterized by mutually determined goals, confidentiality, and respect for the clients' ability ultimately to direct their own lives (Dinkmeyer, Pew, & Dinkmeyer, 1979). A warm and trusting counseling relationship, enhanced by a number of professional techniques, is crucial to effective Adlerian therapy.

Encouragement remains the bedrock of Adlerian intervention, especially in establishing a therapeutic relationship (Dinkmeyer & Losoncy, 1980). Adlerian practice is built on the assumption that clients feel powerless and discouraged. Only when clients change their attitude toward themselves will their behavior change. It is crucial, therefore, to encourage, to accept clients as they are, and to focus on their assets rather than their liabilities. The ultimate goal of such encouragement is to share and analyze the private logic of clients, to persuade them to accept responsibility for living, and to change their self-defeating behaviors (Nikelly & Dinkmeyer, 1972).

A common pitfall in such a therapeutic relationship is that clients often expect their therapists to respond to them as do other people in their lives. If clients feel misunderstood or unloved by others, for example, they may expect the therapist to behave in the same way. They may even create situations that unconsciously invite the therapist to respond negatively. Aware of subtle sabotages, Adlerian therapists use them to better understand how their clients typically elicit responses from others.

On yet other occasions clients may attempt to make the counselor more powerful than themselves. They may want to relinquish symptoms but not underlying causes of those symptoms. Or they may look to the counselor to perform a "miracle." The Adlerian therapist understands, however, that an effective relationship can be built only if the counselor refuses to be caught by the vanity of believing that miracles can be performed (Dinkmeyer, Dinkmeyer & Sperry, 1987).

Lifestyle Investigation

Since Adler believed that our ultimate goal is superiority or perfection, he uncovered ways for individuals to strive for that goal. Each of us develops a unique pattern of behavior, characteristics, and habits that help us reach our goal. In other words, every person develops a distinctive **lifestyle,** a basic orientation toward life, a psychological map, that becomes a guide for action.

> Parents who most need advice are the [ones] who never come for it.
> —Alfred Adler

Our psychological lifestyles are a repertoire of specific behaviors that help us to deal with the demands of living (Mosak, 1972; Mullis, Kern, & Curlette, 1987). All of us, according to Adler, have unique lifestyles that enable us to compensate for inferiority feelings and strive toward superiority. Like two pine trees, one growing in a valley, another on a mountaintop, each of us develops distinctively. Although both are the same kind of tree, each shows a distinct style of life, with adaptation "expressing itself and molding itself in an environment" (Adler, 1956, p. 173).

Adler's concept of lifestyle is composed of four elements: the *self-concept,* or view of the self "as is"; the *self-ideal,* or self as one would like to be; the *picture of the world,* one's model or "myth" about why things work as they do outside of oneself; and one's *ethical convictions.* Since this map determines the choices we make, it determines who we are (Mosak, 1989). Unless challenged to change, clients may persist in reading an inappropriate map, in always trying to please others, for example. Adlerians systematically explore their clients' lifestyles and unravel their secrets by focusing on the "three entrance gates to mental life": birth order, early memories, and dreams.

Birth Order   Although no two children are born into the same environment, the position of the child within the family, as well as the atmosphere of the family, plays a significant role in the client's development and behavior (Bohmer & Sitton, 1993; Curtis & Cowell, 1993; Gates, Lineberger, Crockett, & Hubbard, 1988; Shulman & Nikelly, 1972). The family constellation includes more than a list of family members. It also includes descriptions of each person in the family, their respective personalities, their relationships with each other, and the dynamics of interpersonal power and influence.

Birth order, the interval between siblings, is part of the family constellation and a major influence on the creation of a person's style of life. Adlerians know that siblings, though living in the same house with the same parents, do not have identical social environments. Being older or younger than one's siblings and being exposed to parental attitudes that have evolved as a result of

7.2 | What's Your Lifestyle?

Everyone achieves meaning out of life by interpreting his or her existence. A person's lifestyle, according to Adler, is the platform from which these interpretations are made. A person's lifestyle is a basic orientation to life. It is the cognitive framework from which a person selects the specific behaviors which enable him or her to cope with life. It includes the individual's unique views on how security, belonging, superiority, perfection, or completion can be achieved. All behavior is understandable if seen in the light of the individual's *private logic,* the key to that individual's lifestyle (Dinkmeyer, Pew, & Dinkmeyer, 1979). By age four or five, the lifestyle is pretty well in place, and new experiences are fitted into it rather than used to form it. It remains essentially unchanged throughout life, unless challenged by some overwhelming experience or adjusted through therapy. Mosak (1972, pp. 78–80) has identified 14 probable behaviors associated with commonly observed lifestyles:

1. The *getter* exploits and manipulates life and others by actively or passively putting others into his service. He may use charm, shyness, temper, or intimidation as methods of operation.
2. The *driver* is the person in motion: overconscientiousness and dedication to goals rarely permit rest. Underneath, such a person nurses a fear that he is a "zero."
3. The *controller* is either a person who wishes to control life or one who wishes to ensure that life will not control him. He generally dislikes surprises, controls his spontaneity, and hides his feelings since all of these may lessen his control. As substitutes, he favors intellectualization, rightness, orderliness, and neatness.

---

the arrival of each additional child create different conditions that greatly influence one's personality (Claxton, 1994; Narayan, 1990; Perlin & Grater, 1984; Shulman & Mosak, 1977).

Since parents typically devote a considerable amount of time and attention to their first child, the *firstborn* is in a unique and enviable situation. Often the firstborn has a happy, secure existence—until, that is, the appearance of the second child. Suddenly she or he is no longer the primary focus of attention, and the child, in Adler's terms, becomes "dethroned." No matter how hard the firstborn tries, things will never be the same. Although all firstborns feel this shock, this altered position in the family, those who are younger or who have been pampered will experience an even greater loss.

Adler found that oldest children are often oriented toward the past, locked in nostalgia, and pessimistic about the future. Having learned at one time the advantages of power, they remain concerned to gain power all their lives. As a result, firstborn children become conscientious and scrupulous and long for positions of authority. Adler viewed the only child, in essence, as a firstborn who never forfeits the priesthood (Byrd, DeRosa, & Craig, 1993).

4. The person who needs to be *right* elevates himself over others who he manages to see as wrong. He scrupulously avoids error. Should he be caught in an error, he rationalizes that others are more wrong than he.
5. The person who needs to be *superior* may refuse to participate in any activity he cannot "win."
6. The person who needs to be *liked* tries to please everyone all the time. Particularly sensitive to criticism, he is crushed when he does not receive universal and constant approval. He sees the evaluations of others as the measure of his worth.
7. The person who needs to be *good* prefers to live by higher moral standards than anyone else. Sometimes these standards are higher than God's, since the "good" person sometimes expects God to forgive "sins" in him that he cannot forgive in others.
8. The person who *opposes* everything, especially life's demands of him, really stands for something.
9. Everything happens to the *victim,* who may be characterized by feelings of nobility, self-pity, or resignation.
10. The *martyr* is similar to the victim except that whereas the victim merely "dies," the martyr "dies" for a cause. His goal is nobility and his vocation is injustice collector.
11. The *baby* finds a place in life through charm, cuteness, and exploitation of others.
12. The *inadequate* person acts as if he cannot do anything right. Through his default, he binds others to him as servants.
13. The person who *avoids feelings* may fear his own spontaneity because it might move him in directions he has not thoroughly planned.
14. The *excitement seeker* despises routine and repetitive activities, seeks novel experiences, and revels in commotion.

By the time the *second-born* child arrives, the element of novelty is greatly reduced and parents are typically less anxious and more relaxed in their child rearing. From the beginning, the second-born finds in the older sibling a pace-setter: a model or a threat against which to compete. So significant is this competitive spur, that the second child usually begins speaking at an earlier age than the older child. Adler also found that second-borns are not only more competitive and ambitious but more optimistic about the future as well. If, however, the older sibling excels in everything, the second-born may fail to incorporate competitiveness into his or her lifestyle and may eventually give up trying to succeed.

The youngest or *last-born* child never faces the shock of dethronement. Spurred on by the need to surpass older siblings, last-borns often develop remarkably fast, turning into high achievers in whatever work they undertake as adults. If the youngest child remains the baby of the family, however, and is spoiled or pampered, the opposite may take place. Unaccustomed to striving and struggling, this pampered

> There is no greater evil than the pampering of children.
>
> —Alfred Adler

youngster may find it difficult to cope as an adult (Barry & Blane, 1977; Miller & Maruyama, 1976).

Without attempting to rigidly force a client into one of these birth or-der positions, Adlerian therapists simply consider the likelihood of certain styles of life developing as a result of one's position within the family. But they do not expect that our lifestyles automatically result from our place in the family constellation (Dewey, 1972; Dinkmeyer, Pew, & Dinkmeyer, 1979).

Early Recollections   From early childhood most adults carry memories that appear to have little importance. According to Adler, however, these seemingly insignificant recollections are an excellent guide to uncovering peoples' lifestyles. To Adlerians, **early recollections** encapsulate our present philosophy of life. People remember particular, presumably inconsequential events from childhood because these memories reinforce their basic view of life (Bishop, 1993). Whether these early recollections are of real events or fantasies makes little difference; in either case our adult lives revolve around what was per-ceived in these remembered incidents.

Adler contended that people remember those events from their child-hood that are consistent with their present view of life (1931). Early mem-ories are extraordinarily significant, then, because they have been preserved for years and thus reveal personality and lifestyle. For Adlerians these memories are "an X-ray into the human mind" (Manaster & Corsini, 1982, p. 188).

Adlerian therapists obtain these early recollections by saying, for example, "Think as far back as you can and tell me your earliest memory from your childhood years." If this fails to elicit a recollection, the therapist might ask clients to close their eyes, think back to their childhood, and describe what they see. Clients may even be coached by being asked to recollect their friends, their school days, or holidays (Nikelly & Verger, 1972). The therapist looks, not for general memories, but for actual recollections; not for, "We used to go to the beach a lot every summer when I was a child," but for "I remember traveling across a bridge with my family in a new station wagon."

While Adler insisted that these recollections must be interpreted within the context of each client's life, he found some commonalties. Memories of danger or punishment, for example, might suggest a tendency toward hos-tility, while memories of the birth of a sibling indicate a continued sense of dethronement. Once Adler asked more than 100 physicians for their early recollections. A majority of them recalled either an illness or a death in the family—most likely a factor that helped to lead them into a career of com-bating sickness.

The process of collecting early recollections is simple and generally non-threatening to clients. Most often, clients freely give the therapist as many memories as desired, typically about six. The therapist writes down the recol-lections and begins to look for specific details and themes connecting each of the memories, especially themes that might illuminate the client's perspective

7.3 | Voices, Glances, Flashbacks: Our First Memories

Patrick Huyghe

"The earliest memory that I have is of waking up one morning with blood on my pillow and being extremely frightened."

"I don't remember how old I was, but I distinctly remember the joy of digging both hands into the dirt and stuffing it into my mouth."

"My first memory is of a chocolate birthday cake with white frosting and pink trim, and a little wooden train chugging around it."

Think back, for a moment, to your earliest memory. It is probably not your doctor's hands in the delivery room, or even your precarious first step. More likely, the tantalizing event occurred several years later. Perhaps you recall the birth of a sibling or the death of a family member or pet. Many first memories are of mundane events or images: sitting on the stairs, having a picture taken, eating a bowl of cereal.

That first childhood memory is notoriously hard to pin down. To be certain that you are in fact remembering, you must avoid the influence of family photographs and stories, which you may unintentionally substitute for true memories. While the distinction between memory and memento is easy to understand, in practice it is often hard to make. And even when you do manage to summon up an early experience, you may find it difficult to date accurately.

Or it may not have happened at all. Child psychologist Jean Piaget used to tell of a memory at the age of 2 in which he was nearly kidnapped as his nurse was wheeling him down the street in Paris. His recollection included the fact that the nurse's face was scratched by the kidnappers during the fracas. But when he was in his teens, the nurse confessed that she had fabricated the entire story.

Our earliest childhood memories have a magical quality about them, if for no other reason than their being the apparent beginnings of our conscious lives. These "islands in the sea of oblivion," as the novelist Esther Salaman called them, have fascinated psychologists for more than a century, and their studies of the phenomenon indicate that most people's early memories are remarkably similar on the surface.

"Almost all of our earliest memories are located in the fourth year of life, between the third and fourth birthdays" [italics added], psychologist John Kihlstrom of the University of Wisconsin says. His survey of 314 high school and college students, conducted with Columbia University psychologist Judith Harackiewicz, found that *most early recollections are visual, many in color* [italics added]. Their content, however, varies widely, and seems to fall into three broad categories: trauma, transition and trivia. Other studies have shown that the *first memories of women appear to date back somewhat further than those of men, but the difference,*

(continued)

7-3 | Voices, Glances, Flashbacks: Our First Memories (continued)

which is no more than a few months, may be due to earlier brain development among girls. [italics added]

The pioneers of psychoanalysis attached great significance to first memories. Freud believed that they could open the secret chambers of a person's inner life. Alfred Adler, originator of the Individual Psychology school, said, "The first memory will show the individual's fundamental view of life." *Adler believed that childhood memories have a great diagnostic value, regardless of whether they are real or imaginary, because of their unique capacity for revealing a person's attitude toward self, others and life in general.* [italics added] Interestingly, Adler, who conceived of the inferiority complex, had a vivid first memory of sitting on a bench, sidelined by disease, watching his brother play.

In their autobiographies, various public figures show their tendency to fasten onto early experiences that are important to them. Golda Meir's earliest recollection, which she thought might have been a dream, was of a group of Jews being trampled by cossack horses in czarist Russia. The earliest memories of Seymour Papert, the creator of the LOGO computer language for children, center on wheels, mechanical devices and figuring out what things do and how they work. *Albert Einstein remembered receiving a magnetic compass at about the age of 4 or 5 and being awed by the needle's urge to point north.* [italics added]

"Some people think that these early experiences may somehow form personality, and that's why they get remembered," Kihlstrom says, "but I don't think that's right." Do our memories make us, or do we make our memories? "I think that personality leads to selectivity of memory," Kihlstrom says. "People remember things that are consistent with the concept they have of themselves."

Considering the novelty and richness of the first several years of life, it is perhaps surprising that adults have so few early recollections. This apparent amnesia has been a puzzle to psychologists ever since Freud observed it in his patients at the turn of the century.

The phenomenon, which he labeled infantile or childhood amnesia, applies only to our memories about the self, not to our memory for words or recognizable objects and people. Freud believed that we lose contact with most of our autobiographical memories from the first six years because as children, during the Oedipal phase, we repress anxiety-evoking memories of sexuality and aggression. All that remains, he noted, are "screen memories," memories that are totally lacking in feeling.

"Childhood amnesia does exist, but it's not necessarily Oedipal," contends Emory University psychology professor Ulric Neisser. "The child forgets everything about the self, not just sexual or aggressive memories. We begin to remember our life pretty well only from about the age of 5 or 6 because that's when we go to school and develop an organized structure for our lives."

But if schooling does allow children to better encode episodes for later retrieval, it would seem to follow that children who attend nursery school or other prekindergarten schools should have more early memories than those who did not. So far there haven't been any studies, however, to confirm this intriguing hypothesis.

"The evidence that the phenomenon of childhood amnesia even exists is mostly anecdotal," Kihlstrom says. Some people claim to have memories that date back before the age of 3, and most surveys of childhood memories indicate that there is no age when continuous, uninterrupted memories consistently begin. We are simply less likely to retain a memory as more time elapses from the event.

So perhaps what we call childhood amnesia is really no different from normal forgetting. "After all," says David Rubin, a researcher in human memory at Duke University, "childhood was a long time ago, and perhaps the reason we don't remember much of it is because we have just normally forgotten it."

People often assume that they cannot remember anything before about age 3, not because they have forgotten, but because they were incapable of storing memories in the first place. The evidence for this is conflicting. "If you look at a 3- or 4-year-old in action," Neisser says, "you will see a person who remembers quite a lot, in the sense that you can ask a 4-year-old about things that happened the year before and get very intelligent answers. It's not that they have no memory, but when they become 10 or 12 or 20, they don't remember those things much anymore."

Psychologist Marion Perlmutter and her associates at the University of Michigan have been assessing the mnemonic abilities of preschool children in both experimental and naturalistic settings since the mid 1970s. In one study, she and psychologist Christine Todd examined the conversations between young children and adults to determine, among other things, the length of time children could retain information. They found that children between 35 months and 38 months old could remember events that had occurred more than seven-and-a-half months previously. The older children, those between 45 months and 54 months old, recalled episodes that had occurred as much as 14 1/2 months ago.

Perlimutter was particularly impressed by the fact that in some cases the children "demonstrated a verbal recall for events that occurred prior to the time that they were speaking extensively." Her findings contradict some psychologists'

(continued)

7.3 | Voices, Glances, Flashbacks: Our First Memories (continued)

long-held notion that children's autobiographical memory develops with language ability.

The study of memory in children who aren't yet speaking relies on the evidence of habituation and other forms of conditioned learning. In a study with psychologist Daniel Ashmead, Perlmutter asked parents to keep a diary recording the actions of their 7-, 9- and 11-month-old infants that revealed the use of memory. "Albert eating lunch," one typical entry reads. "Handed Dorine [the babysitter] his glass. Dorine saw it was empty and filled it. He did the same for me several days ago. Twice during one meal he handed me his glass. Each time it was empty. Each time I filled it."

While all the infants in the study showed some spontaneous memory, such episodes were less frequent among the youngest infants. Perlmutter also found that older infants were more likely to reveal actual memory, rather than to just respond to a familiar environmental cue. "We think that this is evidence of something like recall memory beginning to appear in the older infants," she says.

When a child is between 8 and 12 months old, a change does seem to occur in memory abilities. Some psychologists see the change as a transition from conditioned recognition and response to recall memory, but others, such as Daniel Schacter and Morris Moscovitch of the University of Toronto, suggest that two different memory systems are at work. They refer to these systems as early and late memories.

Schacter and Moscovitch compared the performance of two groups: amnesiacs, who have an impaired memory system, and very young infants, who have not yet fully developed a memory system. They used a simple task that Piaget made famous in 1954. Piaget had observed that 7- to 8-month-old infants can easily find an object when it is hidden at the same location all the time. But after several successful searches at that location, many infants continue to search there even after seeing the object hidden someplace else.

"The amnesiac remembers where you put the object in the first place," Schacter says, "but then gets tripped up when you switch locations, just like the infant." But while amnesiacs continue to make the error, infants stop making it as they approach their first birthday. Schacter thinks that the appearance of a late memory system may explain this improvement. "The neural machinery that underlies the ability to remember the past may be in place within a year of birth. Any further developments in memory are probably the result of building up the knowledge base and integrating this machinery with other cognitive functions."

Studies of visual and auditory memory have shown that even the youngest of infants are consistently more responsive to novel stimuli than to familiar stimuli. These observations have led many psychologists to conclude that infants have a memory capacity from birth.

"Infants are able to encode and retain some information about their visual world from the first hours of life," Perlmutter says. Other researchers have shown that premature infants, with an average gestational age of 35 weeks, can discriminate between novel and familiar stimuli.

Despite evidence for early infant memory, psychologists have been reluctant to date the origins of memory before birth. Prebirth memory remains largely uncharted territory, and even those who willingly concede the possibility that the fetus has the rudimentary capacity to encode experience will cry foul at the claims for prebirth memories.

"On one level the subject is very, very controversial," Rubin explains, "but on another level it's totally dull. Why should the act of birth increase your learning abilities?"

Research by Anthony DeCasper at the University of North Carolina at Greensboro strongly implies the existence of prebirth memory. In his study, a newborn infant could choose to hear a recording of its mother's voice or that of another woman by sucking on a nipple in a particular way. Infants as young as 30 hours consistently chose their mothers' voices.

It is very likely that they recognized their mothers' voices from what they heard in the womb. As Rubin points out, "The acoustics are there. There are studies in which microphones have been placed in the uterus of sheep and the sound is not muffled as much as you might think."

But in general, claims for birth and prebirth memories are regarded with suspicion by psychologists, most of whom tread more traditional ground in trying to answer the question, "When does autobiographical memory begin?"

Katherine Nelson, a developmental psychologist at the Graduate School of the City University of New York, has studied the question of early memories in connection with "scripts" that children have for familiar events. These scripts refer to the way children have organized their acquired knowledge in terms of general events. According to her theory, children have scripts for such familiar routines as eating dinner at home and going to the supermarket. This script-building appears by age 1, or earlier.

"The drive to build up these scripts seems to come out of a biological need to understand what is going on," Nelson says. "So the child doesn't need language or anything else; all that is needed is the background of experience."

(continued)

7.3	**Voices, Glances, Flashbacks:** **Our First Memories** (continued)

While these scripts help children remember general events, they can also block or override memories of specific experiences. Nelson found that while 3- and 4-year-old children can produce reasonably good general accounts of dinner at home, they have difficulties producing an account of a specific dinner. They will speak about "what happens" rather than "what happened." Perhaps this explains why children insist upon routines, she says.

Nelson speculates that certain memories are lost as children enter specific experiences into their more general scripts. Unique events, like going to the circus, may be more memorable because they haven't been repeated or overridden by other similar experiences. "But after a while, if you don't go to the circus, you will forget about it, because it's not adaptive to hold onto that memory if it's not going to tell you anything about the future," Nelson says.

By the time children are 2 or 3, speech has developed and memory begins to show signs of social construction. "Children are also taught to remember by their parents," Nelson says, "when they say such things as 'Do you remember when we went to the store last week and you said such and such?' So their memory becomes at least partially formulated in terms of language. *At about the age of 3, significant variations of emotionally involving events begin to create a memory string that is uniquely human and social. That's when autobiographical memory begins.*" [italics added]

Although Nelson's view of early memory development does not pretend to explain the multitude of phenomena involved in memory, it certainly ties up a lot of loose ends regarding autobiographical memory. If, as she says, memory proceeds from the accumulation of single novel experiences, repeated and built into scripts, and then to unique events capable of being shared, it should be easy to see why we, as adults, cannot remember specific autobiographical memories before about the fourth year of life. Such memories could not form until a significant general base of event knowledge had been established. And this, of course, would take a number of years to build up. The reason that early memories are so elusive may be that the process of gaining autobiographical memories is like other developmental processes, something learned with time.

From: *Psychology Today,* September 1985, pp. 48–52.

7.4 | Exploring Your Earliest Memories

Adler viewed early recollections as "the most trustworthy way of exploring personality."

As you explore your own earliest recollections for themes you may find it helpful to complete the following sentence stems as if all you knew about life were contained in your early memory.

Men are . . .
Women are . . .
Life is . . .

In addition, the following questions can be useful in helping you discover what your earliest recollections say about your personality:

1. Who is present? (Mom, Dad, sibs, friends, strangers, etc.)
2. Who is not present? (Dad)
3. How are different people portrayed? (basic thoughts and feelings)
4. What is the world like? (friendly, hostile, cooperative, exciting)
5. What is your role or behavior? (helping, passive, sick, dependent)
6. What is the outcome of your behavior? (successful, good effects, punished)
7. What is your primary social attitude? ("I" or "We")
8. What is your dominant emotion? (happy, worried, fearful, guilty, proud)
9. What is your primary motive? (gain attention, hold power, be left alone, help)
10. What is the underlying theme in a single sentence? (Life is . . .)

on life (Nikelly & Verger, 1972; Watkins, 1985). Although Adler never suggested that such early memories are the sole determinants of behavior, he found that they provide glimpses into events that help shape clients' beliefs about life and its demands.

Dreams While Freud interpreted dreams as wish fulfillments, Adler believed that clients use dreams to rehearse how they might deal with problems in the future. Pointing out that people often cannot recall the specific events of a dream but do remember its mood, Adler further suggested that the moods experienced in a dream might set the stage for the next day's activities (Mosak & Dreikurs, 1973). Adler also used dreams as an indicator of therapeutic progress. While brief dreams with little action might reflect a passive approach to dealing with problems, dreams seem to become increasingly active as treatment proceeds and as patients begin to experiment with a more active lifestyle. In fact, some

> Since I cannot prove a lover . . . I am determined to prove a villain.
> —Shakespeare

Adlerians use the clients' dreams to guide them in deciding when to terminate therapy (Rosenthal, 1959).

While Adlerians often use dreams as a therapeutic strategy, they usually use them to confirm observations that have already been made concerning the family constellation and early recollections (Manaster & Corsini, 1982). Since dreams are a manifestation of people's lifestyles, Adler insisted that they never be interpreted in isolation.

Developing Self-Understanding

By asking open-ended questions that allow clients to explore previously unnoticed patterns in their lives, Adlerian counselors try to help clients develop insight. Since interpreting the answers often takes the form of intuitive guesses, the ability to empathize is especially important. The counselor must be able to sympathize with clients before discovering the reasons for their behavior. At other times, interpretations are based on the counselor's knowledge of ordinal position in the family constellation. However, the Adlerian counselor never puts clients in a position that requires them to accept the therapist's interpretation. The counselor's respect for the clients is never compromised.

Through Adlerian counseling, clients come to recognize that faulty ways of thinking have resulted in unrealistic goals and that actions directed toward attaining these goals are self-defeating (Dinkmeyer, Pew, & Dinkmeyer, 1979). Such insight requires both encouragement and confrontation. It is the general tone of encouragement set during the rapport-building stage of therapy that allows the practitioner to confront the clients about their goals and behavior. Only as a result of this confrontation can patients gain insight that leads to behavioral change (Dreyfus & Nikelly, 1972).

Reorientation

Adlerian interventions, or helping techniques, are fundamentally action-oriented. In early stages of the intervention, the practitioner identifies with and reveals the counselees' failed patterns of thinking, feeling, and acting. Once clients decide on the kind of person they want to become and the kinds of relationships they wish to establish, they can begin to shift from insight to practice. Old patterns of behavior are shed while they become oriented to new, more active ways of being that are especially encouraged in this final phase of therapy. With the help of the practitioner, clients decide what behaviors will help them reach their goals. Often the therapist employs a number of specific techniques that help clients translate their goals into actions.

> I should compare [the pathological person] to a man who tries to put a horse's collar on from the tail end. It is not a sin, but it is a mistaken method.
>
> —Alfred Adler

Asking "The Question"   As one technique the counselor asks: "What would be different if you were well?" This question allows clients to cut to the heart of how they want to change. For example, a client might respond by saying, "I would be a husband who doesn't complain as much," "I would quit my job and start a business of my own," or "I would be able to accept my son despite what he has done." Clients are often asked "the question" during the initial stages of therapy, but it is appropriate to ask it at any time.

Paradoxical Intention   Using this technique, therapists encourage their clients to exaggerate, practice, or perform the symptoms or behaviors they are attempting to avoid or overcome. Clients who complain of being unable to sleep, for example, may be instructed to stop trying and concentrate on remaining awake, and constant nail biters may be instructed to stop once every two hours during the day and bite their nails intentionally. Each evening they may be asked to spend at least three minutes biting their nails in front of a mirror.

Acting "As If"   Sometimes clients claim they would do thus and so if they had a certain quality or trait. When this occurs, Adlerians often instruct their clients to act "as if" they possess that desired quality, as if they were the ideal persons they see in their dreams (Gold, 1979). They may be asked to role-play a situation and act as if they are the person they want to become. If clients want to overcome shyness and be more assertive, for example, the counselor might assign them to "act" assertively for one day next week. This technique is based on the assumption that clients change behavior when they are able to elicit different responses from others. They learn that change is less hazardous than they thought and may be rewarding.

Spitting in the Client's Soup   Adler borrowed the concept of "spitting in the client's soup" from a dirty practice he witnessed in a private school dining hall. By spitting in their neighbor's soup, boys would obtain a second helping for themselves. In a similar way, this therapeutic strategy involves identifying a certain client behavior and, in doing so, ruining the payoff of the behavior for the client. It is a way of besmirching a clean conscience. For example, a mother who always acts superior to her daughter by undercutting her may continue to do so after the behavior is pointed out, but the reward for doing so has disappeared. Like the boys in the dining hall, clients may continue to eat the soup, but it will never taste the same and they can never enjoy it as much.

Catching Oneself   Another technique, "catching oneself," allows clients to become aware of self-destructive behaviors or thoughts without guilt. Often, despite people's strong desire to change a behavior, they may revert to old patterns out of sheer habit. Catching oneself allows clients to pause for a moment and consider other ways of responding. At first the counselor may help in the process, but eventually clients take over this responsibility. With practice, clients catch themselves before they fall into self-defeating behavior.

Push Button   Finally, the so-called "push button" technique encourages clients to realize they have choices in responding or reacting to stimuli in their lives. More specifically, it teaches clients they can create desired feelings by choosing what to think about. In this technique, clients picture alternately pleasant and unpleasant experiences and then notice the emotions accompanying these experiences. By concentrating on their thoughts, they recognize that they can create the feelings they desire. The technique is like pushing a mental button because clients can choose to remember negative or positive experiences. Clients leave the session realizing they can push buttons that will either depress or elate them. They are in control (Mosak, 1989).

APPLICATION

Adlerians function in a variety of settings (private practice, in patient and outpatient settings, schools) and in a variety of modalities (e.g., one-on-one, groups, families). The case of "Pablo," cited by Garfinkle, Massey, and Mendel (1986), illustrates many of the most common Adlerian strategies in working with children.

Pablo, nine years old and a middle child, had a well-behaved older sister and a very bright younger brother. Pablo's parents were separated, and his mother saw in Pablo many aspects of her estranged husband. Her behavior toward Pablo was, needless to say, quite ambivalent, sometimes provocatively loving while at other times punitive.

From an Adlerian perspective, every child strives for belonging in his family in his own unique way. Pablo's style was to reinforce the identification with his father, since he could not compete with his sister's good behavior or his brother's academic excellence. He tried to find his place by continuously misbehaving at home and in school. He also tried to gain recognition by having headaches, through fears of being alone at night, and by crying frequently. He had no friends because he teased the other children, yet he often felt they had wronged him. Pablo's lifestyle was one of discouragement about wanting to belong in a socially useful way, so he drifted toward the useless side of life. His basic mistaken conviction was: "Only if I misbehave or am sick will I be noticed and can find my place."

> The Bible gives us many marvelous psychological hints, and the typical second child is beautifully portrayed in the story of Jacob.
>
> —Alfred Adler

Pablo's behavior and his mother's reaction to it were examined in the exploration and interpretation phases of Adlerian counseling. The counselor formed several hypotheses about the reason for Pablo's behavior and presented them to him: "Could it be that you like the extra attention when you have headaches?" Pablo showed little reaction. "Could it be that you get your headaches when you think the work is hard and you're not sure if you can do it?" Pablo smiled with recognition.

Recognizing this nonverbal cue gave the counselor some tentative ideas about the client's private logic. Later in counseling, in the reorientation stage, the counselor suggested that Pablo's mother focus on her son's strengths and assets rather than berate him for his misbehavior. The counselor reemphasized that Pablo was a discouraged child who needed encouragement to overcome his feelings of inadequacy, and instead of punishing Pablo, she should allow the natural logical consequences of his behavior to flow. For example, if he deliberately sprayed her perfume over the room and spilled her cosmetic lotion, instead of beating him for it, she should teach him how to clean it up and encourage him to replace what had been broken. She could thereby teach Pablo social interest and consideration for others.

A great deal of time was spent discussing alternatives to his having headaches in order to avoid difficult matters. Together with his teacher, the counselor worked out a mutual tutoring program in which he would receive help in reading from a child who would in turn get help from him in math. The teacher also agreed not to call Pablo's mother when he ran out of the room, since that would give him extra attention and would reinforce his attention-getting behavior. As an alternative, she would try to encourage him to cope with his difficulties within the classroom. Pablo was encouraged to stop teasing his classmates and to make new friends. The counselor demonstrated these social skills through role playing with Pablo. The focus in the counseling session was on helping Pablo to belong to a peer group through improved social interactions and concern for others.

CRITICAL ANALYSIS

Few theories are more versatile than Adler's. Its strategies have proven useful in working with children, adolescents, parents, entire families, teacher groups, and other segments of society (Purkey & Schmidt, 1987; Kottman & Warlick, 1990). The Adlerian approach has shown promise in treating conduct disorders, antisocial disorders, anxiety disorders, personality disorders, and some affective disorders (Seligman, 1986). The theory's versatility is also seen in its adaptation to other helping theories and to the public's knowledge and understanding of human interaction. Such concepts as freedom, phenomenology, interpretation of events, life scripts, and personal responsibility are found in existential, Gestalt, rational-emotive, transactional analysis, person-centered therapy, and reality counseling or therapy. Adlerian terms, such as *inferiority complex,* have also become a part of the public's vocabulary.

Another strength of Adlerian therapy is the equalitarian prosocial atmosphere it fosters. Of course, Adler shares the stage with Freud in this regard, since Freud also understood the role of narcissism in neurosis. The critical difference, however, is Adler's challenge to battle self-centeredness by choosing to do something for society, choosing to display social interest. In his last book, *Social Interest,* written before World War II and the atom bomb, Adler said that humankind might be doomed unless it developed more social feelings, nationally and internationally. He warned: "The belief that the cosmos ought to have an interest in the preservation of life is scarcely more than a pious wish" (1939, p. 272).

Few classical theorists have affirmed the importance of understanding diversity within the context of counseling more than Adler. His schema, for example, serves counselors who integrate multicultural perspectives into a single comprehensive theoretical approach (Nicoll, 1993). And Adler's constructs have been shown to have acculturative power among diverse cultural loyalties (Miranda & White, 1993). Adler strove to bring understanding to an important component of people's heritage as individuals. The extensive convergence of social interest with dominant worldviews suggests that he succeeded (Leak, Gardner, & Pounds, 1992). Along these lines, Adler also viewed religious and spiritual values as a part of the global elements of culture. He proposed that counselors who fail to assess their client's diverse religious values risk overlooking potentially important aspects of the client's cultural background and experience (Bishop, 1992).

Adler's theory continues to have an impact on contemporary clinical issues. For example, how a client might cope with physical disability can be understood within an Adlerian framework. The counselor focuses on how the client's lifestyle notions and goals (how the client's personal meaning is attached to the disability) are contributing to, or undermining the acceptance of, adjustment to the disability (Rule, 1984).

> There are no "chance memories."
>
> —Alfred Adler

Adlerian psychology's strengths continue to influence today's counselors, and in a sense, Adler's theory is still ahead of its time (Evans, 1991). But like all theorists of psychotherapy, Adler is not without his critics. Porchaska (1979), for example, questions the very name of Adler's theory: "It is ironic that Adler called his approach individual psychology when in fact he ultimately values social interests over the interests of the individual" (p. 196).

Adler placed emphasis on practice and teaching instead of on theoretical definitions and organization. As a result, a major difficulty with Adler's theory is the lack of systematization in his writings and the vagueness that clouds his constructs. In addition, because he presents so few constructs to explain complex behavior, the application of those constructs, of necessity, is troubled by generalities. Perhaps the vaguest and, therefore, most difficult Adlerian construct to understand is that of the creative self or the **creative power of self**. Although at times it appears to add freedom of choice to the style of life, on other occasions it seems to take on the mystical quality of free will that is totally independent of any prior experiences. The source of this power is unclear. In other words, while Adler's position on the individual's freedom to choose is clear, his explanation of the individual's creative power that permits this freedom is not.

Another limitation of the Adlerian approach to therapy is its lack of a firm research base. For decades, Adlerian therapy has attracted few researchers, the result of which has been a scarcity of empirical studies of either the theory or its effectiveness (Wallace, 1986). In fairness, however, a comparison of research about Adlerian therapy between 1982 and 1990 with research reported between 1970 and 1981 shows that research on Adlerian therapy has increased significantly. And many of these studies have served to validate many of Adler's constructs (Wittmer, 1989). For example, research about early recollections, birth order, social interest, and other studies continues to grow (Watkins, 1992). Also, journals devoted to the Adlerian viewpoint, such as the *Journal of Individual Psychology*, are doing much to rectify the need for a sturdier research base.

CURRENT STATUS

Although Adler's approach to counseling is as venerable as psychoanalysis itself, it remains entirely contemporary. Its vitality is not demonstrated by the number of "Adlerian" practitioners, however. A 1982 survey of more than 400 clinical and counseling psychologists found that less than 3 percent described themselves as "Adlerians" (Smith, 1982). Nevertheless, Adler's approach to therapy hovers over counseling rooms: his ideas and techniques have been integrated wholesale into other approaches to counseling, and contemporary eclectic practitioners shamelessly incorporate his techniques in their work (Burk, 1989).

Freud's ideas may be the most remembered, but Adler's counseling techniques have been the most practiced. Ironically, upon Freud's death an obituary in the London *Times* gave him credit for the term "inferiority complex," and when Carl Jung died, the *New York Times* credited *him* with the term. But it was neither Freud nor Jung, but Adler who originated the concept and coined the term (Kaufman, 1980).

Adler greatly influenced humanistic and existential psychology (Frankl, 1970; Maslow, 1970). Abraham Maslow was influenced by Adler's stress on the creative power of the individual in shaping his or her own life and by his insistence that future goals are more important than past events. "Alfred Adler becomes more and more correct year by year," Maslow wrote (1970, p. 13). And existentialists have stressed the importance that Adler gave to an individual's uniqueness (Ansbacher, 1990; Duncan, 1993).

> For me Alfred Adler becomes more and more correct year by year.
>
> —Abraham Maslow

Carl Roger's emphasis on empathy is likewise an outgrowth of Adlerian therapy. The cognitive approaches to behavior therapy also acknowledge a debt to Adler's pioneering work (Ellis, 1970, 1971; Elliott, 1992). The Adlerian duty of making a contribution to the whole and his emphasis on the role of social interest in countering self-centeredness parallel Erik Fromm's idea of the productive character.

As suggested at the beginning of this chapter, the question is no longer whether one is an Adlerian, but how much of an Adlerian one is (Wilder, 1959). Before Adler's death in 1937, individual psychology had become an international movement with local societies in three dozen nations. Today Adlerian psychology is promoted in America through the North American Society of Adlerian Psychology (NASAP), a membership society that publishes a quarterly journal and a monthly newsletter and which sponsors an annual convention:

The North American Society of Adlerian Psychology
65 East Wacker Place, Suite 400
Chicago, Illinois 60601-7203
(312) 629-8801

The Adler School of Professional Psychology is an accredited graduate school, offering a masters in counseling and a doctorate in psychology. A clearing house of Adlerian books and publications, it also provides a mail order service:

The Adler School of Professional Psychology
65 East Wacker Place, Suite 2100
Chicago, Illinois 60601-7201
(312) 201-5900

The Americas Institute of Adlerian Studies (AIAS) is the postgraduate, professional continuing education provider for counselors:

The Americas Institute of Adlerian Studies (AIAS)
600 North McClurg Court
Suite 2502-A
Chicago, Illinois 60611
(312) 337-5066

AIAS San Diego County
486 Hillway Drive
Vista, California 92084
(619) 758-4658

The AIAS offers three brief courses each year. By completing all three courses along with course requirements, students receive the institute's certification.

SUMMARY

1. *Biography.* Adler (1870–1937) described his childhood as unhappy, growing up with physical and family setbacks. At age 25, he received his medical degree from the University of Vienna and soon went to work in a neighborhood clinic. After the First World War, Adler established guidance clinics for the Vienna school system; this work convinced him of the importance of child-rearing practices. In 1902 Adler was invited to join Freud's discussion group. Adler, however, never considered himself a disciple of Freud, and the two men eventually drifted apart as Adler spoke openly about their differences. Adler formed the Society for Individual Psychology and established his own theory of psychotherapy.

2. *Historical Development.* Adler's thinking was influenced greatly by Hans Vaihinger's "as if" principle. Janet also influenced his thinking on the power of inferiority, while Nietzsche's striving for perfection helped Adler shape his concept of the striving for superiority. Of course, the greatest influence on Adler's thinking was Sigmund Freud, with whom he collaborated for nearly a decade (1902–1911).

3. *View of Human Nature.* Adler viewed people as irreducibly whole, thus the term *individual* psychology. Individuals, according to Adler, experience a sense of inferiority and strive to overcome it. This striving for superiority is what turns a deficiency into an advantage. Adler also believed that expectations and goals for the future motivate human activity and provide the capacity for social interest (an intrinsic concern for others), the most important goal toward which people strive.

4. *Development of Maladaptive Behavior.* According to Adler, maladaptive behavior results from discouraging or disappointing circumstances. When people lose the courage to face life's demands directly, they move from a sense of inferiority to an inferiority complex. Pathological behavior, while not always evident until later years, originates in childhood as a result of the family of origin relationships. Being pampered or neglected as a child, for example, contributes to maladaptive behavior because the child will compensate for either error by manifesting unrealistic striving for personal superiority.

5. *Function of the Therapist.* Adlerian therapists often function as educators who attempt to build on strengths the client already demonstrates. Encouragement is critical as the therapist works to establish and maintain an accepting, caring, cooperative relationship with the client. The work of therapy is viewed as collaborative: The client and counselor are partners, working toward mutually agreed-upon and clearly identified goals. In short, the Adlerian counselor's energy is invested, not in analysis, but encouragement.

6. *Goals of Therapy.* Adlerian therapy seeks to decrease a sense of inferiority in clients and help them encase their social interest. By helping people to contribute, by altering faulty motivations that underlie even acceptable behavior, and by encouraging equality, Adlerians seek to change the lifestyles, perceptions, and goals of their clients.

7. *Major Methods and Techniques.* The most common therapeutic techniques of Adlerian therapy include investigating the client's lifestyle, or basic orientation toward life. This is done systematically by exploring "three entrance gates to mental life." The first of these is birth order, or one's position within the family and the resulting expectations and roles that typically result from it. The second is early recollections that encapsulate one's present philosophy of life. And third is dreams, which, in Adler's view, serve to rehearse how one might deal with problems in the future.

8. *Application.* Many of the most common Adlerian strategies can be seen clearly when working with children. The case of "Pablo," a nine-year-old

middle child is such an example. Together with his teacher, the counselor worked to focus the counseling session on helping Pablo to belong to a peer group through improved social interactions and concern for others.

9. *Critical Analysis*. Adlerian therapy's versatility is evident. It has been proven to work with a wide variety of populations. Its impact on other counseling approaches is also noteworthy. Its emphasis on equalitarian prosocial ideals is another plus. Few classical theorists have affirmed the importance of understanding diversity within the context of counseling more than Adler. However, Adlerian theory has been criticized for placing practice and teaching over definition and organization. As a result, a major difficulty with Adler's theory is the lack of systematization in his writings and the vagueness that clouds his constructs. Another limitation is its lack of a firm research base.

10. *Current Status*. While the number of "Adlerian" practitioners is not staggering, this approach to therapy is integrated to some degree in many of today's counseling approaches. Adler has had a tremendous impact on today's counselors and specialized centers of learning continue to promote his methods and strategies with upcoming practitioners.

Key Terms

Birth order One's position in the family constellation (firstborn, second-born, etc.). To Adler, it was a major factor in the development of personality.

Compensation A motivation to overcome real or imagined inferiority, to strive for higher levels of development through effort and practice.

Creative power of the self The ability of the individual to create an appropriate style of life.

Early recollections A therapeutic assessment technique in which a person's earliest memories are assumed to reveal the individual's primary interest in life.

Fictional finalism The idea that there is an imagined or potential goal that guides an individual's behavior because they act "as if" it were true.

Individual psychology The theory of counseling and method of diagnosis and treatment formulated by Alfred Adler.

Inferiority complex A condition that develops when an individual is unable to compensate for normal inferiority feelings. It is characterized by exaggerated feelings of weakness, including the belief that one cannot overcome one's difficulties through appropriate effort.

Inferiority feelings The source of human striving that is the normal condition of all people.

Masculine protest Behavior motivated by objections to the belief that society regards men as superior to women. It may occur in males or females.

Neglect Failing to give a child sufficient care and attention, thereby creating the belief that the world is a cold and unfriendly place.

Organ inferiority A significant physiological defect, usually of unknown cause, that can trigger strong feelings of inferiority.

Pampering Also known as "spoiling," it is giving a child excessive attention and protection, thereby preventing the development of initiative and independence and creating the impression that the world owes one a living.

Social interest The innate potential of all individuals to cooperate with other people to achieve personal and societal goals.

Striving for superiority The urge toward perfection or completion, the ultimate goal that motivates the individual. Healthy strivings are guided by social interest, whereas pathological strivings ignore the welfare of others.

Style of life, or life style A unique character structure, or a pattern of personal behaviors and characteristics, by which an individual strives for perfection. Four basic styles of life are the dominant, getting, avoiding, and socially useful types.

Superiority complex A condition that develops when an individual overcompensates for normal inferiority feelings. It is a false feeling of power and security that invariably concerns an underlying inferiority complex.

Teleological From the Greek *tele,* meaning *far* or *distant,* an adjective indicating the goal-directness of human behavior.

Suggested Reading

Dinkmeyer, D., Pew, W., & Dinkmeyer, D. (1979). *Adlerian counseling and psychotherapy.* Belmont, CA: Wadsworth.

Orgler, H. (1963). *Alfred Adler, the man and his work: Triumph over the inferiority complex.* New York: Liveright.

Sperber, M. (1974). *Masks of loneliness: Alfred Adler in perspective.* New York: Macmillan.

Stepansky, P. E. (1983). *In Freud's shadow: Adler in context.* New York: Analytic Press.

Sweeney, T. (1981). *Adlerian counseling, proven concepts and strategies* (2nd ed). Muncie, IN: Accelerated Development.

References

Adler, A. (1907). Organic inferiority and its compensation. In H. L. Ansbacher & R. R. Ansbacher (Eds.), *The individual psychology of Alfred Adler.* New York: Harper, 1964.

Adler, A. (1926). The Neurotic Constitution. Freeport: Books for Libraries Press.

Adler, A. (1930). Individual psychology. In C. Murchison (Ed.). Psychologies of 1930. Worcester: Clark University Press.

Adler, A. (1931). *What life should mean to you.* Boston: Little Brown.

Adler, A. (1937). Position in family constellation influences life style. *International*

Journal of Individual Psychology, 3, 211–227.

Adler, A. (1959). *The practice and theory of individual psychology.* Totowa, NJ: Littlefield-Adams.

Adler, A. (1964a). *Problems of neurosis.* New York: Harper & Row.

Adler, A. (1964b). *Social interest: A challenge to mankind.* New York: Capricorn.

Adler, A., & Deutsch, D. (1959). *Essays in individual psychology.* New York: Grove Press.

Ansbacher, H. L. (1983). Individual psychology. In R. J. Corsini & A. J. Marsella (Eds.), *Personality theories, research and assessment.* Itasca, IL.: Peacock.

Ansbacher, H. L. (1990). Alfred Adler's influence on the three leading cofounders of humanistic psychology. *Journal of Humanistic Psychology, 30,* 45–53.

Ansbacher, H. L. (1992). Alfred Adler, pioneer in prevention of mental disorders. *Individual Psychology: Journal of Adlerian Theory, Research and Practice, 48,* 3–34.

Ansbacher, H. L., & Ansbacher, R. (Eds.). (1956). *The individual psychology of Alfred Adler.* New York: Basic Books.

Barry, H., & Blane, H. T. (1977). Birth order of alcoholics. *Journal of Individual Psychology, 62,* 62–79.

Bishop, D. R. (1992). Religious values as cross-cultural issues in counseling. *Counseling and Values, 36,* 179–191.

Bishop, D. R. (1993). Applying psychometric principles to the clinical use of early recollections. *Individual Psychology: Journal of Adlerian Theory, Research and Practice, 49,* 153–165.

Bohmer, P., & Sitton, S. (1993). The influence of birth order and family size on notable American women's selection of careers. *The Psychological Record, 43,* 375–380.

Brink, T. (1985). Individual psychology. In D. Benner (Ed.), *Baker encyclopedia of psychology* (pp. 568–573). Grand Rapids, MI: Baker.

Burk, J. F. (1989). *Contemporary approaches to psychotherapy and counseling: The self-regulation and maturity model.* Pacific Grove, CA: Brook/Cole.

Byrd, B., DeRosa, A. P. & Craig, S. S. (1993). The adult who is an only child: Achieving separation or individuation. *Psychological Reports, 73,* 171–177.

Claxton, R. P. (1994). Empirical relationships between birth order and two types of

parental feedback. *The Psychological Record, 44,* 475–487.

Corsini, R. J., & Wedding, D. (1989). *Current psychotherapies* (4th ed.). Itasca, IL: Peacock.

Curtis, J. M., & Cowell, D. R. (1993). Relation of birth order and scores on measures of pathological narcissism. *Psychological Reports, 72,* 311–315.

Dewey, E. A. (1972). Family atmosphere. In A. G. Nikelly (Ed.), *Techniques for behavior change* (pp. 41–48). Springfield, IL: Charles C. Thomas.

Dinkmeyer, D., Dinkmeyer, D., Jr., & Sperry, L. (1987). *Adlerian counseling and psychotherapy* (2nd ed.). Columbus, OH: Merrill.

Dinkmeyer, D., & Dreikurs, R. (1963). *Encouraging children to learn.* New York: Hawthorn Books.

Dinkmeyer, D., & Losoncy, L. E. (1980). *The encouragement book: Becoming a positive person.* Englewood Cliffs, NJ: Prentice Hall.

Dinkmeyer, D., Pew, W., & Dinkmeyer, D. (1979). *Adlerian counseling and psychotherapy.* Monterey, CA: Wadsworth.

Dreyfus, E. A., & Nikelly, A. G. (1972). Existential-humanism in Adlerian psychotherapy. In A. G. Nikelly (Ed.), *Techniques for behavior change* (pp. 13–20). Springfield, IL: Charles C. Thomas.

Duncan, L. (1993). A contextual theory of counseling. *TCA Journal, 21,* 55–68.

Ellenberger, H. (1970). *The discovery of the unconscious: The history and evolution of dynamic psychiatry.* New York: Basic Books.

Elliott, J. E. (1992). Compensatory buffers, depression, and irrational beliefs. *Journal of Cognitive Psychotherapy, 6,* 175–184.

Ellis, A. (1970). Tribute to Alfred Adler. *Journal of Individual Psychology, 26,* 11–12.

Ellis, A. (1971). Reason and emotion in the individual psychology of Adler. *Journal of Individual Psychology, 27,* 50–64.

Evans, T. D. (1991). How far can you go and still be Adlerian? *Individual Psychology: Journal of Adlerian Theory, Research and Practice, 47,* 541–547.

Forer, L. (1977). Bibliography of birth order literature in the '70s. *Journal of Individual Psychology, 33,* 122–141.

Frankl, V. E. (1970). Fore-runner to existential to existential psychiatry. *Journal of Individual Psychology, 26,* 38.

Freud, S. (1914). On narcissism: An introduction. London: Hogarth Press, Vol. 14. Paperback reprint: *General psychological theory.* New York: Collier, 1963.

Furtmuller, C. (1964). Alfred Adler: A biographical essay. In H. L. Ansbacher & R. R. Ansbacher (Eds.), *Superiority and social interest.* Evanston, IL: Northwestern University Press.

Garfinkle, M. I., Massey, R. F., & Mendel, E. (1987). Two cases in Adlerian child therapy. In Belkin, G. S., *Contemporary Psychotherapies* (2nd ed.). Monterey, CA: Brooks/Cole.

Gates, L., Lineberger, M. R., Crockett, J., & Hubbard, J. (1988). Birth order and its relationship to depression, anxiety, and self-concept test scores in children. *Journal of Genetic Psychology, 149,* 29–34.

Gold, L. (1979). Adler's theory of dreams: An holistic approach to interpretation. In B. B. Wolman (Ed.), *Handbook of dreams: Research, theories, and applications.* New York: Litton.

Greever, A., Tsen, S., & Friedland, B. (1973). Development of the social interest index. *Journal of Consulting and Clinical Psychology, 41,* 454–458.

Kaplan, H. B. (1986). A guide for explaining social interest to laypersons. *Journal of Individual Psychology, 28,* 122–129.

Kaufman, W. (1980). *Discovering the mind: Vol. 3. Freud versus Adler and Jung.* New York: McGraw-Hill.

Kottman, T., & Warlick, J. (1990). Adlerian play therapy. *Journal of Humanistic Education and Development, 28,* 125–132.

Leak, G. K., Gardner, L. E., & Pounds, B. (1992). A comparison of Eastern religion, Christianity, and social interest. *Individual Psychology: Journal of Adlerian Theory, Research and Practice, 48,* 53–64.

Manaster, G. J., & Corsini, R. J. (1982). *Individual psychology: Theory and practice.* Itasca, IL: Peacock.

Maslow, A. (1970). Tribute to Alfred Adler. *Journal of Individual Psychology, 26,* 13.

McGuire, W. (Ed.). (1974). *The Freud/Jung letters.* Princeton, NJ: Princeton University Press.

Miller, N., & Maruyama, G. (1976). Ordinal position and peer popularity. *Journal of Personality and Social Psychology, 33,* 123–131.

Miranda, A. O., & White, P. E. (1993). The relationship between acculturation level and social interest among Hispanic adults. *Individual Psychology: Journal of Adlerian Theory, Research and Practice, 49,* 76–85.

Mosak, B., & Mosak, H. H. (1975). *A bibliography of Adlerian psychology.* Washington, DC: Hemisphere Publishing.

Mosak, H. (1972). Lifestyle. In A. G. Nikelly (Ed.), *Techniques for behavior change* (pp. 77–81). Springfield, IL: Charles C. Thomas.

Mosak, H. (Ed.). (1973). *Alfred Adler: His influence on psychology today.* Park Ridge, NJ: Noyes Press.

Mosak, H. (1989). Adlerian psychotherapy. In R. Corsini (Ed.), *Current psychotherapies* (3rd ed., pp. 65–116). Itasca, IL: Peacock.

Mosak, H. (1991). "I don't have social interest": Social interest as construct. *Individual Psychology: Journal of Adlerian Theory, Research and Practice, 47,* 309–320.

Mosak, H., & Dreikurs, R. (1973). Adlerian psychotherapy. In R. Corsini (Ed.), *Current psychotherapies* (pp. 35–83). Itasca, IL: Peacock.

Mosak, H. H., & Mosak, B. (1985). *A bibliography of Adlerian psychology* (Vol. 2). Washington, DC: Hemisphere Publishing.

Moschetta, P. V. (1993). Encouraging social interest between married partners. *Individual Psychology: Journal of Adlerian Theory, Research and Practice, 49,* 399–405.

Mullis, F. J., Kern, R. M., & Curlette, W. L. (1987). Life-style themes and social interest: A further factor analytic study. *Individual Psychology, 43,* 339–352.

Narayan, C. (1990). Birth order and narcissism. *Psychological Reports, 67,* 1184–1186.

Nicoll, W. G. (1993). Multiple systems counseling: An integrative and extension of Adlerian and systems theories. *Individual Psychology: Journal of Adlerian Theory, Research and Practice, 49,* 132–152.

Nikelly, A. G. (1971). Fundamental concepts of maladjustment. In A. G. Nikelly (Ed.), *Techniques for behavior change.* Springfield, IL: Charles C. Thomas.

Nikelly, A. G., & Dinkmeyer, D. (1972). The process of encouragement. In A. G. Nikelly (Ed.), *Techniques for behavior change* (pp. 97–101). Springfield, IL: Charles C. Thomas.

Nikelly, A. G., & Verger, G. (1973). Current Adlerian Therapies. Comprehensive psychiatry. (Vo. 14) (pp. 41–48).

O'Connell, W. E. (1965). Humanistic identification: A new translation for Gemeinschaftsgefuhl. *Journal of Individual Psychology*, 21, 44–47.

Orgler, H. (1963). *Alfred Adler, the man and his work: Triumph over the inferiority complex*. New York: Liveright.

Parrott, L. (1992). Earliest recollections and birth order: Two Adlerian exercises. *Teaching of Psychology*, 19(1), 40–42.

Perlin, M., & Grater, H. (1984). The relationship between birth order and reported interpersonal behavior. *Journal of Individual Psychology*, 40, 22–28.

Porchaska, J. O. (1979). *Systems of psychotherapy: A transtheoretical analysis*. Homewood, IL: Dorsey Press.

Purkey, W. W., & Schmidt, J. J. (1987). *The inviting relationship*. Englewood Cliffs, NJ: Prentice Hall.

Roazen, P. (1975). *Freud and his followers*. New York: Knopf.

Rosenthal, H. R. (1959). *The final dream: A criterion for the termination of therapy*. In A. Adler & D. Deutsch (Eds.), Essays in individual psychology (pp. 400–409). New York: Grove Press.

Rule, W. (Ed.). (1984). *Lifestyle counseling for adjustment to disability*. Rockville, MD: Aspen Systems.

Rule, W. R. (1987). Acceptance and adjustment to disability: An Adlerian orientation. In G. L. Gandy, E. D. Mertin, R. E. Hardy, & J. G. Cull (Eds.), *Rehabilitation counseling and services: Profession and process* (pp. 219–233). Springfield, IL: Charles C. Thomas.

Seligman, L. (1986). *Diagnosis and treatment planning in counseling*. New York: Human Sciences Press.

Shulman, B. H., & Mosak, H. M. (1977). Birth order and ordinal position: Two Adlerian views. *Journal of Individual Psychology*, 33, 114–121.

Shulman, B. H., & Nikelly, A. G. (1972). Family constellation. In A. G. Nikelly (Ed.), *Techniques for behavior change* (pp. 35–40). Springfield, IL: Charles C. Thomas.

Silverman, N. N., & Corsini, R. J. (1984). Is it true what they say about Adler's individual psychology? *Teaching of Psychology*, 11, 188–189.

Smith, D. (1982). Trends in counseling and psychotherapy. *American Psychologist, 37*, 802–809.

Sperber, M. (1974). *Masks of loneliness: Alfred Adler in perspective*. New York: Macmillan.

Stepansky, P. E. (1983). *In Freud's shadow: Adler in context*. New York: Analytic Press.

Stone, M. (1993). Balancing the self with the marital system. *Individual Psychology: Journal of Adlerian Theory, Research and Practice, 49*, 392–398.

Vaihinger, H. (1911). *The psychology of "as if": A system of the theoretical, practical and religious fictions of mankind*. New York: Harcourt, Brace & World.

Wallace, W. A. (1986). *Theories of counseling and psychotherapy*. Boston: Allyn & Bacon.

Watkins, C. E., Jr. (1985). Early recollections as a projective technique in counseling: An Adlerian view. *AMHCA Journal, 7*, 32–40.

Watkins, C. E., Jr. (1992). Research activity with Adler's theory. *Individual Psychology: Journal of Adlerian Theory, Research and Practice, 48*, 107–108.

Wilder, J. (1959). Alfred Adler's influence. In K. Adler & D. Deutsch (Eds.), *Essays in individual psychology*. New York: Grove Press.

Wittmer, J. M. (1989). Reaching toward wholeness. In T. J. Sweeney (Ed.), *Adlerian counseling: A practical approach for a new decade* (3rd ed.). Muncie, IN: Accelerated Development.

Human will begins in a "no." The "no" is a protest against a world we never made, and it is also the assertion of one's self in the endeavor to remold and reform the world. —**Rollo May**

Existential Therapy

CHAPTER **8**

CHAPTER OUTLINE

Brief Biography
Historical Development
View of Human Nature
Development of Maladaptive Behavior
Function of the Therapist
Goals of Therapy
Major Methods and Techniques
Application
Critical Analysis
Current Status
Summary
Key Terms
Suggested Reading
References

Midway through the 20th century, psychotherapy encountered a puzzling phenomenon. Although social mores had become more permissive than those of the Victorian era, this new liberalism did not seem to alleviate conflicts between the id and superego. Supposedly liberated by the sexual revolution, people were entering psychotherapy in increasing numbers. Suffering from the inability to enjoy their new freedom and self-expression, they were

147

struck with a sense of alienation, emptiness, and self-estrangement. They yearned for meaning and purpose and sought solutions in the offices of their therapists.

Existentialism, which concerned itself with the essence of inner being—with **ontology,** the science of being—promised an answer. Moving away from attempts to recover an unconscious personal past (May & Yalom, 1995), it gave focus to living productively in the present and held out hope for a spiritual awakening, a restoration of the meaning of life (Bugental, 1978).

> The meaning of life always changes but it never ceases to be.
> —Victor Frankl

On the other hand, existential therapy is said to be "plagued by a lack of consistency, coherency, and scrutiny" (Norcross, 1987, p. 41). Since existentialists cannot agree on a theory that fully articulates their ideas, existential therapists approach their profession in a variety of ways. In fact, existentialism does not lend itself to neatly defined models of personality, causes of maladaptive behavior, or treatment strategies. In addition to this criticism, Yalom notes that existential therapy is like "a homeless waif who was not permitted into the better academic neighborhoods" (1980, p. 14). Despite outward diversity and the resistance of academia, existential therapists continue to influence many systems of counseling.

BRIEF BIOGRAPHY

Today the existential approach to counseling is represented by a number of different theorists (e.g., Boss, 1963; Kaam, 1967; Sartre 1953, 1956), but it began with the work of Ludwig Binswanger (1958), a Swiss psychiatrist. Although Binswanger was the first to realize the possibilities of applying the philosophy of existentialism to his day-to-day counseling practice, it was Rollo May, another theorist, who enlarged upon and popularized the work of his predecessor.

Born on April 21, 1909, May was the eldest son of Earl and Matie May, who named him after Little Rollo, a character in a series of nineteenth-century children's books. Growing up in the small town of Ada, Ohio, May grew to detest the name. Throughout his childhood, Little Rollo's exploits in literature were presented to May as the model for proper conduct in life. It was no accident that his father, who valued exercise, subjected his son to a strict regimen of swimming and character building. May's intense dislike for his name remained with him until, as a young adult living in Europe, he learned about a medieval Norman ruler named Rollo the Conqueror (Rabinowitz, Good, & Cozad, 1989).

Since his father was a field secretary for the YMCA, May's family moved from Ohio to Michigan, and it was here that May enrolled at Michigan State College in East Lansing. He and a friend founded a campus magazine, *The Student,* and published an editorial charging the state legislature with using the college to conceal unscrupulous methods for gaining profit. Anticipating dismissal, May left Michigan State and set out for Oberlin College in Ohio. After a brief conference with Oberlin's dean, May was admitted without formal application. With a major in English and minor in Greek history and literature, May received his B.A. degree in 1930.

Despite his lack of proficiency in Greek, May was offered a teaching position at Anatolia College in Salonika, Greece. He accepted the appointment and held the post for three years. During two summer vacations May visited Vienna, where he worked as a secretary for the International School of Art, studied painting in his free time, and more significantly for our purposes, enrolled in seminars conducted by Alfred Adler. It was these summer visits to Vienna that marked the beginning of May's interest in psychotherapy.

> An achievement is a bondage. It obliges one to a higher achievement.
> —Albert Camus

In 1933 May returned to the United States and enrolled in Union Theological Seminary in New York in order to enter the ministry. Following the divorce of his parents, he withdrew from the seminary after his first year to support his younger brothers and sisters in Michigan. Eventually returning to Union, he completed his studies under the German philosopher Paul Tillich, who, like Adler, strongly influenced May's thinking. In 1938 May graduated *cum laude* with a B.D. degree.

May began his ministry in a Congregational parish in Verona, New Jersey. His two years as pastor were disappointing, and he soon enrolled in Columbia University to major in clinical psychology. His studies were cut short, however, by a bout with tuberculosis. Faced with an even chance of surviving, May entered a sanitarium on Saranac Lake in upstate New York, where he remained for 18 months. His struggle with the realities of death reinforced his existential leanings. He was especially impressed with Kierkegaard's explanation of **anxiety** as the result of a threat to one's being. He learned from this experience that he alone had to decide whether he lived or died.

Though not fully recovered, May completed his Ph.D. at Columbia in 1949 at the age of 40. May's doctoral dissertation, *The Meaning of Anxiety,* was a prophetic work. After comparing and synthesizing the existing theories of anxiety, May challenged the popular view that life without anxiety is healthy and argued that anxiety is not only normal but essential to the human condition. His dissertation was published in 1950, and five years later the New York Society of Clinical Psychology recognized his distinguished contribution to the profession and science of psychology. Throughout his career May published, among other works, *Existential Psychology* (1961), *Psychology and the Human Dilemma* (1966), *Man's Search for Himself* (1967), *Love and Will* (1969), *Power and Innocence* (1972), and *The Courage to Create* (1975). He was a visiting professor at Harvard (1965), Princeton (1967), and Yale (1972) and lived out his later years in the San Francisco area, where he wrote about the meaning of myths for modern society. May died of congestive heart failure in October 1994 in his home.

HISTORICAL DEVELOPMENT

As a philosophical movement, existentialism developed in continental Europe during the 19th century from the work of the philosophers Søren Kierkegaard and Fredrich Nietzsche. Although its roots are philosophical, its tenor is often poetic. "Some vision of the good, the true, and the beautiful is essential to a meaningful personal life and a humanistic society" (Partenheimer, 1990, p. 44).

Søren Kierkegaard (1813–1855) lived almost his entire life in Copenhagen. When he was 22, Kierkegaard learned to his dismay that his father had not only cursed God but had seduced his mother before marrying her as well. So deeply did these revelations disturb Kierkegaard that he referred to them in his writings as "the great earthquake."

Partially in response to this crisis, Kierkegaard's many books came to explore the nature of religious faith—more specifically, the meaning of Christianity. Arguing that religious beliefs cannot be supported by rational argument, Kierkegaard believed that true faith is essentially irrational. At its heart, Christianity demands that the believer accept the "absurd": the logical impossibility of God, who is infinite and immortal, being born on earth in Jesus Christ, who was finite and mortal. Religious faith cannot be achieved by an objective examination of the evidence, Kierkegaard argued, but only by a subjective choice, by a so-called "leap of faith." God wants us not to argue *for* Him, but to be obedient *to* Him. Kierkegaard also stressed the virtues of individuality, freedom, responsibility, honesty, and commitment.

Kierkegaard's emphasis on such a subjective commitment provided a provocative stimulus for later counseling theorists (Dopson & Gade, 1981). Although Kierkegaard did not call his philosophy *existentialism*—the term would be applied to his work only some years after his death—he did insist that each person carves out his or her own destiny and that being is the product of action. When existentialism finally took hold as a distinct philosophical movement some 70 years after his death, it was on this framework that all later existentialist thinking was built.

> Is it not things, but the way we view things that is important?
>
> —Seneca

The son and grandson of Protestant ministers, the German philosopher Fredrich Nietzsche (1844–1900) was nevertheless highly skeptical of religion. In *Thus Spake Zarathustra,* he proclaimed, "God is dead," which became a popular theological slogan of the 1960s after an Episcopal bishop wrote a book by that title. Unlike Kierkegaard, Nietzsche believed religion had lost its hold upon people and could no longer serve as the reference point for moral values. The time had come, he said, for people to critically examine their traditional values, which were based on fear and resentment. Associating these values with the Judeo-Christian tradition, Nietzsche repeatedly criticized Christianity in his book *The Antichrist* (1895).

Nietzsche boasted that he was one of the few philosophers who was also a psychologist. His goal and ideal was the passionate individual who learns to control unruly passions and use them in art or in other creative endeavors. So completely should such people accept and **love** their own lives, Nietzsche believed, that they would choose to relive them, with all of their joys and sufferings, an infinite number of times. In 1889 Nietzsche suffered a mental breakdown from which he never recovered.

Kierkegaard and Nietzsche introduced existential thought to Western Europe. It was their work that established the footing for several influential philosophers, including the French writers Albert Camus, Jean-Paul Sartre, and Gabriel Marcel; the German philosophers Karl Jaspers and Martin Heidegger; the Russian religious and political thinker Nicolas Berdyaev; and the Jewish philosopher Martin Buber.

8.1 | I and Thou

In his mid-20s, Martin Buber (1878–1965) began to study Hasidism and wrote prolifically on the philosophy of dialogue and human interaction. *I and Thou* became the title of his best-known book, which was originally published in 1923. In this work, and as further developed and amplified in his later writings, Buber distinguishes between the I-Thou and I-It relationships. The I-Thou relationship is one of mutuality and openness between being and being. The I-It is the contrasting concept, which refers to relations in which nongenuine dialogue takes place and another person is used to satisfy one's own needs.

In therapeutic relations Buber's account of I-Thou allows the greatest opportunity for profound psychological transformation. When one allows the I-Thou relationship to occur, it can have a pervasive influence in a person's life: an "air" of continuous conversation develops; freedom for otherness and difference emerges; one has a sense of the limits of autonomy and identity; one trusts communication and experiences freedom from the ultimate claims of possessions. No matter how alienated one feels in the immediate environment, nonalienated trust moves one's soul.

Buber's description of I-Thou means that the psyche is founded in a nonpersonal relationship that is religious in meaning and that creates psychological well-being through a decentering of the self.

VIEW OF HUMAN NATURE

As the radically divergent approaches of even Kierkegaard and Nietzsche suggest, existentialism is alternately religious, atheistic, and anti-religious. It emphasizes hope and optimism as well as despair and nothingness. While some of its practitioners revel in its philosophical roots, still others are compelled by the therapeutic phenomena of clinical cases (Pervin, 2001). In short, existentialists do not agree on a basic view of human nature (Cogswell, 1993; Kobasa & Maddi, 1977; Maddi, 1980; Pervin, 1960). Despite its diverse interpretations, common threads run throughout all existential perspectives on counseling.

The central focus of existentialism is on the essence of *existence*—on the phenomena that are inherent in the nature of being alive. Almost every existentialist believes we face important and difficult decisions, and the quality of these decisions is limited by our knowledge and by the frames of reference in which these decisions are made (May, 1991). This existential predicament lies at the heart of the human condition. Existentialists believe that life is either fulfilled or constricted by a series of decisions that we make, with no way of knowing conclusively what the correct choices are. Continually we must decide what is true and what is false, what is right and what is wrong, which beliefs to accept and which to reject, what to do and what not to do (von Kaam, 1969).

> I don't like religion much, and I am glad that in the Bible the word is not to be found.
>
> —Martin Buber

Despite the importance of these decisions, existentialists believe no objective standards or rules exist to guide us in making decisions. Because different sources supply conflicting advice, we cannot turn to any specific source for direction. Although each of us, as a result, must decide which standards to accept and which to reject, from another point of view each of us has the need and the ability to make crucial choices. "I prefer to live in a world in which man has the right to make choices, even if they are wrong choices," Frankl writes, "rather than in a world in which no choice at all is left to him" (1967, p. 13).

In the absence of external standards, laws, ethical rules, or traditions, existentialists believe these choices must be made. From the point of view of the so-called **phenomenological** or "here-and-now" perspective, such human choice is wholly subjective. Existentialists, then, emphasize experience as the primary phenomenon in the study of human nature. Both theoretical explanations and overt behavior are secondary to experience itself and its meaning to the person (Owen, 1992).

Only when individuals have learned to make choices and to live with the consequences are they truly free. But because they freely choose, individuals are also fully responsible for their choices. Responsibility is the mirror image of such freedom, the opposite side of the coin. Forced to make choices for themselves, individuals have both freedom and congruent responsibility thrust upon them. As a result they are, in the words of Jean Paul Sartre (1953), "condemned to be free."

Responsibility is the burden that freedom bears. When individuals realize they are completely responsible for their decisions, actions, and beliefs, they are overcome by anxiety. By ignoring or denying their freedom to escape the concomitant responsibility, they attempt to escape this anxiety. But since this rejection actually denies their circumstance, they succeed only in self-deception. Fugitives from freedom are not free, only self-deceived. Existentialists insist that individuals must accept full responsibility for their behavior, no matter how difficult. If people are to live meaningfully and authentically, they must become fully aware of the reality of the human situation and courageously accept it. They must come to terms with being not only of the world but with "being-in-the-world."

"Being human means being engaged and entangled in a situation," writes Frankl. "'Being-in-the-world' is to be confronted with a world whose objectivity and reality is in no way diminished by the subjectivity of that 'being' who is in the world" (1967, p. 138). In short, the objectivity of the world does not impinge on the subjective nature of humankind.

Death, or nonbeing, is also significant to an existential understanding of human nature, for we live on two levels: in a state of forgetfulness of being and in a state of mindfulness of being (Heidegger, 1962). To live in the former state is to live in continual distraction and diversion and thus to be wholly unaware of oneself. It is to be preoccupied with things, abstractions, and diversions. In the latter state, however, individuals are continually aware of being, continually in touch with existence and the world of being. Although this living in awareness of being produces authenticity, it is also fraught with anxiety, which increases when individuals confront the reality of nonbeing or death. An extraordinary sense of accountability is initiated with the realization of death, which urges them on to greater fulfillment or authenticity. In fact, in many ways any experience that diminishes individuality or identity is an anticipation of death, which in turn challenges people to live a fuller, more authentic existence.

Rejecting the concept of causality, Ludwig Binswanger (1963) and Medard Boss (1963, 1977) represent many existentialists' further concentration on **Dasein**—"being there." In a so-called **Daseinsanalysis**—that is, the analysis of our immediate experience—the existentialist therapist will focus on the three levels in which we exist: the **Umwelt,** the physical environment of animate and inanimate objects; the **Mitwelt,** the social environment; and finally the **Eigenwelt,** the inner feelings of our "own world." Together these three levels of existence constitute *Dasein.*

In other words, the existential therapist does not analyze human motivation in terms of past events. *Dasein* motivates us and offers us possibilities that draw us forward. If we are truly authentic, we take responsibility, make choices, free ourselves from domination, and approach our ultimate potential. Failure to be free causes anxiety, and our *Dasein* contracts. Although existentialists do not talk about stages of development, they do believe that *Dasein* develops over time: they do believe that we become free of the influence of others. This is what brings us to true existence.

May (1961) has proposed six essential characteristics that constitute the nature of an authentic person:

1. Humans are centered in themselves. Anxiety is only one method individuals use to protect their own center of existence.
2. Humans are typically in a state of anxiety, in a struggle against that which would destroy their being.

3. Humans are self-affirming; they need to preserve their center. The preservation of this center requires will.
4. Humans can move from centeredness to participation with other beings, but this movement involves risk.
5. Awareness lies on the subjective side of centeredness. Persons are able to be subjectively aware of that with which they are in contact.
6. Self-consciousness is a form of awareness, of knowledge of external dangers and threats, which is unique to human beings. Consciousness

8.2 | Victor Frankl's Search for Meaning

Victor Frankl is best known for his compelling book *Man's Search for Meaning* (1959). In this small volume, Frankl describes his imprisonment in Nazi concentration camps at Auschwitz and Dachau during World War II (1942–1945). While Frankl gives attention to the horrors of the concentration camp, the book is more a testimony to the power of the human spirit and its ability to survive.

Following are some illustrative quotations from Frankl's famous book.

> The most ghastly moment of the twenty-four hours of camp life was the awakening, when at a still nocturnal hour, the three shrill blows of a whistle tore us pitilessly from our exhausted sleep and from the longings in our dreams. We then began the tussle with our wet shoes, into which we could scarcely force our feet, which were sore and swollen with edema. And there were the usual moans and groans about petty troubles, such as the snapping of wires which replaced shoelaces. One morning I heard someone, who I knew to be brave and dignified, cry like a child because he finally had to go to the snowy marching grounds in his bare feet, as his shoes were too shrunken for him to wear. In those ghastly minutes, I found a little bit of comfort; a small piece of bread which I drew out of my pocket and munched with absorbed delight. (p. 50)
>
> We stumbled on in the darkness, over big stones and through large puddles, along the one road leading from the camp. The accompanying guards kept shouting at us and driving us with the butts of their rifles. Anyone with very sore feet supported himself on his neighbor's arm. Hardly a word was spoken; the icy wind did not encourage talk. Hiding his mouth behind his upturned collar, the man marching next to me whispered suddenly: "If our wives could see us now! I do hope they are better off in their camps and don't know what is happening to us."

has to do with our experience with ourselves as subjects who have a world.

To which Frankl (1963) adds a seventh characteristic to May's description of the "existing person":

7. The primary force in our lives is a search for meaning. Each person must have a unique and specific meaning, one that can be fulfilled by that person alone. Our striving toward existence requires will.

> That brought thoughts of my own wife to mind. And as we stumbled on for miles, slopping on icy spots, supporting each other time and again, dragging one another up and onward, nothing was said, but we both know: each of us was thinking of his wife. Occasionally I looked at the sky, where the stars were fading and the pink light of morning was beginning to spread behind a dark bank of clouds. But my mind clung to my wife's image, imagining it with an uncanny acuteness. I heard her answering me, saw her smile, her frank and encouraging look. Real or not, her look was then more luminous than the sun which was beginning to rise.
>
> A thought transfixed me: for the first time in my life I saw the truth as it is set into song by so many poets, proclaimed as the final wisdom by so many thinkers. The truth—that love is the ultimate and the highest goal to which man can aspire. Then I grasped the meaning of the greatest secret that human poetry and human thought and belief have to impart: The salvation of man is through love and in love. I understood how a man who has nothing left in this world still may know bliss, be it only for a brief moment, in the contemplation of his beloved.
>
> In front of me a man stumbled and those following him fell on top of him. The guard rushed over and used his whip on them all. Thus my thoughts were interrupted for a few minutes. But soon my soul found its way back from the prisoner's existence to another world, and I resumed talk with my loved one: I asked her questions, and she answered; she questioned me in return, and I answered. (Frankl, 1959, pp. 58–60)

Frankl maintained a sane response in an insane situation. He paid attention to a crust of bread, he secretly worked on a book, but most of all he thought of his wife. At a more basic level, Frankl found meaning outside the horror of the immediate situation that gave him strength to cope with life's difficult reality. It was here that he found the essence of life and developed logotherapy.

Although Frankl was a student of Freud, he became interested in existentialism in the 1930s through reading such philosophers as Heidegger, Scheler, and Legan. He began formulating his ideas about an existentialist approach to counseling before his death camp experiences, having used the term *logotherapy* as early as 1938. The impact of the concentration camps, however, crystallized Frankl's thoughts about the meaning of life and suffering, and it was partly his determination to share his beliefs that kept him alive.

DEVELOPMENT OF MALADAPTIVE BEHAVIOR

The existential therapist believes that if we fail to live in a state of awareness of our being, even at the risk of anxiety, we will inevitably collapse into maladaptive behavior. But rather than directly confronting and dealing with anxiety, we sometimes lie to ourselves (Stevens, Pfost, & Potts, 1990). We don't want to believe the nature of our predicament, and we attempt to manipulate others into supporting our self-deception. When this occurs, the result is maladaptive behavior (Westman, 1992).

From the point of view of existential psychologists, then, psychopathology is not a difference in degree but in kind. They consider traditional nomenclature, including diagnostic labels, to be alienating and depersonalizing. From an existential perspective, healthy people enjoy a strong *Dasein* and live actively and purposefully in the three levels of existence, *Umwelt, Mitwelt,* and *Eigenwelt* . Maladaptive individuals, on the other hand, lack "authenticity"—that is, they lack meaning and a sense of being-in-the-world. All psychological symptoms, according to the existential therapist, result at some level from decisions that compromise this authenticity.

> I am my choices.
> —Jean-Paul Sartre

Individuals may reject interpersonal relationships (*Mitwelt*), for example, as irreconcilable with their own needs and values (*Eigenwelt*). Or vice versa, constantly attempting to adapt to the wishes of others, maladaptive people may become social chameleons, sacrificing *Eigenwelt* to *Mitwelt*. Alternatively, *Mitwelt* or *Eigenwelt* may be consistently ignored in favor of biological needs (*Umwelt*). On the other hand, sufferers may deny their sexuality (*Umwelt*) in order to conform to parental demands. Whatever the form, such a constriction or loss of *Dasein* ultimately results in self-estrangement, apathy, and an inability to experience existence as real. "The fundamental neurotic process in our day," writes May (1969, p. 75), "is the repression of the ontological sense, the loss of [one's] sense of being."

In *The Divided Self,* R. D. Laing (1959) provides a phenomenological account of a schizoid individual who experiences what he calls a basic "ontological insecurity," a split between the relation with the world and the self. The individual lacks a firm sense of self or identity. Although most people experience similar feelings of uncertainty at times, the maladaptive individual's experience of ontological insecurity is intense and pervasive.

For the existentialist, such maladaptive behavior is fundamentally the result of meaninglessness, of an "existential vacuum," according to Frankl (1967). Substance abuse, marital and family discord, depression, confusion, and self-defeating activity can all develop as a result of perceived meaninglessness (Lantz & Pegram, 1989). Maladaptive behavior is the result of not embracing our freedom and responsibility, of disregarding our true self, of forsaking genuine meaning in life.

FUNCTION OF THE THERAPIST

Regardless of the strategy, the linchpin of existential therapy is the therapist. To help clients restore meaning in their lives, the therapist may use advocacy, empathy, concern, sincere personal interest, reflection, action, environmental modification, or support. Restoration of meaning can occur through work with individuals, families, or even groups (Greenlee, 1990; Lantz & Pegram, 1989; Schwartzberg, 1993).

According to Arbuckle (1975), counselors who view the predicament of individuals from the existential perspective are distinguished by an intellectual flexibility that is not threatened by the ideas and beliefs of others and that does not adhere stubbornly to any one intellectual system, theory, or ideology; by a personality that exemplifies freedom and integrity, which can provide strength to a struggling counselee; and by a recognition that beliefs are ideas that cannot be proven right or wrong but are expressions of faith.

The existential therapist expects the therapeutic responsibility to rest squarely on the client. Therapy is not imposed. Neither is the client viewed as an object to be evaluated, assessed, reported about, programmed for change, or modified. Starting therapy, ending therapy, taking each step in the therapeutic process—all of this is determined in large part not by the therapist but by the clients.

The existential therapist, however, is grounded in the immediate, subjective experience of encountering the client. The emphasis is on a sensitive presence that puts personal needs aside and centers exclusively on the client, on "one existence communicating with another" (May, Angel, & Ellenberger, 1958). To use Martin Buber's well-known phrase, the therapeutic relationship must be an "I-Thou" encounter built on honesty, in which counselors expose their true selves. The counselor's ability to be genuinely human enables clients to become aware of similar qualities in themselves. Through this encounter individuals recognize their potentials. "Encounter is always a potentially creative experience; it normally ensues in the expanding of consciousness, the enrichment of the self" (May, 1994). Nor is this genuine encounter an isolated pocket of intimacy. According to Irvin Yalom, "it exists in one's inner world as a permanent reference point: a reminder of one's potential for intimacy" (1980, p. 404).

Most existential counselors do not believe that individuals are divided into conscious and unconscious dimensions. Too often the so-called unconscious is used to rationalize behavior and evade responsibility, the existential therapist believes, thus avoiding the realities of one's existence. Only when clients embrace this responsibility can therapeutic change occur.

> Man is condemned to be free.
>
> —Jean-Paul Sartre

Usually an existential therapist views the process of this change from six perspectives or angles.

First, clients can change as a result of insight, by understanding personal modes of existing in concert with a developing sense of choice, freedom, and responsibility. The process provides opportunity for seeing and grasping their own potential for existing and exercising choice for, or declining, this way of "being-in-the-world."

Second, change occurs through a process of therapeutic encountering between therapists and clients, a genuine meeting of persons, an open confrontation, a full "being-with-one-another." This risk of an existential clash culminates in transformation and existential growth.

Third, change occurs when clients carry forward their own potential for existing. This is a process of opening up, of actualization, of being, existing, and experiencing one's own potentials.

Fourth, change occurs by means of an internal process of therapeutic encountering between the person and one's own deeper potentials for existing. This internal encounter risks existential clashes and culminates in an integrative meeting, in a welcoming, touching intimacy between patients and their inner potentials.

Fifth, change occurs when clients completely disengage from their own personality structure, identity, or self, and when they enter wholly into a deeper existence or mode of being, into a deeper experiencing. In this process of existential death and rebirth, the innermost core of the person undergoes radical transformation into a new and authentic being.

And, finally, change occurs when clients open up new worlds, when they construct new and changing life situations, when they risk actual new and changing ways of being in worlds of their own construction.

GOALS OF THERAPY

Because the goals of existential therapy emerge from the therapeutic process, they often seem vague and obscure. For example, May asserts, "The aim of therapy is that the patient *experience his existence as real*" (May, Angel & Ellenberger, 1958, p. 85). Corlis and Rabe maintain that the therapist's goals are "to stimulate the patient's willingness to work through pain, to offer help without the jeopardy of undercutting the other's own effort, to offer him strength without dependence" (1969, p. 13). The ultimate goal of existential psychotherapy, according to Phares, is "to help the individual reach a point at which awareness and decision making can be exercised responsibly" (1988, p. 417). With an equally broad stroke, Frey and Heslett say "existential counselors agree with the general goals of most other approaches to counseling and psychotherapy, but seek to embellish these general goals with existential points of view" (1975, p. 43).

While therapists debate the various goals of existential therapy, most would agree that its overarching purpose is to help their clients find purpose and meaning in life. According to Frankl (1963), meaning can be uncovered in three ways: by doing a deed (*creative values*), by experiencing a value (*experiential values*), and by suffering (*attitudinal values*).

> To exist means to-be-in-the-world.
>
> —van Kaam

While there is value in each of these three paths to meaning, the first two can lead to difficulty. The problem with creative values comes, for example, in seeking all of life's meaning through work. Faced with the retirement, illness, or economic recession, maladjusted individuals often lose their elusive sense of meaning. Similarly, people may realize experiential values through a symphony or the intimacy of a friendship, but if they become deaf or their friends move away, meaning becomes a mirage.

As a result, Frankl emphasized attitudinal values for good reason. Unlike creative and experiential values, attitudinal values allow individuals to adjust to things beyond their control, so that they are able to respond to whatever circumstances life brings. The capacity to respond to life's circumstances, even to undeserved suffering, knows no limit. "In the realization of attitudinal values [the individual] is free," writes Frankl. "This freedom knows no conditions, it is a freedom 'under all circumstances' and until the last breath" (1950).

From the point of view of the existential therapist, clients have the capacity for change, which can occur on the twin axes of actualization and integration. The critical word here is "capacity," for existential psychologists do not believe that human beings are the packages of innate drives and desires that characterize most other theories of therapy. There is no biological or biopsychological sequence of growth or development, no force toward becoming mature, no constitutional wellspring pushing or pulling us toward authenticity, spirituality, social consciousness, normality, or health. At the same time, however, the existential therapist recognizes that each person still has the potential to move in the direction of ever increasing actualization and integration (DeCarvalho, 1990).

> Our enemy is as necessary for us as is our friend. Both together are part of authentic community.
>
> —Rollo May

MAJOR METHODS AND TECHNIQUES

Existential therapists are not known for their repertoire of techniques. In fact, some practitioners regard it less as a distinct approach to therapy than as a philosophy of therapy (LeVine, 1993; Osipow, Walsh, & Tosi, 1984; Wallace, 1986). Kemp points out that in existential counseling "technique follows understanding" (1971, p. 18). "Approaching human beings merely in terms of techniques necessarily implies manipulating them," writes Frankl. "Approaching them merely in terms of dynamics implies reifying them, making human beings into mere things" (1967, p. 139). Nor are existential therapists, in general, particularly concerned with issues of transference, countertransference, personal distortions, or defense mechanisms. Far more basic existential issues are freedom, meaning, spirituality, and responsibility (Bylski & Westman, 1991; Payne, Bergin, & Loftus, 1992).

As might be expected, then, the methods used by existential counselors tend to be as varied as the number of practitioners (Osipow & Walsh, 1970). Perhaps more so than any other counselor, the existential therapist will rely on those techniques that are most compatible with his or her personality. In addition, the behavior of counselors can vary considerably during the counseling interview simply because the client and counselor differ at any given moment. And, of course, the training of existential counselors influences the intervention strategies they incorporate into their practice. Those trained in the Freudian approach, for example, may rely heavily on interpretation, while those with a client-centered background will verbally engage their clients.

There are, however, some identifiable characteristics in the practice of existential psychotherapy. Recognizing that the "being" of the counselor is the most dynamic force in the counseling process, the following components of existential therapy are noteworthy.

8.3 | An Existential Focusing Exercise

By Eugene T. Gendlin

Helping a Felt Sense Form

It is possible for a person to focus a little between one communication and the next. Having made a point, and being understood, the person can focus before saying the next thing.

Most people don't do that. They run on from point to point, only talking.

How can you help people stop, and get the felt sense of what they have just said?

This is the second focusing movement. Finding the felt sense is like saying to oneself, "That, right there, *that's* what's confused," and *then feeling it there.*

The focuser must keep quiet, not only outwardly but also inside, so that a felt sense can form. It takes as long as a minute.

Some people talk all the time, either out loud or at themselves inside. Then nothing directly felt can form, and everything stays a painful mass of confusion and tightness.

When a felt sense forms, the focuser feels relief. It's as if all the bad feeling goes into one spot, right there, and the rest of the body feels freer.

Once a felt sense forms, people can relate to it. They can wonder what's *in* it, can feel around it and into it.

When to help people let a felt sense form

When people have said all that they can say clearly, and from there on it is confusing, or a tight unresolved mess, and they don't know how to go on.

Course of Therapy

Like those that follow, the initial therapy session begins with the client's circumstances at the moment and moves on from there. Because this first session can be frightening for the client who does not know what to expect from therapy, it is important that the therapist explores the client's expectations. In response to clients who often enter therapy passively, expecting a quick and painless cure, the therapist may begin by expressing his or her inability to provide simple answers or quick solutions to the inherently difficult facts and possibilities of existence. Rather, existential therapy will entail the painful work of self-discipline and the will to act. This kind of structuring communicates the therapist's faith in the client's abilities and serves to give the client hope.

When there is a certain spot that you sense could be gone into further.

When people talk round and round a subject and never go down into their feelings of it. They may start to say things that are obviously personal and meaningful, but then go on to something else. They tell you nothing meaningful, but seem to want to. In this very common situation, you can interrupt the focuser and gently point out the way into deeper levels of feeling.

FOCUSER: "I've been doing nothing but taking care of Karen since she's back from the hospital. I haven't been with me at all. And when I do get time now, I just want to run out and do another chore."

LISTENER: "You haven't been able to be with yourself for so long, and even when you can now, you don't."

FOCUSER: "She needs this and she needs that and no matter what I do for her it isn't enough. All her family are like that. It makes me angry. Her father was like that, too, when he was sick which went on for years. They're always negative and grumpy and down on each other."

LISTENER: "It makes you angry the way she is, the way they are."

FOCUSER: "Yes. I'm angry. Damn right. It's a poor climate. Living in a poor climate. Always gray. Always down on something. The other day, when I. . . ."

LISTENER: (interrupts:) "Wait. Be a minute with your angry feeling. Just feel it for a minute. See what more is in it. Don't think anything. . . ."

This section originally appeared in *Focusing*. New York: Bantum Books, 1981. Reprinted by permission.

Confrontation of Life Issues

In the world of the existentialist, at least three polarities are fundamental to the human condition: (1) dependence versus independence; (2) rationality versus irrationality; and (3) freedom versus determinism. Knowing that the client who avoids these issues may eventually collapse into an existential crisis (i.e., despair, anxiety, **guilt,** and nothingness), the existential therapist will confront these philosophical alternatives head-on. The resolution of these dilemmas, on the other hand, helps establish purpose and meaning in life. In short, the goal of the existential therapist is to move the client from a psychological to a spiritual plane. For this reason, the most important attribute that a therapist can bring to his or her clients is a "philosophy of life" (Bugental, 1965; Yalom, 1980).

Focusing

While not exclusively existential, Eugene Gendlin developed an approach known as **focusing,** which is often used by existential counselors (1981). This practical method derives from the accidental finding that the difference between successful and unsuccessful therapeutic outcomes is not so much a result of what is achieved by the therapist, but by the client. The crucial difference lies in the client's attitude toward a specific problem—in focusing on and changing one's deepest feelings by discovering what Gendlin calls the "felt sense." "What happens, according to Gendlin, is that from discovering this felt sense, new and changed feelings and aspects of experience emerge . . . and the problem changes." Focusing is not facing painful emotions nor is it an intellectual or analytical process. "When you learn how to focus," writes Gendlin, "you will discover the body finding its own way provides its own answers to many of your problems" (p. 11). One's "felt sense" is actually discovered, then, through awareness of one's body.

Logotherapy

Victor Frankl first set forth his ideas of **logotherapy,** a term derived from the Greek words *logos* (word or meaning) and *therapeia* (healing), in *The Doctor and the Soul* (1955). Logotherapy is a means of providing or experiencing healing through meaning. Responding to people whose "will to meaning" is so frustrated that they develop a sense of meaninglessness, Frankl designed logotherapy to help clients overcome this existential void and find purpose in their lives. This approach seeks to establish responsibility, meaning, and purpose within the context of the I-Thou relationship.

The most common lie is that with which one lies to oneself: lying to others is relatively an exception.

—Friedrich Nietzsche

In contrast to Freud's "will to pleasure" and Adler's "will to power," Frankl characterizes his approach as the "will to meaning." Frankl views human beings as a self-determining and self-actualizing. Because of a spiritual freedom that distinguishes us from the animal world, we possess the innate capacity to transcend environmental factors, whether biological, psychological, or sociological. This spiritual freedom is not so much freedom from oppressive forces as it is the potential for discovering, deciding, and actualizing one's existence. Such freedom cannot be taken from us, and it is this dimension that makes life meaningful and purposeful.

Unlike other existential approaches, however, logotherapy uses several distinctive "techniques," including paradoxical intention, dereflection, and modification of attitudes (Lukas, 1984).

Like Adler, Frankl found great value in **paradoxical intention,** which requires clients to act against their anticipation of fear (Frankl, 1963). The individual who has difficulty sleeping, for example, may be asked to practice staying awake; a client who complains of blushing when speaking before a group would be instructed to try to blush on such occasions. This is a reversal of the client's attitude toward the situation, especially if it is carried out in as humorous a fashion as possible. Paradoxically, the client in our example will usually be unable to blush when she tries to do so. Frankl provides an example of a client, fearful of trembling before his instructor, who was instructed to say to himself: "Oh, here is the instructor! Now I'll show him what a good trembler I am—I'll really show him how nicely I can tremble" (1955, p. 226). Such a reversal brings out a change of attitude toward the symptom, enabling the client to gain some distance from the symptom and view the troubling situation with a degree of detachment (Ascher & Turner, 1979; Solyom, Garza-Perez, Ledwidge, & Solyom, 1972).

Dereflection, the second of these logotherapeutic techniques, is an approach to treating excessive self-observation, obsession, or self-attention. This strategy encourages clients to ignore the problem and direct awareness toward something favorable and pleasant. The clients focus attention away from themselves and onto the real meanings of their existence and the actions that a commitment to those meanings demands. Frankl gives the example of a depressed survivor of the concentration camps who could find no meaning to his suffering or to his life: he had lost his wife and many children to the Nazi ovens and gas chambers. Frankl tentatively asked if it were possible that his suffering might be meant to allow the client "to become worthy of joining them [his family] in heaven" (1955, p. 190). He reported that the individual subsequently dereflected his negative self-obsession and became better able to bear his grief.

A third logotherapeutic approach is to **modify the clients' attitudes,** to change the way they think about their situation, to put new meaning into their predicament. In spite of many positive realities, for example, clients may be pessimistic and negative about their lives. Or perhaps the situation is truly horrific—they may have been terribly burned, for instance—and little can be done to improve the circumstances. In either case, the goal is to help clients change perspective. "This modification of attitudes is most often conducted in a rather direct approach through sharing one's opinions, arguing with the client, or positive suggestions" (Ivey, Ivey, & Simek-Downing, 1987, p. 291). The point is that clients can often do nothing to repair the past or present, but they *can* change the way they think about it. One can find meaning in spite of one's circumstances—even in a concentration camp.

Today traces of these three central techniques—paradoxical intention, dereflection, and change of attitudes—are components of current popular strategies, including cognitive-behavioral therapy, rational-emotive therapy, and family systems theories (Ivey, Ivey, & Simek-Downing, 1987; Lukas, 1984). "Paradoxical intention," according to Ivey et al., "is one of the key 'new' methods that can be used to produce rapid change, yet it was used by Frankl as early as 1929" (1987, p. 290).

APPLICATION

In viewing the case of Mrs. Hutchens, Rollo May illustrates many of the assumptions and principles that have guided him and other existential therapists. A suburban woman in her mid-30s, Mrs. Hutchens suffered from a hysterical tenseness of the larynx so severe that she spoke only with a perpetual hoarseness. May found that the woman believed that if she spoke her mind to people, to her parents in particular, she would be rejected. It was safer to be quiet, she concluded. While May believed that he understood the childhood origins of her problem—her need to protect herself from the belittling remarks of her mother and grandmother—he felt the most important part of the therapy was not his interpretation but rather the client now "existing, becoming, emerging . . . in the room with [him]" (1983, p. 25). May soon realized that his patient, like every human being, was centered in herself, that she was making an attempt to preserve her existence, to protect herself by being excessively in control, by being proper in her behavior, and, most remarkably, by speaking in a hoarse voice.

> He who has a *why* to live for can bear with almost any *how*.
> —Friedrich Nietzsche

In the course of therapy, Mrs. Hutchens revealed she had dreamed that she was searching room by room for a baby in an unfinished house at an airport. When she found the baby, she placed it in a pocket of her robe, only to be seized by anxiety, lest it be smothered. Much to her joy, she found the baby was still alive. Then she had a terrifying thought: "Shall I kill it?"

Analysis revealed that the house was located near an airport where she had learned to fly solo at age 20, an act that asserted her independence from her parents. The baby was her youngest son, with whom she so closely identified that the infant was, in effect, herself—a symbol, that is, of her emerging consciousness, which she considered killing in her dream.

Moreover, approximately six years before Mrs. Hutchens entered therapy, she had abandoned the religious faith of her parents, only to join another denomination that she dared not reveal to her authoritarian parents. During therapy she considered telling them, but whenever May brought up the topic, she became faint. She would report feeling empty inside and would have to lie down on the couch for a few minutes. Finally, she wrote to her parents about her change in religious faith and told them it would accomplish nothing if they tried to change her mind. In the next therapeutic session she told May she felt tremendous anxiety and wondered if she might become psychotic. May said he thought this outcome was highly unlikely.

May interpreted her fainting and attacks of anxiety as attempts to kill her emerging consciousness. She was struggling to accept her hatred of her mother and her mother's hatred of her, to free herself from her mother's painful domination, and to accept responsibility for her own actions and choices, even though they might not always have the best consequences. In brief, Mrs. Hutchens was actively confronting herself in these areas. The result was the opportunity for fuller independence, positive growth, and the development of a healthier life.

CRITICAL ANALYSIS

Few can discount the breadth of existential theory, for it encompasses many of the great philosophical questions of our age. It is an approach that wastes no time on lesser issues; its concepts are all-encompassing, sometimes ambiguous or even paradoxical, but always meaningful.

Reaching into the innermost recesses of human experience, existential psychotherapy has explored aspects of humanity not examined by other theorists. It is a position that has proved highly stimulating to humanistic investigators as well as to members of the general public (McLeod & Ryan, 1993; Tobin, 1990). And while the existential approach has been criticized for being cumbersome or excessively conceptual, it is nonetheless persevering. May's writings, for example, may at times be somewhat awkward, but to his credit he confronts complex issues and does not attempt to oversimplify human personality.

Existential concepts such as being-in-the-world have given practitioners new ways to conceptualize human personality. The existentialists' emphasis on our repressed fear of death and on our sense of alienation and meaninglessness has furthered our understanding of psychopathology and treatment. Existentialists have helped the professional community recognize that humans need and seek meaning, that they are lost without it; that exercising choices brings growth while attempting to escape freedom is debilitating; that humans differ in the experiences they seek and in their interpretations of these experiences (Allman, de la Rocha, Elkins, & Weathers, 1992). For many, the existential approach has breathed new life into psychology.

With its particular focus on personal choice and freedom, existential therapy can be especially useful in helping minority clients deal with multicultural issues. It provides for "cultural relativity," for the ability to understand one's own cultural heritage and world views within the context of other perspectives (Ibrahim, 1985; 1991). With this in mind, ethnic-minority clients facing social limitations, for example, can be encouraged to look at the price they are paying for personal decisions. Through the existential approach some clients, while still recognizing actual discrimination, can be challenged to more objectively separate themselves from their contexts and move beyond imagined limits. They can

If man hasn't discovered something that he will die for, he isn't fit to live.

—Martin Luther King, Jr.

come to recognize they are more than a victim of circumstances, that they are human beings with choices who can transcend culturally learned assumptions. In other words, while accepting some environmental and personal limitations, clients can use the existential approach to exercise some degree of freedom.

While rich in appreciation of the human condition, however, existentialism provides for no systematic presentation of procedure, methodology, or empirical validation of its therapeutic approach. The concepts, which are often highly provocative, are imprecise and hence difficult to define, learn, teach, or research. A variety of definitions are offered for such concepts as anxiety, guilt, intentionality, will, and destiny, and none are operationally defined. Of course, such difficulties and, in fact, existentialism's fundamental lack of coherence lie in the very origins of the approach. Nietzsche and Kierkegaard were both influential in articulating the characteristics of existentialism, but even in the conception there were significant differences between them: while Nietzsche's Zarathustra declared that "God is dead," emphasizing that humankind is ultimately alone, Kierkegaard excoriated those who supposed it possible to generate meaning through observation and reason, and he insisted that all sense and meaning must begin with an initial "leap of faith." And while Jean-Paul Sartre sought to reconcile his existentialist views with Marxism, Albert Camus scathingly denounced Marxist efforts to represent human behavior as deterministic.

Attempts to account for human behavior by means of explanatory generalizations are not welcomed by staunch existentialists; such explanations are possible only for objects and events that are determined, not for those that are free. Attempts to use statistical analyses of human behavior cannot unravel causal effects; they can only make things appear to be determined after the fact. To the thoroughgoing existentialist, such exercises are not scientific; they are merely scholastic. Some radical existentialists can even be anti-intellectual, believing that such intellectual schema victimize people who should be responsible for their own freedom, for constructing their own universe, for engineering their own development. According to existentialists, what is crucial is not science but experience. Staunchly defending his psychology against the charge of being anti-intellectual or antiscientific, however, May points to the sterility of conventional scientific methods and their inability to unlock the ontological character of willing, caring, and acting human beings.

A final noteworthy critique of the existential approach is its lack of educational and training programs. While there may be some validity to the proposition that each existential practitioner is unique, it clearly prohibits the systematic teaching of theory.

CURRENT STATUS

While a mere 4% of the psychotherapists in North America endorse existentialism as their primary orientation (Prochaska & Norcross, 1983), this approach has been a powerful force in changing the face of contemporary psychotherapy. Except perhaps for the classic forms of behavior therapy, existential therapy has been wedded to nearly all major traditions (Norcross,

1987). Thus, most existential therapists are "existential-psychodynamic," "existential family systems," and so forth. World Congresses of Logotherapy have been held since 1980, and Institutes of Logotherapy are gradually developing around the world as therapists on an international scale are adding logotherapeutic insights to their practices. Although few, if any, counseling psychologists would advertise themselves as "logotherapists" or "existentialists," even fewer clients today enter therapy without exposing themselves to the assumptions and approaches of existentialism.

SUMMARY

1. *Biography.* May (1909–1994) grew up in the midwestern United States. He attended Michigan State and graduated from Oberlin College in Ohio with a B.A. in English. Shortly after graduation he taught in Salonika, Greece, and spent two summers in Vienna where he enrolled in seminars conducted by Alfred Adler. After three years abroad, May returned to the United States and enrolled in Union Theological Seminary in preparation for the ministry. After graduating, May's first two years as a pastor were disappointing, and he soon enrolled in Columbia University to major in clinical psychology. His studies were cut short by a bout with tuberculosis but it was during this illness that he read Kierkegaard's works and became interested in existentialism. He eventually completed his Ph.D. and went on to write extensively on existential theory.

2. *Historical Development.* Existential psychotherapy is rooted in the philosophical writings of Kierkegaard and Nietzsche. They introduced existential thought to Western Europe, and their work established the footing for several influential philosophers, including Albert Camus, Jean-Paul Sartre, Martin Heidegger, and Martin Buber.

3. *View of Human Nature.* Existentialism is alternately religious, atheistic, and antireligious. It emphasizes hope and optimism, as well as despair and nothingness. In short, existentialists do not agree on a basic view of human nature. Despite its diversity, however, all agree on the importance of existence, the phenomena that are inherent in the very nature of being alive. Existentialists believe that life is either fulfilled or constricted by a series of decisions that we make, with no way of knowing conclusively what the correct choices are. Existentialists emphasize experience as the primary phenomenon in the study of human nature. Both theoretical explanations and overt behavior are secondary to experience itself and its meaning to the person.

4. *Development of Maladaptive Behavior.* If we fail to live in a state of awareness of our being, according to existential thought, we inevitably develop psychopathology. Of course, this state of being has the potential for great anxiety, which can lead to self-deception and even greater maladaptive behavior. The bottom line is that such maladaptive behavior is fundamentally the result of meaninglessness; maladaptive behavior is the result of not embracing our freedom and responsibility, of disregarding our true self, of forsaking genuine meaning in life.

5. *Function of the Therapist.* The existential therapist is grounded in the immediate, subjective experience of encountering the client. In an effort to restore personal meaning in the life of a client, the existential therapist may use advocacy, empathy, concern, reflection, action, environmental modification, or support. They have a kind of intellectual flexibility that is not threatened by the ideas and beliefs of others and that does not adhere stubbornly to any one intellectual system, theory, or ideology.

6. *Goals of Therapy.* The overarching purpose of the existential approach is to help clients find purpose and meaning in life. More specifically, existentialism attempts to make clients more aware of their existence, elucidate their uniqueness, improve encounters with others, and foster freedom and responsibility. The existential approach strives to help persons move in the direction of ever increasing actualization and integration.

7. *Major Methods and Techniques.* The methods used by existential counselors are varied. However, the typical course of therapy begins with the client's circumstances at the moment. Paradoxical intention, which requires clients to act against their anticipation of fear, is sometimes used. Dereflection is an approach to treating excessive self-observation, obsession, or self-attention. It encourages clients to ignore the problem and direct awareness toward something favorable and pleasant. Modifying one's attitude, changing the way one thinks about a situation, is also a commonly used existential method.

8. *Application.* The case of Mrs. Hutchens illustrates a number of principles Rollo May applied to counseling. This suburban woman in her mid-30s suffered from a hysterical tenseness of the larynx. May found that the woman believed that if she spoke her mind to people, she would be rejected; it was safer to keep quiet. May also observed the patient's fainting spells and anxiety attacks, and he interpreted them as attempts to kill her emerging consciousness. In the end, Mrs. Hutchens was left only to confront herself, and the result was an opportunity for greater independence, positive growth, and the development of a healthier life.

9. *Critical Analysis.* Existential therapy must be commended for its breadth and its focus on issues other approaches have avoided. It is a position that has proven to be highly stimulating and rewarding. The existentialists' emphasis on our repressed fear of death and on our sense of alienation and meaninglessness has furthered our understanding of psychopathology and treatment. Existentialists have helped the professional community recognize that humans need and seek meaning. It is an approach that also lends itself to working with ethnic-minority clients. It provides cultural relativity by helping to understand one's own cultural heritage within the context of other perspectives. Still, existentialism provides no systematic presentation of procedure, methodology, or empirical validation of its therapeutic approach.

10. *Current Status.* While only a small percentage of today's counselors label themselves primarily as existentialists, this approach has been a powerful force in changing the face of contemporary psychotherapy. It has been incorporated in almost every major therapeutic tradition.

Key Terms

Anxiety Apprehension caused by a threat to some value deemed essential to the existence of one's personality. Since death is an absolute and inevitable aspect of existence, a certain amount of anxiety is a natural characteristic of being human.

Attitude modification To put new meaning into a client's predicament by facilitating a change in perspective.

Daimonic Innate benign and illicit forces capable of dominating one's entire personality, such as sex, passion and eros, procreation, self-affirmation, destructiveness, rage, hostility, and the quest for power. Psychological health requires that the daimonic be accepted and integrated into consciousness.

Dasein A conscious and unconscious sense of oneself as a distinct, autonomous, and responsible entity existing in the world of physiological and physical surroundings (*Umwelt*), other people (*Mitwelt*), and one's own self (*Eigenwelt*). A strong Dasein is essential to the healthy personality.

Daseinsanalysis A method of existential psychotherapy developed by Medard Boss that focuses on the individual's existence or his specific way of "being-in-the-world."

Dereflection A technique of counteracting obsessive ideation or hyperreflection by helping the client stop thinking about the problem.

Eigenwelt The world of relationship to oneself and to one's own potentials and values. One of the three simultaneous and interrelated modes of being-in-the-world.

Focusing A technique for introspection and change that identifies how a client talks about his or her experiencing.

Guilt Regret resulting from the impossibility of fulfilling all of one's innate potentials (a denial of *Eigenwelt*), of relating perfectly to others (a denial of *Mitwelt*), and of always recognizing our communion with nature (a denial of *Umwelt*).

Intentionality The capacity of human beings to have a conscious and unconscious sense of purpose and behave teleologically.

Logotherapy An existential approach to psychotherapy developed by Victor Frankl shortly after World War II. It accents the capacity of each person to exercise the power of choice and experience healing through meaning.

Love A delight in the presence of another person and a readiness to affirm that person's values and development as much as one's own.

Mitwelt The world of relationship to other people. One of the three simultaneous and interrelated modes of being-in-the-world.

Ontological characteristics Those qualities that are distinctively and definitively human, including Dasein, anxiety, guilt, intentionality, love, and care.

Ontology The science of existence or being.

Paradoxical intention A technique for directing a client to do something contrary to one's actual instructions; the success of the directive is due to one not being able to force that which is involuntary.

Phenomenological An attitude of respect for the dignity and integrity of each person's experience and an approach or methodology for studying the personal meanings of experience.

Umwelt The world of internal and external objects, which forms our physiological and physical environment. One of the three simultaneous and interrelated modes of being-in-the-world.

Will The conscious capacity to move toward one's self-selected goals. It is the more self-evident aspect of intentionality.

Suggested Reading

Becker, E. (1973). *The denial of death.* New York: Free Press.

Frankl, V. E. (1963). *Man's search for meaning.* Boston: Beacon Press.

May, R. (1981). *Freedom and destiny.* New York: Norton.

May, R. (1991). *The cry for myth.* New York: Norton.

Reeves, C. (1977). *The psychology of Rollo May.* San Francisco: Jossey-Bass.

Yalom, E. D. (1980). *Existential psychotherapy.* New York: Basic Books.

References

Allman, L. S., de la Rocha, O., Elkins, D., & Weathers, R. S. (1992). Psychotherapists' attitudes toward clients reporting mystical experiences. *Psychotherapy, 29,* 564–569.

Arbuckle, D. S. (1975). *Counseling and psychotherapy.* Boston: Allyn and Bacon.

Ascher, L. M., & Turner, R. M. (1979). Controlled comparison of progressive relaxation, stimulus control, and paradoxical intention therapies for insomnia. *Journal of Consulting and Clinical Psychology, 47,* 500–508.

Becker, E. (1973). *The denial of death.* New York: Free Press.

Binswanger, L. (1958). The case of Ellen West. In R. May, E. Angel, & H. Ellenberger (Eds.), *Existence: A new dimension in psychology and psychiatry* (pp. 237–364). New York: Basic Books.

Binswanger, L. (1963). *Being-in-the-world.* New York: Basic Books.

Boss, M. (1963). *Psychoanalysis and Daseinsanalysis.* New York: Basic Books.

Boss, M. (1977). *Existential foundations of medicine and psychology.* New York: Aronson.

Bugental, J. F. T. (1965). *The search for authenticity.* New York: Holt Rinehart and Winston.

Bugental, J. F. T. (1978). *Psychotherapy and process: The fundamentals of an existential-humanistic approach.* Reading, MA: Addison-Wesley.

Bylski, N. C., & Westman, A. S. (1991). Relationships among defense style, existential anxiety, and religiosity. *Psychological Reports, 68,* 1389–1390.

Cogswell, J. F. (1993). Walking in your shoes: Toward integrating sense of self with sense of oneness. *Journal of Humanistic Psychology, 33,* 99–111.

Corlis, R. B., & Rabe, P. (1969). *Psychotherapy from the center: A humanistic view of change and of growth.* Scranton, PA: International Textbook.

DeCarvalho, R. J. (1990). The growth hypothesis and self-actualization: An existential alternative. *Humanistic Psychologist, 18,* 252–258.

Dopson, L., & Gade, E. (1981). Kierkegaard's philosophy: Implications for counseling. *Personnel and Guidance Journal, 60,* 148–152.

Frankl, V. E. (1955). *The doctor and the soul: An introduction to Logotherapy.* New York: Knopf.

Frankl, V. E. (1963). *Man's search for meaning.* Boston: Beacon Press.

Frankl, V. E. (1967a). Logotherapy and existentialism. *Psychotherapy: Theory, Research and Practice, 4,* 138–142.

Frankl, V. E. (1967b). *Psychotherapy and existentialism: Selected papers on Logotherapy.* New York: Simon & Schuster.

Frey, D. H., & Heslett, F. E. (1975). *Existential theory for counselors.* Boston: Houghton Mifflin.

Gendlin, E. (1981). *Focusing.* New York: Bantam Books.

Greenlee, R. W. (1990). The unemployed Appalachian coal miner's search for meaning. *International Forum for Logotherapy, 13,* 71–75.

Heidegger, M. (1962). *Being and time.* New York: Harper & Row.

Ibrahim, F. A. (1985). Effective cross-cultural counseling and psychotherapy: A framework. *The Counseling Psychologist, 13,* 625–638.

Ibrahim, F. A. (1991). Contribution of cultural worldview to generic counseling and development. *Journal of Counseling and Development, 70,* 13–19.

Ivey, A. E., Ivey, M. B., & Simek-Downing, L. (1987). *Counseling and psychotherapy* (2nd ed.). Englewood Cliffs, NJ: Prentice Hall.

Kemp, C. G. (1971). Existential counseling. *The Counseling Psychologist, 2,* 2–30.

Kobasa, S. C., & Maddi, S. R. (1977). Existential personality theory. In R. J. Corsini (Ed.), *Current personality theories.* Itasca, IL: Peacock.

Laing, R. D. (1959). *The divided self.* London: Tavistock.

Lantz, J., & Pegram, M. (1989). Casework and the restoration of meaning. *Social Casework: The Journal of Contemporary Social Work,* 549–555.

LeVine, P. (1993). Morita therapy and its divergence from existential psychotherapy: A proposal for adopting a Morita-based philosophy for use in counseling and psychotherapy. *International Bulletin of Morita Therapy, 6,* 47–58.

Lukas, E. (1984). *Meaningful living.* Cambridge, MA: Schenkman.

Maddi, S. R. (1980). *Personality theories: A comparative analysis* (4th ed.). Chicago: Dorsey Press.

May, R. (1953). *Man's search for himself.* New York: NAL.

May, R. (1961). *Existential psychology.* New York: Random House.

May, R. (1966). *Psychology and the human dilemma.* New York: Norton.

May, R. (1967a). *The art of counseling.* Nashville: Abington.

May, R. (1967b). *Man's search for himself.* New York: The American Library.

May, R. (1969). *Love and will.* New York: Dell.

May, R. (1972). *Power and innocence.* New York: Dell.

May, R. (1975). *The courage to create.* New York: W. W. Norton.

May, R. (1977). *The meaning of anxiety* (Rev. ed.). New York: W. W. Norton.

May, R. (1983). The case of Mrs. Hutchens. In The discovery of being: Writings in existential psychology (pp. 24–34). New York: W. W. Norton and Co.

May, R. (1991). *The cry for myth.* New York: W. W. Norton.

May, R. (1994). The Meaning of Anxiety. New York: W. W. Norton & Company.

May, R., & Yalom, I. D. (1995). Existential psychotherapy. In R. J. Corsini & D. Wedding (Eds.), *Current psychotherapies* (5th ed., pp. 262–292). Itasca, IL: Peacock.

May, R., Angel, E., & Ellenberger, H. (Eds.). (1958). *Existence.* New York: Simon & Schuster.

McLeod, J., & Ryan, A. (1993). Therapeutic factors experienced by members of an outpatient therapy group for older women. *British Journal of Guidance and Counseling, 21,* 64–72.

Nietzsche, F. (1972). The antichrist. Salem, NH: Ayer. (Reprint of 1930 ed.)

Norcross, J. (1987). A rational and empirical analysis of existential psychotherapy. *Journal of Humanistic Psychology, 27,* 41–68.

Osipow, S. H., & Walsh, W. B. (1970). *Strategies in counseling for behavior change.* Englewood Cliffs, NJ: Prentice Hall.

Osipow, S. H., Walsh, W. B., & Tosi, D. J. (1984). *A survey of counseling methods.* Homewood, IL: Dorsey Press.

Owen, I. R. (1992). Applying social constructionism to psychotherapy. *Counseling Psychology Quarterly, 5,* 385–402.

Partenheimer, D. (1990). Teaching literature toward a humanistic society. *Journal of Humanistic Education and Development, 29,* 40–44.

Payne, I., Bergin, A. E., & Loftus, P. E. (1992). A review of attempts to integrate spiritual and standard psychotherapy techniques. *Journal of Psychotherapy Integration, 2,* 171–192.

Pervin, L. (2001). Handbook of Personality (2nd ed.). New York: Guilford Press.

Pervin, L. A. (1960). Existentialism, psychology, and psychotherapy. *American Psychologist, 15,* 305–309.

Phares, E. J. (1988). *Clinical psychology: Concepts, methods, and profession* (3rd ed.). Pacific Grove, CA: Brooks/Cole.

Prochaska, J., & Norcross, J. (1983). Contemporary psychotherapists: Characteristics, practices, theories, and attitudes. *Psychotherapy: Theory, Research and Practice, 20,* 620–627.

Rabinowitz, F. E., Good, G., & Cozad, L. (1989). Rollo May: A man of meaning and myth. *Journal of Counseling and Development, 67,* 436–441.

Sartre, J. P. (1953). *Existential psychoanalysis.* Chicago: Gateway.

Sartre, J. P. (1956). *Being and nothingness.* New York: Philosophical Library.

Schwartzberg, S. S. (1993). Struggling for meaning: How HIV-positive gay men make sense of AIDS. *Professional Psychology Research and Practice, 24,* 483–490.

Solyom, L., Garza-Perez, J., Ledwidge, B. L., & Solyom, C. (1972). Paradoxical intention in the treatment of obsessive thoughts: A pilot study. *Comprehensive Psychiatry, 13,* 291–297.

Stevens, M. J., Pfost, K. S., & Potts, M. K. (1990). Sex-role orientation and the willingness to confront existential issues. *Journal of Counseling and Development, 68,* 414–416.

Tillich, P. (1952). *The courage to be.* New Haven, CT: Yale University Press.

Tobin, S. A. (1990). Self psychology as a bridge between existential-humanistic psychology and psychoanalysis. *Journal of Humanistic Psychology, 30,* 14–63.

von Kaam, A. L. (1967). Counseling and psychotherapy from the viewpoint of existential psychology. In D. S. Arbuckle (Ed.), *Counseling and psychotherapy: An overview.* New York: McGraw-Hill.

von Kaam, A. L. (1969). *Existential foundations of psychology.* New York: Doubleday.

Wallace, W. A. (1986). *Theories of counseling and psychotherapy: A basic issues approach.* Boston: Allyn and Bacon.

Westman, A. S. (1992). Existential anxiety as related to conceptualization of self and of death, denial of death, and religiosity. *Psychological Reports, 71,* 1064–1066.

Yalom, E. D. (1980). *Existential psychotherapy.* New York: Basic Books.

There is one best school of therapy. It is the school of therapy you develop for yourself . . . —**Carl Rogers**

Person-Centered Therapy

CHAPTER **9**

By the middle of the 20th century, two major psychological views of humanity had emerged: the Freudian perspective, which viewed people as victims of repressed sexual and aggressive instincts, and the behavioristic perspective, which derived personality from the stimulus-response mechanism in human behavior. Taken to an extreme, behaviorists thought of individuals as little more than complex laboratory animals responding to their environment.

Many psychologists found it difficult to accept either of these explanations of human nature, for neither made any allowance for free will, human dignity, or cognitive processes. Behavior was controlled, not by personal choices, but the impulses of the id or by learning histories. In response to these concerns, a third approach to understanding human behavior began to develop: the *humanistic approach*. Unlike other counseling theories, this approach assumes that we are largely responsible for our own actions, that we have the power to determine our own destiny. At almost any given moment, we can choose our actions because we have free will.

During the 1960s and 1970s the cultural preoccupation with individuality and personal expression provided fertile soil for the growth of this humanistic perspective. As a result this "third force" in American psychology caught on rapidly among many psychotherapists and with the public. People began talking about "getting in touch with feelings," "letting it all hang out," and "tuning in." While this psychedelic terminology may have advanced the growth of the humanistic approach in popular culture, however, it was Carl Rogers who planted the seeds of this movement.

BRIEF BIOGRAPHY

Born January 8, 1902, in a suburb of Chicago, Carl Ransom Rogers was the product of Midwestern America. He grew up in a close-knit, pragmatic, Protestant family dedicated to Christian principles and the virtues of hard work—so dedicated, in fact, that Rogers would later recall his feelings of guilt and "wickedness" while drinking his first bottle of soda pop (Kirschenbaum, 1979). A precocious child, Rogers "read incessantly" (Rogers, 1961a, p. 6). He loved reading the Bible and adventure stories; the *Encyclopedia Britannica* taught him to play chess. When he entered school, young Rogers was promptly advanced to second grade.

The Rogers family was well off, living on a 300-acre farm that included a clay tennis court (Kirschenbaum, 1979, p. 10). Carl's father, a contractor and civil engineer, employed a manager to implement the latest scientific farming methods. It was here that Rogers began exploring science, studying books on agriculture, for instance, and breeding night-flying moths. Familiar with the scientific method by age 14 he read volumes about testing the effectiveness of various fertilizers and animal feeds. Rogers learned how to design experiments and how to conduct statistical tests of his own hypotheses (Rogers, 1961a), and thus he developed an abiding respect for the scientific method.

> Freud fails to do justice to the positive aspect of life. He only knows the lust of release, not the pleasure of tension.
>
> —Kurt Goldstein

As an undergraduate at the University of Wisconsin, which his mother, father, two older brothers, and sister had attended, Rogers majored in agriculture and history. During this time he became involved with student religious groups, and when he "heard the call" during his sophomore year he committed himself to Christian ministry (Roberts, 1985). A year later he was one of 12 American students who traveled to Peking, China, for the World Student Christian Federation Conference. In 1924 he graduated from college.

Carl Rogers married Helen Elliott, an art major who was gentle, straightforward, and open-minded. Rogers later credited their two children, David and Natalie, with "teaching me far more about individuals, their development, and their relationships, than I could ever have learned professionally" (Rogers, 1961b, p. 12). David later became an administrator in a medical center, and Natalie worked with her father as a cotherapist in encounter groups.

Although his father offered to pay all expenses if Rogers would go to Princeton, his son declared his independence and moved to the more liberal Union Theological Seminary in New York, where he enrolled in the usual courses in scripture and theology. A turning point for his life was a course in "Working with Individuals," in which the professor brought psychologists and psychiatrists as guest lecturers. For the first time, Rogers considered helping people, not as an ordained minister, but as a psychologist. After two years at Union, he transferred across the street to Columbia University Teachers College, where he earned his Ph.D. in clinical and educational psychology in 1931.

For 12 years after leaving Columbia, Rogers immersed himself in practical clinical work with the Society for the Prevention of Cruelty to Children in Rochester, New York. During the summers he taught courses at Columbia and the University of Rochester. His first book, *Clinical Treatment of the Problem Child* (1939), finally brought Carl Rogers to the attention of a search committee at Ohio State University, which appointed him full professor in 1940.

Although Rogers had absorbed the views of Freud, his own clinical experience and experimental research failed to confirm these views, and he gradually began to rely less on traditional psychoanalysis and more on his own thinking. In 1942 his ideas on counseling were published in *Counseling and Psychotherapy*. During subsequent years Rogers held teaching and administrative positions at the University of Chicago (1945–1957) and the University of Wisconsin (1957–1962). In 1964 he became a resident fellow at the Western Behavioral Sciences Institute. In 1968 he helped found the Center for Studies of the Person in La Jolla, California, an experimental "psychological community" in which social and behavioral scientists and others undertook a variety of training, research, and social projects (Meador & Rogers, 1984). Here Rogers remained until, following surgery for a broken hip, he died at the age of 85 on February 4, 1987.

Among Rogers' most noteworthy works is *Client-Centered Therapy* (1951), which thrust him into the professional spotlight and gave him uncontested prominence in the field of human understanding. His *On Becoming a Person* (1961), which he wrote in three weeks, further solidified his professional stature. Until the end of his life, Rogers continued to be a productive writer. He authored several books after the age of 65, including *Freedom to Learn* (1969), *Carl Rogers on Encounter Groups* (1970), *Becoming Partners: Marriage and Its Alternatives* (1972), *Carl Rogers on Personal Power* (1977), *A Way of Being* (1980), and *Freedom to Learn for the 80s* (1983).

HISTORICAL DEVELOPMENT

"It would seem quite absurd to suppose that one could name a day on which client-centered therapy was born," Carl Rogers has said. "Yet I feel it is possible to name that day and it was December 11, 1940" (Kirschenbaum, 1979, p. 112). On this date Rogers, then a professor at Ohio State University, delivered a speech at the University of Minnesota on "Newer Concepts in Psychotherapy." In his address, Rogers described the pitfalls of traditional approaches to counseling, especially their heavy reliance on advice, exhortation, suggestion, ordering, forbidding, and intellectualized interpretation. Having criticized the older methods, many of which were still in practice by members of his audience, Rogers went on to describe the "newer practices."

"The aim of this newer therapy," he said, "is not to solve one particular problem, but to assist the individual to grow, so that he can cope with the present problem and with later problems in a better integrated fashion." In response Rogers was both praised and criticized by the puzzled professionals in his audience. "I was totally unprepared for the furor the talk aroused," he said afterwards. In the ensuing clamor, Rogers realized he had delivered an address that was radical and significantly original.

Shortly thereafter Rogers presented his thoughts to a larger audience in *Counseling and Psychotherapy: Newer Concepts in Practice* (1942). Actually Houghton Mifflin, which had published his previous *Clinical Treatment of the Problem Child*, was reluctant to publish the second, fearing that the publisher would not recoup its investment. Only after Rogers threatened to take his manuscript elsewhere did the publisher reluctantly agree to publish it. Selling well over 100,000 copies in English and translated into numerous languages, *Counseling and Psychotherapy* has had a major, if not revolutionary, effect on the field of psychotherapy.

> A musician must make music, an artist must paint, a poet must write if he is to be ultimately at peace with himself.
>
> —Abraham Maslow

The Rogers methods and perspective were a reaction to what he has often labeled "counselor-centered therapy," in which the therapist administers tests, asks questions, makes a diagnosis, and suggests courses of action for the so-called "patients" to follow. The greater the responsibility that clients—as he came to call them—could take for their healing, both in and out of therapy, the more effective and long-lasting the therapy would be, Rogers believed. In Farson's (1975) words, Rogers's assertions made him "a quiet revolutionary."

One of the changes Rogers urged upon his colleagues may appear rather inconsequential on the surface but connotes the heart of his new therapy. Rogers used the term *client* instead of the traditional *patient,* which seemed to him to indicate a "sick" person who expects a cure from the doctor. Since psychiatry had emerged from the medical profession, the term *patient* had been accepted without much thought or question. To Rogers, however, the term *client* implied a different locus of control. Clients, he believed, might consult a professional who has helping skills, but the control remains with them. They make their own decisions.

Initially termed **nondirective counseling,** this new therapeutic approach was named *client-centered counseling* in 1951 as a means of emphasizing Rogers's positive focus on human capacities (Rogers, 1951). Although Rogers realized, of course, that it was impossible for anyone to be absolutely nondirective, during this period he emphasized the importance of the clients' world as they saw it (Zimring & Raskin, 1992). "The individual," wrote Rogers, "exists in a continually changing world of experience of which he is the center" (Rogers, 1951, p. 483). In other words, how the client sees reality is more important than the reality itself; perception, more important than fact. This manner of thinking was rooted in applied **phenomenology** (Rychalk, 1973), which contends that what we are and what we do reflect our subjective experience of the world and ourselves. External reality can be known only through the inner reality of personal experience (Jones & Butman, 1991). With a profound respect for the client's perception of reality, Rogers focused on experience as the ultimate authority in understanding life: "It is to experience that I must return again and again; to discover a closer approximation to truth as it is in the process of becoming in me. Neither the Bible nor the prophets—neither Freud nor research—neither the revelations of God nor man—can take precedence over my own direct experience" (Rogers, 1961b, pp. 23–24). In fact, this emphasis on experience led some to develop techniques such as focusing (Gendlin, 1981), which helps people "get in touch" with their experience.

In 1974 the name of Rogers's program was once again changed to **person-centered counseling** (Meador & Rogers, 1984), marking the beginning of yet another historic period in the development of this theory. During this period Rogerian principles found a broad range of applications in teaching, administration, organizational behavior, marriage, parenting, and interpersonal relations. In his own classroom at the University of Chicago, for example, Rogers began to shift the responsibility for learning and grading to his students. He simply offered himself as a learning resource. "I ceased to be a teacher," wrote Rogers. "It wasn't easy. It happened rather gradually, but as I began to trust students, I found they did incredible things . . ." (1983 p. 26). In *Freedom to Learn* (1969), Rogers applied this approach to a "person-centered" education to all educational levels.

Reluctant to turn his students into "Rogerians" (Cain, 1987) and wanting to facilitate the process of becoming more self-directed, until 1980 Rogers initially discouraged the institutionalization of person-centered therapy. In the late 1970s, however, Rogers surrendered to international pressure and officially organized. In the first issue of the *Person-Centered Review,* he explained his rationale for becoming more institutionalized as a counseling movement: "There has . . . developed a large number of people in many nations—therapists, teachers, business people, doctors, social workers, researchers, lay people, pastors—who have a strong interest in the continuing development of a client-centered/person-centered approach" (Rogers, 1986, p. 4).

VIEW OF HUMAN NATURE

Person-centered therapy holds an optimistic view of human personality and focuses on present rather than past experience. Focusing on the inner experience of persons rather than on observable behavior, it holds that behavioral change evolves from within the person rather than through the manipulation of the environment. Unlike the Freudian approach, person-centered therapy views people as basically good and trustworthy.

Rogers emphasized an inherent tendency of people to grow and move in healthy directions, to develop their capacities to the fullest. He defined this directional leaning, this **actualizing tendency,** as "the inherent tendency of the organism to develop all its capacities in ways which serve to maintain or enhance the organism" (1959, p. 196). Because this actualizing tendency creates the inner urge for fulfillment, it is the primary motivating force of every human being.

The actualizing tendency is guided by what Rogers called the **organismic valuing process,** an inherent capacity to choose that which will enhance us and reject that which does not. This innate drive serves as a pathfinder. Presumed to be an infallible and instinctive compass for guiding choice and action, the organismic valuing process determines or reveals that which will provide inner fulfillment.

An avid gardener, Rogers often suggested that, in the same way plants grow well when conditions are favorable, so persons have a tendency to flourish when their circumstances support growth. Rogers believed that human beings possess this guiding tendency to actualize themselves and the capacity to do so. Given the proper conditions, the capacities for normal growth and development could be released in every human being. Rogers's counseling theory simply attempts to specify the conditions that allow this developmental process to occur.

> I had expressed an idea whose time had come.
>
> —Carl Rogers

Rogers recognized, of course, that human beings can perpetuate great evil—that they are capable of deceit, hatred, and cruelty—but he believed that these propensities are the result of negative "conditions of worth" imposed on children by family and society (Moreira, 1993). This negative side of the personality, which is not inborn but acquired, is a defensive reaction to an environment that is perceived as dangerous and threatening. Given the opportunity, this defensiveness will diminish, Rogers believed, and individuals will behave in ways that are trustworthy, reliable, constructive, and good. On the other hand, when this defensive reaction overwhelms individuals, they are alienated from their own inherent goodness', this negative reaction to the environment leads to maladaptive behavior.

DEVELOPMENT OF MALADAPTIVE BEHAVIOR

Blessed with a drive toward actualization and an inerrant organismic valuing process to guide them, children still need acceptance and positive regard from others. If this need for acceptance is met, according to Rogers, children begin to define their sense of self in accordance with their own experience rather than in terms of how others see or expect them to be. Unpolluted by distortions caused by other persons' judgments, a **self-concept** allows the organismic valuing process to continue to function as a trustworthy guide. Well-being, then, is seen as congruence between what one wants to become, what one perceives one's self to be, and what one actually is.

Unfortunately, the emotional climate and healthy progression Rogers idealizes is an uncommon commodity in American families; few individuals escape childhood without some kind of experience that distorts the self-concept. Even with good parents, most of us experience limited conditions of worth; we are loved conditionally, not unconditionally. We allow the expectations of parents or significant others to mold our ideal selves, and we develop a self-concept based on how well our experiences match those expectations. Children learn to falsify their perceived selves in order to maintain parental love and protection. Without fail, this leads to a distorted self-concept that quickly warps the organismic valuing process and leads to "problems in living" (Rogers, 1942a).

Rogers suggested that a number of values learned at school, church, or the home may be incompatible with organismic experiencing: that sexuality is wrong, for instance, unquestioning obedience to authority is good, making money is important, unstructured learning is a waste of time, it is improper for men to cry or hug each other, and women should not be independent or assertive (Nye, 1992). Such thoughts, feelings, and behaviors approved by significant others may vary so radically from the experiences approved by the person's own organismic valuing process that an almost complete disassociation develops. Initially this unhealthy development results in anxiety; eventually it causes people to collapse into maladaptive behavior.

In summary, maladaptive behavior results when persons become more externally than internally oriented. When our passion becomes whatever will gain us acceptance from others, we are tempted to distort our feelings to match the expectations of others. We ask "How *should* I be feeling?" rather than "How do I actually feel?" This incongruity between what we really are and what we are trying to be gives birth to psychological pain and maladjustment (see Figure 9.1).

Figure 9.1 | Congruity and incongruity depend on the relationship between the real self and the ideal self.

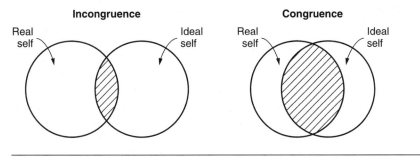

FUNCTION OF THE THERAPIST

Since the person-centered therapist's role is rooted in *being,* not *doing* (McLeod & McLeod, 1993), the major task of the therapist is to provide a climate of safety and trust, which will encourage clients to reintegrate their self-actualizing and self-valuing processes. The therapist accomplishes this by encouraging the psychotherapeutic conditions—the so-called *therapeutic triad*—of accurate empathic understanding, congruence, and unconditional positive regard (these will be explained in detail under "Methods and Techniques").

Rogerians believe that each of these qualities is rooted in the personhood of the therapist (Levant & Shlien, 1984). Although they can be learned as counseling skills, they must spring from the very being of the counselor to be used effectively. Seldom, if ever, does the Rogerian counselor give advice, interpret, or teach the client. Based on a fundamental disrespect of others, such strategies, it is argued, foster dependency and thwart the development of any meaningful sense of autonomy. Unlike therapists who "do something to" the client, the person-centered therapist cultivates the soil in which the client's hidden drive to grow and develop can be nurtured and released. Only through the proper characteristics and competencies of the therapist, then, can the client move toward greater congruence.

> To share something that is very personal with another individual and [not have it be] received and understood . . . makes some individuals psychotic.
> —Carl Rogers

As a result, the person-centered therapist is nonauthoritarian, and formal assessment of the client's problems in the form of psychological testing is considered to be inappropriate and unnecessary. The few techniques in person-centered therapy are secondary to the therapist's attitudes, sensitivities, and skills.

GOALS OF THERAPY

"To be that self which one truly is," a phrase Rogers borrowed from the Danish philosopher-theologian Søren Kierkegaard, is the singular goal of our lives. The goal of person-centered therapy is to facilitate this process. Habitual modes of impressing others, lying to ourselves, and distorting our perceptions all cause us to lose contact with our true selves. Person-centered therapy strives to create an environment safe enough to eliminate the need for these facades.

The aim of person-centered therapy, then, is not so much to solve problems (Rogers, 1977) as to assist clients in their growth process, so they are equipped as human beings who are **fully functioning,** who are able to cope effectively with current and future problems. They live in a way that most fully expresses and develops their potential as human beings while mutually supporting growth in others. According to Rogers (1980a, p. 117), fully functioning persons are increasingly open to experience, increasingly accepting of their own feelings, and capable of living in the present from moment to moment. Since they are increasingly free to make choices and act on them spontaneously, they are trusting of self and of human nature and are capable of balanced and realistic expressions of affection and aggression. Increasingly, they are active and nonconformist.

The goals of person-centered therapy can be thought of as two processes that occur concurrently: first, moving away from the self one is not, and, second, moving toward one's true self.

Moving Away from the Self One Is Not

Person-centered therapy initially strives to help clients relinquish self-concealment and phoniness so that they might gradually dismantle their false selves. The therapist seeks to emancipate individuals from "oughts" and "shoulds" that imprison them in behaviors designed to meet the expectations of others: the father who wants his son to grow up to take over the family business, the mother who would be proud to have her son become a doctor, the teacher who labels a

> Call a client a patient, and he is liable to act like one.
>
> —Carl Rogers

young person as a daydreamer. Whatever the source of these expectations, most of us unwittingly adopt external specifications for the kind of person we "ought" to be or "should" become. Our need for acceptance and love, from a parent or a peer group, locks us into a pattern of behavior that we mistakenly come to accept as our own true self. Person-centered therapy gradually chips away at the "oughts" and "shoulds" that form the artificial self.

To help clients move away from their phony selves, person-centered therapy fosters a nonconformist way of being. The therapist allows them to ignore the pressures of parents, teachers, friends, and the surrounding culture, which defines what a beautiful person wears, what a popular person drives, and so on. Fully functioning persons resist the attempts of Madison Avenue and mass culture to dictate what they should buy and who they should become. Therapy attempts to release people from such cultural imprisonment, so that they might use their own minds.

Person-centered therapy tries to eliminate the unhealthy need to please others. This false sense of self begins to develop in children, when youngsters become obsessed with pleasing their mothers and fathers, and for some this urge to please becomes a characteristic way of relating to others throughout life. Of course, it can't be done, and as people escalate their attempts to please everyone, the drive to please is self-defeating. In the process of moving away from their false selves, clients gradually give up trying to please the counselor and the significant others in their lives. They no longer allow themselves to be in bondage to persons who are not significant to their lives. This does not imply that fully functioning individuals are selfish. While they will do things to please others, they will not *become* someone else just to please others. As healthy people, they are true to the essence of their own selves.

Moving Toward One's True Self

As clients discard their emotional armor, they open themselves to others and the pleasures that come with being authentic. In fact, the goal of person-centered therapy is to move away from what one is not and toward what one

9.1 | Self-Actualization

Central to Rogers's theory is the motive toward actualization (Bozarth & Brodley, 1991). People have an inherent need to enhance themselves by becoming the best self their inherited natures will allow them to be. The term **self-actualization** was first introduced to psychology by Kurt Goldstein (1939), who studied brain-damaged soldiers following World War I. Goldstein was struck with the fact that these individuals, despite an injured nervous system, still had an integrity and wholeness about their personalities.

Rogers theorized that **fully functioning** people, guided by their organismic valuing processes, epitomize psychological health. Actually, the person Rogers described is an ideal. However, some individuals come close to the goal of being fully functioning or self-actualizing. Abraham Maslow is well known for his contribution to self-actualization. He identified several characteristics of self-actualizing people. For example, he found that they perceive reality accurately and accept themselves and others. They have a continued freshness of appreciation, are spontaneous, discriminate between means and ends, and have a deep desire to help humankind. Self-actualizing people are creative and have a philosophical sense of humor. Maslow also made it clear that these individual are not perfect.

The following scale attempts to help measure your own level of actualization. For each of the following statements, indicate the extent to which the statement applies to you, using this four-point scale:

---

is meant to be. The antithesis of defensiveness, this "openness" allows fully functioning people to be receptive to feelings that may have been denied for years. Openness allows us to be moved emotionally and experience reality more accurately. This accurate perception of reality is a universally accepted criterion of mental health.

As clients move toward their true selves, finally free of inhibitions and rationalizations, increasingly they come to trust their own experience. Comfortable with its impulses and intuitions, the true self is equally confident in its judgments and beliefs. Einstein, for example, must have known that his thinking represented a serious departure from traditional scientific assumptions, yet he trusted his own judgment more than that of his colleagues. This approach is not reserved for geniuses, however; according to Rogers, it is the goal of all who enter person-centered therapy.

People who are becoming fully functioning never "arrive." They are continually in process. The notion that we can someday reach a permanent state of being that is free from unpleasantness is pure fantasy. Those who are mov-

1 = Disagree
2 = Disagree somewhat
3 = Agree somewhat
4 = Agree

_____ 1. I do not feel ashamed of any of my emotions.
_____ 2. I feel I must do what others expect of me.
_____ 3. I believe that people are essentially good and can be trusted.
_____ 4. I feel free to be angry at those I love.
_____ 5. It is always necessary that others approve of what I do.
_____ 6. I don't accept my own weaknesses.
_____ 7. I can like people without having to approve of them.
_____ 8. I fear failure.
_____ 9. I avoid attempts to analyze and simplify complex domains.
_____ 10. It is better to be yourself than to be popular.
_____ 11. I have no mission in life to which I feel especially dedicated.
_____ 12. I can express my feelings even when they may result in undesirable consequences.
_____ 13. I do not feel responsible to help anybody.
_____ 14. I am bothered by fears of being inadequate.
_____ 15. I am loved because I give love.

To calculate your score, first reverse the values for items 2, 5, 6, 8, 9, 11, 13, and 14. In other words, for those items: 1 = 4, 2 = 3, 3 = 2, 4 = 1. Next, add the values for all 15 items. The higher the score, the more self-actualized you are said to be at this point in your life. The average score for females is 46 and the average score for males is 45 (both have a standard deviation of 5).

This test is a short form of a measure of self-actualization developed by Jones and Crandall (1986). Reprinted with permission.

ing toward their real selves, who accept the complexity of human relationships, who do not deny their ambivalent or contradictory feelings—these fully functioning human beings accept this perennial condition of flux. They accept the fact that they will never "have it all together." Having abandoned the goal of solving all their problems, they focus not on product but on process. According to Rogers, these are the people who manage to weather the vicissitudes of life, who live with zest.

As a by-product of perceiving oneself, not as being, but as becoming, fully functioning individuals accept others who also are in process. They do not criticize others for not being what they "ought" to be. Just as we do not fault the water for being wet, Rogers pointed out, borrowing an analogy from Abraham Maslow, so fully functioning persons do not judge others for being who they are.

MAJOR METHODS AND TECHNIQUES

The traditional counseling relationship is "coercive," as Rogers put it, and it was never more than superficially effective for him. As a therapist he recalled trying hundreds of different ways of curing his clients before realizing that, in order to help, he must begin by no longer doing anything *to* them. Instead of explaining the causes of their problems or prescribing actions for them to take, Rogers discovered that they improved when he simply accepted and appreciated them as valuable human beings. In other words, when he created a relationship built on unconditional acceptance, his clients seemed to find ways to help themselves. As a result, person-centered therapy boldly asserts that the client, not the therapist, should be at the heart of psychotherapy, for only the client has the resources for becoming more aware of the obstacles to personal growth. Once awareness dawns, light floods all the dark corners. All person-centered methods lead to this end.

Rogers's therapeutic work led him to identify three "necessary and sufficient" conditions for growth and change in personality (1957): *congruence, unconditional positive regard,* and *accurate empathic understanding.* These three conditions are interrelated and may be best understood as general attitudes conveyed toward a client. When these conditions are fully present, persons become fully functioning, showing optimal maturity and adjustment.

> There are as many "real worlds" as there are people!
>
> —Carl Rogers

Congruence

For a client to grow, a therapist must be genuine and transparent (Rogers, 1980b), a state of realness that Rogers called **congruence,** because he wanted to emphasize the perfect match between a therapist's inner experiences and his or her observable outward actions. Without playing the role of a counselor or trying to hide behind a facade of professionalism, the therapist must exhibit an openness to his or her own inner experiences during the therapy hour. "I am more effective when I can listen acceptantly to myself, and can be myself," said Rogers, without trying to act "as though I were something I am not" (1961a, pp. 16–17). If a client relates an experience that is depressing or that arouses sadness, for example, the therapist need not smile benignly to disguise his or her true feelings. Even an experienced therapist might admit to the client, "I find myself saddened because you are touching on feelings that remind me of my own life" (Rogers, 1959). While sharing such feelings expresses genuineness and value to clients, the successful practitioner never becomes so spontaneous, of course, that he or she is burdened with impulsively shared experiences that do not directly relate to creating the necessary conditions of change (Rogers, 1980b).

Nor does a person-centered therapist depend on a secret strategy; he or she is neither defensive nor evasive. These therapists are what they seem to be. If a therapist is uncomfortable with some aspect of the client relationship but does not admit it, the discomfort acts as a shield against authenticity and creates **incongruence,** which keeps the therapist from being fully present in the counseling relationship and hinders unconditional positive regard.

9.2 | The Q-Sort Technique

When psychotherapy is effective, the patient experiences a reduction in the incongruence between the real and ideal selves, a reduction that can be assessed by means of the Q-sort technique. The Q-sort technique requires the client to sort a set of 100 or so statements descriptive of personality into a series of nine categories (piles) varying from "most descriptive" to "least descriptive" of the person. Each card in a Q-sort deck contains a statement such as the following:

> Has a wide range of interests.
> Is productive; gets things done.
> Is self-dramatizing; is histrionic.
> Is overreactive to minor frustrations; is irritable.
> Seeks reassurance from others.
> Appears to have a high degree of intellectual capacity.
> Is basically anxious. (Block, 1961, pp. 132–136)

In sorting the statement-containing cards in a Q-sort deck, the respondent is directed to make his or her choices in such a way that a certain number of statements fall in each category, so the resulting frequency distribution of statements across categories has a predetermined shape, usually normal. To approximate a normal distribution for a Q-sort of 100 statements, Block (1961) recommends instructing sorters to place the following numbers of statements into categories 1 through 9: 5, 8, 12, 16, 18, 16, 12, 8, 5. The response to each statement in a Q-sort instrument is assigned an integer ranging from 1 to 9, depending on the category assigned to the statement by the respondent. The results obtained from different sorts or sorters can then be related by computing correlation coefficients between different sorts.

To assess the changes in self-concept resulting from psychotherapy, clients make before-and-after Q-sorts of a series of statements describing their feelings and attitudes. In a series of studies conducted by Rogers and Dymond (1951), each person was directed to make separate Q-sorts according to his or her "real self" and "ideal self." The results showed that, compared with "no-therapy" groups, differences between the "real" and "ideal" self-sorts of clients who had undergone therapy decreased.

Unconditional Positive Regard

Everyone needs positive regard, and most of us receive it, but only *if* we measure up to what others want us to be. Only if we meet people's specific conditions of worth will they accept and value us. The emphasis lies on the word *if,* because **positive regard** involves a contingent: "If you do as I want you to do, then I will value you as important. If you don't, then I won't." Often, then, we avoid whatever is judged by others as "worthless" and seek out what others judge as more worthy. That is, we learn to act in ways that significant people in our lives value, even if this results in our distorting our personal experiences to conform to their pressure. All of this acting is the price we are willing to pay in order to receive positive regard.

In person-centered therapy, however, the client's worth is not dependent on others' expectations. There are no conditions of worth that the client must meet to qualify for the therapist's acceptance: no expectations that clients should do the "right" thing or be what they "should" be, no distinction between those aspects of personality that are judged to be "more or less worthy of positive regard than any other" (Rogers, 1959, p. 208). Clients do not need to earn approval, since they are freely given **unconditional positive regard**—that is, the experience of receiving warmth, respect, sympathy, acceptance, caring, and trust from others simply for being who they are (Rogers, 1959). Unconditional positive regard is a kind of love, says Rogers, "providing we understand the word love as equivalent to the theologian's term *agape,* and not in its usual romantic and possessive meanings" (1962, p. 422). This allows clients to feel unconditionally prized, valued, accepted, worthwhile, and trusted simply for being who they are.

> The good life is a direction, not a destination.
>
> —Carl Rogers

Unconditional positive regard for people means respecting them, regardless of the different values the counselor might place on certain behaviors. The therapist does not judge behavior as being positive or negative. Rather, regardless of their beliefs or behaviors, clients find acceptance, defined here as a deep and genuine caring for the client as a person without reservations, conditions, judgments, or evaluations (Rogers, 1961b, 1980a, 1964). This is not to suggest that everything people do or say needs to be approved. Rogers was careful to distinguish the individual as a person and the individual's freely chosen values and behaviors. A therapist may disapprove of a client's alcoholism, for example, while accepting him or her as a person. Even though the therapist might wish the client would behave differently, the client is not rejected but accepted. Clients who experience such unconditional positive regard draw a profound conclusion: Since someone who knows all their faults cares about them despite those faults, they must be worth something.

Empathic Understanding

The third ingredient of person-centered therapy is empathy, the capacity to enter the place of other human beings and understand the world from their perspective. Practitioners are almost universally agreed that the use of empathy is vital to counseling (Cramer, 1993; Egan, 1994; Fielder, 1950; Gladstein, 1983; Hackney, 1978; Truax & Mitchell, 1971). Through **empathic understanding** the therapist, while maintaining objectivity, adopts the clients' **internal frame of reference,** viewing reality through their eyes. Delving beneath the surface of the clients' words and actions, empathic understanding perceives inner feelings, attitudes, meanings, and motives. Although a counselor never fully understands what individuals are experiencing internally, the therapist attempts to understand all that is possible. It is as if the person-centered therapist were the client, although Rogers is quick to warn that the therapist must never lose sight of the *as if* quality in the relationship.

Empathy is distinct from sympathy. The sympathetic therapist stands on the shore and throws out a lifeline to someone who is drowning. The empathic counselor plunges beneath the surface, dives into the water to help the person who is struggling. The empathic counselor enters the client's experience while maintaining an objective capacity to understand the experience accurately. While clients may talk about factual information, the person-centered counselor empathizes with and "listens" to the feelings beneath the surface: to the body language, the facial expressions, and the fluctuations in the voice.

> My garden supplies the same intriguing question I have been trying to meet all my professional life: What are the effective conditions for growth?
>
> —Carl Rogers

To facilitate this empathic understanding, the person-centered therapist feeds back or "reflects" to his or her clients, as accurately as possible, the feelings they are expressing. It is an attempt to let clients know that they are accepted as persons, that they have been heard and understood (Barrett-Lennard, 1988). Avoiding explanations, questions, and advice, the counselor has done more than listen to words. When the therapist responds to clients with accurate reflection, they are moved forward by the interaction; their world is changed by the very act of being heard

9.3 | Encounter Groups

Rogers was largely responsible for the growth of "the group movement." From the late 1960s to the middle 1970s, he all but abandoned individual counseling in favor of **encounter groups,** or "T-groups." Rogers, with missionary zeal, wanted to bring enhanced psychological health to greater numbers of people so he developed these groups where people could learn more about themselves and how they relate to, or encounter, one another.

The typical encounter group ranged in size from 8 to 15 persons, meeting from 20 to 60 sessions. The group meets with no structure or agenda and no "leader." The people who run encounter groups are called *facilitators.* Their job is to establish an atmosphere in which the group members can easily express themselves and thus achieve self-insight.

The evidence for the effectiveness of encounter groups is mostly anecdotal, in which people report that they feel better and more aware of their true nature (Rogers, 1970). A review of research on encounter groups showed they can lead to negative as well as positive psychological experiences (Hartley, Roback, & Abramowitz, 1976; Newman & Lovell, 1993). Encounter groups are no longer as popular as they were when Rogers first promoted them, but they are still used by some of his followers.

(Gendlin, 1970). In this way, empathic understanding is the vehicle for both positive regard and congruence. Thus, empathy communicates to clients that they are worth understanding, that their inner hopes and private fears have value.

When clients become convinced that another person values them, they begin to value themselves. Like congruence and unconditional positive regard, empathy gives them the freedom to become fully functioning human beings.

> I have no methods, all I do is accept people.
> —Paul Tournier

APPLICATION

Even though Rogers was devoted to research throughout his career, the years he spent researching his therapeutic procedures at the University of Chicago were among his most productive. During this time he documented many case studies, including that of Mrs. Oak. In her late 30s, feeling unattractive, frustrated, and generally miserable, Mrs. Oak entered the Counseling Center at the University of Chicago. In addition to difficulties with her husband, Mrs. Oak was deeply disturbed by her relationship with her teenage daughter, blaming herself for her daughter's recent, serious illness. Mrs. Oak was a dependent, passive person who felt rejected both at home and in social groups.

During the early stages of therapy, she talked mostly of other people. When she spoke about herself, it was as if she were an object, someone burdened with problems and puzzled as to the causes of her unhappiness. Although she had unrealistically high aspirations and a strong need to be perfect in nearly everything she did, she felt at the same time uninteresting, rebellious, useless, and deeply conflicted over her sexual identity. Finding her to be shy, nondescript, and very nearly incoherent, her therapist wrote that she expressed herself in "jumbled analogies, half-sentences, and incomplete thought" (Rogers, 1954, p. 164). As therapy progressed, Mrs. Oak became less problem-oriented, better able to express herself, and more self-confident.

Once she realized that the therapist cared for her, she began to experience herself in a more positive way. "She gradually became aware of the fact that, though she had searched in every corner of herself, there was nothing fundamentally bad but, rather at heart she was positive and sound" (Rogers, 1954, p. 263). At the end of 40 counseling sessions, Mrs. Oak had experienced considerable change in her self-concept. Although still in conflict over her sexuality, still somewhat pessimistic and depressed, she seemed to herself to be more self-sufficient, less threatened by people, more integrated or whole. Even in the absence of further psychotherapy, she was nevertheless confident that she would continue to make progress.

Mrs. Oak, however, did receive more psychotherapy. Seven months later she returned for follow-up testing and at that time decided to resume counseling in order to clear up a few matters. As Rogers (1951, p. 195) stated, "There is little likelihood that any therapy is . . . complete." Subsequently, Mrs. Oak received eight additional therapy sessions, after which she soon took a job and improved her relationship with her daughter. No longer striving to be perfect, she was content to relax and enjoy life.

| 9.4 | **Comparing Problem-Centered Versus Person-Centered Approaches** |

Counselor: I noticed that you stated you enrolled in Psychology 411 [study-habits course] because you didn't know how to study well enough—uh—and then I checked over the problem list, and I saw that you went rather heavy on—you're worried about low grades and poor memory and so on. How well did you do in high school?

Student: Well, I was just an average student.

Counselor: And what major did you select?

Student: Ah, you mean—

Counselor: In high school, you took college preparatory or commercial?

Student: It was an academic course. I took languages and English and history.

Counselor: What course did you like the best? [Student presumably answers; later in session counselor summarizes:]

Counselor: It seems to me that your problem is that you want to learn more about yourself. We'll be getting all these tests back, and there are those [study] projects, and the way we do, I see you each week at this time and you'll begin to get a little better picture—And then I'll help you check it and I'll tell you if it's right—(Laugh)

Student: Mm-hm.

Counselor: So we can work it out. I would suggest—I would more or less work this project out because you say you are having difficulties concentrating. . . .

Student: I haven't written to my parents about this at all. In the past they haven't been of any help to me in this respect, and if I can keep it away from them as much as possible, I'll do so. But there's a slight matter of grades to explain, and they're not good, and I don't know how I'm going to explain without telling them about this. Would you advise me to tell them about it?

Counselor: Suppose you tell me a little more about what you had thought about it.

Student: Well, I think I'm compelled to, because—

Counselor: It's a situation you've really got to face.

Student: Yes, there's no use getting around it, even if they can't take it the way they should, because I've already flunked my gym course, I just haven't come. . . .

Counselor: It will be fairly hard for you to tell them.

Student: Yes. Oh, I don't know if they're going to sort of condemn me. I think so, because that's what they've done in the past. . . .

Counselor: You feel that they'll be unsympathetic and they'll condemn you for your failures.

Student: Well my—I'm pretty sure my father will. My mother might not. He hasn't been—he doesn't experience these things; he just doesn't know what it's like. . . .

Counselor: You feel that he could never understand you?

Source: From Rogers, 1942a, pp. 116–117, 135–136.

Taping these conversations on a thin thread of wire, well in advance of modern recording tape, Rogers was among the first therapist-researchers to record the psychotherapeutic relationship. Along with the willingness to use this new technology, Rogers committed his therapeutic process to scientific scrutiny. What follows in the side bar are fragments of two recorded counseling interviews with college students. The left column contains the transcript of a "patient" and a therapist who view therapy as a structured, problem-centered activity under the direct control of the therapist. The right column contains the transcript of a similar interview between a "client" and a counselor who recognizes that the therapeutic process is very much person-centered.

The differences between these two session excerpts are easily discernible. Any Rogerian would be quick to point out that if the feelings of the client are mentioned at all in the left-hand transcript, they are talked about rather than genuinely experienced. In the second transcript, in the right-hand column, the client is encouraged to express feelings, and every reply of the counselor is an attempt to respond, not to the informational aspects of the situation, but to the emotional content of the client's statements.

According to Rogers, this person-centered approach need not be limited to individual counseling sessions. Its principles have been widely used in resolving many different kinds of potentially polarized relationships, such as play therapy, marriage and family counseling, human relations training with para-professional helpers, institutional change, labor-management disputes, race-relations, and encounter groups, which Rogers was largely, though not solely, responsible for promoting (Raskin & Rogers, 1995).

CRITICAL ANALYSIS

Perhaps Rogers's greatest strength is his unequivocal respect for persons, his insistence on viewing people holistically and as purposeful, and his reliance on his clients. No theorist before Rogers had the confidence to step outside the role of expert and to place trust and responsibility in the hands of clients. But while Rogers is to be commended for emphasizing the person, any student of therapy will inevitably ask how it is that clients can supply accurate self-appraisals. Critics say Rogers is naively optimistic, but he insists that he does "not have a Pollyanna view of human nature" (1961a, p. 27). Rogers argues that therapists are making a mistake when they assume they know what clients are thinking or why they act a certain way. But there are times, even under good circumstances, when clients are unable or unwilling to provide the therapist with accurate information for these judgments. This leads to an even weightier critique of Rogers's basic assumption: that people are basically good and that we are the sole masters of our own destiny. Personal wholeness assumes primacy; it becomes a moral imperative, possibly at the expense of appreciation of our responsibilities to others. With the self assuming a position of supreme importance, Rogers's individualistic and relativistic philosophy can lead to inflated notions of the self. Although this is more a theological than an empirical question, many 20th-century Americans find the fundamental premise of this theory difficult to accept. In particular, it seems doubtful that an inherently peaceful and cooperative species, as Rogers would have it, would so frequently engage in war, crime, and other destructive behaviors solely because of introjected, pathological conditions of worth.

On a more pragmatic and clinical level, many practitioners do not agree that it is preferable to dispense with interpretations and rely wholly on genuineness, empathy, and unconditional positive regard.

Personality is a
process, not an onion.
—Paul Wachtel

Others warn that in some instances—telling a narcissistic but vulnerable client, for example, that constant self-preoccupation is provoking boredom and anger—such genuineness might well be damaging (Kahn, 1985, p. 901).

Despite these criticisms, most agree that Rogers has made significant strides toward creating a counseling theory with explicitly stated concepts and verifiable hypotheses. While there are problems with measuring some of his concepts, Rogers has received the justifiable respect of many of his peers for stimulating serious research in the practice of psychotherapy. Rogers valued constructing an approach that was empirically based, and in fact no model of therapy has been more extensively researched than his own (Goodyear, 1987; Seligmen, 1986).

One need only consider the global impact of person-centered therapy and its significant contributions to cross-cultural counseling in order to find still further testimony to the impact of his theory. "Our international family consists of millions of persons world-wide whose lives have been affected by Carl Rogers's writings and personal efforts as well as his many colleagues who have brought his and their own innovative thinking and programs to many corners of the earth," writes David Cain (1987, p. 149), summing up the influence of Rogers's approach to cultural diversity. In many respects person-centered psychotherapy provides an ideal foundation for working with ethnically diverse clients (Freeman, 1993; Hayashi, Kuno, Osawa, & Shimizu, 1992; Hill-Hain & Rogers, 1988; Patterson, 1985), and it has proven just as helpful in teaching constructive therapeutic behavior in diverse settings (Fink, 1990; Yau, Sue, & Hayden, 1992).

Despite these significant contributions, the limitations of person-centered therapy, marked mostly by its reductionist nature, have become equally obvious (Usher, 1989). In an attempt to ease racial tension and aggression, for example, Rogers discusses the possibility of reducing these tensions by engaging the concerned parties with each other under facilitative group conditions (Rogers, 1977). Yet these principles, which are used with troubled individuals in therapy, are no match for the more complex set of historical, political, economic, and cultural factors that have preserved the status quo. While sensitive communication under facilitative conditions could be an important beginning in trying to resolve discrimination in the job market, a racial conflict, or any other factor keeping minority groups in bondage, it is clearly not enough. Person-centered therapy may be useful for working out certain kinds of problems in middle-class adjustment, but it is not wholly adequate for dealing with the myriad of serious psychological and social disturbances.

In treating clients with physical disabilities, person-centered therapy has similar strengths and weaknesses. As one might expect, advocates of Rogerian intervention argue that disabled individuals are psychologically affected, not by the disability per se, but by its subjective impact and the personal attitudes associated with it. Early in counseling, therefore, clients can profit from gaining insight into their perceptions and feelings of being disabled, and come to accept their disability emotionally without devaluing themselves or resorting to defensive maneuvers. Most experts would undoubtedly value the counselor's providing and communicating early facilitative conditions, such as personal warmth and empathic understanding, to assist their clients with a disability and to establish a more positive self-concept. But the later phases of such a counseling process require more active and direct involvement than the person-centered approach permits. Among its limitations in such rehabilitation settings are a reluctance to set specific goals, an aversion to diagnose and evaluate or even to give advice, a lack of concern with the external environment, an orientation toward process rather than an outcome, and a tendency to overlook client behavior or skill development (See, 1985).

CURRENT STATUS

Nevertheless, other than Freud and Adler, no single psychologist has more significantly influenced the actual practice of counseling and psychotherapy than Carl Rogers. Whether explicitly or implicitly, his strategies are integrated into the work of almost every contemporary practitioner. Beyond that, the language of professional caring that Rogers pioneered has become embedded in the vocabulary of everyday conversation. "Whole person," "awareness," "potentials," "growth," "self-concept," "realness," "spontaneity," and "process" have all become staples of the terminology we use to describe our condition. More than any other individual, Rogers is responsible for the popularity of such concepts.

> When I accept myself as I am, then I change.
> —Carl Rogers

Several generations of practitioners have observed Carl Rogers demonstrate person-centered therapy—his expression of genuineness, unconditional positive regard, and empathic understanding—in numerous filmed and videotaped presentations. Observing Rogers has led practitioners to what Burke (1989, p. 278) calls an "unfortunate confusion of style with substance," so that imitations of Rogers may have replaced the genuine practice of his theory. After all, to the untrained eye Rogers's therapeutic style, including his reflections and his "Mm-hms" and "Un-huhs," can seem passive and artificial. Taken to the extreme, these mannerisms can become more the subject, of parody than of therapy.

Still, many counseling psychologists and many "eclectic" counselors today report being strongly influenced by person-centered therapy (Baradell, 1990; Miller & Foxworth, 1992; Warner, 1991; Watkins, 1993; Watkins, Lopez, Campbell, & Himmell, 1986). The person-centered approach is used in everything from career counseling (Miller, 1991) to treatment of breast cancer

(Burton, Parker, & Wollner, 1991). Not surprisingly, Rogers is ranked at the top of most lists of psychologists who have made the greatest impact in the field of counseling and psychotherapy (Smith, 1982). So pervasive has been Rogers's effect on counseling that many of his ideas now seem like self-evident truths. "They have become so ingrained in counseling," say Gelso and Fretz (1992, p. 267), "that many counselors forget they ever came from Rogers!"

Despite Rogers's watershed influence, however, most psychologists today do not claim person-centered therapy as their primary theoretical orientation. Regarding it as necessary but not sufficient, counselors treat the Rogerian approach as a foundation upon which they must build other therapeutic skills (Cain, 1988). One of the reasons for this may be that Rogers himself opposed the formation of a person-centered "school" of counseling that would grant certificates and set standards for membership. He viewed this kind of institutionalization as leading to a narrow, dogmatic perspective, which would ultimately be counterproductive. During the 1980s, however, person-centered therapists took the initiative and developed the Association for the Development of the Person-Centered Approach, founded by David Cain, whose purpose is to foster innovation in therapy, education, and supervision. The association has more than 250 members. Dedicated to promoting the work of Rogers and his pioneering spirit, *The Person-Centered Review,* the association's quarterly newsletter, features articles on the current state of theory applied to practice and reviews relevant research.

Since the person-centered approach takes a relatively short time to master and since it emphasizes listening skills, it is the basis for much of today's counselor training. Cain (1990), however, believes that in order for person-centered therapy to be viable in the future, its practitioners will need to focus more directly on drug abuse, child abuse, divorce, and other contemporary issues.

SUMMARY

1. *Biography.* Rogers (1902–1987) grew up in a well-to-do, conservative, Midwestern family. He read voraciously as a child and developed a precocious respect for the experimental method. Rogers majored in agriculture and history at the University of Wisconsin and as a sophomore he committed himself to Christian ministry. After the Union Theological Seminary, he transferred to Columbia where he eventually earned his Ph.D. in clinical psychology. Rogers immersed himself in practical clinical work and after publishing his first book, he was invited to teach at Ohio State University. Following professorships at the University of Chicago and then the University of Wisconsin, in 1968 he founded the Center for Studies of the Person in La Jolla, California, where he died at age 85.

2. *Historical Development.* The origins of person-centered therapy can be found in reaction to what Rogers often called "counselor-centered therapy," in which the therapist administers tests, asks questions, and suggests courses of action for the client. Rogers's revolutionary approach took on

such subtle changes as using the term *client* instead of *patient,* and it was he who first called his approach "nondirective counseling," later changing it to "person-centered counseling," as a means of emphasizing its positive focus on human capacities.

3. *View of Human Nature.* Rogers viewed people through an optimistic lens, seeing human nature as basically good. He emphasized an inherent tendency of people to grow and move in healthy directions. For Rogers, this *actualizing tendency* was the primary motivating force of every human being. It is guided by what he called the *organismic valuing process,* an inherent capacity to choose that which will enhance a person and reject that which will not. The actualization drive creates the inner urge for fulfillment, and the organismic valuing process determines or reveals what will provide that inner fulfillment. Given the proper conditions, Rogers believed the capacities for normal growth and development could be released in every human being.

4. *Development of Maladaptive Behavior.* Distortions in the self-concept quickly warp the organismic valuing process and lead to maladaptive behavior. Rogers suggested that learned values, thoughts, feelings, and behaviors may differ so radically from the experiences approved by the person's own organismic valuing process, that an almost complete dissociation develops. The bottom line is that this leads to being more externally than internally oriented, and thus individuals contort feelings to match the expectations of others. This incongruity gives birth to psychological pain and maladjustment.

5. *Function of the Therapist.* The role of the person-centered therapist is rooted, not in doing, but in being. The major task of the therapist is to provide a climate of safety and trust, which will encourage clients to reintegrate their self-actualizing and self-valuing processes. The therapist accomplishes this through accurate empathic understanding, congruence, and unconditional positive regard. Although these skills can be learned, to be effective, they must spring from the very being of the counselor. The person-centered therapist is nonauthoritarian, seldom, if ever, giving advice, making interpretations, or teaching their clients.

6. *Goals of Therapy.* Person-centered therapy does not seek to solve problems, but to facilitate a process in which clients can know who they really are and become fully functioning human beings. It strives to eliminate the need for impressing others, lying to oneself, or distorting perceptions. Person-centered therapy tries to eliminate the unhealthy need to please others and to move toward increasingly trusting one's own experience.

7. *Major Methods and Techniques.* Rogers's therapeutic work led him to identify three "necessary and sufficient" conditions for growth and change in personality: congruence (in which therapists' inner experiences and their observable outward actions match), unconditional positive regard (the client's worth is not dependent on others' expectations and approval), and empathic understanding (the therapist enters the place of the clients and

understands the world from their perspective, adopting the clients' internal frame of reference).

8. *Application.* Rogers was the first to expose the practice of counseling to audio recording. He made great use of this technology and as a result developed thorough case studies during the formulation of his theory. The case of "Mrs. Oak" is one example that illustrates just how Rogers used the three essential ingredients to bring about a truer sense of one's self and greater autonomy. A comparison of Rogerian transcript with a more problem-solving approach reveals the stark difference between counselor-centered and client-centered approaches to therapy.

9. *Critical Analysis.* The respect of person-centered therapy for the individual and its reliance on the client is most admirable. Trusting clients to be responsible has its advantages. However, this approach leads many to ask how clients can supply accurate self-appraisals, and the underlying philosophical assumption that people are fundamentally good raises many questions among critics. Few can argue with the global impact and contributions to cross-cultural counseling of person-centered therapy. While it is not a complete answer to these circumstances (especially after the initial facilitation processes), it certainly provides a foundation for working with many ethnically diverse clients.

10. *Current Status.* Several generations of practitioners who have been trained in Rogerian strategies report being strongly influenced by the person-centered approach, especially eclectic counselors. Despite Rogers's significant influence, however, most psychologists do not claim person-centered therapy as their primary theoretical orientation. One of their reasons for regarding the approach as necessary rather than sufficient may be that Rogers opposed the formation of a person-centered "school" of counseling that would grant certificates and set standards for membership.

Key Terms

Actualizing tendency The inherent tendency of human beings to develop all of their potential, to become the best that their inherited natures will allow them to be.

Conditional positive regard Accepting another person only if that individual meets one's own standards.

Congruence A healthy state of unison between one's total organismic experience and a self-concept that is free of conditions of worth. It is one of the three basic conditions for therapeutic effectiveness.

Empathy The act of accurately understanding the client's world from the client's perspective. It is one of the three basic conditions for therapeutic effectiveness.

Encounter group A small group of relatively well-adjusted individuals that, through intense interaction, allows individuals to discover more about themselves and how they relate to others.

Experience Everything, including thoughts, needs, and perceptions, going on within the individual that is presently within awareness.

Fully functioning Describes individuals who are using their capacities and talents, realizing their potential, and moving toward complete knowledge of themselves and their full range of experiences.

Genuineness Being truly oneself in relationship with others. It is one of the three basic conditions for therapeutic effectiveness.

Ideal self The self-concept an individual would like to have, including aspirations, moral ideals, and values.

Incongruence A schism between one's total organismic experience and a self-concept burdened by conditions of worth, resulting in a state of inner tension and confusion.

Internal frame of reference The realm of experience that is available to the awareness of a person at a given moment.

Introjection Incorporating the standards of another person within one's own personality.

Nondirective therapy Psychotherapy in which the client leads the way by expressing feelings, defining problems, and interpreting behavior, while the therapist cultivates a warm and accepting atmosphere in which the client can clarify his or her process rather than directing it.

Organismic valuing process The inherent capacity to choose that which will enhance our well-being and reject that which does not.

Person-centered approach The phrase Rogers later used in place of "nondirective" because it more accurately reflected his approach.

Phenomenology An approach to understanding personality that emphasizes the importance of understanding the individual's subjective experiences, feelings, and private concepts.

Positive regard Giving selective attention to the client's verbal and behavioral assets.

Self-actualization The tendency to actualize that portion of experience represented by the self-concept.

Self-concept A collection of learned perceptions about one's abilities and characteristics.

Significant other An important source of positive regard, such as a parent.

Unconditional positive regard The acceptance of another person without conditions of worth; one of the three essential characteristics of the successful therapeutic relationship.

Warmth The primarily nonverbal (e.g., vocal tone, posture, facial expression) means of expressing care in a therapeutic relationship.

Suggested Reading

Kirschenbaum, H., & Land-Henderson, V. (Eds.). (1989b). *The Carl Rogers reader.* Boston: Houghton Mifflin.

Rogers, C. R. (1954). The case of Mrs. Oak: A research analysis: In C. R. Rogers and R. F. Dymond (Eds.), *Psychotherapy and personality change: Co-ordinated research studies in the client-centered approach* (pp. 259–348). Chicago: University of Chicago Press.

Rogers, C. R. (1961b). *On becoming a person.* Boston: Houghton Mifflin.

Rogers, C. R., & Dymond, R. F. (1951). *Psychotherapy and personality change.* Chicago: University Press.

References

Baradell, J. G. (1990). Client-centered case consultation and single-case research design: Application to case management. *Archives of Psychiatric Nursing, 4,* 12–17.

Barrett-Lennard, G. T. (1988). Listening. *Person-Centered Review, 3,* 410–425.

Bozarth, J. D., & Brodley, B. T. (1991). Actualization: A functional concept in clientcentered therapy. *Journal of Social Behavior and Personality, 6,* 45–59.

Burke, J. F. (1989). *Contemporary approaches to psychotherapy and counseling: The self-regulation and maturity model.* Pacific Grove, CA: Brooks/Cole.

Burton, M. V., Parker, R. W., & Wollner, J. M. (1991). The psychotherapeutic value of a "chat": A verbal response modes study of a placebo attention control with breast cancer patients. *Psychotherapy Research, 1,* 39–61.

Cain, D. J. (1987). Carl R. Rogers: The man, his vision, his impact. *Person-Centered Review, 2,* 283–288.

Cain, D. J. (1988). Roundtable discussion: Why do you think there are so few person-centered practitioners or scholars considering that literally thousands of persons throughout the world attest to the enormous impact Carl Rogers has had on their personal and professional lives? *Person-Centered Review, 3,* 353–390.

Cain, D. J. (1990). Celebration, reflection and renewal: 50 years of client-centered therapy and beyond. *Person-Centered Review, 5,* 357–363.

Cramer, D. (1993). Therapeutic relationship and outcome seen by clients in first and third session of individual therapy. *Counseling Psychology Quarterly, 6,* 13–15.

Egan, G. (1994). *The skilled helper* (5th ed.). Pacific Grove, CA: Brooks/Cole.

Farson, R. (1975). Carl Rogers, quiet revolutionary. In R. I. Evans (Ed.), *Carl Rogers: The man and his ideas* (pp. xxviii–xliii). New York: Dutton.

Fielder, F. (1950). The concept of the ideal therapeutic relationship. *Journal of Consulting Psychology, 45,* 659–666.

Fink, J. (1990). Can psychotherapeutic competence be taught? 14th International Congress of Medical Psychotherapy: Training in medical psychotherapy; Cross-cultural diversity. *Psychotherapy and Psychosomatics, 53,* 64–67.

Freeman, S. C. (1993). Client-centered therapy with diverse populations: The universal within the specific. *Journal of Multicultural Counseling and Development, 21,* 248–254.

Gelso, C. J., & Fretz, B. R. (1992). *Counseling psychology.* Fort Worth, TX: Harcourt Brace Jovanovich.

Gendlin, E. T. (1970). A short summary and some long predictions. In J. Hart and T. Tomlinson (Eds.), *New directions in client-centered therapy.* Boston: Houghton-Mifflin.

Gendlin, E. T. (1981). *Focusing.* New York: Everest House.

Gendlin, E. T. (1988). Carl Rogers (1902–1987). *American Psychologist, 43,* 127–128.

Gladstein, G. A. (1983). Understanding empathy: Integrating counseling, developmental, and social psychology perspectives. *Journal of Counseling Psychology, 30,* 467–482.

Goldstein, K. (1939). *The organism.* New York: American Book Company.

Goodyear, R. K. (1987). In memory of Carl Ransom Rogers. *Journal of Counseling and Development, 65,* 523–524.

Hackney, H. (1978). The evolution of empathy. *Personnel and Guidance Journal, 57,* 35–38.

Hartley, D., Roback, H. B., & Abramowitz, S. I. (1976). Deterioration effects in encounter groups. *American Psychologist, 31,* 247–255.

Hayashi, S., Kuno, T., Osawa, M., & Shimizu, M. (1992). The client-centered therapy and person-centered approach in Japan: Historical development, current status, and perspectives. *Journal of Humanistic Psychology, 32,* 115–136.

Hill-Hain, A. & Rogers, C. (1988). Cross-cultural challenges of facilitating person-centered groups in South Africa. *Journal for Specialists in Group Work, 13,* 62–69.

Jones, A., & Crandall, R. (1986). Validation of a short index of self-actualization. *Personality and Social Psychology Bulletin, 12,* 63–73.

Jones, S. L., & Butman, R. E. (1991). *Modern psychotherapies.* Downers Grove, IL: InterVarsity Press.

Kahn, E. (1985). Heinz Kohut and Carl Rogers: A timely comparison. *American Psychologist, 40,* 893–904.

Kirschenbaum, H. (1979). *On becoming Carl Rogers.* New York: Delta.

Kirschenbaum, H., & Land-Henderson, V. (Eds.). (1989a). *Carl Rogers: Dialogues.* Boston: Houghton Mifflin.

Kirschenbaum, H., & Land-Henderson, V. (Eds.). (1989b). *The Carl Rogers reader.* Boston: Houghton Mifflin.

Levant, R., & Shlien, J. M. (Eds.) (1984). *Client-centered therapy and the person-centered approach: New directions in theory, research, and practice.* New York: Praeger.

McLeod, J., & McLeod, J. (1993). The relationship between personal philosophy and effectiveness in counsellors. *Counselling Psychology Quarterly, 6,* 121–129.

Meador, B., & Rogers, C. (1984). Person-centered therapy. In Raymond J. Corsini (Ed.), *Current psychotherapies* (3rd ed.). Itasca, IL: Peacock.

Miller, M. J. (1991). A thought or two on the future of research in career counseling. *Journal of Employment Counseling, 28,* 4–7.

Miller, M. J., & Foxworth, C. L. (1992). Validating a subscale for assessing aspects of the person. *College Student Journal, 26,* 436–439.

Moreira, V. (1993). Beyond the person: Merleau-Ponty's concept of "flesh" as (re)defining Carl Rogers' person-centered theory. *Humanistic Psychologist, 21,* 138–157.

Newman, J., & Lovell, M. (1993). A description of a supervisory group for group counselors. *Counselor Education and Supervision, 33,* 22–31.

Nye, R. D. (1992). *Three psychologies: Perspectives from Freud, Skinner, and Rogers* (4th ed.). Pacific Grove, CA: Brooks/Cole.

Patterson, C. H. (1985). *The therapeutic relationship: Foundations for an eclectic psychotherapy.* Pacific Grove, CA: Brooks/Cole.

Raskin, N. J., & Rogers, C. (1995). Person-centered therapy. In Raymond J. Corsini & Danny Wedding (Eds.), *Current psychotherapies* (5th ed.). Itasca, IL: Peacock.

Roberts, R. C. (1985). Carl Rogers and the Christian virtues. *Journal of Psychology and Theology, 13,* 263–273.

Rogers, C. R. (1931). *Measuring personality adjustment in children nine to thirteen years of age.* New York: Teachers College.

Rogers, C. R. (1939). *Clinical treatment of the problem child.* Boston: Houghton Mifflin.

Rogers, C. R. (1942a). *Counseling and psychotherapy.* Boston: Houghton Mifflin.

Rogers, C. R. (1942b). Some observations on the organization of personality. *American Psychologist, 2,* 358–368.

Rogers, C. R. (1951, November). "Client-centered" psychotherapy. *Scientific American, 66*–74.

Rogers, C. R. (1954). The case of Mrs. Oak: A research analysis. In C. R. Rogers & R. F. Dymond (Eds.), *Psychotherapy and personality change: Co-ordinated research studies in the client-centered approach* (pp. 259–348). Chicago: University of Chicago Press.

Rogers, C. R. (1957). The necessary and sufficient conditions of therapeutic personality change. *Journal of Consulting Psychology, 21,* 95–103.

Rogers, C. R. (1959). A theory of therapy, personality and inter-personal relationships, as developed in the client-centered framework. In S. Koch (Ed.), *Psychology: A study of a science* (Vol. 3, pp. 184–256). New York: McGraw-Hill.

Rogers, C. R. (1961a). Actualizing tendency in relation to "motives" and to consciousness. In M. R. Jones (Ed.), *Nebraska Sym-*

posium on Motivation (pp. 1–24). Lincoln: University of Nebraska Press.

Rogers, C. R. (1961b). *On becoming a person.* Boston: Houghton Mifflin.

Rogers, C. R. (1962). The interpersonal relationship: The core of guidance. *Harvard Educational Review,* 416–429.

Rogers, C. R. (1964). Toward a science of the person. In T. W. Wann (Ed.), *Behaviorism and phenomenology* (pp. 109–140). Chicago: University of Chicago Press.

Rogers, C. R. (1965). Dealing with psychological tensions. *Journal of Applied Behavioral Science, 1,* 6–24.

Rogers, C. R. (1967). Autobiography. In E. G. Boring & G. Lindzey (Eds.), *A history of psychology in autobiography* (Vol. 5, pp. 343–384). New York: Appleton-Century-Crofts.

Rogers, C. R. (1969). *Freedom to learn: A view of what education might become.* Columbus, OH: Charles Merrill.

Rogers, C. R. (1970). *On encounter groups.* New York: Harper and Row.

Rogers, C. R. (1972). *Becoming partners: Marriage and its alternatives.* New York: Delacorte Press.

Rogers, C. R. (1977). *On personal power: Inner strength and its revolutionary impact.* New York: Delacorte Press.

Rogers, C. R. (1980a). *A way of being.* Boston: Houghton Mifflin.

Rogers, C. R. (1980b). Client-centered psychotherapy. In A. M. Freeman, H. I Kapplan, & B. J. Sadock (Eds.), *Comprehensive textbook of psychiatry* (3rd ed., Vol. 2, pp. 2153–2167). Baltimore, MD: Williams & Wilkins.

Rogers, C. R. (1983). *Freedom to learn for the 80s.* Columbus, OH: Merrill.

Rogers, C. R. (1986). A commentary from Carl Rogers. *Person-Centered Review, 1,* 3–5. As quoted in *History of psychotherapy: A century of change,* by D. K. Freedheim (Ed.), 1992, p. 651. Washington, D.C: American Psychological Association.

Rogers, C. R., & Dymon, R. F. (1951). *Psychotherapy and personality change.* Chicago: University Press.

Rogers, C. R., Gendlin, E. T., Kiesler, D. J., & Truax, C. B. (1967). *The therapeutic relationship and its impact: A study of psychotherapy with schizophrenics.* Madison: University of Wisconsin Press.

Rogers, C. R., & Stevens, B. (1968). *Person to person: The problem of being human.* Lafayette, CA: Real People Press.

Rychalk, J. (1973). *Introduction to personality and psychotherapy.* Boston: Houghton Mifflin.

See, J. D. (1985). Person-centered perspective. *Journal of Applied Rehabilitation Counseling, 16,* 15–20.

Seligmen, L. (1986). *Diagnosis and treatment planning in counseling.* New York: Human Sciences Press.

Smith, D. (1982). Trends in counseling and psychotherapy. *American Psychologist, 37,* 802–809.

Truax, C., & Mitchell, K. (1971). Research on certain therapist interpersonal skills in relation to process and outcome. In A. E. Bergin & S. L. Garfield (Eds.), *Handbook of psychotherapy and behavior change: An empirical analysis.* New York: Wiley.

Usher, C. H. (1989). Recognizing cultural bias in counseling theory and practice: The case of Rogers. *Journal of Multicultural Counseling and Development, 17,* 62–71.

Warner, R. E. (1991). A survey of theoretical orientations of Canadian clinical psychologists. *Canadian Psychology, 32,* 525–528.

Watkins, C. E. (1993). Person-centered theory and the contemporary practice of psychological testing. *Counselling Psychology Quarterly, 6,* 59–67.

Watkins, C. E., Lopez, F. G., Campbell, V. L., & Himmell, C. D. (1986). Contemporary counseling psychology: The results of a national survey. *Journal of Counseling Psychology, 33,* 301–309.

Yau, T., Sue, D., & Hayden, D. (1992). Counseling style preference of international students. *Journal of Counseling Psychology, 39,* 100–104.

Zimring, F. M., & Raskin, N. J. (1992). Carl Rogers and client/person-centered therapy. In D. K. Freedheim (Ed.), *History of psychotherapy.* Washington, DC: American Psychological Association.

Without frustrations there is no need, no reason, to mobilize your resources, to discover that you might be able to do something on your own. —Fritz Perls

10 CHAPTER | Gestalt Therapy

Even in some of life's most trivial tasks we seek resolution and closure. We want the incomplete to be completed, the unfinished to be finished. Tension is not released until "the case is closed." An unfinished line of a familiar song or musical score—the first four notes of Beethoven's Fifth Symphony, for instance—won't allow our mind to rest until the lost is found, until the next four notes have been played. Perhaps you may have noticed the same need for visual closure. Consider these images. In the upper image, at any given moment two faces or a vase can be seen, but not simultaneously. Although they can be perceived separately, the removal of one changes the perception of the other. Only together are they complete. Similarly, when we turn to the lower image, our brain attempts to make sense out of the ink blotches on this page, to organize the black ink into images that make sense. Just as it works at filling in the gaps of a song or filling in a blank space to complete an image, even so it works at assembling the pieces until a coherent picture is formed.

While dining in a German cafe, Kurt Lewin observed this phenomenon, this need for closure, in the way waiters went about their work. Although waiters could remember the details of a customer's bill for a considerable stretch of time, he noticed that once it had been paid, they were often unable to recall any of the data, or even the total. As long as the bill remained unsettled, the tension in the incomplete transaction facilitated recall. Payment completed the transaction, which brought about closure, thus dissipating the tension and erasing the memory. Whether it is such a transaction, a song, or a visual image, our minds demand what the Germans call **gestalt,** a complete and meaningful whole. The word *gestalt* has no precise English equivalent, but words such as "form," "structure," "configuration," "essence," and "whole" begin to translate its meaning.

Gestalt therapy is built on this premise, on a theory of perception known as **Gestalt psychology,** which has proposed the radical hypothesis that the whole is psychologically greater than the sum of its parts. It maintains that psychological phenomena can be understood, not when broken down into primitive perceptual elements, but only when viewed as organized, structured wholes (Osborn, 1991; Banks & Krajicek, 1991). Even the stars in the sky are grouped into wholes, into constellations such as the Big Dipper and the Southern Cross, not simply because we enjoy painting pictures in the night sky, but because we possess this fundamental need to make things whole.

> Gestalt therapy is, in a very real sense, a Gestalt.
>
> —E. W. L. Smith

Even before the founder of this approach to therapy was born, Gestalt psychology was emerging in Berlin, initially as a theory of perception. The system of therapy that eventually grew out of Gestalt principles, such as "closure," emphasizes working with the whole person (Graumann, 1989). The focus is phenomenologic, dealing with the present rather than the past, with process rather than product. There is very little analysis. To Gestaltists, analyzing is mere intellectualizing rather than action leading to change. These concepts and their application to counseling were pioneered by Frederick Perls, who was also known for his dramatic ways and inimitable character.

BRIEF BIOGRAPHY

Born in Berlin in 1893, Frederick Solomon "Fritz" Perls was the middle child and only son of middle-class Jewish parents. Although he remembered his childhood as happy, Frederick's parents often fought bitterly. He loved his mother but lost respect for his father, a traveling wine salesman who drank heavily and whose primary avocation, from Perls's viewpoint, was to become Grand Master of the Freemasons. He and his younger sister, Grete, were always close, but his dislike for his older sister, Elsie, grew so intense and long-lasting that he experienced only minimal emotion when he learned she had died in a concentration camp (Perls, 1972).

As a child Perls was unruly, misbehaving at home and causing trouble in school. However, he loved to read and was an excellent student. He earned his M.D., with a specialization in psychology, from Frederick Wilhelm University—just in time to join the German army as a medic in World War I.

After the war Perls began psychoanalytic training at both the Vienna and Berlin Institutes of Psychoanalysis. He was especially influenced by his own analyst, Wilhelm Reich, but he also worked with Otto Fenichel and Karen Horney (Rice & Greenberg, 1992). He later took a position at the Institute for Brain Injured Soldiers in Frankfort where he worked with Kurt Goldstein, and it was here that Perls first learned to view humans not as the sum of their separate parts but as complete entities.

When Hitler's anti-Semitic policies in Germany during the 1930s became intolerable, Perls left for Amsterdam. Carrying only 100 marks (about $25) hidden in his cigarette case, he crossed the German-Dutch border with his wife, Laura, and their two-year-old daughter. They lived for a year in Amsterdam in a small attic apartment under conditions, much like those of Anne Frank, that Perls (1972) would remember as "utter misery."

Anticipating the rising tide of Facism in Europe, Perls fled Holland in 1934, barely ahead of the Nazis and emigrated to South Africa where he established the South African Institute for Psychoanalysis. In Johannesburg he and his wife, Laura, built a strong practice, and he served as director of this institute for about 10 years. As the first traditional, trained analyst in South Africa, his success provided an affluent lifestyle: servants, a nursemaid for the children, tennis courts, a swimming pool, an iceskating rink, cars, even an airplane.

In 1936 Perls attended an international psychoanalytic congress in Czechoslovakia, where he finally met Freud. The long-awaited meeting lasted less than four minutes, however, and took place entirely in the doorway to Freud's room, leaving Perls feeling neither welcomed nor appreciated. Thereafter, Perls dedicated himself to proving Freud and psychoanalysis wrong. Returning to South Africa from the congress, the humiliated Perls was convinced that he needed no one, either personally or professionally, to support him or his views. This return to Africa from Czechoslovakia marked the emergence of Gestalt therapy (Litt, 1978).

With the rise of apartheid in 1946, Perls left South Africa to make his home in New York, where he joined his wife and Paul Goodman in founding the New York Institute for Gestalt Therapy. Eventually becoming dissatisfied with New York life in general and with life with Laura in particular, he separated from his wife, lived in several cities, and eventually became instrumental in the development of the Esalen Institute in Big Sur, California. An actor at heart, Perls loved to parade his ideas before the public. For the last 10 years of his life he conducted popular experimental workshops at Esalen and across the country.

> I believe that I am the best therapist for any type of neurosis in the States, maybe in the world. How is that for megalomania.
>
> —Fritz Perls

In 1969, the year before his death, Perls founded a "gestalt community" at Cowichan on Vancouver Island, British Columbia, as a center where therapists could study for several months at a time. In March 1970, Perls died in a Chicago hospital, where a large crowd of anxious followers gathered for a six-day vigil preceding his death. Because of their grief and intensity, a police guard was called to keep them at bay.

Perls recounted many of the more personal moments of his life in the autobiographical book *In and Out of the Garbage Pail* (1972), a free-floating, poetic, often playful autobiography that provides hundreds of glimpses into his unique personal life.

HISTORICAL DEVELOPMENT

The distinguished roots of Gestalt therapy reach back into the 19th century, to the very beginning of psychology as a discipline. The German word *gestalt* was first used in a psychological context in 1890 by the Austrian psychologist and philosopher Christian von Ehrenfels (1859–1932). He argued that there is a gestalt or quality of form, absent in any of the parts but present in the whole of a structure (Rock & Palmer, 1990; Saariluoma, 1992).

In 1912 three young German psychologists who were particularly interested in human perception joined forces to found the Berlin Gestalt School. These three friends—Max Wertheimer (1880–1943), Kurt Koffka (1886–1941), and Wolfgang Köhler (1887–1967)—reacted against the stark behaviorism of Watson and the narrow framework of Wundt's introspective analysis. Out of their work came such precepts as the **Principle of Closure,** (Figure 10.1A) which describes our need to complete unfinished figures; the **Principle of Proximity,** (Figure 10.1B) which suggests that the relative distance of stimuli from each other within the perceptual field determines how they are seen; and the **Principle of Similarity,** (Figure 10.1C) which causes us to group stimuli together, if they appear similar within our perceptual field.

Figure 10.1A | The Principle of Closure

We add the missing pieces to see the completed figure of a cat or dog.

Figure 10.1B | Principle of Proximity

We organize visual stimuli based on their distance from one another.

Figure 10.1C | Principle of Similarity

We group elements that appear similar.

Wertheimer, Koffka, and Köhler spent considerable time between World War I and World War II describing principles of behavior that help explain how the human mind seeks to make sense of the vast array of stimuli that calls for attention and, more broadly, how we perceive and thus how we learn (Sarris, 1989; Yontef, 1982). Most significantly, these three men reasoned that an individual should be understood as a "meaningful whole."

Years later, when Perls sought to recover something of the original holism of these three Germans who had studied perception, he often returned to his favorite example of water, H_2O, which loses its "gestalt" and ceases to be water once it is broken down into hydrogen and oxygen. He applied the various principles of Gestalt formation to the perceptions of one's own feelings, a contribution that subsequently blossomed into the birth of Gestalt therapy (Wallen, 1970).

Perls distinguished individuals' perceptions of themselves, of their feelings, and of their relationships in terms of the Gestalt dichotomy of figure and ground. Gestalt therapy seeks a smooth transition between those sets of experiences that are the **figure,** that are immediately in the focus of awareness, and those that form the **ground,** or background. This is the basic premise of Gestalt psychology and an important contribution to Perls' Gestalt therapy.

> Gestalt therapy is really permission to be creative.
>
> —J. Zinker

Another important historical influence on Gestalt therapy was the existential movement in philosophy and psychology. Gestalt therapy's emphasis on such concepts as the expansion of awareness, freedom, the immediacy of experience, and the here and now all demonstrate its close relation to existentialism. Nowhere is this influence more clearly seen than in the controversial "Gestalt prayer" that reads, in part: You are you, and I am I, and if by chance we find each other, it's beautiful. If not, it can't be helped.

VIEW OF HUMAN NATURE

Perls believed that people develop in relation to their environment, and he distinguished three stages in this development. During the earliest, the *social stage,* the infant depends upon others for nearly everything; in general, this stage is characterized by an awareness of others but little awareness of self. During the *psychophysical stage,* we become more aware of what is self and what is nonself; during this stage the self and self-image develop through the process of adaptation, acknowledgment, and support. Very few people reach the third or **spiritual stage.** Kempler (1973) describes the spiritual stage as movement from awareness that is sensory sensing to awareness that is extrasensory sensing. In sum, the Gestalt view of human nature, which is further influenced by Eastern philosophy, is existential and humanistic. The fundamental assumptions of these several world

> If you are in the now, you are creative, you have your eyes and ears open, like every small child, you find a solution.
>
> —Fritz Perls

views are evident in the basic assumptions that Gestalt theory makes about human nature.

Organism-Environment Field

People perceive their environment as a total unit of meaning, in which the whole is perceived in one of two ways: as figure, where stimuli are attended to, and as background, or simply ground, where there is no attending to stimuli. Since our most pressing needs determine the figure that comes into focus, our foreground continually shifts as one foreground flows into another (Korb, Gorrell, & Van De Riet, 1989). A healthy person focuses "sharply on one need (the figure) at a time while relegating other needs to the background. When the need is met—or the Gestalt is closed or completed—it is relegated to the background and a new need comes into focus (becomes the figure)" (Thompson & Rudolph, 1988, p. 66). This ceaseless, constantly changing flow of gestalts or patterns is the basis of human experience. In any given situation what is "foreground" for one person may not be for another, making each of us unique. This idea of the figure and the ground is the linchpin of Gestalt therapy.

> Wherever we go we take a kind of world with us.
> —Fritz Perls

Organismic Self-Regulation

The flow of individual experience is far from random. What becomes foreground for an individual is based upon his or her current needs. And Gestaltists believe that what human beings need is wholeness and completeness in life. When we are functioning freely, we make contact with the environment in ways that meet the needs of the organism.

Psychological Homeostasis

Given the environment we are in at any particular time, we attempt to meet these personal needs as best we can. Just as living organisms seek a balance between salt and water or between acid and alkali, so are we regulated by our own psychological rheostat that seeks **homeostasis**, an equilibrium or balance between ourselves and our environment. When we become thirsty, getting a drink comes into the foreground; when we become lonely, finding other people to be with comes into the foreground. Through psychological homeostasis our most pressing needs come to the foreground to help us maintain balance in our lives.

Awareness

To achieve balance and satisfaction, we have the capacity to become aware of our environment. This **awareness**, which determines what is "right for us," is a vital part of our human nature. Awareness gives us a sense of direction and motivation to become more fully who we are. It clarifies what our most pressing need is and the options we have to meet that need. Only when we are fully aware of our organism and our environment do we have choice and freedom. With that choice and freedom we can contact, act on, or interact with our environment to meet our needs. Without this awareness we would not form a gestalt, resulting in dissatisfaction.

There are other ways to conceptualize Gestalt therapy's understanding of human nature. Passons (1975), for instance, lists several related or further assumptions about the nature of humanity that form the framework for the Gestalt approach. Gestalt therapists believe that we are a composite whole made up of interrelated parts, none of which—body, emotions, thoughts, sensations, and perceptions—can be understood outside the context of the whole person. At the same time, we are also part of our own environment and cannot be understood apart from it. The implication is that we are creatures of our environment, and that as such, we are neither "good" or "bad." Gestaltists further believe we have the potential to be fully aware of all sensations, thoughts, emotions, and perceptions, and we are capable of making choices because of this awareness. Only then will we have the capacity to govern our own lives effectively, to choose how to respond to external and internal stimuli, for instance, so that we are acting on our world rather than

10.1 | The Moral Precepts of Gestalt Therapy

The moral precepts of Gestalt therapy have been described by several writers (Korb, Gorrell, & Van De Riet, 1989; Naranjo, 1970). The experience that underlies this set of injunctions is aliveness, "radiance" (Hycner, 1987), or "inspiration" (Jourard, 1964). The precepts are:

- Live now (i.e., be concerned not with the past or the future but with the present).
- Live here (i.e., be concerned with that which is present and not with that which is absent).
- Accept yourself as you are.
- Stop imagining (i.e., experience only the real).
- Stop unnecessary thinking (i.e., be oriented toward hearing, seeing, smelling, tasting, and touching).
- Express directly—do not explain, judge, or manipulate.
- Be aware of both the pleasant and the unpleasant.
- Reject all "shoulds" and "oughts" that are not your own.
- Take complete responsibility for your actions, thoughts, and feelings.
- Surrender to being what you really are.
- Keep the memories of the past and the concern about the future in perspective.
- Be available to an open dialogue with the persons, ideas, things, and institutions in which your life is lived.
- Use the word *appropriate* as a touchstone for your choices.

reacting to it. Counselors trained in Gestalt therapy also believe that we cannot truly experience the past and the future; we can only experience ourselves in the present.

In short, Perls concluded that we are self-directed and must take responsibility for our own lives. According to Perls, all needs stem from, and are grounded in, this basic need to actualize oneself, to become whole (Perls, 1969a). Gestaltists believe that a healthy personality is the result of a person's experiences forming a meaningful whole, a gestalt. It occurs when there is a smooth transition between those sets of experiences that are immediately in the focus of awareness and those sets that are in the background.

> Don't push the river; it flows by itself.
>
> —Fritz Perls

DEVELOPMENT OF MALADAPTIVE BEHAVIOR

According to Gestalt theory, people develop psychological problems in several ways. They can either lose contact with the environment and the resources in it or become so overinvolved with the environment that they lose touch with the self. Some people fail to put aside unfulfilled needs or unexpressed feelings, while others may become fragmented or scattered in many directions. Others may experience what Perls labeled the conflict between the "topdog" (what one thinks one should do) and the "underdog" (what one wants to do). Still others may have difficulty handling the dichotomies of life such as love/hate and pleasure/pain. All of these difficulties keep us from being aware of who we really are.

Although Perls (1970) never developed a systematic or formal theory of maladaptive behavior, he identified five layers of neurosis that potentially interfere with our being authentically in touch with ourselves: the phony, the phobic, the impasse, the implosive, and the explosive. At the *phony layer* we pretend to be something we are not. We play a variety of games and act out various roles. Only when we become more aware of our game playing can we become more honest, open, and in touch with unpleasantness and pain. At the *phobic layer* individuals attempt to avoid recognizing aspects of the self they would prefer to deny. People who experience this layer of awareness are afraid that if they acknowledge who they really are and present it to others, they will be rejected. Below this phobic layer is the *impasse layer*, in which people are adrift in a sea of helplessness and dread, with no sense of direction, leaving them to wonder how they are going to make it in the environment. The fourth and fifth layers, the *implosive* and *explosive*, often go together. At these layers people may frequently feel vulnerable to feelings. Yet, as they peel back the layers of defensiveness built up over the years, they become alive in an explosion of joy, sorrow, or pain that leads to being authentic. When a person reaches this point, the present can be experienced most fully.

Conflicts such as these are usually the result of an inability to bring together individual needs and environmental demands, so that people can be fully present in the now. Passons (1975) provides a Gestalt lens for viewing the styles of maladaptive behavior that can develop from the inability to reconcile the needs of

Lose your mind and come to your senses.
—Fritz Perls

self with the demands of our environment. He divides the kinds of problems individuals experience into six areas. *Lack of awareness* is a problem for people with rigid personalities who move though their daily lives with an uneasy feeling of nonfulfillment. Those who manipulate their environment rather than take charge of their own selves are said to exhibit a *lack of self-responsibility*. Or we can *lose contact with the environment* in one of two ways: either by becoming so rigid that no input from the environment is accepted or by needing so much approval that the self becomes lost in trying to incorporate everything from the environment. Individuals can fail to complete necessary tasks in one of two ways: an *inability to complete unfinished business* prevents them from dealing with current situations, while a *denial of needs* causes them to lose the productive energy of the needs they disown. *Dichotomizing dimensions of the self* occurs when people perceive themselves at one end of a possible continuum, a self-perception that results in an internal conflict, leaving them divided.

Of course, when one is completely incapable of determining the boundaries between one's self and the environment, the result is an anxious state of temporal insecurity (Burke, 1989). "And now here comes the neurotic," wrote Perls in one of his last works (1976), "tied to the past and to outmoded ways of acting, fuzzy about the present because he sees it only through a glass darkly, tortured about the future because the present is out of his hands" (p. 44).

In short, from the point of view of the Gestalt therapist, people become maladjusted when they fail to use their own capacity for self-regulation and spend their energy on acting helpless, depending upon others, or manipulating the environment in countless other ways.

FUNCTION OF THE THERAPIST

In his section of the well-known film *Three Approaches to Psychotherapy*, which documents how Rogers, Ellis, and Perls treat a client named Gloria (Shostrom, 1965), Perls demonstrated the function of the Gestalt therapist. After a preliminary statement in which Perls said the therapist is "like an artist bringing something out which is hidden," he began the interview by stating that Gloria and he would be talking for a brief time. Gloria responded that she was very nervous and afraid of talking, to which Perls immediately replied, "You say you are afraid, but you are smiling." Launching into a series of confrontations with the client about the incompatibility of fear and smiling, not once did he ask Gloria what she would like to talk about. In this brief interview Perls demonstrated how Gestalt therapists provoke clients into awareness, on the premise that the clients who are aware will solve their own problems in their own time (Dolliver, 1991; Dolliver, Williams, & Gold, 1980; McClure, Merril & Russo, 1994).

The role of the Gestalt therapist, then, is an extremely active one. Without taking the responsibility for change within the client, the therapist acts as a catalyst for change. As Perls says, "The therapist is a directive leader and orchestrates all aspects of the therapeutic interactions, with the advice and consent of the client who is working" (Perls, 1976, p. 86). In this context, the word "orchestrate" is especially interesting; Kempler (1973) compares the therapist to a "composing maestro" and the client to an "accomplished musician," both of whom meet to combine their talent and skill (p. 266).

One of the major functions of the Gestalt therapist is to frustrate the clients' demands for support and help, so they are forced to rely on their own resources (Little, 1986). Perls calls this a "safe emergency." Of course, the clients may resist this transition from external to internal support; at this point, when clients are unable to manipulate the counselor into solving their problems, an **impasse** occurs. Because of the threatening prospect of relying only on themselves, the clients become immobilized and are unable to experience feelings (Harman, 1975; Zinker, 1978).

> The underdog is the Mickey Mouse. The topdog is the Super Mouse.
>
> —Fritz Perls

When such an impasse occurs, the therapist provides a "safe emergency," which allows their clients to feel safe enough to work toward self-support. Since it is easier to keep things the way they are, most clients are reluctant to go beyond the impasse. In order to permit them to get in touch with and work through their patterns of frustration, it is therefore the goal of the therapist to compel clients to face and deal with this impasse (Fagan, 1970).

The Gestalt therapist views change, then, through a paradoxical lens. Gestalt theory holds that change and growth take place, not when one tries to be what one is not, but when one becomes what one is. Gestalt therapy is about the process of "being what one is and not a process of striving to become" (Kempler, 1973, p. 262). Change and growth occur in clients not as a result of coercion, persuasion, or interpretation, but only when they fully own what they are doing and how they are doing it. Paradoxically, it is through standing still and becoming aware of ourselves, just as we are, that we grow and expand our boundaries. Significantly, this philosophy holds true for the therapist as well: to be authentic, the Gestalt therapist must try to be, not a better therapist, but who he or she is at the moment (Tyson & Range, 1987). For these several reasons, Gestalt therapists do not make use of standardized assessment instruments, such as psychological tests, nor do they diagnose their clients according to classification standards. They spend their time trying to be who they are and helping their clients do the same.

GOALS OF THERAPY

One of the most significant goals of Gestalt therapy is helping individuals assume responsibility for themselves rather than relying on others to make decisions for them. As Prochaska (1979) contends, the "ideal outcome of Gestalt therapy is the clients' discovery that they do not and never really did need a therapist" (p. 164). Gestalt therapy aims to challenge its clients to move from "environmental support" to "self-support," in order to mobilize their own resources for dealing with the environment effectively and to make creative adjustments that permit the self to respond to environmental pressures and to inner needs.

Another goal of Gestalt therapy is that clients become complete and integrated, so that they function as a systematic whole that consists of feelings, perceptions, thoughts, and a physical body whose processes cannot be divorced from its more psychological components. Integration means bringing together all of the parts of a person that have been disowned. When our emotions and behavior match, little energy is wasted, and we are more capable of responding appropriately to meet our needs. This often comes about through what Köhler (1973) called the "Aha!" experience. Like Archimedes, whose discovery of the principle of the displacement of water by mass was so immediate that he dashed stark naked from his bath into the streets, crying out "Eureka!" we suddenly see and understand what had long eluded us in a climactic moment that is powerful and immediate. With such an "Aha!" experience, the energy that was previously directed toward the playing of roles is released for our self-regulating capabilities. This process of integration is ongoing. "Integration is never completed," Perls (1971) pointed out. "Maturation is never completed. It's an ongoing process forever and ever. . . . There's always something to be integrated; always something to be learned" (p. 64).

Another basic goal of Gestalt therapy is to help clients become aware of the present, which Perls (1969a) viewed as both necessary and sufficient for change to occur. In fact, Perls claimed that "awareness per se—by and of itself—can be curative" (p. 16). Seeking to avoid the Scylla of what Perls referred to as "obsessive remembering of the past" and the Chybardis of the "anxious anticipation of the future," the counselor is always intent on cultivating awareness within clients. Latner (1973) maintains that "the point of therapy is not to make solutions, it is to make the problem-laden present more actual by increasing the patients' awareness" (p. 211).

> Very few people go in therapy to be cured, but rather to improve their neurosis.
>
> —Fritz Perls

Gestalt therapy helps clients become aware of what they do by letting the experience of "the now" flow through all of their senses. By fully experiencing the present moment, clients can eliminate self-manipulation, environmental control, and other factors that interfere with this natural self-regulating process and allow **organismic self-regulation** to take over. As a result, Gestalt therapy must focus on the **here and now**—not the there and then—the essence of which, according to Perls (1970), is summed up in the formula: Now = Experience = Awareness = Reality. "The past is no more and the future not yet," Perls wrote. "Only the now exists" (p. 14). People become anxious, Perls suggested, because they leave the security of the present and become preoccupied with the future, frequently expecting things to go wrong.

Anxiety, for Gestaltists, is the gap between now and then, between the present and the past or the present and the future (Phares, 1988). Living with a focus on the future often results in failing to see what is at hand and to focus on either the past or the future inevitably immobilizes us in the present. Our inclinations to daydream about better times to come or to worry about what might happen can only be dealt with by "presentizing" them into current awareness (Passons, 1975).

The Gestalt therapist also attempts to help clients identify and resolve *unfinished business:* earlier thoughts, feelings, and reactions that still affect their functioning. Unfinished business interferes with life in the present. Children, for example, may have been taught to deny and distort their own emotional reactions ("Wipe that scowl off your face and say you are sorry!"), causing them to lose touch with their "intuitive" instincts and to deny their needs. In these circumstances, the "figure" (needs) never clearly emerges from the "background" (all the competing needs), and thus we are left with the unfinished business of discovering our true emotions. As we begin to see everything incorrectly, this process weighs us down and keeps us from acting in accordance with our genuine feelings. It distorts the sensory-perceptual field and stimuli we receive in other contexts (Perls, 1969a). Very often, unfinished business takes the form of not forgiving our parents for a variety of reasons. This failure to attend to figure-ground relationships in the present can stem from a variety of other factors as well: our tendencies to dwell upon incomplete experiences, for example, to return to and relive these experiences, or to carry around unresolved emotions regarding them.

Simpkins and Yontef (1984) provide three descriptive therapeutic principles that sum up the goals of Gestalt therapy. The *I and Thou* principle describes the horizontal relationship between client and therapist, which is characterized by addressing someone directly (even if absent) instead of talking about that person to the counselor. The *What and How* principle, which emphasizes clients' increasing awareness of what they do and how they do it, occurs through direct and immediate sharing of observations and through exercises and feedback. The *Here and Now* principle refers to the importance placed on present experience for both clients and therapists.

MAJOR METHODS AND TECHNIQUES

Gestalt therapy is not verbal, but primarily experiential; it is about doing rather than saying. Because the focus is on the here and now, Gestalt therapy is particularly intent on providing opportunities for "creative experimentation," and some of counseling's most innovative techniques emerge from out of this therapeutic approach (Covin, 1977; Perls, Hefferline, & Goodman, 1972). Few other major theories present such a diverse array of evocative techniques.

Gestalt therapy often begins with laying down the general "rules" of therapy (Levitsky & Perls, 1970). At the outset it is understood that communication is to be between equals—one talks with, rather than at—and it is in the present tense, since looking either backward or forward is discouraged. In fact, clients are to focus continually on immediate experience. In order to encourage acceptance of responsibility, clients use "I" rather than "it" language, and in order to encourage them to talk to rather than about someone, they are not permitted to engage in gossip. Since questions are often covert means of stating opinions rather than seeking information, questions are similarly discouraged.

> The healthy person, with the present as reference-point, is free to look backwards or ahead as occasion warrants.
>
> —Fritz Perls

The steps in the Gestalt helping process are fourfold: expression, differentiation, affirmation, and choice and integration. Through *expression* clients are encouraged to tell who they are as fully as possible, even becoming aware of gestures, breathing, voice tone, and facial expressions. In order to keep them in the "now" and maintain responsibility, clients are urged to preface their expressions with the phrase, "Now I am aware. . . ."

Once expression has begun, the gestalt therapist begins to experiment with techniques that lead to *differentiation,* so that clients can differentiate among the parts of their inner conflict. They might be encouraged, for example, to exaggerate their facial expression and in so doing, they may become more aware of their "angry part."

The third, crucial stage in Gestalt therapy, *affirmation,* occurs when the client is encouraged to identify with "all the parts" that are emerging into awareness. It is here that the Gestalt therapist will allow clients to fully express their pent-up emotions.

In the final stage, *choice and integration,* the client comes to say, "I am responsible for my frustration and resentment." As Perls (1976, p. 79) put it, "responsibility is really response-ability, the ability to choose one's reactions," and it comes about only when we relinquish our defenses and allow ourselves to become aware of our true feelings and motivations. In this stage an internal integration brings a sense of peace and is a sign of a "completed gestalt."

Dream Work

Perls described dreams as "messages" that represent the person's place at a certain time (Bernard, 1986). Unlike psychoanalysts, however, Gestalt counselors do not interpret dreams; dream work is experiential rather than analytical. Clients present dreams and are then directed to experience what it is like to be each part of the dream. Every image in a dream is believed to represent an alienated, disowned, discordant, or projected part of the self.

The therapist assists clients in understanding their dreams by drawing attention to the order in which the images are played, by helping clients deal with avoidance and resistance in playing the parts, and by suggesting when clients might relate the images and feelings of the dream to current life situations. Reporting the dream in the present tense, as though the dream were occurring now, allows clients to grow more in touch with the multiple aspects of the self and thus to reclaim and integrate the alienated parts of their personality. For example, the therapist might ask clients to "become" the automobile they are dreaming about. On the other hand, clients who experience repetitive dreams are encouraged to realize that unfinished business is being brought into awareness and that they need to take care of the message. In sum, the goal of Gestalt dream work is to help clients come into contact with, own, accept responsibility for, or empower themselves to interact in a different or similar way with the images in the dream—all of which is an attempt to heighten self-awareness and journey on the "royal road to integration," as Perls called it (1969a, p. 66).

Converting Questions to Statements

Perls found that questions, which seem to be helpful and supportive, frequently represent passivity, laziness, lack of personal involvement, manipulation, and cajoling. Often the therapist will ask clients to turn their questions into statements in order to help them take responsibility for their thoughts. Since clients can use questions to camouflage their real thoughts and keep the focus of attention off themselves, this technique heightens the effectiveness of communication. For example, the client who asks, "Do you really believe that?" is generally saying, "I don't think you believe that." Similarly, "Aren't you really saying something else?" more accurately means, "I believe you are saying something else." Forcing clients to convert their questions into statements like this helps them declare their own belief systems and forces them to take responsibility.

10.2 | The Gestalt Workshop

Some Gestalt therapy and a good deal of training in Gestalt therapy is conducted in workshops, which are scheduled for a finite period, some for as short as one day. Weekend workshops may range from 10 to 20 or more hours. Longer workshops range from a week through several months in duration. A typical weekend workshop membership consists of one Gestalt therapist and 12 to 16 people. Given longer periods (ranging from one week up to a month or longer), as many as 20 people can be seen by one therapist. Usually if the group is larger than 16 participants, cotherapists are used.

Because workshops have a finite life and because limited hours are available to the participants, there is usually high motivation to "work." Sometimes, rules are established so that no one can work a second time until every other participant has had an opportunity to work once. At other times, no such rules are set. Thus, depending on their willingness, audacity, and drive, some people may get intense therapeutic attention several times during a workshop.

Although some workshops are arranged with established groups, most assemble people for the first time. As in ongoing groups, the ideal practice is to screen patients before the workshop. An unscreened workshop requires a clinician experienced with the range of severe pathology and careful protection for possibly vulnerable group members. Confrontive or charismatic Gestalt styles are particularly likely to exacerbate existing mental illness in some participants.

Yontef, G. M., & Simkin, J. S. (1989). Gestalt therapy. In R. J. Corsini & D. Wedding, (Eds.), *Current Psychotherapies*. Itasca, IL: F. E. Peacock. Reprinted with permission.

Use of Personal Pronouns

When clients are talking about themselves, the Gestalt therapist also encourages the use of *I* instead of words like *it, you,* or *we.* Rather than saying, "It takes a long time to write a term paper," for example, the client is urged to say, "I take a long time to write a term paper." Such first-person expressions help clients to own and thus to control their behavior, which facilitates the perception of the self as an active, dynamic agent rather than a passive, acted-upon object.

Assuming Responsibility

Clients are also encouraged to conclude all expressions of feelings or beliefs with, "And I take responsibility for it." Sometimes clients are encouraged to assume responsibility by asking them to change *can't* to *won't* or by changing *but* to *and.* For example, the statement, "I want to go to graduate school but I haven't applied anywhere" sounds different when one coordinating conjunction is exchanged for another: "I want to go to graduate school and I haven't applied anywhere." By changing the *but* to *and,* the client is verbalizing responsibility. This assumption of responsibility helps clients see themselves as possessing internal strength, rather than relying on external controls.

Playing the Projection

When clients project something onto another person, the counselor will ask them to play the role of the other person. For example, when a client says to the counselor, "I have the feeling you don't really like me," the counselor may ask him or her to play the role of the therapist and to express what he or she believes the counselor is feeling. By entering into the world of others, by empathizing with them, by discovering that their projection may be off target, clients discover how much of their image of others, and thus of their self-image, is colored by their own insecurities. In this example, the client recognizes that his or her feelings toward the counselor are being projected in a way that affects what he or she believes the counselor is feeling.

Empty Chair

To help clients retrieve parts of themselves they are either unaware of or have denied, Gestalt therapists often give clients the opportunity to role-play the way they would like to behave toward another person (Greenberg, 1979). This is accomplished by asking them to picture that person sitting across from them in the empty chair. Clients are then asked to speak the part of the other person and, by moving back and forth from chair to chair, to carry on a dialogue with that person. In the case of a teenager who is upset with his mother, for instance, the counselor will ask him to respond from the

Don't worry about tomorrow; for tomorrow will worry about itself.
    —Matthew 6:34

perspective of his parent by physically moving to the designated chair, which contributes to his awareness that his mother may see things from a different perspective than he does. This technique can also be used when clients rehearse new roles that will be tried outside of the counseling session, in order to strengthen their belief that they can carry out the new behavior. This method is not recommended, however, for those who are severely disturbed emotionally (Bernard, 1986).

Making the Rounds

In group therapy Gestalt therapists often "make the rounds" of each member of the group, especially when a particular theme or feeling expressed by clients should be faced by every person. The client may say, for example, "Nobody understands me." The client is then encouraged to personalize this sentence by saying, "You don't understand me" to each person in the group, adding remarks about each group member as appropriate. This rounds exercise is flexible and may include nonverbal and positive feelings as well. By participating in it, clients become more aware than before of inner feelings.

Exaggeration

By heightening unwitting movements or gestures, clients can become more aware of the inner meaning of their behaviors. For example, the therapist may notice that every time a woman mentions her male friend she agitates her right foot. She, in turn, will be prompted to move her foot even faster, exaggerating the movement as if the foot had a life and voice of its own. In doing this, the client may begin to realize that this particular mannerism points to her frustration with her friend's behavior toward her. Exaggeration may also be used when clients offer a significant statement in a casual or feeble manner, indicating a lack of awareness of its importance. If they say mildly, "I'm angry with him," they would be asked to repeat the statement again and again with amplified movement, loudness, and emphasis. This helps clients achieve better contact with themselves.

Confrontation

At times the Gestalt therapist will point out incongruent behaviors and feelings to clients. For example, clients who report being happy about hearing seemingly satisfying personal news, but fail to smile while talking about it, are functioning incongruently. People who are happy typically express it, in part, through their smile. Confrontation involves asking clients *what* and *how* ques-

In Gestalt therapy
change is not planned,
programmed, or
coerced. It is allowed.
—William R. Passons

tions, such as: "What is happening within you that keeps
you from expressing your happiness with a smile?" *Why*
questions are avoided because they lead to an avoidance
of feeling, defensiveness, explanations, and intellectualization. According to Gestalt theory, trouble occurs because of an overdependency on intellectual experience
(Simkin, 1975).

May I Feed You a Sentence?

Sometimes implicit attitudes or messages are implied in what the client is
saying. In "may I feed you a sentence," the therapist asks if clients will repeat a certain sentence given by the counselor that attempts to make explicit
their underlying assumptions. In other words, the therapist proposes a sentence for clients "to try on for size." If the counselor is correct in interpreting the underlying message, clients will gain insight by rehearsing the
sentence.

10.3 | Common Gestalt Techniques

Gestalt counselors employ a wide assortment of powerful tools designed to increase
client awareness and help them "experience" rather than intellectualize. The following list shows several common techniques, along with the client behavior each
attempts to address (Passons, 1975).

CLIENT CONCERN OR DEFICIT	GESTALT VERBALIZATION
• Ambivalence toward a situation	Ask the client to omit qualifiers like "may" or "possibly."
• Not listening to self	Ask: "Are you listening to what you are saying?"
• Lack of experiencing own behavior	Ask questions of "How" and "What" rather than "Why."
• Distorted messages through question-asking	Say: "Please change the question to a statement."
• Improper word use	Have client change passive voice to active voice; change *need* to *want*; change *have to* to *choose to*; change *can't* to *won't*.
• Depersonalization of self	Have client change *we* to *I*; change *it* to *I*.
• Unaware of affect	Say: "Stay with that feeling."
• Unaware of reactions of others or self	Ask client to say: "I'm aware that I ____;" or "I'm aware that you ____."
• Unaware of *Now* experience or involvement	Ask: "What are you aware of now?"

APPLICATION

Gestalt therapy, with **adaptation** to particular situations, can be used among a wide variety of clinical populations. The following excerpt, from the pages of *Gestalt Therapy Verbatim* (Perls, 1969a), provides one of the best first-hand accounts of how Perls applied his theory in a "dream work seminar" with Beverly. Pay particular attention to how Perls probes her to externalize her feelings, to center herself, and to get in touch with the games or gimmicks she is using to hide behind.

BEVERLY: I guess I'm supposed to say something. I don't have any interesting dreams. Mine are sort of patent.

PERLS: Are you aware that you're defensive? . . . I didn't ask you in only to bring dreams.

BEVERLY: You asked for them last night and I was afraid that would disqualify me. If I could manufacture a few . . .

PERLS: Now you have a very interesting posture. The left leg supports the right leg, the right leg supports the right hand, the right hand supports the left hand.

BEVERLY: Yeah. It gives me something to hang onto. And with a lot of people out there you kind of get some stage fright. There are so many of them.

PERLS: You have stage fright and there are people outside. In other words you're on stage.

BEVERLY: Yeah, I suppose I feel that way.

PERLS: Well, what about getting in touch with your audience? . . .

BEVERLY: Well they look very good. They have wonderful faces.

PERLS: Tell this to them.

BEVERLY: You have very warm faces, very interested, very interesting . . . with— with a lot of warmth.

PERLS: So then shuttle back to your stage fright. What do you experience now?

BEVERLY: I don't have any more stage fright. But my husband doesn't look at me.

PERLS: So go back to your husband.

BEVERLY: You're the only one that looks self-conscious. Nobody else looks self-conscious at me. [*Laughter*] You sort of feel like you're up there don't you? Or sort of like your youngster's up there? . . . Now? [*From audience, yells*] Answer!

HUSBAND: She's the one who's up there, and she's trying to place me up there.

PERLS: [*To husband*] Yah. You've got to answer. [*To Beverly*] You have to know what I feel.

BEVERLY: Well, he doesn't usually answer. Did you want him out of character? [*Much laughter*]

PERLS: So, you are a clobberer.

BEVERLY: You need an ashtray.

PERLS: "I need an ashtray." [*Perls hold up his ashtray.*] She knows what *I* need. [*Laughter*]

BEVERLY: Oh, no—you have one. [*Laughter*]

PERLS: Now I get stage fright. [*Laughter*] I always have difficulties in dealing with "Jewish mothers." [*Laughter*]

BEVERLY: Don't you like "Jewish mothers"?

PERLS: Oh, I love them. Especially their matzo-ball soup. [*Laughter*]

BEVERLY: I'm not a gastronomical Jewish mother, just a Jewish mother. [*Chuckles*] I don't like gefilte fish either. I guess I'm a pretty obvious Jewish mother. Well that's not bad to be. That's all right. Matter of fact, that's good to be.

PERLS: What are your hands doing?

BEVERLY: Well, my thumbnails are pulling at each other.

PERLS: What are they doing to each other?

BEVERLY: Just playing. I do this often. See, I don't smoke, so what else are you gonna do with your hands? I doesn't look good to suck your thumbs.

PERLS: That's also the Jewish mother. She has reasons for everything. [*Laughter*]

BEVERLY: [*Jokingly*] And if I don't have one I'll make one up. [*Chuckles*] The ordered universe. What's wrong with being a Jewish mother?

PERLS: Did I say there's something wrong with a Jewish mother? I only say I have difficulties in dealing with them.

There is a famous story of a man who was such an excellent swordsman that he could hit even a raindrop, and when it was raining he used his sword instead of an umbrella. [*Laughter*] Now there are also intellectual and behavioristic swordsmen, who in answer to every question, statement, or whatever, hit it back. So whatever you do, immediately you are castrated or knocked out with some kind of replay— playing stupid or poor-me or whatever the games are. She's perfect.

BEVERLY: I never realized that.

PERLS: You see? Again the word. Playing stupid. I want once more to restate what I said earlier. Maturation is the transcendence from environmental support to self-support. The neurotic, instead of mobilizing his own resources, puts all his energy into manipulating the environment for support. And what you do is again and again manipulate me, you manipulate your husband, you manipulate everybody to come to the rescue of the "damsel in distress."

BEVERLY: How did I manipulate you?

PERLS: You see, again. This question, for instance. This is very important for maturation—change your questions to statements. Every question is a hook, and I would say that the majority of your questions are inventions to torture yourself and torture others. But if you change the question to a statement, you open up a lot of your background. This is one of the best means to develop a good intelligence. So change your question to a statement.

BEVERLY: Well, th—that implies that, ah, there's a fault to me. Didn't you intend it so? . . .

PERLS: Put Fritz in that chair and ask him that question.

BEVERLY: Don't you like Jewish mothers? Did you have one that you didn't like?

PERLS: Well, I like them. They're just a very difficult lot to deal with.

BEVERLY: Well, what makes them so difficult?

PERLS: Well, they're very dogmatic and very opinionated and inflexible and the box that they construct for themselves to grow in is a little narrower than man. They're less easy to therapize.

BEVERLY: Does everybody have to be subject to your therapy?

PERLS: No. [*Laughter*]

BEVERLY: [*To Perls*] Did you ever switch chairs like this with yourself?

PERLS: [*Laughing*] Oh yes—Oh! Even I get sucked in! [*Laughter*]

BEVERLY: You said you had problems with Jewish mothers. [*Laughter*]

HUSBAND: Do you understand now why I didn't answer? [*Laughter and applause*]

PERLS: That's right, because you see how a Jewish mother doesn't say "You need an ashtray." [*Laughter*] Okeh. Thank you.

Traditionally, Gestalt therapy has been considered most effective with anxious, phobic perfectionists and with depressed clients, those who are "overly socialized, restrained, constricted individuals" (Shepherd, 1970, pp. 243–245). However, current practice of Gestalt therapy includes treatment of a much wider range of problems (e.g., Bryant, Kessler, & Shirar, 1992; Dolliver, 1981; Jessee & Guerney, 1981; Kastner & Neumann, 1986; Lawe & Smith, 1986; Tyson & Range, 1987). Gestalt therapy has also been used for crisis intervention, adults in poverty programs, school problems, psychosomatic disorders, psychotics, multiple personality disorders, couples, and almost any group imaginable. Unfortunately the literature, while providing examples, provides little explication of necessary alteration in the focus of Gestalt therapy in these diverse settings.

CRITICAL ANALYSIS

One of the most appealing features of Gestalt therapy is its holistic emphasis on the integration of fragmented parts of the personality. By underscoring the importance of awareness, authenticity, confrontation, encounter, immediacy, personal responsibility and risk taking, Gestalt therapy, more than any other approach, stresses the unity of mind, body, and feelings.

Exploring inconsistencies between what is said and what is done has similarly opened up many untapped therapeutic avenues and reveals Gestalt therapy's unusually insightful analysis of the games we play in our interpersonal relationships. The methods of confronting and directly encountering "unfinished business" also hold equal intuitive appeal. While few therapists will go as far as does the Gestalt therapist to frustrate the neurosis, they generally agree that control issues are central to the process of change and healing. Many of us would rather "confirm our neuroses," Perls correctly observed, rather than confront our inevitable tendency to deny, distort, or disown parts of ourselves.

A significant concern over Gestalt therapy, however, is its questionable outcomes. Perls argued that persons are essentially organisms with strong needs, and in any given day the primary task is to see to it that these organismic needs are met. Meeting one's own current organismic needs in a constructive, creative, and healthy fashion is the ultimate goal of Gestalt therapy. The problem is that, depending on one's perspective, this could result in either greater self-integration or in hedonism. That is, it is a matter of intense debate as to whether or not Gestalt therapy is capable of leading to more responsible ethical and moral behavior in the larger social context. Since it is the view of Gestalt therapy that our wants and needs assume a position of absolute primacy, our accountability to others is inevitably of secondary importance. The fully functioning person is the one who is fully alive and aware, who meets his or her biological needs in an adult and responsible fashion, and who is not dependent on others to meet these needs. In short, the approach tends to glorify individuality, which can readily lead to a low estimation of the value of relationships. For the Gestalt therapist, self-sufficiency is the preeminent virtue.

> A Gestalt therapist does not use techniques; he applies himself in and to a situation with whatever professional skill and life experiences he has accumulated.
>
> —Laura Perls

Still others commonly raise questions, not about the games played by clients, but about those played by Gestalt therapists. Few counselors doubt that the techniques of Gestalt therapy are powerful tools, but they raise questions of possible misuse or abuse of these tools in a power game controlled by the therapist. The possibility for the counselor to enter into an unhealthy relationship of power with clients or to avoid dealing with his or her own countertransference problems seems inevitable. To be fair, this is a concern in all therapeutic approaches. The issue seems more glaring in the Gestalt approach, however, and it reminds clinicians of the importance of timing, tact, and sensitivity, as well as personal and professional competencies.

When Gestalt therapy turns its attention to the treatment of diverse populations, the approach offers some beneficial elements. To begin with, any activity that helps clients become more integrative can be employed in Gestalt therapy. Since this approach is not limited to a few techniques, it is flexible enough to dismantle cross-cultural barriers. In other words, its techniques can be customized in ways that a client can perceive and interpret from a distinct culture.

Unfortunately, therapists using Gestalt techniques with clients of other cultures must first consider the hazards that are bound to accompany its use. Some cultures, for example, are more emotionally reserved, and the intensity of Gestalt techniques is destined to lead, at best, to resistance and, at worst, to premature termination of therapy. Also, in some cultures that consider personal expression and public exposure to be disgraceful rather than cathartic, the Gestalt approach only increases a sense of shame and adds to an already heavy burden (McGoldrick, Pearce, & Giordano, 1982; Serok & Levi, 1993). The Gestalt approach, therefore, is only flexible within rather narrow parameters, which are defined by the confrontive role of the counselor, the intensity of the client's emotional experience in therapy, and the highly individualistic philosophy which the Gestalt approach encourages. Paradoxically, then, while the Gestalt therapist welcomes any techniques that heighten awareness and bring about wholeness, he or she may appear to hold in contempt any social system or lifestyle that does not open itself to doing so.

In treating clients with physical disabilities, Gestalt therapy is particularly useful for those who are in the denial or hostility phases of adaptation. By mildly confronting and clarifying inconsistencies and discrepancies between verbal and nonverbal messages and behaviors, for example, counselors can engage clients who deny the permanence or severity of disabilities such as spinal cord injuries. With this approach, clients may also be asked to project into the future their difficulties related to their disability, thereby allowing them to deal with their denial in a less threatening life context (Allen, 1985). For clients containing internalized anger, empty chair work or role playing can help them gain awareness of inner conflicts and of unfinished business, which may include a lost body part or function. Writing a farewell letter expressing grief, anger, and ambivalence toward the loss can also help clients to become more aware of inner conflicts and to assimilate and ultimately accept the new reality.

> Permit yourself to express with full emotional force all the kicking, pounding and screaming of a child's tantrum.
>
> —Fritz Perls

Like all approaches, Gestalt therapy has its advantages and disadvantages. One further critique needs to be addressed: Gestalt purists tend to be unconcerned with larger questions of meaning and purpose in life. Perhaps it is true that too many "why" questions, especially in the psychotherapeutic context, can be a means of avoiding more important issues, but this does not erase the fact that we have a compelling need to ask such questions. The ability to know, to properly understand, is at least as crucial as the imperative of Gestalt therapy to be fully alive, to living a life of integrity and value.

CURRENT STATUS

The impact of Gestalt therapy on the field of counseling has been significant. As an experiential therapy, it has provided a provocative challenge to earlier theoretical approaches such as psychoanalysis. The turbulence of the late 1960s and the early 1970s, with the focus of these years on "doing your own thing," welcomed Gestalt therapy with open arms, and the approach was propelled into widespread recognition. It can be said, however, that although Gestalt therapy captured the *zeitgeist*, the spirit of the age, it failed to take hold.

Nevertheless, though seldom recognized by academic psychologists, Perls's impact cannot be ignored. His contributions to the human growth and human potential movements in the United States are crucial. Thousands of people have participated in the workshops and seminars offered by more than 50 Gestalt training centers across the country. But the Perls era of Gestalt therapy is over, and few Gestalt "purists" remain. In a survey of a large sample of counseling psychologists (Watkins, Lopez, Campbell, & Himmell, 1986), for example, less than 5 percent of the participants claimed Gestalt therapy as either their primary or secondary theoretical orientation. Some argue that Gestalt therapy's decline in popularity is due, in part, to its lack of a research base. Gestalt therapy has never truly been supported by empirical study. Few outcome studies have been conducted to support its effectiveness, and it has not received the respect of academicians (Epstein, 1988; Simkin, 1978). Cadwallader (1981) argues, for example, that Perls and his followers have accepted emotion and intuition in the place of intellect.

> The dream is the royal road to awareness and integration.
> —Fritz Perls

Despite the waning popularity of Gestalt therapy, the Gestalt approach continues to influence the field of counseling. Many therapists from different theoretical modes use the techniques created by Perls and other Gestaltists (Burke, 1989). There are more than 60 Gestalt therapy institutes throughout the world, and the *Gestalt Journal* is devoted to publishing articles on Gestalt therapy. Although no national Gestalt therapy organization exists, the following institutes and training centers are among the most well-known:

Gestalt Institute of Cleveland
1588 Hazel Drive
Cleveland, OH 44106

Gestalt Training Center
P.O. Box 2189
La Jolla, CA 92038

Gestalt Therapy Institute of Los Angeles
620 Venice Boulevard
Venice, CA 90291

Gestalt Institute of San Francisco
1790 Union Street
San Francisco, CA 94123

New York Institute for Gestalt Therapy
7 West 96th Street
New York, NY 10025

Gestalt Institute of the Southwest
7700 Alabama Street
El Paso, TX 79904

SUMMARY

1. *Biography.* Frederick Perls (1893–1970) grew up as the only son in a German family. He was an unruly child but loved to read and was an excellent student. He earned his M.D. from Frederick Wilhelm University and soon joined the German army as a medic. After World War I, Perls began psychoanalytic training and eventually took a position in Frankfort working with Kurt Goldstein, who taught him to view the human being as a complete entity rather than the sum of its separate parts. During the 1930s Perls fled the Nazis, eventually emigrating to South Africa where he and his wife, Laura, built a strong practice. But it was after a meeting with Freud in 1936 that Perls moved to New York, where he founded the Institute for Gestalt Therapy and dedicated himself to proving Freud wrong.

2. *Historical Development.* The origins of Gestalt therapy are found in three Germans whose work Perls studied: Wertheimer, Koffka, and Köhler. Perls saw an individual's perceptions in terms of the Gestalt dichotomy of figure-ground and established his theory on that premise. Another important historical influence on Gestalt therapy was the existential movement in philosophy and psychology.

3. *View of Human Nature.* Perls believed that people develop in relation to their environment, and he divided this development into the social, psychophysical, and spiritual stages. His existential and humanistic perspective viewed people as self-directed; he believed they must take responsibility for their own lives. Gestaltists believe that a healthy personality is the result of a person's experiences forming a meaningful whole (i.e., gestalt). This occurs when there is a smooth transition between those sets of experiences that are immediately in the focus of awareness and those that lie in the background.

4. *Development of Maladaptive Behavior.* In Gestalt theory people develop maladaptive behavior, characterized by a lack of awareness, self-responsibility, contact with environment, and denial of needs, when they fail to use their own capacity for self-regulation and spend their energy on acting helpless, depending upon others, or manipulating the environment in countless ways. The result is an anxious state of temporal insecurity originating when the self is unable to determine the boundaries between the individual and the environment.

5. *Function of the Therapist.* The role of the Gestalt therapist is to serve as a catalyst for change without assuming the responsibility for change within the clients. As a result, the Gestalt therapist plays an active role that often frustrates the clients' demands for support and help, forcing them to rely on their own resources. The Gestalt therapist also views change through a paradoxical lens, holding that change takes place, not when one tries to be what one is not, but when one becomes what one is. Thus, to be authentic, the Gestalt therapist must try to be who he or she is at the moment rather than the goal of becoming a better therapist.

6. *Goals of Therapy.* Gestalt therapy tries to help individuals assume responsibility for themselves, rather than relying on others to make decisions for them. It tries to facilitate a process in which clients can become complete

and integrated, functioning as a systematic whole that consists of feelings, perceptions, thoughts, and a physical body whose processes cannot be divorced from its more psychological components. This goal is often reached through an "Aha!" experience, in which we suddenly see and understand what had long eluded us.

7. *Major Methods and Techniques.* Perls's work led him to identify many therapeutic techniques, all of which are experiential rather than verbal. Gestalt therapy is about doing rather than saying. After laying a foundation of general "rules" of therapy (e.g., communication is to be between equals in the present tense), a therapist may choose from a smorgasbord of methods: dream work, converting questions to statements, using personal pronouns, assuming responsibility, playing the projection, the empty chair, making the rounds, exaggeration, and confrontation.

8. *Application.* Perls often demonstrated his therapeutic approach in open workshop settings. In his work *Gestalt Therapy Verbatim,* he provides many first-hand accounts of how Gestalt therapy can be applied to a variety of situations. The case of "Beverly" is one example that illustrates just how Perls probed a client to encourage her to externalize feelings, to center herself, and to get in touch with the games or gimmicks behind which she was hiding.

9. *Critical Analysis.* Gestalt therapy features a holistic emphasis on the integration of fragmented parts of the personality. More than any other theory, it stresses the unity of mind, body, and feelings. It has enormous intuitive appeal, but its intended outcomes raise questions. With its strong emphasis on individuality, relationships are in danger of being relegated to a seconary status. The preeminent virtue is self-sufficiency. The Gestalt approach offers some benefits to cross-cultural counseling (e.g., its techniques can help dismantle some cross-cultural barriers) but also has many limitations (e.g., it can lead to resistance or greater shame). Nevertheless, in treating people with physical disabilities, Gestalt therapy has been found quite useful.

10. *Current Status.* As an experiential approach, Gestalt therapy has provided a provocative challenge to other theoretical approaches, but is it seldom recognized by academic psychology. In many respects, the Perls era of Gestalt therapy is over. Due in part to its lack of a research base, there are few Gestalt purists. Despite its waning popularity, however, the Gestalt approach continues to influence the field of counseling as its strategies are integrated into other approaches.

Key Terms

Acknowledgment Individuals discover themselves and develop a sense of self and appreciation through acknowledgment.

Adaptation In this process the individual discovers personal boundaries and differentiates self from nonself.

Aggression The organism's means of contacting its environment to satisfy its needs and of meeting resistance to the satisfaction of its needs. Its purpose is not destruction, but simply overcoming resistance.

Approbation A process through which people develop splits in their personalities and create a self-image (a notion of self based on external standards). Approbation interferes with the development of a sound and healthy notion of self.

Awareness The process of observing and attending to your thoughts, feelings, and actions, including body sensations as well as visual and auditory perceptions. It is seen as a flowing panorama that constitutes your "now" experience.

Closure The Gestalt concept that the mind synthesizes the missing parts of a perceived image and, in effect, closes the gap between the reality and the desired "picture."

Figure That which occupies the center of a person's attentive awareness; that which now commands a person's attention.

Gestalt German word meaning shape, figure, configuration, totality, or whole.

Gestalt psychology An approach that focuses on the dynamic organization of experience into patterns of configurations. This viewpoint came into prominence as a revolt against structuralism, which analyzed experience into static, atomistic sensations, and also against the equally atomistic approach of behaviorism, which dissected complex behavior into elementary conditioned reflexes.

Ground The part of the perceptual field that is not "figure" is identified as ground. Taken together, figure and ground constitute a gestalt.

Here and now An emphasis on understanding present feelings as they occur in an ongoing treatment, with little or no emphasis on past experience.

Homeostasis The tendency for living organisms to find equilibrium or balance between themselves and their surrounding environment.

Impasse The situation in which progress in the treatment process has ceased, and failure is imminent. This situation occurs when further insight is not forthcoming or when the process is blocked by extreme resistance.

Introjection The uncritical acceptance of other people's concepts, standards of behavior, and values. The person who habitually introjects does not develop his or her own personality.

Organismic self-regulation The process by which an individual, confronted by either an external demand or an internal need, strives to reduce tension by maintaining the organismic balance between demands and needs.

Projection The process by which the individual places in the outside world the parts of the personality that the organism refused (or is unable) to identify.

Proximity The Gestalt principle that states that objects or stimuli that are close together will be perceived as a unity. For example, a series of unconnected lines in a neon sign become a word or sentence.

Retroflection The process by which some function that was originally directed from the individual toward the world changes direction and is bent back towards the originator. The result is a split between the self as doer and the self as receiver.

Self The creative process that leads the person to actualizing behaviors by responding to emergent needs and environmental pressures. The fundamental characteristic of the self is the formation and distinction of gestures.

Self-image The part of the personality that hinders creative growth by imposing external standards.

Similarity When stimuli in the perceptual field causes us to group similar things together.

Suggested Reading

James, M., & Jongeward, D. (1971). *Born to win: Transactional analysis with Gestalt experiments*. Reading, MA: Addison-Wesley.

Korb, M. P., Gorrell, J., & Ban De Reit, V. (1989). *Gestalt Therapy: Practice and Theory* (2nd Ed.). New York: Pergamon Press.

Latner, J. (1973). *The Gestalt therapy book*. New York: Bantam.

Passons, W. R. (1975). *Gestalt approaches in counseling*. New York: Holt, Rinehart & Winston.

Perls, F. (1969). *Gestalt therapy verbatim*. Moab, UT: Real People Press.

Perls, F. (1969). *In and out of the garbage pail*. Moab, UT: Real People Press.

Van Diert, V., and Korb, M. (1980). *Gestalt therapy: An introduction*. New York: Pergamon Press.

References

Allen, H. A. (1985). The Gestalt perspective. *Journal of Applied Rehabilitation Counseling, 16,* 21–25.

Banks, W. P., & Krajicek, D. (1991). Perception. *Annual Review of Psychology, 42,* 305–331.

Bernard, J. M. (1986). Laura Perls: From ground to figure. *Journal of Counseling and Development, 64,* 367–373.

Burke, J. F. (1989). *Contemporary approaches to psychotherapy & counseling: The self-regulation and maturity model.* Pacific Grove, CA: Brooks/Cole.

Bryant, D., Kessler, J., & Shirar, L. (1992). *The family inside: Working with the multiple.* New York: W. W. Norton.

Cadwallader, E. H. (1981). Values in Fritz Perls' Gestalt therapy: On the dangers of half-truths. *Counseling and Values, 28,* 192–201.

Covin, A. B. (1977). Using Gestalt psychodrama experiments in rehabilitation counseling. *Personnel and Guidance Journal, 56,* 143–147.

Dolliver, R. H. (1981). Some limitations in Perls' Gestalt therapy. *Psychotherapy, Research and Practice, 8,* 38–45.

Dolliver, R. H. (1991). Perls with Gloria re-reviewed: Gestalt techniques and Perls's practices. *Journal of Counseling and Development, 69,* 299–304.

Dolliver, R. H., Williams, E. L., & Gold, D. C. (1980). The art of Gestalt therapy or "What are you doing with your feet now?" *Psychotherapy: Theory, Research and Practice, 17,* 136–140; 142.

Epstein, W. (1988). Has the time come to reha-
bilitate Gestalt theory? *Psychological Research, 50*, 2–5.

Fagan, J. (1970). The task of the therapist. In J.
Fagan & I. L. Shepherd (Eds.), *Gestalt
therapy now*. Palo Alto, CA: Science and
Behavior Books.

Graumann, C. F. (1989). Gestalt in social
psychology. *Psychological Research, 51*,
75–79.

Greenberg, L. S. (1979). Resolving splits: Use of
the two chair technique. *Psychotherapy:
Theory, Research and Practice, 16*,
316–324.

Harman, R. L. (1975). A Gestalt point of view
on facilitating growth in counseling. *Personnel and Guidance Journal, 53*,
363–366.

Hycner, R. (1987). An interview with Erving
and Miriam Polster. *The Gestalt Journal,
10*(2), 27–66.

Jessee, R. E., & Guerney, B. G. (1981). A comparison of Gestalt and relationship enhancement treatments with married
couples. *American Journal of Family
Therapy, 9*, 31–41.

Jourard, S. (1964). *The transparent self*. Princeton, NJ: D. Van Nostrand.

Kastner, M., & Neumann, M. A. (1986). A
model combining two psychotherapeutic
approaches in group psychotherapy. *Psychotherapy, 23*, 593–597.

Kempler, W. (1973). Gestalt therapy. In R.
Corsini (Ed.), *Current psychotherapies*
(pp. 251–286). Itasca, IL: F. E. Peacock.

Köhler, W. (1973). *The mentality of apes* (2nd
ed.) (E. Winter, Trans.). New York: Harcourt Brace & World. (Original work
published 1927).

Korb, M. P., Gorrell, J., & Van De Riet, V.
(1989). *Gestalt therapy: Practice and theory* (2nd ed.). New York: Pergamon Press.

Latner, J. (1973). *The Gestalt therapy book*.
New York: Bantam Books.

Lawe, C. F., & Smith, E. W. (1986). Gestalt
processes and family therapy. *Individual
Psychology, 42*, 537–544.

Levitsky, A., & Perls, F. S. (1970). The rules
and games of Gestalt therapy. In J. Fagan
& I. L. Shepherd (Eds.), *Gestalt therapy
now*. Palo Alto, CA: Science and Behavior Books.

Litt, S. (1978). Fritz Perls and Gestalt therapy.
American Psychologist, 33, 958–959.

Little, L. F. (1986). Gestalt therapy with parents
when a child is presented as the problem.
Family Relations, 35, 489–496.

McClure, B. A., Merrill, E., & Russo, T. R.
(1994). Seeing clients with an artist's eye:
Perceptual simulation exercises. *Simulation and Gaming, 25*, 51–60.

McGoldrick, M., Pearce, J. K., & Giordano, J.
(1982). *Ethnicity and family therapy*. New
York: Guilford.

Naranjo, C. (1970). Present-centerdness: Technique, prescription, and ideal. In J. Fagan
& I. Shepherd (Eds.), *Gestalt therapy
now*. Palo Alto, CA: Science and Behavior
Books.

Osborn, D. (1991). A return to Piaget: Guidelines for counselors. *TACD Journal, 19*,
13–19.

Passons, W. R. (1975). *Gestalt approaches in
counseling*. New York: Holt, Rinehart and
Winston.

Perls, F. S. (1969a). *Gestalt therapy verbatim*.
Moab, UT: Real People Press.

Perls, F. S. (1969b). *In and out of the garbage
pail*. Moab, UT: Real People Press.

Perls, F. S. (1970). Four lectures. In J. Fagan &
I. L. Shepherd (Eds.), *Gestalt therapy now*.
Palo Alto, CA: Science and Behavior
Books.

Perls, F. S. (1976). *The Gestalt approach and
eye witness to therapy*. New York: Bantam
Books.

Perls, F. S., Hefferline, R. F., & Goodman, P.
(1972). *Gestalt therapy: Excitement and
growth in the human personality*. New
York: Souvenir Press.

Phares, E. J. (1988). *Clinical psychology: Concepts, methods, and profession* (3rd ed.).
Pacific Grove, CA: Brooks/Cole.

Prochaska, J. O. (1979). *Systems of psychotherapy: A transtheoretical analysis*.
Homewood, IL: Dorsey Press.

Rice, L. N., & Greenberg, L. S. (1992). Humanistic approaches to psychotherapy. In
D. K. Freedheim (Ed.), *History of psychotherapy: A century of change*. Washington, DC: American Psychological
Association.

Rock, I., & Palmer, S. (1990, December). The
legacy of Gestalt psychology. *Scientific
American*, 84–90.

Saariluoma, P. (1992). Do visual images have
Gestalt properties? *Quarterly Journal of
Experimental Psychology, 45*, 399–420.

Sarris, V. (1989). Max Wertheimer on seen motion: Theory and evidence. *Psychological Research 51*, 58–68.

Serok, S., & Levi, N. (1993). Application of Gestalt therapy with long-term prison inmates in Israel. *Gestalt Journal, 16*, 105–127.

Shepherd, I. L. (1970). Limitations and cautions in the Gestalt approach. In J. Fagan & I. L. Shepherd (Eds.), *Gestalt therapy now* (pp. 234–238). Palo Alto, CA: Science and Behavior Books.

Shostrom, E. L. (Producer). (1965). *Three approaches to psychotherapy: Part 2. Frederick Perls* [Film]. Orange, CA: Psychological Films.

Simkin, J. S. (1975). An introduction to Gestalt therapy. In F. D. Stephenson (Ed.), *Gestalt therapy primer*. Springfield, IL: Thomas.

Simkin, J. S. (1978). Gestalt therapy and the psychological abstracts. *American Psychologist, 33*, 705–706.

Thompson, C. D., & Rudolph, L. B. (1988). *Counseling children* (2nd ed.). Pacific Grove, CA: Brooks/Cole.

Tyson, G. M., & Range, L. M. (1987). Gestalt dialogues as a treatment for mild depression: Time works just as well. *Journal for Clinical Psychology, 43*(2), 227–231.

Wallen, R. (1970). Gestalt therapy and Gestalt psychology. In J. Fagan and I. L. Shepherd (Eds.), *Gestalt therapy now*. Palo Alto, CA: Science and Behavior Books.

Watkins, C. E., Lopez, F. G., Campbell, V. L., & Himmell, C. D. (1986). Contemporary counseling psychology: The results of a national survey. *Journal of Counseling Psychology, 33*, 301–309.

Yontef, G. M. (1982). Gestalt therapy: Its inheritance from Gestalt psychology. *Gestalt Theory, 4*, 23–39.

Yontef, G. M., & Simkin, J. S. (1989). Gestalt therapy. In R. J. Corsini & D. Wedding (Eds.), *Current psychotherapies*. Itasca, IL: F. E. Peacock.

Yontef, G. M., & Simkin, J. S. (2000). Gestalt therapy, In Corsini, R. J. & Wedding, D. Current psychotherapies, Itasca, IL: F. E. Peacock.

Zinker, J. (1978). *Creative process in Gestalt therapy*. New York: Random House.

There is no hope for the human race, but there is hope for individual members of it. —**Eric Berne**

11 CHAPTER | **Transactional Analysis**

During a single day, each of us negotiates our way through a myriad of interactions. Some negotiations are instantaneous, like greeting the doorman, who returns the civility with a nod of recognition, and some negotiations, such as a first date or a request for a raise, have higher stakes and are more carefully sculpted. Daily life is a series of such negotiations.

These commonplace interactions are the concern of transactional analysis. Developing a language that is neither couched in theoretical concerns nor veiled in obtuse terminology, or TA as it is commonly called, seeks to take the mystery out of counseling. Indeed, the basic ideas of TA have long been accessible to the general public through two landmark books that remained on the national best-seller list for more than a year: Eric Berne's *Games People Play* and Thomas A. Harris's *I'm OK—You're OK*.

BRIEF BIOGRAPHY

Born in Montreal, Quebec, in 1910, as a young lad Eric Lennard Bernstein often accompanied his father, a general practitioner of medicine, on his house calls. Eric admired his father's devotion to his patients and his lack of concern for money. Unfortunately, his father died at the age of 38, when Eric was barely nine years old. Eric's desire to help others was born of his admiration for his father and nurtured on the memory of his happy relationship with him. Eric dedicated his first book to his father with these words: "He lived in dignified poverty as a country physician." As an adult, Eric inscribed an epigraph on his father's grave that read, "David Hillel Bernstein, M.D., a humane and conscientious physician. . . . He loved his neighbor as himself and did no wrong." Fortunately, Eric's mother was a professional writer and editor, and she supported Eric and his younger and only sister after their father's death.

Inspired by the memory of his father, Eric followed his footsteps through medical school at McGill University, receiving his M.D. in 1935. Eric soon married his first of three wives, became a U.S. citizen, and, in an accommodation to anti-Semitism, dropped the Lennard from his name and shortened Bernstein to Berne.

After his psychiatric residency at Yale University School of Medicine, Berne began psychoanalytic training at the New York Psychoanalytic Institute, a traditional Freudian stronghold that taught classical methods. His training, however, was cut short by World War II, which sent Berne to the U.S. Army Medical Corps in 1941, where he practiced medical psychiatry in several military hospitals.

After his discharge from the Army in 1946, Berne settled at the Veterans Administration Hospital in San Francisco and soon established a private practice in Carmel, California. It was there that he separated from his first wife and completed his first work, *The Mind in Action* (1947). He also resumed psychoanalytic training at the San Francisco Psychoanalytic Institute under Eric Erikson, who insisted that Berne not remarry until after the analysis was finished. Berne obliged, but did remarry in 1949 and fathered two children, as in his first marriage.

For more than 15 years, Berne pursued credentialing as a psychoanalyst without ever achieving official recognition. Indeed, he was humiliated and devastated when the San Francisco Institute said he was not yet ready and would need at least three or four years of further personal analysis and training. This rejection propelled him into the development of his own orientation to psychotherapy. Turning his back on the obtuseness that seemed to be endemic in the classical method, Berne sought a more "rational" approach to therapy. He turned to the experiences he used in conducting group therapy during the war and gravitated toward a common-sense style, which characterizes his approach (Steiner, 1974).

Eric Berne was single-minded and passionate in his vision for a new form of psychotherapy. Although he published many articles and monographs, he continued to insist that "there is only one paper to write which is called 'How to Cure Patients'—that's the only paper that's really worth writing if you're really going to do your job."

Berne built a study in his house away from the noise of his children. In 1950 he imposed a demanding schedule on himself, typically beginning on Monday and concluding on Sunday, which he followed until his death. Biographers describe him as indefatigable (Cheney, 1971). Most of his productive life he practiced in his two offices in Carmel and in San Francisco. His schedule was controlled and predictable: on Monday mornings he saw patients in Carmel; Tuesdays he counseled in San Francisco; Wednesdays he lectured at the University of California School of Medicine; Thursdays he was at Stanford or working with private clients or, later in the day, conducting a TA seminar in Monterey; and on Fridays he wrote, after which there was the inevitable game of poker in the evening. Weekends were devoted to more writing.

> I'm a head mechanic—that's all I am.
> —Eric Berne

After a second divorce in 1964, Berne increased his writing time. Friends attributed the early wreck of his third marriage, and perhaps his untimely death at age 60, to his frenetic work habits. At the time of his death, Berne was working on six different books. In fact, he called for page proofs and worked on them for three hours the day before suffering a fatal heart attack in 1970.

HISTORICAL DEVELOPMENT

Berne's long association with psychoanalysis helped form the ideas that eventually became Transactional Analysis. While Berne denied any intentional borrowing from Freud, he admitted to thinking of psychoanalysis as "the core and transactional analysis as the apple" (Holland, 1973, p. 354).

But the roots of TA extend beyond its Freudian soil. Roots may also be found, for example, at McGill University in the neurological research on the brain conducted by Dr. Wilder Penfield. It was he who taught Berne (1952) that there is a neurological basis for the assumption that people exist in different ego states simultaneously and that these states are connected to memories. Alfred Adler, whose lifestyle so closely parallels Berne's own script, also influenced

Berne's theorizing (Simoneux, 1977). Berne's concern with feeling "not-OK" is strikingly similar to Adler's concept of feeling inferior. And when he turned to Carl Rogers, of course, Berne found a colleague who also rejected the Freudian diagnostic model and accepted the client as a problem-solving person. These assorted influences—Freud, Adler, and Rogers—were mixed, merged, and synthesized into transactional analysis.

Although Berne's first paper on TA was published in 1957, it took several years before the movement achieved public recognition. From the beginning, however, Berne strove to make his theory accessible. He wanted nothing to do with fancy language or "jazz," as he called it. After listening patiently to an elaborate report studded with jargon, Berne would often say, "That is all well and good. All I know is the patient is not getting cured" (Steiner, 1974, p. 14). At his seminars he banned theoretical jargon, which he labeled "bright ideas," polysyllabic vocabulary ("glossing over"), and hypothetical examples ("distractions"). He preferred short words, short sentences, short meetings, short presentations— and, partly in reaction to his long years of psychoanalysis, short cures.

Dusay (1977) describes the formulation of TA as proceeding through four successive phases. In the first phase (1955–1962), influenced by his clients' descriptions of behaving as a child, as a parent, and as an adult, Berne developed the concept of ego states. In the second phase (1962–1966), he concentrated on ideas about transactions and games. During this period the International Transactional Analysis Association was created (1964), and Berne published the best-seller *Games People Play*. In the third phase (1966–1970), Berne explored the reasons some individuals choose to play certain games in life; and in the fourth phase (from 1970), he studied action and energy distribution.

TA was the first therapy the lay public could understand. People soon began talking about "Child," "Parent," and "Adult" and about "games" and "scripts" as they described themselves in relationships. The diagrams, circles, and arrows that Berne used to explain interactions between people became increasingly commonplace in counseling offices, classrooms, management seminars, even Sunday School classes (Burke, 1989; Jongeward, 1973; Oden, 1974), and TA enjoyed wide appeal and great popularity. Unlike other casualties of the 1960s and 1970s, however, it has managed to survive its popularity and, in combination with other techniques, it is still considered a significant approach to counseling and psychotherapy.

VIEW OF HUMAN NATURE

Berne believed that basic psychological hungers motivate people to transcend patterns of behavior that begin early in life. "People are born princes and princesses and then their parents kiss them and turn them into frogs" (Steiner, 1974, p. 2), he once wrote. According to Berne, we transcend or overcome our "froggyness" by means of basic psychological hungers, especially by three fundamental needs: stimulus hunger, structure hunger, and position hunger.

Stimulus hunger is the need to be acknowledged or affirmed by others both psychologically and physically. Berne believed all persons have this basic need to be recognized, this need to receive **strokes,** whether positive (e.g., a smile) or negative (e.g., a frown). So powerful is the need for these strokes, which he described as basic units of social interaction essential for life, that individuals deprived of positive reinforcement will actually seek **negative strokes** (Wollams & Brown, 1979). A child who misbehaves, for example, in order to receive the attention of parents may be punished, but he or she is still receiving strokes. Such strokes result in the collection of either good or bad feelings, which Berne called **stamps,** which can be cashed in when enough of them are collected. Individuals might collect enough bad feelings from failing grades, for instance, to justify their quitting school, or enough **positive strokes** about studying hard to take time off to attend a party (Gladding, 1992).

> Of all those who preceded TA, Alfred Adler comes the closest to talking like a script analyst.
>
> —Eric Berne

   Structure hunger refers to how we maximize the number of strokes we receive. The question "What do you say after you say hello?" distills Berne's thoughts about how we use time to maximize the number of strokes we receive. Berne (1972) identifies several options. Some individuals will withdraw, escaping into the safety of the self to avoid risk. The most restrictive and least rewarding way to structure time, in this mode of withdrawal it is necessary to live on "stored" strokes or to fantasize "artificial" strokes. Others engage in so-called **rituals** and **pastimes,** interactions based on greetings, pleasantries, and other low-risk, non-involving social conversations (e.g., "How are you?" "I'm fine, thanks"). While these rituals provide some strokes, the yield is low. Still others will take up **activities,** time structured in terms of goals, work, and hobbies that typically bring strokes from others. And still others play **games,** which are interactions based on unwritten rules designed to create payoff. Usually covert and dishonest, these games typically generate negative payoffs, and Berne considered them to be the most common disturbance factor in interpersonal behavior. In contrast, **intimacy** is a method of structuring designed to bring people together. Based on honest, open mutual relationships, such intimacy is as a result both the most risky and the most rewarding approach to increasing strokes.

   Position hunger is the need to have our fundamental decisions about life validated and affirmed—to be told, as Berne put it, that we're either OK or not OK. It is a reflection of intrinsic self-worth. Early in life one makes basic decisions about the self: "I'm OK" or "I'm not OK." Once this decision about the self has been made, it provides a script for the ways in which a person structures time and seeks strokes.

Structure of Personality

According to Berne and his followers, personality is composed of three conscious or preconscious **ego states:** the Parent, the Adult, and the Child (Figure 11.1). Each ego state is an organized psychological system of feelings, thoughts, and behaviors (Drego, 1993), and each is distinct and mutually exclusive (Figure 11.1).

   The **Parent ego** is the tape-recorder-like composite of childhood memories, an audible record of how parents and significant others—parents and parent

Figure 11.1 | Ego States

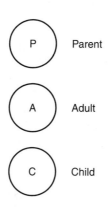

substitutes—acted, thought, and felt about us in childhood. This mind-set is filled with values, injunctions, shoulds, oughts, and behaviors the individual has internalized from significant others during childhood. Under the influence of such prohibitions, permissions, and nurturing messages, people behave as they believe their parents would want them to behave. Depending on the kinds of messages that the Parent has internalized, then, the Parent ego can be subdivided into the **Nurturing Parent,** the composite of messages that were loving, supportive, and accepting, and the **Critical Parent,** the composite of messages that were rejecting, controlling, and judgmental.

> Maybe the reason people go into psychiatry is that they are not required to do very much except to have staff conferences to explain why they can't do very much.
>
> —Eric Berne

The second ego state, the **Adult ego,** is the computer-like processor of information from both the other two ego states as well as the external world. It acts to regulate the activities of the Child and Parent, mediating between them. Since its function is to test reality and since it is focused on data processing, probability estimating, and decision making, it does not deal with feelings but with facts. In fact, the Adult ego state is void of feelings. Its ultimate function is to present situations in an organized and intelligent way.

A further distinction between the Adult state and those of the Parent and Child is that only in the Adult state do we possess a kind of "psychic energy" that Berne labeled **free energy.** This free energy is willed and deliberately enacted. Usually the Adult is thought of as a reservoir of free energy, while the Parent and the Child are composed of so-called **unbound energy,** which is active but expressed without conscious choice and is therefore not under deliberate control. Another state of psychic energy, according to Berne, is **bound energy,** which holds the potential for activity (i.e., it is available) but inactive (Shapiro, 1969).

The third ego state, that of the **Child**—the "child-within"—is the little boy or girl portion of us that never grows up. This ego state is not about being childish, but about being childlike: about the fun-loving part of most individuals that is alternately inquisitive, affectionate, selfish, mean, playful, whiny, and manipulative. The Child ego state, which typically emerges in response to a communication from a Parent ego state (Clark, 1991), functions in two distinct forms. The **Natural Child** (or *Free Child*) strives for total freedom to do whatever it wants whenever it wants—to be loving, affectionate, creative, aggressive, rebellious, or spontaneous. An uninhibited responder to the world, the Natural Child can also be intuitive and sensitive to nonverbal messages.

On the other hand, the **Adapted Child** denies or ignores its own instincts and tries desperately to please parents by conforming to their demands. It uses compliance and procrastination to deal with feelings that will prevent reprimand from the Parent. As a result, the Adapted Child duplicates the original reactions individuals have toward parents during childhood, including such feelings as guilt, fear, anger, and frustration. Negotiating between the Natural Child and the Adapted Child is the emerging Adult in the Child, called the **Little Professor.** This childlike parallel to the Adult ego state is the source of intuition, creativity, and manipulation.

Gladding (1992) points out that these several ego states function simultaneously. He provides the example of a woman who observes an attractive man and goes through the following self-dialogue: "He is really good looking and well spoken [Adult], but he's probably stuck up [Critical Parent], although I've heard he's very sensitive [Nurturing Parent]. I wonder how I could attract him and get him to notice me [Natural Child]. I had better stop looking and get back to work or my boss will get mad at me [Adaptive Child]" (p. 126).

Although TA does not favor one ego state over another, the theory stresses the importance of being able to balance responses appropriately. TA also proposes that people are generally in one ego state or another. This functioning ego state can be identified by the content and expressions (especially nonverbal) of what we think, feel, say, and do.

Students often compare TA ego states with the three Freudian psychic structures: the id being the Child; the ego, the Adult; the superego, the Parent. But Berne believed that all three structures are intrinsic to the ego and that, while Freud deemed only the ego to be conscious, all three ego states are conscious or potentially so. While it may be initially tempting to compare Freud's and Berne's three-part concept, the overlap is not accurate (see Figure 11.2).

Figure 11.2 | Freud's Psychic Structure vs. TA Ego States

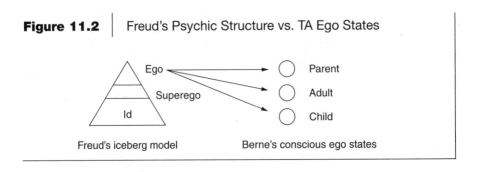

DEVELOPMENT OF MALADAPTIVE BEHAVIOR

Maladaptive behavior, according to Berne, is the result of confused ego states. This confusion occurs when a person vacillates between ego states without completing their transaction. When a young man is ineffective in maintaining a romantic relationship (an Adult function) because of lapses into inappropriate humor during potential times for romance (the Child), he is experiencing fuzzy ego boundaries and is blocking the free-flowing interaction among ego states. This person suffers from a *boundary problem*.

Blocking, Contamination, and Exclusion

The two major boundary problems in TA are blocking and contamination. **Blocking** occurs when too much unbound or active energy is located in the Parent and/or Child, and the boundaries among ego states are too rigid and impermeable to deal with this excess energy (Figure 11.3).

Blocking can lead to a dissociated condition in which individuals feel estranged from themselves, out of control. "I feel as though I'm in a dream," they may say, or "I feel that I'm doing this mechanically." When such a blocking of ego states occurs, people may seem peculiar and behave inappropriately. People who compulsively clean, for example, may be blocking the free energy of the Adult ego state. As a result they are tirelessly propelled by the unbound energy of their Parent. In its extreme form, blocking may lead to multiple personality disorder, in which the individual assumes alternate personalities, such as those of Dr. Jekyll and Mr. Hyde.

Contamination, on the other hand, occurs when one's boundaries break down, when they become too labile, too permeable to the unbound energy of the Parent and/or Child. The ego states invade and take command of each other and thereby create confusion—just the opposite of blocking (Figure 11.4). When the Parent takes over the Adult's rationality and judgment, for instance, the individual becomes highly legalistic and judgmental (Critical Parent). A Child contamination occurs when past experiences are incorrectly identified as

Figure 11.3 | Blocking

Figure 11.4 | Contamination

Contamination is the result of permeable ego boundaries

current reality ("I'm a klutz"). A double contamination has occurred when the beliefs of the Parent ("everyone is bad") and the experiences of the Child ("I feel bad") invade the ego state of the Adult ("I am bad"). This may be the most common form of ego contamination (Shilling, 1984).

Exclusion takes place when one or two ego states dominate a personality. While the constant Parent will be directive and authoritarian, for instance, the constant Adult may be devoid of feeling, and the constant Child will only want to play and to entertain others. It must be remembered, however, that no exclusion is total. The degree of intensity varies in time and place.

Games

In addition to boundary problems, maladaptive behavior can result from "the games people play." Berne used the term *game* because it suggests the idea of a contest that involves players, rules, moves, and predictable outcomes. Berne (1967, p. 125) defined a psychological game as a "recurring set of transactions, often repetitive, superficially rational, with a concealed motivation; or more colloquially, a series of transactions with a gimmick." On the surface, games appear to be **complementary transactions,** but they have a concealed motivation. The actual message of these games is an **ulterior transaction,** and its real motivation is the predictable payoff or "gimmick" with which it concludes (Goldhaber & Goldhaber, 1976; Summerton, 1992).

This game playing is anything but enjoyable; it is serious and tragic. Games are not played for recreation; they are played compulsively over and over again. Every game, according to Berne (1964, p. 48), is "basically dishonest, and the outcome has a dramatic, as distinct from merely exciting, quality." Games occur when persons turn to others for confirmation of their negative, "not OK" position, and the result is the avoidance of intimacy.

While intimacy is immensely rewarding, the difficulty is that it is spontaneous and thus involves considerable risks. It can be quite threatening. Since predictability outweighs the rewards of the risk, we settle for a lesser reward to be certain of achieving it. Rather than allowing unpredictable intimacy to occur, some people predetermine the outcome of their transactions by engaging in ulterior and crossed transactions, which ensure a predictable outcome. As the saying

> Information is of no value for its own sake, but only because of its personal significance.
> —Eric Berne

goes, a bird in the hand is worth two in the bush. For these people, it is better to be negatively discounted than to take the risk of not counting at all. This overwhelming fear of not being recognized or acknowledged by others leads people to the pain and isolation of playing games.

Berne has analyzed numerous interaction games and, in his customary fashion, has labeled them with commonsense, straightforward names. One of the most common games people play is "Why Don't You—Yes But." It is typically played like this:

A: "My husband always insists on doing our own repairs, and he never does anything right."

B: "Why doesn't he take a course in carpentry?"

A: "Yes, but he doesn't have the time."

B: "Why don't you buy him some good tools?"

A: "Yes, but he doesn't know how to use them."

B: "Why don't you have your building done by a carpenter?"

A: "Yes, but that would cost too much."

B: "Why don't you just accept what he does the way he does it?"

A: "Yes, but the whole thing might fall down."

Good players of "Why Don't You—Yes But" are able to wear people down. They give up because there is always one more problem, one more rejoinder.

Among other popular games that Berne describes is "Seduction," which is played by a male and female who flirt with each other until one turns down the other, leaving both feeling slightly uncomfortable. "Uproar" is played by two persons who get increasingly angry until one or both cries "uproar." Although the game could have been stopped at any time by either player, the fracas continues with increasing decibels of sound until it finally ends in an uproar. Another game, called "Cops and Robbers," is played by those who dare people in authority to catch them, although the players leave clues about where they can be found. In a game called "Blemish," players do not feel comfortable with a new person until they have found his or her imperfection or foible, which can be as trivial as a style of dress. And individuals whose chief preoccupation is with the question "How will I look?" often play the game "Look How Hard I Tried." If they are late, for example, they will take pains to arrive out of breath with a story that justifies their lateness.

People play these kinds of games with different degrees of vigor. Berne (1964) lists three levels of intensity: first degree games are socially acceptable; second degree games leave no permanent scars and the players would rather conceal the consequences; while third degree games, which are played for high stakes, usually lead to the emergency room, the courtroom, or the morgue.

Rackets

Each of us assumes a life position regarding our own OKness and the OKness of others. As another means of convincing themselves that they are "not OK" and to justify their never taking risks with real intimacy, people often develop habitual ways of feeling that Berne called **rackets.** Originating in the experiences we had growing up as children, these rackets are the unpleasant chronic feelings we hold on to after game playing. They are the feelings we get from the strokes we received when we acted in certain ways and observed how our parents responded. Eventually, these feelings become a basic part of our life script, a veritable collection of rackets: the guilt racket, the depression racket, the worry racket, to name a few. Of course, these habitual feelings are inauthentic—that is, they are wholly unrelated to reality as currently experienced.

> Was it a friend or foe that spread these lies? Nay, who but infants question in such wise? 'Twas one of my most intimate enemies.
>
> —Dante Gabriel Rossetti

Injunctions

Injunctions can also contribute significantly to maladaptive behavior. Typically the signals that children pick up from their parents' internal Child are "don't" messages that tell children what they need to do to be recognized. Since these messages stem from the parents' own anxiety, frustration, and unhappiness, they are often nonverbal, usually inferred from observation, but nonetheless powerful. According to Mary Goulding (1987), we decide as children to accept certain injunctions or to challenge them. The basic list of common injunctions (Goulding, 1987; Goulding & Goulding, 1979) include: don't be, don't succeed, don't be you, don't be sane, don't be well, don't belong. When children decide to accept them, these injunctions result in patterns of maladaptive behavior. But with help, these injunctions can be identified and rejected.

FUNCTION OF THE THERAPIST

The TA counselor works at being a catalyst for enabling clients to mobilize their resources (Dusay & Dusay, 1989). Acting very much like a "teacher, trainer, and resource person with heavy emphasis on involvement" (Harris, 1967, p. 239), the therapist explains key concepts such as structural analysis, transactional analysis, script analysis, and game analysis. In addition the counselor employs various techniques to help clients make full and effective use of all three ego states and to live game-free lives with intimate, rewarding relationships.

The TA therapist takes a significant amount of time to do both structural and transactional analysis. **Structural analysis** involves recognizing the influence of each ego state on thinking and behaving, so that people who are psychologically healthy can activate any one of the ego states whenever it is deemed appropriate. By identifying which ego state is in power at any given point in time, we are better able to understand our own behavior and the behavior of others (George & Cristiani, 1990; Knox & Lichtenberg, 1991).

But transactions are units of social action as well (Berne, 1963), and **transactional analysis** is concerned with diagnosing ego states that emerge in a social interchange. TA therapists explore three kinds of transactions. The first of these, **complementary transactions,** occur when the lines of communication are parallel. An example of a complementary transaction is when one person encounters another and provides a *transactional stimulus*—an opening statement—from the Adult ego state and the listener responds with an appropriate reply also from the Adult state.In the terminology of TA, this reply is known as a *transactional response.* The key to such transactions is that the transactional response be appropriate, whether Adult to Adult or Parent to Child and then Child to Parent. As long as transactions are complementary, communication can proceed smoothly and indefinitely (Figure 11.5).

When Linda asks, "What time is it?" she is speaking as an Adult, and Roy's parallel response, "I think it's about 9:30," completes a complementary transaction. Or, similarly, Child to Child, one friend says to another, "Let's party!" and the friend appropriately responds, "Party on!" At other times, of course, it may be utterly appropriate for the Child to complain to the Parent—the spouse coming home from a hard day at the office, for instance—and for the Parent to respond to the Child with a hug and words of comfort.

Crossed transactions, however, are a different story. When the lines of communication are crossed, communication is broken off, and the relation typically shuts down. The most common crossed transaction occurs when an Adult-Adult transactional stimulus is coupled with a Parent-Child or Child-Parent response (Figure 11.6). Unless the respondent is able to mobilize his or her Adult to complement the Adult in the other person, deadlock is inevitable, and the transaction concludes with one or both of the parties feeling hurt, angry, or misunderstood.

When a student asks a professor, "How is this different from the concept we discussed yesterday?" he or she is speaking from the Adult ego state, and it

Figure 11.5 | Complementary transactions

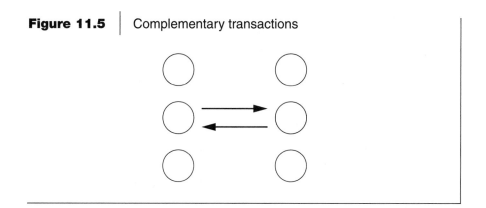

Figure 11.6 | Crossed transactions

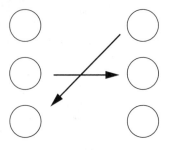

is not appropriate for the professor to play the role of the Parent and angrily ask, "Where have you been for the past hour? Surely you heard what I just said!" Similarly, when Jerry says, "I am soo hungry! I'm like way starving!" he is speaking Child to Child, and a crossed transaction occurs when Alex's measured response is Adult to Adult: "You might consider a small nutritional snack to suppress your appetite." Such crossed transactions often occur out of negligence or preoccupation.

Ulterior transactions, which occur when more than two ego states operate simultaneously, are equally problematic. In ulterior transactions, one message is usually sent on a social level, usually Adult-Adult, while an implied subtext is sent on an unspoken level in another ego state (Figure 11.7). For example, when Julie the Adult solicitously asks her friend an overt question, "Are you sure you don't want to go out with him again?" the covert question may be coming from the Parent: "Don't you think it's about time you quit being so nit-picky and go out with a guy more than once?!"

In both structural and transactional analysis, the competent TA therapist is genuine. Berne was aware that his therapeutic approach could lead counselors into assuming a phony facade or even becoming disingenuous. To help his students understand just how important the quality of genuineness is for the

Figure 11.7 | Ulterior transactions

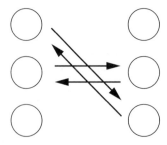

therapist, Berne labeled several unhealthy, nongenuine styles that professionals might develop (1966, p. 357). There is, for example, "Phallus in Wonderland,"

Achievement is not the
most important thing.
Authenticity is.

—James & Jongeward

who is fascinated by clients and what happens to them. The counselor who seemingly knows everything is "The Delegate," with the "whole weight of psychoanalytic tradition behind him." Experimenting with clients, "The Smiling Rebel" tends to keep secret what's on his or her mind, while "The Jargon Junk Juggler" enjoys using large words that nobody understands. The therapist who gets along slowly, rescues somewhat, and never gets upset is "The Patient Clinician," and "The Conservative," who is so bland and passive that nothing much happens, is even less effective. And then there is "The Hypochondriac," afraid to try anything new because of his or her concern for comfort.

GOALS OF THERAPY

The fundamental goal of transactional analysis is to help clients achieve autonomy (Berne, 1964; James and Jongeward, 1971), which means assuming responsibility for one's own actions or feelings, taking control of one's life, planning and directing one's own destiny, and throwing off any perceptions that are inappropriate for living here and now. In other words, TA helps to free one's Adult from the influence of the Child and Parent, allowing the Adult the autonomy to be in control of decision making (James, 1977).

Autonomy is characterized by three qualities. Awareness, a realistic understanding of one's world, "requires living in the here and now," says Berne (1964, p. 179), "and not in the elsewhere, the past or the future." Second, spontaneity, the ability to express emotion in an uninhibited, game-free fashion, allows us to choose which ego state we want to express. Intimacy, the capacity to share love and closeness with others, can occur only when all games have been discarded and only when we truly relate to each other with unguarded acceptance and warmth.

Life Positions

Another goal of TA is to help clients analyze their relationships—that is, their transactions. This involves determining the predominant **life position** one has taken, since it causes a given transaction to go one way or another. Harris (1967) suggests that all of these life positions are intentional, that we decide what we are willing to compromise in order to satisfy our needs or our stimulus hunger. These decisions lead to the position we take toward ourselves and others. According to Harris (1969), individuals choose one of four basic life positions:

- "I'm OK—you're OK": These people have formed a self-concept, are acknowledged as individuals, and have a positive self-identity as well as a positive image of others.

- "I'm OK—you're not OK": These people have a positive self-image, but see everyone else as the enemy who threatens their existence. This position is paranoid because of the distrust it requires.
- "I'm not OK—you're OK": These people blame themselves for everything that goes wrong and are drowning in guilt. They view themselves as polluted, and they feel unworthy of positive feedback from significant people in their lives. This depressive position is the most prevalent in contemporary society.
- "I'm not OK—you're not OK": These people have a poor self-image and harbor hostility and anger toward the outside world. This position is futile. Prisons, psychiatric hospitals, and morgues are filled with people in this basic life position (Wollams & Brown, 1979).

The goal of TA is to replace each of the three maladaptive life positions with the healthy "I'm OK, you're OK" position, which is "the *most* reality oriented" (Oden, 1974, p. 83). It is the original state of the baby at birth, and TA is optimistic about the human ability to recapture this birthright. "We do not drift into a new position," Harris writes (1967, p. 50). "It is a decision we make. In this respect it is like a conversion experience."

Scripts

These life positions are acted out in **scripts,** which are the dramas that tie together the games and transactions of our lives. A script is "a person's ongoing program for his life drama which dictates where he is going with his life and how he is to get there. It is a drama compulsively acted out, though his awareness of it may be vague" (James and Jongeward, 1971, p. 65). A life script is built uniquely on how one answers three questions: Who am I? What am I doing here? Who are all those others?

This idea of a life script may be illuminated by the "Parable of the Eagle." James and Jongeward (1971) tell of an eagle who had grown up among chickens and did not know his true identity. A passing naturalist said, "It has the heart of an eagle and surely it can learn to fly." He took the eagle to the top of a mountain, saying, "You belong to the sky and not the earth. Stretch forth your wings and fly." The eagle hesitated, looked back toward the barnyard, began to tremble, and slowly stretched his wings. At last, with a triumphant cry, he soared away into the heavens. James and Jongeward call those who discover their real potential, "winners."

> Preparation of the therapist must precede preparation of the patient.
>
> —Eric Berne

MAJOR METHODS AND TECHNIQUES

"The basic interest of transactional analysis," wrote Eric Berne (1972), "is the study of ego states" (p. 11) on which most TA methods focus. These TA methods have been applied to numerous clinical problems and settings (Jensen,

11.1 | The OK Corral

Franklin Ernst (1973) uses this concept in a grid diagram, colloquially called "The OK Corral."

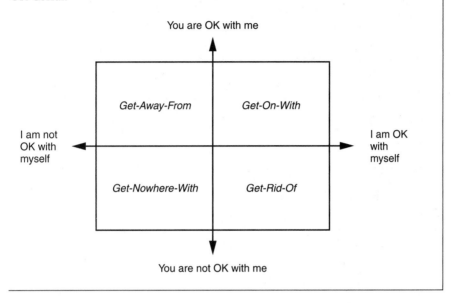

You are OK with me

Get-Away-From   Get-On-With

I am not   I am OK
OK with   with
myself   myself

Get-Nowhere-With   Get-Rid-Of

You are not OK with me

Baker, & Koepp, 1980): to treating personality disorders, for instance (Bonds-White, 1984), to trauma survival (Jacobs, 1991), asthma (Lammers, 1990), adult children of divorce (Silvestri, 1992), physical disability (Chapeau, 1992), eating disorders (Martin, 1990, Rumney & Steckel, 1985), childhood anxiety (LaFreniere & Dumas, 1992), family relationships (James, 1984), and group processes (Nykodym, Longenecker, & Ruud, 1991).

Contracting

TA typically begins with the client and therapist initiating a **contract,** which includes a statement about what the client hopes to achieve in counseling, a statement about what the counselor will do to facilitate the process, and some specific criteria for knowing when the goal has been achieved. This strategy helps to prevent the client from shifting total responsibility to the counselor and establishes positive expectations. "A contract is an agreement between counselor and client which specifies the goals, stages, and conditions of treatment" (Wollams & Brown, 1979, 221).

The contract must meet several specific requirements (Dusay and Steiner, 1971; Hansen, Stevic, & Warner, 1982). At the outset both the counselor and the client, through Adult-Adult transactions, must mutually agree on the objectives.

Second, the contract must call for mutual considerations: the counselor must give of his or her professional skill and time, and the client must give of his or her time and effort as well. Third, the contract defines the competencies of both parties. The counselor identifies the skills that will be applied in the situation, and the client commits his or her mind, time, and energy toward fulfilling the contract. Finally, the objective(s) of the contract must be within ethical limits.

Structural Analysis

In structural analysis clients are taught to identify their ego states and to become aware of how they function. During this initial, highly didactic stage of therapy, clients learn the terminology of TA. They are encouraged to read TA literature and to attend TA workshops (Friday, 1977). At this time, the counselor often makes use of audiovisual devices to demonstrate the ways in which the ego state functions. The purpose of structural analysis is to help clients look at the developmental history of each of their ego states and at their innate capacity for expression. The counselor may even "give permission" to their clients to express all of their ego states.

One way of assessing how much energy exists in the five functional ego states of any person—Critical Parent, Nurturing Parent, Adult, Free Child, and Adapted Child—is through the use of an *egogram* (Dusay, 1972; Dusay & Dusay, 1989). Essentially a portrait of psychological energy, an egogram is constructed on a bar graph with five positions, each of which represents an ego state (Figure 11.8). Because each person has a distinct and unique personality, the five psychological forces differ within each individual.

Ideally, a psychologically healthy individual will produce an egogram that is shaped like a bell curve. A person with such an egogram is capable of Adult-to-Adult transactions, is more likely to become a Nurturing rather than a

Figure 11.8 | Example of an Egogram

Egogram of a person who responds mostly from the Adult ego state.

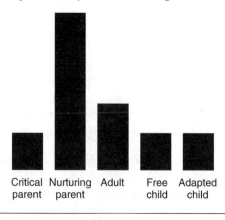

Critical parent   Nurturing parent   Adult   Free child   Adapted child

Critical Parent, and exhibits the acceptance and aliveness of the Free Child rather than the passivity and resentment of the Adapted Child (Burke, 1989).

Functional Analysis

Less didactic than the first stage, the next stage of therapy is still insight-oriented. Functional analysis describes transactions, whether complementary, crossed, or

> The patient must undertake the task of living in a world in which there is no Santa Claus.
>
> —Eric Berne

ulterior. It describes the way people use their ego states to relate to themselves and others. Wollams and Brown (1979) outline three fundamental rules of communication that clients learn during this stage: first, as long as transactions remain complementary, communication may continue indefinitely; second, wherever the transaction is crossed, a breakdown in communication results and something different is likely to follow; and third, the outcome of the transactions will be determined not on the social but on the psychological level.

Game Analysis

Wollams and Brown (1979) have identified five methods of analyzing the dynamics of game playing: (1) formal game analysis involves exploring the "advantages" of playing specific games; (2) drama triangle analysis involves focusing on the various game positions of Persecutor, Rescuer, or Victim (Karpman, 1968) as illustrated in the diagram in Figure 11.9. (3) transactional game diagramming diagnoses ego states with an emphasis on the psychological level of communication; (4) symbiosis diagramming identifies the preferred ego states of each player; and (5) Formula G describes the flow of a game and the steps it will take once the initial moves are begun.

Script Analysis

TA therapists believe poor transactions, rackets, and games are not random occurrences but are patterned toward a desired end. Created in order to achieve this end, scripts are written at an early age, usually by parents, and they often consist of grand injunctions against certain healthy life developments (e.g., Don't Feel, Don't Get Close). Scripts may also be defined in terms of a life-theme

Figure 11.9 | Drama Triangle

cliché, such as Getting Even, Being Helpful, Carrying My Cross, or Looking for the Pot of Gold. In addition, scripts may be understood in terms of childhood mythologies or fairy tales. TA therapists believe that adults live out literary metaphors from childhood that symbolize their lives. While Snow White, for instance, spends her life waiting for her prince to come along to remove her from difficulties, Cinderella sighs and waits for the invitation to arrive. In the meanwhile, the golden-haired Prince spends his life looking for Sleeping Beauty, while Peter Pan simply refuses to grow up (Karpman, 1968).

Other kinds of scripts set out considerably more negative patterns of interaction (Gladding, 1992, p. 130): the *never script,* which forbids one to do what one wants because the parent forbids it; the *until script,* which requires waiting until a certain time to do something before one can have a reward; the *always script,* which compels its subject to repeat the same activity over and over again; the *after script,* which expects difficulty after a certain event; and the *open-ended script,* which involves not knowing what one is supposed to do after a given time.

The analysis of scripts like these requires a detailed exploration of the decisions clients have made about their life positions. In this process, clients are made to understand their life positions and to make decisions that allow them to adjust their scripts: to rid themselves of self-defeating behavior and to achieve more autonomy, spontaneity, and intimacy. Often such analysis leads to learning about early childhood scripts that are updated for contemporary situations (Goulding & Goulding, 1979).

> What was once decided can be undecided.
> —T. A. Harris

In addition, Claude Steiner (1984) talks about our need for *emotional literacy* as a rationale for changing past life scripts. Emotional literacy is the ability to experience all of one's emotions with appropriate intensity and to understand what is causing these feelings. The systematic steps toward this emotional understanding include asking the client for permission to explore feelings, providing strokes, making a feeling/action statement ("I feel . . . about . . ."), in which emotion and action are closely tied, and ensuring that the feeling/action statement is heard by the other.

Redecision

A major branch of contemporary TA is Mary McClure Goulding's and Robert L. Goulding's "redecision school" (Barnes, 1977). Practitioners who follow the classical TA work of Berne do counseling with the Parent primarily on an intellectual level as they identify and change scripts. But the Gouldings believe individuals can change their own scripts through redecision, an emotional, intellectual, and behavioral process that takes place in the Child with the support of the Adult and Parent. This approach emphasizes self-direction and incorporates concepts and techniques from Gestalt therapy and other techniques.

Goulding and Goulding (1979) use redecision "scenes" to change life scripts. As a means of freeing up the Child, the client and therapist select a real or imaginary scene and then act it out, allowing the client to make or remake decisions about which scripts to live out and which to abandon.

Group Therapy

The preferred form of treatment for TA-based programs, however, appears to be the group setting. The counselor observes individuals as they interact in a quasi-natural and spontaneous way with a group, which typically numbers about eight individuals who meet once a week for two hours. This provides rich and immediate data on which to illustrate and demonstrate the TA approach as it applies to interpersonal situations.

In a TA group the leader assumes the role of teacher to a greater extent than in most other forms of group therapy. The leader may begin a group session with a general introduction to TA concepts, or it may be a traditional group therapy situation in which members take turns discussing personal problems while others offer help and suggestions. In any event the leader focuses on both verbal and nonverbal behavior as members interact about their individual problems. As "transactions" within the group emerge, the leader uses them as data to illustrate various types of interactions (Berne, 1968; Freedman, 1993), often using a chalkboard to diagram transactions among the members.

APPLICATION

To a large extent, then, TA has focused its attention on nonclinical applications such as social and organizational situations, often at the expense of providing substantial case material. The following case study of "Mrs. Enatosky," however, from Eric Berne's *Transactional Analysis in Psychotherapy* (1961), is considered a classic TA counseling situation. While it does not represent every aspect of the TA approach, it is distinctly TA and it illustrates many of Eric Berne's major counseling applications.

Mrs. Enatosky, a 34-year-old high school graduate whose husband was a mechanic, complained initially of "depressions" of sudden onset. She had previously been in Alcoholics Anonymous, hypnosis, and psychotherapy combined with Zen and yoga. Berne noted that she showed a special aptitude for transactional analysis and soon began to exert social control over the games that went on between herself and her husband, and herself and her son. Berne's formal diagnosis was "schizo-hysteria." The case will now be reviewed session by session with excerpts in Berne's own words:

> I'm not interested in progress. . . . I want to cure people.
>
> —Eric Berne

April 1

The patient arrived on time for her initial interview. She stated that she had been an alcoholic for ten years and had been cured by Alcoholics Anonymous. She dated the onset of her drinking from her mother's psychosis when she was nineteen. She said that her depressions began at the same time. A preliminary search for traumatic events elicited that her father drank heavily and that her parents separated when she was seven years old. The medical history revealed headaches, and numbness of one arm and leg.

The history-taking was carefully planned so that at all times the patient seemed to have the initiative and the therapist at most was curious rather than formal or openly systematic in gathering information. This means that the patient was not required to play a game of psychiatric history-taking.

April 8

The neurologist suspected cervical arthritis, but did not recommend any specific treatment. The patient spontaneously mentioned wanting approval and rebelling "like a little girl," as some "grown-up part" of her judged it. She said the "little girl" seemed "childish." It was suggested that she let the "little girl" out, rather than try to clamp down on her. She replied that that seemed brazen. She sees the two most important "parents" in her life as her husband and her father. She is seductive toward her husband and recognizes that she was the same with her father.

The patient's special aptitude for structural analysis is already evident. She herself makes the separation between "the little girl" and "a grown-up part" and recognizes the compliance of "the little girl" toward certain people whom she relates to her parents. It was only necessary, therefore, to reinforce this trichotomy in a non directive way. With many other patients this might not have been undertaken until the third or fourth session, perhaps even later.

April 15

She resents people who tell her what to do, especially women. This is another reaction to "Parents." She mentions a feeling of "walking high." It is pointed out that this is the way a very small girl must feel, that this is again the child. It was emphasized that there was no mysterious or metaphysical aspect to these diagnostic judgments.

The patient has now experienced some of the phenomenological reality of the child and has added to the behavioral, social, and historical reality she established in the previous interviews. The indications, therefore, are favorable for treatment with transactional analysis.

April 22

"This week I've been happy for the first time in fifteen years. I don't have to look far to find the child, I can see it in my husband and in others too. I have trouble with my son." The game with her son was clarified in an inexact but timely and illustrative way in terms of parent (her disapproval and determination), child (her seductiveness and her sulkiness at his recalcitrance), and adult (her gratification when he finally did his work). It was hinted that an adult approach (good reason) rather than a parental approach (sweet reason) might be worth a try. The patient is now involved in transactional analysis proper and the idea of social control has been suggested.

April 28

She reports that things work better with her son. As the session ends she asks: "Is it all right to be aggressive?" Answer: "You want *me* to tell you?" She understands the implication that she should decide such things on adult grounds rather than asking parental permission, and replies: "No, I don't." During this session some of the elements of her script are elicited. It gives the therapist an opportunity to decline to play and to reinforce her adult. The patient has made such good progress in understanding structural and transactional analysis that she is already considered adequately prepared for fairly advanced group therapy. The group she is to enter consist largely of women.

May 4

She liked the group but it made her uncomfortable during the rest of the week. She related some memories, including homosexual play during childhood. The experience in the group has activated sexual conflicts, and this is the first indication of their nature.

May 11

She felt highly excited on leaving the group meeting. "Things are better at home. I can kiss my son now and my daughter for the first time came and sat on my lap." The analysis of her family games had resulted in the establishment of some adult social control. It is evident that this improved control has been perceived by her children and for the first time in a long while they had the feeling that she can maintain her position and they react accordingly. An experience in the group later this week rather clearly showed her need for parental figures in some of her games. There was a new patient in the group, a male social worker, and she was very much impressed by his occupation. She asked him what they were supposed to do there. It was pointed out that she knew more than he did, since it was his first meeting and her third.

May 18

She has visited her mother only once in the past five or six years and it was suggested that it might be advisable for her to do that again. This suggestion was very carefully worded so as to be adult rather than parental. Any implication that she was a bad girl for not visiting her mother had to be avoided. She was able to understand the allure of such a visit as an exercise for her adult and as a means of preventing further difficulties between her parent and her child if her mother should die. The good reception of this suggestion was manifested by her bringing up new information. Her husband never washes his hair and always has a good excuse, which she accepts.

May 18

She said she has always been more afraid of sick animals than of sick people. This week her cat was sick, and for the first time she was not afraid of him. Once when she was little her father hit her, and her dog jumped on him, whereupon he gave the dog away. The import of this is not clear. Her maintenance of social control with the sick cat is evidence that a visit to her mother may be possible in the near future.

June 1

She wonders: "Why do I exist? Sometimes I doubted my existence." Her parents' marriage was a shotgun wedding and she has always felt that she was unwanted. The patient is now involved with existential problems. Her adult has evidently always been shaky because her child has implanted doubts about her existence, her right to exist, and the form in which she exists.

June 8

She describes her husband's alcoholic game. At AA she was told that she should bless him and comfort him, and that made her sick. She tried something different. "One day I said I would call the ambulance for the hospital, since he didn't appear to be able to take care of himself, so he got up and didn't drink again." He said he was only trying to help her stay sober by drinking himself. This comes up because he was drinking heavily last week and she had pain in her shoulders and wanted to hit him, but told him off instead. It appears from this that their secret marriage contract is based partly on the assumption that he will drink and she will function as a rescuer. This session helped to clarify for the patient the structure of her marriage and also emphasized the amount of time and effort that is required to keep marital games going, and equally, the amount of energy involved in their repression without conscious control.

July 6

There has been an interval of a month for summer vacation. She has some olfactory illusions. She thinks she smells gas in the office, but decides it is clean soap. During her recent yoga training, she developed imagery which was almost eidetic. She would see gardens and wingless angels with sparkling clarity of color and detail. Her existential doubts are less disturbing. These phenomena, and the auditory manifestations she had previously mentioned, are not necessarily alarming. They point to childhood restitutive tendencies related to a deeply disturbed relationship between her and her parents. The conventional approach would be to give her "supportive" treatment and help her repress this psychopathology and live on top of it. Structural analysis offers another possibility that requires some boldness: to allow this disturbed child to express herself and profit from the resulting constructive experiences.

July 13

She told her husband she was going to finger paint and he got angry and said: "use pastels!" When she refused, he started to drink. She recognizes what happened here was a game of "Uproar" and feels some despair at having been drawn into this. She says, however, that if she does not play "Uproar" with him then *he* will feel despair, and it is a hard choice to make.

July 20

She is losing interest and feels tired. She reveals some family scandals she has never mentioned to anyone before and states now that her drinking did not begin after her mother became psychotic, but after these scandals. At this session a decisive move was made. The patient habitually sits with her legs in an ungainly exposed position. She complains that the men also made passes at her. She doesn't understand why, since she did nothing to bring this on. She was informed of her exposed position and expressed considerable surprise. At the subsequent group meeting she was silent most of the time. At the price of sacrificing the possibilities of normal family life, the patient has obtained a multitude of gains, primary and secondary, by playing games with her husband and other men and women.

August 10

The therapist returns after a two-week vacation. The confrontation has been successful. The patient now describes an assault by her father in her early puberty while her stepmother pretended to be asleep. She relates this "assault" to her own seductiveness. This situation she discusses at some length, eliciting her feeling that sex is dirty or vulgar. She says she has always been very careful sexually with her husband because of this feeling and has tried to avoid sex with him for this reason. She understands that the games she plays with him are an attempt to avoid sex, as she feels she cannot let go enough to enjoy it and it is merely a burden to her.

August 17

The patient announces that this is her last session. She no longer fears that her husband will think she is dirty or vulgar if she acts lusty. During the week, she approached him differently and he responded with gratified surprise. For the last few days he has come home whistling for the first time in years. She also realizes something else. She has always felt sorry for herself and tried to elicit sympathy and admiration because she is a recovered alcoholic. She recognizes this now as a game of "wooden leg." She feels ready at this point to try it on her own. She reports that she is drawing instead of finger painting, doing what she wants; she feels this isn't wrong, it's like learning to live. "I don't feel sorry for people any more, I feel they ought to be able to do this too if they went about it right. I no longer feel I'm below everyone, although that feeling isn't completely gone. I don't want to come to the group any more; I'd rather spend the time with my husband. It's like we're starting to go with each other again when he comes home whistling. It's wonderful. I'll try it for three months and if I feel bad I'll call you." She was asked directly whether structural analysis helped and whether game analysis helped and in each case replied: "Oh, yes!" She added: "Also the script. For example, I said my husband had no sense of humor and you said 'Wait a minute, you don't know him and he doesn't know you because you've been playing games and acting out your scripts, you don't know what either of you is really like.' You were right because now I've discovered that he really has a sense of humor and that not having it was part of the game."

In summing up the work he conducted with Mrs. Enatosky, Berne states: "Although in some current thinking the course of this case may not indicate that the improvement is stable, it requires only one assumption to take a more optimistic view, and that assumption is borne out by experience; namely, that playing games and playing through one's script are optional, and that a strong adult can renounce these in favor of gratifying reality experiences. This is the actionistic aspect of transactional analysis."

11.2 | **Psychic Borderlines**

Erica E. Goode

Lavinia's dreams are vivid. In one, she is swimming, pursued by a man with a knife. She can feel the metal of the blade piercing her skin and see her blood filtering red in the bluegreen water. An artist in her late 20s, Lavinia is creative and vulnerable, passionate and flexible, free-wheeling and unguarded. Her world is fluid: Thoughts and feelings run together, and at times she is uncertain where she leaves off and another person begins. Even as a child, she was extremely sensitive—not only to other people's feelings, but to violent images, even to loud noises. "I can't keep things out," she says.

In the language of a new personality theory proposed by Temple University psychiatrist Ernest Hartmann, Lavinia is a person with very *"thin boundaries"; the invisible membrane separating her from the outside world is highly permeable, more akin to gossamer than to iron* [italics added]. Charles, on the other hand, a 40-year-old businessman, has very "thick" boundaries. He is methodical and solid, his life a grid of precisely drawn lines. Charles dreams he is "in a room, squarish in shape, with concrete walls on three sides." He often speaks in engineering metaphors. In college, he had friends, he says, but he was never very close to them, and now "my only friend is my wife." Charles remembers his childhood only vaguely. Opening his eyes in the morning, he is instantly awake.

Psychic Poles

Lavinia and Charles, described in Hartmann's recently published book, *Boundaries in the Mind* (Basic Books, $23), are extremes. Lavinia is probably perceived by others as somewhat "flaky"; Charles, as unusually rigid. They scored at the poles of the Boundary Questionnaire, the test Hartmann developed to measure what he calls a "basic and neglected dimension of personality." But most people, Hartmann says, fall somewhere in between, exhibiting "thickness" or "thinness" in more moderate forms.

Hartmann, of course, is not the first to divide the world into character types. Ever since the Greek philosopher and physician Empedocles sorted the personalities of his fellow citizens into the categories of air, earth, fire and water, there has been no shortage of ingenious ways to pigeonhole human variation. Swiss psychoanalyst *Carl Jung drew a basic distinction between introverts and extroverts* [italics added]. Psychologist *William James preferred the dichotomy of tough-minded and tender-minded.* [italics added]. And more recently, Americans have been able to divide themselves, often by merely filling in the blanks on a personality test, into *Type A's and Type B's,* "sharpeners" and "levelers," *right brains and left brains,* to name only a few [italics added].

Such systems for carving up the personality pie are not free from scientific controversy. Filling out a questionnaire, critics point out, is rarely a substitute for the complexities of life. And research based on personality tests, notes the *Oxford Companion to the Mind,* has "had little impact on the development of psychology, whether in the clinic or the lab." Yet bringing order to the chaos of individual differences is intuitively appealing. And Hartmann's studies have generated interest among clinicians, who recognize in his work their patients, their friends and even themselves. "It's an intriguing hypothesis," says Cornell University psychiatrist Robert Michels, "with confirmation awaited."

Hartmann, whose interest in "boundaries" grew out of his research on sleep and dreaming, argues that his theories may prove more useful than previous attempts at personality taxonomy. For one thing, he says, the notion of boundaries cuts across many levels of human experience: There are boundaries between the states of sleep and waking, between thinking and feeling, between the conscious, rational processes of the ego and the chaotic unconscious world of the id.

Defensive Barricades

Repression and other psychological defense mechanisms can serve as boundaries to painful memories or unwanted feelings. (Freud himself, Hartmann points out, talked of "ego boundaries.") And in our daily interactions with partners, parents and co-workers, we constantly negotiate our boundaries, allowing people to come closer or preventing their approach.

But Hartmann goes further. The concept of boundaries, he believes, reflects something basic about the organization of the brain—a link missing from most personality theories. With its complicated interplay of nerve pathways and messenger chemicals, the brain both brings things together—integrating sensory information and mental processes—and keeps them apart, creating barriers that are protective and allowing the business of consciousness to proceed in an orderly fashion. Certain drugs—LSD, for example—can alter the efficiency of these processes. People's tendencies toward thickness or thinness, Hartmann speculates, may in some way relate to differences in functioning at the biological level.

In studying the responses of more than 2,000 people who have taken the Boundary Questionnaire, Hartmann finds that people differ greatly in the permeability of their boundaries. To a large degree, he says, "thickness" or "thinness" stretches across sensory, interpersonal and mental realms. A person who scores as "thin" on the test, for example, is likely to agree that he is "unusually sensitive to loud noises and to bright lights," and also that he feels "unsure of who I am at times" and that "sometimes I don't know whether I am thinking or feeling." *Women, on the whole, have thinner boundaries than men* [italics added], Hartmann's studies indicate. People with thicker boundaries are more likely to be married but enjoy their sex lives less than "thinner" people. Those with porous boundaries report more symptoms of illness and

(continued)

11.2 | **Psychic Borderlines** (continued)

are much more likely to dream vividly and recall their dreams upon waking. *Everyone's boundaries, says Hartmann, tend to thicken with age* [italics added].

The permeability of boundaries seems to have little to do with more traditional measures of mental illness. A thin personality may be creative, open to experience, a bit wacky and prone to unusual dreams, Hartmann finds, but not necessarily psychologically disturbed. Yet being either very thick or very thin has its risks: *"Having boundaries that are too thick and solid,"* he says, *"makes you incapable of relationships and deprives you of dreams and fantasies. But having no boundaries at all is very dangerous"* [italics added]. Indeed, the subjects with very thin boundaries in Hartmann's studies often plunged deeply into destructive relationships; one woman said she *could not leave her physically abusive boyfriend because he was "part of her"* [italics added]. *And though thin boundary individuals appear no more prone to mental illness than others, extreme thinness of boundaries is characteristic of people who suffer the mental disintegration of schizophrenia or the volatile mood swings and identity confusion that clinicians label "borderline personality disorder."*

Childhood Origins

Many people with thin boundaries say they have been that way for as long as they can remember, Hartmann reports. And studies indicate that even children as young as 3 or 4 show differences in boundary thickness. But are thick or thin boundaries

---

CRITICAL ANALYSIS

TA brings several advantages to the counseling field. It is conducive to short-term treatment, works well in a large variety of settings, can easily be adapted to group counseling, and provides opportunities even in brief treatment for developing effective problem-solving skills along with insight and personality change (Jensen, Baker, & Koepp, 1980). It is an approach that even counselors who do not view themselves primarily as TA practitioners can integrate into their therapeutic work (Massey, 1990). The combined use of TA and Gestalt therapy has been especially powerful (James & Jongeward, 1971; O'Hearne, 1992).

Since so much of our meaningful life experience is interpersonal, it is a major strength of TA that it is one of the only approaches that illuminates interpersonal, as opposed to intrapsychic, reality. This, coupled with TA's creative, catchy, and intuitively appealing terminology is perhaps its greatest strength. Berne intended that his approach have practical value for the client and be accessible to the masses, that its concepts should be easily grasped and applied. Once people have learned the system and become

> Do as I say and as I do, but don't be as I am!
> —Eric Berne

present at birth? There is scant evidence one way or the other, but the psychiatrist speculates that heredity plays some role, because the permeability of boundaries seems to run in families and shows a pattern characteristic of other genetically influenced traits. Thin boundary adults remember reacting unusually strongly, even as children, to quite normal traumatic events, such as the death of a pet or the birth of a sibling. Yet learning probably contributes, too. Some adults with thick boundaries, for example, recall great pressure to "catch up" to an older sibling.

Though boundary differences emerge early, they do not appear immutable. Hartmann and his colleagues have found that mental and emotional permeability can change over time. Individuals with extremely thin boundaries, for example, sometimes develop thickness as protection against their vulnerability. And through long-term psychotherapy or psychoanalysis, the psychiatrist says, boundaries can shift, the thick person becoming more flexible, the thin person tougher and more thick-skinned.

Thick or thin, most people seem quite content to remain that way. Indeed, many have a sense of superiority about their approach to life. The thick research subjects Hartmann interviewed invariably assumed that the psychiatrist, like them, had thick boundaries. Thickness, they opined, was unquestionably the way to be, and they saw thinness as "weird and crazy." Similarly, thin subjects viewed thickness as "stolid, dull and dumb." Surely, as a creative scientist, Hartmann must have thin boundaries too, they said.

Has he taken the Boundary Questionnaire? Of course he has. "I come out in the middle," the psychiatrist says. "But a bit on the thin side of average."

Source: *U.S. News & World Report,* January 20, 1992, p. 57–59.

more aware of their self-defeating patterns, they can almost immediately understand previously baffling interactions.

More broadly, TA therapists have taken specific actions to make their approach sensitive to particular cultural needs, and as a result TA has experienced some success in applying itself to cross-cultural contexts. Berne's script types, for example, have been applied to Chinese myths (Chan, 1991) and to police work in Israel (Elaad, 1993). TA has also called for a continuous highlighting of ethical codes in different cultures (Chang, 1994, Pizer, 1994). When considering TA in a multicultural context, it must be pointed out that it also offers a structured approach that deals head on with issues of power and control. And since in the dominant mainstream culture people of color often experience a sense of powerlessness, TA, with its emphasis on personal responsibility, can provide a means for a stronger sense of empowerment and increased personal power (Hlongwane & Basson, 1990). In addition, the contract used in the TA approach can serve as a means of preventing therapists from imposing their cultural values in a multicultural context.

There is, of course, a negative side to the accessibility of TA language: it can be used to excess, creating a barrier to the outsider, and there is a tendency to confuse labeling with counseling. The reader of TA literature is bombarded with phrases, concepts, lists, clichés, in-group language, and abbreviations that can baffle even the most ardent devotee. A hearty dose of second-degree games, second-order functional analyses of structural diagrams, Parent-in-Child ego states, drama triangles, and so forth can be particularly challenging. Perhaps more so than any other approach, TA is encumbered by an extraordinary number of "passwords" and awkward idiomatic expressions. The real danger is that we mistakenly believe that we have understood or explained something just because we have labeled it.

As a result, the jargon of TA may often serve as a stumbling block, being foreign to many ethnic-minority groups and consequently cumbersome to implement. Berne obviously loved colorful language and frequently used myths and metaphors in his approach. Yet, while he claimed that TA vocabulary had basically only five words (Parent, Adult, Child, game, and script), *What Do You Say After You Say Hello?* lists nearly 100 terms in its glossary, and *Principles of Group Treatment* lists 127 terms. While TA therapists assert that their approach is simple and easy to understand, many clients have difficulty with the complexity of some of its concepts, such as crossed transactions. Consequently, before therapists challenge the life scripts of ethnic-minority clients, great care must be taken to build a trusting relationship that does not take the language of TA for granted.

A final critique of the TA approach must point out that it doesn't seem to appreciate the mysterious, conflicted dimensions of human life. In many respects, the TA therapists treat clients as objects. Rather than beginning with trust, they begin with a contract; rather than attempting to understand the clients, they teach the language of TA so that their clients can understand them. The risk, then, is that TA counselors focus more on states, transactions, and scripts than on persons.

CURRENT STATUS

In the 1960s the best-seller *Games People Play* propelled TA into such a groundswell of popularity that critics inevitably dismissed it as a fad. Instead, TA matured and shows no signs of fading. Thirty years later TA has developed an increasingly stable body of data, has its own respected professional journal, *Transactional Analysis,* and may be considered an important part of the background of a well-trained counselor. There are now more than 14,000 members in the International Transactional Analysis Association (Ivey, Ivey, & Simek-Downing, 1993).

To be certified as a clinical member of the International Transactional Analysis Association (ITAA), the candidate must hold a regular current membership, pay dues and fees, and complete a training program of no less than one year, which includes 50 hours of advanced TA training, 50 hours of supervision of direct clinical service, 150 hours of clinical application, and participation in various TA seminars and other presentations.

Psychiatrists know many therapeutic procedures but less about what in a particular procedure is therapeutic.

—Eric Berne

To be certified as a clinical teaching member of ITAA, a candidate must hold a current clinical membership, pay fees and membership dues, complete a training program of no less than two years in association with three sponsoring Teaching Members, and hold a graduate degree in a "healing arts profession" or six years of full-time experience in the field of counseling.

The therapeutic approach developed by Eric Berne is both simple and profound. Although it is accessible to all counselors, it is understood fully only by those who are thoroughly trained. Regardless of its impact, however, TA is clearly past its heyday. In a survey of more than 400 clinical and counseling psychologists, less than 1 percent identified TA as their basic theoretical orientation (Smith, 1982). A survey of major American psychological and psychiatric journals between 1980 and 1986 indicates that research using TA is being published almost exclusively in a journal and newsletter dedicated entirely to transactional analysis. Still, TA interventions and the theories that underlie them continue to be included in all major counseling textbooks, and it is part of the eclectic repertoire of many practitioners.

SUMMARY

1. *Biography.* Born in Montreal, Quebec, Berne (1910–1970) grew up admiring his father who was a physician devoted to his patients. After his father's early death, Berne entered medical school, became a U.S. citizen, and soon entered the Army Medical Corps as a psychiatrist. After World War II, Berne moved to San Francisco and resumed psychoanalytic training under Eric Erikson. Never achieving official recognition by the psychoanalytic association, however, Bern developed his own orientation to psychotherapy, transactional analysis, which he called a more "rational" approach. He wrote many papers and books, including *Games People Play.*

2. *Historical Development.* The origins of TA can be found in a wide variety of sources. Berne merged, mixed, and synthesized the approaches of Freud, Adler, and Rogers especially. From the beginning, Berne strove to make his theory accessible and he succeeded. The diagrams that Berne used to explain interactions between people have become increasingly commonplace in counseling offices, classrooms, and management seminars.

3. *View of Human Nature.* For Berne, people are motivated primarily by basic psychological hungers to transcend patterns of behavior that begin early in life: stimulus hunger (the need to be acknowledged or affirmed by others); structure hunger (how we use time to maximize the number of strokes we receive), and position hunger (the need to have our fundamental decisions about life validated and affirmed). Personality is composed of three conscious or preconscious ego states, each an organized

psychological system of feelings, thoughts, and behaviors: the Parent, the Adult, and the Child.

4. *Development of Maladaptive Behavior.* Psychopathology, according to Berne, is the result of confused ego states. This confusion occurs when a person vacillates between ego states without completing their transaction (i.e., blocking the free flowing interaction among ego states). In addition, maladaptive behavior can result from playing games, a recurring set of transactions with a concealed motivation. Games occur when persons turn to others for confirmation of their negative "not OK" position, and the result is the avoidance of intimacy.

5. *Function of the Therapist.* The TA counselor works at being a catalyst for enabling clients to mobilize their resources. Acting very much like a teacher, the therapist explains key concepts such as structural analysis, script analysis, and game analysis. In addition the therapist helps clients make full and effective use of all three ego states, to live game-free.

6. *Goals of Therapy.* The fundamental goal of TA is to help clients achieve autonomy—that is, to assume responsibility for their own actions or feelings, to take control of their lives, to plan and direct their own destiny, and to throw off any perceptions that are inappropriate for living here and now. In other words, TA helps to free one's Adult from the influence of the Child and Parent. Another goal of TA is to help clients analyze their relationships by discovering their predominant life positions (e.g., "I'm OK—you're OK").

7. *Major Methods and Techniques.* TA typically begins with a contract between client and therapist, which includes statements about what the client hopes to achieve and what the counselor will do, as well as specific criteria for knowing when the goal has been achieved. Structural analysis is then employed to identify the client's ego states and to become aware of how they function. Functional analysis is a didactic method used to describe transactions to the client. Game analysis looks at the methods of game playing in which a client might be involved. And script analysis examines the person's life direction, which is usually set at an early age.

8. *Application.* TA does not provide an abundance of case material. Nonetheless, the case of "Mrs. Enatosky," a 34-year-old who had previously been in AA, illustrates many of Berne's applications. Berne noted that she showed a special aptitude for TA, and she soon began to exert social control over the games that occurred between herself and her husband and between herself and her son.

9. *Critical Analysis.* TA is conducive to short-term treatment and works well in a variety of settings. The use of TA and Gestalt therapy together has been especially helpful to many. It is one of the only approaches that illuminates interpersonal, as opposed to intrapsychic, reality. But while TA's language has made it accessible to a lay audience, it can be used to excess and the terminology threatens to create a barrier rather than a bridge. Cross-culturally, TA has shown some initiative in being sensitive to particular cultural needs and may lead to a greater sense of empowerment for minorities, but the TA jargon may also serve as a stumbling block for ethnic-minority groups.

10. *Current Status.* TA enjoyed a national groundswell of popularity in the 1960s and has been furthered by a body of data and a respected professional journal. Although it is often integrated into the work of a wide variety of therapists, few practitioners today would identify TA as their primary theoretical orientation. Nevertheless, its interventions continue to be used by many eclectic practitioners.

Key Terms

Activities Any work or other goal-oriented behavior is an activity. In activity, the individual sets up a situation in which the accomplishment of the task brings the needed strokes.

Adapted Child Becomes more controlled by interacting with Parents.

Adult ego state Best characterized as being concerned with facts. It acts as an assimilator of information and is mature.

Child ego state Composed of all the feelings and ways of behaving that were experienced during the early years of childhood.

Complementary transaction Sometimes called a *parallel transaction,* it is one in which stimulus and response vectors are parallel so that only two ego states are involved, one from each person.

Conditional stroke A stroke given for *doing* something.

Contamination One of two ego-state boundary problems. It occurs when the prejudicial or irrational ideas and attitudes of the Parent or the archaic feelings of the Child interfere with the logical, clear thinking of the Adult.

Contract An agreement between counselor and client that specifies the goals, stages, and conditions of treatment.

Controlling parent Opinionated, powerful, strongly protective, principled, punitive, demanding, in charge.

Critical parent Rejecting, controlling, judgmental.

Crossed transaction Occurs when the vectors are not parallel, or more than two ego states are involved.

Discounting Involves ignoring or distorting some aspect of internal or external experience. One may discount the existence of a problem, the significance of a problem, the change possibilities of a problem, or one's own personal abilities. Selling short.

Drama triangle A triadic interaction in which one person acts as persecutor, another as rescuer, and the third as victim, as occurs occasionally in love relationships.

Ego state States of mind and their related patterns of behavior as they occur in nature.

Exclusion This boundary problem exists when one or more ego states are effectively prevented from operating.

Filtered stroke A stroke that is distorted or containing nonrelevant information.

Game A series of "duplex transactions," which lead to a switch and a well-defined, predictable payoff that justifies a not-OK or discounted position.

Injunction A type of negative parenting behavior, edicts that require children to behave in certain prescribed ways. They are usually "don't" messages.

Intimacy A candid, game-free relationship with mutual, free giving and receiving without exploitation.

Life position Early in life, people experience a need to take a position regarding their own intrinsic worth and that of others. There are four life positions: I'm OK, you're OK', I'm OK, you're not OK', I'm not OK, you're OK', I'm not OK, you're not OK.

Little Professor The part of the Child ego state that is the forerunner of Adult reasoning.

Natural Child This part of the Child ego state contains the young, impulsive, untrained, emotionally expressive child.

Negative stroke A painful stroke carrying a "You're not OK" message and resulting in unpleasant feelings for the receiver.

Nurturing Parent Caring, concerned, forgiving, reassuring, permissive, warmly protective, and worried.

Parent ego state Consists of a collection of mental tapes from significant others who had some kind of power relationship with the person.

Pastime A semi-ritualized conversation in which people share opinions, thoughts, or feelings about relatively safe topics that don't require them to act.

Position hunger The need to have one's basic decisions about life confirmed constantly—decisions about the "OKness" of oneself and the world.

Positive stroke A pleasurable stroke carrying a "You're OK" message and resulting in good feelings for the receiver.

Racket A habitual process (usually of complementary transactions) by which a person interprets or manipulates the environment to justify a life position of not-OKness.

Rituals Highly stylized and predictable ways of exchanging low-involvement, low-risk strokes such as greetings.

Script A personal life plan that each individual forms by a series of decisions early in life in reaction to his or her interpretation of the important things happening in his or her world.

Stamps Feelings or strokes collected to justify some later behavior.

Stimulus hunger The universal need for stimulation or stroking.

Stroke A unit of attention providing stimulation to a person.

Structure hunger People's need to use their time in ways that maximize the number of strokes they can receive.

Symbiosis Two or more individuals behave as though they form a whole person; coming together.

Transaction An exchange of strokes between two persons, consisting of a stimulus and a response between specified ego states.

Transactional analysis Psychotherapy that focuses on characteristic interactions that reveal internal "ego states" and the "games people play" in social situations.

Ulterior transaction A transaction that contains both an overt (social) and a covert (psychological) message. They may be either angular or duplex. An angular transaction involves three ego states and occurs when messages are sent simultaneously from one ego state of the initiator to two ego states of the respondent. A duplex transaction involves four ego states, two in each person. During the course of a duplex transaction, two sets of complementary transactions occur simultaneously, one on the social level and one on the psychological level.

Unconditional stroke Given for *being,* they pertain to conditions that occur naturally and do not require special effort.

Withdrawal The most limiting and least rewarding way of structuring time. People who structure time by withdrawing live on strokes stored from the past or fantasized in the future.

Suggested Reading

Berne, E. (1961). *Transactional analysis in psychotherapy.* New York: Grove Press.

Berne, E. (1963). *The structure and dynamics of organizations and groups.* Philadelphia: Lippincott.

Berne, E. (1964). *Games people play.* New York: Grove Press.

Berne, E. (1972). *What do you do after you say hello?* New York: Grove Press.

Harris, T. (1967). *I'm OK—You're OK: A Practical Guide to Transactional Analysis.* New York: Harper & Row.

Harris, T. (1985). *Staying OK.* New York: Harper & Row.

References

Barnes, G. (1977). *Transactional analysis after Eric Berne: Teachings of three TA schools.* New York: Harper & Row.

Berne, E. (1947). *The mind in action.* New York: Simon & Schuster.

Berne, E. (1961). *Transactional analysis in psychotherapy.* New York: Grove Press.

Berne, E. (1963). *The structure and dynamics of organizations and groups.* Philadelphia: Lippincott.

Berne, E. (1964). *Games people play.* New York: Grove Press.

Berne, E. (1966). *Principles of group treatment.* New York: Oxford University Press.

Berne, E. (1968). *Principles of group treatment.* New York: Grove.

Berne, E. (1972). *What do you say after you say hello?* New York: Grove Press.

Bonds-White, F. (1984). The special it: Treatment of the passive-aggressive personality.

Transactional Analysis Journal, 14, 180–190.

Burke, J. F. (1989). *Contemporary approaches to psychotherapy and counseling: The self-regulation and maturity model.* Pacific Grove, CA: Brooks/Cole.

Chan, D. W. (1991). Berne's script types and Chinese myths. *Transactional Analysis Journal, 21,* 220–226.

Chang, V. N. (1994). A transactional analysis decision-making model and ethical hierarchy. *Transactional Analysis Journal, 24,* 15–20.

Chapeau, T. (1992). Transactional analysis and rehabilitation: An integrative approach to disability. *Transactional Analysis Journal, 22,* 234–242.

Cheney, W. D. (1971). Eric Berne: biographical sketch. *Transactional Analysis Journal, 1,* 14–22.

Clark, B. D. (1991). Empathic transactions in the deconfusion of Child ego states. *Transactional Analysis Journal, 21,* 92–98.

Drego, P. A. (1993). Paradigms and models of ego states. *Transactional Analysis Journal, 23,* 5–29.

Dusay, J. M. (1972). Egograms and the constancy hypothesis. *Transactional Analysis Journal, 1,* 34–44.

Dusay, J. M. (1977). The evolution of transactional analysis. In G. Barnes (Ed.), *Transactional analysis after Eric Berne: Teachings and practices of three TA schools* (pp. 32–52). NY: Harpers College.

Dusay, J. M., & Dusay, K. M. (2000). In R. J. Corsini & D. Wedding (Eds.), *Transactional Analysis* (6th ed., pp. 405–453). Itasca, IL: F. E. Peacock.

Dusay, J. M., & Steiner, C. (1971). Transactional analysis in groups. In H. I. Kaplan and B. J. Sadock (Eds.), *Comprehensive group psychotherapy.* Baltimore, MD: Williams & Wilkins.

Elaad, E. (1993). Detection of deception: A transactional analysis perspective. *Journal of Psychology, 127,* 5–15.

Ernst, F. H. (1973). Psychological rackets in the OK corral. *Transactional Analysis Journal, 3,* 19.

Freedman, L. D. (1993). TA tools for self-managing work teams. *Transactional Analysis Journal, 23,* 104–109.

Friday, P. J. (1977). A TA 101: Does it make a difference? *Transactional Analysis Journal, 7,* 176–177.

George, R. L., & Cristiani, T. S. (1990). *Counseling theory and practice* (3rd ed.). Englewood Cliffs, NJ: Prentice Hall.

Goldhaber, G. M., & Goldhaber, M. B. (1976). *Transactional analysis: Principles and applications.* Boston: Allyn and Bacon.

Goulding, M. M. (1987). Transaction analysis and redecision therapy. In J. K. Zeig (Ed.), *The evolution of psychotherapy* (pp. 258–299). New York: Brunner/Mazel.

Hansen, J. C., Stevic, R. R., & Warner, W. R., Jr. (1982). *Counseling: Theory and process* (3rd ed.). Boston: Allyn and Bacon.

Harris, T. (1967). *I'm OK—You're OK.* New York: Avon.

Hlongwane, M. M., & Basson, C. J. (1990). Self-concept enhancement of Black adolescents using transactional analysis in a group context. *School Psychology International, 11,* 99–108.

Holland, G. A. (1973). Transactional analysis. In R. Corsini (Ed.), *Current psychotherapies.* Itasca, IL: F. E. Peacock.

Ivey, A. E., Ivey, M. B., & Simek-Downing, L. (1993). *Counseling and psychotherapy: Integrating skills, theory, and practice* (3rd ed.). Englewood Cliffs, NJ: Prentice Hall.

Jacobs, A. (1991). Aspects of survival: Triumph over death and loneliness. *Transactional Analysis Journal, 21,* 4–11.

James, J. (1984). Grandparents and family script parade. *Transactional Analysis Journal, 14,* 18–28.

James, M. (1977). *Techniques in transactional analysis for psychotherapists and counselors.* Reading, MA: Addison-Wesley.

James, M., & Jongeward, D. (1971). *Born to win: Transactional analysis with gestalt experiments.* Reading, MA: Addison-Wesley.

Jensen, S. M., Baker, M. S., & Koepp, A. H. (1980). TA in brief psychotherapy with college students. *Adolescence, 15,* 683–689.

Jongeward, D. (1973). *Everybody wins: TA applied to organizations.* Reading, MA: Addison-Wesley.

Karpman, S. B. (1968). Fairy tales and script drama analysis. *Transactional Analysis Bulletin, 7,* 39–43.

Knox, P., & Lichtenberg, J. (1991). Order out of chaos: A structural analysis of group therapy. *Journal of Counseling Psychology, 38,* 279–288.

LaFreniere, P., & Dumas, J. E. (1992). A transactional analysis of early childhood anxiety and social withdrawal. *Development and Psychopathology, 4,* 385–402.

Lammers, W. (1990). From cure to care: Transactional analysis treatment of adult asthma. *Transactional Analysis Journal, 20,* 245–252.

Martin, F. E. (1990). The relevance of a systemic model for the study and treatment of anorexia nervosa in adolescents. *Canadian Journal of Psychiatry, 35,* 496–500.

Massey, R. F. (1990). Berne's transactional analysis as a neo-Freudian/neo-Adlerian perspective. *Transactional Analysis Journal, 20,* 173–186.

Nykodym, N., Longenecker, C. O., & Ruud, W. N. (1991). Improving quality of work life with transactional analysis as an intervention change strategy. *Applied Psychology: An International Review, 40,* 395–404.

Oden, T. A. (1974). *Game free: A guide to the meaning of intimacy.* New York: Harper & Row.

O'Hearne, J. (1992). How and why do transactional-gestalt therapists work as they do? *American Journal of Psychology, 4,* 163–172.

Penfield, W. (1952). Memory mechanisms. *Archives of Neurology and Psychiatry, 67,* 178–198.

Pizer, I. (1994). Ethics in Europe. *Transactional Analysis Journal, 24,* 60–63.

Rumney, A., & Steckel, T. (1985). Growing up and getting dependency needs met as an adult: Reparenting in anorexia nervosa. *Transactional Analysis Journal, 15,* 55–61.

Shapiro, S. B. (1969). Critique of Eric Berne's contributions to subself theory. *Psychological Reports, 25,* 283–296.

Shilling, L. E. (1984). *Perspective on counseling theories.* Englewood Cliffs, NJ: Prentice Hall.

Silvestri, S. (1992). Treating adult children of divorce: A model based on redecision therapy. *Transactional Analysis Journal, 22,* 164–173.

Simoneux, J. (1977). Adlerian psychology and TA. In M. James (Ed.), *Techniques in Transactional Analysis for psychotherapists and counselors.* Reading, MA: Addison-Wesley.

Smith, D. (1982). Trends in counseling and psychotherapy. *American Psychologist, 37,* 802–809.

Steiner, C. (1974). *Scripts people live: Transactional analysis of life scripts.* New York: Grove Press.

Steiner, C. (1984). Emotional literacy. *Transactional Analysis Journal, 14,* 162–163.

Summerton, O. (1992). Game analysis in two planes. *Transactional Analysis Journal, 22,* 210–215.

Wollams, S., & Brown, M. (1979). *The total handbook of transactional analysis.* Englewood Cliffs, NJ: Prentice Hall.

The world of the mind steals the show. Behavior is not recognized as a subject in its own right. In psychotherapy, for example, the disturbing things a person does or says are almost always regarded merely as symptoms, and compared with the fascinating dramas which are stated in the depths of the mind, behavior itself seems superficial indeed. —B. F. Skinner

12 CHAPTER | Behavior Therapy

After years of living close to civilization, grizzly bears in Yellowstone National Park have lost their fear of humans. Before this region was so heavily populated by tourists and the garbage they leave behind, the bears avoided human contact. But recently the bears have become accustomed to people, and an alarming number of human fatalities has been the result. This is not only a terrible human tragedy, but the bears involved in such attacks must be destroyed. Because of this, there is concern that grizzly bears may become extinct.

Specialists have tried a number of strategies to protect the grizzlies, all to no avail. Even when trapped and transported deep into the wild, these fearless bears will return to human habitats. More recently, however, officials have begun a promising, new program to reestablish fear of humans in these animals. Once trapped and caged, a human delivers a brief, electric shock to the bear in order to associate humans with pain and thus teach bears, once again, to fear people. It's working. These bears quickly learn to associate people with pain and are far more likely to stay away from humans.

What does protecting grizzly bears have to do with behavior therapy, you may be asking. Actually, the principle used in protecting this endangered species, "learning by association," is basic to the process of learning in humans as well as animals. Perhaps you have received a ticket for speeding on the freeway. If so, you can probably pinpoint the spot, and even months later you still slow down as you near that location. You have associated it with an expensive penalty. **Behavior therapy** is built on the principle of association as well as a vast assortment of other laws of learning (e.g., shaping, punishment, and reinforcement). In the theory and techniques of behavior therapy you will discover a treatment strategy distinct from all others, an approach that is precise in its application and thoroughly grounded in its reliance on research.

BRIEF BIOGRAPHY

Behavior therapy, unlike other theories in this book, is not closely identified with any single person. It has several important proponents: O. H. Mower (1947), A. Salter (1949), H. G. Jones (1956), V. Meyer (1957), H. J. Eysenck (1959), J. D. Krumboltz (1966), A. J. Yates (1958, 1980), and Arnold Lazarus (1958, 1971, 1989) are some of the most influential. But it is largely through the successive work of three psychologists that behavior therapy came to be. It was B. F. Skinner's creative ideas that allowed the behavioral approach to grow into a major force in psychology and give behavioral therapy a solid platform. Joseph Wolpe launched a vigorous program of research and training in behavior therapy, making it the most empirically validated approach to psychotherapy. And Albert Bandura stimulated the behavior therapy movement by drawing on social psychology as a source of innovative therapeutic strategies, opening the way for other theorists and researchers to expand the boundaries of behavior therapy.

B. F. Skinner

Burrhus Frederic Skinner was born on March 20, 1904, in Susquehanna, a small railroad town in northeastern Pennsylvania. His childhood was spent, as he described it, in a warm, stable family environment. His father was a lawyer; his mother, according to Skinner, was rigid with high moral standards. While growing up, Skinner was an avid builder of things—sleds, rafts, seesaws, slingshots, blowguns, water pistols, scooters, wagons, model airplanes. He even built a gadget that confronted him with a sign in his bedroom closet whenever he failed to hang up his clothes (Skinner, 1976).

Skinner majored in English at a small liberal arts school in New York State, Hamilton College. After graduating in 1926, he attempted to make his mark as a writer of short stories. He even received encouragement from the noted poet Robert Frost. Gradually, however, he gave up in literary attempts and came to realize that he was intensely interested in human behavior but "had been investigating it in the wrong way" (Skinner, 1976, p. 291). In the fall of 1928, Skinner entered Harvard University and began studying psychology. After earning a Ph.D. in 1931, he stayed on at Harvard for five years doing research. He then took a teaching position at the University of Minnesota and later became chair of the Department of Psychology at Indiana University. In 1948 he returned to Harvard as a professor where he remained the rest of his career (Nye, 1992).

Skinner's first important book was *The Behavior of Organisms*, published in 1938. Among his later works are *Walden Two* (1948), *Science and Human Behavior* (1953), *Verbal Behavior* (1957), *The Technology of Teaching* (1968), *Beyond Freedom and Dignity* (1971), *About Behaviorism* (1974), and *Recent Issues in the Analysis of Behavior* (1989).

Skinner has been described as the most influential psychologist of this century and in one study (Goodell, 1975), 82 percent of college students could identify him. Skinner's last public appearance was on August 10, 1990, when he gave the keynote address at the opening ceremony of the American Psychological Association's annual convention. He died eight days later in Cambridge, Massachusetts, at age 86, of complications from leukemia.

Joseph Wolpe

Born in Johannesburg, South Africa, in 1915, Joseph Wolpe received his medical degree from the University of Witwaterstrand in South Africa.

Although his initial work was psychoanalytically focused, by 1944, Wolpe was moving away from this approach in search of something more effective and began reading the work of Pavlov. By the late 1940s he had also been exposed to the writings of Hull and Mary Cover Jones. The learning principles he discovered in his study became the basis for Wolpe's landmark work, *Psychotherapy by Reciprocal Inhibition* (1958). Wolpe not only developed specific therapy techniques but provided numerous case histories with outcome data in support of the efficacy of this "systematic desensitization" approach. At the University of Witwaterstrand in South Africa, Wolpe met frequently with several colleagues and students who were excited about this new and effective way to treat anxiety and phobias. Arnold Lazarus and Stanley Rachman were among those in this group. They later helped to spread Wolpe's systematic desensitization technique to England and the United States, where Wolpe himself moved in 1963.

In 1966, Wolpe, by then at Temple University School of Medicine in Philadelphia, launched a program of research and training in behavior therapy. The same year, a nonprofit clinic and training center called the Behavior Therapy Institute and headed by Arnold Lazarus opened in Sausalito, California; a new book, *Behavior Therapy Techniques*, by Wolpe and Lazarus (his colleague at Temple), appeared; and the following year Wolpe and behavior therapy were introduced to the nation's intelligentsia by an article in the *New York Times Magazine*.

Albert Bandura

Born December 4, 1925, Albert Bandura grew up in the tiny hamlet of Mundare in northern Alberta, Canada. His parents were wheat farmers of Polish heritage, but little is known about his early life. We do not have an autobiographical statement from his own pen, nor has any other biographer contributed much information about Bandura's life. We do know, however, that Bandura was 1 of 20 students in a high school that had only two teachers and few resources. As a result, Bandura learned early to rely on his own academic initiative. After graduating from high school, Bandura got a summer job on a highway crew, patching holes in the Alaska highway and then matriculated at the University of British Columbia in Vancouver. From there he chose the University of Iowa for graduate study because of its emphasis on learning and rigorous experimentation. Even then Bandura was interested in the application of learning theory to clinical phenomena. It was at Iowa that Bandura met his future wife, Virginia.

Following completion of his Ph.D. in clinical psychology in 1952, Bandura joined the faculty at Stanford University. Under the influence of Robert Sears he began investigation of interactive processes in psychotherapy and on the family patterns that lead to aggressiveness in children. The work on familial causes of aggression, with Richard Walters, his first graduate student, gave rise to the emphasis on the central role of modeling influences in personality development and eventually culminated in their book, *Social Learning and Personality Development* (1963).

Bandura describes himself as conducting a multifaceted research program aimed at clarifying aspects of human capability that should be emphasized in a comprehensive theory of human behavior. His 1986 book, *Social Foundations of Thought and Action*, represents an effort to develop such a comprehensive theory. Professor Bandura is also known for *Principles of Behavior Modification* (1969) and his popular *Social Learning Theory* (1977). Today, Bandura continues to influence the field of behavior therapy in the post he has held at Stanford for more than 40 years.

HISTORICAL DEVELOPMENT

Behavior therapy has been described as having "a long past but a short history" (O'Leary & Wilson, 1987, p. 1), meaning that while many of its techniques have been in use for countless years, behavior therapy as a systematized approach dates back to only the 1950s. To understand this relatively new approach, however, one must begin with its "long past."

The beginnings of behavior therapy can be found in two converging historical events: the rise of behaviorism and the development of the experimental method in psychology (Wilson, 1989). **Behaviorism,** as a philosophy, is a metaphysical view based on *naturalism,* which assumes that the universe is composed exclusively of matter and energy, and hence there are no such things as supernatural entities. Human qualities such as "mind," "unconscious," "soul," or "will" are in this view presumed either not to exist or to be understandable by the same physical laws that explain the rest of existence. Behaviorism's embrace of naturalism gave rise to the implication that all behaviors are caused by factors outside of themselves; all behavior is viewed as caused by events in the environment (Sechrest & Smith, 1994).

The leading figure in this movement was John B. Watson, professor at Johns Hopkins University, who directly challenged the prevalent "introspectionist" theories like psychoanalysis and proposed that such "mentalistic" approaches were unscientific and irrelevant. For Watson, psychology would only make a significant contribution if it were to follow after the natural sciences in dealing exclusively with the study of overt behavior. He sought to discredit ideas like unresolved Oedipal strivings and id-ego conflicts by proving that a phobia could be induced solely through external forces. Watson presented an 11-month-old infant named Albert with a tame white rat and then crashed a hammer against a steel bar held just behind Albert's head. After only seven repetitions of this traumatic sequence, Albert was conditioned: He now showed a strong fear of the rat alone and also generalized his fear to other furry animals such as rabbits (Samelson, 1980; Watson, 1913, 1919, 1924). By the mid-1920s Watson carried his thinking into crusading perspectives. With examples like Albert, Watson postulated that behavior could be controlled scientifically and that the place of traditional religious mores could be replaced by experimental ethics.

> I am sometimes asked, "Do you think of yourself as you think of the organisms you study?" The answer is yea. So far as I know, my behavior at any given moment has been nothing more than the product of my genetic endowment, my personal history, and the current setting. That does not mean that I can explain everything I do or have done.
>
> —B. F. Skinner

In his book *Behaviorism* (1924), Watson stated: "Give me a dozen healthy infants, well formed . . . and I'll guarantee you to take any one at random and train him to become any type of specialist I might select" (p. 82).

In addition to the rise of behaviorism, experimental research on the psychology of learning also contributed to the development of behavior therapy. This is an approach based on a view known as *logical positivism,* under which everything that exists is empirically verifiable. From this perspective, if the material universe, understandable only as matter and energy operating according to universal laws, is all that is, then human beings are material beings only and hence explainable by natural laws. In a sense, the experimental method was putting behaviorism's philosophy into practice. This was first evident in 1879 when Wilhelm Wundt set up the first psychological laboratory in Leipzig, Germany. He decided to dispense with mental faculties and supernatural concepts such as the human soul and concentrate his attention on experience as the appropriate subject of psychology. But it was Russian physiologist Ivan Pavlov's turn-of-the-century experiment demonstrating classical conditioning principles, as revealed in the salivation responses of dogs, that was the most seminal event in the catalyst for this experimental movement in psychology. Around the same time in the United States E. L. Throndike was developing his famous law of effect, in which he described how behavior was learned according to principles of reward and punishment, and Mary Cover Jones (1924) demonstrated how counterconditioning can be employed to help children overcome phobic reactions. In the late 1930s, B. F. Skinner elaborated the principles of instrumental learning with his work on operant conditioning. As with Pavlov and Watson, Skinner (1938) carried out innumerable experiments on animals to establish his behavioristic psychology. In 1932 he introduced what is now known as the *Skinner box,* with which he studied the learning habits of pigeons and rats and in a dramatic display revealed that through proper reinforcement, pigeons could even learn to play ping-pong. Eventually Skinner's studies were also transposed to human learning, as described in his books *Walden Two* (1948) and *Beyond Freedom and Dignity* (1971), where the so-called freedom and dignity of humankind are viewed simply as products of reinforcement.

The work of Ivan Pavlov, with his salivating dogs, John Watson's discovery that phobias could be induced by scaring infants, and B. F. Skinner's fascination with teaching pigeons to play ping-pong are important milestones in the development of behavioristic thinking (Kanfer & Goldstein, 1980). But it was Joseph Wolpe (1958) who first translated those early research efforts into action techniques for promoting systematic client change. In 1958 he wrote one of the most important books in the development of behavior therapy, *Psychotherapy by Reciprocal Inhibition.* Until that time, no practitioner had systematically presented learning principles to the practice of counseling. Wolpe used a combination of classical conditioning theory and Clark Hull's then-popular learning theory as the basis for his work. Anxiety was learned through conditioned reactions in Wolpe's view, and he devised several techniques to extinguish this anxiety. The most widely cited and used of these was Wolpe's systematic desensitization which continues to be a powerful behavioral treatment today (discussed later in this chapter).

It was not until the advent of systematic desensitization that behavior therapy as we know it today began to emerge. The term *behavior therapy* was introduced independently by three groups of researchers. Skinner and Lindsley (1954) referred to their use of operant conditioning principles with chronic schizophrenics as behavior therapy; Eysenck (1959) used the term in applying "modern learning theory" to treatment strategies; and Arnold Lazarus (1958) coined the term behavior therapy to refer to the addition of objective laboratory procedures to traditional psychotherapeutic methods. In this respect, Lazarus felt that behavior therapy is but one part of a total picture that could include certain elements of traditional psychotherapy with validated techniques from any source.

After its birth in the late 1950s, behavior therapy grew quickly in the 1960s as a significant alternative to psychodynamic approaches, causing John D. Krumboltz, a strong proponent and popularizer of this new therapy, to write *Revolution in Counseling* (1966). Behavioral strategies such as the token economy were applied to institutional settings (Ayllon & Azrin, 1968), and by 1969, Albert Bandura published the tremendously influential *Principles of Behavior Modification,* in which he describes the importance of behavioral modeling—learning by observing others and then being reinforced for performing as the model does. Concurrent with these developments were the formation of the Association for Advancement of Behavior Therapy and the emergence of several journals devoted exclusively to behavior therapy. In the 1970s behavior therapy gained widespread acceptance and by the 1980s, behavioral approaches were being refined and undergoing significant revisions, enough to make a common definition of behavior therapy next to impossible (Farkas, 1980; Follette & Houts, 1992; Masters, Bursh, Hollon, & Rimm, 1987; Ross, 1985). By the end of the decade behavior therapy had basically split into three main theories: respondent learning (emphasizing Pavlov and Watson's findings), operant conditioning (emphasizing Skinner's approach), and social modeling (emphasizing Bandura's vicarious learning). However, there are few purists in any of these schools; counselors who employ a behavioral approach usually integrate aspects of each of these theories.

> All of life is nothing other than the realization of one purpose: the preservation of life itself, the tireless labor of which may be called the general life instinct.
> —Ivan Pavlov

VIEW OF HUMAN NATURE

Despite the diversity of thought among behavior therapists, certain characteristics can be identified as basic to the overall approach. To begin with, the individual is seen as a product of his or her experience. Therefore, in the behavior therapy approach, people are neither good nor bad; they are essentially neutral. Because the "laws of learning" are emphasized, behavior therapists are less likely to emphasize commonalities of experience (e.g., stages of development and self-actualization) and instead focus on the way in which learning can lead to the development of practically any pattern of human behavior imaginable, depending upon the person's learning history and biological potential. One implication of this is that behavior therapists tend not to employ a standard diagnostic nomenclature, which is judged to be rooted more in theory than reality.

The behavioral view of human nature is generally interactional—that is, it gives serious consideration to both personal and environmental determinants of human behavior. To the behavior therapist *inter*psychic views of personality underemphasize the pervasive effect that external events have upon persons. They believe instead that the behavior originates primarily from *intra*psychic causes.

Most behavior therapists would also argue that humans are basically hedonistic in nature. Therefore, behavior therapy is maximally responsive to requests to end or decrease personal suffering and to promote growth toward greater pleasure and enjoyment of life. Behavior therapists have no model of optimal human functioning toward which clients are led.

DEVELOPMENT OF MALADAPTIVE BEHAVIOR

From the behavior therapy perspective psychopathology is defined as behavior that is disadvantageous or dangerous to the individual and/or to other people. Certain environmental circumstances shape the development of maladaptive behavior. Insufficient reinforcement, for example, occurs when a person acts but does not receive a reward. On the other hand, reinforcement for maladaptive actions is also a possibility. This occurs when an individual is reinforced for negative behavior. The child who tells the truth about misbehaving and is immediately punished versus the child who lies about bad behavior and avoids punishment is an example.

Another cause of maladaptive behavior from the behavioral perspective is the reliance on a single, self-defeating reinforcer such as food, smoking, alcohol, or other addictive behaviors to cope with problems in life. Excessive punishment in place of positive reinforcement to control behavior can also lead to pathological behavior. For when punishment is used, anxiety and fear may develop (Krumboltz & Thoresen, 1976).

Insufficient cues to predict consequences occurs when individuals do not know when certain behavior is appropriate. In other words, individuals may be unaware of the effect their behavior may have on others and on themselves, or they may incorrectly anticipate others' behaviors. This often results from poorly designed contingencies of reinforcement, punishment, or inappropriate generalizations, such as little Albert's fear of rabbits. A more clinical example might be a person who has one or two unpleasant experiences with her boss, for example, and becomes hostile and fearful toward all authority figures. The person then takes on a defensive stance with authorities and evokes true negative reactions from other authority figures she meets, thereby perpetuating the faulty belief and self-defeating behavior (Marks, 1994).

From a Skinnerian perspective, maladaptive behavior is often shaped through reinforcement. For example, a child may engage in temper tantrums because the parents have reinforced such behavior with attention and concern. Or a busy parent may fail to respond to the child's polite request and answer only louder and louder calls, thereby shaping the child in the direction of becoming irritatingly noisy. According to Skinner (1953, p. 98), "[Such] differential reinforcement supplied by a preoccupied or negligent parent is very close to the procedure we should adopt if we were given the task of conditioning a child to be annoying." A shy child, on the other hand, may be regarded by a well-meaning but misguided teacher who pays close attention to shy pupils only when they isolate themselves from their classmates and sulk.

Perhaps the most painful of all maladaptive behaviors stems from an overly severe set of self-standards and the resulting attempt to avoid guilt or external punishments through excessive self-criticism. "There is no more devastating punishment than self-contempt," writes Bandura (1977, p. 141, 154). "Linus, the security-blanketed member of the 'Peanuts' clan, also alluded to this phenomenon when he observed, 'There is no heavier burden than a great potential.'" Of course, Bandura differs from Skinner in his understanding of maladaptive behavior by attributing considerable importance to inner, cognitive causes of psychopathology.

> Neurotic habits are distinguished by their resistance to extinction in the face of their unadaptiveness.
>
> —Joseph Wolpe

"Many human dysfunctions and ensuing torments stem from problems of thought. This is because, in their thoughts, people often dwell on painful pasts and on perturbing futures of their own invention. . . . They drive themselves to despondency by harsh self-evaluation. . . . And they often act on misconceptions that get them into trouble." (Bandura, 1986, p. 515)

FUNCTION OF THE THERAPIST

A behavior therapist may take on one of several roles, depending on the client's goals, but generally a counselor who takes a behavioral approach is active in counseling. He or she serves as a consultant in behavior change, a supporter and motivator in the process of change, a resource in clarifying the problem and designing change strategies, and a model of more functional behavior (Gilliland, James, & Bowman, 1989). He or she may even work with people in the client's environment who are assisting in the behavioral change process.

To better understand the function of the behavior therapist, one can study the four major steps most behavior therapists take in the process of working with a client (Blackham & Siberman, 1971; Kazdin, 1978; Krumboltz, 1966). To begin with, the behavior therapist attempts to accurately and concretely define the problem. Thus, the therapist asks the client to specify when, where, how, and with whom the problem arises. The counselor may benefit from actually observing the problem behavior, but that is not absolutely necessary. It should be noted, by the way, that while counselors using a behavioral approach differ widely regarding the use of psychological tests and diagnoses, most rarely use paper-and-pencil personality profiles and instead attempt to measure the client's behavior and action. Next, the therapist conducts a developmental history of the client. In other words, the therapist tries to learn how the client has handled past circumstances and whether the presenting problem might be organically based.

After defining the problem and taking a developmental history, behavioral counselors help clients establish specific goals, breaking down large goals into small, achievable units. Counselors also set up learning experiences for clients

12.1 | **B. F. Skinner on Counseling**

In interviewing B. F. Skinner, Mary Harrington Hall asked about his view of clinical psychology and psychotherapy. Here is what he said.

Skinner: Well, they won't get anywhere if they don't get results. And you can't get results by sitting around and theorizing about the inner world of the disturbed. I want to say to those people: get down to the facts. But they seem to be threatened by facts. Operant conditioning—the proper arrangement and management of contingencies of reinforcement—has been fantastically successful with a number of problems of disordered behavior.

Take autistic children, for example. Our success in that area is a real threat, you see, to the people who think that the problem is something about the inner life, or the lack of identity, or alienation, or whatever all those things are that these kids are supposed to be suffering from.

What they are suffering from in fact is very bad schedules of reinforcement. That is something you can change for them, but this is not done. And you really can't expect mentalistic psychologists to do things like that; their approach just simply destines them to inadequacy and failure.

Oh, but they are so sincere. They want to understand the boys, to sit and talk and gain their confidence, and all of this stuff. Meanwhile, there is a very simple way in which you can begin to get them to behave in a very respectable way and to learn the kinds of skills that will give them a chance to be effective citizens.

Take the problem in correctional institutions, for example. One of our people recently took over one of the buildings in a training school for boys and organized it on the basis of a point-reinforcement system. The boys were paid for their work, and they had to buy everything except basics. For free they could get the basic diet and a place to sleep in the dormitory, but anything else they had to buy. And the most points were given for learning something interesting with the help of teaching machines, or without. They got points for learning.

Don't you see, that's the point. It made them discover for the first time that they could learn something, and that learning something was valuable. This is a very important thing. Most of them had been convinced by our school systems that they were stupid. They discovered that they really weren't. It's remarkable, surprising, it really works! How very different it is from hand-holding and getting to know the boys.

Source: Hall, M. H. (1967). The behavioral view: A conversation with B. F. Skinner. In P. Chance & T. G. Harris (Eds.), *The best of Psychology Today* (p. 535). New York: McGraw-Hill.

to develop any needed skills (Krumboltz & Thoresen, 1976). For example, if a parent wants to avoid losing his or her temper with a son or daughter, the parent must first define what losing one's temper is and then make incremental steps toward reaching the major goal.

Finally, the behavioral therapist must determine the best methods for change. Several behavioral methods may be effective in helping a client reach desired goals, and some may work better than others in any client's particular case. Therefore, the therapist must continually assess the effectiveness of selected methods and modify ones that are not working or try new ones.

GOALS OF THERAPY

Essentially, the goal of behavior therapy is to extinguish the client's identified maladaptive behavior and to introduce or strengthen adaptive behavior that can serve as a replacement and enable him or her to live a productive, happy life (Thoresen, 1969). The key to reaching this goal has nothing to do with uncovering psychological conflicts and everything to do with helping the client *learn* new behaviors. In behavior therapy, change comes simply through modifying one's behavior.

To more accurately understand the goals of behavior therapy, one must view the process of change through the three behavioral lenses of learning, three paradigms that can stand alone but are often integrated: respondent learning, operant conditioning, and social modeling.

Respondent learning was discovered by Pavlov, and it is evident when a stimulus that is neutral is paired with a stimulus that has an effect until the neutral stimulus begins to elicit the same effects as the primary stimulus. Using Pavlov's experiments with dogs, the bell becomes a **conditioned stimulus,** in that just like the food, it elicits salivation in the dog. The dog's response to the food is called an **unconditioned response;** its response to the bell, once the bell becomes a conditioned stimulus, is called a **conditioned response.** Behavior then is a function of a stimulus. This reduces considerably the complex factors influencing human reactions to situations and allows the behaviorist to focus on a specific problem as a reaction to a given set of stimuli. From this paradigm, the goal of behavior therapy is to pair stimuli that strengthen healthy behavior; it is to make adaptive generalizations. For example, the female client who has grown up with a destructive father has learned specifically to not trust her father. She may generalize her father's behavior to all men (making them a conditioned stimulus). Thus, learning to differentiate among stimuli becomes an important goal from the perspective of respondent learning (Wilson, 1995).

In **operant conditioning** a behavior occurs and some event follows the behavior that is reinforcing. This **positive reinforcement** increases the chance that the behavior will reoccur in the future. If a counselor, for example, responds favorably when a client practices a relaxation exercise, and if such a favorable response is followed by the client performing the exercise more and more, the counselor's response is said to be a **positive reinforcer.** In like fashion, **negative reinforcement** is anything that increases the probability of a response as a result of avoiding something negative that would have occurred had the behavior not been emitted (Rasnake, 1993). An example of this would be a client whose avoidance of flying in airplanes is strengthened by the relief that comes from avoiding such activity. A similar concept, **punishment,** refers to the aversive consequences of a response and is often followed by a decrease in that response. For example, a child who is spanked by a parent after asking questions would likely decrease his or her questioning. It is important to note that in operant conditioning, if no reinforcement is ever given, the probability of behavior change is unlikely. Thus from this perspective, the goal of therapy is to find reinforcers that strengthen adaptive behavior.

The third form of learning, **social modeling,** or *vicarious learning* as it is sometimes called, occurs independently of reinforcement when a person sees another's behavior that "teaches" him or her a new way of behaving. This approach was put forth by Albert Bandura (1977), who theorized that almost all important learning takes place through a social modeling approach that emphasizes the self-regulation of behavior and de-emphasizes the importance of external reinforcers. Bandura points out that millions of people, watching and imitating others at Toastmasters Clubs, have overcome their fear of public speaking. Commercials featuring admired athletes and celebrities are also vivid examples of the potency of imitative learning. From this perspective, the goal of therapy is to provide the client with models that strengthen adaptive behavior.

> There is no scientific evidence for the Freudian conception of neurosis. . . . A neurosis is just a habit—a persistent habit of unadaptive behavior, acquired by learning.
>
> —Joseph Wolpe

The specific goals of behavior therapy vary with each client, but in all cases, the general goal is to create new conditions for learning to ameliorate problem behaviors.

MAJOR METHODS AND TECHNIQUES

Because the quality of the counseling relationship is de-emphasized in behavior therapy, and because the main priority of this approach is the resolution of the client's symptoms, the behavioral therapist relies heavily on a large repertoire of techniques to deal with client problems. Unlike other therapeutic schools, techniques in the behavioral approach must be effectively supported by empirical research as measured against specifiable ends. In fact, any technique that can be demonstrated to change behavior may be incorporated into a behavioral treatment plan, according to Arnold Lazarus (1989). He advocates the use of diverse techniques, regardless of their theoretical origin. Intervention methods associated with behavior therapy are so varied that the *Dictionary of Behavior Therapy Techniques* (Bellack & Hersen, 1987) contains descriptions of more than 150 techniques. The methods described in this section, therefore, are only a sample portion of the strategies available to the behavior therapist: behavioral assessment, positive reinforcement, token economies, assertiveness training, modeling, relaxation training, systematic desensitization, and flooding. These techniques are representative of some of the most common and effective techniques in the evolving field of behavior therapy.

Behavioral Assessment

Behavior therapists often begin work with clients by using a behavioral assessment developed to collect specific information about the client's presenting problem and accompanying behavior (Nelson & Barlow, 1981). After asking about the problem, the therapist would attempt to get as specific and concrete as possible by asking the client questions such as: "If I were watching you in this situation, what would I see you do?" The goal is to understand what the client does in particular situations. The purpose of behavioral interviewing is to identify the target behavior and the controlling variables and to plan an appropriate intervention strategy. And while the therapist can work to define the presenting problem concretely, understanding its antecedents and consequences, the client may not be ready to reveal the true problem at the beginning of the behavioral assessment. For this reason a global assessment is sometimes used in which several structured interviews assess employment, sleep, stress, and relationships (Lazarus, 1971). This allows the therapist to use information derived from the structured interview along with the initial description of the presenting problem to develop a more accurate picture of the problem.

Behavioral assessment may include the use of questionnaires and interviews with significant others (Nelson & Barlow, 1981). Self-monitoring is another often-used assessment tool in which the client is asked to record his or her thoughts, feelings, and behaviors as they happen. This can provide valuable information in completing an accurate picture of the client's behavior. The bottom line of behavioral assessment is that specificity is necessary to develop individualized treatment plans (Galassi & Perot, 1992).

> At a recent cocktail party . . . [I] was cornered by an inquiring lady who expressed considerable puzzlement over adolescents' fascination for unusual and bizarre styles. The lady herself was draped with a sack, wearing a preposterous object on her head, and spiked high heel shoes that are more likely to land one in an orthopedic clinic, than to transport one across the room to the olives.
> —Albert Bandura

Positive Reinforcement

This is probably the most widely used and most successful of all the behavior modification techniques. It involves providing a reward for positive behavior. The reward can be anything ranging from a token that can be used to purchase goods, to a star in one's book, to a verbal compliment, to a smile. The principle underlying positive reinforcement is that the tendency to repeat a response to a given stimulus will be strengthened as the response is rewarded. The key to successful positive reinforcement is selecting a reinforcer that will indeed strengthen the desired behavior. It is therefore necessary for the counselor to test out reinforcers, and one of the best ways of doing this is simply by asking the client what will best serve as a reward.

Token Economies

Token economies can be applied to shape behavior when approval and other intangible reinforcers do not work. Under this system, appropriate behavior may be reinforced with "tokens" that can be later exchanged for desired objects or privileges. Tokens can be used to obtain candy and toys or to participate in certain programs. The advantages of using a token economy are that tokens do not lose their incentive value and they are a concrete measure of the person's motivation to change certain behaviors. Tokens also give the person receiving them the opportunity to decide how to use them.

Assertiveness Training

The major tenet of **assertiveness training** is that a person should be free to express thoughts and feelings appropriately without feeling undue anxiety (Alberti & Emmons, 1982). The technique is especially helpful for timid clients and basically consists of counterconditioning their social anxiety and reinforcing their assertive behavior. The main method of assertiveness training is **behavior rehearsal,** in which the therapist helps the client practice behaving more assertively. The client is first taught that everyone has the right of self-expression and how aggressive, passive, and assertive actions differ. The client and therapist then begin rehearsing assertive situations, and the therapist offers feedback regarding the client's performance. Eventually the client is able to transfer the rehearsal to real situations where his or her behavior can become more adaptive with some assertiveness.

Modeling

Modeling is used to help a client acquire desired responses or to extinguish fears through observing the behavior of another person. This observation can be presented in a live modeling demonstration, in symbolic form through written and media-taped models, or via the client's own imagination. Through live modeling the counselor can demonstrate a behavior by role-playing, taking the part of the client and showing him or her a different way to respond or behave. A client who wishes to acquire self-expression skills, for instance, may benefit from seeing the counselor demonstrate such skills in role-played situations. Of course, live models other than the counselor can be equally effective. In fact it is best to select a model who is quite similar to the client in age, gender, ethnic background, social status, and so on. Researchers have found that arranging conditions so that clients hear or see themselves performing the desired response on tape can be a powerful learning tool (Hosford & deVisser, 1974).

While live models are often the best form for vicarious learning (Perry & Furukawa, 1980), they are often difficult to use because of the lack of control in ensuring their systematic demonstration of the desired behavior. To remedy this, many counselors make use of symbolic models through audiotapes or videotapes in which a desired behavior is introduced and presented. For example, the client who wants to improve his or her ability to make public speeches can read about successful people and their ability to overcome struggles in learning to become effective speakers, or the client can listen to an audiotape or watch a videotape on the same subject. Yet another way of using modeling as a technique in therapy is to have the client imagine a model performing a desired behavior or activity (Cautela, 1976). For example, if a client wants to be more vulnerable with his or her spouse, the client and therapist would develop a situation or scene to imagine. In this scene the client would be performing new behaviors (e.g., freely talking about his or her feelings) with favorable consequences. Of course, the favorable outcome must be something that is realistic and within the client's reach.

Relaxation Training

The most common form of relaxation training used by behavior therapists is called **progressive relaxation,** or muscle relaxation. It is used to treat a wide variety of disorders, including headaches, psychosomatic pain, hypertension, and other anxiety related problems. The basic premise of relaxation training is that muscle tension exacerbates anxiety and as a result individuals experience a reduction in felt anxiety by learning to discriminate between tense and relaxed muscle groups and relax them upon cue. The procedure involves training clients to successively tense and relax various muscle groups in their bodies while the counselor directs their attention to pleasant sensations. The training needs to occur in a quiet environment, and the counselor uses a quiet soothing tone of voice when delivering the relaxation instructions. Each step in the process of alternating tension and relaxation of each muscle group takes about 10 to 15 seconds, with a 10- to 15-second pause between each of the steps. The entire procedure takes 20 to 30 minutes. After going through the procedure several times with the counselor's assistance, clients are encouraged to practice it on their own, daily if possible.

In using relaxation training, it is important for counselors to remember that many clients have developed a state of chronic muscular tension that may not disappear after only one or two attempts at muscle relaxation. Also, some clients may need more or less time to tense and relax muscles; others may prefer much less dialogue from the counselor. The point is that successful use of this technique requires that the counselor apply the procedure with each client in an individualized way.

Systematic Desensitization

This anxiety-reducing technique is based on the learning principles of classical conditioning and was developed by Joseph Wolpe (1958, 1982). **Systematic desensitization** involves the pairing of a neutral event or stimulus with a stimulus that already elicits fear. Desensitization employs counterconditioning, substituting one type of response for another, to progressively lower the client's level of fear. In a relatively relaxed state, the client is exposed, step-by-step, to increasingly stronger stimuli until what used to bring about fear can now be experienced in a state of relaxation.

The procedure itself involves three basic steps and, on average, takes about 10 to 30 sessions to complete, depending on the client, the problem, and the intensity of the anxiety. There are three basic steps in desensitization: training in deep muscles relaxation (discussed previously), constructing a hierarchy of emotionally provoking situations, and progressively pairing the items on the hierarchy with a state of relaxation in the client.

Hierarchy construction involves identifying various situations that evoke fear or anxiety. It involves situations the client has already experienced or anticipates experiencing in the future and usually consists of 10 to 20 different items arranged by the client in graduated order from the lowest or least anxiety-provoking to the highest. The following is an example of a hierarchy constructed to eliminate the fear of snakes:

See the word "snake" in a book.
See a picture of a snake in a book.
Hear someone talk about snakes.
See a live snake in the zoo.
See a dead snake as you walk down the road.
See a live snake as you drive down the road.
See a live snake as you walk down the road.
Touch a dead snake on the road.
Touch a live snake held by someone else.
Hold a dead snake.
Hold a live snake.

Once the hierarchy has been constructed and the client has been trained in muscle relaxation, the counselor and client are ready to begin the pairing process. This starts with the counselor and client agreeing on a signal the client can use to let the counselor know if and when he or she is experiencing any anxiety during the pairing (usually the raising of an index finger). A state of relaxation is then induced for the client, and the counselor asks the client to imagine the first item on the hierarchy. The scene is presented for about 10 seconds, assuming the client does not signal anxiety prior to this time, and concludes when the counselor says something like, "Now stop imaging that scene." This is done several times until the client can imagine that scene without sensing any anxiety. Once this is achieved, the counselor moves up the hierarchy presenting the next scene until it can be imagined with no anxiety. Each desensitization session involving the pairing process typically begins with the last item successfully completed during the previous session and ends with a non-anxiety item. The pairing process is usually terminated in each session after successful completion of three to five hierarchy items. Because the pairing process may occur over several weeks, it is important for the counselor to keep accurate written notations about each item as it is presented to the client (Goldried & Davison, 1976).

12.2 | **A Diary of Self-Modification**

Israel Goldiamond

A distinguished teacher of behavior modification calmly explains how he turned a tragic automobile accident into a personal triumph.

One autumn afternoon in 1970, I found myself lying on my back, watching a white cloud moving slowly across a blue sky. My leg was bent back under my arm, totally devoid of feeling. I suspected, lying there on the grass near my wrecked car, that I might have suffered a spinal injury. Soon an ambulance arrived to take me to a nearby hospital, where I underwent surgery. A few weeks later I transferred to a rehabilitation hospital in the large city where my wife and I live. The hospital was to be my home for the next eight months.

During my hospitalization I observed my own behavior as a patient, as well as the behavior of my fellow patients. These observations did not occur in an intellectual vacuum, but in the context of my previous work as a psychologist. My approach to observation stemmed from the *experimental analysis of behavior,* or what might be called functional behaviorism. According to this viewpoint, if certain patterns of behavior occur on certain occasions, it may be because certain consequences can be observed to follow. On these occasions, the consequences are contingent on the behavior and maintain it. By understanding and changing these relations we can understand and change the behavior. This approach, when applied to clinical and classroom problems, is named *behavior modification;* when applied to courses of study, it is *programmed instruction;* and when applied to physiological problems, it is *biofeedback.*

In our laboratory and clinic at the University of Chicago, my colleagues and I have been applying behavior analysis to emotional and other problems of hospital outpatients. Our program required self-analysis and self-control. We train the patient to discover and change the contingencies, the environmental conditions, that govern his behavior. By finding out what these contingencies are, the patient can analyze and understand his own responses.

When I awoke in the intensive-care unit after surgery, I realized that if I wanted to get back to the work I enjoy, work that I feel is important, I would have to exert the same type of self-control and analysis we had been applying in our clinic. I would have to specify the outcomes I wished to attain, discover the existing behaviors which were relevant to these outcomes, and develop a program to convert my current repertoire of behaviors to the desired repertoire. I would have to discover the contingencies governing my own behavior.

The patients enrolled in our self-control clinic must keep daily logs of their behaviors and other events, so I assigned myself this task as well. I kept a meticulous account of my physical abilities and progress. I made graphs. I described muscle movements. I recorded medications, surgery and X-rays. I noted some exercises I had imposed on myself ("9:15–9:20 a.m., shrugged shoulders 10 times"). Much later, I noted that when a person crawls forward the right arm and the left leg move together, but when he crawls backward the right arm and right leg move together.

I also recorded my own emotions—elation, annoyance, etc., and the contingencies responsible for producing them. Usually the contingencies were quite clear, but in one case they were not. Then the records I had kept proved to be valuable in clarifying them.

The problem was sleeplessness. The staff had to log-roll me every two hours during my sleep so that I would not develop skin ulcers, but I always fell asleep again. One evening in February I was unable to fall asleep for two hours after the final log-roll. The next night I was sleepless for four hours, the next for six, and on the fourth and fifth nights I was totally sleepless. My nurse attributed my mounting sleeplessness to mounting anxiety. What was I thinking about that kept me awake? Was I worried? What about?

Of course I was worried. If one can't sleep, one is liable to worry about it, and many of my thoughts were not pleasant; there is no reason why one's thoughts should be pleasant when one is lying sleepless in a hospital. But, as I have taught outpatients in our self-control program, emotions do not cause behavior. Contingencies determine both emotions and behavior. The solution had to be that something was keeping me awake at night. The nurse could find nothing in her record so I look in mine. For the past four months I had been taking 40 milligrams of Valium (a tranquilizer and muscle relaxer) every day. This is a high dosage, and I had been told to kick it at my convenience, as I had previously kicked similar medications. I asked for 30 milligrams one day, and on the next day, the one preceding my first sleepless period, I switched to zero. My pattern of sleeplessness fit one of the many withdrawal symptoms that can occur upon termination of Valium treatment. When I discovered this, I promptly reinstated myself on a low dosage and began to sleep soundly all night. During the following month, I gradually faded the medication out completely.

Ongoing Professionalism

I kept up my professional activities while I was hospitalized. Even though I was immobilized, I conferred with a grant committee in my hospital room. By the start of the spring quarter, I was making weekend visits home, where I resumed my graduate seminar. When a small skin ulcer appeared on a buttock, I simply conducted class lying on my other side on the living room couch. I ran the laboratory

(continued)

12.2   A Diary of Self-Modification (continued)

and clinic from my hospital room, with research assistants, staff, students and colleagues constantly there during visiting hours. One weekend I addressed the annual banquet of the Association for Precision Teaching. I also took on a new client in a self-control weight program. My new roommate, John McWethy, editor of the Midwest edition of *The Wall Street Journal* and a severely impaired quadriplegic, caught my bad habits. He began to run his office from the same room and has since resumed his duties.

Resumption of my professional life was critical to me. Since doing so required that I participate in the rehabilitation program at the hospital, I participated above and beyond the call of duty. In other words, there was a contingency relation between my participation in the rehabilitation program and the resumption of my professional activities.

Problems as Goals

My laboratory office is on the second floor of a museum. To get there I go down a loading ramp to the basement, where there is a freight elevator. This requires that I telephone in advance to make sure the basement doors are open and the elevator is available. If calling every day became bothersome, I would arrange to arrive at definite hours so that my arrival could be anticipated, as is the arrival of visitors to the museum every morning when the guards unlock the main gates. The visitors too are dependent, in their case on the guard's completion of his duly appointed rounds.

Recently a nurse asked me to discuss the various difficulties of being disabled, because some patients were "not realistic about them." I declined indignantly. It is far more sensible, useful and fulfilling to define problems in terms of goals and ways to program getting them.

When the professional refers to a patient as being "unaware of," "not realistic about," or "repressing" his problem it is often the professional who is being unrealistic. If I choose not to discuss my pains, problems, and infections, it is not because I am unaware, unrealistic, or repressing. At times I am painfully aware of them, and I mean that literally. If a patient does not "face up" to these issues, it may be because he is facing, or trying to face, in a different direction, one that can help him achieve his goal.

The Crumbling Contingencies

Seated in my wheelchair, I very often feel a discomfort in my seat. I might call it pain. This occurs most frequently when I am not working. Now one way to talk about this is to say that because I am not working my attention has turned to my seat, and I feel discomfort. Either way I get sympathy and support, but neither approach is particularly helpful. A third way to talk about it is to say that the reason I am not working is because the contingencies which maintain productive work are absent or crumbling. The discomfort in my butt is a signal to me that something is lacking contingency-wise. My butt is apparently more sensitive to this state of affairs than is my intellect.

It follows that when I start to feel the discomfort, I should immediately attend to the contingencies before they break down completely. I should set up working conditions so that my writing can progress. True, I will not get sympathy, but my behavior will get the same support of my colleagues, which maintained it at a high rate before, and which I valued then and value now.

Reaction to one's own injury is supposed to cause depression. By considering apathy, depression or aggression as inevitable developmental stages in injury (or aging or illness), the professional staff can avoid asking how their actions might have been causal. The hospital told my wife to expect me to be profoundly depressed. When she protested that I was not depressed, the staff greeted the news with great skepticism.

Press the Right Levers

I submit that when depression does arise in the ill or disabled, it may be because consequences which used to be critical maintainers of behavior are no longer available, or the cost of obtaining these consequences may suddenly have become very high. A solution is to program actively either alternative consequences or alternative behavior patterns.

This viewpoint leads us to reinterpret the nature of a patient's symptoms. The question is, what contingencies are now governing the patient's behavior? Far from indicating pathology, the patient's behavior may actually be the most sensible one possible, given the particular reinforcement contingencies in effect. We know that a laboratory pigeon will peck at a disk, even though all previous pecks have produced electric shock, as long as he also occasionally gets food after a peck, an unshocked response. We do not say that the pigeon is masochistic. His behavior is quite sensible. The pigeon is always right (Goldiamond, 1973).

Flooding

While systematic desensitization seeks to minimize anxiety by pairing small doses of it with a deep relaxation, **flooding** maximizes the anxious state of the client. The person who fears flying, for example, might be asked to imagine being on a plane high above the ocean, without first going through a hierarchy of scenes. While the client's anxiety becomes extremely high while using the flooding technique, it usually dissipates and is eventually extinguished if the client stays with the scene long enough. The same strategy can be used, as can systematic desensitization, in real-life scenarios. For example, the counselor may actually make a plane trip with the client, encouraging him or her until the anxiety subsides. The principle is that anxiety will disappear if not reinforced. Of course, this method is clearly anxiety-provoking, and the client must also be in good physical condition to undergo such intense treatment. Inexperienced counselors should not try flooding without supervision.

> The time seems to have come when psychology must discard all reference to consciousness; when it need no longer delude itself into thinking that it is making mental states the object of observation.
>
> —John B. Watson

APPLICATION

Considerable research has shown different forms of behavior therapy effective in the treatment of numerous clinical problems in different populations (Kazdin & Wilson, 1978). For example, behavior therapy has been effectively applied to the treatment of anger (Moore & Shannon, 1993), obsessive compulsive disorders (Fals & Lucente, 1994; Roth & Church, 1994), phobias (Emmelkamp, 1974; Emmelkamp, Brilman, Kuipers, & Mersch, 1986; Emmelkamp & Wessels, 1975; Stern & Marks, 1973; Turner, Beidel, Cooley, & Woody, 1994), depression (Gardner & Oei, 1981; Hersen, Bellack, Himmelhoch, & Thase, 1984; Jacobson, Fruzzetti, Dobson, & Whisman, 1993; Lewinsohn, 1975; Rehm, 1977; Taylor & McLean, 1993; Thase, Reynolds, Frank, & Simons, 1994; Wilson, 1982; Wilson, Goldin, & Charboneau-Powis, 1983; Zeiss, Lewinsohn, & Munoz, 1979), alcoholism (Baker & Cannon, 1979; Cannon & Baker, 1981; Elkins, 1980; Olson, Ganley, Devine, & Dorsey, 1981), sexual dysfunctions (Clement & Schmidt, 1983; Crowe, Gillan, & Golombock, 1981; Hartman & Dally, 1983; Obler, 1973), paraphilias (Brownell & Barlow, 1976; Brownell, Hayes, & Barlow, 1977; Evans, 1970; Levin, Barry, Camaro, Wolfinsohn, & Smith, 1977; Maletzky, 1980; Quinsey, Bergersen, & Steinman, 1976), marital distress (Babcock & Jacobson, 1993; Emmelkamp, Van der Helm, MacGillavry, & Van Zanten, 1984; Jacobson, 1984; Kelly & Halford, 1993; O'Leary & Turkewitz, 1978), and childhood disorders (Bijou, Birnbrauer, Kidder, & Tague, 1966; Bornstein & Kazdin, 1985; Craighead, 1982; Masters, Burish, Hollon, & Rimm, 1987; Ross, 1981; Wolf, Risley, & Mees, 1964). Behavior therapy has been used successfully in hospital and prison settings, in rehabilitation counseling, and in special education environments. It also has broad applicability to problems in education, medicine, and community living (Liberman, Van Putten, Marshall, & Mintz, 1994).

The following case, written by Joseph Wolpe, illustrates two fundamental behavioral strategies: systematic desensitization and assertiveness training. It is the case of Mr. B., who is suffering from numerous somatic symptoms and has developed an obsession with his wife's sexual involvement with another man prior to their marriage. Dr. Wolpe picks up the case from here:

> Mr. B. was a 31-year-old advertising salesman who four years previously had begun to notice himself [becoming] increasingly anxious in social and business situations from which it was difficult to get away. Within a few months, even five minutes in the office of a client would produce considerable anxiety accompanied by a strong desire to urinate. If he went out and relieved himself, the urge would return after a further five minutes, and so on. The only circumstances that could be associated with the onset of Mr. B.'s neurosis were the unsettlement of having moved to a new house in town, and his concern at the unexpected break-up of the marriage of close friends whom he had regarded as ideally mated. His only previous neurotic phase had been a brief one that had occurred upon moving to a new school at the age of 16. This could conceivably have conditioned anxiety to "new places." The Fear Survey Schedule revealed very high anxiety to the following stimulus classes: strange places, failure, strangers, bats, journeys especially by train, being criticized, surgical operations, rejection, planes, being disapproved of, losing control, looking foolish, and fainting.
>
> Mr. B.'s early history was quite conventional. A feature of interest was a strong religious training with marked emphasis on "the good and the bad." Churchgoing had played a prominent part in his childhood and adolescence. In his middle teens he had come to resent it, but had never outwardly rebelled. He had done well in school and got on well with both classmates and teachers. He had been trained in journal advertising, but was now engaged in advertising salesmanship, which he greatly liked.
>
> At 18 he had met his wife who attracted him by her intelligence, good looks, and responsiveness to his jokes. The courtship was broken by Mr. B. after she revealed that she had had an affair two years earlier. On reflection, he condoned the episode, and at the age of 20 married her. The relationship turned out to be a very congenial one, and sexually very satisfying to both; but Mr. B. was never really able to divest himself of the painful idea that he had been "dealt a dirty card."
>
> At the second session, Mr. B. described how embarrassing and incapacitating he found his neurotic anxiety and the associated urge to urinate. Anxiety was greater in the presence of unfamiliar people and if there was no easy access to a toilet. Other factors that increased it were the importance of the occasion and the importance of the other person. On the whole, there was more anxiety in anticipation of a meeting than at the meeting itself. Since it was evident that a desensitization program would need to be undertaken, relaxation training was started at this interview.
>
> At his next session, five days later, Mr. B. reported that he had practiced relaxing, and that by means of it had been able to desist from urinating while at home for a period of six and a half hours despite quite a strong urge. Relaxation training was now extended, and the general desensitization

strategy worked out. It was apparent that the duration of interviews with his clients was an important factor determining the strength of Mr. B.'s anxiety. It was therefore decided to treat an "interview" hierarchy, using a time dimension for its easy quantifiability. I started the desensitization by having him imagine himself scheduled to a very brief meeting (of two minutes' duration) with the manager of an important firm. The first scene was presented to him as follows: "Imagine that you have just entered the office of a manager who has a rule that no representative is permitted to spend more than two minutes in his office." By the third presentation this scene produced no anxiety, and scenes of meetings of four minutes and six minutes were then presented in succession.

In subsequent interviews, the duration of these meetings was progressively extended, until by the ninth he could imagine being with an executive for 60 minutes without anxiety. He now found himself much better at real meetings and social situations. While visiting relatives, he urinated only three times in five hours. However, his anticipatory anxiety was almost as bad as ever. There was some measure of it several hours before a prospective meeting, but it became much more noticeable 30 minutes to one hour beforehand, and then increased rather steeply. At the ninth interview, then, desensitization of anticipatory anxiety was started. Anxiety decreased to zero in two to three presentations of each of the following scenes:

1. In his office, 60 minutes before visiting a client.
2. In his office, 30 minutes before visiting a client and preparing to leave.
3. Twenty minutes before visiting a client, entering his car to allow ample time.
4. In his car on the way to a client ten minutes before the appointed time.
5. Emerging from his car at the premises of the client's office, with eight minutes in hand.
6. Entering the waiting room of the client's office six minutes before the appointed time.
7. Announcing himself to the client's secretary five minutes before the appointed time.

At his tenth interview, a week later, Mr. B. reported considerably less anxiety in relation to anticipated business meetings. He had for the first time in many months taken his wife to a downtown restaurant. During the 25-minute ride to that restaurant he had not, as in the past, had to stop to relieve himself in a rest room. At first slightly anxious in the restaurant, he had become almost entirely calm after the first ten minutes. Desensitization to the anticipation of interviews was continued to the point that he could calmly imagine himself in the client's waiting room two minutes before he was to be called in. This hierarchy was finally disposed of at the next session. Now Mr. B. spontaneously reported that he felt far greater confidence in all respects. He had been going out to get new business—at first feeling some strain, but later increasingly comfortably. He had spent one and a half hours with a new and imposing manager of an important new client firm, with hardly any anxiety before or during the interview. He was no longer bothered at going into strange places because it no longer mattered whether or not he knew where the toilet was. For the same reason, he had ceased to fear using trains, airlines, buses, and other public transportation.

Attention was now turned to Mr. B.'s difficulty in asserting himself with strangers. Assertive behavior was instigated. To facilitate it, he was desensitized to one relevant situation—telling a waiter "This food is bad." Anxiety disappeared at the second presentation. Two weeks later, at his 14th interview, B. stated that he was expressing himself where required with increasing ease. For example, he had immediately and effectively spoken up at a drugstore when another customer was taken ahead of him out of turn. He had become more and more comfortable making business calls, citing as an example a one-and-three-quarter-hour interview with a particular executive. He commented that three months earlier he would in the course of so long a period have had to go out to urinate about 20 times. However, he still had to push himself to do some of the things he had become inured to avoiding.

From this point onward, the main focus of therapy was his distress about his wife's premarital affair. First, it was mutually agreed that Mr. B.'s reactions were irrational. Then, an attempt was made to employ imagery . . . having Mr. B. project himself back to the time of his wife's affair and imagine that he was in the next room while she was amorously engaged with her lover in a hotel. He was to force the connecting door open and beat up the paramour. In doing this, it was supposed that angry emotions would be counterpoised to the anxiety that this image ordinarily evoked. Mr. B. was enjoined to practice this imaginary sequence 50 to 100 times a day. He felt himself making progressive improvement for about two weeks, when he stated that his obsession was about 20 percent less in incidence and 40 percent less in emotional intensity. But continuing the drill for a further four weeks yielded no further benefit . . . .

I decided, therefore, to tackle the problem by systematic desensitization. In order to desensitize Mr. B. to this long-past situation, I employed images from a fictitious film supposed to have been taken of his wife's premarital amorous activities by a hidden camera in her family's living room. Relaxed and with his eyes closed, Mr. B. was asked to imagine that his wife was sitting on a couch with her lover who kissed her and then put his hand on one of her breasts over her dress for exactly five seconds. He felt no anxiety at this. A fair amount of anxiety was evoked by the next scene in which the duration of contact was made eight seconds, but at the third presentation of this scene anxiety disappeared. Two presentations were required to remove anxiety from him imagining the hand over the breast for 10 seconds, and five for 20 seconds.

At the following session, six weeks later, Mr. B. again felt anxiety to the 20-second hand contact, but it disappeared at the third presentation. Two weeks later, he reported that his feelings toward his wife were more detached and that he was thinking of her less. In general his thoughts were turning away from the past and toward the present and future. Mr. B. stated that "having got over the hump last time," he no longer cared what his wife had done in the past. Recovery from the obsession (as well as the other problems) had endured at last contact three years later.

CRITICAL ANALYSIS

In critiquing behavior therapy, one must begin by understanding that its major appeal is to those who prefer a coherent conceptual framework rather than an approach based more on intuition, anecdotal evidence, and personal preference. In other words, a primary strength of behavior therapy has to be its commitment to systematization, objectivity, evaluation, and an exceptionally good research base. It demystifies the process of counseling and makes it possible for clients and outside evaluators to assess in a measurable way its level of accountability.

Behavior therapy deals directly with specific symptoms and thus is often able to assist clients more rapidly than some approaches. It provides clients with an understanding of the treatment process by supplying them with concrete information about their role in that process and their level of progress through it. It also provides them with useful information about the reinforcements in their environment that maintain both adaptive and maladaptive behaviors.

Another strength of the behavioral approach is its abundance of available techniques and their applicability to a variety of settings. Its methods are constantly being evaluated and improved, and new techniques evolve and are tested. In fact, between 1970 and 1980, the number of behavior therapy interventions available to counselors more than doubled (Groden & Cautela, 1981).

On the negative side, behavior therapy does not deal with the total person, only his or her behavior. Critics contend that many behaviorists have taken the person out of personality and replaced it with an emphasis on laws that govern actions in specific environments. They ignore clients' personal history and unconscious, treating them more like pigeons than people. In other words, behavior therapy is too simple in its explanation of complex human interactions and its application is too mechanical (Erwin, 1992).

Although behavior therapists have been productive in evaluating the efficacy of various techniques, relatively little attention has been devoted to the therapeutic process (Milne, Cowie, Gormly, & White, 1992). Therapists' qualities have been found, at least in one study (Ford, 1978), to account for more variance in treatment outcome than therapy type. To be fair, many behavior therapists are careful to establish rapport with their clients and to make counseling a collaborative effort, but the fact that some behaviorists do not initially stress the relationship with the client has hurt the approach's image with other therapists and the public. Some even see behavior therapy as inhumane, particularly when practiced in institutions such as mental hospitals and prisons. The 1971 film, *A Clockwork Orange,* which depicted cruel, enforced behavioral control, was the image many had of behavior therapy. Some even equated it with brainwashing and torture (Turkat & Feuerstein, 1978). Of course, behavior therapists (Wolpe, 1981) have argued that it is inherently humane in that the role of the therapist is to teach clients the means to reach their goals. The truth is that promoters of behavior therapy have always seen the need for a good therapist/client relationship (e.g., Goldfried & Davison, 1976; Wolpe, 1958); it is just that research articles and theoretical work, in contrasting this new approach with traditional ones, did not emphasize the therapeutic relationship. The image of behavior therapy, however, seems to have changed as it has ma-

Twenty-five hundred years ago it might have been said that man understood himself as well as any other part of his world. Today he is the thing he understands least.

—B. F. Skinner

tured—the Clockwork Orange image is not as prevalent as it was initially—but contemporary behavior therapy must continue to balance its demonstrated effectiveness with sensitivity to the human aspects of its work.

When it comes to multicultural counseling, behavior therapy has some clear advantages. To begin with, since it does not place emphasis on lengthy introspection, emotions, and past history but, rather, on changing behaviors, behavior therapy can more quickly help the ethnic minority client who has a specific behavioral problem. Behavior therapy, since it is a problem-solving approach, is not as likely to get bogged down in extraneous material that increases the likelihood of confusion and misunderstanding between client and therapist. Behavior therapy also allows for flexibility and adaptation of its techniques. This can be a tremendous plus in working with ethnic-minority clients. Since it does not force all clients into the same treatment program, it offers room to consider the unique background and needs of individual clients. On the downside, ethnic-minority clients who are functioning at relatively high levels but who are searching for meaning, purpose, or a better sense of identity within a particular culture will find little solace through behavior therapy. It simply does not take into account these issues unless they can be directly related to behavior.

CURRENT STATUS

Behavior therapy is no longer a radical alternative, it is part of the establishment. In only a few decades, an unknown and simplistic application of conditioning principles to the treatment of specific problems has become a highly sophisticated and generally accepted approach to a broad spectrum of individual disorders and societal concerns. Behavioral principles have been assimilated into the mainstream of therapeutic counseling to the extent that even insight-oriented counselors regularly use many of the techniques, including goal setting, assertiveness training, relaxation training, and other methods of skill acquisition (Hundert, 1994; Kavanagh, 1994).

Behavior therapy today, however, is more complex than when it was practiced in the 1970s. It is now much broader than its original conception, more diverse with regard to theory, techniques used, and behaviorists' views on what the field should encompass (Adelsberg, 1994). It's becoming more comprehensive in its therapeutic scope and considerably more sophisticated in its efforts to maintain therapeutic gains. In spite of its broadening, or perhaps because of it, approaches to therapy that integrate a behavioral perspective continue to grow.

In the early 1960s there was not a single professional journal devoted exclusively to research on behavioral approaches in clinical psychology. Now there are more than a dozen, the most influential of which are *Behavior Research and Therapy, Journal of Applied Behavior Analysis, Behavior Therapy, Behavior Modification, Behavioral Assessment,* and *European Journal of Behavior Analysis and Modification.*

Similar growth has occurred in the publication of textbooks and handbooks dealing with behavior modification. The first book with "behavior therapy" in the title was Eysenck's *Behavior Therapy and the Neuroses,* published in 1960. Today there are hundreds of books about behavior therapy.

SUMMARY

1. *Biography.* B. F. Skinner (1904–1990) spent most of his professional life at Harvard. He has been described as the most influential psychologist of this century, and he certainly set the stage for the development of behavior therapy. Joseph Wolpe (1915–) received his medical degree in South Africa and after studying Pavlov, rebelled against his psychoanalytic training and devoted his career to an empirical approach to psychotherapy. He is best known for devising systematic desensitization. Albert Bandura (1925–) has taught psychology his entire career at Stanford University where he has developed a broader perspective on behavior therapy by bringing in a social learning component.

2. *Historical Development.* The beginnings of behavior therapy can be found at the crossroads of the rise of behaviorism as a philosophical view (due in great part to John B. Watson) and empiricism as a growing method in psychology (due in great part to Pavlov and Skinner). With the advent of systematic desensitization in the 1950s, however, behavior therapy came into its own and grew quickly during the 1960s as an alternative to psychodynamic approaches.

3. *View of Human Nature.* Behavior therapists view humans as products of their experience. People are neither good nor bad. But the behavior therapist does view humans as hedonistic in nature, responding to requests to end or decrease personal suffering or to promote greater pleasure and enjoyment in life. Behavior therapists have no model of optimal human functioning toward which clients are led.

4. *Development of Maladaptive Behavior.* Psychopathology, from the behavioral perspective, is defined as behavior that is disadvantageous or dangerous to the individual and/or to other people. It can result from insufficient cues to predict consequences or from inadequate reinforcement. One of the most painful of all maladaptive behaviors stems from an overly severe set of self-standards and the resulting excess of self-criticism.

5. *Function of the Therapist.* The behavior therapist is generally very active in counseling. He or she serves as a consultant, a supporter, a resource, and a model. Functionally, the behavior therapist facilitates a process involving four major steps: accurately defining the problem, gathering a developmental history of the client, establishing specific goals, and determining the best methods for change.

6. *Goals of Therapy.* The goal of behavior therapy is to extinguish the client's identified maladaptive behavior and to introduce or strengthen adaptive behavior that can serve as a replacement and enable him or her to live a productive life. The key to reaching this goal is learning new behaviors. This relies on three paradigms that can stand alone but are often integrated

in this approach: respondent learning, operant conditioning, and social modeling.

7. *Major Methods and Techniques.* Since its task is to resolve client symptoms, there are literally dozens and dozens of behavior therapy techniques. Some of the most common methods include behavioral assessment (specifying an individualized treatment plan), positive reinforcement (reward for positive behavior), token economies (using tokens to be exchanged for desired objects or privileges), assertiveness training (enabling clients to more freely express thoughts and feelings), modeling (learning through observing the behavior of another), relaxation training (discriminating between tense and relaxed muscle groups to relax upon cue), systematic desensitization (pairing of a neutral stimulus with one that already elicits fear), and flooding (maximizing the anxious state of a client for eventual extinction).

8. *Application.* Research has shown different forms of behavior therapy effective in treating anger, obsessive-compulsive disorders, phobias, depression, alcoholism, sexual dysfunctions, paraphilias, marital distress, and childhood disorders. It has been used successfully in a wide variety of settings. The case of "Mr. B." summarized by Joseph Wolpe illustrates the effectiveness of systematic desensitization and assertiveness training.

9. *Critical Analysis.* Behavior therapy provides a relatively coherent conceptual framework of psychotherapy. It is committed to systematization, objectivity, evaluation, and a solid research base. It provides clients with an understanding of the treatment process and also supplies the practitioner with an abundance of effective techniques. Behavior therapy, however, is criticized for not dealing with the total person. Critics also point to the relatively little attention the behavioral approach has devoted to the therapeutic process. While behavior therapy offers some advantages to multicultural counseling, it lacks relevance for the ethnic-minority client who is searching for a better sense of identity within a particular culture.

10. *Current Status.* After only a few decades, behavior therapy is now part of the professional therapeutic establishment. It is also much more sophisticated than its founders might have imagined, encompassing a broad spectrum of individual disorders and societal concerns. It is more diverse in its theory, techniques, and views. Approaches to therapy that integrate a behavioral perspective continue to grow.

Key Terms

Assertiveness training Semistructured training approach characterized by its emphasis on acquiring assertiveness skills through practice. Assertiveness skills enable one to stand up for one's rights and beliefs more effectively.

Behavior modification A term referring specifically to Skinnerian methods for changing behavior, ones that need not necessarily involve psychopathology.

Behavior rehearsal Therapeutic technique that consists of acting out short exchanges between client and counselor in settings from the client's life. The aim of such rehearsing is an effective preparation for the client to deal with a real "adversary," so that the anxiety that the latter evokes may be reciprocally inhibited.

Behavior therapy An approach to psychotherapy that seeks to change particular "target" behaviors and/or symptoms of the client, rather than trying to alter some unobservable or unconscious inner state.

Behaviorism An approach to psychology that regards only actual behavior as suitable to scientific study.

Conditioned response The response to the conditioned stimulus.

Conditioned stimulus A previously neutral stimulus that acquires positive or aversive properties through conditioning.

Conditioning, classical (respondent conditioning) A simple form of learning first demonstrated by Ivan Pavlov, wherein a conditioned stimulus (e.g., light) becomes capable of eliciting a particular conditioned response (salivation) by being repeatedly paired with an unconditioned stimulus (food).

Conditioning, operant Operant conditioning is a theory of learning derived from the work of B. F. Skinner. The essential difference between operant and classical conditioning is that in operant conditioning, the unconditional stimulus follows some predetermined behavior when that behavior occurs spontaneously. In this procedure, the unconditioned stimulus is called a *reinforcer.*

Counterconditioning A technique in which the experimenter (or therapist) presents an unconditioned stimulus that elicits an unconditioned response incompatible with the conditioned response and thus inhibits the conditioned response. For example, relaxation (UR) is incompatible with fear (CR).

Desensitization Behavioral technique through which anxiety may be reduced by using relaxation as the counterconditioning agent. Graded anxiety-producing stimuli (in the anxiety hierarchy) are repetitively paired with a state of relaxation, until the connection between those stimuli and the response of anxiety is eliminated.

Extinction The process of removing an unwanted response by failing to reinforce it.

Flooding Therapeutic technique in which repeated presentation of the conditioned stimulus without reinforcement brings about extinction of the conditioned response. It differs from desensitization in that no counterconditioning agent is used.

Hierarchy A list of stimuli on a theme, ranked according to the amount of anxiety they produce. The hierarchy provides the therapist with a graded set of anxiety-producing stimuli to present to the client in conjunction with a counterconditioning agent to remove the anxiety attached to the stimuli.

Modeling Demonstrating a behavior by role-playing.

Negative reinforcer A stimulus that increases the probability of a response when removed following that response, such as an electric shock or disapproval.

Operant conditioning A behavior occurs and some event follows the behavior that is reinforcing.

Positive reinforcer A stimulus such as food or approval that increases the probability of a response when presented following that response.

Progressive relaxation A common form of relaxation training used to treat a wide variety of disorders, including headaches, psychosomatic pain, hypertension, and other anxiety related problems.

Punishment An interactional behavior involving the application of an aversive event as a result of the individual's engaging in a particular behavior. Punishment, the converse of reinforcement, is applied only to those behaviors that are to be eliminated.

Reinforcement A specified event that strengthens the tendency for a response to be repeated.

Reinforcement, negative Form of conditioning involving the removal of an aversive event as a result of the appearance (or disappearance) of the target behavior.

Reinforcement, positive Form of conditioning in which the individual receives something pleasurable or desirable as a consequence of his or her behavior.

Respondent learning Learning when a neutral stimulus is paired with a stimulus that has an effect and the neutral stimulus begins to elicit the same effects as the primary stimulus.

Social modeling Learning which occurs when a person sees another's behavior, independent of reinforcement.

Systematic desensitization A form of behavior therapy, devised by Joseph Wolpe, wherein the client imagines a hierarchical sequence of feared stimuli and inhibits the resulting anxiety by practicing previously taught techniques of muscular relaxation. Alternatively, *in vivo* desensitization may be used with clients who are unable to imagine the feared situations vividly enough to feel anxious.

Token economy A detailed and complicated form of behavior therapy, based on Skinnerian operant conditioning, wherein desirable behaviors are followed with conditioned positive reinforcers (such as plastic tokens) that can later be exchanged for more primary reinforcers chosen by the client.

Unconditioned response An automatic, unlearned response elicited by an unconditioned stimulus.

Unconditioned stimulus A stimulus that automatically elicits a particular (unconditioned) response, without any learning or conditioning being necessary.

Suggested Reading

Bandura, A. (1969). *Principles of behavior modification.* New York: Holt, Rinehart and Winston.

Krumboltz, J. D. (Ed.) (1966). *Revolution in counseling: Implications of behavioral science.* Boston, MA: Houghton Mifflin.

Skinner, B. F. (1971). *Beyond freedom and dignity.* New York: Knopf.

Wolpe, J., & Lazarus, A. A. (1966). *Behavior therapy techniques.* New York: Pergamon Press.

References

Adelsberg, M. (1994). The integration of behavioral principles and a psychodynamic viewpoint in the treatment of adolescents on an intermediate inpatient unit. *Psychiatric Quarterly, 65,* 135–147.

Alberti, R. E. & Emmons, M. C. (1982). *Your perfect right: A guide to assertive behavior* (4th ed.). San Luis Obispo, CA: Impact.

Ayllon, T., & Azrin, N. H. (1968). *The token economy: A motivational system for therapy and rehabilitation.* New York: Appleton-Century-Crofts.

Babcock, J. C., & Jacobson, N. S. (1993). A program of research on behavioral marital therapy: Hot spots and smoldering embers in marital therapy research. *Journal of Social and Personal Relationships, 10,* 119–135.

Baker, T. B., & Cannon, D. S. (1979). Taste aversion therapy with alcoholics: Techniques and evidence of a conditioned response. *Behavior Research and Therapy, 17,* 229–242.

Bandura, A. (1969). *Principles of behavior modification.* New York: Holt, Rinehart & Winston.

Bandura, A. (1977). *Social learning theory.* Englewood Cliffs, NJ: Prentice Hall.

Bandura, A. (1986). *Social foundations of thought and action: A social cognitive theory.* Englewood Cliffs, NJ: Prentice Hall.

Bandura, A., & Walters, R. (1963). *Social learning and personality development.* New York: Holt, Rinehart & Winston.

Bellack, A. S., & Hersen, M. S. (Eds.). (1987). *Dictionary of behavior therapy techniques.* New York: Pergamon.

Bijou, S. W., Birnbrauer, J. S., Kidder, J. D., & Tague, C. (1966). Programmed instruction as an approach to the teaching of reading, writing, and arithmetic to retarded children. *Psychological Record, 16,* 505–522.

Blackham, G. J., & Siberman, A. (1971). *Modification of child behavior.* Belmont, CA: Wadsworth.

Bornstein, P., & Kazdin, A. E. (Eds.). (1985). *Handbook of clinical behavior therapy with children.* Monterey, CA: Brooks/Cole.

Brownell, K. D., & Barlow, D. H. (1976). Measurement and treatment of two sexual deviations in one person. *Journal of Behavior Therapy and Experimental Psychiatry, 7,* 349–354.

Brownell, K. D., Hayes, S. C., & Barlow, D. H. (1977). Patterns of appropriate and deviant sexual arousal: The behavioral treatment of multiple sexual deviations. *Journal of Consulting and Clinical Psychology, 45,* 1144–1155.

Cannon, D. S., & Baker, T. B. (1981). Emetic and electric shock alcohol aversion therapy: Assessment of conditioning. *Journal of Consulting and Clinical Psychology, 49,* 20–33.

Cautela, J. R. (1976). Behavior therapy and self-control: Techniques and implications. In C. Franks (Ed.), *Behavior therapy: Appraisal and status* (pp. 323–340). New York: McGraw-Hill.

Clement, U., & Schmidt, G. (1983). The outcome of couple therapy for sexual dysfunctions using three different formats.

Journal of Sex and Marital Therapy, 9, 67–78.

Craighead, W. E. (1982). A brief clinical history of cognitive-behavior therapy with children. *School Psychology Review, 11,* 5–13.

Crowe, M. J., Gillan, P., & Golombock, S. (1981). Form and content in the conjoint treatment of sexual dysfunction: A controlled study. *Behavior Research and Therapy, 19,* 47–54.

Elkins, R. L. (1980). Covert sensitization treatment of alcoholism: Contributions of successful conditioning to subsequent abstinence maintenance. *Addictive Behavior, 5,* 67–89.

Emmelkamp, P. M. G. (1974). Self-observation versus flooding in the treatment of agoraphobia. *Behavior Research and Therapy, 12,* 229–237.

Emmelkamp, P. M. G., Brilman, E., Kuipers, H., & Mersch, P. P. (1986). The treatment of agoraphobia: A comparison of self-instructional training, rational emotive therapy and exposure in vivo. *Behavior Modification, 10,* 37–53.

Emmelkamp, P. M. G., & Wessels, H. (1975). Flooding in imagination vs. flooding in vivo: A comparison with agoraphobics. *Behavior Research and Therapy, 13,* 7–16.

Emmelkamp, P. M. G., Van der Helm, M., MacGillavry, D., & Van Zanten, B. (1984). Marital therapy with clinically distressed couples: A comparative evaluation of system-theoretic, contingency contracting and communication skills approaches. In K. Hahlweg & N. Jacobson (Eds.), *Marital therapy and interaction.* New York: Guilford.

Erwin, E. (1992). Current philosophical issues in the scientific evaluation of behavior therapy theory and outcome. *Behavior Therapy, 23,* 151–171.

Evans, D. R. (1970). Subjective variables and treatment effects in aversion therapy. *Behavior Research and Therapy, 8,* 147–152.

Eysenck, H. J. (1959), Learning theory and behavior therapy. *British Journal of Medical Science, 105,* 61–75.

Eysenck, H. J. (1960). *Behavior therapy and the neuroses: Readings in modern methods of treatment derived from learning theory.* New York: Pergamon Press.

Fals, S., & Lucente, S. (1994). Treating obsessive-compulsive disorder among substance abusers. *Psychology of Addictive Behaviors, 8,* 14–26.

Farkas, G. M. (1980). An ontological analysis of behavior therapy. *American Psychologist, 35,* 364–374.

Follette, W. C., & Houts, A. C. (1992). Philosophical and theoretical problems for behavior therapy. *Behavior Therapy, 23,* 251–262.

Ford, J. D. (1978). Therapeutic relationship in behavior therapy: An empirical analysis. *Journal of Consulting and Clinical Psychology, 46,* 1302–1314.

Galassi, J. P., & Perot, A. R. (1992). What you should know about behavioral assessment. *Journal of Counseling and Development, 70,* 624–631.

Gardner, P., & Oei, T. S. (1981). Depression and self-esteem: An investigation that used behavioral and cognitive approaches to the treatment of clinically depressed clients. *Journal of Clinical Psychology, 37,* 128–135.

Gilliland, B. E., James, R. K., & Bowman, J. T. (1989). *Theories and strategies in counseling and psychotherapy* (2nd ed.). Boston: Allyn & Bacon.

Goldiamond, I. (1973). A diary of self-modification. *Psychology Today.* November, 188.

Goldried, M. R., & Davison, G. C. (1976). *Clinical behavior therapy.* New York: Holt, Rinehart & Winston.

Goodell, R. (1975, August). The visible scientist. *APA Monitor, 1,* 8.

Groden, G., & Cautela, J. R. (1981). Behavior therapy: A survey of procedures for counselors. *Personnel and Guidance Journal, 60,* 175–179.

Hartman, L. M., & Dally, E. M. (1983). Relationship factors in the treatment of sexual dysfunction. *Behavior Research and Therapy, 21,* 153–160.

Hersen, M., Bellack, A. S., Himmelhoch, J. M., & Thase, M. E. (1984). Effects of social skill training, amitripty-line, and psychotherapy in unipolar depressed women. *Behavior Therapy, 15,* 21–40.

Hosford, R., & deVisser, L. (1974). *Behavioral approaches to counseling: An introduction.* Washington, DC: American Personnel and Guidance Press.

Hundert, J. (1994). The ecobehavioral relationship between teachers' and disabled preschoolers' behaviors before and after supervisor training. *Journal of Behavioral Education, 4,* 75–91.

Jacobson, N. S. (1984). A component analysis of behavioral marital therapy: The relative effectiveness of behavior exchange and communication/problem-solving training. *Journal of Consulting and Clinical Psychology, 52,* 295–305.

Jacobson, N. S., Fruzzetti, A. E., Dobson, K., & Whisman, M. (1993). Couple therapy as a treatment for depression. *Journal of Consulting and Clinical Psychology, 61,* 516–519.

Jones, H. G. (1956). The application of conditioning and learning techniques to the treatment of a psychiatric patient. *Journal of Abnormal and Social Psychology, 52,* 414–419.

Jones, M. C. (1924). The elimination of children's fears. *Journal of Experimental Psychology, 7,* 383–390.

Kanfer, F. H., & Goldstein, A. P. (1980). *Helping people change* (2nd ed.). New York: Pergamon Press.

Kavanagh, D. J. (1994). Issues in multidisciplinary training of cognitive-behavioral interventions. *Behavior Change, 11,* 38–44.

Kazdin, A. E. (1978). Behavior therapy: Evolution and expansion. *The Counseling Psychologist, 7,* 34–37.

Kazdin, A. E., & Wilson, G. T. (1978). *Evaluation of behavior therapy: Issues, evidence and research strategies.* Cambridge, MA: Ballinger.

Kelly, A., & Halford, W. K. (1993). Adapting behavioral therapy to the needs of a secondary marriage: A case evaluation. *Behavioral Psychotherapy, 21,* 115–125.

Krumboltz, J. D. (Ed.). (1966). *Revolution in counseling: Implications of behavioral science.* Boston: Houghton Mifflin.

Lazarus, A. A. (1958). New methods of psychotherapy: A case study. *South African Medical Journal, 32,* 660–663.

Lazarus, A. A. (1971). *Behavior therapy and beyond.* New York: McGraw-Hill.

Lazarus, A. A. (1989). *The practice of multimodal therapy.* Baltimore, MD: John Hopkins University Press.

Levin, S. M., Barry, S. M., Camaro, S., Wolfinsohn, L., & Smith, A. (1977). Variations of covert sensitization in the treatment of pedophilic behavior. A case study. *Journal of Consulting and Clinical Psychology, 45,* 896–907.

Lewinsohn, P. M. (1975). The behavioral study and treatment of depression. In M. Hersen, R. M. Eisler, & P. M. Miller (Eds.), *Progress in behavior modification* (Vol. 1). New York: Academic Press.

Liberman, R. P., Van Putten, T., Marshall, B. D., & Mintz, J. (1994). Optimal drug and behavior therapy for treatment-refractory schizophrenic patients. *American Journal of Psychiatry, 151,* 756–759.

Lindsley, O. R., Skinner, B. F., & Solomon, H. C. (1953). *Studies in behavior therapy.* Status Report 1. Waltham, MA: Metropolitan State Hospital.

Maletzky, B. M. (1980). Assisted covert sensitization. In D. J. Cox & R. J. Daitzman (Eds.), *Exhibitionism: Description, assessment and treatment.* New York: Garland.

Marks, I. M. (1994). Behavior therapy as an aid to self-care. *Current Directions in Psychological Science, 3,* 19–22.

Masters, J. C., Burish, T. G., Hollon, S. D., & Rimm, D. C. (1987). *Behavior therapy* (3rd ed.). San Diego, CA: Harcourt Brace Jovanovich.

Meyer, V. (1957). The treatment of two phobic patients on the basis of learning principles. *Journal of Abnormal and Social Psychology, 55,* 261–266.

Milne, D., Cowie, I., Gormly, A., & White, C. (1992). Social supporters and behavior therapists: Three studies on the form and function of their help. *Behavioral Psychotherapy, 20,* 343–354.

Moore, K. J., & Shannon, K. K. (1993). The development of superstitious beliefs in the effectiveness of treatment of anger: Evidence for the importance of experimental program evaluation in applied settings. *Behavioral Residential Treatment, 8,* 147–161.

Mower, O. H. (1947). On the dual nature of learning—A reinterpretation of "conditioning" and "problem solving." *Harvard Educational Review, 17,* 102–148.

Nelson, R. O., & Barlow, D. H. (1981). Behavioral assessment: Basic strategies and initial procedures. In D. H. Barlow (Ed.), *Behavioral assessment of adult disorders* (pp. 13–43). New York: Guilford.

Nye, R. D. (1992). *The legacy of B. F. Skinner.* Pacific Grove, CA: Brooks/Cole.

O'Leary, K., & Wilson, G. (1987). *Behavior therapy: Application and outcome* (2nd ed.). Englewood Cliffs, NJ: Prentice Hall.

O'Leary, K. D., & Turkewitz, H. (1978). The treatment of marital disorder from a behavioral perspective. In T. J. Paolino & B. S. McCrady (Eds.), *Marriage and marital therapy*. New York: Brunner/Mazel.

Obler, M. (1973). Systematic desensitization in sexual disorders. *Journal of Behavior Therapy and Experimental Psychiatry, 4,* 93–101.

Olson, P. P., Ganley, R., Devine, V. T., & Dorsey, G. C. (1981). Long-term effects of behavioral versus insight-oriented therapy with inpatient alcoholics. *Journal of Consulting and Clinical Psychology, 49,* 866–877.

Perry, M. A., & Furukawa, M. J. (1980). Modeling methods. In F. H. Kanfer & A. P. Goldstein (Eds.), *Helping people change* (pp. 131–171). New York: Pergamon Press.

Quinsey, V. L., Bergersen, S. G., & Steinman, C. M. (1976). Changes in physiological and verbal responses of child molesters during aversion therapy. *Canadian Journal of Behavioral Science (Montreal), 8,* 202–212.

Rasnake, L. K. (1993). Treatment acceptability research: Relevance to treatment selection decisions. *Child and Adolescent Mental Health Care, 3,* 31–47.

Rehm, L. P. (1977). A self-control model of depression. *Behavior Therapy, 8,* 787–804.

Ross, A. O. (1981). *Child behavior therapy.* New York: Wiley.

Ross, A. O. (1985). To form a more perfect union: It is time to stop standing still. *Behavior Therapy, 16,* 195–204.

Roth, A. D., & Church, J. A. (1994). The use of revised habituation in the treatment of obsessive-compulsive disorders. *British Journal of Clinical Psychology, 33,* 201–204.

Salter, A. (1949). *Conditioned reflex therapy.* New York: Farrar, Straus.

Samelson, F. J. B. (1980). Watson's Little Albert, Cyril Burt's twins, and the need for a critical science. *American Psychologist, 35,* 619–625.

Sechrest, L., & Smith, B. (1994). Psychotherapy is the practice of psychology. *Journal of Psychotherapy Integration, 4,* 1–29.

Skinner, B. F. (1938). *The behavior of organisms: An experimental analysis.* New York: Appleton-Century-Crofts.

Skinner, B. F. (1948). *Walden two.* New York: Macmillan.

Skinner, B. F. (1953). *Science and human behavior.* New York: Macmillan.

Skinner, B. F. (1957). *Verbal behavior.* New York: Macmillan.

Skinner, B. F. (1968). *The technology of teaching.* New York: Appleton-Century-Crofts.

Skinner, B. F. (1971). *Beyond freedom and dignity.* New York: Knopf.

Skinner, B. F. (1974). *About behaviorism.* New York: Knopf.

Skinner, B. F. (1976). *Particulars of my life.* New York: Alfred A. Knopf.

Skinner, B. F. (1989). *Recent issues in the analysis of behavior.* Columbus, OH: Merrill.

Skinner, B. F., & Lindsley, O. R. (1954). *Studies in behavior therapy, status reports II and III.* Norfolk, VA: Office of Naval Research Contracts.

Stern, R., & Marks, I. M. (1973). Brief and prolonged flooding: A comparison in agoraphobic patients. *Archives of General Psychiatry, 28,* 270–276.

Taylor, S., & McLean, P. (1993). Outcome profiles in the treatment of unipolar depression. *Behavior Research and Therapy, 31,* 325–330.

Thase, M. E., Reynolds, C. F., Frank, E., & Simons, A. D. (1994). Response to cognitive-behavioral therapy in chronic depression. *Journal of Psychotherapy Practice and Research, 3,* 204–214.

Thoresen, C. E. (1969). The counselor as an applied behavioral scientist. *Personnel and Guidance Journal, 47,* 841–848.

Turkat, I. D., & Feuerstein, M. (1978). Behavior modification and the public misconception. *American Psychologist, 33,* 194.

Turner, S. M., Beidel, D. C., Cooley, M. R., & Woody, S. R. (1994). A multicomponent behavioral treatment for social phobia. *Behavior Research and Therapy, 32,* 381–390.

Watson, J. B. (1913). Psychology as the behaviorist views it. *Psychological Review, 20,* 158–177.

Watson, J. B. (1919). *Behavior from the standpoint of a behaviorist.* Philadelphia: Lippincott.

Watson, J. B. (1924). *Behaviorism.* New York: Norton.

Wilson, G. T. (1989). Behavior therapy. In R. Corsini & D. Wedding (Eds.), *Current psychotherapies* (4th ed., pp. 241–284). Itasca, IL: Peacock.

Wilson, G. T. (1995). Behavior therapy. In R. Corsini & D. Wedding (Eds.), *Current psychotherapies* (5th ed., pp. 197–228). Itasca, IL: F. E. Peacock.

Wilson, P. H. (1982). Combined pharmacological and behavioral treatment of depression. *Behavior Research and Therapy, 20,* 173–184.

Wilson, P. H., Goldin, J. C., & Charboneau-Powis, M. (1983). Comparative efficacy of behavioral and cognitive treatments of depression. *Cognitive Therapy and Research, 7,* 11–124.

Wolf, M. M., Risley, T. R., & Mees, H. L. (1964). Application of operant conditioning procedures to the behavior problems of an autistic child. *Behavior Research and Therapy, 1,* 305–312.

Wolpe, J. (1958). *Psychotherapy by reciprocal inhibition.* Stanford, CA: Stanford University Press.

Wolpe, J. (1981). Behavior therapy versus psychoanalysis: Therapeutic and social implications. *American Psychologist, 36,* 159–164.

Wolpe, J. (1982). *The practice of behavior therapy* (3rd ed.). New York: Pergamon Press.

Wolpe, J., & Lazarus, A. A. (1966). *Behavior therapy techniques.* New York: Pergamon Press.

Yates, A. J. (1958). The application of learning theory to the treatment of tics. *Journal of Abnormal and Social Psychology, 56,* 175–182.

Yates, A. J. (1980). *Biofeedback and the modification of behavior.* New York: Plenum.

Zeiss, A. M., Lewinsohn, P. M., & Munoz, R. F. (1979). Nonspecific improvement effects in depression using interpersonal skills training, pleasant activity schedules, or cognitive training. *Journal of Consulting and Clinical Psychology, 47,* 427–439.

*You are today where your thoughts have brought you; you
will be tomorrow where your thoughts take you.* —**James Allen**

Rational-Emotive Therapy and Other Cognitively Based Theories

CHAPTER **13**

CHAPTER OUTLINE

Brief Biography
Historical Development
View of Human Nature
Development of Maladaptive Behavior
Function of the Therapist
Goals of Therapy
Major Methods and Techniques
Application
Other Cognitively Based Theories
Critical Analysis
Current Status
Summary
Key Terms
Suggested Reading
References

The comedian Mel Brooks tells the story of a crotchety grandfather who had
troubled his family for years with an annoying, compulsive habit. He tore paper
into bits and scattered the little pieces wherever he went. For years the family
dragged him to world-renowned psychoanalysts, Adlerian therapists, existential
therapists, and so on—all to no avail. The man would not stop tearing paper.
Finally, the family turned to an obscure, off-beat therapist. With the anxious family looking on, this modern therapist put his arm around the patient's shoulder

and said, "Let's take a little walk." The doctor walked with the old man from one end of the tiny office to the other, all the while whispering in his client's ear. Finally they stopped, and the doctor told the family: "You can take him home now. He's cured."

The man didn't tear paper for days. A year went by, and the habit still had not returned. The family was amazed and grateful but remained curious about this new therapeutic technique. Finally they telephoned the therapist and begged him to repeat what he had said to the grandfather. The miracle worker said, "I told him, 'Don't tear paper.'"

More and more clients are seeking out commonsense therapeutic approaches that provide rapid and verifiable results. As a result, cognitive therapeutic strategies that emphasize logic and reason have become increasingly attractive. After all, who wouldn't want the benefits of simple problem-solving techniques that involve a short-term commitment and a minimal amount of angst?

The pioneer of these methods has been alternately described as "abrasive, impatient, and lacking in . . . social graces" and as "brilliant, sensitive, perceptive, humorous, and stimulating" (Weinrach, 1980, p. 152). His rugged language is more often found in a bar than a classroom. Despite his rough edges, or perhaps because of them, Albert Ellis blazed the trail for a new kind of counseling strategy known today as *rational-emotive therapy*, which remains one of the most popular contemporary approaches to counseling.

This chapter explores the history, theory, and application of Ellis's therapeutic technique, which is the most widely recognized cognitive approach, but it also presents other cognitively based therapeutic approaches that have made significant contributions to the counseling field.

BRIEF BIOGRAPHY

Albert Ellis, the founder and moving force behind rational-emotive therapy, was born into a devout Jewish family in Pittsburgh, Pennsylvania, in 1913. When he was four, his family moved to New York, where he grew up on the mean streets of the Bronx. Although his father was often absent, Ellis describes him in mostly positive terms, remarking that he acquired his intelligence, drive, and persistence from his father and his independent and often idiosyncratic behavior from his mother (Wiener, 1988). Describing her method of parenting as "benign neglect," Ellis credits his early independence of thought to his parents' hands-off approach to child-rearing (Dryden, 1989). At age five Ellis almost died from tonsillitis and later suffered from diabetes (Dryden, 1989; Morris & Kanitz, 1975). By age seven Ellis was largely on his own (Weinrach, 1980).

Ellis was 12 when his parents divorced. It was then that he questioned much of his early religious training and gave up plans to be a teacher of Hebrew. Instead he became a self-described "probabilistic atheist," one who does not believe that God exists but would accept empirical evidence to the contrary.

Even as a young adolescent in junior high school, Ellis dreamed of becoming a novelist. He planned to work as an accountant and save enough money to retire at age 30 to devote his time entirely to writing. And in fact he did complete a baccalaureate degree in business administration in 1934 at City College of New York. Despite the ravages of the Depression, Ellis was gainfully employed in business until the mid-1940s. When he was not working, he wrote fiction, but his literary efforts were disappointing. After eight of his novels were rejected by publishers, Ellis decided to study psychology and write nonfiction. Ellis received a master's degree in 1943 and a Ph.D. in clinical psychology in 1947 from Columbia University. After earning his doctorate, Ellis became senior clinical psychologist at the New Jersey State Hospital and taught part-time at Rutgers University.

> There's nothing either good or bad but thinking makes it so.
> —Shakespeare

Inevitably, Ellis became interested in psychoanalysis. Since institutions that specialized in psychoanalytic training admitted only medical professionals, Ellis was hard-pressed to find the training he desired. He finally succeeded in obtaining personal analysis for three years from the Karen Horney group. By the middle 1950s, however, Ellis's faith in psychoanalysis had deteriorated. Although his patients were gaining psychoanalytic insight and understanding, they seemed to continue in their dysfunctional behavior. Becoming increasingly more active and more directive with his patients, Ellis soon began practicing his own unique approach to therapy.

Ellis's original passion for writing would appear to have been rekindled by his study of psychology. He has served as editor for 10 journals, written more than 600 articles, produced numerous films and tapes, and published 50 books, some of which have been written for the general public, including *How to Live with a "Neurotic"* (1957) and *The Intelligent Woman's Guide to Dating and Mating* (1979). His writings for professional therapists include *A Guide to Rational Living* with Robert A. Harper (1961), *Humanistic Psychotherapy* (1974), *Overcoming Resistance* (1985), and *Rational-Emotive Couples Therapy* (1989).

Today Ellis lives in New York City, where he sees as many as 80 clients each week and supervises up to 80 group sessions. He also gives about 200 workshops annually. Requests for his lectures, consultations, seminars, professional conferences, and personal appearances on radio and television continue unabated (Weinrach, 1980).

HISTORICAL DEVELOPMENT

The origins of rational-emotive therapy can be traced to the philosophy of Stoicism in ancient Greece, which distinguished an act from its interpretation.

According to the Stoics, we are not so much disturbed by what happens to us, as by how we *interpret* what happens to us.

While Greek Stoics like Epictetus and Marcus Aurelius planted the seeds of cognitive therapy, it wasn't until recently that they were cultivated. From the teachings of Alfred Adler and through personal and clinical experiences, Albert Ellis came to agree with the ancients that we are truly less influenced by the event itself than by what we choose to think about the event. Given this fundamental premise, Ellis developed a humanistic theory of psychotherapy that "squarely places man in the center of the universe and of his own emotional fate and gives him full responsibility for choosing to make or not to make himself seriously disturbed" (Ellis, 1973, p. 10).

Men are disturbed not by things, but by the views which they take of them.

—Epictetus

Ellis's contemporary theory has flourished within the context of what is sometimes called the *cognitive revolution,* a scientific revolution that has assembled research in physiology, philosophy, linguistics, computer science, medicine, and various other areas of psychology (Dobson, 1988a, 1988b). There was more research in human cognition in the 1960s and 1970s, writes Hunt (1982), than throughout all the previous history of scientific study.

Despite Ellis's original training and diligent practice of psychoanalysis, he remained dissatisfied when his patients' perfectionist and self-condemning behaviors remained unchanged. It was about this time that Ellis began studying learning theory, which he applied in his clinical practice. Although all the pieces of Ellis's therapeutic montage were not yet in place, his therapeutic effectiveness improved.

Ellis quietly observed that his patients' behaviors were not so much the singular result of their social learning and conditioning as of their attitude and perceptions. A hunch led Ellis to a new hypothesis. He discovered that his patients' dysfunctional behavior resulted from a predisposition to retain tenacious and irrational ideas and thoughts. Although to some, this assumption may have seemed little more than a classical commonplace, it motivated Ellis's to work diligently toward a rational approach to psychotherapy (Ellis, 1993).

In recounting the beginnings of his theory, Ellis talks about his own decision to cope with profound shyness and fear of approaching women during his undergraduate days. As Ellis tells it, it was only by making himself extremely uncomfortable that he finally became comfortable in approaching women. Indeed, for one month he forced himself to approach and talk with more than 100 unfamiliar women in the Bronx Botanical Gardens, until he could do so comfortably. As he wryly explained, recalling the episode, his successful conquest of his social phobia was scarcely a matter of reinforcement: he managed to arrange for only a single date, and she never showed up. Nevertheless, he had taken action in the face of irrational doubts and fears.

Based as much on a philosophical as a psychological model, then, Ellis explained his new and radical approach to psychotherapy in a series of articles that culminated with the publication of *Reason and Emotion in Psychotherapy* in 1962. The therapeutic technique that emerged would come to be known as *rational-emotive therapy,* usually designated by its now-familiar acronym, RET. During his methodological pilgrimage, Ellis claims to have progressed from an improvement rate of 60 percent in 100 sessions with psychoanalytic techniques to 90 percent in only 10 or so sessions, due to this new approach (Ellis, 1979a).

VIEW OF HUMAN NATURE

Although Ellis believes that we are persistently buffeted by the unpredictable currents of living, he does not maintain that we are victims of the storms about us. Rather, he claims, we have final dominion over much of the pleasure and pain that come from circumstances beyond our control. Since RET emphasizes

Reason is a light that
God has kindled in the
soul.

—Aristotle

that one's thoughts affect, and often create, one's feelings, the attention of the therapist is on the thought processes (Ellis, 1990). Although this theory does not ignore the emotional aspects of the human condition—the human psyche is considered to be intricately composed of both thoughts and feelings—it is nevertheless our thoughts that are central to RET's view of human nature. As a result, the efficacy of RET stems from our capacity to think rationally.

Ellis often summarized his view of human nature by means of a so-called *A-B-C theory* of our behavior (Grieger, 1986a, 1986b). People frequently come to therapy because of a *consequence* (C), an emotional or behavioral condition that is disturbing them. It is common for them to attribute their emotional or behavioral consequence to an *activating event* (A)—an external event, such as a financial setback, a fight with a friend, or a person's own thoughts or behavior—as if there were some necessary and invariable causal relationship between A and C. But according to Ellis, people are not disturbed by the events themselves, but by the *beliefs* (B) they hold about those events (Figure 13.1).

From the point of view of RET, whenever the client is disturbed or dysfunctional at point C (the emotional consequence), it is not because of what is happening at point A (the activating event). Rather "it is because of his own irrational and unvalidating suppositions at point B (his belief system)" (Ellis, 1971, p. 6). For example, if clients feel depressed at point C, it is not because they have been rejected by someone or have failed an exam at point A, but because they are convincing themselves of irrational beliefs at point B (e.g., "I'll never have a girlfriend" or "I'm stupid"). Ellis stresses that the A-B-C theory

Figure 13.1 | A-B-C Theory

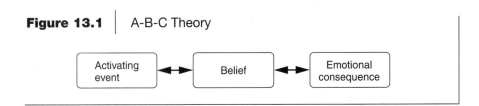

"is central to the whole field of RET and cognitive-behavior therapy and has an enormous amount of research that solidly supports it" (Ellis, 1977a, p. 3).

While the A-B-Cs of RET are central to its approach to personality, Ellis (1979a, 1979b, 1979d) makes several further assumptions about human nature as well. RET embraces a "soft determinism," which allows human beings to resist only with great difficulty the strong pressures that surround them. Although human nature is, to some extent, determined by these extraordinary biological and social pressures, the fact remains that we do have free will and can create our own worlds. Ellis does not believe that human beings are good or evil, angels or devils; they are simply human beings, nothing more. Nevertheless, they are born with inner conflicting tendencies. They have a strong tendency to be reasonable and to find fulfillment while also being drawn to act irrationally and to thwart their own growth. One of the strongest human, innate tendencies is to be influenced by family and by culture.

Patterson (1980) notes several additional assumptions about the nature of humanity that are foundational to the cognitive approach to therapy. Most importantly, the RET therapist believes that individuals are uniquely rational and irrational. When they behave and think rationally, they are effective, happy, and competent. When they are irrational, however, they think illogically, resulting in psychological disturbance. And since thought and emotion accompany one another—since emotion is, in effect, biased, prejudiced, highly personalized, irrational thought—this is an emotional disturbance as well.

Such irrational thinking originates in early illogical learning, which children acquire from their parents and culture. In the process of growing up, children are taught to think and feel certain things about themselves and others. When emotions such as love and joy are associated with the idea of "this is good," they become positive human emotions; when emotions such as anger or depression become associated with "this is bad," they become negative emotions. As a result, it is not the situation, but that which we have been taught to associate with it—our perceptions of it—that make it negative or unpleasant.

We talk ourselves into this negative frame of mind, Ellis emphasizes. After all, human beings are verbal animals; we think in symbols and in language. Continuing states of emotional disturbance, then, are the result of self-verbalization, and they are determined, not by external circumstances or events, but by our perceptions and attitudes toward these events, which are incorporated in our internalized discussion of them. Disturbed individuals perpetuate this disturbance, maintaining illogical behavior by internally verbalizing irrational ideas and thoughts. And since thinking accompanies emotion, if the emotional disturbance persists, irrational thinking necessarily persists as well.

But we are not victims of our circumstances, of past conditioning. In the same way in which people have been talked into—and have talked themselves into—their maladjustment, so they can talk and think their way out again. They can think and work until they actually make themselves different. The RET counselor believes, then, that people have the capacity to confront their value systems and reindoctrinate themselves with different beliefs, ideas, and values. Moreover, they have vast untapped resources for actualizing their potentials and

13.1 | **Talking to Yourself**

They say there's nothing wrong with talking to yourself, but when you start answering back, it's time to worry. They're wrong. Talking aloud to yourself in public isn't a sign of mental health, but holding an internal dialogue is quite normal and very useful. In fact, inner conversations have a powerful impact on emotional well-being and motivation. Becoming aware of exactly what you are saying to yourself about your self can help you understand why you react the way you do to events and people in your life. It can also give you a handle on controlling your moods repeating your successes and short-circuiting your shortcomings.

Positive self-talk can do a lot to give you the confidence that frees you to serve, and to use your talents to the fullest. If public speaking makes you nervous, use your inner voice to reassure yourself: "You can do it. You've done it well before. Why else would they have asked you to do it again?" Behind your nervousness may well be negative thoughts such as: "There are 300 people out there! I'll never hold their attention." Since self-talk has a way of becoming self-fulfilling prophecy, negative thinking can spell trouble. That's why it's important to monitor your inner voice.

Take the case of a 39-year-old mother who has persistent feelings of depression. Her inner voice tells her: "I'm lost. I feel like such a failure. I know I should be more patient with my kids, but they're such losers. I've given up even talking to them. It's just not fair. My friends' kids are perfect but mine are a mess and so is my life." These ruminations are a garbage bag of negatively loaded words and labels ("failure," "losers"); errors in the way she processes information ("My friends' kids are perfect"); faulty assumptions ("It's not fair"—neither, of course, is life), and guilt-inducing expectations ("I should . . .").

This mother needs to identify these errors and distortions and develop a more accurate internal dialogue ("I know I'm not a perfect mother, but nobody is perfect. I do the best I can with my kids and they're not perfect either. But, if I work on being more patient and communicating better, maybe the problems we've been having can be worked out"). The revised self-talk improves her mood and motivation, diffuses her anger and directs her toward actions that can address some of her difficulties. This can eventually lead to positive changes in her behavior that improve her relationship with her family.

The real power of self-talk lies in how it changes behavior. Simply correcting your internal programming will improve your mood, but it won't do the most important job. The ultimate purpose of examining what is going on inside your head is to change actions that are self-defeating. Thinking correctly does alter your negative moods, but enduring change comes only with modifying your behavior.

(continued)

13.1 | **Talking to Yourself** (continued)

If, for example. your self-talk tells you, "I can't break up this relationship because I can't stand being alone, even though the relationship is harmful to me," you're likely to stay locked in the same unhappy situation. To make your self-talk more accurate, you might say, "I feel anxious about breaking up and facing the idea that I might be alone for awhile. But if I really want to give myself a chance for the kind of relationship that will make me happy, I must let go of the one I'm in."

Now comes the clincher: To activate the full power of your self-talk, you must follow the path that your new, accurate inner messages point. To find the behavior that goes with your new self-talk, ask yourself these questions: What behavior has my erroneous self-talk generated? How has it hindered me from reaching my goals? What actions does my corrected self-talk suggest? How will my life be better when I change? When and how will I start to change?

Accurate self-talk should enable you to know how your behavior needs to change. And behavior is what counts. As an old proverb advises: "To know but not to act is not to know at all."

Adapted from "The Power of Self-Talk," by Harriet B. Braiker, *Psychology Today* (December 1989).

for changing their personal and social destinies. According to Ellis, they have the power to understand their limitations, to change views and values that were uncritically accepted as a child, and to challenge self-defeating tendencies.

Therefore, the goal of counseling is to enable clients to reorganize their perceptions and thought processes, so that their thinking becomes logical and rational. Only then can they truly understand how illogical (senseless) and **irrational** (without mental clarity) are their self-verbalizations. And only then can they begin to attack their negative and self-defeating thoughts. Ultimately, the goal is to clarify their thinking so self-verbalizations become more logical and efficient and are no longer producing negative emotions and self-defeating behavior.

DEVELOPMENT OF MALADAPTIVE BEHAVIOR

The **cognitive** approach to psychopathology is based on the straightforward assumption that people are both "inherently rational and irrational, sensible and crazy" (Weinrach, 1980, p. 154). Because humans are self-conscious creatures, they observe their disturbance and then make themselves disturbed all over again about being disturbed (Burns & Nolen, 1992). Ellis believes this starts early. Children learn irrational beliefs and they continue to reindoctrinate themselves until the beliefs are entrenched in their thinking patterns.

This theory is based on the premise that maladaptive behavior results from a number of major illogical ideas that are held and perpetuated until a new way of thinking is learned. These illogical ideas and thoughts are designated as "inappropriate" or "self-defeating" and result in feelings of worthlessness, depression, rage, anxiety, mania, or self-pity (Ellis & Grieger, 1977; Garamoni et al., 1992; Russell, 1992).

According to Bard (1980, p. 23), the RET counselor will look for a number of symptoms as evidence of maladaptive behavior. Some clients may report an abusive lifestyle, such as taking drugs, that threatens to shorten the span of enjoyable living. More broadly, they may become preoccupied with short-range enjoyment at the expense of long-range satisfaction. Or they may turn their back on the future altogether, refusing to acquire knowledge, for instance, which might increase their ability to maximize future enjoyment. Others tend to repeat actions, such as making themselves anxious when there is no real danger, which tend to generate immediate and unnecessary discomfort and pain. Still others may fail to cultivate innate capacities for different satisfactions, thus subjecting themselves to frequent periods of boredom, inertia, or dissatisfaction.

> As he thinketh in his heart, so is he.
> —Proverbs 23:7

Whatever the symptoms, Ellis (1962) found that specific, commonly occurring irrational beliefs typically lead to "various kinds of emotional disturbance" (Ellis, 1984a, p. 266). Following are some of the more common irrational beliefs.

Being loved and approved by virtually every significant person in our world is necessary for happiness and fulfillment. The need to be loved by everybody is an unattainable goal that renders people less self-directing and more insecure and self-defeating.

To be worthwhile, one should be thoroughly adequate, fully competent, and high achieving in all possible respects. This is another impossibility. People who base their worth on achievements, who turn every situation into a test, can never enjoy what they are doing. They are predestined to a sense of inferiority and constant fear of failure.

Certain people are bad, wicked, or villainous and should be severely blamed and punished. Everyone makes mistakes as a result of stupidity, ignorance, or emotional disturbance. Drawing the worst out of everyone, this blame-and-punishment approach often leads to unacceptable behavior and increased emotional disturbance.

It is awful and catastrophic when conditions are not the way one would very much like them to be. No situation is ever entirely perfect. Even in the best of circumstances, there is always something more that could be done. Treating an event as catastrophic will not change the event; in fact, it makes things worse. If people don't like the situation, they can try to change it, but if it cannot be changed, mature people will learn to adjust, to accept those things beyond their control. Under such circumstances, frustration is normal, of course, but prolonged stress over matters that cannot be altered is illogical.

Unhappiness is caused externally; therefore people have little or no ability to control their sorrows and disturbances. The reality is that most outside events perceived as harmful are only psychologically harmful. The events cannot hurt unless they are allowed to hurt. Psychological hurt is a bilateral experience, demanding the cooperation of people's attitudes and reactions. When someone is unkind, rejecting, or annoying, for example, we disturb ourselves by perceiving their words and behavior as negative. Only when we realize that disturbances consist of our own perceptions and judgments, does the locus of control shift from the other to ourselves.

If something is or may be dangerous or frightening, one should be terribly concerned about it and should keep dwelling on the possibility of its occurring. Thinking about something doesn't change it; in fact, obsessive concentration on the problem may evolve into a self-fulfilling prophecy, turning clients into victims of their own obsessions.

It is easier to avoid difficulties and responsibilities than to face them. On the other hand, turning our backs on troubles does not solve them either. Usually the difficulty remains, until it eventually looms larger, so that it must be dealt with anyway.

People need to be dependent on someone stronger than themselves. Everyone depends on others to some extent, but overdependency leads to a loss of independence, individualism, and self-expression, resulting in insecurity and an inability to learn.

One's personal history is an all-important determiner of one's present behavior; because if something once strongly affected one's life, it will always have a similar effect. While the past may influence the present, it does not necessarily determine it; often it is used as an excuse to avoid changing our present behavior.

One should be personally upset over other people's problems and conditions. Beyond a general humanitarian concern, there is little to gain from dwelling on other people's problems. Usually they have nothing to do with us and therefore should not seriously concern us. Even if there is a concern because of family connections or filial relationship, we are not upset by the behavior but by our perception of the other's behavior, and mature people are able to control their own perceptions. In point of fact, getting upset usually prevents us from accurately understanding the circumstances into which others have fallen and keeps us from effectively helping them to resolve their problems.

There is always a right, precise, and perfect solution to human problems, and it is catastrophic if this perfect solution is not found. The perfect solution does not exist. The search for the final answer, the definitive solution, produces only anxiety and leaves us feeling dissatisfied and empty.

In summary, Goldfried (1988) holds that the two most common irrational beliefs involve approval from others (e.g., "If I am not liked and approved by others, that is terrible and I am no good") and perfection (e.g., "If I don't consistently do a perfect job, then I am no good").

Despite the fact that we are born with the potential to be rational and logical, Ellis (1973) believes that each of us, but especially the child, is gullible and highly suggestible to these various kinds of irrational thoughts. According to Ellis, these examples of "crooked thinking" are the result of distortions during childhood that have been reinforced by contemporary events and associations. "No matter what a person's past history may be, or how his parents, teachers, and other early associates may have helped him to become emotionally disturbed, he only remains disturbed because he still believes some of the unrealistic and illogical thoughts which he originally imbibed" (Ellis & Harper, 1975, p. 50).

FUNCTION OF THE THERAPIST

Intentionally attempting to *lead* patients to a healthier perspective, the rational-emotive therapist is unequivocally directive. In keeping with his view that all psychotherapies are to some degree authoritarian, Ellis (1962, 1967) openly favors therapist's providing a high degree of direction to the clients. He does not mince words on this issue. An irrational belief, he writes, "can be elicited and demolished by any scientist worth his or her salt, and the rational-emotive therapist is exactly that: an exposing and nonsense-annihilating scientist" (1988, p. 199).

Therefore the RET therapist, while accepting of the client, is quite verbal, often challenging or confronting clients, even in the first few sessions. To help them face their illogical thinking as quickly as possible, the therapist will use persuasion and debate in attacking clients' self-defeating patterns even at the outset of counseling (Harrell, Beiman, & Lapointe, 1986). However, he or she will not spend much time exploring the morbid details of the past, of who did what to whom, which are little more than a smoke screen, hiding the real issue of irrational thinking.

The task of the RET counselor is to help clients to straighten out crooked, irrational thinking, to rid themselves of illogical ideas, and to replace them with logical thoughts. Ellis (1973) calls this process, which begins by showing clients how and when they are irrational, **Insight Number 1.** **Insight Number 2** occurs when clients understand and are convinced that they feed their own emotional disturbance by reindoctrinating themselves with the same repetitious, irrational ideas. **Insight Number 3** allows clients to fully acknowledge that ridding themselves of their disturbances depends on their willingness to challenge their beliefs and develop new ways of thinking.

> In the world of minor lunacy the behavior of both the utterly rational and the totally insane seems equally odd.
>
> —J. K. Galbraith

To accomplish this, the rational-emotive therapist must thoroughly understand belief systems and clearly distinguish rational and irrational beliefs if he or she is to lead clients to this new perspective. Rational beliefs, which are consistent with reality, can be supported with hard evidence and can be corroborated by a group of objective observers. Since irrational beliefs, such as those listed previously, are inconsistent with reality, they are not based on evidence. Both rational and irrational beliefs represent the clients' evaluation of "reality," but they lead to different consequences. Irrational beliefs lead to dysfunctional emotional consequences, which interfere with the clients' goals.

Although Ellis (1962) urges the therapist to attempt to understand the clients' world views, to see from their frame of reference, he believes it is harmful for the therapist to actually feel clients' disturbances or believe their irrationalities. "Indeed, it is precisely the therapist's ability to comprehend the patient's immature behavior without getting involved in or believing in it that enables him to induce the patient to stop believing in or feeling that this behavior is necessary" (p. 115).

GOALS OF THERAPY

Thus, the goal of RET is to "teach" clients to analyze and to correct their distortions of reality, to distinguish their irrational from their rational beliefs, so that they can challenge their irrational beliefs. The result is the reduction or elimination of undesirable emotions (Cohen, 1987). At this juncture, Ellis extends his A-B-C paradigm to include D, E, and F (Figure 13.2): after (A) teaching clients to recognize activating events, (B) corresponding beliefs, and (C) the emotional and behavioral consequences of these beliefs, the goal of RET is to teach a variety of ways (D) to *dispute* the emotional beliefs and (E) to discriminate or attend to new emotional and behavioral *effects,* (F) resulting in new *feelings.*

Disputation, which requires clients to challenge their irrational beliefs, aims to eliminate those beliefs and substitute them with a new, more rational philosophy. If disputation is effective, it will be apparent in diminished emotional distress. The ultimate goal is to increase clients' awareness of these new effects and thus motivate them to continue using the disputational process in a self-directed manner, even after therapy is terminated.

In addition to disputing irrational thoughts, the cognitive approach has several additional goals, according to Ellis (1979c, 1984b). First of all, RET urges clients to assume responsibility for their lives and work out their own problems. The goal is a self-directed life in which they can be true to themselves and at the same time aware of others. If therapy is successful, clients will accept themselves as they are, not as they wish they were. Only then can they become comfortable with themselves and find the courage to take risks. RET seeks to teach that worth does not depend on what they do or on the opinions of others.

> The whole world is a comedy to those who think, a tragedy to those who feel.
>
> —Horace Walpole

They will become more accepting, more tolerant as well, allowing others to make mistakes without judging them and freeing themselves from both in-

Figure 13.2 | A-B-C and D-E-F

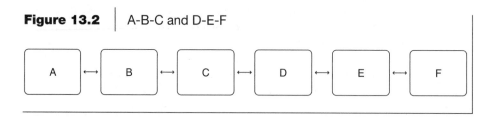

ternal and external condemnation. They will find that it is possible to like people without liking what they do. Accepting themselves and accepting others, they will be able to accept random chance as a reality of life. Through RET therapy, clients will learn to deal with uncertainty and chance with calmness. They realize they can enjoy life in an imperfect world and still be mentally healthy. Healthy clients are also logical and objective and thus generally open minded: open to change, open to engaging in meaningful commitments to both people and activities. RET therapists work to help clients turn their perspective outward and to absorb themselves in other-directed pursuits.

MAJOR METHODS AND TECHNIQUES

RET consists of three general modes or phases, the cognitive, emotive, and behavioristic, each accompanied by its own set of techniques. During the *cognitive phase* the counselor will present the cognitive rationale for the therapy to the client. As Ellis has pointed out, an RET therapist can begin each therapeutic session by asking clients, "What problems have you been bothering yourself about?" During this initial stage clients are told they can learn to control their emotions by learning to become aware of their underlying thoughts and by learning to substitute alternative thoughts. The *emotive phase* of cognitive therapy is devoted to helping the clients become aware of their thoughts. This is often done by asking clients to write down their troublesome thoughts. During the final *behavioristic phase* clients are trained to verbalize alternative cognitions and to change their behavior.

The following are some of the techniques used by RET and other cognitive therapists during these three phases.

Identifying Beliefs

The RET therapist is aware that clients often report their irrational beliefs as *feelings* and therefore have trouble responding to the counselor's questions about what thoughts influenced their emotional consequence. When clients do not know what they are thinking, counselors facilitate the identification of irrational beliefs by asking questions such as: If you bugged yourself, what would you hear? Suppose you were tape-recording. What is going on in your mind? Can you replay the tape? Tell me what it says.

Once clients begin to identify their irrational beliefs, the counselor can help group them into themes. The student who receives a C on an examination, for example, thinks he or she is an academic failure, a classic illustration of the theme of **all-or-nothing thinking.** Clients tend to categorize matters in terms of black or white, yes or no, for or against: a conversation that is less than perfect is a total failure. Others will engage in **mind reading:** making inferences about how people feel and think, imagining, for instance, that the president doesn't like people, that no one can get in to see him because he tells the Secret Service to keep them away. **Over generalization,** seeing a single event as a never-ending pattern of defeat, is another theme that commonly emerges in RET sessions. Typically, clients overgeneralize by using the words *always* or *never,* e.g., "I am always in the wrong place at the wrong time." Still others will engage in **discounting,** rejecting positive experiences by insisting they "don't count." The perfectionist who earns high marks in a class will discount his or her experience by saying, "anyone could have done it."

Further themes that RET therapists look for include **magnification,** exaggerating the importance of problems and shortcomings ("With my IQ I can never get a really good job"); **emotional reasoning,** assuming that negative emotions reflect the way things really are ("I feel guilty so I must be guilty"); and **self-blame,** taking personal responsibility for events that are beyond one's control ("If I had not made him get up he never would have been in the wreck").

Disputing

Disputation of irrational beliefs occurs in two stages. The initial, more specific stage requires a meticulous sentence-by-sentence examination and challenge of any irrational belief reported by the client. The second, general stage seeks to develop an alternate, more rational way of thinking. This disputation can take one of three forms: cognitive, imaginal, and behavioral. Regardless of the form(s) used, all disputations challenge the irrational beliefs of the clients and ask them to produce evidence to support the beliefs (Dryden, 1986; Dryden & Ellis, 1988; Ellis, 1982).

Cognitive disputation uses persuasion and direct questioning: Can you prove it? How do you know? If that is true, what's the worst that can happen? How would that be so terrible? Where's the evidence? As long as you believe that, how will you feel? (Walen, DiGuiseppe, & Wessler, 1980, pp. 97–99). Of course disputation can make some clients defensive, but the RET counselor is taught to be professionally sensitive to their responses.

Imaginal disputation, which is sometimes called *rational-emotive imagery,* is based on the assumption that the emotional consequences of clients' imaginings are similar to those produced by real stimuli. This technique is used to provide safe opportunities for trying new ways of thinking (Ellis 1984a, 1985, 1986b, 1989; Maultsby, 1975, 1984; Maultsby & Ellis, 1974). Using this technique, the therapist asks clients to imagine themselves in a problematic situation they dread. Once they have been guided into the feelings of that moment, they are asked to change their fear to mild apprehension, their anger to mild irritation, their depression to sadness, and so on. In other words, they are asked to imagine themselves feeling or behaving differently in this situation. As soon as clients receive the image of different feelings and behavior, they are instructed to signal to the counselor, who then asks them to notice what they are saying or thinking to themselves in order to produce those different emotions. These are the kinds of sentences or beliefs, the counselor will point out, that they need to use in real-life situations to produce different effects. For maximum results Maultsby (1984) recommends clients use this intervention on their own several times daily for at least a week or two to create positive habits leading to greater internal control of emotions.

Finally, *behavioral disputation* challenges clients to alter their irrational beliefs by behaving in different ways, a crucial step toward adopting a more rational philosophy. Behavioral disputation usually takes the form of reading books—bibliotherapy—and systematic homework assignments that include both written and *in vivo* practice (McMullin, 1986).

Countering

Countering asks clients to identify "counters" for each of their significant irrational beliefs and then to argue against these beliefs. Thus it provides for "thinking or behaving in an opposite direction, arguing in a very assertive fashion, and convincing oneself of the falsity of a belief" (McMullin & Giles, 1981, p. 6). McMullin and Giles (1981, pp. 67–68) have outlined several "rules" that must be followed in making use of this strategy. First of all, counters must be directly *opposite* to the false belief. For example, if the irrational belief is "I'm a failure if my wife leaves me," a directly opposite counter would be, "My wife's behavior is independent of my own success and accomplishments." Second, counters must be *believable* statements of reality. While it might be reasonable to conclude, "I don't need to get straight As in high school to get a reasonably good job after graduation," it is neither reasonable nor believable to conclude, "I don't have to go to high school to get a reasonably good job."

Furthermore, the RET therapist will urge clients to develop as *many* counters as possible in order to counteract the effects that the irrational beliefs have produced over time. Since lengthy, long-winded statements are easily forgotten, it is equally important that these counters be *concise,* capable of being summarized in a few words, and that they be stated with *assertive and emotional intensity.* They should not be said in a mechanical or unconvincing way. Finally, of course, it is essential that the clients create and *"own"* these counters. Because clients are likely to be more invested in counters that they themselves generate, the counselor's role in developing counters needs to be limited to coaching. As a result, effective countering is often highly idiosyncratic among different people.

Rational Self-Analysis

The cognitive practitioner will often ask clients to engage in *rational self-analysis,* which allows them to apply the A-B-C theory to their situations and which helps them to actively dispute their own irrational beliefs. After all, realizing that A does not cause C is not enough. Not even accepting responsibility for disturbing emotions and self-defeating behavior is enough. Only the repeated investigation and disputation of irrational beliefs and the earnest practice of new and actualizing behaviors are likely to bring about positive change in thoughts, feelings, and behaviors. Typically, this procedure will ask clients to complete daily homework assignments. The format in Figure 13.3 is often used to facilitate this exercise.

13.2 | **Emotional Control Card**

To practice rational-emotive imagery an **emotional control card** is sometimes used (Sklare, Taylor, & Hyland, 1985). This wallet-sized card contains four emotionally debilitating categories (anger, self-criticism, anxiety, and depression), a list of inappropriate feelings, and a parallel list of appropriate feelings:

Inappropriate or Self-Destructive Feelings	*Appropriate or Nondefeating Feelings*
Anger—Feelings of resentment, anger, madness, fury, rage	*Irritation*—Feelings of (mild or intense) irritation, displeasure, annoyance, frustration; anger at people's acts but not at their persons
Self-criticism—Feelings of humiliation, shame, embarrassment, inadequacy; discounting self as a person	*Criticism of one's behavior*—Feelings of (mild or intense) regret, sorrow, displeasure, doubt; criticism of one's behavior but not of one's total self
Anxiety—Feelings of anxiety, nervousness, hypertension, panic, helplessness, horror	*Concern*—Feelings of (mild or intense) concern, caution, vigilance; tension about one's performance but not about one's self
Depression—Feelings of depression, worthlessness, undeservingness, guilt, self-doubting	*Sadness*—Feelings of (mild or intense) sadness, sorrow, regret, discontentment, displeasure; feeling that one is a person who has performed badly but is not a bad person

In a potentially troubling situation, a client may refer to the card and change the quality of feelings about that situation. At the next session with the counselor, the client discusses the use of the card in cognitively restructuring thoughts to make them rational.

Source: From "An Emotional Control Card for Inappropriate and Appropriate Emotions in Using Rational-Emotive Imagery" by Albert Ellis, 1986, *Journal of Counseling and Development, 65*, p. 206. Reprinted with permission.

To help clients debate irrational thinking, they can be encouraged to ask a variety of questions: Is my thinking here based on fact? Will my thinking here best help me protect my life and health? Will my thinking best help me achieve my short- and long-term goals? Will my thinking here best help me avoid my most unwanted conflict with others? Will my thinking best help me habitually feel the emotions I want to feel?

Figure 13.3 | Example of Rational Self-Analysis Homework Form

	Activating Event	Consequence	Belief	Disputation	Effects
Date & Time	Situation	Emotions	Automatic thought	Rational response	Outcome
2/19 8:00	studying counseling theories	confusion, frustration, anxiety	"I feel so stupid. I'll never be a good counselor since I already feel lost"	"Just because I don't understand everything about these theories doesn't make me stupid. Almost every introductory student feels overwhelmed."	relief, mild tension

Action Homework

In addition to rational self-analysis, specific **action homework** may also encourage clients to dispute their irrational ideas behaviorally. Since clients are often asked to do the very thing they fear most, these assignments nearly always involve some degree of risk. Clients who demand self-perfection, for example, may be instructed to select three tasks during the following week that they will intentionally do poorly. Those who anticipate the rejection of others are told to collect at least three rejections a day for three consecutive days and to note their self-talk immediately after each attempt. Others who have difficulty asking for help are assigned to request a helping hand once a day for five days in a row.

These kinds of homework assignments share several important characteristics: "consistency, specificity, systematic follow-through, and large steps" (Walen, DiGiuseppe, & Wessler, 1980). That is to say, the homework must be consistent with the work of the session in which it is assigned. It needs to be both clear and concise. It expects that clients will follow through with their assignments in structured, systematic ways that will be reported at the beginning of the next session. And it calls for large steps, which are considered more effective in cognitive restructuring than gradual shaping.

Heightening Awareness

The RET therapist can also help clients become more aware of the *effects* of the A-B-C-D-E-F model through the use of numerical ratings and self-recording.

For example, on a scale from 1 to 100—with 1 being "not intense distress" and 100 being "very intense distress"—clients are asked to record levels of emotional distress during actual situations they experience outside of counseling. The counselor may also rely on both self-reports and on significant others to observe the clients' new and different behaviors or responses.

> The soul of God is poured into the world through the thoughts of men.
> —Ralph Waldo Emerson

Humor

Because the rational-emotive practitioner believes clients' problems stem from an exaggerated sense of the significance of unfortunate events, he or she will sometimes use humor to show clients how to "lighten up" and view their difficulties in the light of day (Ellis, 1977b, 1987a; Fry & Salameh, 1987; Mahoney, 1988).

In fact, the Institute for Rational-Emotive Therapy has produced an RET songbook and cassette recording entitled "A Garland of Rational Songs," featuring lyrics actually sung by a spirited Albert Ellis. Sometimes Ellis prescribes these "rational-humorous songs" to his clients, to highlight the absurdity of their irrational beliefs. Often clients are encouraged to sing the tunes to themselves or to each other in a group setting (Ellis, 1977b, 1987b). Sung to the tune of "I'm Just Wild about Harry," one of the most memorable lyrics of the RET collection is "I'm Just Wild about Worry":

> Oh, I'm just wild about worry
> And worry's wild about me!
> We're quite a twosome to make life gruesome
> And filled with anxiety!
> Oh, worry's anguish I curry
> And look for its guarantee!
> Oh, I'm just wild about worry
> And worry's wild about
> Never mild about,
> Most beguiled about me!

Lyrics by Albert Ellis, Copyright 1977–1988 by Institute for Rational-Emotive Therapy.

APPLICATION

Part of what makes RET so stimulating is the effect of the therapist, especially when the therapist is Albert Ellis himself. Although a transcript cannot completely capture the essence of rational-emotive therapy, the following case portrays much of the dramatic momentum associated with its application. The client is a 26-year-old male, a commercial artist, who is homophobic. He has graduated from college, is doing well at his work, and has a steady girlfriend. Nevertheless, he is terribly afraid of becoming homosexual and is often obsessed with the idea. Whereas the pace of some approaches to this kind of issue would be quite slow, Ellis zeros in on the irrational, illogical thinking that has led to the obsession and quickly attempts to dismantle it. What follows are excerpts and adaptations from the sessions Ellis had with this client, interjected with Ellis's own commentary on the case.

THERAPIST: What's the main thing that's bothering you?

CLIENT: I have a fear of turning homosexual—a *real* fear of it!

THERAPIST: A fear of *becoming* homosexual?

CLIENT: Yeah.

THERAPIST: Because "*if* I become a homosexual—," what?

CLIENT: I don't know. It really gets me down. It gets me to a point where I'm doubting every day. I do doubt everything, anyway.

THERAPIST: Yes. But let's get back to—answer the question: "If I were a homosexual, what would that make me?"

CLIENT: [*Pause*] Less than a person?

THERAPIST: Yes. Quite obviously, you're saying: "I'm bad *enough*."

CLIENT: That's right.

THERAPIST: Now, why did you just say you don't know?

CLIENT: Just taking a guess at it, that's all. It's—it's just that the fear really gets me down! I don't know why.

THERAPIST: [*Laughing*] Well, you just *gave* the reason why. Suppose you were saying the same thing about—we'll just say—stealing: You hadn't stolen anything, but you *thought* of stealing something.

CLIENT: [*Silence*]

THERAPIST: If you believed that: "If I stole it, I would be a thorough jerk"—would you think of it often? occasionally?

CLIENT: I'd think of it often.

THERAPIST: That's right! As soon as you say, "If so-and-so happens, I would be a thorough jerk!" you'll get *obsessed* with so-and-so. And the reason you're getting obsessed with homosexuality is this nutty belief, "If I *were* a homosexual, I would be a total jerk!" Now, look at that belief for a moment, and let's admit that if you were a homosexual, it would have real disadvantages. Let's assume *that*. But why would you be a thorough jerk if you were a homosexual? Let's suppose you gave up girls completely, and you were with guys. Now, why would you be a thorough jerk?

CLIENT: [*Mumbles incoherently' is obviously having trouble finding an answer.*]

THERAPIST: Think about it for a moment. The reason you're obsessed is the same reason you'd be obsessed with anything. I see people who are obsessed with five thousand different things. But in every single case, just about, I can track it down; and they're saying, "*If* I were so-and-so—" For example, "if I got up and made a public speech and fell on my face, I'd be a jerk!" "If I went to school and failed, I'd be a jerk!" "If I tried for a better job and failed, I'd be a jerk!" Now, you're doing the same thing about homosexuality: "If I ever *did* fail heterosexually and become a homosexual, I'd be an utter worm!" Now that will obsess you with homosexuality.

CLIENT: And that obsession brings me to doubt myself.

THERAPIST: Well—no. It's part of your general obsession. Your real obsession is: "If (1) I failed at something big, like heterosexuality, and (2) other people didn't like me—they really didn't like me—then I'd be no good!" Now, as a *subheading* under that, you've got the homosexuality. Your general fear is of being worthless—isn't it?

CLIENT: Yeah.

THERAPIST: And you don't only have it in the homosexual area—that's only dramatic and outstanding.

"Although I, as the therapist, know very little about the client, I size him up quickly and decide to take a chance, on the basis of RET theory, and to try to get at one of the main cores of his problem quickly: his terrible feelings of inadequacy. I know fully that I may be barking up the wrong tree, and am prepared to back down later if I turn out to be mistaken. But I know, on the basis of considerable prior evidence, that there is an excellent chance that I may be right; and I want, by taking that chance, to try to save the client a great deal of time and pain. So I not only immediately try to educate him about his own magical beliefs in wormhood and its connection with his fear of homosexuality, but I also try to show him how human beings, in general, easily think the way he does and how so many of them, no matter what their abilities and talents, wind up by hating themselves because of this type of crooked thinking. I am thus exceptionally educational in the first minutes of this first session—just as, presumably, any good teacher would be."

CLIENT: [*Pause*] I mean, I—sit there and I try to prove what a homosexual is. Then I try to prove what a heterosexual is. And then I try to prove what *I* am. And to try to prove what *you* are, as a person—

THERAPIST: Yeah?

CLIENT: —is very hard to do.

THERAPIST: Because there is no way of doing it—except by some *definition*: "that if I were completely heterosexual, or if I were a *great* supervising artist, or if I were an Adonis, *then* I'd be a good guy!" That's the only way you can *prove* yourself: by some arbitrary definition of accomplishment.

CLIENT: Yeah, I kept, like—in the other therapy, I kept using the words *abnormal* and *homosexual*.

THERAPIST: Meaning—but what you mean is, "*If* I were abnormal—if everybody is normal but me—I'm no good!" Is that what you mean?

CLIENT: Yeah, I do mean that.

THERAPIST: But let's suppose that, now. Let's just suppose that. Let's suppose that ninety-nine out of one hundred guys are normal—which is not true, but we'll deliberately suppose it—and they all are with girls and having a ball and marrying and having children; and you're the one out of a hundred who can't do that, who really is homosexual. All you can do is go after boys, and you can't make it with girls. You're impotent; you just can't make it with girls. We'll deliberately assume that. Therefore, statistically you're abnormal. Right? 'Cause you're one out of a hundred, and they can do things that you can't do. Now, why would you be a no-goodnik? Not why would you be abnormal—we're just assuming that you would be; now why would you be a no-goodnik if that were so: you were the one out of a hundred who couldn't make it heterosexually?

CLIENT: Well—maybe fear of loneliness.

THERAPIST: That's why it would be *inconvenient:* because they'd get along with girls, and you wouldn't. So therefore you might be lonely. Though that's not true either: you might have a lot of homosexual guys. But let's suppose you're lonely. Now, why would you be a *louse* because you're lonely? Not why would you be failing? Because we're assuming you'd be failing. They're succeeding heterosexually; you're not. Now why would you be a louse?

CLIENT: For not falling in with what they're doing.

THERAPIST: But that's a definition! Now let's suppose the opposite, incidentally—that ninety-nine out of one hundred guys just about made it with girls—they got a girl here and they got a girl there, and they sort of succeeded—but you were outstanding, and you really were very good looking and bright and sexy, and girls just fell all over you. Now that would be *abnormal*, statistically. Right?

CLIENT: [Pause] It would be.

THERAPIST: Why would you be a jerk *then*? You'd be one out of a hundred!

CLIENT: So I'm going by the use of a definition?

THERAPIST: That's right! "That I have to be super good. Then I'm okay. But if I'm super bad—one out of a hundred on the bad side—then I'm a louse!" That's your definition. See? Now, is a definition—does a definition prove anything about a fact? Because it is a definition, and if you want to feel you're a jerk, you can feel you're a jerk. But does it really prove you are a jerk—if you can only get there by definition?

CLIENT: I dunno.

THERAPIST: Because it can really get absurd. I, for example, could say: "I'm a tuba." And you say, "You're a tuba? Well, how did you become a tuba? Prove it!" And I say, "Well, I'm going around oomp-oomp-oomp-bah. Therefore I'm a tuba!" Now does that prove I'm a tuba!

CLIENT: No.

THERAPIST: What does it prove? It does prove something. What?

CLIENT: That you're not one. You may want to be one—

THERAPIST: Yes, that I *think* I am a tuba. That's what it proves. Because if I'm going to go around acting like a tuba, whether I am or not, I think I am a tuba. But it never proves I *am*, you see. Therefore, if you go around acting as if you are a jerk, it doesn't prove you *are* one; but it does prove that you *think* you are. And that's the story of your life! "If I'm not at *least* as good as others, and preferably much better, I *define* myself as an utter lowlifer! A skunk!" Right?

CLIENT: Yes, that's true.

"I, as the therapist, keep belaboring a single point here, until I am fairly sure that the client is getting it. For this is one of the main cores of RET: to show the client that his anxieties are *not* caused by his failing to achieve some goal that he wishes to achieve, but by his *demanding* that he achieve it. I feel, with practically all my clients, that if I can get over to them this single point, especially in one of the early sessions, that I have something of almost inestimable value: namely, the idea that *they* create their anxieties and other upsets, and they almost invariably do so by a single major irrational idea: the idea that they *must have* or *need* what they want. If they see this, then no matter what they are anxious, guilty, depressed, or angry about, they have a simple way of quickly discovering the *real* cause of their disordered emotion—their own demandingness—and of starting to challenge and attack it right away."

CLIENT: So as long as I keep thinking of a human being not being a jerk and yet one who makes mistakes, as long as I keep proving it to myself that that's all there is, and if I work at that, within time the problem will just leave. And I don't even think I'll have to work at it.

THERAPIST: Right.

CLIENT: I think it will just come now. So I see it more and more, yet I still have these lags of going back to a jerk. It's so much—so much more secure. But it makes for misery! And a lot of it. Something I don't need! But now that I've gotten over the problem, I really get along with my girl friend a lot better, and everything else. I've noticed that.

THERAPIST: Right.

CLIENT: And—I enjoy it more!

THERAPIST: Yes, because you're not spending the time doubting.

CLIENT: Yeah.

"At the end of this eighth session, the client feels that he is doing so well that he decides on a two-week instead of a one-week gap between sessions. He continued therapy for five subsequent sessions, then felt that he wanted to try it on his own. A follow-up report, six months after therapy ended, showed that he was no longer obsessed with sexual ideas, and was continuing to get along better than ever with his girl friend."

OTHER COGNITIVELY BASED THEORIES

While rational-emotive therapy is the most widely known approach to cognitive therapy, it is not the only approach. About the same time that Albert Ellis was perfecting his therapeutic techniques, Aaron Beck, a Philadelphia psychiatrist, developed a cognitive theory based on the rationale that the way people feel and behave is determined by how they structure their experience. In investigating Freud's theory of depression as "anger turned inward," for example, Beck found little support for it. Instead, Beck discovered that depression was caused more by how patients processed information at a cognitive level. Based on his research, Beck (1975) developed a cognitive theory of depression that has subsequently become more comprehensive and is applied to other therapeutic issues.

Beck's cognitive therapy is brief (typically no more than 16 sessions), present-centered, active, directive, and problem-oriented. In these ways it resembles RET, and Beck notes these similarities as well as Ellis's influence on

the development of cognitive and behavioral therapies in general. Unlike RET, however, cognitive therapy does not assume that the client has "irrational beliefs" and that the disorder will be corrected by modifying these beliefs

> Men are apt to mistake the strength of their feeling for the strength of their argument. The heated mind resents the chill touch and relentless scrutiny of logic.
> —William Gladstone

through persuasion. Rather, the therapist and client work collaboratively to find and understand the "dysfunctional" cognitive thoughts and underlying assumptions that are contributing to the client's problems. Beck calls this work *collaborative empiricism*, and it is built on a technique he calls *Socratic dialogue*. Thus, therapists carefully develop a series of questions that they ask clients to promote learning. The purpose of this questioning is to help the client arrive at logical conclusions.

Beck, also in contrast to RET, theorized that each psychological disorder has its own, unique cognitive content. For example, people suffering from panic disorders show different cognitive content from those experiencing depression, obsessive-compulsive disorders, and paranoid problems. Whatever the therapeutic issue, Beck helps his clients to generalize and project less often, so that they might become more realistic in their interpretation of events. Unlike Ellis, Beck does not try to dispute beliefs; instead, he employs specific profiles and treatment plans. In addition, Beck is more exploratory than Ellis (Beck, 1991), and he has a more positive attitude toward religion as well (Weinrach, 1988).

Beck has delineated several kinds of systematic errors in reasoning (cognitive distortions) that appear when people are in distress. *Selective abstraction* involves conceptualizing a situation on the basis of a detail taken out of context.

Overgeneralization involves abstracting a general rule from a few instances and applying it too broadly. *Arbitrary inference* entails drawing conclusions in the absence of supporting evidence. *Personalization* entails attributing blame for some event to oneself without any evidence.

As director of the Center for Cognitive Therapy at the University of Pennsylvania Department of Psychiatry, Beck has found his emphasis on "dysfunctional" thinking to be a highly effective means of achieving structured, active, short-term treatment (Beck, 1975, 1976, 1987, 1993; Beck & Emery, 1985; Beck, Rush, Hollon, & Shaw, 1979; Beck, Rush, Shaw, & Emery, 1979; Beck & Weishaar, 1989; DeRubeis & Beck, 1988; Haaga & Davison, 1986; Rush, Beck, Kovacs & Hollon, 1977; Weinrach, 1988).

Beck's cognitive approach is only one of several alternatives to RET. Another method, commonly referred to as *cognitive-behavioral therapy,* has emerged from the work of Albert Bandura's social learning and self-efficacy theory (1977, 1986) and Donald Meichenbaum's cognitive behavior modification or stress-inoculation training (1977, 1985). The work of Bandura and Meichenbaum evolved from out of traditional behaviorism. However, while true behaviorists look to external factors as the ultimate cause of behavior, the cognitive-behavior practitioner believes that some human behavior is caused by internal or mental events. And while behaviorists focus greatly on conditioning as the explanation for all behavior, cognitive-behavioral practitioners assume that behavior transcends operant and classical conditioning, that it is more complex than pure reinforcement. As one might expect, the cognitive-behavior therapist believes that thoughts are equally important contributors to behavior (Beutler et al., 1991; Meichenbaum, 1986; Meichenbaum & Cameron, 1982).

According to Meichenbaum (1977), the cognitive-behavioral therapist will encourage clients to become aware of how they think, feel, and behave in order to interrupt the scripted nature of their behavior, so that they can evaluate their behavior in various situations. Like RET, this approach assumes that distressing emotions are typically the result of irrational thoughts. Unlike RET, however, cognitive-behavior therapy is more integrated into the discipline of psychology, less dogmatic, and more scientific in its formulations (Emery, 1981; Jones & Butman, 1991; Wiser & Goldfried, 1993). Perhaps it is this that accounts for the therapist-client relationship being less personal than in many other approaches. The task of the therapist is to "act as a diagnostician, educator and technical consultant" to remedy dysfunctional cognitions (Kendall & Bemis, 1983, p. 566).

The practice of cognitive-behavior therapy features short-term interventions directed toward specifically defined targets. There are three major types of such interventions: *coping skill training,* in which clients are assisted in developing behavioral and cognitive skills for dealing with challenging situations;

13.3 | The Prince of Reason: An Interview with Albert Ellis

RE: You were trained initially in the Rogerian tradition of therapy, which is entirely non-directive, Then you shifted to Freudian psychoanalysis. How did you end up developing your own very directive technique?

AE: I was trained in Rogerian therapy at Columbia University, but I didn't buy it so I never practiced it. I had used eclectic therapy and behavior therapy on myself at the age of 19 to get over my fear of public speaking and my terror of approaching young women in public. So I'd used other forms of therapy on myself, and I started to use those with clients. But I thought foolishly that Freudian psychoanalysis was deeper and more intensive than other, more directive forms of therapy, so I was trained in it and practiced it. Then I found that it intensively went into every irrelevancy under the sun—and that it didn't work.

RE: Freudian therapists do a lot of listening and very little persuading.

AE: Right, and that was one of the reasons I eventually gave up being an analyst. You had to be too passive and not speak up, and you couldn' t give homework to clients. While I was still an analyst, I wrote several articles criticizing psychoanalysis, but the analysts weren't listening to my objections. So I finally quit psychoanalysis after practicing it for six years.

RE: What's an irrational belief, and how can it interfere with our normal functioning?

AE: If something is irrational, that means it won't work. It's usually unrealistic. People are terrified of other people or difficult projects because they tell themselves that they could fail or be rejected. Failure can lead to sorrow, regret, frustration, and annoyance—all healthy, negative feelings without which people couldn't exist. But then they add, "I absolutely must succeed and must be loved by significant persons, and if I don't, it's terrible and I'm no good." Those are irrational beliefs. As long as people keep them, they'll be terrified of life and will put themselves down when they get rejected.

RE: So there's a certain level of belief that isn't harmful.

AE: Yes, like when we say that something that we're encountering is bad. We don't like it.

RE: Then people add another level of belief—the "must" level—which is harmful. The rational belief is one that's closer to the facts, and the irrational belief includes imperatives like "must," "should" and "ought."

AE: Yes. Rational beliefs bring us closer to getting good results in the real world.

RE: Psychoanalysis can take decades, but you became known for producing rapid change. How did you achieve this?

(continued)

13.3 | The Prince of Reason: An Interview with Albert Ellis (continued)

AE: My rational emotive behavior therapy (REBT) was one of the very few therapies that was originated partly or largely because I wanted to be brief and efficient. And therefore right from the start I was active and directive. I tried to show people some central masturbatory core to their philosophy and to get them to work at changing it cognitively, emotionally, and behaviorally.

RE: How did REBT develop?

AE: I started to call myself a "rational therapist" in January 1955; later I used the term "rational emotive." Now I call myself a "rational emotive behavior therapist." But from the start, I always included philosophic techniques as well as experiential, emotional, and behavioral techniques. At first I did REBT myself. Then I taught it to a few of my friends who were psychotherapists. And then I began, in 1956, to start teaching it to others. In 1959, I got a great big Ampex tape recorder and recorded specific sessions that I had with people and started sending samples to other therapists. That year I also established the Institute for Rational Living, which later became the Institute for Rational Emotive Therapy and then the Albert Ellis Institute, which trains therapists and gives them certificates in REBT.

RE: How did the profession react to REBT?

AE: I was ostracized by most of the psychological, psychiatric, and social professions. Therapists said REBT was superficial. It won't work. They wrongly said it has no "feeling" aspects. Some said it wasn't behavioral, although it was very behavioral. Critics said all kinds of things about it and objected philosophically and otherwise to it. But essentially they said it wouldn't work.

RE: Who were the most vocal critics?

AE: One was Fritz Perls. Whenever we were on a symposium together, he would say, "I'm bored. It's too rational. It has no feeling." Many psychoanalysts refused to let me speak at their meetings. They were exceptionally vigorous because I had previously been an analyst and they were very angry at my flying the coop. Practically every other kind of therapist was opposed to REBT.

---

cognitive restructuring, which attempts to directly modify maladaptive thought patterns; and *problem-solving training,* in which people expand their general capacity for understanding and facing challenging problems (Dobson & Block, 1988; Neimeyer & Feixas, 1990).

Considerable research using strategies from cognitive approaches has supported its theoretical foundation (Beck, 1993). The broad application of the theory and strategies bolsters the claim of cognitive therapy as a robust system of treatment. Consider the myriad of clinical situations to which it has been effectively applied in recent years: panic disorder (Barlow, 1990; Telch et al., 1993),

RE: You and the thousands of therapists you've trained and influenced have used REBT with perhaps millions of people. What evidence do you have that it works?

AE: In my very first paper on what we now call REBT, I outlined 11 common irrational beliefs. Later I added 30 or 40 more common irrational ideas. Beginning in the 1960s, many studies showed that people who hold what we call irrational beliefs are significantly more disturbed than when they don't hold them, and the more strongly they hold them, the more disturbed they tend to be. We started doing outcome studies, and then later Aaron Beck and Donald Meichenbaum began to do them, and now there are probably 2,000 or more studies on the effectiveness of cognitive behavior therapy, which I originated. The studies tend to show that when people change their irrational beliefs to undogmatic flexible preferences, they become less disturbed.

RE: Are there any particular populations that are more resistant to this technique?

AE: The psychotics, naturally. They don't think straight. And severe personality disorders take much longer to treat than people who are neurotic.

RE: Does your technique work better with men than with women?

AE: There's no evidence whatsoever that men are more rational than women or that men are more willing to surrender their irrational beliefs. Both sexes seem to be equally irrational and equally benefit from REBT and cognitive behavior therapy.

RE: Rogers' approach and your approach seem to be miles apart.

AE: But they're also similar in one respect. We both had the idea—which I think we each got from Paul Tillich's book *The Courage To Be*—that humans can always accept themselves unconditionally. But Rogers thought that he could get people to accept themselves just by listening to them and being nice to them, and I don't think that's enough. I think nine out of ten people who go through Rogerian therapy conclude wrongly that "I'm okay because my therapist approves of me." But that' s conditional love. I get people to truly accept themselves unconditionally, whether or not their therapist or anyone loves them. Self-esteem is the greatest sickness known to man or woman because it's conditional. "When I do well and am loved by significant others, then I'm okay." Rogers would have been opposed to that as an endpoint of therapy, but he didn't have a good technique for showing people how to get beyond it. In REBT, we give clients unconditional acceptance but we also teach them how to give it to themselves.

insomnia (Morin, Kowatch, Barry, & Walson, 1993), bulimia nervosa (Hom & Giles, 1991; Jones, Peveler, Hope, & Fairburn, 1993; Wilson, Eldgredge, Smith & Niles, 1991), marital conflict (Denton, 1991; Epstein, Baucom, & Rankin, 1993; Montag & Wilson, 1992), rape victims (Foa, Rothbaum, Riggs, & Murdock, 1991), kleptomania (Schwartz & Hoellen, 1991), social phobia (Bruch, Heimberg, & Hope, 1991), schizophrenia (Liberman & Green, 1992), sexual abuse (Deblinger, McLeer, & Henry, 1990), job-related distress (Barkam

& Shapiro, 1990), and depression (Addis & Jacobson, 1991; Beardslee, et al., 1992; Burns & Nolen, 1992; Propst et al., 1992; Thase & Simon, 1992).

CRITICAL ANALYSIS

The cognitive approach to therapy is one of the most effective and easily learned methods of counseling. Few would disagree that it is a largely successful means of preventing clients from seriously passing judgment on themselves based on some inconsequential or superficial aspect of their behavior, and this within a relatively short time period. The economy and efficiency of this approach are just as impressive. Since the cognitive approach fits instinctively with the rational aspect of human beings, it has generated a significant amount of bibliotherapeutic material and positive research findings.

Despite its many contributions to the field of counseling, however, RET and similar cognitive approaches present a number of critical concerns. To begin with, the almost exclusive focus of RET on cognition has been criticized for simplifying the complexity of the human experience and ignoring the client's history. The A-B-C model may be attractive, but it may also be misleading: its linear and simple components may not always fit neatly into the complex emotional and cognitive environment that characterizes most people. The point is that in evaluating RET for its breadth of methods, one quickly sees that it is one of the narrower approaches. In combination with other behavioral approaches, however, this critique of RET begins to diminish.

> Humans are highly suggestible, impressionable, vulnerable, and gullible.
>
> —Albert Ellis

Another criticism of RET is that it attempts to implement a truly "value-less" approach to therapy. Ellis (1978, p. 40) clearly states that "RET posits no absolutistic or invariant criteria of rationality." Paradoxically, the very article (Ellis, 1977a, p. 55) that proclaims value openness concludes with a list of particular values and goals that clients "need to seek" if they want to obtain happiness and minimize emotional disturbance. Again refusing to arbitrarily identify the criteria by which therapists might distinguish rational from irrational thoughts, Ellis has argued elsewhere that "rational thoughts . . . are defined in RET as those thoughts that help people to live longer and happier, particularly by . . . choosing for themselves certain . . . happiness-producing values, purposes, goals" (Ellis & Bernard, 1986, pp. 5–6). But to judge the efficacy of a belief, based on the criterion of whether it produces "happiness-producing values" on the one hand or an irrational or inappropriate effect on the other, is clearly an invitation to circular reasoning. After all, how does one recognize an inappropriate effect except by the irrationality of the belief that produced it? And on what basis does the therapist determine a belief to be irrational, unless it is the effect that it produces? If one has a depressive reaction to a belief that "My physician says I am seriously ill, and that is awful," an RET therapist cannot conclude that this reaction is excessive except by having a predetermined notion of exactly how upset one can legitimately be in such circumstances. Ellis has attempted to overcome this problem by defining an inappropriate emotional response as one that impedes rather than helps people overcome the obstacle that is causing their distress. The question remains, however: Who determines what emotions help and what emotions hurt our growth?

When it comes to therapy from a multicultural perspective, RET and other cognitive-behavioral therapies have fundamental advantages and disadvantages. The most obvious contribution of these therapies to multicultural counseling is their challenge to examine how one's thinking determines to a large extent how one feels and what one does. This is a near-universal human experience that transcends many cultural barriers (Beutler, Mohr, Grawe, Engle, et al., 1991; Rihani, 1987). Indeed, some have suggested that particular ethnic-minority cultures may even be more receptive to the directive style of RET than North Americans, who view counseling as a more exploratory and democratic process (Waxer, 1989). It has also become clear that the cognitive approach is frequently used in training practices around the world (Deane, 1992; Lloyd & Bhugra, 1993; Page, 1993). The difficulty is that the cognitive approach can easily misconstrue as "irrational" the values of ethnic-minority clients that are related to their particular world view. In addition, this approach may neglect the fact that many irrational environments in which clients reside and that exist beyond the counseling office continue to foster and reinforce irrational thoughts and maladaptive behaviors. When working with minority clients, the cognitive therapist needs to exercise considerable care to avoid these dangers.

A critique of the cognitive approach to counseling must also take into account its frequently effective work with physically disabled clients. There is often a need for the counselor working with disability-related interventions, for example, to confront and interrupt the client's unrealistic and negative beliefs and expectations concerning the disability and its implications. The cognitive approach can further help clients to disassemble seemingly insurmountable problems into smaller and more manageable units (Halligan, 1983).

A final comment must be made concerning Ellis's bombastic style, which can become unnecessarily intertwined with one's understanding of how RET is practiced. There are many styles of doing rational therapy, however, and there are gentle, respectful ways to aid the process of cognitive change. It is vital in studying RET to separate the habits and manner of Ellis as a therapist from his ideas.

CURRENT STATUS

In recent years RET has come to enjoy wide acceptance. While the approach certainly has its critics, Ellis has consistently countered attacks with a hearty spirit and with "innumerable studies" providing empirical evidence (Ellis, 1977b, p. 3). In general, research exploring the A-B-C theory is supportive (DiGuiseppe, Leaf, & Linscott, 1993; DiGiuseppe, Miller, & Trexler, 1979; Ellis, 1979c, 1983; Engels, Garnefski, & Diekstra, 1993; Folkins, 1970; Geer, Davison, & Gatchel, 1970; Hajzler & Bernard, 1991; Jordan & Kempler, 1970; McGovern & Silverman, 1986; Oei, Hansen, & Miller, 1993; Silverman, McCarthy, & McGovern, 1992; Steffy, Meichenbaum, & Best, 1970; Valins, 1970). The evidence shows that emotional difficulties do tend to be associated with specific irrational ideas (Dua, 1970; Haaga & Davison, 1989; Lipsky, Kassinove, & Miller, 1980; Moleski & Tosi, 1976; Reardon & Tosi, 1977;

Rimm & Litvak, 1969; Tosi & Carlson, 1970; Tosi & Eshbaugh, 1976; Tosi & Reardon, 1976; Velten, 1968). Today, a great deal of research on RET routinely appears in the *Journal of Rational Emotive and Cognitive-Behavior Therapy*.

Two nonprofit institutes have been established by Ellis to promote RET: the Institute for Rational Living, a scientific and educational foundation established in 1959, and the Institute for Rational-Emotive Therapy, an institution for professional training and clinical services established in 1968. With headquarters in New York, these institutes have branches in several cities in the United States and other countries. The Institute for Rational-Emotive Therapy offers several levels of training, including Primary and Intermediate Certificates, an Associate Fellowship, and a Fellowship. All levels involve instruction, individual supervision, and written and oral examinations. A register at the Institute for Rational-Emotive Therapy lists hundreds of psychotherapists who have received training in RET. In addition to therapists who have received formal training in RET, hundreds of others follow cognitive approaches. To obtain further information or a catalog of RET workshops and publications, contact:

> The individual's primary problem has to do with his construction of reality.
>
> —Aaron Beck

Institute for Rational-Emotive Therapy
45 East 65th Street
New York, NY 10021–6593
Telephone: (212) 535–0822

Some years ago, Aaron Beck asked, "Can a fledgling psychotherapy challenge the giants in the field—psychoanalysis and behavior therapy?" (Beck, 1976, p. 333). Since asking that question, substantial empirical support has accumulated and thousands of practitioners subscribe to a form of cognitive therapy, making the cognitive approach one of the most popular modes of psychotherapy.

SUMMARY

1. *Biography.* Albert Ellis (1913–) grew up in New York, where as a young adolescent he dreamed of becoming a novelist. In 1934 he graduated from City College of New York with a BA in business administration. In his spare time, Ellis wrote fiction, but his literary efforts did not pay off. After eight of his novels were rejected by publishers, Ellis decided to study psychology and eventually earned his Ph.D. in clinical psychology from Columbia University. Ellis began practicing psychoanalysis but eventually became more active and directive with his patients, gradually developing his own approach to therapy.

2. *Historical Development.* Although the origins of RET can be traced as far back as ancient Greece, the approach more recently stems from cognitive learning theory. Despite Ellis's original training and practice of psychoanalysis, he remained dissatisfied with this approach and hypothesized that

his patients' behaviors were influenced by their attitudes and perceptions. This hypothesis motivated Ellis to work diligently toward a rational approach to psychotherapy.

3. *View of Human Nature.* Ellis holds that human nature has the potential to control much of the pleasure and pain that seemingly results from life's circumstances. According to Ellis, the human psyche is intricately entwined with thoughts and feelings. Ellis's view of human nature can be summarized in his formulation of the A-B-C theory, which suggests that people come to therapy because of a disturbing consequence (C), which is attributed to an activating event (A), as if there were a causal relationship. According to Ellis, however, people are not disturbed by events themselves, but by the beliefs (B) they hold about those events.

4. *Development of Maladaptive Behavior.* Because humans are self-conscious creatures, they observe their disturbance and then make themselves disturbed all over again about being disturbed. Maladaptive behavior, therefore, results from a number of illogical ideas (e.g., being loved and approved by everyone is necessary for happiness) that are held and perpetuated until a new way of thinking is learned. These illogical ideas result in feelings of worthlessness, depression, rage, anxiety, mania, or self-pity. Although we are born with the potential to be rational, we become illogical because of distortions during childhood and the contemporary reinforcement of those distortions.

5. *Function of the Therapist.* In RET the therapist is unequivocally verbal and directive, intentionally attempting to lead the patient to a healthier perspective. By using persuasion and debate to attack self-defeating patterns, the therapist works as quickly as possible to help clients face their illogical thinking. Exploring the details of the past is only a smoke screen, hiding the real issue of irrational thinking. The process for the RET therapist, then, centers on showing clients how and when they are irrational.

6. *Goals of Therapy.* The ultimate goal of RET is to "teach" clients to analyze and correct their distortions of reality. It aims to help clients separate their rational from their irrational beliefs. Then the identified irrational beliefs are challenged; that is, the client is brought to a point of disputing irrational emotional beliefs. RET aims to eliminate the irrational beliefs and substitute them with a new, more rational philosophy. If this disputation is effective, it will be apparent in the diminished emotional distress, and it will result in clients assuming more responsibility for their own lives.

7. *Major Methods and Techniques.* RET consists of three general phases. In the cognitive phase the therapist presents the rationale for therapy to the clients. The emotive phase is devoted to helping clients become aware of their thoughts. During the behavioristic phase clients are trained to verbalize alternative cognitions and to change their behavior. During each of these phases, techniques such as disputation, countering, and action homework may be used.

8. *Application.* A transcript cannot completely capture the role that Ellis's personality plays in how he applies RET, but the case of a 26-year-old male commercial artist who is homophobic portrays much of its dramatic momentum. In this case, Ellis quickly taps into the client's irrational, illogical thinking and through disputation quickly attempts to dismantle it. After eight sessions, the client's obsession is relieved.

9. *Other Cognitively Based Theories.* While RET is the most widely known cognitive approach, it is not the only one. Aaron Beck also developed a highly effective cognitive theory based on the rationale that the way people feel and behave is determined by how they structure their experience. Emphasizing "dysfunctional" thinking, he tries to help clients become more realistic in their interpretation of events by projecting less often. Donald Meichenbaum has inaugurated a cognitive-behavioral approach, which emphasizes that clients need to become aware of how they think, feel, and behave in order to interrupt the scripted nature of their behavior so that they can evaluate their behavior in various situations.

10. *Critical Analysis.* The cognitive approach to therapy is a proven short-term strategy for preventing clients from seriously passing judgment on themselves based on some inconsequential aspect of their behavior. But it has been criticized for simplifying the complexity of human experience and for trying to implement a truly "valueless" approach to therapy. Concerning multicultural counseling, the cognitive approach is capable of transcending many cultural barriers but runs the risk of misconstruing as "irrational" the values of ethnic minority clients that are related to their particular world view.

11. *Current Status.* In recent years RET and other cognitive approaches have come to enjoy wide acceptance. Much of its following and support can be attributed to the empirical evidence which undergirds its efforts. Also, Ellis's two nonprofit institutes, with headquarters in New York, promote RET in many areas. Thousands of practitioners subscribe to a form of cognitive therapy today, making it one of the most popular modes of psychotherapy.

Key Terms

Action homework Assignments designed to encourage clients to dispute their irrational ideas behaviorally. These assignments nearly always involve some degree of risk since clients are often asked to do the very thing they fear most.

All-or-nothing thinking Seeing things in black or white, yes or no, for me or against me categories. If a conversation is anything less than perfect, is it seen as a total failure? Example: A student who receives a C on a single exam thinks he is an academic failure.

Cognitive Characteristic of putting importance on purpose, knowing, understanding, thinking, and reasoning in behavior.

Countering A technique whereby clients are asked to identify "counters" for each of their significant irrational beliefs and then to argue against these beliefs. In other words, countering involves arguing in an assertive fashion and convincing oneself of the falsity of a belief.

Discounting Rejecting positive experiences by insisting they "don't count." Example: Earning high marks in a class are discounted by saying, "anyone could have done it."

Emotion control card A wallet-sized card containing four emotionally debilitating categories (anger, self-criticism, anxiety, and depression), a list of inappropriate feelings, and a parallel list of appropriate feelings. It is used in practicing rational-emotive imaging.

Emotional reasoning Assuming that negative emotions reflect the way things really are. Example: "I feel guilty so I must be guilty."

Emotive Having to do with emotion-provoking stimuli.

Insight Number 1 What Ellis calls showing clients how and when they are irrational.

Insight Number 2 What Ellis calls convincing clients that they maintain their own emotional disturbance by reindoctrinating themselves with the same repetitious irrational ideas.

Insight Number 3 What Ellis calls leading clients to a full acknowledgment that ridding themselves of their disturbances depends on their willingness to join in challenging their beliefs and in developing new ways of thinking.

Irrational Characterized by being influenced or guided by "crooked" thinking.

Magnification Exaggerating the importance of problems and shortcomings. Example: "With my IQ I can never get a really good job."

Mind reading Making inferences about how people feel and think. Example: "The president doesn't like people; no one can get in to see him because he tells the Secret Service to keep them away."

Overgeneralization Seeing a single event as a never-ending pattern of defeat by using the words *always* or *never* when thinking about it. Example: "I am always in the wrong place at the wrong time."

Rational Characterized by being influenced or guided by reason.

Self-blame Taking personal responsibility for events that are beyond one's control. Example: "If I had not asked to go shopping, he never would have been in the wreck."

Self-efficacy A comprehensive sense of one's own capability, effectiveness, strength, or power to attain desired results.

Social learning A modified form of behaviorism that stresses the importance of cognitive processes as causal agents in behavior. Albert Bandura is the leading contemporary exponent of this point of view.

Suggested Reading

Ellis, A. (1962). *Reason and emotion in psychotherapy*. New York: Lyle Stuart.

Ellis, A., & Dryden, W. (1987). *The practice of rational-emotive therapy*. New York: Lyle Stuart.

Ellis, A., & Grieger, R. (1977). *Handbook of rational-emotive therapy* (Vol. 1.) New York: Springer.

Ellis, A., & Grieger, R. (1986). *Handbook of rational-emotive therapy* (Vol. 2.) New York: Springer.

References

Addis, M. E., & Jacobson, N. S. (1991). Integration of cognitive therapy and behavioral marital therapy for depression. *Journal of Psychotherapy Integration, 1,* 249–264.

Bandura, A. (1977). Self-efficacy: Toward a unifying theory of behavioral change. *Psychological Review, 84,* 191–215.

Bandura, A. (1986). *Social foundations of thought and action*. Englewood Cliffs, NJ: Prentice Hall.

Bard, I. (1980). RET in practice. Edison, NJ: Resolute Press.

Barkam, M., & Shapiro, D. A. (1990). Brief psychotherapeutic interventions for job-related distress: A pilot study of prescriptive and exploratory therapy. *Counseling Psychology Quarterly, 3,* 133–147.

Barlow, D. H. (1990). Long-term outcome for patients with panic disorder treated with cognitive-behavioral therapy. *Journal of Clinical Psychiatry, 51,* 17–23.

Beardslee, W. R., Hoke, L., Wheelock, I., Rothberg, P. C., (1992). Initial findings on preventive intervention for families with parental affective disorders. *American Journal of Psychiatry, 149,* 1335–1340.

Beck, A. T. (1975). *Depression: Causes and treatment*. Philadelphia: University of Pennsylvania Press.

Beck, A. T. (1976). *Cognitive therapy and emotional disorders*. New York: International Universities Press.

Beck, A. T. (1987). Cognitive therapy. In J. K. Zeig (Ed.), *The evolution of psychotherapy* (pp. 149–178). New York: Brunner/Mazel.

Beck, A. T. (1991). Cognitive therapy: A 30-year retrospective. *American Psychologist, 46,* 368–375.

Beck, A. T. (1993). Cognitive therapy: Past, present, and future. *Journal of Consulting and Clinical Psychology, 61,* 194–198.

Beck, A. T., & Emery, G. (1985). *Anxiety disorders and phobias: A cognitive perspective*. New York: Basic Books.

Beck, A., Rush, A., Hollon, S., & Shaw, B. (1979). *Cognitive therapy of depression*. New York: Guilford.

Beck, A., Rush, A., Shaw, B., & Emery, G. (1979). *Cognitive therapy of depression*. New York: Guilford Press.

Beck, A. T., & Weishaar, M. E. (1989). In R. J. Corsini & D. Wedding (Eds.), *Current psychotherapies* (4th ed., pp. 285–320). Itasca, IL: Peacock.

Beutler, L. E., Engle, D., Mohr, D., Daldrup, R. J., (1991). Predictors of differential response to cognitive, experiential, and self-directed psychotherapeutic procedures. *Journal of Consulting and Clinical Psychology, 59,* 333–340.

Beutler, L. E., Mohr, D. C., Grawe, K., Engle, D., et al. (1991). Looking for differential treatment effects: Cross-cultural predictors of differential psychotherapy efficacy. *Journal of Psychotherapy Integration, 1,* 121–141.

Bruch, M. A., Heimberg, R. G., & Hope, D. A. (1991). States of mind model and cognitive change in treated social phobics. *Cognitive Therapy and Research, 15,* 429–441.

Burns, D. D., & Nolen, S. (1992). Therapeutic empathy and recovery from depression in cognitive-behavioral therapy: A structural equation model. *Journal of Consulting and Clinical Psychology, 60,* 441–449.

Cohen, E. D. (1987). The use of syllogism in rational-emotive therapy. *Journal of Counseling and Development, 66,* 37–39.

Deane, F. P. (1992). Pretreatment expectations of New Zealand clients receiving cognitive-behavioral psychotherapy: Comparison with a North American sample. *International Journal of Social Psychiatry, 38,* 138–149.

Deblinger, E., McLeer, S. V., & Henry, D. (1990). Cognitive behavioral treatment for sexually abused children suffering post-traumatic stress: Preliminary findings. *Journal of the American Academy of Child and Adolescent Psychiatry, 29,* 747–752.

Denton, W. H. (1991). The role of affect in marital therapy. *Journal of Marital and Family Therapy, 17,* 257–261.

DeRubeis, R. J., & Beck, A. T. (1988). Cognitive therapy. In K. S. Dobson (Ed.), *Handbook of cognitive-behavioral therapies* (pp. 273–306). New York: Guilford Press.

DiGuiseppe, R. A., Leaf, R., & Linscott, J. (1993). The therapeutic relationship in rational-emotive therapy: Some preliminary data. *Journal of Rational Emotive and Cognitive Behavior Therapy, 11,* 223–233.

DiGiuseppe, R. A., Miller, N. J., & Trexler, L. D. (1979). A review of rational-emotive psychotherapy outcome studies. In A. Ellis & J. M. Whiteley (Eds.), *Theoretical and empirical foundations of rational-emotive therapy* (pp. 218–235). Pacific Grove, CA: Brooks/Cole.

Dobson, K. S. (Ed.). (1988a). *Handbook of cognitive-behavioral therapies.* New York: Guilford Press.

Dobson, K. S. (1988b). The present and future of the cognitive-behavioral therapies. In K. S. Dobson (Ed.), *Handbook of cognitive-behavioral therapies* (pp. 387–414). New York: Guilford Press.

Dobson, K. S., & Block, L. (1988). Historical and philosophical bases of the cognitive-behavioral therapies. In K. S. Dobson (Ed.), *Handbook of cognitive-behavioral therapies* (pp. 3–38). New York: Guilford Press.

Dryden, W. (1986). Vivid methods in rational-emotive therapy. In A. Ellis & R. Grieger (Eds.), *Handbook of rational-emotive therapy* (Vol. 2, pp. 221–245). New York: Springer.

Dryden, W. (1989). Albert Ellis: An efficient and passionate life. *Journal of Counseling and Development, 67,* 539–546.

Dryden, W., & Ellis, A. (1988). Rational-emotive therapy. In K. S. Dobson (Ed.), *Handbook of coaviorgnitive-behal therapies* (pp. 214–272). New York: Guilford Press.

Dua, P. S. (1970). Comparison of the effects of behaviorally oriented action and psychotherapy reeducation on introversion-extroversion, emotionality, and inter-external control. *Journal of Counseling Psychology, 17,* 567–572.

Ellis, A. (1962). *Reason and emotion in psychotherapy.* New York: Lyle Stuart.

Ellis, A. (1967). Rational-emotive psychotherapy. In D. Arbuckle (Ed.), *Counseling and psychotherapy.* New York: McGraw-Hill.

Ellis, A. (1969). A weekend of rational encounter. In A. Burton (Ed.), *Encounter: The theory and practice of encounter groups.* San Francisco: Jossey-Bass.

Ellis, A. (1971). *Growth through reason.* Hollywood, CA: Wilshire Books.

Ellis, A. (1973). *Humanistic psychotherapy: The rational-emotive approach.* New York: Julian Press.

Ellis, A. (1977a). The basic clinical theory of rational-emotive therapy. In A. Ellis & R. Grieger (Eds.), *Handbook of rational-emotive therapy* (Vol. 1, pp. 3–34). New York: Springer.

Ellis, A. (1977b). *A garland of rational songs.* New York: Institute for Rational-Emotive Therapy.

Ellis, A. (1979a). The practice of rational-emotive therapy. In A. Ellis & J. Whiteley (Eds.), *Theoretical and empirical foundations of rational-emotive therapy* (pp. 61–100). Pacific Grove, CA: Brooks/Cole.

Ellis, A. (1979b). Rational-emotive therapy. In A. Ellis & J. M. Whiteley (Eds.), *Theoretical and empirical foundations of rational-emotive therapy* (pp. 1–6). Pacific Grove, CA: Brooks/Cole.

Ellis, A. (1979c). Rational-emotive therapy: Research data that support the clinical and personality hypotheses of RET and other modes of cognitive-behavior therapy. In A. Ellis & J. M. Whiteley (Eds.), *Theoretical and empirical foundations of rational emotive therapy* (pp. 101–173). Pacific Grove, CA: Brooks/Cole.

Ellis, A. (1979d). The theory of rational-emotive therapy. In A. Ellis & J. Whiteley (Eds.), *Theoretical and empirical foundations of rational-emotive therapy* (pp. 33–60). Pacific Grove, CA: Brooks/Cole.

Ellis, A. (1979e). Toward a new theory of personality. In A. Ellis & J. Whiteley (Eds.), *Theoretical and empirical foundations of rational-emotive therapy* (pp. 7–32). Pacific Grove, CA: Brooks/Cole.

Ellis, A. (1982). Rational-emotive family therapy. In A. M. Horne & M. M. Ohlsen

(Eds.), *Family counseling and therapy*. Itasca, IL: Peacock.

Ellis, A. (1984a). Is the unified-interaction approach to a cognitive-behavior modification a reinvention of the wheel? *Clinical Psychology Review, 4,* 215–217.

Ellis, A. (1984b). Maintenance and generalization in rational-emotive therapy. *The Cognitive Behaviorist, 6,* 2–4.

Ellis, A. (1985). *Overcoming resistance: Rational-emotive therapy with difficult clients.* New York: Springer.

Ellis, A. (1986a). Rational-emotive therapy. In I. L. Kutash & A. Wolf (Eds.), *Psychotherapist's casebook* (pp. 277–287). San Francisco: Jossey-Bass.

Ellis, A. (1986b). Rational-emotive therapy and cognitive behavior therapy: Similarities and differences. In A. Ellis & R. Grieger (Eds.), *Handbook of rational-emotive therapy* (Vol. 2, pp. 31–45). New York: Springer.

Ellis, A. (1987a). The evolution of rational-emotive therapy (RET) and cognitive behavior therapy (CBT). In J. K. Zeig (Ed.), *The evolution of psychotherapy* (pp. 107–132). New York: Brunner/Mazel.

Ellis, A. (1987b). The impossibility of achieving consistently good mental health. *American Psychologist, 42,* 364–375.

Ellis, A. (1988). *How to stubbornly refuse to make yourself miserable about anything—yes, anything!* New York: Lyle Stuart.

Ellis, A. (1989). Rational-emotive therapy. In R. J. Corsini & D. Wedding (Eds.), *Current psychotherapies* (4th ed., pp. 197–238). Itasca, IL: Peacock.

Ellis, A. (1990). Rational and irrational beliefs in counselling psychology. *Journal of Rational-Emotive and Cognitive-Behavior Therapy, 8,* 221–223.

Ellis, A. (1993). Reflections on rational-emotive therapy. *Journal of Consulting and Clinical Psychology, 61,* 199–201.

Ellis, A., & Bernard, M. E. (1986). What is rational-emotive therapy (RET)? In A. Ellis & R. Grieger (Eds.), *Handbook of rational-emotive therapy* (Vol. 2, pp. 3–30). New York: Springer.

Ellis, A., & Dryden, W. (1987). *The practice of rational-emotive therapy.* New York: Lyle Stuart.

Ellis, A., & Grieger, R. (1977). *Handbook of rational-emotive therapy* (Vol. 1). New York: Springer.

Ellis, A., & Grieger, R. (1986). *Handbook of rational-emotive therapy* (Vol. 2). New York: Springer.

Ellis, A., & Harper, R. (1975). *A new guide to rational living* (Rev. ed.). Hollywood, CA: Wilshire Books.

Ellis, A., Sichel, J., Yeager, R., DiMattio, D., & DiGiuseppe, R. (1969). *Rational emotive couples therapy.* New York: Pergamon Press.

Ellis, A., & Whiteley, J. M. (Eds.). (1979). *Theoretical and empirical foundations of rational-emotive therapy.* Pacific Grove, CA: Brooks/Cole.

Ellis, A., & Yeager, R. J. (1989). *Why some therapies don't work.* Buffalo, NY: Prometheus Books.

Emery, G. (1981). *A new beginning: How you can change your life through cognitive therapy.* New York: Simon & Schuster (Touchstone Books).

Engels, G. I., Garnefski, N., & Diekstra, R. F. (1993). Efficacy of rational emotive therapy: A quantitative analysis. *Journal of Consulting and Clinical Psychology, 61,* 1083–1090.

Epstein, N., Baucom, D. H., & Rankin, L. A. (1993). Treatment of marital conflict: A cognitive-behavioral approach. Special Issue: Marital conflict. *Clinical Psychology Review, 13,* 45–57.

Foa, E. B., Rothbaum, B. O., Riggs, D. S., & Murdock, Tamera B. (1991). Treatment of post traumatic stress disorder in rape victims: A comparison between cognitive-behavioral procedures and counseling. *Journal of Consulting and Clinical Psychology, 59,* 715–723.

Folkins, C. H. (1970). Temporal factors and the cognitive mediators of stress reaction. *Journal of Personality and Social Psychology, 14,* 173–184.

Fry, W. R., Jr., & Salameh, W. A. (Eds.). (1987). *Handbook of humor and psychotherapy.* Sarasota, FL: Professional Resource Exchange.

Garamoni, G. L., Reynolds, C. F., Thase, M. E., Frank, E. (1992). Shifts in affective balance during cognitive therapy of major depression. *Journal of Consulting and Clinical Psychology, 60,* 260–266.

Geer, J. H., Davison, G. C., & Gatchel, R. L. (1970). Reduction of stress in humans through non-veridical perceived control of aversion stimulation. *Journal of Personal-*

ity and Social Psychology, 14, 731–736.

Goldfried, M. R. (1988). Application of rational restructuring to anxiety disorders. *The Counseling Psychologist, 16,* 50–68.

Grieger, R. M. (1986a). From a linear to a contextual model of the ABCs of RET. In A. Ellis & R. Grieger (Eds.), *Handbook of rational-emotive therapy* (Vol. 2, pp. 59–80). New York: Springer.

Grieger, R. M. (1986b). The process of rational-emotive therapy. In A. Ellis & R. Grieger (Eds.), *Handbook of rational-emotive therapy* (Vol. 2, pp. 203–212). New York: Springer.

Haaga, D. A., & Davison, G. C. (1986). Cognitive change methods. In F. H. Kanfer & A. P. Goldstein (Eds.), *Helping people change: A textbook of methods* (3rd, ed., pp. 236–282). New York: Pergamon Press.

Haaga, D. A., & Davison, G. C. (1989). Outcome studies of rational-emotive therapy. In M. E. Bernard & R. DiGiuseppe (Eds.), *Inside rational-emotive therapy.* San Diego, CA: Academic Press.

Hajzler, D. J., & Bernard, M. E. (1991). A review of rational-emotive education outcome studies. *School Psychology Quarterly, 6,* 27–49.

Halligan, F. G. (1983). Reaction depression and chronic illness: Counseling patients and their families. *The Personnel and Guidance Journal, 61,* 401–406.

Harrell, T. H., Beiman, I., & Lapointe, K. (1986). Didactic persuasion techniques in cognitive restructuring. In A. Ellis & R. Grieger (Eds.), *Handbook of rational emotive therapy* (Vol. 2, pp. 213–220). New York: Springer.

Hom, P. H., & Giles, T. R. (1991). Performance-based intervention for non-purging bulimia: Some implications for the treatment of binge eating and obesity. *Psychology and Health, 5,* 183–191.

Hunt, M. (1982). *The universe within.* New York: Simon & Schuster.

Jones, R., Peveler, R. C., Hope, R. A., & Fairburn, C. G. (1993). Changes during treatment for bulimia nervosa: A comparison of three psychological treatments. *Behaviour Research and Therapy, 31,* 479–485.

Jones, S. C. & Butman, R. E. (1991). Modern psychotherapies. Downer's Grove, IL: Intervarsity Press.

Jordan, B. T., & Kempler, B. (1970). Hysterical personality: An experimental investiga-tion of sex-role conflict. *Journal of Abnormal Psychology, 75,* 172–176.

Kendall, P., & Bemis, K. (1983). Thought and action in psychotherapy: The cognitive-behavioral approaches. In M. Hersen, A. Kazdin, & A. Bellack (Eds.), *The clinical psychology handbook* (pp. 565–592). New York: Pergamon.

Liberman, R. P., & Green, M. F. (1992). Whither cognitive-behavioral therapy for schizophrenia? *Schizophrenia Bulletin, 18,* 27–35.

Lipsky, M. J., Kassinove, H., & Miller, N. J. (1980). Effects of rational-emotive therapy, rational role reversal, and rational-emotive imagery on the emotional adjustment of community mental health center patients. *Journal of Consulting and Clinical Psychology, 48,* 366–374.

Lloyd, K., & Bhugra, D. (1993). Cross-cultural aspects of psychotherapy. *International Review of Psychiatry, 5,* 291–304.

Mahoney, M. J. (1988). The cognitive sciences and psychotherapy: Patterns in a developing relationship. In K. S. Dobson (Ed.), *Handbook of cognitive-behavioral therapies* (pp. 357–386). New York: Guilford Press.

Maultsby, M. C. (1975). *Help yourself to happiness.* New York: Institute for Rational-Emotive Therapy.

Maultsby, M. C. (1984). *Rational behavior therapy.* Englewood Cliffs, NJ: Prentice Hall.

Maultsby, M. C., & Ellis, A. (1974). *Technique for using rational-emotive imagery.* New York: Institute for Rational-Emotive Therapy.

McGovern, T. E., & Silverman, M. (1986). A review of outcome studies of rational emotive therapy from 1977 to 1982. In A. Ellis & R. Grieger (Eds.), *Handbook of rational-emotive therapy* (Vol. 2, pp. 81–102). New York: Springer.

McMullin, R. E. (1986). *Handbook of cognitive therapy techniques.* New York: Norton.

McMullin, R. E., & Giles, T. R. (1981). *Cognitive-behavior therapy.* New York: Grune & Stratton.

Meichenbaum, D. (1977). *Cognitive behavior modification: An integrative approach.* New York: Plenum.

Meichenbaum, D. (1985). *Stress inoculation training.* New York: Pergamon Press.

Meichenbaum, D. (1986). Cognitive behavior modification. In F. H. Kanfer & A. P. Goldstein (Eds.), *Helping people change: A textbook of methods* (pp. 346–380). New York: Pergamon Press.

Meichenbaum, D., & Cameron, R. (1982). Cognitive-behavior therapy. In G. T. Wilson & C. M. Franks (Eds.), *Contemporary behavior therapy: Conceptual and empirical foundations* (pp. 310–338). New York: Guilford Press.

Mischel, W. (1973). Toward a cognitive social learning reconceptualization of personality. *Psychological Review, 80,* 252–285.

Moleski, R., & Tosi, D. J. (1976). Comparative psychotherapy: Rational-emotive therapy versus systematic desensitization in the treatment of stuttering. *Journal of Consulting and Clinical Psychology, 44,* 309–311.

Montag, K. R., & Wilson, G. L. (1992). An empirical evaluation of behavioral and cognitive-behavioral group marital treatments with discordant couples. *Journal of Sex and Marital Therapy, 18,* 255–272.

Morin, C. M., Kowatch, R. A., Barry, T., & Walton, E. (1993). Cognitive-behavior therapy for late-life insomnia. *Journal of Consulting and Clinical Psychology, 61,* 137–146.

Morris, J. B. & Kanitz, F. (1975). Rational emotional therapy. New York: Houghton Mifflin.

Neimeyer, R. A., & Feixas, G. (1990). The role of homework and skill acquisition in the outcome of group cognitive therapy for depression. *Behavior Therapy, 21,* 281–292.

Oei, T. P. S., Hansen, J., & Miller, S. (1993). The empirical status of irrational beliefs in rational emotive therapy. *Australian Psychologist, 28,* 195–200.

Page, A. C. (1993). To whom should cognitive-behavior therapies be taught? *Australian Psychologist, 28,* 51–54.

Patterson, C. H. (1980). *Theory of counseling and psychotherapy* (3rd ed.). New York: Harper & Row.

Propst, L. R., Ostrom, R., Watkins, P., Dean, T., et al. (1992). Comparative efficacy of religious and nonreligious cognitive-behavioral therapy for the treatment of clinical depression in religious individuals. *Journal of Consulting and Clinical Psychology, 60,* 94–103.

Reardon, J. P., & Tosi, D. J. (1977). The effects of rational stage directed therapy on self concept and reduction of psychological stress in adolescent delinquent females. *Journal of Clinical Psychology, 33,* 1084–1092.

Rihani, S. (1987). Irrational ideas among Jordanians and Americans: A cross-cultural study of Ellis' theory of rational-emotive therapy. *Dirasat, 14,* 73–102.

Rimm, D. C., & Litvak, S. B. (1969). Self-verbalization and emotional arousal. *Journal of Abnormal Psychology, 74,* 181–187.

Rush, A. J., Beck, A. T., Kovacs, M., & Hollon, S. (1977). Comparative efficacy of cognitive therapy and pharmacotherapy in the treatment of depressed outpatients. *Cognitive Therapy and Research, 1,* 17–37.

Russell, L. A. (1992). Comparisons of cognitive, music, and imagery techniques on anxiety reduction with university students. *Journal of College Student Development, 33,* 516–523.

Schwartz, D., & Hoellen, B. (1991). "Forbidden fruit tastes especially sweet": Cognitive-behavior therapy with a kleptomaniac woman: A case report. *Psychotherapy in Private Practice, 8,* 19–25.

Silverman, M. S., McCarthy, M., & McGovern, T. (1992). A review of outcome studies of rational-emotive therapy from 1982–1989. *Journal of Rational-Emotive and Cognitive-Behavioral Therapy, 10,* 111–186.

Steffy, R. A., Meichenbaum, D., & Best, J. A. (1970). Aversive and cognitive factors in the modification of smoking behavior. *Behavior Therapy and Research, 8,* 115–125.

Telch, M. J., Lucas, J. A., Schmidt, N. B., Hanna, H. H., et al. (1993). Group cognitive-behavioral treatment of panic disorder. *Behaviour Research and Therapy, 31,* 279–287.

Thase, M. E., & Simons, A. D. (1992). Cognitive behavior therapy and relapse of nonbipolar depression: Parallels with pharmacotherapy. *Psychopharmacology Bulletin, 28,* 117–122.

Tosi, D. J., & Carlson, W. A. (1970). Dogmatism and perceived counselor attitudes. *Personnel and Guidance Journal, 48,* 657–660.

Tosi, D. J., & Eshbaugh, D. M. (1976). The personal beliefs inventory: A factor-analytic study. *Journal of Clinical Psychology, 32,* 322–327.

Tosi, D. J., & Reardon, J. P. (1976). The treatment of guilt through rational stage directed therapy. *Rational Living, 11,* 8–11.

Valins, S. (1970). The perception and labeling of bodily changes as determinants of emotional behavior. In P. Black (Ed.), *Physiological correlates of emotion.* New York: Academic Press.

Velten, E. A. (1968). A laboratory task for induction of mood states. *Behavior Research and Therapy, 6,* 473–482.

Walen, S., DiGuiseppe, R., & Wessler, R. (1980). *A practitioner's guide to RET.* New York: Oxford University Press.

Waxer, P. H. (1989). Cantonese versus Canadian evaluation of directive and nondirective therapy. *Canadian Journal of Counselling, 23,* 263–272.

Weinrach, S. G. (1980). Unconventional therapist: Albert Ellis. *Personnel and Guidance Journal, 59,* 152–160.

Weinrach, S. G. (1988). Cognitive therapist: A dialogue with Aaron Beck. *Journal of Counseling and Development, 67,* 159–164.

Wilson, G. T., Eldredge, K. L., Smith, D., & Niles, B. (1991). Cognitive-behavioral treatment with and without response prevention for bulimia. *Behavior Research and Therapy, 29,* 575–583.

Wiser, S. L., & Goldfried, M. R. (1993). Comparative study of emotional experiencing in psychodynamic-interpersonal and cognitive-behavioral therapies. *Journal of Consulting and Clinical Psychology, 61,* 892–895.

A therapy that leads all patients toward reality, toward grappling successfully with the tangible and intangible aspects of the real world, might accurately be called . . . Reality Therapy. —**William Glasser**

14 CHAPTER | **Reality Therapy**

Many counselors, disillusioned with a perceived ineffectiveness of unconditional positive regard, wary of approaches involving the unconscious, and put off by the presumption that behavioral techniques are inhumane, have looked for a viable alternative to these methods. They have sought a straightforward theoretical approach that could make a practical difference in people's lives, and many have found that alternative in reality therapy.

Reality therapy holds that people can do something about their fate if they consider themselves and their environment realistically. In a sense it is a straightforward, action-oriented, pragmatic approach to counseling that is relatively uncomplicated and easy to understand (Osipow, Walsh, & Tosi, 1984). Although it seems simple, proponents of reality therapy remind us that "simple" should not be mistaken for "simplistic."

Reality therapy is based on an explanation of brain functioning known as **control theory.** This theory accounts for human behavior, not on the basis of past conflicts, external stimuli, or rational thinking, but on the principle that we act in an attempt to fulfill our current needs: belonging, power, pleasure, freedom, and survival. Actions, thoughts, emotions, and even human physiology are continuously generated to fulfill these generic needs and specific wants. Some behavior is helpful; some, ineffective or harmful. Through the process of reality therapy clients learn to travel on a more effective path, to make more realistic choices, in order to satisfy their needs—a journey often unseen by clients in the beginning of therapy. In a trusting environment in which they can define and express their needs and wants, they are able to self-evaluate and choose alternatives leading to a more effective life.

Like other approaches we have examined in this text, reality therapy is largely the product of a single person, Dr. William Glasser.

BRIEF BIOGRAPHY

William Glasser was born in Cleveland, Ohio, on May 11, 1925, the third and youngest child of Ben and Betty Glasser. Little has been written about Glasser's childhood, which he speaks of as being relatively uneventful and happy. Graduating from Cleveland Heights High School, where he played cornet in the band and developed a lasting interest in sports, he majored in chemical engineering at Case Institute of Technology. While still a student, he married Naomi Judith Silver. After graduation he pursued a Ph.D. in clinical psychology, but after his advisors rejected his dissertation, he gained admission to medical school at Western Reserve University. In 1953 he received his M.D. degree at the age of 28. He completed a psychiatric residency at UCLA in 1957, spending the last year of his residency at the West Los Angeles Veterans Administration Hospital. In 1961 he became board-certified.

While in residency, Glasser became increasingly pained over the disjunction between the Freudian methods he had studied and approaches that truly seemed to help the patient. Increasingly disillusioned with the efficacy of traditional psychoanalytic procedures, Glasser began experimenting with alternative treatments. In 1962 Glasser joined the staff of an institute for adolescent girls in Ventura, California. Three years later he published *Reality Therapy: A New Approach to Psychiatry*, which made ample use of his experiences at the Ventura school in order to illuminate the details of his therapeutic approach. In 1969 he published with considerable success *Schools Without Failure*, which applied the principles of reality therapy to the school setting (Parish, 1988).

Glasser was married to his wife, Naomi, for more than 40 years before she died in 1994. Their three children have followed in their father's footsteps: one in counseling, another in teaching, a third in medicine. Naomi Glasser has also contributed to her husband's work by editing two important texts that explain how reality therapy is done: *What Are You Doing?* (1980) and *Control Theory in the Practice of Reality Therapy* (1989). Dr. Glasser continues to lecture around the globe on his ideas.

Two of Dr. Glasser's most recent books are *Reality Therapy in Action* (2000), and *Counseling with Choice Theory* (2001). At the present time, Dr. Glasser is focusing much of his attention on a new project to create a "Choice Theory Community" in Corning, New York. Twenty thousand people in the city of Corning, New York have embraced a five-year training and restructuring program to remove External Control Psychology from all systems in local businesses, community organizations, and government agencies. The people of Corning, New York are attempting to replace External Control Psychology with Choice Theory. This may be the first time in the history of the world that a whole community has embraced a new psychology. The project has been underway since 1997.

HISTORICAL DEVELOPMENT

Although the presupposition that justifies reality therapy is an earlier account of brain functioning called control theory, the two phrases *control theory* and *reality therapy* are now sometimes used interchangeably. Norbert Wiener, a Harvard University mathematician who formulated many of the principles that have been subsumed under control theory, has described the importance of feedback to both engineering and biological systems (1948) as well as the sociological implications for human beings (1950).

Central to Glasser's approach is his belief in the potential for and the necessity of individuals to choose their own direction. One writer argues that the roots of this notion can be found in Ralph Waldo Emerson's concept of "self-reliance" (Croll, 1992); others have suggested that Alfred Adler's model of psychotherapy is a direct ancestor of reality therapy (Rozsnafsky, 1974; Whitehouse, 1984). But when asked about the historical development of reality therapy, Glasser is more likely to point to his basic dislike of and objections to psychoanalytic therapy, which focuses primarily on neurosis and mental illness. Rejecting the medical model of mental illness developed by his Freudian colleagues, Glasser began to argue that patients are not ill, but weak. Only if patients' abilities were strengthened, he thought, could they function as healthy members of society.

14.1 | Understanding Control Theory

Wubbolding (1988) has provided a standard summary of Glasser's control theory as it applies to counseling and psychotherapy.

1. *Human beings are born with five needs:* belonging, power (competence, achievement, recognition, and self-esteem), fun or enjoyment; freedom or independence (autonomy), and survival. These needs are general and universal. Along with wants, which are specific and unique for each person, they serve as the motivators or sources of all behavior.

2. *The difference between what a person wants and what he perceives he is getting (input) is the immediate source of specific behaviors at any given moment.* Thus, reality therapy rests on the principle that human behavior springs from internal motivation, which drives the behavior moment to moment (Wubbolding, 1988). Another consequence of this principle is that human behavior is not an attempt to resolve unconscious, early childhood conflicts. The sources of effective behaviors ("I'll do it," positive symptoms, negative symptoms, and negative addictions) are current, internal, and conscious.

3. *All human behaviors are composed of doing (acting), thinking, feeling, and physiology.* Behaviors are identified by the most obvious aspect of this **total behavior.** Thus, someone counseled for poor grades in school is seen with a presenting action problem. People are labeled psychotic because the primary and most obvious aspect of their total behavior is dysfunctional thinking. Depression, anger, resentment, and fear are most obvious in other persons, so their behavior is called a feeling behavior. The most obvious component of others' behavior is the physiological element, including heart disease, high blood pressure, and other ailments. Because behavior is total, made up of four components, and because it is generated from within, it is useful to see behavior not as static but as ongoing. Therefore, total behavior is often expressed in "ing" words. Feelings, for example, are described as "depressing," "guilting," and "anxiety-ing." Another implication of this principle is that all behavior has a purpose. Human choices are not aimless or random. They are all teleological; in other words, they serve a purpose to close the gap between the perception of what a person is getting and what he or she wants at a given moment.

4. *Human behavior, originating from within, means that human beings are responsible for their behaviors.* In other words, we are all capable of change. This change is brought about by choosing more effective behaviors. The aspect of human behavior over which we have the most direct control is that of acting and secondarily that of thinking. Therefore, in counseling and psychotherapy, the focus is on changing total behavior by discussing current actions along with the evaluation of their effectiveness in fulfilling needs and current wants, the evaluation of their realistic attainability, and current perceptions or viewpoints along with their helpfulness to the individual.

5. *Human beings see the world through a perceptual system that functions as a set of lenses.* At a low level of perception, the person simply recognizes the world, gives a name to objects and events, but does not make a judgment about them. At a high level of perception, the person puts a positive or negative value on the perception. Exploring the various levels of perception and their helpfulness is part of the counseling process.

> You cannot help men permanently by doing for them what they could and should do for themselves.
>
> —Abraham Lincoln

While Glasser was in the valley of doubt, Dr. G. L. Harrington, his teacher at UCLA, was having his own troubled thoughts about the merits of psychoanalysis as a curative science. Since Harrington believed that there is no significant proof that psychoanalysis has any curative powers, he too was seeking a more effective psychotherapy. Harrington's doubts inspired Glasser to develop what finally emerged as reality therapy. Glasser gives full credit for many of his ideas to his supportive and sympathetic teacher.

Actually, the ever-practical Glasser arrived at his treatment theory at least in part because he was not optimistic about starting a private practice. Glasser knew that his open resistance to the psychoanalytic approach during his residency at UCLA would not make him a top choice for referral among his former professors. Yet these were the very referrals on which he would need to rely if he were to succeed as a beginning psychiatrist. Believing referrals would not be forthcoming, Glasser gave up the idea of starting a private practice in favor of a position as head psychiatrist at a youth facility operated by the state of California for female delinquents, the Ventura School for Girls. It was here that Glasser had the freedom to practice his treatment strategies without hindrance. He began using techniques he had developed earlier—techniques that met with such amazing success that Glasser (1965) managed to cut recidivism in the institution to an unheard-of 20 percent.

Shortly after publishing *Reality Therapy* in 1965, Glasser founded the Institute of Reality Therapy in Canoga Park, California, to train human service professionals in his new therapeutic approach. Glasser also joined with California educators to apply the principles of reality therapy to both the ghetto schools of Watts and the more affluent schools of Palo Alto.

So successful were Dr. Glasser's efforts in education that he soon began lecturing extensively on reality therapy throughout the United States and Canada. He has worked with communities and school districts to establish teacher training centers and has served as consultant for courts, police bureaus, and welfare departments. His frequent appearances on television and his writings, which have been translated into numerous languages, have carried the practical message of reality therapy around the world.

VIEW OF HUMAN NATURE

Reality therapy assumes that every person wants to be different—to feel somehow separate and distinct from every other living being—and it underscores this desire by identifying the unique needs of the individual. "No matter where the search may go, no other person exists who thinks, looks, acts, and talks exactly as we do" (Glasser & Zunin, 1979, p. 292). This intrinsic and inherited need to be unique transcends cultures and is the driving force for all behavior (Peterson & Woodward, 1992).

According to Glasser, during the first six years of our lives, we develop either a negative or positive identity. People with a positive self-image believe that they are worthwhile, that there is at least one other person in the world who cares about them (Glasser & Wubbolding, 1995). "When a man acts in such a way that he gives and receives love, and feels worthwhile to himself and others, his behavior is right and moral," writes Glasser (1965, p. 57). People with positive identities tend to associate with other people who also have positive identities.

Negative identities are formed by individuals who do not think well of themselves and who, as a result, also have problems caring about other people. Characterized by irresponsible and self-defeating behavior that hurts themselves and others, these people engage in behavior that often denies reality (Protheroe, 1992). "In their unsuccessful effort to fulfill their needs," Glasser (1965, p. 219) argues, "no matter what behavior they choose, all patients have a common characteristic: they all deny the reality of the world around them." According to Glasser (1981), this denial and the formation of a negative identity leads to maladaptive behavior.

> Conventional psychiatry wastes too much time arguing over how many diagnoses can dance at the end of a case history.
> —William Glasser

As a result reality therapy views identity through one's behavior. Unlike behavioristic theory that focuses on a stimulus-response paradigm, reality therapy measures behavior against the objective standard of reality, with which individuals are either in consonance or dissonance.

DEVELOPMENT OF MALADAPTIVE BEHAVIOR

Reality therapists reject the medical model, arguing against the existence of nearly all forms of mental illness. According to Glasser (1984), mental illness is not like a case of the measles: It is not so much something that happens to individuals as it is an attempt to deal with external events and to maintain control. That is to say, people choose mental illness. Despite heavy criticism, Glasser ignores biology as a factor in mental illness and instead views maladaptive functioning as the consequence of irresponsibility. Problems arise when people are not taught, or do not accept, responsibility for their behavior. When some people refuse to accept or ignore that responsibility, the price they pay is high: no longer feeling worthwhile, they establish a "failure identity."

In contrast, in order to have a **success identity** and feel worthwhile, healthy individuals will conscientiously maintain a satisfactory standard of behavior. "To do so," Glasser says, "we must learn to correct ourselves when we do wrong and to credit ourselves when we do right. If we do not evaluate our behavior . . . we do not act to improve our conduct where it is below our standards, we will not fulfill our need to be worthwhile and we will suffer" (1965, p. 10).

> To belabor the whys of a plan's failure is to reinforce failure identity.
> —William Glasser

There was a time when human behavior, according to Glasser, was controlled by the "old brain" needs of survival. In contemporary times, however, our behavior is associated with "new brain" needs for belonging, power, freedom, and pleasure. People have images of these needs, and these images in their minds behave according to whether or not their needs are being satisfied. Thus, personal actions are based on perceptions. "Our behavior is our constant attempt to control perceptions," Glasser writes (1981, p. 53). In his model of maladaptive behavior, Glasser posits individuals who *create* behaviors, then, including mentally disturbing ones such as delusions and hallucinations, in order to create an identity for themselves that meets their expectations.

FUNCTION OF THE THERAPIST

The reality therapist is an educator and attaches direct values to behavior, measuring clients' success or failure in treatment against their ability to meet these values (Thatcher, 1987). For the reality therapist, responsibility serves as a foundational value. "Responsibility is considered the basic concept of reality therapy and is defined as the ability to meet one's needs without depriving others of the ability to meet theirs" (Rachin, 1974, p. 47).

Because the reality therapist believes that a change in behavior must precede a change in identity, the focus is on changing irresponsible, self-defeating behavior. If, according to Glasser, "we are what we do," in order to change "who we are" (identity), we must change "what we do" (behavior). That is, change in identity follows change in behavior (Glasser & Wubbolding, 1995). The reality therapist's task is therefore to help clients identify and change self-defeating behavior.

As might be expected, Glasser (1965) describes the role of the reality therapist in concrete terms. The work of the therapist is difficult because a "firm emotional relationship" must be built with clients who have failed to establish such relationships in the past. However, the therapist is "aided by recognizing the patient is desperate for involvement and suffering because he is not able to fulfill his needs" (p. 21). In fact, the therapist's participation is the "major skill of doing reality therapy." The counselor needs to be tough, interested, warm, understanding, sensitive, and genuine. In order to provide clients with examples of responsible behavior, the therapist must fulfill his or her own needs and be willing to talk about personal struggles. In short, he or she must provide clients with a genuine person who cares. "Unless the requisite involvement exists between the responsible therapist and the irresponsible patient, there can be no therapy" (Glasser, 1965, p. 21). In the counseling relationship, then, the counselor's role is to communicate warmth, understanding, and concern.

Nevertheless, the reality therapist must withstand clients' requests for sympathy or a "justification of his actions no matter how the patient pleads or threatens" (p. 22). Irresponsible action must never be condoned. The therapist must also be "willing to watch the patient suffer, if that helps him toward responsibility" (p. 22). Glasser also writes that therapists must "never be frightened or rebuffed by the patient's behavior" (p. 23).

Assuming the warm, caring mind-set of this therapist, Glasser characterizes the function of the reality therapist in several ways (Glasser, 1965; Glasser & Wubbolding, 1995). First of all, the focus is on behavior, and since the past cannot be changed, the focus is on behavior in the present tense. Although the counselor will not punish clients for failure, they must finally learn to identify their irresponsible patterns of behavior before being open to change. Once this self-defeating behavior is identified, the counselor will assist clients in developing a plan to change behavior. It is important for this plan to be in writing. Finally, making it clear that excuses are unacceptable, the counselor will help clients to make a commitment to carry out their plan.

Because interviews with clients are likely to take place in settings other than the typical counseling office, with its carpet, desk, and bookshelves, the personhood of the reality therapist is vitally important. In fact, reality therapy is often practiced in such atypical places as schools, street clinics, and prisons; it take place on the playground, with young people in a delinquent detention center, or in a prison yard with inmates. The circumstances often determine the therapy in these settings. These varied environments require a reality therapist to be a consistent model of personal responsibility, in or out of the counseling office (Clagett, 1992).

GOALS OF THERAPY

Because clients are unable to achieve a healthy identity without becoming aware of their behavior, the overarching goal of reality therapy is to help them to identify and change their self-defeating behavior. In fact, Glasser believes that clients have more control over their behavior than over their thinking or feeling responses. To this end, reality therapy seeks to help clients interact constructively by accepting the reality of their existence, by developing a keen sense of responsibility, and by making appropriate choices. Unlike clients in existential therapy, however, individuals in reality therapy do not create their own existence and destiny through such choices. Instead, they conform to standards of reality in order to behave and thus to live more productively and harmoniously.

Glasser (1976) lists several criteria for behavior that is suitable and healthy. First of all, the behavior has such real, specific value for the clients that they believe their lifestyles will improve if they practice the behavior. Clients should be able to engage in this behavior without being self-critical and without being competitive. And they should be able to accomplish this behavior on their own without an extraordinary amount of mental effort.

The final, broad goal of enabling clients to live productive, harmonious lives is realized through three separate but interwoven procedures, according to Glasser. First, the counselor helps clients face reality head on and then helps them test their behavior against that reality. Second, without rejecting them as people, the counselor rejects their unrealistic behavior. And finally, the counselor teaches them better ways to fulfill their needs within the parameters of reality. In these several ways the reality therapist strives to help clients clarify their life goals, to identify what they want in life. After examining the obstacles that lie in the path of those

> We constantly gripe, complain, and struggle with reality.
> —William Glasser

goals, the therapist will then help clients to discover the personal assets and environmental supports that will facilitate the successful completion of their goals.

Only when clients assume responsibility for their personal behavior, only when they manage to meet their personal needs without hurting themselves or others, can it be said that they have made progress toward reaching their goals (Wubbolding, 1975).

MAJOR METHODS AND TECHNIQUES

Glasser (1965) conceives of the process of reality therapy in eight general steps that therapists can very flexibly apply in helping clients face reality and become more responsible. At the outset of therapy it is crucial that the therapist *be involved,* that he or she establish a caring rapport within the context of a professional helping relationship and that the therapist remain positive and emphasize the clients' strengths. **Involvement** allows the therapist to find out what clients really want and whether the "want" is possible. Second, the therapist will *focus on behavior,* not on feelings. Because the clients' behavior is presumed to be an attempt at some form of control, a means of satisfying a want or need, the therapist then needs to persuade them to own up to what they are doing now and to deal with evasions and abstractions. Third, it is essential that the therapist *focus on the present* to help clients realize that what they are doing is ineffectual. This is not to be viewed as a callous judgment by the therapist; it is simply a means of subordinating clients' histories to the present, so that they can examine what they are doing now. Next, *make a plan.* Functioning as a resource for solutions and as a concrete planner, the therapist helps clients to devise a plan to more effectively control their lives. Nevertheless, the effective therapist knows that he or she can never solve anything for clients; that is the clients' work. And it is the clients, not the therapist, who must learn to evaluate their behavior to know if what they are doing is helping their situation.

But such a plan is not worthwhile, Glasser believes, unless the therapist manages to get a **commitment** from clients to carry it out. Clients with failure identities are particularly reluctant to commit to change. At this point, the therapist will brook *no excuses,* which are always part of the ineffectual patterns of the past. Reality therapists are interested in the future and maintain an attitude of "no excuses." Even if the plan is failing, the emphasis needs to lie, not on dissecting the old plan, but on developing a new strategy for success. This the therapist can, and should, accomplish without being punitive. The therapist needs to *eliminate punishment,* which usually involves another person controlling the client's life. Natural consequences are punishment enough. We are better motivated, then, if we are able to do things without the fear of being punished. Finally, the effective therapist will *never give*

> I went to the woods because I wished to live deliberately, to front only the essential facts of life, and see if I could not learn what it had to teach, and not, when I came to die, discover that I had not lived.
>
> —Henry David Thoreau

up. To give up is to be controlled by the client's ineffectual behavior, Glasser writes, so the therapist must always look toward the possibility of change.

Glasser does not rely on these procedures as a "cookbook" for therapeutic intervention. If ideas from other theoretical orientations can help clients confront reality, practitioners of reality therapy will use those techniques as well. Wallace (1986) and Wubbolding (1988, 1991) note a number of strategies, often shaped by a therapist's personality, that are used as part of the approach in reality therapy.

Structuring

Reality therapists help clients to *structure* their expectations, to understand the nature, limits, and goals of therapy. This structuring helps clients adjust their expectations and gives them a realistic hope for change. Providing clients with confidence in their therapist, it lets them know their therapist values their well-being. Simple descriptions of the counseling process or brief explanations—discussing fees, for example, or talking about the expected number of sessions—may help alleviate the anxiety clients feel. In fact, Glasser (1965) suggests that setting a predetermined time limit or stipulating the number of sessions may motivate clients to focus better and work more intensely. By helping clients accept the responsibility for their behavior and by allowing them to face the reality of their situation, structuring encourages them to remain in therapy so that they can continue to face reality.

Confrontation

Confrontation is inevitable in reality therapy. At the outset of therapy clients will be immediately confronted with present reality, and eventually they will need to face the question: Is what I am currently doing right or wrong for me? Most confrontations in reality therapy are reflected by a variety of questions that call clients to action and that place responsibility for the action squarely on their shoulders. These questions will confront clients with the issue of how they plan to meet their goals or with whether or not they are truly committed to meeting their goals at all. Clients are also confronted with the consequences of their actions, whether internal (e.g., feeling depressed) or external. This critical aspect of reality therapy teaches individuals what they can expect when they act in certain ways. Sometimes clients are even confronted with a contract requiring their signature as evidence of their commitment.

Contracts

While verbal agreements, confirmed with a handshake, may suffice for some clients, a written contract signed by both clients and their therapist further reinforces a commitment to follow through. An ongoing reminder of the specific sequence and schedule in the clients' plans, a signed contract provides concrete evidence of their intention to change their behavior. Once the conditions of a written contract are fulfilled, it serves as a record of people's capacity to work responsibly and successfully to meet their goals.

Instruction

In reality therapy clients will inevitably need specific skill development to implement their course of action. If the therapist is competent to teach the desired skill, he or she will use time in the therapy sessions to instruct the client; if not, clients may be referred for skill instruction elsewhere. Whatever the alternative, as long as both the therapist and the clients assume mutual responsibility in the learning process, reality therapy will not avoid providing whatever instruction is needed for clients to meet their goals.

Skillful Questioning

A major intervention in reality therapy centers on the question: "Does your present behavior enable you to get what you want now, and will it take you in the direction you want to go?" (Glasser, 1989). The practitioner of reality therapy helps clients to evaluate their behavior by asking a number of direct questions, such as: Is what you are doing helping or hurting you? Is what you are doing now, what you want to be doing? Is your behavior working for you? Is what you are doing against the rules? Is what you want realistic or attainable? How committed are you to the therapeutic process, and to changing your life? (Wubbolding, 1988). Direct questions like these begin to highlight the importance of choice. Wubbolding (1988) notes that such skillful questioning not only allows the therapist to enter the client's world, where he or she can gather important information, but also helps clients take more effective control of their lives.

Emphasizing Choice

By emphasizing the freedom of clients to live by their own personal standards, reality therapy keeps the responsibility for their behavior on themselves. In order to sharpen this emphasis on personal **responsibility,** the counselor will often turn adjectives into verbs. Instead of saying clients are angry, for instance, as if anger were an inescapable situation, he or she will use verbs such as "angering" or "bullying," which highlight clients' responsibility for this frame of mind. Or instead of having a headache, clients are said to be "headaching." The emphasis here is on personal choice. In changing adjectives and nouns, which describe attributes or states of being, to active verbs, individuals can finally begin to understand that they are "choosing to depress." As a result fewer choices will be made that result in depression. The emphasis is on positive, constructive actions that stem from choosing to live by standards of reality (Glasser, 1989).

> The therapist must teach the patient that therapy is not primarily directed toward making him happy.
> —William Glasser

Role Playing

When clients are struggling to put to practice recently acquired skills, the reality therapist may turn to role playing techniques that help "presentize" clients' behavior and that allow them to rehearse events that cause their anxiety. During a role playing activity, clients learn to prepare for the consequences of their behavior, including their feelings, while performing the activity. Difficulties in interpersonal relationships are often relieved through role playing specific situations with the reality therapist (Cockrum, 1993).

Support

Clients with a "failure identity," who have learned to expect failure, often need encouragement in anticipating successful outcomes of their efforts. As they put their new plans into action, support can assist them in achieving an optimistic outlook. Once they see that their therapist encourages and supports them, that he or she believes in them, their motivation and self-efficacy increases. Inevitably the therapist's trust and support communicates a sense of self-worth, and it is this growing feeling of being worthwhile that gives clients more energy to live responsibly.

Constructive Debate

A client's self-concept can be enhanced through constructive debate. When therapist and clients challenge one another's ideas and values, it demonstrates that they have values worth defending, that what they have to say is worthwhile and is taken seriously. Through constructive debate, clients learn they can contribute meaningfully to the therapeutic process. Their voice is significant.

Humor

Knowing that clients can be brought closer to reality through the therapeutic use of humor, the reality therapist will occasionally use humor in a sensitive manner. Used appropriately, humor can help clients gain a healthy ability to laugh at themselves and to become less introspective and more objective. When humor is used improperly, however, when it is sarcastic, punitive, or demeaning, it will dismantle whatever trust, confidence, and credibility has been established (Saper, 1987). Such inappropriate humor will certainly undermine the process of reality therapy.

Self-Disclosure

Requiring equal and active participation of both client and therapist, reality therapy is a collaborative effort. As a result reality therapists will share personal experiences and struggles and will open themselves up to reveal their humanity, even to the point of questioning their own values or uncovering their own weaknesses. When therapists make themselves vulnerable, clients feel less vulnerable. Such appropriate self-disclosure brings clients closer to reality.

Positive Addictions

Glasser encourages his clients to choose **positive addictions** that lead to more satisfactory ways of living, such as jogging, movies, meditation, or visiting with friends, anything that might help them reach a "healthy high." Of course, our world offers the opportunity for negative or positive addictions, but, according to Glasser, our addiction and our fate is up to us. We are in control of our addictions; we can choose pain or we can choose joy (Glasser, 1976).

Assessment

While the counselor in reality therapy makes little attempt to test, diagnose, interpret, or otherwise assess clients, he or she does evaluate their progress toward desired goals. Although the basic requirement on the part of the client is responsibility, almost any constructive, responsible change in clients' behavior is defined as a step in that direction. Termination of therapy is warranted, "if the patient can act in increasingly responsible ways, resolve crises and adjustment problems through accepting that he is responsible for himself and his behavior and that he can fulfill his needs without hurting himself or other people" (Glasser & Zunin, 1979, p. 327).

APPLICATION

Reality therapy has been effectively applied to a wide variety of clinical issues, including suicidal ideation (Lester, 1994), school discipline and motivation (Benshoff, Poidevant, & Cashwell, 1994; Parish, 1992), self-esteem (Williamson, 1992), alcohol abuse (Barrett, 1992; Honeyman, 1990; Hulbert, 1992; Peacock, 1992), drug abuse (Mickel, 1993; Reuss, 1985), anxiety (Udry, 1992), mental illness (Garner, 1983), burnout (Edelwich, 1980; Wubbolding, 1979), grief recovery (Stanwood, 1992), exercise initiation (Hart, 1992), sexual offenders (Stanton, 1992), neurolinguistic hypnosis (Ignoffo, 1994), and autonomy training (Newton, Brack, & Brack, 1992).

While reality therapy has been used to treat effectively a variety of clients, William Glasser illustrates the essentials of his approach—involvement, rejection of irresponsibility, relearning, and so on—in the following case. Glasser is quick to point out, however, that the application of his theory does not follow a static formula; it is uniquely determined by the personality of each client. The following are Glasser's own words in describing how he applied his approach to "Pat."

A wealthy, young, overindulged, satisfactorily married mother of two whose only obvious problem was overweight, Pat is typical of the fairly responsible patients whom the psychiatrist sees. Extremely pleasant, with an agile, intelligent mind, she was skeptical of psychiatry yet hopeful that perhaps through therapy she might gain more from her life. Notwithstanding her material well-being, she felt that there was much she was missing.

The first part of reality therapy with Pat was difficult for both of us as I tried to create involvement between us and she tried to understand what I was driving at. Expecting to discuss her childhood, she found it difficult to understand that I was not particularly interested in historical material. Attempting at times to talk about her dreams and unconscious mind, she found me equally uninterested. Restricting the discussion to the present seemed sterile to her because her life was the rather humdrum existence of the rich suburban housewife who had difficulty in filling her days. Nevertheless we did find much to discuss about the current status of her large, complex family and also about books, plays, movies, and current events. Stimulated to think about what was going on in the world outside of her limited existence, she enjoyed our discussions, but she continually questioned the therapy and the lack of progress toward a better life.

Her favorite diversion was to take me to task for not helping her to reduce. In addition to her own direct comments, she quoted her husband as saying he could not see one apparent benefit from therapy. According to him she was as fat and difficult to live with as ever. To these attacks on my therapeutic skill I would answer that psychotherapy does not reduce people, that it does not make them happier, and it does not solve their problems. If she wanted to reduce, she was free to do so and I would encourage her, but weight reduction was not my responsibility. I emphasized that if she wanted to change she had to come regularly because I knew that we had to become involved before anything could happen. I did not care what she talked about as long as it had to do with the present. I had to stress both that she must come and that I could do little directly for her because I did not want her to become involved with me as a dependent. Without magic to help her, I would stay with her until the problems she came for were solved. As with every patient, I let her know that I was there as a person who would not desert her or give her false hope.

Discussing her rather irresponsible existence in which she did everything to please herself only, Pat seemed to revel in the long descriptions of her childish behavior toward her husband, her family, and even some other friends. It was very important to her to tell me how much better she would be if she could act in a more mature way, but how she absolutely would not do so. She was anxious for me to tell her to do something different, which I was tempted to do, but I refrained because I knew she was trying to cast me in the role of reformer so that she could reject me as she had rejected everyone else who had tried to correct her.

Therapy continued slowly, little seemed to be happening, yet the relationship was growing. Unable to make me assume a role she could reject, she began to develop some respect and trust for me and what I was doing. Although she started to come late in an effort to show how little she cared, she did come. I paid no attention to her lateness, or to her insincere apologies or excuses. Finally, one day during a rather innocuous conversation she burst out and said, "There's nothing you can do to make me responsible." Here was a remarkable statement because I had never mentioned the word responsibility to her. Nevertheless, the months of subtle pressure had had their effect. She was now very slightly on the defensive, because she was beginning to understand what I was trying to do. I was able to increase the pressure on her to change by discussing my work with the delinquent girls. When I pointed out how similar she was to these girls, she readily agreed, saying, "If you help them so much why can't you help me?" To this little pleasantry I replied, "because I can't lock you up. If I could, you know as well as I do that you would change." Not denying my claim, she countered by stating that all I had was these two hours a week in the office and that's all I ever would have. Since I had no control it was up to her. I added, "I'll wait, I have all the time in the world."

Next, Pat attacked my fees by saying that they were too low, another depreciation of my worth. She said she could afford more, other psychiatrists were getting larger fees, why didn't I ask more. I answered her charge by asking if therapy had helped her. When she replied that it hadn't, I said that considering my ineffectiveness I could hardly charge more, I wasn't worth it. Having thus passed the test of avarice, I was not again challenged on my fees. Through this gambit and countless others we became more deeply involved. She tried everything to prove me irresponsible. I responded by admitting any apparent shortcomings but never giving up. All her efforts were really directed toward having me commit one of two fatal errors—giving up or giving in. Either one would have finished therapy.

After almost a year, we began to be more involved; I could point out her irresponsibilities. My regular presence and my stand for greater responsibility encouraged her to take a chance and change. During the whole of the second year she slowly became more responsible. Although the change was not dramatic, she was less self-centered and more able to give to others, especially to her husband and children, who needed her far more than she was originally able to admit to herself. She felt a keener sense of achievement and she lost fifty pounds. She tried to credit me with the weight loss, but as I refused to take the blame for her inability to lose earlier, I refused to take the credit then.

It was a difficult, though rewarding, case. With her intelligence and energy, Pat certainly had great capacity for more worthwhile behavior within her immediate surroundings, and perhaps she will have a chance to do more in the larger world. In the final part of therapy we were both groping toward the goal of even greater responsibility.

CRITICAL ANALYSIS

The strengths of reality therapy are quite apparent. To begin with, it has great versatility. It can be applied to many different populations—children, adolescents, adults, and the aged—and in almost any setting that emphasizes mental health and adjustment, such as hospitals, schools, prisons, and crisis centers (Glasser, 1989). In addition, Glasser's approach is concrete. Both counselor and clients are able to assess how much progress is being made and in what areas, especially if a goal-specific contract has been drawn up. If clients are doing well in modifying one behavior and not another, increased attention can be given to the underdeveloped area. Another strength of reality therapy is that it has successfully challenged the medical model of psychotherapy, providing a refreshing alternative to pathology-centered approaches to counseling.

> The therapist freely gives praise when the patient acts responsibly and shows disapproval when he does not.
> —William Glasser

Reality therapy, however, is not without its pitfalls. For example, it has been criticized for exaggerating observable behavior traits, while ignoring other valuable therapeutic concepts like the unconscious. Linked to this shortcoming is Glasser's view that all forms of mental illness are attempts to deal with external events—in short, that people choose mental illness. The result is, of course, a reluctance to consider the biological factors that contribute to mental illness, a stance that critics find naive or even irresponsible. In addition, reality therapy makes little allowance for the need of some clients to resolve past events. A traumatic experience, for example, may need to be dealt with in the context of treatment.

And more than some approaches, reality therapy has the potential to be misused by practitioners who are insufficiently involved with their clients, who settle for general goals, force a plan on the client, or proceed too quickly to commitment (Wubbolding, 1975). In other words, reality therapy runs the risk of being abused in the hands of an authoritarian counselor, the "expert" who is frantically straightening everyone else out. While Glasser believes that in reality therapy the counselor should not judge clients' behavior—that the counselor is to support them in their personal exploration of values—an overzealous practitioner could easily impose values on clients. While this is always a potential danger, it is perhaps most hazardous when applying reality therapy within a cross-cultural context.

In fact, when practiced appropriately, Glasser's approach readily lends itself to cross-cultural counseling in a number of ways. Since its focus is on acting and thinking rather than on identifying and exploring feelings, and since it is not burdened with a great deal of technical jargon, many ethnic-minority clients can find the rational emotive approach relatively inviting. Not surprisingly, then, reality therapy is taught in many countries. The Institute for Reality Therapy has ties to Japan, Korea, Ireland, Norway, the United Kingdom, Australia, New Zealand, Hong Kong, Singapore, and the former Yugoslavia (Glasser & Wubbolding, 1995).

Since it is up to clients to determine what they want, reality therapy has the potential to help ethnic-minority clients integrate into their lives desirable "foreign" values and practices, while allowing them to retain their ethnic values and identity. However, since the approach depends considerably on effective two-way communication, it does have limitations in helping clients who, for any reason, cannot adequately express their needs. Some ethnic-minority clients are reluctant to say what they need; their culture has not reinforced an assertive stance and they may have been socialized to think more socially than personally.

Glasser's emphasis on personal freedom gives rise to yet a further caution in applying reality therapy to ethnic-minority clients: his radical view on one's ability to choose may cause the therapist not to comprehend fully the ways in which social forces have systematically repressed members of minority groups. A brutal fact of life for many minorities, discrimination is a real barrier that prevents minority clients from getting what they want.

In terms of counseling diverse populations, reality therapy can work effectively with people adjusting to a disability and with their ensuing rehabilitation as well. During the early phases of counseling, for example, clients are required to learn and face the reality of their disabilities, which are never to be used as excuses for personal failures and dependency. Then they are provided with the means of living within the framework of their disabilities (Ososkie & Turpin, 1985; Walker, 1987). In later phases of adaptation, the reality therapist may further assist clients in setting time-limited personal, social, and vocational goals and in teaching and practicing community-based problem-solving and decision-making skills.

CURRENT STATUS

Although Glasser's thinking has expanded through the years, he has remained true to the basic constructs of his early methods and theory. Already in 1981, for instance, in *Stations of the Mind,* Glasser built a comprehensive picture of the workings of the "internal world" of the mind, which can be understood only by how we relate to external reality. And in 1984, in *Take Effective Control of Your Life,* Glasser revealed the importance of control theory, which enables people to avoid problems that require professional help and to take more effective charge of their lives.

Since 1965 reality therapy has achieved a substantial following, especially among teachers and youth guidance counselors, substance abuse treatment counselors, and rehabilitation counselors. Today reality therapy is recognized as an effective therapeutic approach that has been successfully applied in school settings, correctional institutions, psychiatric hospitals, convalescent homes, vocational rehabilitation centers, psychiatric clinics, and social service settings (Bassin, Bratter, & Rachin, 1976; Bratter, Bratter, Radda, & Steiner, 1993; Cohen & Sordo, 1984; Edens & Smryl, 1994; Evans, 1984; Heuchert, 1989; Vogt, 1985). Between the years of 1970 and 1990, eighty-two doctoral dissertations were written on this therapeutic approach (Franklin, 1993).

> Ideas have to be wedded to action.
> —Henry Miller

The Institute for Reality Therapy offers seminars that lead to certification for practitioners of reality therapy. The 18-month training program consists of workshops, supervised practice, video and audio taping, small-group practice, feedback, and other experiences. More than 4,500 people have completed the reality therapy certification process worldwide (Glasser & Wubbolding, 1995). Further information on these training programs can be obtained through: the Institute for Reality Therapy, 7301 Medical Center Drive, Suite 407, Canoga Park, CA 91307, Telephone: (818) 888-0688, or the Center for Reality Therapy, 777 Montgomery Road, Cincinnati, OH 45236, Telephone: (513) 561-1911.

Launched in 1981, the *Journal of Reality Therapy* is devoted to publishing articles concerning research, theory, and practical applications of reality

14.2 | **Reality Therapy with Rape Victims**

By Margaret J. McArthur

In a rape victim group, members have an opportunity to learn how others with similar experiences have been able to recover and work through similar problems. The peer support from members all along the continuum of recovery gives an individual a sense of hope (Roth, Dye, & Lebowitz, 1988). This instillation and maintenance of hope is crucial in all forms of psychotherapy (Yalom, 1985). Group therapy is extremely effective when the members have similar problems, but are at different stages of resolution (Kaltenbach & Gazda, 1975). Collective problem-solving in a peer support group is presumed to be very effective (Coates & Winston, 1983).

Reality therapy groups provide individuals greater opportunities for involvement, both in having others care for them and in providing opportunities for them to care for many others. The group assists the individual in making value judgments about whether or not previous behavior is working. The group is a tremendous resource when individuals make plans, offering ideas without advising. Commitment to a group is a powerful motivator, and peer support aids the individual in successfully completing her or his plan. The never-ending support of a nonpunishing group of peers is vital in achieving a success identity.

Rape has an impact on the sense of self, effecting a loss of self-esteem, creation of guilt and shame, mistrust in interpersonal relationships and distorted perceptions of self-worth. Because of this massive injury to the self, rape victims may very quickly become isolated and lonely. They may experience their pain in any of the modes previously listed: disturbances of emotions, behavior problems, disturbances of thoughts, or somatic complaints. While other therapeutic approaches for rape victims focus on alleviating symptoms of psychiatric illness, reality therapy treats the sense of self. The intrusive thoughts, feelings, and actions a rape victim experiences may lead her to believe she is going crazy (Rose, 1986). Other frameworks reinforce this belief by placing a value judgment on her symptoms of illness. In contrast, reality therapy changes the point at which this value judgment is made, moving the assessment up to step three in the process of asking the victim to determine for herself if what she is doing is moral, legal, and is working to fulfil her needs. Reality therapy teaches the victim she is not crazy, but that she may be having difficulty in meeting her basic needs. Emphasis in reality therapy is on effective and ineffective behavior, not on the signs and symptoms of mental illness. Reality therapy offers the victim opportunities to regain self-esteem, resolve guilt and shame, rebuild trusting relationships, and renew her sense of self-worth by changing the point at which value judgments are made.

(continued)

14.2 | **Reality Therapy with Rape Victims** (continued)

Loss of the sense of competence results in loss of self-esteem for rape victims. Reality therapy helps rebuild lost self-esteem. The rape victim is given opportunities to make plans to meet her needs, plans in which she can succeed and feel powerful over her environment again. When she succeeds, her success identity is reinforced. She regains mastery over her environment.

Loss of self-determination creates guilt and shame. Control was taken away from the victim at the time of the rape, but control over her behavior is now back in her hands. The feelings of helplessness and loss of control reported by rape victims may lead to depression as Seligman's learned helplessness model suggests (1985). Many victims appear to use what happened as an excuse for acting out, isolating themselves from others and withdrawing into depression. Victims often develop a passive life-style because of chronic feelings of helplessness and powerlessness (Goodman & Nowak-Scibelli, 1985). They feel their lives are out of their control. The reality therapy group actively confronts this passive style in a warm, supportive atmosphere. The group doesn't allow excuses for acting out or isolative behavior. The responsibility for the victim's behavior is not with the family who doesn't understand or the assailant who has ruined her life forever. The opportunity for making a success of her life, for becoming a survivor instead of a victim, is hers. Reality therapy by no means attempts to minimize the real pain and loss of the victim, but does help the victim to see that her behavior is no longer under someone else's control. Now, it is up to her to continue to choose how this event will affect her behavior and life-style. Reality therapy reinforces her responsibility for fulfilling her needs and, in doing so, returns her sense of self-determination.

Following rape, the victim may have difficulty trusting others. She is sensitive to the reactions of others. Sensing their discomfort, she may want to withdraw and isolate herself. Women who have shared similar traumas quickly develop empathic rap-

therapy in field settings. During the past 15 years, more than 200 essays, articles, and research studies have been published on the applications of reality therapy. For further information on this journal, contact: *Journal of Reality Therapy,* 203 Lake Hall, Boston-Bouve College, Northeastern University, 360 Huntington Avenue, Boston, MA 02115.

Never content to allow his approach to remain without constant scrutiny, additions, and changes, Dr. Glasser continues to be a quite active student, especially of educational systems. In fact, many of today's school districts are looking to his work in formulating curricula and school policies.

port (Sadock, 1983). Members in rape groups form a common bond around their experience. However so-called crazy may seem their thoughts, feelings, and behaviors, they soon learn they are common to others. Reality therapy groups require involvement with other victims, as involvement with others is proposed to be the key to developing a success identity. Along with this involvement comes recognition and respect for themselves and others. They begin to trust others as they realize they are not alone. Members realize they are able to help others, because they understand each other's problems. In helping others they find a sense of purpose and belonging that restores their own self-esteem. They are able to rediscover the dignity they lost. They begin to meet their needs to love and be loved while giving and receiving support from others.

Evans (1978) says a supportive, non-punishing atmosphere is necessary for maintaining a healthy ego after rape. Those to whom the rape victim discloses herself may be critical and nonsupportive. Reality therapy groups pride themselves on being supportive and nonpunishing. The affirmation a victim receives in a reality therapy group allows for a return of feelings of self-worth and begins the repair of her distorted self-perception.

The role of the leader in a reality therapy group for rape victims is the same as in any reality therapy group. The leader serves as a model of a responsible person (Kaltenbach & Gazda, 1975). The leader becomes highly involved with each group member, and focuses on here-and-now behavior and relationships. The leader assists members clearly to define what they want, to make value judgments at the right time, and to make plans for which success is guaranteed. In addition, the leader rewards successes, makes sure no excuses are accepted, and helps the group guard against criticism. In teaching the group the principles of reality therapy, the members are able to learn new behavior, accept responsibility, and ensure long-lasting, successful life-styles. The fact that reality therapy is a simple, straightforward technique for meeting one's needs makes it possible for individuals to continue to use reality therapy as a self-help coping strategy once the group has ended.

SUMMARY

1. *Biography.* Glasser (1925–) was born in Cleveland, Ohio, and his early years were characterized by a happy childhood in a loving family. He majored in chemical engineering and after graduation pursued a Ph.D. in clinical psychology. However, when Glasser's advisors rejected his dissertation, he gained admission to medical school and received his M.D. degree from Western Reserve University in 1953 and completed a psychiatric residency at UCLA in 1957. During this time, Glasser became disillusioned with the efficacy of traditional psychoanalytic procedures and began experimenting with alternative methods of treatment.

2. *Historical Development.* The origins of reality therapy are found in Glasser's basic dislike of the psychoanalytic approach, which focuses primarily on neurosis and mental illness. Glasser rejected the medical model of mental illness and argued that the patient is weak, not ill. Glasser's teacher G. L. Harrington spurred him on in his unorthodox beliefs and his rejection of the medical model. Eventually taking a position as head psychiatrist at a youth facility for female delinquents operated by the state of California, Glasser was finally free to practice his treatment strategies without hindrance. After he cut recidivism dramatically in the institution, he began writing about his unique approach.

3. *View of Human Nature.* Reality therapy assumes everyone wants to be different and has an intrinsic and inherited need to feel somehow separate and distinct from every other living being. Glasser defines two kinds of identity—positive and negative—which he views through behavior, testing it against reality. Individuals function either in consonance or dissonance with reality.

4. *Development of Maladaptive Behavior.* According to Glasser, a person chooses mental illness. He ignores biology as a factor in mental illness and instead views maladaptive functioning as the consequence of irresponsibility. According to Glasser, individuals must maintain a satisfactory standard of behavior if they are to have a *success identity,* feel worthwhile, and avoid forms of maladaptive behavior.

5. *Function of the Therapist.* Viewing responsibility as a foundational value, the therapist attempts to help clients change irresponsible behavior. To do so the therapist works to build a solid emotional relationship with the client by being tough, interested, warm, understanding, sensitive, and genuine. The bottom line is that the reality therapist must be an excellent example of responsible behavior.

6. *Goals of Therapy.* The primary goal of reality therapy is to help clients identify and change self-defeating behavior, to help them make appropriate choices, and to develop a sense of responsibility. Reality therapy strives to help clients clarify what they want in life and then examine obstacles that stand in the way of their reaching what they want.

7. *Major Methods and Techniques.* Glasser outlines eight general procedures that therapists can apply in helping their clients face reality and become more responsible: establishing a caring rapport, focusing on behavior (not feelings), focusing on the present (not the past), making a specific plan, getting a commitment, accepting no excuses, eliminating punishment, and never giving up. In addition, the reality therapist may employ a variety of techniques such as writing a contract with the client, role playing, and finding positive addictions.

8. *Application.* Reality therapy has been applied to a wide variety of clinical issues, but the essentials of Glasser's approach can be illustrated in the case of "Pat," a wealthy, young, overindulged, satisfactorily married mother of two. It is a typical case in that it begins with Glasser investing in Pat and then helping her become responsible for what she wants, weight reduction.

The therapy continued slowly as Pat was unable to make Glasser assume a role she could reject. This helped her develop some respect and trust in the process and eventually come to accept that only she could make herself responsible. After almost a year, Glasser could point out Pat's irresponsibilities and truly encourage her to take a chance and change. Pat felt a keener sense of achievement and she lost 50 pounds.

9. *Critical Analysis.* Reality therapy has great versatility with applications to different populations and in a variety of settings. It is also goal-specific, allowing for accessible monitoring of progress. Another strength is that it provides a refreshing alternative to pathology-centered approaches. On the other hand, reality therapy does not validate other valuable concepts like personal history and the unconscious as well as biological factors contributing to mental illness. However, when reality therapy turns to ethnic-minority clients, it offers an approach that is free from jargon and relatively inviting. Since the approach leaves it to the client to determine what he or she wants, it allows ethnic-minority clients to retain their ethnic identity and values while integrating other desired values and practices.

10. *Current Status.* Glasser's thinking on reality therapy continues to expand and is being undergirded more firmly by control theory. The research base continues to grow with a steady stream of doctoral dissertations being written on reality therapy. The Institute for Reality Therapy offers seminars that lead to certification for its practitioners, and there is a journal devoted to publishing articles on reality therapy. Today Glasser's approach is being successfully applied in schools, correctional institutions, hospitals, clinics, and social service settings while Dr. Glasser continues to be active in writing about his unique approach to counseling.

Key Terms

Autonomy The condition of accepting responsibility for one's own life instead of relying on others.

Commitment Staying with one's plan to make productive change.

Control theory Glasser's view that humans are internally motivated and behave to control the world around them according to their own purpose.

Involvement The therapist's interest in and caring for the client.

Paining behaviors Choosing misery by developing symptoms (such as depressing or anxieting) because these seem to be the best behaviors available at the time.

Perceived world The reality that we experience and interpret subjectively.

Picture album The perceptions and images we have of how we can fulfill our basic psychological needs.

Positive addiction A route for gaining psychological strength, such as running and meditation.

Psychological needs The psychological needs for belonging, power, freedom, and fun.

Reality therapy Developed by William Glasser, an approach to counseling that holds that people can do something about their fate if they consider themselves and their environment realistically.

Responsibility The act of satisfying one's needs in ways that do not interfere with others' fulfilling of their needs.

Self-evaluation Clients' assessment for current behavior to decide whether it is working and if what they are doing is meeting their needs.

Success identity The state in which effective need-fulfilling behaviors are mastered.

Total behavior The integrated components of doing, thinking, feeling, and physiology. Control theory assumes that all elements of behavior are interrelated.

Suggested Reading

Glasser, N. (Ed.). (1989). *Control theory in the practice of reality therapy: Case studies.* New York: Harper & Row.

Glasser, W. (1965). *Reality therapy: A new approach to psychiatry.* New York: Harper & Row.

Glasser, W. (1969). *Schools without failure.* New York: Harper & Row.

Wubbolding, R. E. (1988). *Using reality therapy.* New York: Harper & Row.

References

Barrett, C. (1992). Substance abuse: A window of opportunity. *Journal of Reality Therapy, 11,* 20–21.

Bassin, A., Bratter, T. E., & Rachin, R. L. (Eds.). (1976). *The reality therapy reader: A survey of the work of William Glasser.* New York: Harper & Row.

Benshoff, J. M., Poidevant, J. M., & Cashwell, C. S. (1994). School discipline programs: Issues and implications for school counselors. *Elementary School Guidance and Counseling, 28,* 163–169.

Bratter, B. I., Bratter, T. E., Radda, H. T., & Steiner, K. M. (1993). The residential therapeutic caring community. *Psychotherapy, 30,* 299–304.

Clagett, A. F. (1992). Group-integrated reality therapy in a wilderness camp. *Journal of Offender Rehabilitation, 17,* 1–18.

Cockrum, J. R. (1993). Teaching role playing and critiquing. *Journal of Reality Therapy, 12,* 70–75.

Cohen, B., & Sordo, I. (1984). Using reality therapy with adult offenders. *Journal of Offender Counseling, Services & Rehabilitation, 8,* 25–39.

Croll, M. (1992). The individualist roots of reality therapy: A textual analysis of Emerson's "self-reliance" and Glasser's reality therapy. *Journal of Reality Therapy, 11,* 22–26.

Edelwich, J. (1980). *Burn-out.* New York: Human Sciences Press.

Edens, R. M., & Smryl, T. (1994). Reducing disruptive classroom behaviors in physical education: A pilot study. *Journal of Reality Therapy, 13,* 40–44.

Evans, D. B. (1984). Reality therapy: A model for physicians managing alcoholic patients. *Journal of Reality Therapy, 3,* 20–26.

Franklin, M. (1993). Eighty-two Reality Therapy doctoral dissertations written between 1970–1990. *Journal of Reality Therapy, 12,* 76–83.

Garner, A. (1983). Living with mental patients. *Journal of reality therapy, 2,* 27–31.

Glasser, N. (Ed.). (1980). *What are you doing? How people are helped through reality therapy.* New York: Harper & Row.

Glasser, N. (Ed.). (1989). *Control theory in the practice of reality therapy: Case studies.* New York: Harper & Row.

Glasser, W. (1961). *Mental health or mental illness?* New York: Harper & Row.

Glasser, W. (1965). *Reality therapy: A new approach to psychiatry.* New York: Harper & Row.

Glasser, W. (1969). *Schools without failure.* New York: Harper & Row.

Glasser, W. (1972). *The identity society* (Rev. ed.). New York: Harper & Row.

Glasser, W. (1976). *Positive addiction.* New York: Harper & Row.

Glasser, W. (1981). *Stations of the mind.* New York: Harper & Row.

Glasser, W. (1984). *Take effective control of your life.* New York: Harper & Row.

Glasser, W. (1990). *The quality school.* New York: Harper & Row.

Glasser, W. (2000). *Reality Therapy in Action.* New York: HarperCollins.

Glasser, W. (2001). *Counseling with Choice Theory.* New York: HarperCollins.

Glasser, W., & Iverson, N. (1966). *Reality therapy in larger group counseling, A manual of procedure and practice.* Los Angeles: Reality Press.

Glasser, W., & Wubbolding, R. E. (1995). Reality therapy. In *Current psychotherapies* (5th ed.). Itasca, IL: Peacock.

Glasser, W., & Zunin, L. (1979). Reality therapy. In *Current psychotherapies.* Itasca, IL: Peacock.

Hart, E. A. (1992). Using reality therapy for exercise initiation. *Journal of Reality Therapy, 12,* 24–31.

Heuchert, C. M. (1989). Enhancing self-directed behavior in the classroom. *Academic Therapy, 24,* 295–303.

Honeyman, A. (1990). Perceptual changes in addicts as a consequence of reality therapy based group treatment. *Journal of Reality Therapy, 9,* 53–59.

Hulbert, R. J. (1992). The Iowa therapeutic community model of chemical dependency treatment. *Journal of Substance Abuse Treatment, 9,* 389–393.

Ignoffo, M. (1994). Two compatible methods of empowerment: Neurolinguistic hypnosis and reality therapy. *Journal of Reality Therapy, 13,* 20–25.

Lester, D. (1994). Psychotherapy for suicidal clients. *Death Studies, 18,* 361–374.

McArthur, M. J. (1990). Reality therapy with rape victims. *Archives of Psychiatric Nursing, 4,* 360–365.

Mickel, E. (1993). Parent Assistance Workshops (P.A.W.S.) reality based intervention for the crack exposed child. *Journal of Reality Therapy, 12,* 20–28.

Newton, F. B., Brack, C. J., & Brack, G. (1992). Autonomy training: A structure group experience. *Journal of College Student Development, 33,* 371–373.

Osipow, S. H., Walsh, W. B., & Tosi, D. J. (1984). *A survey of counseling methods.* Homewood, IL: Dorsey.

Ososkie, J. N., & Turpin, J. O. (1985). Reality therapy in rehabilitation counseling. *Journal of Applied Rehabilitation Counseling, 16,* 34–38.

Parish, T. S. (1988). Why reality therapy works. *Journal of Reality Therapy, 7,* 31–32.

Parish, T. S. (1992). Ways of assessing and enhancing student motivation. *Journal of Reality Therapy, 11,* 27–36.

Peacock, J. A. (1992). Using RT/CT to enhance alcohol use/abuse awareness. *Journal of Reality Therapy, 12,* 19–23.

Peterson, A. V., & Woodward, G. D. (1992). Basic needs—competitive or complementary: A statistical study of psychological needs. *Journal of Reality Therapy, 11,* 41–45.

Protheroe, D. (1992). Reality therapy and the concept of cognitive developmental stages. *Journal of Reality Therapy, 12,* 37–44.

Rachin, R. L. (1974). Reality therapy: Helping people help themselves. *Crime and Delinquency, 20,* 45–53.

Reuss, N. (1985). Alternatives to cocaining. *Journal of Reality Therapy, 4,* 8–11.

Rozsnafsky, J. (1974). The impact of Alfred Adler on three "free-will" therapies of the 1960s. *Journal of Individual Psychology, 30,* 65–80.

Saper, B. (1987). Humor in psychotherapy: Is it good or bad for the client? *Professional Psychology: Research and Practice, 18,* 360–367.

Stanton, D. T. (1992). Treating sexual offenders: Reality therapy as a better alternative. *Journal of Reality Therapy, 12,* 3–10.

Stanwood, D. L. (1992). Grief and the process of recovery. *Journal of Reality Therapy, 12,* 11–18.

Thatcher, J. A. (1987). Value judgments: A significant aspect of reality therapy. *Journal of Reality Therapy, 7,* 23–25.

Udry, E. M. (1992). Interventions for the anxious and depressed: Suggested links between control theory and exercise therapy. *Journal of Reality Therapy, 12,* 32–36.

Vogt, S. (1985). Reality therapy in a convalescent home. *Activities, Adaptation & Aging, 6,* 55–59.

Walker, G. (1987). Rehabilitation counseling with dual diagnosis clients. *Journal of Applied Rehabilitation Counseling, 18,* 35–37.

Wallace, W. A. (1986). *Theories of counseling and psychotherapy: A basic issues approach.* Boston: Allyn & Bacon.

Whitehouse, D. (1984). Adlerian antecedents to reality therapy and control theory. *Journal of Reality Therapy, 3,* 10–14.

Wiener, N. (1948). *Cybernetics.* New York: Wiley.

Wiener, N. (1950). *The human use of human beings: Cybernetics and society.* Boston: Houghton Mifflin.

Williamson, R. S. (1992). Using group reality therapy to raise self-esteem in adolescent girls. *Journal of Reality Therapy, 12,* 37–44.

Wubbolding, R. E. (1975). Practicing reality therapy. *Personnel and Guidance Journal, 53,* 164–165.

Wubbolding, R. E. (1979). Reality therapy as an antidote to burn-out. *American Mental Health Counselors Association, 1,* 39–43.

Wubbolding, R. E. (1988). *Using reality therapy.* New York: Harper & Row.

Wubbolding, R. E. (1991). *Understanding reality therapy.* New York: HarperCollins.

The supreme happiness of life is the conviction that we are loved. —**Victor Hugo**

Marriage and Family Therapy

CHAPTER **15**

CHAPTER OUTLINE

Historical Development
The Circumplex Model of Marriage and Family
Other Models of Marriage and Family Therapy
The Family Life Cycle
The Goals of Marriage and Family Therapy
Marriage and Family Interventions
Application
Critical Analysis
Current Status
Summary
Key Terms
Suggested Reading
References

Albert Einstein, whose theoretical physics opened the way for the atomic bomb, was asked what new weapons might be employed in World War III. He shook his head. After several long moments he said, "I'm not sure. But there isn't any doubt what weapons will be used in World War IV."

"And what are those?" an interviewer asked.

"Stones and spears," said Einstein.

Einstein was one of the great scientists of all time—best known for his theory of relativity, which he advanced when he was only 26 years old. It revolutionized scientific thought and made matter and energy no longer distinct, but exchangeable. He found power in relationships within the cosmos. Einsteinian physics superseded Newtonian physics. Einstein, needless to say, was a big thinker. He and other physicists proved that each person is a representation of the whole and that each profoundly affects the system as a whole. Einstein and scientists who followed him demonstrated that the elements of the stars are in our bones, that we are more energy than mass, more process than "stuff," and that we are all mutually influenced by all humankind.

A hundred times a day I remind myself that my inner and outer life depend on the labors of other men, living and dead, and that I must exert myself in order to give in the same measure as I have received and am receiving.

—Albert Einstein

Einstein's connectedness view of the cosmos is reflected dramatically through the lens of marriage and family therapy. Through this modality people cannot ignore how much we really do need each other.

The family is a system pulsing with energy. "You know how when you put your hand on something like a radio that is plugged in and you can feel the energy going through it?" asks Paul Pearsall. "That's like our family. You can feel our energy when we're together" (1990, p. 185). However, not until recently did psychotherapy begin to understand and use this synergistic energy of the family to its advantage in therapy.

HISTORICAL DEVELOPMENT

While the beginnings of marriage and family counseling can be traced to the 1940s and '50s, its real growth did not flourish until the late 1970s and '80s (Foley, 1989; Becvar & Becvar, 1988). The stage was set for this entirely new way of conceptualizing and working with couples and families by a number of unrelated influences.

First, the biologist Ludwig von Bertalanffy (1968) devised a theory of living organisms, including couples and families, that viewed them as interacting components mutually affecting one another. The focus of the theory of the family is on the interaction of the parts, which influences the system as a whole.

One of the main concepts introduced by this new theory is **circular causality,** the idea that tenets are related through a series of interacting feedback loops. When viewing the family through this lens, dysfunction is shifted away from an individual and put on the total family unit itself.

If you cannot get rid of the family skeleton, you may as well make it dance.

—George Bernard Shaw

Another influence on family theory in the 1950s came from a group of pioneering studies in the area of schizophrenia. Don Jackson (1957) and Gregory Bateson (Bateson, Jackson, Haley, & Weakland, 1956) at the Mental Research Institute in Palo Alto, California, Theodore Lidz (Lidz, Cornelison, Fleck & Terry, 1957) at Yale, and Murray Bowen (Bowen, 1960) at the National Institute of Mental Health all observed how couples and families functioned upon learning that a family member was diagnosed as schizophrenic.

Their observations led to the formation of concepts like the **double bind** where a person receives two contradictory messages at the same time and is unable to follow both. For example, a child might be told by a father, "Always stand up for your rights, no matter who, no matter what!" But that child is also told by the father, "Never question my authority; I am your father and what I say goes!" Such contradictions provide fertile soil for maladjustment.

These research groups also coined the term **pseudomutuality** to describe the facade of family harmony that covers underlying tension. For example, many children of alcoholics grow up in households that appear totally "normal" from the outside. However, children in these homes grow up without a childhood. Out of such homes, four family member roles crop up again and again:

- **Heroes** pick up the responsibilities abandoned by the alcoholic and spouse and, in essence, run the family, doing the chores and caring for siblings.
- **Scapegoats** respond to their negative environment with defiance and anger. They become the "losers," the family's James Dean.
- **The lost child** fades into the family woodwork, preferring his or her own world to the troubled atmosphere at home.
- **Mascots** are the jokers in the family. They are the ones who take laughter as an analgesic to their pain.

The establishment of the American Association of Marriage Counselors in 1942, which is now the **American Association of Marriage and Family Therapists (AAMFT)**, also opened the way for this new emphasis on the total family. Founders of the association identified three entities to be considered in every relationship: two persons and one couple.

These influences—interacting components, the facade of family harmony and the three entities—combined with the emergence of group counseling, the growth of the child guidance movement, and other post World War II changes, set the stage for the growth of contemporary marriage and family therapy (Fox, 1976). Since its inception, family therapy has had an explosive impact on the mental health scene, not only as a technique but as a theoretical approach to counseling.

For example, whereas in 1973 there existed only one journal in the field of family counseling, there are now dozens of therapy journals dedicated to marriage and the family published in multiple languages. The AAMFT has more than 27,000 members today, and there are more than 1,500 training programs in marriage and family therapy.

Family therapy is one of the most popular counseling specializations—and with good reason. Gurman and Kniskern (1981) report that approximately 50 percent of

> If a woman peels an onion; if a man reads a newspaper or watches television; if there is dust or no dust on the furniture; if a parent kisses or does not kiss his child when he comes home; if the family has eggs or cereal for breakfast, orange juice or no orange juice, and so on through all the "trivia" of everyday life—this is significant to me, if for no other reason than that the commonplaceness proves the family sane.
>
> —Jules Henry

all problems brought to counselors are related to marriage and family issues. Spouse abuse, underachieving students, relational conflict, unemployment, career indecision, rebellion, sibling rivalry, parenting difficulties, and self-concept issues are just a few entries on the long log of problems families bring to counseling.

THE CIRCUMPLEX MODEL OF MARRIAGE AND FAMILY

Many of the key concepts explained in marriage and family theories can be subsumed under the **circumplex model** of marital and family functioning described by David Olson and his colleagues (Olson, Russell, & Sprenkle, 1983; Olson, Sprenkle, & Russell, 1979). For this reason, this model is worthy of a closer look.

The circumplex idea "emerged from a conceptual clustering of over fifty concepts developed to describe marital and family dynamics" (Olson, 1989, p. 8). The model assumes that a marital or family system needs enough **cohesiveness** (togetherness) to give members a sense of identity and belonging and enough **adaptability** (change) to balance family needs for flexibility and stability.

Olson (1979, 1986) describe cohesion as the emotional bonding that family members have toward one another. The cohesion dimension occurs along a continuum that lies between **enmeshment** at one extreme and **disengagement** at the other. Moderate or "balanced" levels of cohesion are considered most conducive to effective marital and family functioning. For example, with balanced cohesion, family members can be alone (separated) and also connected. They do not live at either extreme.

Extreme family types (disengaged or enmeshed) have only a small behavioral repertoire and are thus constricted in their ability to cope effectively.

A disengaged relationship is characterized by extreme emotional separateness and little involvement among family members, who "do their own thing."

In the enmeshed relationship, there is an extreme amount of emotional closeness. Loyalty is demanded. Persons are irrationally dependent on each other. There is little private space. Their energy is focused primarily inside the marriage or family. There are few outside interests. Many couples and families who come for treatment fall into one of these extremes, disengaged or enmeshed.

The strength of a marriage or a family is dependent on its ability to adjust. Adaptability in Olson's model is defined as the ability to change power structure, role relationships, and rules in response to stress.

The four levels of adaptability range from rigid (very low) to structured (low to moderate) to flexible (moderate to high) to chaotic (very high). As with cohesion, the central levels of adaptability (structured and flexible) are more conducive to marital and family functioning, while the extremes are problematic. See Figure 15.1.

Figure 15.1 | The Circumplex Model

Source: From Life Innovations Inc., David H. Olson, President, Minneapolis, MN.
Copyright © 1979 (rev. 1986). Reprinted by permission.

Adaptability/flexibility has become an important consideration in therapy. The major goal of marriage and family therapy in the 1950s was balance, as in the analogy of a thermostat that keeps the temperature within a prescribed range (Jackson, 1957). More recently, the goal has been to "push" the marital and family system beyond its equilibrium to a point where it must accommodate by making substantial changes, thereby functioning at a new level (Dell, 1982).

OTHER MODELS OF MARRIAGE AND FAMILY THERAPY

Some theories used in individual counseling (e.g., the person-centered approach, Gestalt therapy, Adlerian counseling, reality therapy, and transactional analysis) are also used with couples and families (Horne & Passmore, 1991). However, several approaches are uniquely designed for marriage and family counseling. In fact, while Goldenberg and Goldenberg (2000) identified seven theoretical viewpoints and corresponding approaches to family therapy, Levant (1984) identified more than 20 distinct schools of marriage and family therapy. So many overlapping theories borrow and combine techniques and terminology that separating them into discrete entities without distorting them is difficult. For our purposes, we will explore a few of the most popular, beginning with the structural approach and the strategic approach. Each of these approaches and the ones described later in this section have been influenced by systems theory, although they evidence it in different ways.

Structural Therapy

Salvador Minuchin (1974) is often identified as the founder of the structural school of family counseling. Individuals in a family develop patterns of relatedness with each other, and these patterns constitute a structure that allows the family to respond to the needs of individual family members as well as to external environmental demands. Family therapies fitting the structural model focus on these present patterns of interpersonal communication (verbal and nonverbal) among family members.

Minuchin (1974) put it this way: "Family structure is the invisible set of functional demands that organizes the way family members interact. A family is a system that operates through transactional patterns. Repeated transactions establish patterns of how, when, and to whom to relate, and these patterns underpin the system" (p. 51). Structures are rarely made explicit and can only be observed when the family is in action. Put another way, these structures are mutual expectations that change only when someone no longer abides by the structures. Ideally, the structures in a family are dynamic, capable of changing while continuing to hold the system together.

> Psychotherapy has been handicapped by the nineteenth-century concept of man as a hero. . . . We have created a generation of sleuths who are looking for psychodynamic clues to the emotional crime.
>
> —Salvador Minuchin

The goal of **structural therapy** is to transform dysfunctional family structures by creating disequilibrium.

This approach advocates attempts by the therapist to disrupt the homeostasis of the dysfunctional family so they will reorganize. In Minuchin's (1974) own words: "The therapist's job is to manipulate the family system toward planned change" (p. 140). The goal is to make a new structure, a new therapeutic system (Minuchin, Montalvo, Guerney, Rosman & Schumer, 1967).

Strategic Therapy

Jay Haley (1973) and the Milan Group (Selvini-Palazzoli, Boscolo, Cecchin, & Prata, 1978) are often associated with this highly active and problem-focused school of family therapy.

Rather than attempting to alter family structures, the problem-focused school attempts to resolve the presenting problems through a variety of creative and often "paradoxical" (seemingly opposite) therapeutic directives that have no obvious bearing on the problem or existing family structures. Its practitioners assume the family will sort out new relational structures as a result of symptomatic change.

Instead of viewing family communication in a linear way, Haley uses a dynamic feedback system in which erroneous inference breeds new erroneous communications. According to Haley (1976), problems really represent the crystallization of patterns of communication, and phobias or periods of depression, for example, are really interpersonal maneuvers that fit into the power patterns of the family. The dysfunctional quality of the family becomes apparent when it attempts to adjust to the transitions occurring in the life cycles of all families. Families move through the life cycle by means of established patterns of action and communication. When those patterns are inadequate to the developmental challenge, a crisis occurs, evidenced in the creation or exacerbation of the problems of one or more family members. Strategic counselors take a systemic view of problem behaviors and focus on the process rather than the content of dysfunctional interactions.

It is not necessary for the counselor to choose between the structural and strategic approaches. They hold ideas in common and complement each other with their respective focuses. These two family therapies agree on certain principles (Stanton, 1981):

- People affect and are affected by their family contexts.
- Families have predictable developmental stages and crises that are helpful in diagnosis.
- A client's symptoms are maintained by the family system.

- When an individual changes, the family system changes: or, when the context changes, the individual changes.
- Techniques from a variety of theories are useful.
- Emphasis in counseling is placed on the present rather than the past.
- Work should be centered primarily on resolving the presented symptoms.
- The family counselor accepts responsibility for facilitating change.
- Interpretations are used more for labeling and diagnosis than for promoting insight.
- Behavioral tasks and homework are assigned to family members.
- Counseling is usually brief, often lasting less than six months.

Most modern family therapists who emphasize these two approaches tend to recognize that each model captures part of the truth and that each offers useful guidelines. Stanton (1981) recommends that counselors begin structurally to diagnose, analyze, and test boundaries and rules, since this approach is more direct and comprehensible. They can move to strategic intervention once they have encountered resistance, defensiveness, or confusion. Then it may be effective to revert back to structural theory to pull together any loose ends. Stanton says that in this way one can *think* structurally and *work* strategically.

Other Approaches

Goldenberg & Goldenberg (2000) point out that the psychodynamic view planted the seeds for yet a different approach to family therapy known as **object relations.** The fundamental contention of this approach is the need for a satisfying relationship with some "object" (i.e., another person). From the object relationships perspective, we bring memories of loss or unfulfillment from childhood into current dealings with others, seeking satisfaction but sometimes contaminating family relations in the process. Thus, this approach argues that people unconsciously relate to one another in the present based largely on expectations formed from their past. The job of the family therapist, therefore, is to help family members become aware of those unresolved objects from their families of origin.

Another well-known approach to family therapy is **experiential family therapy.** Made popular by Virginia Satir and Carl Whitaker, experiential family therapy proposes that troubled families need a "growth experience" derived from an intimate interpersonal experience with an involved therapist. Experiential therapists contend that they can help families best when they are authentic and honest with their own expressions. For Virginia Satir, building self-esteem and learning to communicate effectively were essential therapeutic goals. Carl Whitaker attempted to free families to activate their innate growth process by proving their own covert world of symbolic meanings. Both variations represented by Satir and Whitaker are based upon humanistic and systemic foundations that attempt to change negative interactions while making their emotional connections stronger.

Murray Bowen identified with *transgenerational family therapy,* in which family members are tied to each others' thinking, feeling, and behavior. Those persons with the strongest affective connection with the family are most vulnerable to personal emotional reactions to family stress. **Differentiation** of the self—becoming more independent—is correlated with the ability to resist being overwhelmed by emotional reactivity in the family. The more differentiation, the less likely the individual is to experience personal dysfunction. The most vulnerable child, according to Bowen (1978), is the most attached child. The child's level of differentiation is low and he will select as a marital partner someone who is also poorly differentiated in her family. And the least differentiated of their children will marry someone equally undifferentiated, and so on—thus, the term *transgenerational.* Bowen believed that in severe cases schizophrenia could result after several generations of increased attachment.

> Not long ago, it was expected that a therapist would be closeted along with one person who would talk at length about himself and his fantasies. Today, a therapy session . . . is full of action and emotion as the therapist shifts people from chair to chair and guides the action among the participants.
>
> —Jay Haley

Ivan Boszormenyi-Nagy (1987) is also identified with transgenerational family therapy. He emphasizes the ethical dimensions in family relationships extending over generations. His focus is on trust, loyalty, entitlements, and indebtedness. The patterns of relating within a family that are passed down from generation to generation, according to Boszormenyi-Nagy, are the keys to understanding the individual within the context of family functioning.

THE FAMILY LIFE CYCLE

Many marital and family therapists view the developmental stages of family life as a key component in understanding the family as a system (Carter & McGoldrick, 1988; Haley, 1973; Solomon, 1973). This developmental outlook notes that certain predictable marker events or phases occur in all families, regardless of structure or composition, compelling each family to deal in some manner with these events. The **family life cycle** is the name given to the stages a family goes through as it evolves through the years. Becvar and Becvar (1988) outline a nine-stage cycle that begins with the unattached adult and continues through retirement.

Stage	Emotion	Stage-Critical Tasks
1. Unattached adult	Accepting parent-offspring separation	a. Differentiation from family of origin
		b. Development of peer relations
		c. Initiation of career
2. Newly married	Commitment to the marriage	a. Formation of marital system
		b. Making room for spouse with family and friends
		c. Adjusting career demands
3. Childbearing	Accepting new members into the system	a. Adjusting marriage to make room for child
		b. Taking on parenting roles
		c. Making room for grandparents
4. Preschool-age child	Accepting the new personality	a. Adjusting family to the needs of specific children
		b. Coping with energy drain and lack of privacy
		c. Taking time out to be a couple
5. School-age child	Allowing child to establish relationships outside the family	a. Extending family/society interactions
		b. Encouraging the child's educational progress
		c. Dealing with increased activities and time demands

Stage	Emotion	Stage-Critical Tasks
6. Teenage child	Increasing flexibility of family boundaries to allow independence	a. Shifting the balance in the parent-child relationship
		b. Refocusing on mid-life career and marital issues
		c. Dealing with increasing concerns for older generation
7. Launching center	Accepting exits from and entries into the family	a. Releasing adult children into work, college, marriage
		b. Maintaining supportive home base
		c. Accepting occasional returns of adult children
8. Middle-aged adult	Letting go of children and facing each other	a. Rebuilding the marriage
		b. Welcoming children's spouses, grandchildren into family
		c. Dealing with aging of one's own parents
9. Retirement	Accepting retirement and old age	a. Maintaining individual and couple functioning
		b. Supporting middle generation
		c. Coping with death of parents, spouse
		d. Closing or adapting family home

Source: From Dorothy Stroh Becvar, Raphael J. Becvar, *Family Therapy: A Systemic Integration.* Copyright 1988 by Allyn & Bacon.

Marriage and family therapists need to be aware of the different stages of development within the family (Wilcoxon, 1985). For instance, family stress tends to be highest at the transition points between stages, and dysfunction is most likely to appear in a family when there is an interruption or dislocation in the unfolding life cycle. The therapist's role is to help remobilize the family life cycle, so that normal developmental progress can continue. Carter and McGoldrick (1988) stress that the developmental tasks for nontraditional families, such as those headed by single parents or

Parents are in the beginning the prime givers. The children are at first mainly receivers, but, across time, they also make significant returns in kind.
—Nathan Ackerman

blended families, must also be considered. Family life cycles, it should be noted, sometimes vary by (1) gender (Carter & McGoldrick, 1988), (2) culture (Hines, 1988), and (3) socioeconomic status (Fulmer, 1988).

It should also be noted that some writers have described developmental schema focusing entirely on the marital life cycle. Campbell's (1980) approach includes five stages: (1) romance, (2) power struggle, (3) stability, (4) commitment, and (5) co-creation.

THE GOALS OF MARRIAGE AND FAMILY THERAPY

The obvious goal of marriage and family therapy is to reduce problems. This is achieved by intervention focused on changing the family system. As Goldenberg (1983, p. 297) has summarized, "the focus of family therapy is on changing the system . . . so that each member experiences a sense of independence, uniqueness, and wholeness while remaining within the context and security of the family relationship." The basic assumption is that the current family system dynamics are helping to maintain these symptomatic behaviors. In other words, the current pattern of interaction in the family needs to be changed before the symptoms or presenting problems will be alleviated.

Unhealthy systems resist change. They tend to be static (Minuchin, 1974). In unhealthy family systems, members often project the tension between two members within the system (such as marital conflict) onto a third member of the system (such as the adolescent daughter who takes on an identity as the "rebellious one" or as "the bulimic") rather than dealing more directly with the real issues at hand. This phenomenon of projection is called triangulation. The two members who have the problem triangle a third party into their problem. Healthy systems are less rigid and able to evolve, flex, and change without triangulation attempts.

Marriage and family therapies ultimately are in the business of building strong healthy families. According to researchers Stinnett and DeFrain (1985), families that are most successful, happy, and strong are (1) committed to each other, (2) appreciate each other, (3) spend time together, (4) have good communication patterns, (5) have a high degree of religious orientation, and (6) are able to deal with crisis in a positive manner.

While a list that characterizes the healthy family could be almost endless, most professionals agree that the following half-dozen qualities are essential. The healthy family:

1. *Responds positively to challenges and crises.* Instead of denying or distorting reality, this family draws on their individual and collective resources to develop adaptive and healthy coping strategies. When these families are un-

able to find the resources within, they readily admit problems and seek help elsewhere.

2. *Has a clearly articulated world view,* sometimes expressed in terms of a specific religious commitment. This undergirds their moral development, altruistic endeavors, and sense of history and heritage.

3. *Communicates well.* They know how to listen actively by expressing their thoughts and feelings clearly, and they manage the inevitable differences of opinion that occur in a family system. These families have a well-developed repertoire of conflict management skills.

4. *Chooses to spend time together in a variety of tasks,* including both planned and spontaneous activities. They know how to enjoy each other when they play or work. They can work hard together toward a common goal or enjoying a day off.

> Family life is too intimate to be preserved by the spirit of justice. It can be sustained by a spirit of love which goes beyond justice.
>
> —Reinhold Niebuhr

5. *Makes promises and honors commitments to one another.* The marital and familial tasks and responsibilities are taken seriously. There is a sense of belonging and respect for individual differences. The family is seen as the context for the development of a strong sense of self-esteem and personal security.

6. *Knows how to express love and appreciation for one another.* Family members know and respect one another. They are caring, compassionate, respectful, tolerant, and trusting (Jones & Butman, 1991, p. 353).

 ## FACES III

This scale is designed to measure two main dimensions of family functioning: cohesion and flexibility. It is the result of Dr. David H. Olson's research on the systematic assessment and treatment of families and is based on his Circumplex Model of family functioning. A full description of his work and the Circumplex Model can be found on the Web site www.lifeinnovations.com.

Describe your family now: (sample of items)

_____ 1. Family members ask each other for help.
_____ 6. Different persons act as leaders in our family.
_____ 9. Family members like to spend free time with each other.
_____ 14. Rules change in our family.

For more information about FACES III or to order it, visit the Web site: www. lifeinnovations.com.

Reprinted with permission from David H. Olson, Ph.D., Professor Emeritus, University of Minnesota, Life Innovations, P.O. Box 190, Minneapolis, MN 55440.

MARRIAGE AND FAMILY INTERVENTIONS

To facilitate change and break dysfunctional patterns, marital and family therapists access a number of interventions. **Reframing** is an example. This technique involves relabeling problems by viewing them in a more positive light. Instead of seeing a wife as nagging her husband to pick up his clothes, for example, she is seen as valuing a pleasant and orderly home for her family. Reframing changes the context in which a behavior happens, thus inviting new responses from family members. In other words, reframing changes the meaning attributed to a behavior without changing the behavior, and this altered perspective changes the family system.

Boundary setting can be used within a family relationship to bring about more flexibility. It generally involves building "walls" between people to establish lines of separation, or "bridges" to allow more permeable boundaries and connection. In the counseling session, spatial arrangements, such as seating parents next to each other or moving chairs farther apart, creates boundaries. Monitoring communication so one person speaks at a time can help an enmeshed couple or family create a permeable but more rigid boundary to establish each person's individuality. Other boundary-setting activities may involve family tasks such as establishing rules regarding an adolescent's need for privacy.

Family **sculpting** is an intervention that involves asking a family member to physically position herself or himself and other family members into a formation that metaphorically represents the family relationships. The family member may then reposition family members to represent an ideal image of the family. The therapist may ask each family member to describe what it's like in their sculpted position. This intervention can metaphorically represent various aspects of a relationship and help family members become more aware of hidden system dynamics (Papp, 1976).

A **genogram** is a three-generational family tree used to help family members and counselors detect patterns of family functioning that have been passed from generation to generation. Murray Bowen (1978) calls this **multigeneration transmission**. A genogram helps display significant issues in a graphic manner to unveil the impact of one's family history on the present. See Figure 15.2 of the Fonda Family genogram.

This complex and crowded genogram reveals such important details as:

- Multiple marriages are common in this family.
- Both of Henry Fonda's first two wives committed suicide.
- Henry Fonda separated from his second wife, Jane's mother, only a few months before she committed suicide. He had already started an affair with his third wife, Susan Blanchard, whom he married eight months later.
- At the time of the third marriage (in fact, during the honeymoon), Peter Fonda, Jane's brother, shot himself (and nearly died).

Figure 15.2 Fonda Family Genogram

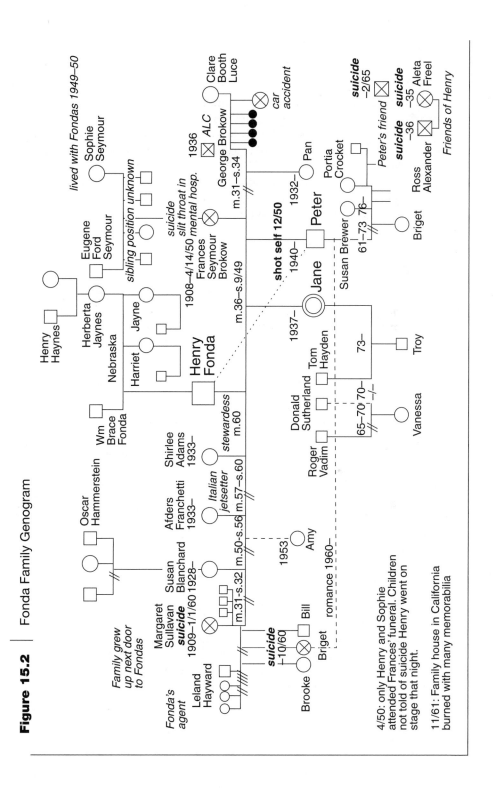

Family grew up next door to Fondas

Fonda's agent

lived with Fondas 1949–50

sibling position unknown

suicide slit throat in mental hosp.

shot self 12/50

Italian jetsetter *stewardess*

romance 1960–

suicide –1/60

suicide –2/65

suicide –36

suicide –35

Peter's friend

Friends of Henry

car accident

Margaret Sullavan 1909–1/1/60 **suicide**

Oscar Hammerstein

Susan Blanchard 1928–

Afders Franchetti 1933–

Shirlee Adams 1933–

Henry Haynes

Herberta Jaynes

Eugene Ford Seymour

Sophie Seymour

Clare Booth Luce

ALC

George Brokow 1936

Frances Seymour Brokow 1908–4/14/50

Wm Brace Fonda

Nebraska

Harriet   Jayne

Henry Fonda

m.36–s.9/49   m.31–s.34

m.31–s.32   m.50–s.56   m.57–s.60   m.60

Leland Hayward

Brooke   Bill

Briget

1953   Amy

Jane   1937–

Peter   1940–

Pan   1932–

Susan Brewer

Portia Crocket

Ross Alexander

Aleta Freel

Donald Sutherland

Tom Hayden

Roger Vadim

73–

65–70   70– –/–

Troy

Vanessa

61–73   76–

Briget

4/50: only Henry and Sophie attended Frances' funeral. Children not told of suicide Henry went on stage that night.

11/61: Family house in California burned with many memorabilia

379

- Henry Fonda had two close friends who committed suicide. His son, Peter, fell in love with Briget Hayward the year that she killed herself, and also had a friend who committed suicide.

The **powergram** (Stuart, 1980) is a method for clarifying the power balance in a marital relationship. Decisions in a marriage may be made along a continuum of power balance, which will vary among couples and with each spouse. (1) Couples are asked to read a list of categories couples commonly use in making decisions. (2) They are then asked to identify how decisions in these areas are currently made. (3) Couples are asked to indicate how they would like decisions in the different areas to be made ideally. The therapist helps couples compare their expectations and negotiate their desired changes.

APPLICATION

Most family therapists presuppose an average level of intelligence and education on the part of adult members of the family. Family therapy tends to be short-term treatment, usually several months in length, with a focus on resolving specific problems such as eating disorders, difficulties with school, or adjustments to bereavement or geographical relocation. It is not normally used for long-term or intensive restructuring of severely dysfunctional families.

In family therapy sessions, all members of the family and the therapist (though there may be more than one therapist with this modality) are present at most sessions. The therapist seeks to analyze the process of family interaction and communication as a whole; he or she does not take sides with specific members. The therapist may make occasional comments or remarks intended to help family members become more conscious of patterns or structures that had been previously taken for granted. Family therapists who work as a team also model new behaviors for the family through their interactions with each other during sessions.

Family therapy is often recommended in the following situations:

- Blended families with adjustment difficulties.
- Families with problems across generational boundaries. These would include problems caused by parents sharing housing with grandparents or children being reared by grandparents.
- Treatment of a family member with schizophrenia or multiple personality disorder (MPD). Family therapy helps other family members understand their relative's disorder and adjust to the psychological changes that may be occurring in the relative.
- Families that deviate from social norms, such as common-law relationships or gay couples rearing children. These families may not have internal problems but may be troubled by outsiders' judgmental attitudes.
- Families with members from a mixture of racial, cultural, or religious backgrounds.

- Families where the identified patient's problems seem inextricably tied to problems with other family members.

Whatever the specific situation, problems are treated by changing the way the system works rather than trying to "fix" a specific member, commonly referred to as the **identified patient,** or IP. The IP is the family member with the symptom that has brought the family into treatment. The concept of the IP is used by family therapists to keep the family from using him or her as a way of avoiding problems in the rest of the system (i.e., scapegoating).

Family therapists may be either psychiatrists, clinical psychologists, or other professionals certified by a specialty board in marriage and family therapy. They will usually evaluate a family for treatment by scheduling a series of interviews with the members of the immediate family, including young children, and significant or symptomatic members of the extended family. This process allows the therapist(s) to find out how each member of the family sees the problem and to form first impressions of the family's functioning. Family therapists typically look for the level and types of emotions expressed, patterns of dominance and submission, the roles played by family members, communication styles, and the locations of emotional triangles. They will also note whether these patterns are rigid or relatively flexible.

Preparation also usually includes drawing a genogram to depict the significant persons and events in the family's history by uncovering intergenerational patterns of behavior, marriage choices, family alliances and conflicts, the existence of family secrets, and other information that sheds light on the family's present situation.

Results of family therapy vary, but in good circumstances, they include greater insight, increased differentiation of individual family members, improved communication within the family, loosening of previously automatic behavior patterns, and resolution of the problem that led the family to seek treatment. The following "case of Maria" will illustrate (Capuzzi & Gross, 1999).

Presenting Problem

Juanita Van Pelt (age 8) was suspended by Roosevelt Elementary School for stealing money from her classmates. Juanita was suspended along with two other classmates, both of whom had a long history of discipline problems despite their young age. This suspension was Juanita's first. After the suspension, Roosevelt's school counselor, Domingo Chavez, held a conference with Juanita's mother, Maria Van Pelt (age 32). He reported to Maria that Juanita had recently committed several disciplinary infractions, something they had not seen before in Juanita. Maria acknowledged that she was having problems at home with both Juanita and Norberto, Juanita's brother. Mr. Chavez noted that the kindergarten teacher was concerned that Norberto (age 6) always seemed sullen and uncooperative.

In talking with Maria, Mr. Chavez sensed that she was feeling overwhelmed with her children's problems. He asked if she had considered counseling to work on these problems. Maria said that she had, in fact, consulted her physician and that this doctor had given her a referral to a respected psychiatrist located downtown. However, Maria reported that she had not followed up on this referral due to the cost and travel involved. Also, she commented that her faith was very important to her and she was unsure if the psychiatrist would respect her faith. Mr. Chavez suggested to Maria that an alternative existed. He reminded her that since Maria was a school district employee, she could take advantage of the services offered by the school district's employee assistance program (EAP). Mr. Chavez said that currently the EAP allowed six counseling sessions per year at no cost. Also, he noted that Catholic Social Services was one of the contracted EAP providers. Maria went home and immediately called the Catholic Social Services office at her local parish, St. Gregory's. She scheduled an appointment for herself, Juanita, and Norberto for the following Tuesday.

Therapists

Mrs. Mesa and Sr. Benedict were the cotherapists assigned to work with Maria and her children. They are both staff therapists with the diocese's Catholic Social Services. Mrs. Mesa possesses a national certification in family therapy. Sr. Benedict holds a national certification as an art therapist and has worked extensively with families.

Family Demographics and History

Maria and her children live in a blue-collar neighborhood of Tucson, Arizona. Maria's former husband, Mark Van Pelt (age 33), is a civil engineer. He lives in Boston and has no direct contact with Maria or his two children. Maria works as a junior high math and science teacher. Also living in Tucson are Maria's parents, Jose Maria Flores (age 52) and Rosa Flores (age 51), and Mark's parents, Joe (age 54) and Babs (age 50). Both sets of grandparents interact periodically with Maria and her children, but these relationships are very strained. In addition to these grandparents, all of Maria's siblings live in Tucson. These include Juan (age 31), Enrique (age 30), Ernesto (age 29), and Bonita (age 28). Maria's relationships with her siblings are tension-filled. Especially painful to Maria is Bonita's refusal to talk to her. In contrast to the present, Maria and Bonita were close as children.

Maria's marriage outside her faith caused intense familial discord. This discord exposed subtle tensions and power alliances that existed in the Flores family. Only Ernesto attended Maria's wedding. Bonita blames all current interpersonal conflicts in the Flores family on Maria and her "disloyalty" to the family. Following the lead of Maria's father, the Flores family maintains a strong covert adherence to a rule of not directly addressing personal problems such as family conflict (i.e., a "no talk" rule). The one exception to this rule is the sacrament of confession with the parish priest. Otherwise, the Flores family views sharing personal problems as a sign of weakness. Maria's genogram appears in Figure 15.3.

Family Therapy Process

Intake Interview   Maria arrived 15 minutes early for her appointment and brought Juanita and Norberto as planned. Norberto sucked his thumb during the interview. Juanita was quiet and appeared to believe she was being punished. In the intake interview, Maria spoke of her financial fears, frustrations with parenting, and sense of alienation from her parish and family.

Case Conceptualization and Treatment Planning   Mrs. Mesa and Sr. Benedict diagnosed Maria as suffering from late-onset Dysthmic Disorder. The therapists conceptualized this disorder as a posttraumatic symptom. The specific traumas in Maria's case were the psychological and physical battering from Mark, her family's rejection of her because of her out-of-faith marriage, and her perception that she could not fully participate in the sacramental life of her parish because she was divorced. Mrs. Mesa and Sr. Benedict decided that their family therapy work would need to occur on three levels: Maria's immediate family (i.e., Maria, Juanita, and Norberto), Maria's family of origin, and Maria's parish family. The therapists prioritized the

Figure 15.3 | Maria Van Pelt's Genogram

addressing of Maria's traumas in the following order: (1) family-of-origin level, (2) parish family level, and (3) immediate family level. The therapists felt that Juanita's and Norberto's acting out was a symptom of the children's vicarious traumatization, which took place and was maintained by living in a family system with a parent who was a trauma victim. Mrs. Mesa and Sr. Benedict believed that if they could adequately address Maria's traumas, they could remediate the family structures that maintained Juanita's and Norberto's problematic behaviors.

To address Maria's alienation from her family of origin, the two therapists proposed that Maria bring her parents and siblings to the next session. Maria cried and stated that she doubted if they would all come, because "We don't talk about problems in the family." Sr. Benedict proposed that she call each family member and invite him or her to come to the next session. Maria thought they might consider an invitation from Sr. Benedict, and she eagerly gave her permission. Sr. Benedict did call the family members, and after some persuading they all agreed to come. Mrs. Flores's sister agreed to baby-sit Juanita and Norberto during the sessions.

Trauma survivors such as Maria pose intense challenges for family therapists (Balcom, 1996). Unfortunately, most trauma treatment techniques are oriented toward individual or group work. However, art has been shown to be effective with both family dysfunctions (Sobol, 1982) and trauma resolution (Appleton, 1993). Haley (1976) held that metaphor was a basic means of family communication, and Sobol (1982) drew upon this idea in designing her family therapy interventions. She chose art because its inherent metaphorical qualities can facilitate productive family communication—specifically, by permitting family members to express and represent problems in a less destructive way than do words or action. Mrs. Mesa and Sr. Benedict decided that they would ask members of the Flores family to participate in a series of drawing tasks and then use the information obtained through the art products to set goals and plan directives. They felt that art tasks could help "restructure" the Flores family system, specifically by restructuring that system through reconnecting family members via culturally powerful symbols. As in narrative therapy approaches, the metaphor that would emerge from the Flores family's art processes would help family members to rediscover their deep interconnectedness to each other.

Session 1

The first session involved building a working relationship with the members of the Flores family and engaging them in a series of art tasks to help them begin to express themselves.

Building Working Alliances   Mrs. Mesa and Sr. Benedict have both worked extensively with Latino families. This experience influences the selection and application of their interventions. For instance, they initiated *La platica* (i.e., small talk) with family members at the initial session. *La platica* is an essential part of creating a working relationship with Latino families.

Combining Strategic Family Therapy with Art   Both Mrs. Mesa and Sr. Benedict were worried about the Flores family's covert "no talk" rule. They designed a series of four art tasks to help the family members begin to express themselves. The first drawing task eased the family into the art-making process by introducing the material with a warm-up process (individual free drawing). The second and third drawings focused specifically on the problems and resolutions identified by each family member. The final art process put the entire family together to create a family mural on one piece of paper. Through the art task sequence, the family was moved from a distant to a closer physical proximity. At the end of the family art process, the therapists reviewed all of the drawings with the family. The assignments given for each of the tasks were:

- "Make an individual free drawing of anything that comes to mind."
- "Make an individual drawing of why you think you are here."
- "Make an individual drawing of how you would like the 'problem' to change."
- "Now together, make a joint mural about your family."
- "At this time we will review the drawings you have made."

Sr. Benedict often used this series of tasks with families like Maria's that maintained structure by covert communication norms. The use of such tasks allows a family therapist to do the following:

- Elicit metaphorical information for planning future intervention.
- Provide drawing tasks that disrupt dysfunctional family communication patterns (e.g., a family's covert "no talk" rule).
- Help family members express themselves free of covert familial communication norms.

Given the tension present in the family system, each member of the Flores family welcomed Sr. Benedict's initial suggestion that they start out by working on their own drawing. The therapists had a wide array of drawing materials available for the family members to use, including oil and chalk pastels and felt marker pens.

Free Drawing Art Task   Maria's free drawing was a weeping, pregnant image of the Virgin. In high school, Maria and Bonita were members of their parish's Legion of Mary. They enjoyed belonging to this group because of a strong devotion to Our Lady rooted in Latino cultures (i.e., Marianismo).

After 20 minutes, Mrs. Mesa had the family members stop their drawings and share them with the whole family. Maria showed her drawing of the Virgin. The family was moved to tears by Maria's expressive representation of the Virgin. Without words, they surrounded Maria. Bonita even took Maria by the hand. Sr. Benedict read these nonverbal behaviors as a sign that the family had moved to some new level of communication, a new level that contained acknowledgment of, and empathy for, Maria's suffering. To concretize this new connection to Maria, Sr. Benedict directed the other family members to add to Maria's drawing through the production of a joint mural.

Family Mural Art Task   After the mural was completed, Mrs. Mesa asked each family member to discuss the feelings the mural evoked about the family. At this point, Bonita asked Maria why her drawing of Our Lady was weeping. Maria hesitated and then looked toward her mother. In a halting voice, Maria replied that the Virgin weeps for Maria because the Virgin understands the sorrow of pregnant, unmarried women. Then Maria walked over and knelt in front of her mother. Maria began to weep uncontrollably. Rosa looked at her and softly said, "This is why you married Mark and left the family." Maria nodded yes, and Rosa kissed her on the forehead in reconciliation.

Sessions 2 Through 5

The next four sessions involved rebuilding family connectedness and "trying on" new styles of communication. Again, Sr. Benedict used art tasks to facilitate culturally salient modes of communication. Despite this work, Maria's full reentry to her familial life remained blocked by her belief that as a divorced woman, she should not participate in the sacramental life of her parish. This left Maria feeling marginalized in the Flores family. Sr. Benedict corrected Maria's mistaken notion that divorced persons could not receive communion. He also set up an appointment for Maria with a member of her own community who does marriage tribunal work. This sister would help Maria to receive a marriage annulment so that she would become free to remarry in the Church.

  During one of these middle sessions, the art tasks served as a potent stimulus for self-discovery. Maria's chalk pastel drawing recounted her strong devotion to the Blessed Sacrament during her high school years. Maria shared how this devotion had helped her weather the typical turmoils of adolescence. Mrs. Mesa helped Maria negotiate with her parents to baby-sit Juanita and Norberto three times a week so she could spend an hour meditating in the Perpetual Adoration Chapel at St. Gregory's. Later, Maria reported to Mrs. Mesa that these hours were meaningful to her and gave her a sense of peace she had not felt in a long time.

Session 6: Termination

As Maria began to reenter full family and parish life, her dysthymia lifted and she began to have more energy for her work and her children. By the final session of family therapy, Maria reported that neither Juanita nor Norberto was having any disciplinary problems in school. Also, the renewed consistency of Maria's parenting had begun to help her build a productive relationship with Joe and Babs Van Pelt. Mrs. Mesa and Sr. Benedict worked with Maria to help her outline the boundaries she wanted to set in her relationship with the Van Pelts.

CRITICAL ANALYSIS

Family therapy requests the therapist to give up the nonjudgmental stance developed in most of the conventional individual psychotherapies covered in this book. With this approach, a change in family functioning comes about through a therapist who is supportive and nurturing at times and challenging and demanding at others. These therapists move quickly in and out of emotional involvements without losing track of family interactions and patterns (Goldenberg & Goldenberg, 2000). This personal vulnerability can be seen as an asset or liability, depending on one's personal views of the counselor role.

In critiquing marriage and family therapy, one must underscore the chief risk it involves—the possible unsettling of rigid personality defenses in individuals or couple relationships that had been fragile before the beginning of therapy. Because the therapist is called upon to take a personal stance within this context, family therapy holds the potential to dismantle what stability a person might have. Of course, there is undeniable truth behind the notion that sometimes things have to get worse before they can get better.

Contemporary family therapists have begun to examine spirituality not just as a special topic, but as it is interwoven in all aspects of people's lives, from family heritage and congregational affiliations to belief systems, rituals, and practices. It has also considered how gender, cultural background, ethnicity membership, and social class shape the behavioral patterns of family members. Each of these factors must be considered. The experience of being male or female, for example, shapes and in turn is shaped by one's economic status and cultural background. Today's approach to family therapy emphasizes gender sensitivity, being careful not to reinforce sexist or patriarchal attitudes. Contemporary family therapists pay attention to differences in power and status not only within families, but in society in general. Why? Because cultural specificity calls for an understanding of the extent to which family members are influenced by such factors as ethnic background to ascertain the role they play in the presenting problem (Kliman, 1994; McGoldrick, 1998).

Overall results from surveys based mainly on efficacy studies indicate that clients receiving family therapy did significantly better than untreated control group clients. In certain cases, a combination of therapeutic modalities (i.e., individual therapy along with family therapy) may work best (Pinsof, Wynne, & Hambright, 1996). Still, some families are not considered suitable candidates for family therapy. They include:

- Families in which one, or both, of the parents is psychotic or has been diagnosed with antisocial or paranoid personality disorder.

- Families whose cultural or religious values are opposed to, or suspicious of, psychotherapy.
- Families with members who cannot participate in treatment sessions because of physical illness or similar limitations.
- Families with members with very rigid personality structures. Here, members might be at risk for an emotional or psychological crisis.
- Families whose members cannot or will not be able to meet regularly for treatment.
- Families that are unstable or on the verge of breakup.

Still, family therapy is certainly the treatment of choice for many problems with the family.

CURRENT STATUS

Family therapy continues to grow in popularity, and families will most likely use family therapy with even greater frequency in the future because, in addition to being effective, it is a relatively short-term approach that is solution oriented and deals with immediate problems. Its preventive quality also invites accessibility to individuals who don't wish to be perceived as pathological.

Today, family therapy is fully recognized by practitioners from most every perspective. Since its founding in 1942, the American Association of Marriage and Family Therapists (AAMFT) has grown significantly to more than 27,000 members and has been involved with the problems, needs, and changing patterns of couples and family relationships. The association facilitates research, theory development, and education. Members develop standards for graduate education and training, clinical supervision, professional ethics, and the clinical practice of marriage and family therapy. The AAMFT hosts an annual national training conference each fall and a week-long series of continuing education institutes in the summer. It publishes the *Journal of Marital and Family Therapy* and *Family Therapy News*.

The International Association of Marriage and Family Counselors (IAMFC) is another organization that promotes excellence in the practice of family counseling by creating and disseminating publications and media products, providing a forum for exploration of family-related issues, involving a diverse group of dedicated professionals in its activities, and emphasizing collaborative efforts. IAMFC is a division of the American Counseling Association.

SUMMARY

1. *Historical Development.* Relative to other modalities covered in this text, the roots of marriage and family therapy do not run deep, and its establishment can be drawn from a number of unrelated influences. The biologist Ludwig von Bertalanffy, for example, with his theory of circular causality, devised a theory of living organisms that viewed them as inter-

acting components mutually affecting one another. Another influence on family theory in the 1950s came from a group of pioneering studies in the area of schizophrenia. The establishment of the American Association of Marriage Counselors in 1942, which is now the American Association of Marriage and Family Therapists (AAMFT), also opened the way for this new emphasis on the total family.

2. *The Circumplex Model of Marriage and Family.* Devised by David Olson and his colleagues, the circumplex idea emerged from clustering more than 50 concepts developed to describe marital and family dynamics. The model assumes that a marital or family system needs enough *cohesiveness* (togetherness) to give members a sense of identity and belonging and enough *adaptability* (change) to balance family needs for flexibility and stability. The cohesion dimension occurs along a continuum that lies between *enmeshment* at one extreme and *disengagement* at the other.

3. *Other Models of Marriage and Family Therapy.* With more than 20 distinct schools of marriage and family therapy being identified, many overlapping theories borrow and combine techniques and terminology. Two established and fairly representative approaches are the structural approach (identified with Salvador Minuchin) and the strategic approach (identified with Jay Haley and the Milan Group). Both have been influenced by systems theory, although they evidence it in very different ways. Most modern family therapists tend to recognize that each model of family therapy captures part of the truth and that each offers useful guidelines.

4. *The Family Life Cycle.* Every family goes through stages as it evolves through the years. Becvar and Becvar outline a nine-stage cycle that begins with the unattached adult and continues through retirement. Family stress tends to be highest at the transition points between stages, and dysfunction is most likely to appear in a family when there is an interruption or dislocation in the unfolding life cycle. The therapist's role is to help remobilize the family life cycle, so that normal developmental progress can continue. The developmental tasks for nontraditional families, such as those headed by single parents or blended families, must also be considered.

5. *The Goals of Marriage and Family Therapy.* The focus is on changing the system so that each member experiences a sense of independence, uniqueness, and wholeness while remaining within the context and security of the family relationship. The basic assumption is that the current family system dynamics are helping to maintain these symptomatic behaviors. In other words, the current pattern of interaction in the family needs to be changed before the symptoms or presenting problems can be alleviated. Unhealthy systems resist change. Marriage and family therapies ultimately are in the business of building strong healthy families.

6. *Marriage and Family Interventions.* To facilitate change and break dysfunctional patterns, marital and family therapists access interventions such as *boundary setting* (which can be used to bring about more flexibility),

family *sculpting* (which can metaphorically represent various aspects of a relationship and help family members become more aware of hidden system dynamics), and a *genogram* (a three-generational family tree used to help family members and counselors detect patterns of family functioning that have been passed from generation to generation).

7. *Application.* Family therapists presuppose an average level of intelligence and education on the part of adult members of the family. Family therapy tends to be short-term treatment, usually several months in length, with a focus on resolving specific problems such as eating disorders, difficulties with school, or adjustments to bereavement or geographical relocation. It is not normally used for long-term or intensive restructuring of severely dysfunctional families.

8. *Critical Analysis.* Effective family therapists move quickly in and out of emotional involvements without losing track of family interactions and patterns. Yet, this personal vulnerability can be seen as an asset or liability, depending on one's personal views of the counselor role. Results from surveys based mainly on efficacy studies, indicate that clients receiving family therapy did significantly better than untreated control group clients. While it has its limits, family therapy is certainly the treatment of choice for many problems with the family.

9. *Current Status.* Practitioners of family therapy continue to increase, as represented by its current professional organization memberships. It is likely to be used with even greater frequency in the future because, in addition to being effective, it is a relatively short-term approach, solution oriented, and deals with immediate problems. Its preventive quality also invites accessibility to individuals who don't wish to be perceived as pathological. The future of family therapy looks bright.

Key Terms

AAMFT The American Association of Marriage and Family Therapists, a professional group of more than 27,000 members.

Adaptability A concept from the circumplex model that represents change that allows a family to balance its needs for flexibility and stability.

Blended family Formed by the remarriage of a divorced or widowed parent; it includes the new husband and wife, plus some or all of their children from previous marriages.

Boundary setting Can be used within a family relationship to bring about more flexibility; it generally involves building "walls" between people to establish lines of separation or "bridges" to allow more permeable boundaries and connection.

Circular causality The idea that tenets are related through a series of interacting feedback loops.

Circumplex model The clustering of more than 50 concepts describing marital and family dynamics.

Cohesiveness Concept from the circumplex model that represents togetherness, where family members have a sense of identity and belonging.

Differentiation The ability to retain one's identity within a family system while maintaining emotional connections with the other members.

Disengagement Extreme independence within the circumplex model of family cohesiveness.

Double bind Involves a person receiving two contradictory messages at the same time and being unable to follow both.

Enmeshment One extreme of overdependence within the circumplex model of family cohesiveness.

Experiential family therapy Based upon humanistic and systemic origins, this approach contends that therapists can help families best when they are authentic and honest with their own expressions, thus building self-esteem within family members and making their emotional connections stronger.

Extended family field Person's family of origin plus grandparents, in-laws, and other relatives.

FACES III Scale designed to measure two main dimensions of family functioning: cohesion and adaptability.

Family life cycle The name given to the stages a family goes through as it evolves through the years.

Family sculpting Intervention that involves asking a couple or family member to physically position themselves and other family members into a formation that metaphorically represents the family relationships.

Family systems theory An approach to treatment that emphasizes the interdependency of family members rather than focusing on individuals in isolation from the family. This theory underlies the most influential forms of contemporary family therapy.

Genogram Three-generational family tree used to help family members and counselors detect patterns of family functioning that have been passed from generation to generation.

Heroes Family members who pick up the responsibilities abandoned by the alcoholic spouse or parent and, in essence, run the family, doing the chores and caring for children or siblings.

Homeostasis The tendency of a family system to maintain internal stability and resist change.

Identified patient (IP) Family member in whom the family's symptom has emerged or is most obvious.

Lost child Family member who fades into the family woodwork, preferring their own world to the troubled atmosphere at home.

Mascots The jokers in the family; they are the ones who take laughter as an analgesic to their pain.

Multigeneration transmission Term coined by Murray Bowen to describe how a genogram helps display significant issues in a graphic manner to unveil the impact of one's family history on the present.

Nuclear family Basic family unit, consisting of father, mother, and their children.

Object relations Psychodynamic approach to family therapy that argues that people unconsciously relate to one another in the present based largely on expectations formed from their families of origin.

Pseudomutuality Describes the facade of family harmony that covers underlying tension.

Scapegoats Family members who respond to their negative environment with defiance and anger. They become the "losers," the family's James Dean.

Strategic therapy Highly active and problem-focused school of family therapy. Rather than attempting to alter family structures, this problem-focused approach attempts to resolve the presenting problems through a variety of creative and often "paradoxical" directives that have no obvious bearing on the problem or existing family structures.

Structural therapy Associated with Salvador Minuchin, in this approach, a family develops patterns of relatedness with each other, and these patterns constitute a structure that allows the family to respond to the needs of individual family members and to external environmental demands.

Triangling Process in which two family members lower the tension level between them by drawing in a third member.

Suggested Reading

Carter, B., & McGoldrick, M. (1988). *The changing family life cycle* (2nd ed.). New York: Gardner.

Friedman, E. H. (1985). *Generation to generation: Family process in church and synagogue.* New York: Guilford Press.

Goldenberg, I., & Goldenberg, H. (2000). *Family therapy: An overview* (5th ed.). Pacific Grove, CA: Brooks/Cole.

McGoldrick, M. (Ed.). (1998). *Re-visioning family therapy: Race, culture, and gender in clinical practice.* New York: Guilford Press.

Minuchin, S. (1974). *Families and family therapy.* Cambridge, MA: Harvard University Press.

Napier, A. Y., & Whitaker, C. A. (1988). *The family crucible.* New York: Harper & Row.

Walsh, Froma (Ed.). (1999). *Spiritual resources in family therapy.* New York: Guilford Press.

References

Appleton, V. (1993). An art therapy protocol for the medical trauma setting. *Art therapy journal of the American Art Therapy Association, 10*, 71–77.

Balcom, D. (1996). Interpersonal dynamics and treatment of dual trauma couples. *Journal of Marital and Family Therapy, 22*(4), 431–442.

Bates, M., Johnson, C. D., & Blaker, K. E. (1982). *Group leadership: A manual for group counseling* (2nd ed.). Denver: Love.

Bateson, G., Jackson, D. D., Haley, J., & Weakland, J. (1956). Toward a theory of schizophrenia. *Behavioral Science, 1*, 251–264.

Beck, A. P. (1974). Phases in the development of structure in therapy and encounter groups. In D. Wexler & L. Rice (Eds.), *Innovations in client-centered therapy*. New York: Wiley.

Becvar, D. S., & Becvar, R. J. (1988). *Family therapy: A systematic integration*. Boston: Allyn & Bacon.

Bertalanffy, L. von. (1968). *General systems theory: Foundations, development, application*. New York: Brazillier.

Boszormenyi-Nagy, I. (1987). *Foundations of contextual therapy: Collected papers of Ivan Boszormenyi-Nagy*. New York: Brunner/Mazel.

Bowen, M. (1960). A family concept of schizophrenia. In D. D. Jackson (Ed.), *The etiology of schizophrenia*. New York: Basic Books.

Campbell, S. (1980). *The couple's journey*. San Luis Obispo, CA: Impact Press.

Capuzzi, D., & Gross, D. R. (1999). *Counseling and psychotherapy* (2nd ed.). New York: Merrill.

Carter, B., & McGoldrick, M. (1988). *The changing family life cycle* (2nd ed.). New York: Gardner.

Childers, J. H., & Couch, E. (1989). Myths about group counseling: Identifying and challenging misconceptions. *Journal for Specialists in Group Work, 14*, 105–111.

Corey, G. (1983). Group counseling. In J. A. Brown & R. H. Pate, Jr. (Eds.), *Being a counselor: Directions and challenges*. Monterey, CA: Brooks/Cole.

D'Alelio, W. A., & Murray, E. J. (1981). Cognitive therapy for test anxiety. *Cognitive Therapy and Research, 5*, 299–307.

Dell, P. F. (1982). Beyond homeostasis: Toward a concept of coherence. *Family Process, 21*, 21–41.

Driver, H. (1958). *Counseling and learning through small group discussions*. Madison, WI: Monona.

Foley, V. D. (1989). Family therapy. In R. J. Corsini & D. Wedding (Eds.), *Current psychotherapies* (4th ed., pp. 455–502). Itasca, IL: Peacock.

Fox, R. E. (1976). Family therapy. In I. B. Weiner (Ed.), *Clinical methods in psychology*. New York: Wiley-Interscience.

Fulmer, R. (1988). Lower-income and professional families: A comparison of structure and life cycle process. In B. C. Carter & M. McGoldrick (Eds.), *The changing family life cycle* (2nd ed., pp. 545–578). New York: Gardner Press.

Galassi, J., & Galassi, M. (1984). Promoting transfer and maintenance of counseling outcomes: How do we do it and how do we study it. In R. Brown & R. Lent (Eds.), *Handbook of counseling psychology*. New York: Wiley.

Goldenberg, H. (1983). *Contemporary clinical psychology* (2nd Ed.). Monterey, CA: Brooks/Cole.

Goldenberg, I., & Goldenberg, H. (2000). *Family therapy: An overview* (5th ed.). Pacific Grove, CA: Brooks/Cole.

Grebstein, L. C. (1986). An eclectic family therapy. In J. C. Norcross (Ed.), *Handbook of eclectic psychotherapy* (pp. 282–319). New York: Brunner/Mazel.

Gruen, W. (1977). The stages in the development of a therapy group: Telltale symptoms and their origin in the dynamic group forces. *Group, 1*, 10–25.

Gurman, A. S., & Kniskern, D. P. (Eds.) (1981). *Handbook of family therapy*. New York: Brunner/Mazel.

Haley, J. (1973). *Uncommon therapy*. New York: Norton.

Haley, J. (1976). *Problem-solving therapy*. San Francisco: Jossey-Bass.

Hanson, J. C., Warner, R. W., & Smith, E. M. (1980). *Group counseling: Theory and process* (2nd ed.). Chicago: Rand McNally.

Hines, P. M. (1988). The family life cycle of poor black families. In B. C. Carter & M. McGoldrick (Eds.), *The changing family life cycle* (2nd ed., pp. 513–544). New York: Gardner Press.

Horne, A. M., & Passmore, J. L. (1991). Family counseling & therapy (2nd ed.). Itasca, IL: F. E. Peacock.

Jackson, D. (1957). The question of family homeostasis. *Psychiatric Quarterly Supplement, 31,* 79–90.

Kliman, J. (1994). The interweaving of gender, class, and race in family therapy. In M. P. Mirkin (Ed.), *Women in context: Toward a feminist reconstruction of psychotherapy.* New York: Guilford Press.

Levant, R. F. (1984). *Family therapy: A comprehensive overview.* Englewood Cliffs, NJ: Prentice Hall.

Lidz, T., Cornelison, A., Fleck, S., & Terry, D. (1957). Intrafamilial environment of schizophrenic patients II: Marital schism and marital skew. *American Journal of Psychiatry, 20,* 241–248.

Lubin, B. (1976). Group therapy. In I. B. Weiner (Ed.), *Clinical methods in psychology.* New York: Wiley-Interscience.

MacKenzie, K. R., & Livesley, W. J. (1990). A developmental model for brief group therapy. *International Journal of Group Psychotherapy, 37,* 101–115.

Maslow, A. H. (1970). *Motivation and personality* (2nd ed.). New York: Harper & Row.

Maynard, P. K., & Olson, D. H. (1987). Circumplex model of family systems: A treatment tool in family counseling. *Journal of Counseling and Development, 65,* 502–504.

McGoldrick, M. (Ed.). (1998). *Re-visioning family therapy: Race, culture, and gender in clinical practice.* New York: Guilford Press.

Minuchin, S. (1974). *Families and family therapy.* Cambridge, MA: Harvard University Press.

Minuchin, S., Montalvo, B., Guerney, B., Rosman, B., & Schumer, F. (1967). *Families of the slums.* New York: Basic Books.

Ohlsen, M. M. (1977). *Group counseling* (2nd ed.). New York: Holt, Rinehart & Winston.

Olson, D. H. (1986). Circumplex Model VII: Validation Studies and Faces III. *Family Process, 25,* 377–381.

Olson, D. H., Russell, C., & Sprenkle, D. (1983). Circumplex model of marital and family systems: IV. Theoretical update. *Family Process, 22,* 69–83.

Olson, D. H., Sprenkle, D., & Russell, C. (1979). Circumplex model of marital and family systems: I. Cohesion and adaptability dimensions, family types and clinical applications. *Family Process, 18,* 3–15.

Papp, P. (1976). Family choreography. In P. J. Guerin (Ed.), *Family therapy: Theory and practice* (pp. 465–479). New York: Gardner Press.

Pearsall, P. (1990). *The power of the family.* New York: Doubleday.

Pinsof, W. M., Wynne, L. C., & Hambright, A. B. (1996). The outcomes of couple and family therapy: Findings, conclusions and recommendations. *Psychotherapy, 33,* 321–331.

Ritter, K. Y. (1982). Training group counselors: A total curriculum perspective. *Journal for Specialists in Group Work, 7,* 266–274.

Roth, D., Bielski, R., Jones, M., Parker, W., & Osborne, G. (1982). A comparison of self-control therapy and combined self-control and antidepressant medication in the treatment of depression. *Behavior Therapy, 13,* 133–144.

Rutan, J. S., & Alonso, A. (1978). Some guidelines for group therapists. *Group, 2,* 4–13.

Selvini-Palazzoli, M., Boscolo, L., Cecchin, G., & Prata, G. (1978). *Paradox and counter-paradox.* New York: Aronson.

Sobol, B. (1982). Art therapy and strategic family therapy. *American Journal of Art Therapy, 21,* 23–31.

Solomon, M. A. (1973). A developmental, conceptual premise for family therapy. *Family Process, 12,* 179–188.

Stanton, M. D. (1981). One integrated structural/strategic approach to family therapy. *Journal of Marital and Family Therapy, 10,* 427–439.

Stuart, R. B. (1980). *Helping couples change.* New York: Guilford Press.

Tuckman, B. W. (1965). Developmental sequence in small groups. *Psychological Bulletin, 63,* 384–399.

Wilcoxon, S. A. (1985). Healthy family functioning: The other side of family pathology. *Journal of Counseling and Development, 63,* 495–499.

Beginning counselors should become familiar with the basic theories of many approaches. Only then can you make the informed choices necessary to create, integrate, and structure your personal method. —Scott T. Meier and Susan R. Davis

16 CHAPTER | Conclusion: Comparing the Major Therapeutic Theories

Once considered the exclusive province of the very rich and the very disturbed, psychotherapy now reaches throngs of people who are not only afflicted with severe mental illness but everyday people who suffer from the problems associated with "normal" living. The demand for therapy has increased 400 percent in the last three decades, and more than 80 million people, at a cost of more than $4 billion annually, seek psychotherapy.

The wide variety of therapeutic options has become such an establishment in contemporary society, it's easy to forget that it was not always so. In 1920 there was one basic theory of psychotherapy, Sigmund Freud's psychoanalysis. Over the next two decades, several versions of neo-psychoanalytic theory emerged and began competing for dominance. Today, literally dozens, if not hundreds (Corsini, 1981; Gabbard, 1995; Herink, 1980), of therapies are striving for recognition. Some say there are almost as many approaches to counseling as there are counselors (Ivey, 1980). It is even possible to buy consumers' guides to today's myriad of therapies (for a brochure on choosing a psychologist, contact the APA Public Affairs Office at 750 First St., N.E., Washington, DC 20002). In this book, however, we have examined the most well-known, most documented, and most reputable approaches: psychoanalytic, Adlerian, existential, behavioral, person-centered, Gestalt, transactional analysis, rational-emotive, and reality therapy. And we have seen that each theory provides a structure or framework from which counselors can work in a systematic fashion. But we are still left with a question: How does a student, or for that matter, a client, choose one theoretical orientation over another?

COMPARING THERAPEUTIC APPROACHES

A well-known study conducted in 1950 found that experienced helpers of different theoretical persuasions tended to have more in common than inexperienced helpers of the same persuasion. These common elements included the relationship dimensions of genuineness, empathic understanding, respect, and acceptance of the client (Fiedler, 1950). More recently, other studies have described the same phenomenon after comparing counselors using different approaches (Lieberman, Yalom, & Miles, 1973; Truax & Carkhuff, 1967).

To help you gain a clearer picture of the various counseling approaches you have studied in this book and to stimulate your thinking about how they compare and contrast, consider the following table (Gladding, 1992; Pietrofesa, Hoffman, & Splete, 1984):

After reviewing the comparison table on pages 398–399, you may have derived several emphases and strategies that cut across therapeutic boundaries. If so, you are not alone. Practitioners have sought commonalties and have found much overlap among the various theories. For example, many of the terms used in transactional analysis stem from psychoanalytic thinking. Gestalt therapy and person-centered therapy both focus on the present and emphasize positive directions and goals of living. One can find many, many similarities between theories. Some have even argued that the various approaches may be emphasizing different aspects of the same process (Patterson, 1980).

They may take different forms when implemented under a different orientation, but some strategies are similar enough to be seen as common factors for therapeutic effectiveness. Notwithstanding theoretical differences, here are some of the overarching factors most frequently noted by practitioners.

1. *Developing an expectancy for change.* Perhaps the most common factor of effective therapy involves raising the client's level of expectance for change. In fact, many therapists attribute the success of psychotherapy more to a heightened expectancy level than to any specific technique. Simply translated, hope seems to cut across therapeutic border lines. It brings about a belief in clients that fosters a curative power. In other words, therapy achieves its success, in part, because of its capacity to generate client's

Comparing Major Therapeutic Theories

	Psychoanalysis	Adlerian	Existential	Person-Centered
View of Human Nature	Emphasizes early childhood and psychosexual development, the unconscious and ego defense mechanisms. Its focus is on biological, deterministic aspects of behavior.	Emphasizes social interests as a primary motivator while focusing on birthorder, family constellation, and lifestyle as major influences on personal growth and development.	Emphasizes a belief in human freedom and choice of lifestyle. The primary focus is on meaning as it relates to anxiety, life, death, and the relevance of individual experience.	Emphasizes the positive, forward-moving and good aspects of human nature and a phenomeno-logical view of the self, which demonstrates a growth orientation if provided with the right conditions.
Role of the Counselor	The counselor encourages transference and exploration of the unconscious. Using interpreta-tion, the counse-lor is viewed as the expert.	The counselor works with the client, modeling, teaching, and assessing the client's situation. Homework is often assigned and encourage-ment is given freely.	The counselor focuses on being authentic and understanding with the client while stressing a personal relationship of shared experience.	The counselor works to cultivate an environment that emphasizes personal warmth, empathy, acceptance, and genuineness.
Goals of Therapy	Goals include making the unconscious conscious, working through unresolved developmental stages, and reconstructing the personality.	Goals include cultivating social interest, correcting faulty assumptions and mistaken goals, and bringing about behavioral change through acting "as if."	Goals include helping clients realize their responsibility, awareness, freedom, and an outward frame of reference.	Goals include self-exploration and acceptance, openness to self and others, self-direction, and a focus on the here and now.
Methods and Techniques	Free association; dream analysis; analysis of transference; analysis of resistance; interpretation.	Empathy, support, collaboration; stressing client responsibility; examination of memories, family constellation.	Inquiringness; acceptance of client uniqueness; confrontation; awareness exercises; and imagery.	Acceptance; clarification; reflection of feeling; positive regard, self-disclosure; open-ended questions

Behaviorism	Gestalt	Rational-Emotive	Transactional Analysis	Reality
Emphasizes that human behaviors are learned and that old behaviors can be extinguished while new ones are established.	Emphasizes the importance of wholeness and completeness in human life while stressing the importance of affect, phenomenology, and antideterminism.	Emphasizes that humans are both inherently rational and irrational; that they can disturb themselves by what they think.	Emphasizes the ego states of Parent, Adult, and Child while stressing the importance of interpersonal integration and analysis of transactions.	Emphasizes that problems occur when people don't take responsibility for behavior and that people need to love and be loved and act in control of their environment.
The counselor serves as a teacher, director, and expert who actively participates in session and assists clients in clarifying goals and modifying behaviors.	The counselor uses an energetic demeanor to emphasize the here and now while helping clients resolve unfinished business.	The counselor is active and directive in teaching, confronting and correcting the client while also concentrating on the ABCs of self-talk.	The counselor contracts with the client for specific change and instructs in the language of interpersonal transactions.	The counselor, being active, practical, and didactic, serves as a model and teacher who focuses on establishing a relationship.
Goals include helping clients modify maladaptive behavior, learn productive responses, establish and achieve specific concrete goals.	Goals include immediacy of experience, making choices in the now, resolving the past, becoming congruent, and growing up mentally.	Goals include putting an end to irrational thinking, eliminating oughts, shoulds, and musts and elimination of self-defeating habits.	Goals include relative attainment of autonomy, increased personal health, becoming more aware, game free, and intimate.	Goals include becoming psychologically strong and rational, taking responsibility, clarifying goals, formulating a realistic plan and eliminating excuses.
Reinforcement; shaping, extinction; self-monitoring; punishment; systematic desensitization; flooding; stress inoculation.	Exercises and experiments; fantasy and role playing; dream work; taking responsibility; confrontation; exaggeration.	Disputing; instruction of emotion construction; imagery; persuasion; logical reasoning; homework assignments.	Treatment contracts; interrogation; illustration and specification; confrontation; often combined with Gestalt techniques.	Focusing; evaluating; making a plan and commitment to follow it; not blaming; role playing; confronting; role modeling.

expectancy of improvement. Part art and part science, psychotherapy profits from the mystique that surrounds both fields. Also, clients often approach therapy with a large emotional investment in making it work, and effective therapy, no matter what modality, capitalizes on this hopeful investment. The perception by a client that "I have been heard and understood and can be helped" can be as important as any other therapeutic intervention. Whatever the means, the objective of therapy is almost always to bring about the kind of change the client expects.

2. *Reducing emotional discomfort.* Most who find their way into a therapist's office are truly unhappy, beleaguered by depression, anxiety, phobias, or some other distress from the long list besetting the human race. Whatever the discomfort, therapists of all stripes are dedicated to alleviating it. Of course, therapists, to greater and lesser degrees, do not strive to eliminate all discomfort; in so doing, they might also eliminate motivation for working toward more lasting change. The challenge is to diminish extreme distress without sapping the client's desire to deal with enduring problems. The therapeutic relationship can be used as a means to this by serving as a buffer against outside hostility. The form this takes will certainly differ among therapists (from direct reassurances to more subtle alliances), but each is using the relationship to reduce the client's emotional discomfort.

3. *Fostering insight.* While Freud focused almost exclusively on bringing about insights from an analysis of unconscious influences, most therapists aim for insight in a general sense of greater self-understanding. By learning why they behave as they do, clients can became empowered to choose a different way of behaving. Therapists of all theoretical persuasions seek to promote self-examination and self-knowledge in their clients. Some deal with a specific type of content while other therapists try to promote insight by asking their clients to examine the implications of specific behaviors.

4. *Encouraging catharsis.* Most therapists encourage their clients to express emotions freely in their presence. Releasing pent-up emotions that the client has not acknowledged brings about a desired cathartic effect whereby the client's pain is eased and the client becomes more comfortable with his or her emotions. Most therapeutic modalities, in their own way, value the understanding that comes from expressing emotions in constructive ways and modifying those emotions that have become so maladaptive that the client's functioning is impaired. However catharsis is brought about, the goal is for the evoked emotions to be reexamined and be made to work for, rather than against, the client.

5. *Providing new information.* Many theoretical approaches involve an educational component, sometimes subtly, sometimes not. In general terms, the therapist provides new information to correct gaps of distortion in a client's understanding or self-knowledge. Misinformation about countless issues can be cleared up relatively quickly in many cases where a therapist adapts a teacherlike role. In some approaches this is accomplished

through providing reading material about a topic, a process known as bibliotherapy (Marx, Gyorky, Royalty, & Stern, 1992). New information, regardless of the theoretical orientation from which it is received, gives clients an added perspective on their issues and allows them to be seen as more solvable.

While there is no one fully acceptable theoretical model of therapy, these therapeutic factors form the backbone of most practitioners' counseling and psychotherapy. As you compose your own integrationist model of therapy, or even if you devote yourself to one primary mode, these fundamentals remain fairly consistent. They may be revealed, emphasized, and altered, in different ways, depending on their theoretical undergirding, but they comprise the factors common to most therapeutic work. These commonalities, by the way, beg the question: Does therapy really work?

DOES PSYCHOTHERAPY WORK?

In 1995 the American Psychological Association commissioned a study to determine how many people seek professional help from a professional psychotherapist or counselor. A random telephone survey revealed that 46 percent of those questioned had seen a mental health professional at some point in their lives. In 1977, a similar survey revealed 33 percent of those queried had sought psychological help. Going back to 1957, the rate was only 13 percent (Cavaliere, 1995). It appears that the stigma associated with seeing a professional is lessening and more people are seeking help. Or, perhaps, it may be that the general population is discovering that help from a counselor can make a difference. Whatever the reason, the increasing numbers cannot necessarily be correlated with therapeutic success. To determine this, other studies are needed and, fortunately, have been conducted for a number of decades.

One of the first studies to consider the effectiveness of counseling was done by Hans Eysenck (1952), who surveyed 19 published reports covering more than 7,000 cases. Eysenck concluded that individual psychotherapy was no more effective against neurotic disorders than no therapy at all: "Roughly two-thirds of a group of neurotic patients will recover or improve to a marked extent within about two years of the onset of their illness whether they are treated by means of psychotherapy or not" (p. 322).

Although Eysenck's conclusions caused a storm of controversy in the psychological community, his study immediately stimulated more research. A later review of the literature done by Meltzoff and Kornreich (1971) found more "good" or acceptable results than did

Eysenck and therefore concluded that psychotherapy is effective and superior to no treatment. Bergin and Lambert (1978) also found evidence of treatment-related improvement. They questioned the "spontaneous recovery" of the control subjects in the studies that Eysenck surveyed, noting that even though they received no formal therapy, many of them did get help from friends, clergy, physicians, and teachers. They concluded that the improvement rate among people in psychotherapy was greater than that of untreated control subjects. Sloane and his colleagues (1975), who compared people who had received psychoanalytic psychotherapy, those who had had behavior therapy, and a control group of people who were on a waiting list for therapy, found that both therapies were superior to the control condition in reducing major symptoms.

In 1977, a dramatically new approach was taken to the effectiveness question. Smith and Glass (1977) reported an averaging of the results of a large number of studies, from which they concluded that the typical therapy client is better off than 75 percent of untreated controls. But is this result due simply to the fact that the clients believed they would be helped, or is it due to the actual treatment itself? Landman and Dawes (1982) concluded that while initiating any treatment will create a small improvement, actually receiving therapy leads to a much greater improvement. In other words, the effects of receiving therapy appear to be due to more than just believing that you are going to get better.

Today, researchers have enough data to refute Eysenck's 1952 charge with conviction. Investigators have repeatedly shown that clients with diverse problems who receive a broad range of therapies improve more than they would with no treatment, with "placebo" treatment, or through spontaneous recovery, and the gains are lasting. A recent University of Pennsylvania study of the major modes of psychotherapy, including dynamic psychotherapy, behavior therapy, and cognitive therapy, concluded that they all had similar outcomes and that 80 percent of the treated patients showed improvement (Gabbard, 1995). An even more comprehensive and recent study published in *Consumer Reports* ("Mental Health: Does Therapy Help?" 1995) provides strong evidence in favor of psychotherapy's effectiveness. The study concluded that most patients who receive psychotherapy benefit from it and that those who receive more benefit more. In examining *Consumer Reports* methodology, Martin Seligman (1995) concluded that the results of the study are quite robust and may provide the most effective answer yet to the question "Does psychotherapy work?" The answer appears to be yes.

> The only therapy is life.
> —Otto Rank

IS ONE THERAPY BETTER THAN ANOTHER?

The global issue of effectiveness raises the question of how the effectiveness of particular theories stack up against one another. Is psychoanalytic therapy, for example, more effective than person-centered therapy? Logically, you might expect that the different approaches to therapy ought to vary in effectiveness.

Several reviews, however, have concluded that there are few differences in the results obtained by various forms of therapy (Casey & Berman, 1985; Cross, Sheehan, & Khan, 1982; DiLoreto, 1971; Garfield, 1983; Michelson, 1985; Smith, Glass, & Miller, 1980). One group of researchers (Luborsky, Singer, & Luborsky, 1975), after reviewing the evidence, quoted the dodo bird who had just judged a race in *Alice in Wonderland:* "Everyone has won and all must have prizes." However, other psychologists question these conclusions; they point out that there is no agreement on appropriate methods for determining the relative effectiveness of different types of therapy (Eysenck, 1985; Piroleau, Murdoc, & Brody, 1983; Shapiro, 1985). It is dismaying that the debate over such an important issue has not yet been resolved, but the debate itself continues to spur careful well-managed studies conducted in the hope of making a breakthrough.

What is clear, however, is that some kinds of psychotherapy appear to be more appropriate for certain kinds of people and problems. Psychoanalytic therapy, for example, seems to be best suited to people seeking extensive scrutiny of themselves or profound self-understanding, relief of inner conflict, or better relationships with others. On the other hand, behavior therapy is probably more appropriate in cases where there is a specific behavioral problem. Desensitization, for example, is most effective with conditioned avoidance responses such as phobias and anxiety disorders. Studies show that cognitive therapy brings moderate relief from unipolar depression as well as panic disorder.

Perhaps more crucial than therapeutic modality in predicting whether psychotherapy is a success for certain clients is the client's motivation. The old joke is true: It takes only one therapist to change a light bulb, but the light bulb has to *want* to change. Another consideration beyond matching a specific therapeutic issue with a specific modality is how the length of treatment may be more important than the type of therapy that is implemented. The *Consumer Reports* survey (1995) found that long-term therapy produced significantly more improvement than short-term therapy. This finding is not without its critics, however. They attribute this to "therapy junkies" who are so committed to therapy as a way of life that they bias the results in this direction. Consider the accompanying article, "Is a Single Session Enough?"

When comparing different therapeutic approaches, one must not lose sight of the fact that not all therapists are created equal. Some counselors are unquestionably more effective than others and the variation in effectiveness depends more on therapists' personal skills than differences in theoretical orientation. Effective therapy, generally speaking, has as much or even more to do with the chemistry between therapist and client and with the strength of the working alliance than it does with the theoretical constructs to which the therapist subscribes. Good, bad, and mediocre therapists are found within each therapeutic approach.

> A little experience often
> upsets a lot of theory.
> —Cadman

With these findings and others, it is no wonder that the followers of particular theories are beginning to ease their boundaries.

16.1 | Is a Single Session Enough?

In keeping with the mood of the times to economize in all things, some therapists are saying that a single session of psychotherapy is enough for most people.

The approach capitalizes on the fact that on average about a third of the people who consult a therapist never return for a second session, making one session the most frequent length of therapy. The advocates of single-session therapy argue that what is so often a person's only therapeutic encounter should be used to maximize its effect. But they also contend that for many, if not most, people, one therapy session can leave them with the tools and the encouragement to handle their problems on their own. For example a single session may be all that is required to give a person the resolve to end a destructive relationship.

"It's not hard to be helpful to somebody in a single session," said Dr. Bernard Bloom, a psychologist at the University of Colorado who is an originator of the approach.

For most psychoanalysts and other psychotherapists who routinely do therapy lasting months or years, the idea seems absurd. And even some therapists who have milder reactions are skeptical.

Typical was the reaction of Dr. Robert Michels, dean at the Cornell Medical School who is a former chairman of the psychiatry department. "In my clinical experience," he said, "a single session of therapy is unlikely to be enough for most patients."

Even so, Dr. Simon Budman, a psychologist at the Harvard Community Health Plan in Boston, said: "There is more single session therapy going on than many therapists realize. I find that 10 to 15 percent of my clients only need a single session."

Recently, Dr. Budman treated a college senior who had been suffering from panic attacks. The first occurred in the initial meeting of a second-semester course, when the instructor asked students to introduce themselves and tell their plans for their future. "He got so panicked, he had to walk out," Dr. Budman said, after which the student became increasingly anxious because of the fear he would have more attacks.

In talking to the student, Dr. Budman discovered that he was worried about his future. "Here it was, the end of his senior year and he was unsure about what he would do next," Dr. Budman said. "I pointed out that it was entirely appropriate for him to be anxious in his situation."

Sometimes, Dr. Budman said, all a person needs to hear is that his or her reaction is normal given the circumstances. Four months after their single meeting, Dr. Budman called the student and found that he had not had any more panic attacks.

Normally, therapists use the first session, or several, to gather information about a client, delaying therapeutic intervention until later. But single-session advocates argue that, in addition, therapists should use the initial session to make interventions and suggestions that can have therapeutic effect. "You can say from the outset, let's see what I can do to be helpful to you in an hour or so," Dr. Bloom said. "When the hour is over, the person can have gotten enough to make a change in his life."

To be sure, even the most enthusiastic supporters of single-session therapy admit limitations. Perhaps the most important is how long a person expects the therapy to last.

"If a client comes in the door expecting long-term therapy, single-session therapy can't work," said Dr. Moshe Talmon, a psychologist at the Kaiser Permanente Medical Center in Hayward, Calif., a leading advocate of the approach. But he said that most first-time patients in community clinics and prepaid medical plans do not expect therapy to last long. Dr. Talmon said most people who go to therapists are appropriate candidates for a single session, especially those who have a specific problem, like family conflicts.

"At the beginning I thought single-session therapy would be most helpful for less severe and acute problems," Dr. Talmon said, "but when a problem is very urgent and painful, people are motivated to change quickly."

Data supporting the single-session treatment has come from a variety of studies, often unexpectedly. For example, one of the earliest was a follow-up of 141 people who had consulted therapists on only one occasion in community clinics in New York City. Done in the 1950s, the study found that two-thirds said they had been helped, though their therapists thought of them as "dropouts."

Indirect evidence of benefit came from a 1979 study of 304 patients in a prepaid medical plan in California. The study found that people who consulted a psychotherapist for a single session had a 60 percent decline in their use of all other medical services over the next five years.

And in recent research, 200 patients who had consulted a therapist just once at a California prepaid medical plan were called several months later; 78 percent said they had got what they wanted out of that single session and felt better about the problem. The research is reported in Dr. Talmon's book *Single Session Therapy*.

Adapted from Goleman, D. (1991, May 2), Therapists say a single session may be enough. *The New York Times*, p. 38.

INTEGRATING THERAPEUTIC APPROACHES

There is a significant trend in counseling to move away from strong loyalty to individual schools of thought and a corresponding move toward integrating different approaches to therapy (Beitman, Goldfried, & Norcross, 1989). Most clinicians used to depend exclusively on one system of therapy while rejecting the utility of all others. This era of fragmentation may be drawing to a close. Since the 1970s, researchers have found that the greatest proportion of psychologists responding to a survey described themselves as *eclectic* in approach (Jensen, Bergin, & Greaves, 1990; Norcross & Prochaska, 1982; Smith, 1982). See Figure 16.1. The relatively new *International Journal of Eclectic Psychotherapy* and the *Society for the Exploration of Psychotherapy Integration* are two indicators that eclecticism is thriving among today's clinicians.

Eclectic means "drawn from many sources." Counselors who embrace this approach are well acquainted with all the theories involved, and they use various theories to match the needs of various clients. Eclectic, however, does not mean the absence of an orientation. Nor does an eclectic orientation permit an ill-defined, inconsistent, or random collection of philosophy, purposes, and techniques. When therapists take this approach, they are sometimes sarcastically referred to as "electric," because they are trying any and every method that "turns them on." Understandably, this kind of counselor can do more harm than good if he or she does not thoroughly understand the theories from which therapy is drawn. A "healthy" eclectic approach requires counselors to have a sound knowledge of the counseling theories used, a basic integrative philosophy of human behavior, and a flexible means of fitting the approach to the client, not vice versa (Cavanagh, 1982). After mastering the various theories, the key is to know what approach to use when, where and how (Harman, 1977).

Figure 16.1

The pooled data from a survey of 415 clinical and counseling psychologists (Smith, 1982) and another survey of 479 clinical psychologists (Norcross & Prochaska, 1982) indicate that the most widely employed approaches to therapy are (in order) eclectic, psychodynamic, behavioral, cognitive, and client-centered approaches.

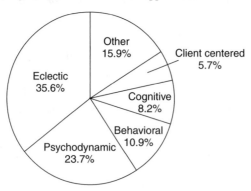

Some scholars advocate a hierarchy of eclectic practices (McBride & Martin, 1990). The first level of eclecticism is termed "syncretism," which is an unsystematic, sloppy process of fitting unrelated clinical concepts together. The second level is "traditional" and incorporates an orderly combination of compatible features into a harmonious whole. The third level is described as "professional" and requires the counselor to master at least two theories before ever trying to make any combinations. The final level of eclecticism is called "theoretical"; it is conceptualized as a type of metatheory that underlies and explains the overall practice of counseling in a unifying manner. Arnold Lazarus (1967, 1971, 1976, 1981, 1985) has done more than any other theorist to provide this kind of encompassing approach to eclecticism.

Lazarus initially defined his approach as "technical eclecticism," but it is now commonly known as *multimodal therapy*. With his approach, therapists use whatever techniques are most appropriate for given problems regardless of the theoretical system from which the techniques are derived. While he carries a strong behavioral emphasis, Lazarus may view behavioral techniques as being appropriate for one type of difficulty, while Gestalt or psychoanalytic procedures are preferred for another.

According to Lazarus, a client's personality is organized by seven modes of functioning, which can be summarized by the acronym BASIC ID: Behavior, Affect, Sensation, Imagery, Cognition, Interpersonal relations, and Drugs. Each of these areas of functioning (with the exception of drugs, which is a form of treatment) may call for different techniques, ranging across several schools of therapy. Treatment focuses on influencing each of these areas of functioning, but the choice of what systematic approach to use with a client depends on where the client is experiencing the most difficulty.

> The important thing is not to stop questioning. Curiosity has its own reason for existing. One cannot help but be in awe when he contemplates the mysteries of eternity, of life, of the marvelous structure of reality. It is enough if one tries merely to comprehend a little of this mystery every day. Never lose a holy curiosity.
>
> —Albert Einstein

Human areas of functioning are interactional, Lazarus believes, and there is a "firing order" by which one mode influences another. The goal of treatment, then, is multifaceted and involves influencing the behavior of the entire person by selectively working in one or two primary areas.

While widely respected, Lazarus's method of trying to achieve a healthy eclecticism should not be viewed as the only way this can be done. In a national survey of psychotherapists (Jensen, Bergin, & Greaves, 1990), it was found that 72 percent of "eclectics" reported using psychodynamic principles within their version of eclectic therapy, 54 percent reported cognitive approaches as their foundation, and 45 percent reported using behavioral methods as their underlying structure for eclecticism (as does Lazarus). The point is that eclectic therapy does not come in only one form; there are analytic eclectics and behavioral eclectics and humanistic eclectics. Eclectic psychotherapy is a diverse orientation that embraces many different combinations fitting the style of individual therapists.

As you examine the various approaches to counseling, it is hoped that you have begun thinking of ways to integrate some of the theories and techniques into your own orientation as a counselor. It is vital for each counselor to discover what systematic approaches work best for him or her as a personal style develops. In your continued studies of professional counseling and psychotherapy, and perhaps as you develop a careful eclectic approach, let me remind you that your choice of techniques should be principled. Your integration of strategies should be based on each individual case rather than on the dictates of a general theoretical system to be imposed on every client. In other words, your integration of strategies should model Lazarus's method of drawing on the combined and complementary wisdom of different theoretical approaches because you understand how each one can be used in given situations and for differing human needs and functions.

16.2   A Call for Help: Telephone Therapy

Reserved parking places and ramps now facilitate access for disabled persons to various public buildings, but many individuals are still unable to take advantage of these advances in "barrier-free" accessibility. Some are too severely ill to be moved short of ambulance transport. Some are so physically incapacitated that the energy needed to go into the community is beyond their own reserves and those of their caregivers. Some are too depressed to even think about leaving their homes or their bedrooms.

The telephone provides a link to psychotherapeutic services for these people. This form of therapy obviously differs from conventional face-to-face therapy and provides challenges for both clients and therapists. A great deal of energy and commitment is required to fulfill the therapeutic contract, and the differences inherent in this mode of therapy sometimes create considerable anxiety. Listening carefully substitutes for visual cues, such as crossed arms, silent tears, or postural changes.

The telephone can also be appropriate for traditional individual psychotherapy, especially in crisis intervention, but it is becoming a capable way of providing significant benefits to people who formerly were barred from services accessible to the majority.

Adapted from Melton, M. C., & Smoyak, S. A. (1992). Telephone therapy. *Journal of Psychosocial Nursing, 30,* 29–32.

THE CHALLENGE OF CONTEMPORARY PSYCHOTHERAPY

When one of the Disney theme parks was opened a few months after Walt Disney's death, an impressed visitor reportedly expressed his appreciation to one of the park's designers. "It is sad that Mr. Disney did not live to see this," the visitor said.

"Oh, but he did see it," the designer replied. "That's why the park is here."

Visionaries like Walt Disney are able to anticipate the future, imagine the possibilities, and then work to make them a reality. The field of professional counseling and psychotherapy needs visionaries—realistic people who understand change, who see possibilities that others miss, and who refuse to dispense yesterday's answers to today's questions.

Contemporary society, often rootless, cynical, and sometimes hopeless, breeds apprehensive apathy. But contemporary counselors cannot allow this toxin to contaminate the field of psychotherapy. Nor can we, as counselors, retreat into a therapeutic cocoon that is dedicated solely to looking inward. For too long, some say, psychotherapy has traced unhappiness and dysfunction to the subjective world of the "interior self." We have been warned of the hazards of gazing perpetually within—that the flip side of self-awareness is self-absorption, narcissism, and the tendency to interpret everything in individual terms.

In their 1985 volume *Habits of the Heart,* for example, University of California at Berkeley sociologist Robert Bellah and his colleagues correlated the spread of the inward psychotherapeutic ethic with the erosion of values, arguing that it "posits an individual who is able to be the source of his own standards" and "denies all forms of obligation and commitment in relationships." Similarly, James Hillman and Michael Ventura, authors of *We've Had a Hundred Years of Psychotherapy—and the World's Getting Worse,* see therapy's emphasis on self-analysis as a holdover from 19th-century individualism, an approach inappropriate to modern society where active social involvement is imperative.

The first years of the twenty-first century are an appropriate time for the next generation of counselors to reassess the field and envision its future. The process of human change and transformation will remain much the same; it will always be arduous, always a matter of steps taken forward, steps back. But we cannot give into the temptation to only look back in order to avoid the future. Our profession cannot afford to withdraw and watch from the sidelines.

The next generation of counselors and psychotherapists must move forward with confidence, squarely facing the challenges our changing society presents. The truth is that the future does not depend so much on the dreams we dream or the plans we conceive. The future depends more on the choices we make. And so I leave you, the next generation of counselors, with a challenge.

> Psychotherapy is the systematic use of a human relationship for therapeutic purposes.
>
> —Hans Strupp

As we have seen throughout the chapters of this book, theories cannot be developed apart from the contexts of the theorists and their backgrounds. The most widely respected and significant counseling theories, therefore, reflect the

16.3   Making Room on the Couch for Culture

The patient seemed psychotic, complaining in a listless ramble, "My soul is not with me anymore—I can't do anything." Seriously disturbed, she had been taken to a psychiatric hospital by her relatives. The psychiatrist who interviewed the woman discovered the problem had begun when she got bad news from her native Ecuador: an uncle she was close to had died unexpectedly.

"I realized that her clinical picture fit a syndrome known in Latin American cultures as 'susto,' or loss of the soul," said Dr. Juan Mezzich, a psychiatrist at the Mount Sinai School of Medicine in Manhattan, who treated the woman. "In facing the tragic news, the soul of the patient departs with the dead person, leaving the person soulless. In our psychiatric terms, we would say she was depressed."

Dr. Mezzich is at the forefront of a new movement in psychiatry to recognize the cultural trappings that patients bring with them, and to shape diagnosis and treatment accordingly. In the last five years the movement, which comes at a time when an increasing proportion of psychiatric patients in America come from an array of cultures, has led to a growing stream of books and scholarly articles on cultural influences in mental health. Virtually every professional convention for psychotherapists now offers a workshop on how culture affects psychiatric problems.

The American Journal of Psychiatry recently published guidelines for psychiatric evaluation that for the first time explicitly recommended that a patient's cultural or ethnic background be considered, including how the patient understands the symptoms he or she is having.

For example, the woman from Ecuador was at first misdiagnosed as psychotic by another psychiatrist. But Dr. Mezzich, who is from Peru, not only knew about the susto syndrome but also devised a treatment for her that drew upon his understanding of her background. "Instead of just giving her antidepressants, I tried an approach based on Hispanic culture," he said. "There, for susto, you would expect to have a mourning ritual to help the person assimilate the loss. So, with her family, we organized a sort of wake where everyone talked about the loss of her uncle and what it meant to them."

The wake "was quite powerful for her," Dr. Mezzich said. "She didn't need any antidepressants, and within a few meetings, including two with her family, her symptoms lifted and she was back participating fully in life once again."

The anthropological study of psychiatric disorders like susto has yielded a fascinating list of syndromes known only in one or another culture, like the sudden, violent outburst known as "amok" in Malaysia, or "koro," the East Asian term for intense anxiety that one's sexual organs will recede into one's body with fatal consequence. Anthropologists say these are not mere ethnographic curiosities. Rather, they say, the syndromes illustrate a broader point, that notions of mental disorder, if not the disorders themselves, are shaped by culture.

Indeed, some disorders of the mind that are well recognized in some cultures simply have no equivalent in Western psychiatry. One such is "taijin kyofusho," a Japanese malady that loosely translates as "fear of people." The name describes a morbid dread that one will do something that will embarrass other people.

"The syndrome revolves around social shame," said Dr. Arthur Kleinman, a medical anthropologist and psychiatrist at Harvard Medical School. "The closest equivalent Western psychiatric diagnosis is social phobia, but that is an anxiety disorder, a fear that people will criticize you. It's not at all the same thing. Japanese clinicians say this psychological problem simply has no parallel in our own culture or diagnostic system— we don't think of the fear of embarrassing other people as a psychological syndrome."

The stamp of culture on mental disorders extends to America itself, Dr. Kleinman asserts. Although it is difficult to see for those immersed in American culture, he contends that there are psychiatric syndromes unique to Western industrialized societies. "Anorexia nervosa seems as culture-bound to America and similar industrialized cultures as amok is to Malaysia," Dr. Kleinman said.

Dr. Spero Manson, a medical anthropologist in the psychiatry department at the University of Colorado Health Science Center and himself a Chippewa, said: "There is simply no such thing as anorexia among native peoples in North America. The over concern with body stereotypes aren't relevant in Indian cultures—the grave concern with slenderness is itself seen as absurd. Native people would be very concerned about a person who was willfully wasting away, but you just don't find it, except perhaps among highly acculturated Indians."

Dr. Kleinman says that although exotic disorders exist most mental health workers will not confront them directly, but rather will have to deal with differences in how patients describe or experience universal problems like depression. "You need to understand the idiom of distress—how a person talks about his problem," Dr. Kleinman said. For Hopi Indians, for example, there are five terms that refer to types of depression. Dr. Manson said the nearest English equivalents were "deep worry," "pouting," "drunken-like craziness," "unhappiness," and "heartbroken."

Most of these categories have only a surface resemblance to psychiatry's concepts of depression, Dr. Manson says. "The term 'heartbroken' translates also as 'heart is dying' or 'spiritual death'—there's really no match for this in the diagnostic manual," Dr. Manson said.

The most common cause of "heartbreak" is a rupture in a close relationship, such as a child being ignored by its mother or the breakup of a teenage romance. The typical reactions range from being shocked and perplexed to feeling despair and exhaustion.

(continued)

16.3 **Making Room on the Couch for Culture**
(continued)

"Depending on which of these sicknesses a Hopi patient thinks he is suffering from, some treatments would make better sense than others," Dr. Manson said. "Heartbreak, for example, has mainly physiological manifestations, like disturbed sleep and loss of appetite. Typically it's treated with herbs, so a medication would make sense. But for unhappiness the appropriate treatment for a Hopi would be a combination of psychotherapy and group support.

"Take a psychiatrist aware only of the standard psychiatric approaches," Dr. Manson continued. "In comes a Hopi patient, and the questions asked and treatment approach taken may mesh poorly at best with that patient's understanding of what should happen. The psychiatrist's lens might lead him to call it major depression, but that imposes another way of thinking about it."

Many of the syndromes specific to one culture refer to some kind of brief psychosis, Dr. Mezzich said. "In countries like India and Egypt, for example, about half of psychiatric patients have a temporary psychotic state, typically a well-recognized syndrome in those cultures, that had no matching diagnosis in American psychiatry until the diagnosis of acute, transient psychosis was added last year," he said.

Not only has the diagnostic manual changed to take account of disorders specific to one culture, the training of mental health workers is also changing.

"At San Francisco General Hospital, we offer residents training on units that are focused on different cultural groups," said Dr. Francis Lu, co-director of the Cultural Competence and Diversity Program at the hospital and a psychiatrist at the University of California. And, for the first time, the national guidelines for training psychiatry residents this year specify that they be trained in assessing any cultural impact on their patients' problems.

Adapted from Goleman, D. (1995, December 5). Making room on the couch for culture. *New York Times*, p. B5.

spirit of the era and region in which the theorists who developed them lived. It is no secret, then, that these theories were developed by white men in Western cultures primarily for middle- and upper-middle-class clients. Thus, it has been up to individual practitioners in contemporary society to shoulder the onus for developing cultural awareness and applicability in the context of these theories (see accompanying article on "Making Room on the Couch for Culture").

Classic counseling theories, as we have seen, do not specifically address the racial, ethnic, and cultural considerations of today's American minority groups.

However, instead of disowning or discarding these traditional therapeutic theories because of their original context, we can work to integrate these theories with cultural considerations. Pedersen (1991) put it succinctly when he stated, "Until and unless the multicultural perspective can be understood as not only generic to all counseling but also increasing the accuracy of counseling, culture will remain an exotic concept" (p. 250). He calls multiculturalism "the fourth force" that will carry the next generation of counselors.

This fourth force will undoubtedly require a redefinition of current theories and a major integration of multicultural considerations into our current theories. A theoretical framework that incorporates multicultural aspects is no longer just a goal, but a necessity. As counselors and therapists, we cannot wait for the evolution of a new theory to do the work for us. The reality of changing demographics of our clientele presents this generation of practitioners with the challenge of integrating multicultural components into theoretical understanding (Ridley, 1995; Wehrly, 1995).

Where will the future of psychotherapy take us? In an attempt to extract and amplify salient counseling trends, 40 experts in the field were asked just that. They predicted that present-centered, structured, and directive techniques would increase in the years to come (Norcross & Freeheim, 1993). Whether they are correct or not, only time will tell, but one thing is certain: All therapies have the ultimate common goal of helping clients reduce their suffering, improve their relationships, and take action to live a more fulfilling life. By facing the future and developing your own approach to counseling—whether it be psychoanalytic, behavioral, person-centered, eclectic, or something else—you will be joining ranks with a diverse group of professionals who are basically headed in the same direction.

> A theory is no more like a fact than a photograph is like a person.
>
> —Ed Howe

References

Beitman, B. D., Goldfried, M. R., & Norcross, J. C. (1989). The movement toward integrating the psychotherapies: An overview. *American Journal of Psychiatry, 146,* 138–147.

Bellah, R. N., Madsen, R., Sullivan, W. M., Swidler, A., & Tipton, M. (1985). *Habits of the heart: Individualism and commitment in American life.* New York: Harper & Row.

Bergin, A. E., & Lambert, M. J. (1978). The evaluation of therapeutic outcomes. In S. L. Garfield & A. E. Gergin (Eds.), *Handbook of psychotherapy and behavior change: An empirical analysis.* New York: Wiley.

Casey, R. J., & Berman, J. S. (1985). The outcome of psychotherapy with children. *Psychological Bulletin, 98,* 388–400.

Cavaliere, F. (1995, June). APA brochure offers tips on choosing a psychologist. *APA Monitor,* p. 9.

Cavanagh, M. E. (1982). *The counseling experience.* Monterey, CA: Brooks/Cole.

Consumer Reports. (1995, November). Mental health: Does therapy help? pp. 734–739.

Corsini, R. J. (Ed.). (1981). *Handbook of innovative psychotherapies.* New York: Wiley.

Cross, D. G., Sheehan, P. W., & Khan, J. A. (1982). Short- and long-term follow-up of clients receiving insight-oriented therapy and behavior therapy. *Journal of Consulting and Clinical Psychology, 50,* 103–112.

DiLoreto, A. O. (1971). *Comparative psychotherapy: An experimental analysis.* Chicago: Aldine-Atherton.

Eysenck, H. J. (1952). The effects of psychotherapy: An evaluation. *Journal of Consulting and Clinical Psychology, 16,* 319–324.

Eysenck, H. J. (1985). *The decline and fall of the Freudian empire.* London: Pelican.

Fiedler, F. (1950). A comparison of therapeutic relationships in psychoanalytic, nondirective and Adlerian therapeutic relationships. *Journal of Counseling and Psychology, 14,* 436–445.

Gabbard, G. (1995). Are all psychotherapies equally effective? *The Menninger Letter, 3,* 1–2.

Garfield, S. L. (Ed.). (1983). Special section: Meta-analysis and psychotherapy. *Journal of Consulting and Clinical Psychology, 51,* 3–75.

Gladding, S. T. (1992). *Counseling: A comprehensive profession.* (2nd ed.). New York: Merrill.

Harman, R. L. (1977). Beyond techniques. *Counselor Education and Supervision, 17,* 157–158.

Herink, R. (Ed.). (1980). *The psychotherapy handbook.* New York: New American Library.

Hillman, J. & Ventura, M. (1993). *We've had a hundred years of psychotherapy—and the world's getting worse.* San Francisco: Harpers.

Ivey, A., with Simek-Downing, L. (1980). *Counseling and psychotherapy: Skills, theories, and practice.* Englewood Cliffs, NJ: Prentice Hall.

Jensen, J. P., Bergin, A. E., & Greaves, D. W. (1990). The meaning of eclecticism: New survey and analysis of components. *Professional Psychology: Research and Practice, 21,* 124–130.

Landman, J. C., & Dawes, R. M. (1982). Psychotherapy outcome: Smith and Glass' conclusions stand up under scrutiny. *American Psychologist, 37,* 504–516.

Lazarus, A. A. (1967). In support of technical eclecticism. *Psychological Reports, 21,* 415–416.

Lazarus, A. A. (1971). *Behavior therapy and beyond.* New York: McGraw-Hill.

Lazarus, A. A. (1976). *Multimodel behavior therapy.* New York: Springer.

Lazarus, A. A. (1981). *The practice of multimodel therapy: Systematic, comprehensive, and effective psychotherapy.* New York: McGraw-Hill.

Lazarus, A. A. (1985). *Casebook of multimodel therapy.* New York: Guilford Press.

Lieberman, M., Yalom, I., & Miles, M. (1973). *Encounter groups: First facts.* New York: Basic Books.

Luborsky, L., Singer, B., & Luborsky, L. (1975). Comparative studies of psychotherapies: Is it true that everyone has won and all must have prizes? *Archives of General Psychiatry, 32,* 995–1008.

Marx, J. A., Gyorky, Z. K., Royalty, G. M., & Stern, T. E. (1992). Use of self-help books in psychotherapy. *Professional Psychology: Research and Practice, 23,* 300–305.

McBride, M. C., & Martin, G. E. (1990). A framework for eclecticism: The importance of theory to mental health counseling. *Journal of Mental Health Counseling, 12,* 495–505.

Meltzoff, J., & Kornreich, M. (1971, July). It works. *Psychology Today,* 57–61.

Mental health: Does therapy help? (1995, November) *Consumer Reports,* 734–739.

Michelson, L. (Ed.). (1985). Meta-analysis and clinical psychology. *Clinical psychology Review, 5,* 1.

Norcross, J. C., & Freeheim, D. K. (1993). Into the future: Retrospect and prospect in psychotherapy. In D. K. Freedman, *History of psychotherapy.* Washington, DC: American Psychological Association.

Norcross, J. C., & Prochaska, J. O. (1982). National survey of clinical psychologists: Affiliations and orientations. *Clinical Psychologist, 35,* 4–6.

Patterson, C. H. (1980). *The therapeutic relationship: Foundations for an eclectic psychotherapy.* Monterey, CA: Brooks/Cole.

Pedersen, P. B. (1991). Concluding comments to the special issue. *Journal of Counseling and Development, 70,* 250.

Piroleau, L., Murdoc, M., & Brody, N. (1983). An analysis of psychotherapy versus placebo studies. *Behavioral and Brain Sciences, 6,* 275–310.

Pietrofesa, J. J., Hoffman, A., & Splete, H. H. (1984). Counseling: An introduction. (2nd ed.). Boston: Houghton Mifflin.

Ridley, C. R. (1995). *Overcoming unintentional racism in counseling and therapy: A practitioner's guide to intentional intervention.* Thousand Oaks, CA: Sage.

Seligman, M. E. P. (1995). The effectiveness of psychotherapy: The *Consumer Reports* study. *American Psychologist, 50,* 965–974.

Shapiro, B. A. (1985). Recent applications of meta-analysis in clinical research. *Clinical Psychology Review, 5,* 13–34.

Sloane, R. B., Staples, F. R., Cristol, A. H., Yorkston, J. J., & Whipple, K. (1975). Short-term analytically oriented psychotherapy versus behavior therapy. *American Journal of Psychiatry, 132,* 373–377.

Smith, D. (1982). Trends in counseling and psychotherapy. *American Psychologist, 37,* 802–809.

Smith, M. L., & Glass, G. V. (1977). Meta-analysis of psychotherapy outcome studies. *American Psychologist, 32,* 752–760.

Smith, M. L., Glass, G. V., & Miller, T. I. (1980). *The benefits of psychotherapy.* Baltimore, MD: Johns Hopkins University Press.

Truax, C., & Carkhuff, R. (1967). *Toward effective counseling and psychotherapy.* Chicago: Aldine.

Wehrly, B. (1995). *Pathways to multicultural counseling competence: A developmental journey.* Pacific Grove, CA: Brooks/Cole.

Divisions of the American Counseling Association

1. Association for Adult Development and Aging (AADA)
2. Association for Assessment in Counseling (AAC)
3. American College Counseling Association (ACCA)
4. Association for Counselors and Educators in Government (ACEG)
5. Association for Counselor Education and Supervision (ACES)
6. Association for Gay, Lesbian and Bisexual Issues in Counseling (AGLBIC)
7. Association for Multicultural Counseling and Development (AMCD)
8. American Mental Health Counselors Association (AMHCA)
9. American Rehabilitation Counseling Association (ARCA)
10. American School Counselor Association (ASCA)
11. Association for Spiritual, Ethical, and Religious Values in Counseling (ASERVIC)
12. Association for Specialists in Group Work (ASGW)
13. Counseling Association for Humanistic Education and Development (C-AHEAD)
14. Counselors for Social Justice (CSJ)
15. International Association of Addiction and Offender Counselors (IAAOC)
16. International Association of Marriage and Family Counselors (IAMFC)
17. National Career Development Association (NCDA)
18. National Employment Counseling Association (NECA)

Divisions of the American Psychological Association

1. Society for General Psychology
2. Society for the Teaching of Psychology
3. Experimental Psychology
4. There is no Division 4
5. Evaluation, Measurement, and Statistics
6. Behavioral Neuroscience and Comparative Psychology
7. Developmental Psychology
8. Society for Personality and Social Psychology
9. Society for the Psychological Study of Social Issues (SPSSI)
10. Psychology and the Arts
11. There is no Division 11
12. Society of Clinical Psychology
13. Society of Consulting Psychology
14. Society for Industrial and Organizational Psychology
15. Educational Psychology
16. School Psychology
17. Counseling Psychology
18. Psychologists in Public Service
19. Military Psychology
20. Adult Development and Aging

21. Applied Experimental and Engineering Psychology

22. Rehabilitation Psychology

23. Society for Consumer Psychology

24. Theoretical and Philosophical Psychology

25. Behavior Analysis

26. History of Psychology

27. Society for Community Research and Action: Division of Community Psychology

28. Psychopharmacology and Substance Abuse

29. Psychotherapy

30. Society of Psychological Hypnosis

31. State Psychological Association Affairs

32. Humanistic Psychology

33. Mental Retardation and Developmental Disabilities

34. Population and Environmental Psychology

35. Society for the Psychology of Women

36. Psychology of Religion

37. Child, Youth, and Family Services

38. Health Psychology

39. Psychoanalysis

40. Clinical Neuropsychology

41. American Psychology-Law Society

42. Psychologists in Independent Practice

43. Family Psychology

44. Society for the Psychological Study of Lesbian, Gay, and Bisexual Issues

45. Society for the Psychological Study of Ethnic Minority Issues

46. Media Psychology

47. Exercise and Sport Psychology

48. Society for the Study of Peace, Conflict, and Violence: Peace Psychology Division

49. Group Psychology and Group Psychotherapy

50. Addictions

51. Society for the Psychological Study of Men and Masculinity

52. International Psychology

53. Society of Clinical Child and Adolescent Psychology

54. Society of Pediatric Psychology

55. American Society for the Advancement of Pharmacotherapy

Name Index

Subject Index

TO THE OWNER OF THIS BOOK:

We hope that you have found *Counseling and Psychotherapy* useful. So that this book can be improved in a future edition, would you take the time to complete this sheet and return it? Thank you.

School and address: _____

Department: _____

Instructor's name: _____

1. What I like most about this book is: _____

_____

_____

2. What I like least about this book is: _____

_____

_____

3. My general reaction to this book is: _____

_____

4. The name of the course in which I used this book is: _____

_____

5. Were all of the chapters of the book assigned for you to read? _____

   If not, which ones weren't? _____

6. In the space below, or on a separate sheet of paper, please write specific suggestions for improving this book and anything else you'd care to share about your experience in using the book.

_____

_____

_____

_____

_____

Optional:

Your name: _____ Date: _____

May Brooks/Cole quote you, either in promotion for *Counseling and Psychotherapy* or in future publishing ventures?

Yes: _____ No: _____

Sincerely,

Les Parrott III

IN-BOOK SURVEY

At Brooks/Cole, we are excited about creating new types of learning materials that are interactive, three-dimensional, and fun to use. To guide us in our publishing/development process, we hope that you'll take just a few moments to fill out the survey below. Your answers can help us make decisions that will allow us to produce a wide variety of videos, CD-ROMs, and Internet-based learning systems to com-plement standard textbooks. If you're interested in working with us as a student Beta-tester, be sure to fill in your name, telephone number, and address. We look forward to hearing from you!

In addition to books, which of the following learning tools do you currently use in your counseling/human services/social work courses?

_____ **Video** _____ in class _____ school library _____ own VCR

_____ **CD-ROM** _____ in class _____ in lab _____ own computer

_____ **Macintosh disks** _____ in class _____ in lab _____ own computer

_____ **Windows disks** _____ in class _____ in lab _____ own computer

_____ **Internet** _____ in class _____ in lab _____ own computer

How often do you access the Internet?
_____

My own home computer is a:

_____

_

The computer I use in class for counseling/human services/social work courses is a:

_____

_

If you are NOT currently using multimedia materials in your counseling/human services/social work courses, but can see ways that video, CD-ROM, Internet, or other technologies could enhance your learning, please comment below:

_____

_____

_____

Other comments (optional):
_____

_____

Name _____Telephone
_____

Address _____

School
_____

BUSINESS REPLY MAIL
FIRST CLASS   PERMIT NO. 358   PACIFIC GROVE, CA

POSTAGE WILL BE PAID BY ADDRESSEE

ATT: _Marketing_

The Wadsworth Group
10 Davis Drive
Belmont, CA 94002

NO POSTAGE
NECESSARY
IF MAILED
IN THE
UNITED STATES

Attention Professors:

Brooks/Cole is dedicated to publishing quality publications for education in the social work, counseling, and human services fields. If you are interested in learning more about our publications, please fill in your name and address and request our latest catalogue, using this prepaid mailer. Please choose one of the following:

☐ social work   ☐ counseling   ☐ human services

Name: _____

Street Address: _____

City, State, and Zip: _____